MANAGING

BUSINESS AND

PUBLIC POLICY

Concepts, Issues & Cases

Second Edition

JOHN D. ARAM

The Weatherhead School of Management
Case Western Reserve University

BALLINGER PUBLISHING COMPANY
Cambridge, Massachusetts
A Subsidiary of Harper & Row, Publishers, Inc.

© 1986 John D. Aram

Library of Congress Cataloging-in-Publication Data

Aram, John D., 1942–
  Managing business and public policy.

  Bibliography: p.
  Includes index.
  1. Industry and state–United States–Case studies. 2. Business
and politics–United States–Case studies. I. Title
HD3616.U47A73 1985   338.973   85-16955
ISBN 0-88730-256-4 (previously published by Pitman
  Publishing Inc., ISBN 0-582-98830-6)

Manufactured in the United States of America

**BALLINGER SERIES IN
BUSINESS AND PUBLIC POLICY**

CONSULTING EDITOR
EDWIN M. EPSTEIN
University of California, Berkeley

CURRENT BOOKS IN THE SERIES:

John D. Aram, *Managing Business and Public Policy: Concepts, Issues and Cases*, 2nd. Ed.

R. Edward Freeman, *Strategic Management: A Stakeholder Approach*

S. Prakash Sethi, Nobuaki Namiki and Carl L. Swanson, *The False Promise of the Japanese Miracle: Illusions and Realities of the Japanese Management System*

Charles S. McCoy, *Management of Values: The Ethical Difference in Corporate Policy and Performance*

Stefanie Ann Lenway, *The Politics of U.S. International Trade: Protection, Expansion and Escape*

Donna J. Wood, *Strategic Uses of Public Policy: Business and Government in the Progressive Era*

Michael Murray, *Decisions: A Comparative Critique*

Contents

Foreword

In an era where there is a surfeit of the written word on virtually every subject, it is incumbent upon an academic editor to explain — even to justify — the introduction of a new series of books into the intellectual marketplace. Potential adopters have every right to ask: how is this series different (and better) than any other series and how are the individual books different (and better) than their competitors?

Scholarship, an ongoing and cumulative process, and research advances of both a conceptual and an empirical nature have occurred in the Business and Public Policy field during the past decade. The rapidity of developments in the American (and international) political economy since the early 1970's have required conscientious students of the field to reexamine and augment the intellectual bases provided by earlier writing. The underlying motivation for the Pitman Series in Business and Public Policy is to provide the most current and creative thinking in the Business and Public Policy area.

More specifically, in developing the Pitman series, Publisher Bill Roberts and I have sought to achieve five objectives:

1. To help shape the emerging field of Business and Public Policy (also known as Business and Society; Business, Government and Society; and Business and its Environment) by offering a collection of high-quality books which expose teacher and student alike to the latest thinking of some of the most creative scholars in this dynamic, complex, multidisciplinary area. We are seeking not merely to synthesize existing thought in this dynamic area of inquiry, but rather, to expand the intellectual borders of the field.
2. To publish: (a) texts which will contribute to the education of present and future business leaders by providing high-quality teaching materials; and (b) scholarly monographs which broaden and deepen our understanding of the Business and Public Policy interface.
3. To generate a series of books which will have intellectual coherence. While each of the individual books will be able to stand on its own feet both as teaching vehicles and as catalysts to scholarly thought, the

books will complement one another — much like the fragments of a mosaic.

4. To provide books which are highly readable and teachable. The dual objectives of facilitating the student's understanding, and the ability of the professor to convey sophisticated concepts lucidly go to the heart of the pedagogical goal of the series.

5. To provide materials which we believe will assist business practitioners, public officials and policy analysts to understand and function more effectively in the Business and Public Policy arena.

In summary, the Pitman series in Business and Public Policy seeks both to present the best of the current thinking in the field and to expand its intellectual borders. Other books in the series deal with such important issues as how the strategic management process enables business organizations to interact more effectively with its multiple stakeholders; the facts and fantasies of the Japanese management "miracle" and its relevance for U.S. business; the interrelation of ethics and values in the management decision process; and the politics underlying the development of U.S. international trade policy in three key sectors of our economy. Forthcoming volumes will deal with the role of public enterprise in the international political economy, the politics of environmental policy in the United States, business political advocacy and its impact on the public policy process, a three-dimensional (legal, political and organizational/economic) perspective of corporate organization, the government-business interface during the Progressive Era, and a political-economy approach to Business and Public Policy.

Few issues have stimulated more controversy in western societies in the post-World War era than that of the appropriate role of business and the state in the operations of advanced industrial societies. Although the local, state and federal levels have been actively involved in the functioning of the economy since the founding of the United States, both the extensiveness and the intensity of this involvement have increased dramatically since 1946. By the mid-1970's there began a re-examination of the respective roles of business firms and governmental bodies in the American political economy. As of the mid-1980's, this internal re-assessment is still in process as is reflected by the ongoing public policy debates surrounding such issues as "Industrial Policy" (ill-defined as this term is) and the appropriate balance among the Regulation-Deregulation-Reregulation to achieve an internationally competitive, socially accountable business sector. Business executives and governmental officials will require an even more analytical and less ideologically-tinged understanding of the roles of "public" and "private" institutions as we move toward the 21st century.

The second edition of John Aram's MANAGING BUSINESS AND PUBLIC POLICY builds upon and enhances the highly successful first edition. It not merely updates its predecessor, but introduces new materials, analyses and cases; reorganizes parts of the book to enhance its coherence and pedagogical effectiveness; and otherwise makes an excellent first edition even better by incorporating the thoughtful suggestions we have received from experts in the field. John offers a highly thoughtful, well-researched and conceptually-coherent examination of the multiple interactions of business and government in the United States. In dealing with such important subjects as the ideological bases of government-business relations, the governance and accountability of the modern large corporation, business impacts upon America's political and social structure, and the economic consequences of governmental interventions in the marketplace, he weaves together his insightful narrative analysis with provocative and well-written cases. The outcome of Professor Aram's efforts is a stimulating and highly original book which renders the complex interactions between governmental and business institutions comprehensible to the conscientious reader and provides a reliable roadmap for teachers guiding their students toward a more sophisticated understanding of these interactions. The cases and text are pedagogically reinforcing to a degree uncommon among previous works on the subject. In addition to its public policy focus, MANAGING BUSINESS AND PUBLIC POLICY has, accordingly, a distinctly managerial orientation which requires readers to place themselves in the positions of business executives and governmental officials to examine these complex situations. The book combines conceptual understanding of the issues with decision-making skills. In its coherence in concept, comprehensiveness in scope, lucidity of argumentation, clarity of exposition, and intellectual creativity, Professor Aram's book achieves the five objectives set forth above which Bill Roberts of Pitman and I have delineated for the series.

Pitman and I are proud to be associated with John Aram in publishing MANAGING BUSINESS AND PUBLIC POLICY and are confident that the Second Edition will make an important contribution to teaching and scholarship in the Business and Public Policy field for the remainder of the 1980's and into the 1990's.

University of California
Berkeley, California
November 1985

Edwin M. Epstein
Consulting Editor

Preface

The several years since the publication of the first edition of this book have witnessed no reduction in the complexity of issues involving business and society. Interdependence between the private enterprise sector and social, economic, and political forces has — if anything — been heightened.

Issues driven by forces external to the firm present challenges to leaders in both the private and public sectors. For example, major consolidation is occurring within the financial services industry and crises within several major banking institutions have led to public intervention. The weakening of the U.S. international competitive position in many manufacturing industries poses a central problem for private firms in those industries and for the economy as a whole. The influence of political action committees appears increasingly to shape governmental action; and the unrelenting advance of technology confronts society with heightened benefits and risks. Changes in these and other areas of the business environment demand the attention and considered response of institutions and their leaders.

Several publicized cases of illegal insider trading by public figures, the apparent misuse of the financial system by an established brokerage firm, and reports of corporate fraud in the defense contracting industry generate serious concerns about the prevailing ethic in business. Credibility of the system becomes strained when respected individuals and institutions appear to take advantage of the public's trust.

Changes in the business environment lead to unfamiliar situations and stimulate new and difficult questions: To what extent should current managers of large, publicly-held firms be allowed to defend against unfriendly takeover attempts?; How can we best balance the efficiency and equity considerations arising from continuing economic transitions among geographic regions and among employment occupations in the United States?; How can we assess the risks to society of major industrial accidents and how can we fully evaluate the costs of preventing them?; How can we best address the domestic disposal of hazardous waste and how best to determine compensation for victims?

As evident from these questions, this book favors a broad definition of the field of business and public policy. Rather than focusing exclusively on social regulation, anti-trust policy or multinational corporations, the writing deals with these and other topics important to the role and practices of corporations today.

The primary goal of the text is to present experiences, studies concepts, issues, and events that help to inform prospective managers about the busines environment. Challenging students to formulate their own analyses and draw their own conclusions on current issues is intended to heighten their sensitivity to the wider context of the firm. This book is intended to encourage students to develop their own perspectives and their own views of the responsibilities, roles, and relationships of business to society.

Exploration of these issues raises important implications for managers. First and foremost, managers must be skilled in reconciling competing short-term demands. More importantly, they need to be skilled in establishing systems and processes in which various groups rely on the long-term and interdependent character of their interests. In short, managers need to be capable of identifying and developing positive-sum or mutual-enhancement relationships among interests that might otherwise revert to debilitating conflict.

A vital, intangible, and creative quality called *leadership* will be a primary requirement of managers in the coming decades. Paraphrasing Oliver Wendell Holmes, Jr., the task of the leader is not only to collect and analyze information, nor only to reason and generalize, but also to idealize and imagine. The chapters of this text attempt to provide material for development of this quality by blending present with past, combining concrete and abstract, and integrating the pragmatic with the ideal. The goal of the book is to assist development of the leadership attitudes and capabilities needed for the future of our business system.

Compared to other areas of study in business, the field of business and public policy encompasses a relatively long time horizon and is substantially more qualitative than quantitative. In addition to economics, this field draws upon political science, sociology, law, and other social sciences as constituent management disciplines. It inquires relatively more into the role of values in decisions than other fields of management training often do. If a manager's performance and that of our entire economic system rest on the ability to integrate private actions and public interests, the study of business and public policy has a vital role to play in management education.

The style and approach of the first edition of the text are continued in the present work. Analysis of relevant issues is given more weight than solely descriptive material. Cases provide relatively unstructured situations calling for a mix of inquiries into public policy and private management problems. Every attempt is made to combine discussion of specifics with, and appreciation of, the general ideas and values to which they relate.

While maintaining this continuity with the prior edition, the present work makes some important additions. First, entirely new introductory and concluding chapters seek to provide more useful frameworks for the material and to focus attention on key issues. Second, a new chapter on the process of public policy development has been added. This discussion (chapter 3) adds an analysis of governmental action, especially legislative, that was absent from the first edition. Also, in addition to general updating of prior material in other chapters, this edition deletes some cases, makes major revisions in several others, and includes five completely new cases. Chapter and case changes attempt to maintain the book as both comprehensive and current.

A number of chapters have been reorganized in this edition. Material on economic and social regulation now appears together as a new Section II, and the three chapters dealing with governance issues appear as Section III. Chapters on differing aspects of economic growth — urban and regional development, innovation and entrepreneurship, and a revised discussion of international issues — are presented as Section IV. Finally, a chapter on corporate political action is combined with a concluding discussion of private sector leadership to form Section V. This reorganization of chapters was developed in response to user feedback. Finally, as with the first edition, an instructor's manual, including discussion of chapter and case discussion questions, is available.

Numerous persons have contributed to the completion of this, as well as the first, edition of the text. Ed Epstein has continued to be a thoroughly supportive colleague in this project. I am grateful to Bob Chatov, Jim McCullough, Tom Bier, Gerhard Mensch, Gerhard Rosegger and Scott Cowen for their help in the first edition, and to Lee Preston and Paul Tiffany for helpful suggestions in developing the present work.

Carol Fritz, Barry Dobson, and Connie George, M.B.A. students at the Weatherhead School of Management during the preparation of the first edition, made important input to numerous chapters and cases, and their presence continues here. In this version other students have been a great help. Jeffrey S. Coomes provided valuable assistance in researching several topics and was instrumental in preparing new case material. Suzanne M. Seifert, in particular, made crucial contributions to this edition. First, her substantial work on the text's cases are evident in the Contents. Moreover, she ably and diligently researched, organized, and drafted revision material in many of the chapters. This edition benefited immensely from her excellent work.

I owe a great deal of gratitude to Peggy Little for her patience, responsive assistance, and expert typing in seeing this material and the new instructor's manual through to completion.

Once again, it has been a pleasure to work with the Pitman team. Bill Roberts, Michael Weinstein, and Susan Badger have played especially valuable roles in assisting my efforts.

Finally, I wish to thank the members of my immediate family for their support and patience in my work on this edition. Dorothy, Bethany, and Jon have each been more than tolerant of my frequent inaccessibility, my preoccupied attention, and my cluttered office. I appreciate their understanding and encouragement.

Chapter 1

The Scope and Focus of Business-Government Relations

In the spring and summer of 1984 Continental Illinois National Bank and Trust Company of Chicago faced impending failure. Ultimately the government intervened with a $4.5 billion loan — the largest ever to a private firm — even though the bank's financial deterioration resulted solely from private, managerial actions. While government leaders were committed to an ideology of the free market, the apparent threat to the stability of the country's financial system implied by the failure of a $41.5 billion bank provided a larger, more overriding concern. In arriving at a course of action government officials and leaders in the private sector confronted a trade-off in their thinking between free market reliance and the stability of the financial system. It was a trade-off not without price.

The near collapse of Continental Illinois came at a time of dramatic change in financial services involving the globalization of markets and the blurring of distinctions between financial and nonfinancial institutions. The presence of electronic technologies and market growth were making government attempts to segment and regulate financial markets by type of institution, such as commercial banking and investment banking, impractical. So confusion abounded.

Continental's experience further complicated matters, but it stimulated a number of recurrent questions in business-government relationships. It also raised doubts concerning the appropriateness of government policy toward a number of other industries that were likewise experiencing internationalization of competition, rapid technological change, and new market potentials. In the face of unprecedented uncertainty and change in banking, the borders between public and private interests were blurred considerably — a not uncommon occurrence in many other industries today.

The search for lessons to shape and direct governmental policy followed the Continental incident. Some observers claim that the bank's failure symbolizes the chaos and disorder present in the nation's banking system as laws against interstate banking and separation of commercial banking and securities underwriting weaken. Allowing these patterns to continue would increase the likelihood of future crises and increase the risk of failure to our financial system. Persons of this view argue for a moratorium on all new bank combinations such as nonbank acquisitions and interstate banking.[1]

In the search for meaning in the aftermath of Continental's rescue, another point of view held that Continental might have escaped difficulty in a deregulated market. Unable to grow by statewide or interstate banking or to enter profitable fields such as securities underwriting, real estate, or insurance, Continental was forced to become involved in risky foreign and energy loans in order to seek its growth objectives.[2] This viewpoint supports orderly deregulation of the banking industry.

Events stimulate reconsideration of the relationship between the public and private sectors and often generate controversies based in differing values, in differing economic interests, or in simply differing assumptions about causes and effects. Out of the ensuing dialogue and debate, certain directions emerge. For example, the Continental incident led to a more equitable system of risk-based deposit insurance premiums as well as to increased financial disclosure requirements and closer monitoring of insured banks.[3] Other questions, such as the future of banking deregulation, take longer and perhaps require more experience to shape a political consensus.

As the events leading up to Continental's financial crisis came to light through press interviews, investigative reports, and congressional hearings, some insight into the internal workings of the corporation was also made possible. A picture of a poor internal environment for decision making emerged, including inadequate definitions of responsibilities and goals, defective executive decision making, and refusal to acknowledge internal warnings made by lower level personnel of impending problems and their recommendations for policy changes.[4]

Continental's board of directors was composed of the chief executive officers (CEOs) of successful and highly considered firms: Borg-Warner Corporation, Jewel Companies, IC Industries Incorporated, Baxter Travenol Laboratories Incorporated, Inland Steel Corporation, FMC Corporation, Dart & Kraft Incorporated, De Kalb AgResearch, Incorporated, American Information Technologies Corporation, and — until April 1983 — Deere & Company. Acknowledging that this board had some of the nation's finest businessmen, *Forbes* magazine asked, "What were they doing for their fees?" "Who was watching the store?"[5]

What do these internal and private matters have to do with public policy? First, they bear upon general topics such as the adequacy of internal control in the firm and the legal relationship of employee to employer, which have been issues debated in public policy in recent years. In addition, wherever private management actions bear significantly upon widely accepted public goals, such as the integrity and performance of the country's economic system, public policy discussion is needed to ensure consistency between private actions and public expectations.

The risk to succeed or to fail is normally assumed by individual investors and employees of a firm in the private enterprise system. Today, however, some firms have become sufficiently dominant — and hence powerful — that their failure may have consequences far beyond the persons immediately involved. Continental Illinois was one example. In 1980 Chrysler Corporation was judged to have been another, as the federal government provided a $1.5 billion loan guarantee. Public policy is inevitably a mixture of economic interests and social values. If the stakes are so high that the failure of a single company might potentially lead to the collapse of the banking system or to economic disaster for a region or industry, then decision making in large, dominant firms — the system of decision making that determines if institutions will succeed or fail — becomes a matter of some public interest.

The case for the presence of a public interest in private actions, however, does not specify how widely accepted social goals are or how critical a single company's actions are in relation to them. These questions involve the substance of the debate. Furthermore, governmental action in a particular area may ultimately be judged to create more problems than it solves: many governmental actions may simply not be efficient and effective responses to a given situation.

In an important way Continental Illinois demonstrates the interdependency of public and private interests in our society. Whether the issue at stake is international competitiveness, tax and fiscal policy, health and safety protection, regional economic development, employee relations, or corporate political activity, the presence of a public interest is often argued in the functioning of the private enterprise system. In each of these areas the interaction of private sector actions with the values and aspirations permeating our society is significant.

The Continental situation demonstrates but one small area of interdependence; however, the types of issues it raises are now commonplace and will be consistent ingredients of managers' careers in the coming decades. The specifics may change, but the fundamental ability to deal with the interrelationships of the social, political, and economic dimensions of the business environment — in short, the public policy environment of the firm — will constitute a salient challenge to the next generation of managers.

This discussion leads us closer to the meaning of *public policy* in this book. So far, *governmental action* has been assumed to coincide with *public policy*. However, the context and broader implications of government action are as important as the action itself. Expectations about the relationship between the private economic sector and other perceived social interests are the important elements that will be abstracted from the presence of governmental action or inaction. Thus the loan to Continental was important primarily as public policy: the acknowledged presence of a public interest in the continuity of a dominant firm in the banking system.

The following section presents a more complete framework for understanding points at which public interests bear upon private management.

FRAMEWORK FOR UNDERSTANDING PRIVATE AND PUBLIC SECTOR INTERACTIONS

A model of the operations of a corporation is presented in Fig. 1.1. In this model a series of management practices involving corporate strategy, management systems, and organization are combined to produce a product or service that, upon entering the market, achieves a certain degree of financial performance. A welcome reception in the marketplace leading to successful financial performance for the firm generates cash, which is utilized by management to continue producing marketable products or services.

When this cycle is working effectively, marketplace success ensures the availability of sufficient cash for the organization to modernize the product, improve the service, increase manufacturing efficiency, or make other improvements necessary to meet the demands of a constantly changing marketplace. A negative cycle, on the other hand, means that the management organization is unable to make the changes in products or services necessary in the marketplace, either owing to insufficient resources resulting from a weak market position or owing to ineffectiveness in the process of management itself.

The critical factors in this model are managerial behavior, and as the figure indicates, executive leadership. In other words responsibility for creating a positive or a negative cycle rests with the senior levels of management, and the aspirations, outlooks, and decisions established by that management determine the effectiveness of the organization.

Organizations are conglomerations of different persons and units often holding conflicting goals. The task of management referred to earlier largely consists of attaining a sense of purpose and a set of values strong enough to enable the organization to function at a high level of effectiveness.

This model simplifies a great number of complex and important aspects of management. Obscured within the general topic of strategy, management systems, and organization reside extensive bodies of techniques and knowledge specific to the various fields of management: operations, finance, accounting and control, supervision, marketing, and other areas. These are especially important to efficiency and effectiveness when individuals and units are working toward common objectives.

Fig. 1.1 presents the operations of the firm schematically as a self-contained system. Of course it is not. Numerous factors external to management's control affect the corporation. Several forces external to the firm — competition, the cost of capital, the effectiveness of boards of directors,

FIGURE 1.1   *Model of the Corporate Process*

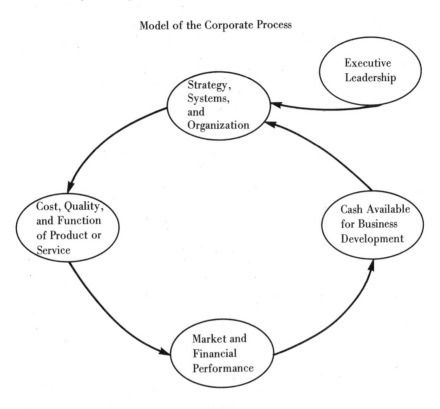

Model of the Corporate Process

and so forth — are identified in Fig. 1.2. These factors represent phenomena outside the internal functions of the firm. Since individual firms, and the private enterprise system as a whole, depend on these external factors, a public interest is often perceived in the interaction between a particular factor and the private enterprise system. Does the country, for example, have sufficient capital formation, manpower, and technology to meet international competition? Let us consider the factors presented in Fig. 1.2 in more detail, discussing the types of considerations often present between a particular factor and the business system.

Industry Competition

The U.S. economic system is founded on the concept that competition requires firms to operate efficiently and to adapt to changes in the marketplace. A large body of public policy called *antitrust* has grown up to address

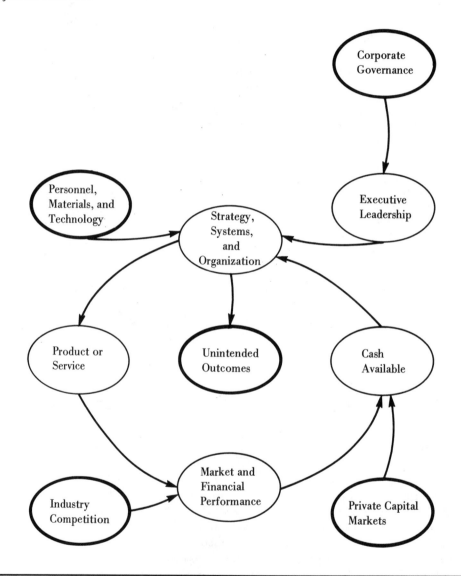

the competitive impact of market structures and trade practices. On the whole this body of legislative, judicial, and regulatory policy attempts to ensure that the economic system fulfills the promise of economic competition. Individual businesspersons may at times feel that antitrust prohibitions offer a defense against the predatory actions of larger, stronger firms. At other times they may seem to be unnecessary and unwelcome restrictions on actions that may truly enhance the functioning of the socioeconomic system. One current realization is that global markets, rather than traditional domestic markets, are an important context for thinking about industry competition. Today's question becomes how to enhance industrial competitiveness in order to participate in worldwide improvements in employment and increase our standard of living.

Capital

Firms typically access external sources of debt and equity in order to finance required fixed assets and working capital. Returns on the firm's financial assets, then, are paid out of the earnings generated by the use of the physical assets purchased. Growth in size of the firm and efforts to compete more efficiently usually require funds generated internally from profit and depreciation to be supplemented by investment from external capital markets.

The cost of private capital is influenced by a host of governmental policies. To the extent government deficits need to be financed, the government is also a borrower in the private capital markets; and the degree of government borrowing is influenced by spending and taxation policies, the level of prosperity in this country and internationally, and this country's willingness to risk increases in inflation by printing money. The exact nature, influence, and interrelations among these factors are themselves subject to continuous analysis and policy debate. Suffice it to say here that, in general, government policy strongly influences the cost of private capital and constitutes a major determinant of the cash available to firms for operations.

Corporate Governance

Smaller firms, which compose the vast majority of U.S. businesses, typically raise their external capital from relatively few sources — a few private investors and direct relationships with a credit institution, usually a bank. The need for capital in larger firms, or in enterprises growing quickly, is often greater than that capable of being provided by such more limited sources, and the firm seeks to market its stock and/or bonds on the public capital markets. In return for receiving considerable investment sums the initial owners reduce their relative ownership share. Many of the largest firms in the United States are almost entirely owned by the general public, although buy outs — returning firms to private ownership — are relatively common today.

Ownership of many of America's largest and most visible companies by the investing public has meant that a broader social or public policy interest has evolved in the system of corporate governance. Typically the owners of the corporation each hold a relatively small portion of the firm and are geographically dispersed and essentially unknown to each other. Yet as owners of the firm they are responsible for hiring, evaluating, and firing management and for seeing that management directs the firm in accordance with their general and specific wishes. If this cannot happen because of the dispersed nature of investors, then management would appear to function unaccountable to anyone, and the integrity and credibility of the institution would be seriously threatened — a potentially dangerous situation for the economic system as a whole. The discussion of how accountability can be established, especially through a group of trustees called a *board of directors,* has come to be an important focus of analysis in the field of business and public policy.

Quality and Availability of Personnel, Materials, and Technology

A large and heterogeneous number of factors that comprise essential ingredients to the effective functioning of the firm are also influenced by public policy. The nation's manpower is shaped by the long-term performance of its educational systems, which are in many cases public and in other cases strongly influenced by public actions. Other topics bearing upon employee-employer relations are also a function of public policy. Minimum wages, collective bargaining and labor relations, provisions for pension fund management, antidiscrimination laws and regulations, and endorsement of employee rights such as protection from unjust dismissal are areas of public-private interaction having influence on personnel and thus on corporate strategies, management systems, and organization.

The availability and cost of material inputs to business are again influenced by various government policies. Actions that involve import quotas or other trade restrictions may increase the cost of goods; others that involve the deregulation of surface transportation appear overall to reduce the cost of materials. Material factors in turn influence the location of suppliers and jobs and in the long run influence the cost and competitiveness of products and services.

Government policy directly influences the investment in, and supply of, new technology in the country by channeling funds to industry, universities, and government laboratories. Patent and copyright policies affect the rates of invention and innovation, as do special provisions of tax law such as the research and development (R & D) tax credit. Innovation — particularly technological innovation — is a driving force behind economic growth and a force to improve the standard of living. While rarely an explicit focus of public policy, governmental actions affect industrial innovation and thus have consequences for the business system.

Unintended Outcomes as a Source of Public-Private Interaction

Fig. 1.2 indicates two outcomes from the operations of a firm. The first is an intended outcome — the cost, quality, and function of a product or service. The second type of result, termed *unintended outcomes,* refers to a large range of interactions of the business system and its environment that become the focus for public policy toward the business system. For example, the following incidents, reported in the business press on a single day, would not be considered atypical:

- Amidst several highly publicized commuter airline crashes, 177 pilots from 16 different airlines were withdrawn from service after the Department of Transportation determined that they were not properly certified.[6]
- At least 25 deaths linked to an antihypertension drug and known to the manufacturer were not reported within the required time period. A major ethical drug firm pleaded guilty to charges of failing to make a timely report on the side effects of an antihypertension drug.[2] In an unprecedented aspect of this case, three former or current employees of the company were charged with the criminal provisions of the Food, Drug, and Cosmetic Act, meaning that they face not only financial penalties but up to one year in prison.[7]
- In the wake of over 2,000 deaths from the accidental leakage of poisonous gases into the surrounding community in Bhopal, India, U.S. Congressmen and administration officials announced an intention to review U.S. policies on the export of hazardous substances.[8]

These examples deal with health and safety issues that arise as unanticipated by-products in the course of doing business. Commercial aircraft do have occasional accidents that may be influenced by lax company policies on pilot training. Certainly a widely supported public interest for ensuring that standards for air safety are developed and maintained could be identified. Likewise, drugs and industrial chemicals can, under certain conditions, threaten life; a public interest also appears to exist here for reducing risk within affordable limits.

Health and safety problems, and a related concern for environmental quality, comprise a large number of unintended outcomes. Literally hundreds of specific problems and controversies could be identified within each of these broad categories. Owing to their common presence in an advanced technological and industrial society, they are frequent issues in the public policy environment of business.

THE SOCIOPOLITICAL ENVIRONMENT OF BUSINESS AND PUBLIC POLICY

Previous sections have presented some dimensions of the role of management and the role of public policy not only in the success of the firm but also in the performance of the private economic system as a whole. Although our framework is growing complex, it is still far too simplified to describe business and public policy relationships adequately. Several final elements need to be added to the discussion before completing this introductory view. Fig. 1.3 includes several dimensions implied in earlier sections and incorporates another level of social and political analysis into our framework.

First, Fig. 1.3 indicates the frequent public policy response to unintended outcomes of economic activity: regulating product safety, setting safety standards in the workplace, or controlling the results of operations such as pollution emission or disposal of hazardous wastes. This, of course, has been an area of considerable governmental action in recent decades. Substantial business expense — fixed investment and operating costs — is required of the private sector to address the unintended outcomes of economic activity. Such requirements in turn channel some of the cash available to the firm into publicly determined uses, as well as influencing the internal strategies, systems, and structures of firms.

Second, the efficient functioning of the private enterprise system generates societalwide benefits. Fig. 1.3 shows this influence with the addition of an outcome entitled "changes in living standards, employment, and quality of life." The task of society as a whole is to organize its public-private relationships and to manage trends so that the performance of the whole system increases living standards, employment, and life quality as rapidly as possible. These results constitute the objectives of the entire system and the long-run end point by which the management of all private and public institutions should be judged.

The final dimension of our growing schema draws attention to the broadest context for understanding public-private relationships and the management of the private firm. This general, contextual factor is referred to as the *ideological, social, and political environment*. These are primarily the values, ideals, and cultural assumptions that underlie a sense of what constitutes the "right" state of affairs and what is to be avoided in a society. Such assumptions, such as the role of individualism, equity, and justice and the relationship of citizen to state, are embedded in the history of the United States. Such cultural assumptions are not always evident and explicit in debating current directions. On an everyday level they are to us more like the surrounding atmosphere: they guide and support all actions but rarely are the object of our direct perceptions.

In a large, heterogeneous, and economically developed society like the United States, differing values and ideals are present and often in conflict. In fact, differing viewpoints on most public policy issues represent

FIGURE 1.3 *Model of the Corporate Process, External Forces, and Sociopolitical Environment*

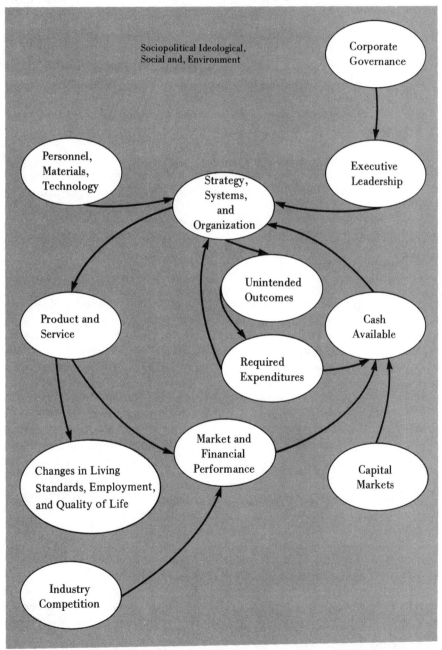

disagreements on underlying values, and differences are resolved through political processes — namely, the distribution and use of power.

The field of business and public policy is replete with controversial issues involving differing values and touching different social interests. Because opposing views on economic questions are only resolved through political processes, an important context for understanding business and public policy is the way that social values and expectations, economic questions, and political decision making intersect. The outer circle in Fig. 1.3 represents the intersection of these general forces.

IMPLICATIONS OF THE FRAMEWORK

This model describes various factors important to the success of the firm. Some lie under the control of the firm's managers; others lie outside the direct influence of the firm. The model leads to the following observations:

1. Governmental action influences the activities of the private enterprise system at numerous points. The functioning of competition, the efficiency of capital markets, and the effectiveness of corporate accountability are large-scale factors vital to the performance of the private market system that have been the focus of public policy. The number and importance of these policy areas reaffirm the interdependence of the private and public sectors.
2. Addressing the unintended outcomes of private activities is another major area of public policy. However, just as there are unintended consequences of private actions, there are also unintended results from governmental policy. In this case, as the public sector attempts to overcome market imperfections in the creation of safety, health, and environmental quality problems, the government influences the use of funds available to the firm and the efforts of managers to create social benefits through improved productivity and new product development. Unintended effects of public policy also illustrate the interdependence of the two sectors.
3. Conflicting value issues underlie our economic system and determine its public policy considerations. Investment and consumption, equity and efficiency, and market process and social justice each need to be balanced in establishing public policy toward business. Such general and abstract questions need to be examined and understood by business leaders.
4. A variety of social and economic interests are influenced by any particular policy question. Consequently the structure and process of political decision making constitute major elements of the managerial environment.
5. The task of management is to perform effectively on multiple levels. The internal workings of the firm are one important context for ex-

ecutive leadership. As other factors bear upon the success of the firm, though, managers are required to adapt the firm to constantly changing circumstances. The ability to address general and vague value issues is paramount, and managers will increasingly be participants in the process of policy analysis and development.

The roles of future managers as they relate to the objectives of this book lead us to the next section which develops this theme more completely.

FOCUS AND OBJECTIVES OF THE BOOK

One characteristic of the field of business and public policy is the absence of settled, resolved questions; few topics are out of bounds for consideration or reconsideration. Rather than a process that has a beginning, a middle, and an end, public policy is continuous and incremental. Assumptions are always open to challenge, and new experience inevitably leads to calls for redirecting governmental action.

Examples of major social change abound: the average age of the population is increasing, service industries rather than traditional manufacturing industries have become the leading source of employment, nearly all industries are deeply affected by global economic competition, major transitions in investment and employment are occurring among regions of the country, problems of social justice and economic equity between age groups, races, and sex groups persist, the effects of modern society threaten supplies of clean water and air. Such changes focus attention on the specific "problems," which are unemployment, loss of international competitiveness, increasing income differentials between rich and poor, preservation of natural resources such as underground water supplies, among others. Sufficient attention to a problem places the issue on the governmental agenda.

Public policy is the surface upon which issues arising from economic and social changes are publicly articulated. A diverse and pluralistic society requires a forum where competing interests and ideals interact to determine the country's direction in countless specific areas.

Given constant change and unending reconsideration of directions, one objective of this book is to prepare future managers to participate in the analysis of policy questions and to help shape the environment of business. A variety of definitions to *the problem* always exist, and multiple criteria are usually relevant for finding solutions. Our effort is to cast issues in fairly broad terms and to stress their long-term and general dimensions. While managers may arrive at any number of recommended actions, the important abilities are to explore diverse criteria for problem definition, to explain the rationale for one's proposed actions, and to maintain an awareness of the multiple consequences of a given action.

Not everyone will agree with a particular problem definition or with specific solutions. Understanding the basis of disagreement, however, holds the promise of refining the discussion and leading to more widely accepted and perhaps more effective outcomes. The first objective of the book, then, is to prepare the manager as a participant in public policy development.

The second objective is to define the manager's role as decision maker and leader within an organization. Just as society as a whole needs to adapt to constant change and transition, so does the manager need to adapt the organization. Public expectations for product performance increase, job loss in a community forces attention to economic strategy, efficient international competitors enter the firm's markets, new laws or court rulings establish fresh ground rules for hiring or releasing personnel, or entry and pricing in the firm's industry is suddenly deregulated. In the face of widespread social, economic, technological, and political changes, the firm must be adaptive. Leadership is demanded that grasps these issues and understands how to forge concepts and management systems to address them. The levers for executing this role — visions, ideals, and processes — are highly intangible. Yet they will determine the success of managing organizational adaptation. The second objective of the book, then, is to prepare managers to adapt their organizations by illustrating the need and showing the possibilities.

TEXT ORGANIZATION

While any organization of topics inevitably fails to reflect the complex interrelationships among issues in the public policy environment of business, a structure for discussion is necessary. Substantive issues in this field are grouped into thematic chapters, and related chapters are grouped into four primary sections.

Today's public policy questions arise in the context of social and cultural traditions in the United States. Our ingrained assumptions about the roles and rights of individuals, for example, lead us to feel much more skeptical about direct governmental guidance of private investment than would citizens of European countries or of Japan. The same sense of individualism and independence seems likely to lead to differing systems of labor management relations and different concepts of the rights of consumers, for instance.

Cultural assumptions and social values influence the definition of *public policy considerations.* They structure the debates, and they shape the country's directions. Consequently our study begins with a broad sweep of business history and the political process in the United States. The role of business in the political system is singled out for attention in this initial section.

These chapters are intended to set the context for examining the more immediate and specific issues of business and public policy in the succeeding chapters. Questions orienting Section I — entitled "The Historical and Political Context of Business" — include:

- What core values are evident in shaping and reshaping today's business-government relationships? How are conflicts between these values expressed in the consideration of public policy toward business?
- What are the significant landmark events in the past course of business-government relations?
- What are the important characteristics of the process of policy-making in the United States? More specifically, how does policy toward business get made?

Section II, entitled "Government Policy in Economic and Social Regulation," addresses economic regulation in the control of market structures and trade practices and social regulation for health and safety objectives. The role of values — fair competition, market efficiency, decentralization of economic power, health and safety — is readily apparent in these topics. Each is a fertile ground for historical discussion and current evaluation, and interesting departures from long-standing traditions are being taken within each field. Questions guiding this survey include the following:

- What economic and social assumptions do our antitrust laws convey? How relevant are these assumptions in today's economic environment? What is our historical experience with applying these laws?
- What are the main points of view in the debate on quality of life? What criteria might be used to decide questions between economics, safety, health, and environmental quality? How should scientific uncertainties influence the discussion?
- What innovative public policies are being evaluated in the area of business regulation?

Section III — "Institutional Management: Governing the Corporation" — casts a conceptual net around questions bearing most directly upon internal decision making in the corporation. This section examines corporate accountability and the role of the board of directors, it reviews the organization and management of auditing and legal professional services in the firm, and it discusses ways of achieving employee-employer integration. Many questions about the firm in society are frequently phrased in terms of ethical behavior. Ethical decision making, a legitimate and important concern for corporate managers, is addressed most directly in the chapters of this section, which pursues these questions:

- What is the origin and the focus of the concern about corporate governance? What has been the rationale and substance of government policy in this area?

- How are auditors and lawyers important to the governance of the firm? How do these professionals represent ethical criteria in management?
- What public policies and corporate practices involve the participation of employees in corporate decision making? How has the law influenced the evolution of employee-employer relationships?

The close tie between social welfare and economic development provides the context for a final grouping of public policy issues. Advancing economic development is an active problem for public and private sector leaders at all levels of society — local and state, national, and international. The nature of the problems in these respective areas and the role of government in each are difficult and yet vital questions before us. The chapters of Section IV — "Public Policy, Private Management, and Economic Development" — derive from the following questions:

- What are the issues and trends in federal, state, and local policies toward regional economic development?
- What role do technological innovation and small business development play in the nation's economic growth? How has government addressed these issues?
- Given an increasingly important global economy, how does government act to assist or impede international trade?
- What are the significant economic, technological, social, and ethical dimensions of direct foreign investment by multinational firms?

Section V, the final section of the book, addresses business leadership in public and private policy development. The first chapter of this section examines corporate political involvement in both electoral and governmental politics; the second is a personal essay summarizing corporate leadership requirements for firm adaptation and social integration. Because both processes apply across the many substantive policy areas discussed in the text, discussion of both has been included in a final section entitled, "Policy Making: Public and Private Roles for Business." The central question in each of these chapters is: What are the roles, responsibilities, and skills for policy making needed by corporations and business leaders in the coming decades?"

DISCUSSION QUESTIONS

1. Select a particular corporation and examine ways in which social expectations and governmental policies both result from and, in turn, influence the firm. Identify particular constraints and opportunities created for the firm by the public policy environment.
2. Describe ways in which you feel the social, economic, or political environment of American business is changing. What demands do these

changes place on corporations and what is the role of the general manager in managing needed adaptation? What needs to occur in the firm and through what process can it come about?

NOTES

1. Jeffrey E. Garten, "Chaos, Not Confidence, Reigns; Congress Must Restore Order," *Wall Street Journal*, May 29, 1984, p. 30.
2. William M. Isaac, "Continental Case Was Handled Well But Shows Need to Push Deregulation," *Wall Street Journal*, May 29, 1984, p. 30; *Congressional Quarterly Weekly Report*, September 15, 1984, p. 2247.
3. Leon E. Wynter, "Formula to Rate a Bank's Riskiness Urged by Treasury," *Wall Street Journal*, January 11, 1985, p. 17.
4. Jeff Bailey, "Continental Illinois Blames 3 Ex-Officers in Report on Penn Square Loan Purchases," *Wall Street Journal*, July 23, 1984, p. 3; Tim Carrington, "Regulators Charged with 'Timid Action on Continental Illinois in House Hearings," *Wall Street Journal*, September 19, 1984, p. 10.
5. Geoffrey Smith, "Who Was Watching the Store?" *Forbes*, July 30, 1984, p. 37–38.
6. Christopher Conte, "U.S. Inspection of Airlines Led to Restrictions," *Wall Street Journal*, December 13, 1984, p. 2.
7. Richard Koenig, "Smith Kline Pleads Guilty to U.S. Charges It Was Slow to Report Drug's Side Effects," *Wall Street Journal*, December 13, 1984, p. 5.
8. Robert S. Greenberger, "Union Carbide Gas Break in India Spurs Debate in Congress on Export Controls," *Wall Street Journal*, December 13, 1984, p.2.

The Historical and Political Context of Business

Each of the thousands of legislative actions, court rulings, and administrative decisions that constitute public policy toward business is anchored in social values and political processes. The purpose of this section is to review the dominant social values and political processes influencing governmental actions. We are concerned with how broad issues bearing upon the private sector are defined and how public-private relations are influenced by large-scale factors.

Chapter 2 traces the contours of business history in the United States, emphasizing the changing character of business-government relations in response to the process of industrialization. Emphasis is placed on the interaction of social, economic and political factors in the business environment. An assessment of current public policies toward business is summarized within the concept of industrial policy.

Changes in business-government relations inevitably result from political processes, and any review of the relationship between these sectors must address policy formulation. Chapter 3 presents a framework for understanding the making of public policy. This framework is applied in two examples of changing public policy toward the private sector. Together, the two chapters of this section serve as context for many of the specific issues and problems discussed in subsequent sections of the book.

Chapter 2

Ideology and Business-Government Relations
An Historical Review

In the late 1700s Thomas Jefferson and Alexander Hamilton, leaders of the infant United States of America, were opponents in a national debate about the role of the federal government in economic matters. It is well known that Jefferson envisioned a decentralized society with an agrarian economy and a limited central government. On the other hand Hamilton favored a stronger and more active government that could stimulate the development of industry: banking, commerce, and manufacturing.

The terms of national discussion today — *environmental quality, import protection, market efficiencies, employee rights, technology policy, reindustrialization, income redistribution* — are different from the terms of debate in the late nineteenth century. However, many of the same questions about the proper role of the public sector remain the focus of controversy. The country's problems have changed and the concepts and tools available to address them are different, but the value issues involved today have much in common with earlier periods.

This chapter reviews the significant strands of ideology comprising the American business system. Ideas and values expressing the aspirations of the society are key to understanding today's managerial environment. Because specific issues and controversies are tied to long-established and abstract beliefs about the proper relationship of business and government, our analysis of the public policy environment begins with a review of early American ideology and its subsequent development.

Individualism is a central value in American society. Religious, political, and intellectual developments in Europe offering the potential for individualism were incorporated into beliefs and American institutions. The chapter's first objective is to show how this value was seeded in the young American Republic and how it has subsequently influenced the development of our business system.

While individualism remains a core value of the society, the process of economic industrialization has stimulated differing interpretations. For example, the concept of justice implied political freedom in the small, agrarian, and relatively homogeneous society of colonial America. Reducing barriers to political freedom enhanced equality; the state's role was to protect political liberty and thereby ensure social justice.

Today, however, in a more diverse and heterogeneous society, *justice* implies social and economic rights as much as it means political freedom. A second objective of this chapter is to review the impact of social and economic change on traditional American values and to examine how traditional values compete in American belief systems today.

These two factors — the value of individualism inherent in the business system and the impact of industrialization on ideology — have influenced major patterns of business-government relations since the founding of the Republic. The historical roles of government and of the business system create constraints and, at the same time, offer potential directions for public policy. A final objective of the chapter is to review major landmarks in the historical relationship between business and government and to outline salient features of the relationship today.

The discussion of these topics is organized by general historical period. First, we examine major intellectual influences prior to and following the establishment of the Republic in the late eighteenth century. This review highlights strands of individualism that will later be important elements of the business creed. It also discusses the forefathers' vision of the government's role in ensuring social order and protecting individual rights.

A second historical slice of this chapter covers the nineteenth century, an important period in the industrialization of the United States. Major social and economic changes took place in that century, and new ideological currents arose to form the American business creed. The nineteenth century witnessed the beginnings of the modern regulative function of the national government as Congress enacted initial pieces of economic legislation dealing with competition, industry concentration, and fair trade practices.

The final section in this historical review summarizes events in the present century. This section reviews major themes of business-government relations and assesses current dimensions of sociopolitical ideology. Today many questions about national goals and about the role of the public sector in the economy are encapsulated in the topic of industrial policy. Discussion in the final section will ask whether business-government relations today constitute an industrial policy.

THE INFANT REPUBLIC: ORIGINS AND EXPRESSIONS OF IDEOLOGY

Many factors would have to be taken into account in a complete review of the origins of America's economic development. The following sections identify several key elements of religious, economic, and political thought that converged to form an ideology from which the role of business later evolved.

Protestant Ethic

America was founded primarily by individuals escaping religious oppression in England; they sought only to live their lives and practice their religion freely. Although fiercely intolerant of deviations from their own beliefs, their great independence and willingness to accept risks and sacrifices characterized the new society.

The substance of the beliefs of the early seventeenth and eighteenth century Americans is often referred to as the *Protestant ethic*. One of the best known and strictest forms of Puritan religion was the doctrine of John Calvin. Calvinists held that man was condemned to depravity and corruption as a result of Adam's fall. A few select persons, however, were chosen by God to be saved. While salvation for these predestined few did not depend on their performing saving works, they could achieve limited atonement for their corrupt natures by following God's will as revealed through the Bible.[1]

Responsibility, diligence, and fulfillment of duty to God were one's life work. Commercial activities were considered a valid means of performing good works; and the Protestant doctrines of hard work, honesty, and responsibility were consistent with successful economic activity. Economic prosperity, in fact, was often considered to be a sign, although not a condition, of predestined salvation. Early Protestant beliefs in responsibility, hard work, and the desirability of wealth offered fertile ground for sowing compatible seeds of thought in science, politics, and economics.

Faith in Science and Empiricism

The seventeenth century intellectual climate saw the development of the belief that human beings could study, decipher, control, and put to their own uses the physical environment. The processes of closely observing physical behavior, of breaking down physical complexity into increasingly detailed classifications, and of constructing general laws of behavior were the methods of the scientific revolution. Its impact was immense; ideologically it fostered faith in human progress, and it reinforced the idea of human freedom by manipulation and control of the physical environment. Practically it encouraged the development and application of technology in work and in the organization of economic enterprise. The belief in science and its applications was undoubtedly a forceful component of American pragmatism — a problem-solving "can do" mentality.

In the United States in the midseventeenth century no figure better represents an integration of philosopher, scientist, businessman, public servant, and statesman than Benjamin Franklin. Benjamin Franklin's life and philosophy express a dominant stream of pragmatism and rationality in the American value system.

The most widely known of all Franklin's writings are the epigrams that constitute his *Poor Richard's Almanac.* A few examples of his wit show the combination of industry, self-reliance, faith in progress, and practical outlook that communicate central American values:

> No gains
> Without pains.
>
> Plough deep while sluggards sleep
> And you shall have corn to
> sell and to keep.
>
> When the well goes dry,
> then we know the worth of water.
>
> No man e'er was glorious
> Who was not laborious.
>
> He that would catch a fish
> must risk his bait.
>
> There was never a good knife
> made of bad steel.[2]

Laws of Nature and Natural Rights

The idea of natural rights forms another critical strand of thought in the tapestry of American ideology. The colonies' break with England and the founding of a new nation were justified by the concept of the natural rights of human beings and the choice to enter, or to withdraw from, a social contract propounded by Rousseau and other political philosophers. American revolutionaries incorporated the related ideas of John Locke about natural human rights and the consent of the governed into the Declaration of Independence. Moreover, Locke's views of the limited role of government influenced the conception and writing of the Bill of Rights. As shown in Insert 2.A from Locke, the role of government is influenced by assumptions about human beings as partial, biased, and largely concerned with their own self-interests. Government's function is to establish and enforce general rules of right and wrong, to ensure individual rights to property, and to adjudicate conflicts among parties overly partial to their narrow interests. Government is justified only on the basis of being able to protect life, liberty, and property better than individuals can ensure these values on their own.

Insert 2.A

FOUNDING CONCEPTS OF HUMAN NATURE AND THE FUNCTIONS OF GOVERNMENT

Seventeenth century British philosopher John Locke believed that a human being by nature had rights to life, political equality, and property. The state should not interfere with these rights, although, owing to man's partial and biased nature, the state needed to protect them. The following quotation reflects Locke's view of the functions and limits of government, a view that influenced Thomas Jefferson and other Founding Fathers of the United States:

> The great and chief end . . . of men uniting into commonwealths, and putting themselves under government, is the preservation of their property: to which in the state of Nature there are many things wanting.
>
> Firstly, there wants an established, settled, known law, received and allowed by common consent to be the standard of right and wrong and the common measure to decide all controversies. For though the law of Nature be plain and intelligible to all rational creatures, yet men, being biased by their interest, as well as ignorant for want of study of it, are not apt to allow of it as a law binding to them in the application of it to their particular cases.
>
> Secondly, in the state of Nature there wants a known and indifferent judge, with authority to determine all differences according to the established law. For every one in that state being both judge and executioner of the law of Nature, men being partial to themselves, passion and revenge is very apt to carry them too far. . . . Thirdly, in the state of Nature there often wants power to back and support the sentence when right and to give it due execution.

SOURCE: John Locke, *Concerning Civil Government* (London: J. M. Dent and Sons, 1924), p. 180. Used with permission.

The Democratic Ideal

The institution of democracy was a central aspiration in the fervor of eighteenth century political liberalism. Faith in the individual, faith in the rule of law, and faith in a secular state were growing elements of European thought that influenced the development of America's democratic political beliefs. America's most outstanding democrat was Thomas Jefferson, author of the Declaration of Independence, third president of the United States, and spokesman for a philosophy of self-government. Jefferson was deeply fearful of tyranny, and he opposed a strong central government in the United States, believing instead that public security could rely on the willingness of every citizen to adopt the defense of the public order as his or her own personal concern.

"Sometimes it is said that man cannot be trusted with the government of himself," said Jefferson. "Can he, then, be trusted with the government of others? Or, have we found angels in the form of Kings to govern him?"[3] The central government, in Jefferson's view, should restrain citizens from injuring each other and otherwise leave them free to pursue their own livelihoods and improvements. State governments are able to administer domestic concerns, and they are the greatest defense against dictatorial tendencies.

To Jefferson, commerce was considered agriculture's handmaiden. Industry and banking were artificial activities; they required centralization of economic and political power, and he deeply distrusted them. Owing to these dangers of industrialization, human virtues and capabilities could best be realized in an agrarian setting.

Jefferson was, above all, a humanist. The opportunity to liberate, enhance, and fulfill the individual provided the justification for democracy, the purpose of a limited government, the reason for strong states' rights, and the value of an agrarian society. "The Jeffersonian theory of democracy was rooted in spiritual and humane, rather than material and economic values," writes political historian Robert McCloskey.

> When he used the term "liberty," the early democrat meant, first of all, freedom of conscience — moral liberty — rather than freedom of business enterprise. His chief interest, in short, was in the right of the individual to realize his moral personality, and not the right to buy and sell and prosper economically.[4]

Mercantilism

As described by historian Louis Hacker, the economy of the colonies was part of a stage of economics known as "mercantilist capitalism" — the view that business, including foreign trade, should be under the complete control of government to achieve maximum state power.[5] Business and government were closely allied in the early American society. Joint stock companies such as the Virginia Company and the Plymouth Company were formed in the seventeenth century to promote settlement, and political power was held by their leaders.[6] In the early days of the Republic private corporations were chartered by national or state legislative action, usually granting monopolies for the development of roads, canals, or bridges. For example, between 1780 and 1801 a total of 317 separate enterprise charters were granted in the states: 66 percent were for enterprises related to transport; 20 percent were for banks or insurance companies; 10 percent were for local public services, such as water supply; and general business corporations constituted less than 4 percent of the total.[7] Corporations, licensed by the states to serve community needs for economic development, were granted monopolies and supervised by the public sector.

While a dominant role of government in economic development was not uncontested, the guiding hand of the central government was a primary element of economic activity in the country's first half century. The most forceful spokesman for development of industry, banking, and commerce as a matter of national policy was Alexander Hamilton, the political foe of Thomas Jefferson. Hamilton advocated a strong central government whose role was to promote industry and commerce actively. Historian Arthur Schlesinger outlines the major components of the Hamiltonian program:

> The essence of Hamilton's policy was to transfer capital to those most likely to make use of it to increase the national productive power. . . . His Report on Manufactures was the first grand expression of the industrial vision of America; and the Hamiltonian program — the United States Bank, the assumption of the state's debts, the protective tariff — was precisely designed to give capital to those who could be relied upon to put it to vigorous use. The task of government, as he saw it, was to guide economic activity while at the same time inciting individual energy.[8]

Until the 1830s the beliefs of Alexander Hamilton in a strong central government and a partnership with business that would promote economic development were strongly influential in national policy.

In summary there was no "business creed" in the days of the early Republic. The founders of the country were initially concerned with freedom from religious oppression and later with political independence from England. New ideas about science and rationality and new doctrines of natural rights contributed to the emergent American value that placed individual liberty on the highest plane. For the most part discussion well into the latter part of the eighteenth century concerned the colonies' relationship to England and ways to prevent political oppression in the new Republic. Only as independence was achieved and principles of the new government were decided did questions of economics begin to move to the foreground of policy issues. Adam Smith's famous *The Wealth of Nations*[9] was published in 1776 and was probably not widely known in the United States until after the turn of the century. Hamilton's influential report on the role of the central government in the development of national wealth through industry was not published until 1791.

The role of business was not an issue in the earliest period of this country's history. State licensing of corporations for monopoly control of trade was an accepted and noncontroversial practice. Economic transactions were small scale and relatively simple; political doctrines and structures were far more widely discussed and disputed. Most important, personal freedom was established as bedrock value upon which fresh ideas and a dynamic and diverse economy could be built.

NINETEENTH CENTURY INDUSTRIALIZATION: CAPITALISM AND THE DEVELOPMENT OF THE AMERICAN BUSINESS CREED

The Rise of Capitalism as a Centerpiece of Economic Ideology

The first third of the nineteenth century was a period of geographic expansion and of the beginnings of an industrial economy. By the end of the century these developments had gained enormous momentum, and the basic structure of what would become the world's largest and most diverse national economy had been established. Industrial development was encouraged by the premises of the Hamiltonian program: creation of efficient transportation through railroads and canals, encouragement in settling the West, tariff protection for developing domestic industries, and creation of a national bank. As the beginnings of economic development were aided by the pragmatism and independence of the American character and by a responsive public sector, economic progress, in turn, had a important influence on political attitudes and business ideology.

Trade and commerce prospered in the early 1800s in the expanding country, and beginnings of basic industries in mining, transportation, and small-scale manufacturing were evident. Economic development was of a magnitude sufficient to influence the configuration of national political forces. By the 1830s an agrarian distrust of growing banking and manufacturing power expressed itself in the populism of Andrew Jackson. Populist sentiment would reemerge periodically to influence public policy in the succeeding years. This movement was a political expression of distrust of unbridled industrialization. It is no accident that Jackson vetoed the renewal of the charter of the Second United States Bank, which had become a symbol of the nascent industrial state. He articulated a new style of business-government relations in which the national government was a counterweight and a control on the impact of industrialization. Commenting on the significant shift in business ideology in the 1830s, Schlesinger wrote:

> The politics of the Jackson period was a traumatic experience for businessmen. The result was to make business reconsider the whole mercantilist assumption that positive government was a good thing. In the new economic system context, businessmen no longer saw an economic need for governmental activism. Under the stern eye of Jackson, they began to discern a belated charm in the Jeffersonian proposition that the government was best which governed least.[10]

The earlier pattern of state licensing of private corporations through legislative action also changed dramatically in this period. A heightened level of business formations and an increasing diversity of economic activity made state control of business impractical and undesirable. By the 1840s most states had moved to general incorporation laws that placed the realm of business more into the sphere of market competition.

Not only had quickening economic activity reduced the role of the state in a growing business system by midcentury, but the precepts of capitalism as an economic ideology had become more widely dispersed and had begun to take root in American intellectual currents. The vision of economic well-being incorporated in the principles of laissez-faire economics outlined by Adam Smith coincided neatly with the pragmatic opportunity offered in America and the values afforded by the American character.

The principles of capitalism are an indisputable, vital element within major Americal ideological foundations. Most important, this concept showed how economic freedom, guided by the single-minded pursuit of self-interest, leads to economic efficiency and growth and to an orderly society. This process, generally referred to as the *invisible hand*, requires each individual to offer something someone will buy, causing the overall mix of goods and services by producers to equal the economic needs of buyers. Economic transactions are direct and simple; when each individual freely sees opportunities and independently adjusts his or her production and consumption, the whole economic system, by definition, enhances the general welfare. Individual decisions are decentralized, private, and voluntary, whereas aggregate benefits are maximized.

Of course, the tenets of capitalism are more extensive than just requirements for economic liberty and the pursuit of self-interest. In addition to property rights, at least four conditions should be added: (1) free prices of goods, labor, and capital, with fluctuations of these serving as signals to persons to allocate their resources and their labor to areas of greatest demand relative to available supply; (2) unhampered physical movement of labor and capital; (3) profit, which provides motivation for risk and innovation, and financial return for successful management of capital; and (4) interfirm competition, which places stringent requirements on the efficiency of individual producers.

The compatibility of the capitalistic economic concept with the following ideological elements is clear: faith in the individual and belief in freedom, progress by control over the physical environment, the sanctity of property and a limited function of government, and the condition of political equality. These elements, although presented as independent strands, were interwoven and mutually compatible; an unusual confluence of ideas converged in the young Republic, forming the basis for an economy that would achieve unsurpassed scale and diversity. All are dimensions of an American ideology perhaps best captured in this single word: *individualism.*

Emergence of the Business Creed

The period of American history from the Civil War through the first decade of the twentieth century has variously been labeled as the "economic takeoff" stage of the U.S. economy or as the "age of enterprise." It was the period of conversion from an agrarian, commercial nation into an urban, industrial nation. An industrial economy was formed — an economy that, in today's more advanced and mature stage, continues to express aspects of large and market-dominant firms formed in this early industralization. It was also the time in which America achieved the responsibilities and problems of a world power that was becoming a symbol of political and economic freedom.

Perhaps there is no better manifestation of the American creed of this period than the imagery and heroism of Horatio Alger: industrious, honest, and optimistic. As a cultural model Alger epitomized the virtues of self-reliance and individualism within the free enterprise system. Popular magazines at the turn of the century expressed similar beliefs and values. Take, for instance, the appeal of the *Saturday Evening Post* in reflecting and interpreting the American business creed. Insert 2.B from the classic *Letters of Post* editor George Lorimer during the magazine's sensational growth in the 1890s illustrates this popularization and idealization of business life.

Insert 2.B

THE BUSINESS ETHOS IN THE LATE NINETEENTH CENTURY

The spirit of business in the age of enterprise, as popularized in George H. Lorimer's *Letters from a Self-Made Merchant to His Son,* was a lively and down-to-earth statement of the American business creed. In the following excerpt the merchant, owner of a Chicago meat-packing business, is mildly

Insert 2.B   *continued*

admonishing his son, Pierrepont, who is undertaking his first sales trip for the company.

Chicago, April 10, 189_

Dear Pierrepont: You ought to be feeling mighty thankful today to the fellow who invented fractions, because while your selling cost for last month was within the limit, it took a good deal of help from the decimal system to get it there. You are in the position of the boy who was chased by the bull — open to congratulations because he reached the tree first, and to condolence because a fellow up a tree, in the middle of a forty-acre lot, with a disappointed bull for company, is in a mighty bad fix.

    I don't want to bear down hard on you right at the beginning of your life on the road, but I would feel a good deal happier over your showing if you would make a downright failure or a clean-cut success once in a while, instead of always just skinning through this way. It looks to me as if you were trying only half as hard as you could, and in trying it's the second half that brings results. If there's one piece of knowledge that is of less use to a fellow than knowing when he's beat, it's knowing when he's done just enough work to keep from being fired. . . . You've got to know your goods from A to Izzard from snout to tail, on the hoof and in the can. You've got to know 'em like a young mother knows baby talk, and to be as proud of 'em as the young father of a twelve-pound boy, without really thinking that you're stretching it four pounds. You've got to believe in yourself and make you buyers take stock in you at par and accrued interest. You've got to have the scent of a bloodhound for an order, and the grip of a bulldog on a customer. You've got to feel the same personal solicitude over a bill of goods that strays off to a competitor as a parson over a backslider, and hold special services to bring it back into the fold. You've got to get up every morning with determination if you're going to go to bed with satisfaction. You've got to eat hog, think hog, dream hog — in short, go the whole hog if you're going to win out in the pork-packing business.

SOURCE: George Horace Lorimer, *Letters from a Self-Made Merchant to His Son* (Boston: Small, Maynard, 1902), pp. 141–43.

The late nineteenth century saw the grafting of a new ideological dimension, "social Darwinism," which has influenced our present ideas of competition and success. In 1859 Charles Darwin published *The Origin of the Species*,[11] which explained the process of evolution through detailed and extensive analyses of animal anatomy, behavior, and distribution. Darwin showed that natural variations occurring within a species are better or more poorly adapted to environmental circumstances and determine the species' chances for survival or extinction.

Social theory based on Darwin's observations of the process of animal evolution stated the inevitability of conflict and competition among social groups. In the last third of the nineteenth century in the United States, sociologist William Graham Sumner widely espoused this view of natural selection in society.[12] In his analysis individuals most fit to survive economic competition would rise to the top of society, and the less fit would gradually become extinct. This view could easily be called upon to justify a notion of class superiority and indifference to the lot of the lower economic sectors of society.

Various tenets of nineteenth century social Darwinism — natural selection and class superiority — are discredited today. This social philosophy, however, did reinforce the sanctity of unrestrained economic action and praised wealth's preference for economic values over humanitarian and social concerns.

At least the *implication* of competition deserves to be highlighted because of its central place in our present ideals for the economic system. Darwin's observation of limited resources and adaptive survival among animal species parallels the individualism basic to laissez-faire economic ideology. "Survival of the fittest," arising from the sphere of biological behavior, became an attractive economic slogan.

The widespread acceptance of social Darwinism signified that competition took hold of the American mind in the explosion of economic activity in the last half of the nineteenth century. The concept of competition, a form of American individualism, has become deeply ingrained in the American mentality and is a cornerstone of public policy toward the business sector, as well as a fundamental tenet of American free enterprise.

The element of social Darwinism in the American business creed is not the only influential view in America of social relations. Another point of view encourages civic participation and fulfillment of responsibilities to the wider community, neighborhood, or even nation. This is the philosophy of *voluntarism* — the notion that individuals have an obligation to contribute to the wider society from whose quality and strength everyone benefits. This value system underlies the development of philanthropic institutions in America and is the basis for a high level of individual voluntary participation in civic organizations.

In another sense this quality has been termed *enlightened self-interest*.

Alexis de Tocqueville, a perceptive observer of the American nation in the 1840s, was intrigued by the maintenance of community within the spirit of individualism. Wary of the selfish and isolating side of American individualism, he observed a widespread instinct to balance personal interests with broader responsibility. He termed this "self-interest properly understood." Although intangible, attitudinal, and perhaps delicate, this dimension offers a context for the ethical practice of early capitalism and a background to the "social responsibility of business" today. De Tocqueville wrote:

> The Americans . . . enjoy explaining almost every act of their lives on the principle of self-interest properly understood. It gives them pleasure to point out how an enlightened self-love continually leads them to help one another and disposes them freely to give part of their time and wealth for the good of the State.

> The doctrine of self-interest properly understood does not inspire great sacrifices, but every day it prompts some small ones: by itself it cannot make a man virtuous, but its discipline shapes a lot of orderly, temperate, moderate, careful, and self-controlled citizens. . . . Every American has the sense to sacrifice some of his private interests to save the rest.[13]

One of the hallmarks of an expanding, urbanizing, increasingly mobile society may be a growing tension between different social values. Acquisitive drives may conflict with humanitarian values; unrestrained self-interest conflicts with enlightened self-interest. At some irreducible level money versus morality may be a conflict inherent in the system.

De Tocqueville's observation of "self-interest properly understood" is probably a workable solution to this inherent dilemma; it offers a means for moderating the pursuit of immediate self-interest with an appreciation for others' needs, and it accepts the importance of a long-term melding of interests. This solution to capitalism's ethical challenge also has the advantage of drawing upon traditional principles of individual initiative and voluntarism, focal dimensions of the traditional American ideology.

However, this ethical stance may weaken as managers are no longer owners of the firm, as a host of intermediaries — salesmen, purchasers, personnel specialists, public relations staff — intervene between managers and the various constituencies of the corporation, and as social and economic factors lead to less direct identification among owners, employees, and particular communities. Persons, not roles, experience social obligations and can act in an enlightened manner; yet modern institutions may be maintained as much by complex role interactions as by stable personal relationships.

Business and Government in the Last Half of the Nineteenth Century

Beginning during the Civil War and continuing in its role in world affairs, the U.S. government stimulated, relied upon, and required a strong, diverse, technically progressive, industrial economy.[14] Demand for armaments, clothing, food, and transportation to create and supply a national defense became a major factor in industrial development. The government's role as purchaser of goods and services had major consequences for business opportunities and economic structure. "War contracts fostered large-scale production," states one analyst of this period, "and their proceeds put large amounts of capital into entrepreneurs' hands."[15] The fiscal role of the federal government was vastly expanded in the Civil War period, permanently altering the role of government in the business environment.

Government support for industrial development took several forms in the second half of the nineteenth century. In addition to a vast expansion of purchased services, government favored industry by erecting high protective trade barriers. The Morrill Tariff Act of 1861 and the McKinley Tariff Act of 1890 were justified as protecting agricultural and manufacturing "infant industries" as well as justified on the grounds of protecting American employment.[16] In addition, the Morrill Act established an extensive and unique program of support for the agriculture industry, including land grant educational programs, public sector agricultural extension services, and agricultural research support.

Prior to and during the Civil War, various states began to exercise power — such as levying taxes and regulating rates in the industries of railroading, insurance, and meat packing. Neither national laws nor judicial rulings were available to guide and standardize the degree of control states should have over private corporations, nor was any mention of corporate rights or obligations made in the Constitution or the Bill of Rights. Laissez-faire capitalism and democracy had been implanted in the agrarian society and were now being swept into an industrial structure. Given the pervasiveness of the corporate institution, a solution to the issue of public and private rights would have to be invented during the industrial expansion of the late 1800s.

The Fourteenth Amendment contained the clause: "nor shall any State deprive any person of life, liberty or property without due process of law." This statement, which declared blacks as citizens of the United States and gave them equal protection of the laws, also came to be interpreted in the courts as a protection of corporate property from state intervention. After giving early support to the concept of state regulation, the Supreme Court reversed itself in several critical cases in the late 1800s and accepted the definition of *person* to include corporations, thus protecting them from state interference.[17]

This series of decisions prevented states from levying corporate taxes or otherwise regulating business activities, holding such actions to be violations of Fourteenth Amendment rights to liberty and property. Insert 2.C illustrates the Supreme Court's reasoning in a case where New York State passed a law to regulate bakers' working hours. Judicial restraint or conservatism was an important factor in American industrial development.

Even as the states were prohibited from regulating industry for a period of time, industrialization saw the beginning of the regulatory function of the federal government. The Interstate Commerce Commission Act of 1887 established regulation of the railroads; and the Sherman Act (1890), Clayton Act (1914), and Federal Trade Commission Act (1914) challenged monopoly market power, anticompetitive mergers, and collusive behavior. These statutes were intended to preserve a concept of competition within a more decentralized economic structure — a structure that had been altered by the dramatic growth of firms and by widespread merger and consolidations among them. Business historian Alfred Chandler argues that it was the small shippers and businessmen in out-of-the-way communities that insisted on government regulation of railroad rates.[18] Similarly, the small manufacturers and general wholesalers, whose businesses were threatened by the market power of large firms, were the advocates of antitrust and trade regulation.

In summary the nineteenth century saw the emergence both of a coherent business philosophy in the United States and an economy of international scale and importance. The process of industrialization created changes in economic scale and scope that influenced a realignment of earlier ideologies. By the early twentieth century the Jeffersonian premise of limited government had been married to Hamilton's desire for a strong industrial state and infused with the ideology of economic capitalism. In varying degrees these ingredients today represent the conservative strand of American ideology. On the other hand Jefferson's belief in moral and social development became fused with Hamilton's reliance on a strong central government to create the modern liberal tradition in American thought.

The liberal and conservative political traditions in America share common values, such as a distrust for centralized power, which perhaps

---

Insert 2.C

JUDICIAL RESTRAINT ON STATE ACTION AT THE TURN OF THE CENTURY: LOCHNER V. NEW YORK

In 1897 the New York state legislature passed a bill limiting hours of work of employees in bakeries to no more than 10 hours a day or more than 60 hours in a week, based on the observation of a substantial incidence of respiratory disease and a generally shortened life-span among bakers. This legislative action also assumed that the state held the power necessary to secure public health, safety, and welfare and to regulate the activities of

Insert 2.C   continued

individuals and businesses to these ends. This particular law was upheld in the New York State court system and was appealed to the U.S. Supreme Court, which decided the case in 1904.

In a 5–4 decision the Supreme Court found the New York labor law unconstitutional. Not only did the law limit the freedom of individuals to work for as long as they might want in the pursuit of their livelihoods, but it violated the right of freedom of contract of business to purchase labor. Although the Court allowed that "reasonable" conditions for state action may exist, it found none in the particular case.

This famous decision is important not only for illustration of the use of the Fourteenth Amendment to limit state regulation of business in this period but also for the contrast it offers with present-day acceptance of public regulation of business for health and safety, legislated by the federal government and suported by the courts. Several excerpts from the majority decision follow:

> The statute necessarily interferes with the right of contract between the employer and employees, concerning the number of hours in which the latter may labor in the bakery of the employer. The general right to make a contract in relation to his business is part of the liberty of the individual protected by the Fourteenth Amendment of the Federal Constitution. Under that provision no State can deprive any person of life, liberty, or property without due process of law. The right to purchase or to sell labor is part of the liberty protected by this amendment. . . .

> There is, in our judgement, no reasonable foundation for holding this [state action] to be necessary or appropriate as a health law to safeguard the public health or the health of the individuals who are following the trade of a baker. . . .

> There must be more than the mere fact of the possible existence of some small amount of unhealthiness to warrant legislative interference with liberty. It is unfortunately true that labor, even in any department, may possibly carry with it the seeds of unhealthiness. But are we all, on that account, at the mercy of legislative majorities? . . . No trade, no occupation, no mode of earning one's living, would escape this all-pervading power, and the acts of the legislative . . . might seriously cripple the ability of the laborer to support himself and his family.

SOURCE: Lochner v. New York, 198 U.S. 45 (1904).

helps to explain why the United States has been relatively invulnerable to the appeals of extreme political parties. The former worries more about concentrated power in private hands, whereas the latter is more concerned with excessive control in the hands of government. Both value individualism, although the liberal favors potential for growth of the disenfranchised individual (often by public intervention), whereas the conservative seeks individual fulfillment in unrestrained economic activity. Transformations of the economy and society have led to realigned expressions of traditional values.

While it is important to identify the spectrum of political beliefs in the United States, particularly concerning the role of the government in economic affairs, it is equally important to point out that through the first third of the twentieth century government played a relatively minor role in the business system. Compared with counterparts such as Germany, Japan, or France, the American government's actions in areas such as trade protection, industry regulation, or sponsorship of the agricultural industry were relatively limited and indirect forms of involvement.

The late nineteenth and early twentieth centuries saw the beginnings of sociopolitical issues, national defense and security, and international competitiveness, which represent major dimensions of business-government relations today. The changing American economy, a global environment much altered by two world wars, and a shifting of world economic power have given rise to questions of whether and how government should assist, control, or decontrol the business system. We now turn to examine business ideology and business-government relations in this modern period.

THE TWENTIETH CENTURY: IDEOLOGY AND THE SHIFTING ROLES OF THE PUBLIC AND PRIVATE SECTORS

Public policy today toward business in part represents an extension of earlier themes. Policies supportive of the business sector — tariff protection, assistance to the agricultural industry, and government procurement — can be readily identified. On the other hand government regulation of the social consequences of industrialization — an agenda initiated in the nineteenth century but deferred until the twentieth — has become widespread and also widely controversial.

These topics, each reviewed briefly below and further developed in succeeding chapters of the book, lead us to the central question of the Jefferson-Hamilton debate in the late 1700s: What should the government's role be in the country's economic system? Although questions of economy and society are exceedingly more complex today, governmental action is an issue in trying to solve modern problems of economic efficiency and growth, social equity, and international competitiveness. To a large extent the question of whether the United States has, or should have, an industrial policy is a relevant point of reference in a review of twentieth century business-government relations.

Direct Governmental Involvement: Policies and Programs

Two striking and somewhat contradictory trends may be observed about direct governmental involvement in the business system. The first is the remarkably minor amount of public ownership in the United States. In many countries of the world, industrialized as well as developing, the public owns basic industries — telecommunications, railroad, and utilities. Although public ownership exists in the United States, it more commonly plays a minor role, with the single exception of the postal service.[19] The American style has relied more on regulating the price and entry conditions of certain industries while leaving them in private hands. Moreover, the environment of deregulation in public policy in the 1970s and 1980s has led to a significant decrease of price and entry control by the public sector.

While the United States has seen a few large-scale experiments with public economic agencies such as the Tennessee Valley Authority, these examples are more notable for their absence in this country. Arguments for governmental industrial policy today typically call for public financing of targeted industries justified by either the need to modernize, the opportunity to export, or the desire to preserve jobs in the face of foreign competition. Note, however, that these arguments favor weaker forms of government involvement than public ownership, a more common form of public action elsewhere.

The second striking feature about the American system is the high degree of government influence on business. This is not involvement due to doctrine, tradition, or intention; rather it is uncoordinated and usually suggests public responses to specific and limited problems. The government *indirectly* supports the business sector. Public sector sponsorship of agricultural research, educational programs, extension work, and price support programs continues to assist the agriculture industry. Large-scale funding of university research contributes to technology-driven industries. The space program, with its great industrial potential, has until recently been entirely public. And development and maintenance of the nation's infrastructure of roads, bridges, ports, and sewers are public functions.

One major area of *direct* business-government integration is procurement; the government's purchase of goods and services from the private sector totaled $166.4 billion in 1984.[20] Government procurement has grown in this century as defense needs have been judged to have increased and as the requirements of the public sector have grown. In 1983 the federal government was budgeted to spend over $43 billion on R & D alone; federal funding of industrial R & D was expected to represent 23.6 percent of that amount.[21] Such funds are spent disproportionately on defense-related projects and support proportionately more technical work at large firms. In 1984 the Defense Department's R & D budget totaled $29.3 billion: approximately 66 percent of the total federal R & D budget.[22] Firms employing over 10,000 employees have consistently received more than 80 percent of the overall federal R & D dollars awarded to industry since 1970.[23] While such patterns do not constitute deliberate "industrial policies," they do characterize a salient dimension of business-government relations.

A number of credit programs, often called *off-budget programs,* exist in support of specific industries or particular issues. Loans at less-than-market rates are provided to the housing industry, for example, through the Federal Home Loan Bank Board or the Veterans Administration Program of low-interest home loans. Other large loan programs involve farming, rural electrification, guaranteed student loans, and the Export-Import Bank.

By 1983 the federal government had committed over $531 billion in loan and credit guarantees through numerous federal lending programs.[24] The large $1.2 billion loan guarantee to Chrysler received headlines for a period, but the less visible credit programs are more typical of continuing business-government relations. Special aid in the form of low-interest loans has been given to companies, and cash benefits have been given to their employees when the firms are judged to have been significantly harmed by foreign competition.

Government assists business in other ways as well. Favorable loan rates are provided to private sector projects having promise of creating employment in urban centers. Not infrequently, the government provides trade protection to industries by administering tariffs or imposing quotas through negotiation with foreign governments.

The programs mentioned above refer to federal programs alone. State and local governments replicate many federal credit and procurement programs and often add others of their own. While the predominance of activities and funds involved pertain to the national government, the public sector at the local level also supports business in numerous ways.

Does this wide range of public programs in support of business mean that the United States has a policy toward industry? Does it say that America intentionally fosters the development of the private sector? On the contrary. This array of activities shows disjointed and unplanned public responses. These programs constitute little more than a collection of actions stimulated by special interests, conflicting ideologies, threatening external events, and largely unproven beliefs about how to solve social problems through public action. Moreover, they often conflict with other ways in which the government restricts or constrains the private sector. While the amount and extensiveness of the government's support for the business sector is immense, it lacks the quality of intentional design or even coordination.

Direct Governmental Constraints: The Regulatory Environment

Earlier we noted that by the late nineteenth and early twentieth century a social agenda was created as a consequence of the process of industrialization in the United States. Given the emergence of a business ideology at this time, the social agenda was largely deferred into the present century. Dramatic change in the role of government occurred in the 1930s. The endorsement of labor organization as a legitimate institution and the passage of securities regulation were two historical events in the changed relationship of the public and private sectors. Since then, social legislation involving worker safety, employee pensions, anti–discriminatory employment practices, truth in advertising and in lending, product safety, air and water pollution, and numerous other subjects has flowed from Washington. There is no doubt that the social agenda generated from the process of industrialization has been fully joined in this century. Insert 2.D illustrates the emergence of a recent regulatory issue — certification of day-care centers — and shows the type of controversy surrounding it. The enormous extent to which society has responded to this social issue serves as a major constraint on the private enterprise sector.

Again, is the development of a large and imposing regulatory environment a matter of coherent public policy? The fragmented, limited, and occasionally conflicting nature of laws and regulations concerning social objectives indicates that public policy is not universally agreed upon here either. Rather than a set of consistently applied principles, the growth of government regulation is a case-by-case, issue-by-issue response to the unintended consequences of our modern industrial economy.

The postponement of the involvement of government until well into this century has, in the analysis of business historian Alfred Chandler, influenced the tenor of business-government relationships. In Chandler's view the adversity between the private and public sectors in America is due to the early establishment of a large managerial hierarchy in business prior to the growth of the civil service during and after the Great Depression. For example, even by 1929 the total number of nonpostal government employees in Washington was about 200,000, substantially less than the employee size of U.S. Steel, General Motors, or Standard Oil of New Jersey at that time. Chandler states that "because two sets of administrative hierarchies grew at different periods of time for different reasons to carry out different functions with different objectives, two quite different cultures appeared."[25] In contrast, public and private administration developed in parallel in Europe and Japan, and a close examination of their industrial history reveals specific factors conducive to a more cooperative relationship.

Chandler's thesis conforms with the ideological pattern emerging at the end of the nineteenth century. The postponed growth of American public administration might, in part, be due to the business ideology that took hold in the nineteenth century. Government entered the picture more

Insert 2.D

DAY-CARE STANDARDS: TO REGULATE OR NOT TO REGULATE

Widely publicized charges of sexual abuse of children in New York and California in mid-1984 led to heightened calls for federal regulation of day-care businesses. Proponents pointed to regulation of many areas of personal safety in our society and to the absence of standards for child care. On the other hand no evidence existed to show that child abuse or neglect was any more prevalent in day care than other youth settings or activities.

The national government's role was anything but clear as some church groups, many state officials, and some parts of the industry strongly opposed federal action.

At least one fact was undisputed by all parties: the dramatic growth of the day-care industry since the late 1970s. Between 1977 and 1984 the number of children five years old or younger whose mothers were employed has grown to 10 million — a 50 percent increase. According to one expert, 52 percent of the mothers of children six years or younger were working outside the home. In 1982, 30,750 places had child care as their primary source of income.

Standards for child care are subject to state regulation and, in many areas, to state licensing. They vary widely. Only an estimated 25 percent of the employees in child-care operations in the United States have had professional training in working with children, and proponents of regulation claim that rapid industry growth has permitted unqualified persons to find employment in this field. Some experts argue that state standards can be sufficiently lax that it is possible to operate without a license at all.

Opponents counter that uniform standards are unnecessary and would be costly. Regulation of supervisor-child ratios and staff qualifications would raise prices considerably, restricting child-care services to higher-income groups. Furthermore, some persons argue that competitive forces of the marketplace would lead businesses with poorer services to fail. In addition, persons at some church-affiliated centers charge that federal regulation would infringe, unconstitutionally, on their religious freedom.

Arguments on the merits and drawbacks of day-care regulation echo many other questions of governmental response to social concerns. Common to numerous other situations, this policy debate is shaped by social and economic changes, and in all probability public opinion would be strongly influenced by the outcomes of several cases of child molestation moving slowly through the courts.

SOURCE: Robert Lindsey, "Increased Demand for Day Care Prompts a Debate on Regulation," *New York Times,* September 2, 1984, pp. 1, 16.

actively in the 1930s in the context of an established business system. At this point actions for social improvement meant an "intervention" into the business system; in seeking social goals government tended to restrict, rather than aid, corporations.

If the 1930s marked a modern period of government activism in the economy, the late 1970s and early 1980s are most significant for a reappreciation for the role of market processes and the weaknesses of government intervention. Industry deregulation in the last decade serves as a significant example of the return to less, rather than more, government involvement in the economy. By the 1970s a serious challenge to the efficiency and effectiveness of the independent commissions primarily in the airline, trucking, shipping, communications, and banking industries had been mounted, and a rather rapid movement to return these industries to the free market swept through the Congress. This movement shows the presence of a powerful intellectual force in the United States supporting the reign of market discipline, and it suggests that any dimension of business-government relations, no matter how long-standing, is open to challenge, reevaluation, and change.

The country has a commitment to assistance and to restraint, and to the values of market efficiency and social equity. The inclusion of multiple values in the American system leads to public policies that are specific rather than general, limited rather than inclusive, and multiple rather than few.

An Emergent Government Role in Macroeconomic Management

The management of the overall economy has risen to the fore in this century as a preeminent dimension of business-government relations. The field of economics has created new understandings of the interrelationship and impact of government spending and interest rates, money supply growth and inflation, and tax rates and economic growth. Government policy has considerable influence on the realization of the nation's goals for low unemployment, price stability, and international competitiveness. Because public policy results from numerous and often conflicting interests, because economic decisions invariably require painful trade-offs, and because economics remains an inexact science, policy directions for macroeconomic management are rarely clear-cut and noncontroversial. The importance of decisions in this area to the business system, as well as the ambiguity that often surrounds policy choices, makes macroeconomic policy the subject of continuing analysis and debate.

The premises of macroeconomic policy that have been followed more or less consistently since the 1930s are generally referred to as *Keynesian* or *demand management policies*. In this view government spending plays a key role in stimulating sufficient demand for goods and services, which draws investment into productive use. The role of the Federal Reserve

Bank is to increase the money supply sufficiently to provide credit for business expansion.

With the U.S. economy seeming to be mired in high inflation, high unemployment, and low economic growth in the 1970s, an alternative series of assumptions about macroeconomic management gradually emerged from the conservative wing of the Republican party. Rather than stimulate demand, the government should encourage an adequate supply of private capital to renew and rebuild the productive sector of the economy. Marginal tax rates should be lowered to allow for savings and investment and to provide incentives for greater personal effort. Inflation should be controlled by tighter management of the money supply, and government spending should be drastically reduced.

Whatever the specific focus of discussion about the proper roles of fiscal and monetary policies, the importance of government decisions in managing the national economy is great. Immediate consequences for businesses that are influenced by these actions include the cost of capital, the value of the dollar on world markets, and the rate of real economic growth. While economic management is not controllable from the standpoint of the individual manager, it is an aspect of government policy with major ramifications for business.

American Ideology in the Late Twentieth Century

Observing American democracy in the first half of the nineteenth century, de Tocqueville saw a close and mutually supportive relationship between liberty and equality. In a relatively simple and small-scale society, these values were considered in solely a political context. In a *political* sense greater equality means greater personal freedom since fewer people are restrained by barriers to equality, such as property, race, or sex restrictions on voting. This identity of equality and freedom in American politics has allowed the nation to push back periodically the barriers to equality in the name of freedom. De Tocqueville's comment that "men will be perfectly equal because they are entirely free."[26] has been taken seriously in the United States.

While equality and freedom may be complementary in a democratic political system, they appear to compete in an *economic* context: economic liberty leads to inequalities of wealth, as the economic context determines winners and losers. On the other hand the enforced economic equality of socialism implies control over all facets of the economy, and a leveling of life conditions among all persons vastly reduces their personal liberties.

Today's economic trade-off between equality and freedom is not simple. *Income transfers* — or the redistribution of income through social security, welfare, and public health insurance for low-income and elderly persons — take income from people who have relatively more and give it to people who have relatively less. This redistribution makes economic conditions more equal than they would have been without the programs. But does it also reduce economic freedom? It certainly appears to reduce the freedom of the people who were taxed, for they lack that amount of transferred income to spend or save as they wish. However, the recipients of the transfer have that amount (or some portion of it, in actuality) more to spend, so their economic freedom seems to be enhanced. In the final analysis economic liberty tends, over time, to lead to inequalities of income. As society attempts to redress this imbalance, the impact of greater equality of economic freedom depends on one's role in the system.

A similarly complex relationship exists between *social equality* (for example, access to educational and employment opportunities) and *personal freedom* (the ability to do what one wants and what one can). In an ideal world, as de Tocqueville saw in American democracy, these values would be mutually reinforcing. But, if the society had at one time created barriers to opportunities based on social characteristics of race, sex, national origin, or religion and wishes to redress this past exclusivity, a different relationship of equality and freedom arises: the effort toward equality only gives one greater freedom if that person had previously suffered discrimination. The corrective process may infringe on the present freedom of access of those who benefited from past inequalities. This, of course, is the social dilemma associated with affirmative action and the possibility of so-called reverse discrimination. While the effect of greater equality on freedom can be said to depend on one's role in the society, the impact on the business system is quite clear: taxation for income transfers and public requirements for equal opportunity reduce the autonomous and discretionary sphere of business decision making and decrease the economic freedom of relatively higher-income groups of organizational members.

CONCLUSION

This overview of American business history has illustrated the origins of the American system, its evolution into an American business system, and the impact of industrialization on central American values and on business-government relations in the United States.

Business-government relations have traveled a circuitous route to the present. In the colonial period and for several decades after independence, economic issues were either nonexistent or played a subordinated role to questions of governmental process and political freedom. When the beginnings of a national economy first began to take shape in the early nineteenth century, partnerships between government and business for economic develoment were dominant. This pattern changed, however, as the country entered a period marked by rapid industrialization, governmental restraint, social conservatism, and the emergence of an American business creed around the core value of individualism.

In some respects the twentieth century represents an extrapolation of the predominant nature of business-government relations in the latter part of the nineteenth century. A low degree of public ownership in the economy, a strong allegiance to unfettered market processes, and a continuing reliance on individualism as expressed in an ideology of economic liberty are consistent elements of the business creed. Similarly, present programs of public support for business through procurement, credit, and infrastructure development are extensions of nineteenth century programs.

On the other hand, the emergent role of government as an interventionist into the business system to protect "public" interests is a new and controversial dimension of public-private relationships. In an economic sense this trend can be seen as an effort to internalize the external costs of private economic activity. In an ideological sense it is an effort to integrate the values of equity and justice with economic progress. Whatever one's specific framework, the process of industrialization appears to generate social issues and perceived problems, unanticipated in an earlier stage of development, to which the public sector has been pressed into responsiveness.

Another new dimension to business-government relations is the influential role of public institutions in the management of the macroeconomy. Again a function of increasing scale and size of domestic and international economies and of advances in the science of economics, the role of the government has to be perceived not only as influential but as vital to the well-being of the business system. Because the "science" of economics remains inexact and policy positions are invariably value laden, questions of macroeconomic management lie at the center of political debate.

The problems of later-stage industrialization — international competition, capital mobility, job loss in many basic industries, inadequate capital formation for industrial modernization, shifting labor markets — have alarmed the nation and led to reexamination of the relationship of government to business. To a large extent, discussion of a national industrial policy originates from a concern about whether our present business system is structured suitably to confront international competition. Not infrequently, recommendations are suggested for various forms of public-private partnerships — concepts that appear borrowed from the early nineteenth century in the business history of this country. Whether models from an earlier chapter in American history find utility today, or what other shape general policies toward business assume, is of course, the central issue of political economy.

Finally, social and economic benefits occurring as consequences of industrialization have in turn influenced the ideological foundations of the country. Jefferson's greatest worry was the intrusion of government on individual rights. His and the others' deep suspicion of centralized government is manifested in the limits of the constitutional powers of the national government. Yet, with an increase in economic scale and the impact of industrialization, new definitions of *individual rights* have arisen, and the government has come to be viewed as guarantor of minimal standards of individual well-being in education, health, housing, income, and other conditions of life. What was conceived as a limited role of government has, on the assigned duty of protecting rights, become much more pervasive. Traditional belief in limited government often conflicts with the aspiration to fulfill modern definitions of individual rights, entitlements, and greater income equality. Although claims for equality have historically played a subordinate role to the principles of individualism and economic liberty, the twentieth century saw the balance even substantially; the tension between individualism and equality constitutes a major challenge to business and society integration.

In summary these currents and crosscurrents of business and public policy in the United States provide a rich context for analysis. The substantive issues addressed in this book — corporate political action, corporate governance, economic and social regulation, public policy, and economic growth — are influenced by intellectual history in defining today's goals, problems, and opportunities.

To this point, the passage of a law, the decision of a court case, and the ruling of an administrative agency have been taken as statements of "public policy." In actuality, though, determining public policy is a much more complicated process. Owing to the impact of governmental decisions on business, the making of public policy assumes considerable importance. The political economy of public policy is a subject of great importance to managers in the American economy, and it is the topic to which we turn in the next chapter.

DISCUSSION QUESTIONS

1. In your view what are the most significant developments in business-government relations across U.S. history? How have social and economic changes influenced the nature of this relationship?
2. Describe today's dominant social and economic ideologies in the United States in your own words. What, if any, tensions exist among these points of view?
3. Identify several specific areas of controversy about the roles of business and government today. What general ideals and values are represented by these various points of view?
4. How are national economic and social ideologies different in any other countries with which you may have experience? What importance do these differences have for business-government relations?

NOTES

1. James D. Hart, *The Oxford Companion to American Literature*, 4th ed. (New York: Oxford University Press, 1965), pp. 129–130.
2. Louis Untermeyer, ed., *Library of Great American Writing* (Chicago: Britannica Press, 1910), pp. 148–51.

3. Thomas Jefferson, "First Inaugural Address," in ibid., p. 218.

4. Robert Green McCloskey, *American Conservatism in the Age of Enterprise* (Cambridge: Harvard University Press, 1951), pp. 2–3.

5. Louis M. Hacker, *The Triumph of American Capitalism* (New York: Simon and Schuster, 1940), pp. 19–21.

6. Edwin M. Epstein, *The Corporation in American Politics* (Englewood Cliffs, N.J.: Prentice Hall, 1969), p. 21.

7. James Willard Hurst, *The Legitimacy of the Business Corporation in the Law of the United States, 1780–1972* (Charlottesville: University of Virginia Press, 1970), p. 110.

8. Arthur M. Schlesinger, *Paths of American Thought* (Boston: Houghton Mifflin, 1970), p. 110.

9. Adam Smith, *An Inquiry Into The Nature and Causes of The Wealth of Nations* (New York: The Modern Library, 1937).

10. Schlesinger, *Paths of American Thought*, pp. 114–15.

11. Charles Darwin, *The Origin of the Species by Means of Natural Selection* (New York: The Modern Library, 1936).

12. McCloskey, *American Conservatism*, pp. 22–71.

13. Alexis de Tocqueville, *Democracy in America*, ed. J. P. Mayer, (Gordon City, N.Y.: Anchor Books, Doubleday, 1969), pp. 525–26.

14. Hacker, *The Triumph*, pp. 401–24.

15. James Willard Hurst, *Law and the Conditions of Freedom in the Nineteenth-Century United States* (Madison: University of Wisconsin Press, 1956), p. 79.

16. Robert F. Wescott, "U.S. Approaches to Industrial Policy," in *Industrial Policies for Growth and Competitiveness*, ed. F. Gerald Adams and Lawrence R. Klein (Lexington, Mass.: Lexington Books, 1983), pp. 91–92.

17. McCloskey, *American Conservatism*, pp. 72–126.

18. Alfred D. Chandler, Jr., "Government versus Business: An American Phenomenon," in *Business and Public Policy*, ed. John T. Dunlop (Cambridge: Harvard University Press, 1980), pp. 5–6.

19. Thomas K. McGraw, "Business and Government: The Origins of the Adversary Relationship," *California Management Review* 26 (Winter 1984):134.

20. Sanford L. Jacobs, "Software Is a Cheap Business to Get Into — But Many Fail," *Wall Street Journal*, April 29, 1985, p. 21.

21. National Science Foundation, *National Patterns of Science and Technology* (Washington, D.C.: U.S. Government Printing Office, February 1984), p. 11.

22. Congressional Budget Office, *Research and Development Funding in the Proposed 1985 Budget: A Special Study* (Washington, D.C.: U.S. Government Printing Office, March 1984), p. 10.

23. National Science Foundation, *Research and Development in Industry, 1981* (Washington, D.C.: U.S. Government Printing Office, January 1982), p. 20.

24. U.S., Bureau of Government Financial Operations, Department of the

Treasury, *Statement of Liabilities and Other Financial Commitments of the U.S. Government as of September 30, 1983* (Washington, D.C.: Government Printing Office, undated), p. 11.

25. Chandler, "Government versus Business," p. 4.
26. De Tocqueville, *Democracy in America,* p. 503.

John D. Aram
Suzanne M. Seifert

Case 2.A

Ideology and Industrial Policy
Lessons From International Competitors

For many years world economic competition was seen primarily in terms of state-owned economies versus market-oriented, private economic systems. In recent years the declining competitiveness of U.S. business relative to the performance of other private economies, particularly Japan and West Germany, has focused attention on comparisons among the industrialized free nations. Within the context of U.S. declining world market shares, lower productivity gains and economic growth rates, and high inflation and unemployment, it is appropriate to reexamine the American strategy for economic development and international competition.

While private ownership of economic means is common to the United States, Japan, and West Germany, substantial differences are evident in the social philosophy of business and in business-government relationships. Several relevant questions arise from such comparisons: Are these differences significant factors in international economic competition? and, Do traditional American arrangements prepare this nation to meet these challenges, or is the United States in need of an ideological overhaul?

A dramatic view of declining American competitiveness had become visible in the early 1980s. The percentage of worldwide manufacturing exports of industrial nations sold by U.S. manufacturers, for example, had fallen from nearly 25 percent in 1960 to 17 percent in 1979.[1] Similarly, foreign penetration of U.S. domestic markets appeared to be on the rise: in 1979 foreign manufacturers held nearly 7 percent of manufacturing sales in the United States, whereas in 1960 they held less than 2 percent.[2]

Several large and visible U.S. industries were particularly hard hit. Dramatic increases in foreign market share occurred between 1960 and 1979[3] in the following major U.S. markets:

	1960 (in percent)	**1979** (in percent)
Automobiles	4.1	20.1
Electrical components	.5	20.1
Consumer electronics	5.6	50.1
Textile machinery	6.6	45.6

Major penetration had been achieved in mature as well as young industries, in industrial and consumer markets, and in high-technology and low-technology industries.

The economies of Japan and West Germany are certainly not without significant problems. However, both nations appear to outperform the U.S. economy on vital indicators. For example, considering personal savings as a percentage of disposable income, Japan led most other industrialized nations in 1982 with a 17.7 percent rate, and Germans had a 14.2 percent savings ratio. In contrast Americans had a 6.2 percent savings ratio.[4] Moreover, the 1982 rates are representative of the preceding ten years for all three countries.[5]

Changes in investment in plant and equipment for these three countries[6] as a percentage of gross national product (GNP) is illustrated by the following table:

	1970 (in percent)	**1979** (in percent)	**1983** (in percent)
Japan	21	15	14.6
Germany	8	9	11.7
United States	10	7	10.7

Japanese corporations invest more heavily than either the U.S. or West German corporations.

Contrasts in productivity gains in manufacturing among these countries share equally dramatic changes. During the 1970s Japan and West Germany significantly outpaced the United States in productivity: between 1973 and 1979 both Japan and West Germany had rates of productivity increases of 4 to 5 percent per year, whereas the rate of increase in the United States was less than 2 percent per year.[7]

These three economies are facing the same world economic environment. In fact Japan and West Germany are even more dependent on volatile imports, such as oil, than is the United States. It is also difficult to assign these differences in performance solely to governmental burden since, for example, the West German government budget is about a third of the country's GNP, whereas the corresponding figure for the United States lies somewhere above 20 percent.

While many avenues might be explored to identify reasons for these differences, one obvious area for examination lies in the contrasting labor practices and in differing styles of public-private relationships. The purpose of this case is to examine briefly Japanese and German practices in these areas and to ask whether these are desirable or even possible directions for American corporations.

IDEOLOGICAL DIFFERENCES

The apparent differences in business relationships with labor and government between the United States and Japan have received a great deal of attention in the media and in the business press. To a lesser extent the West German way of doing things has been in the public eye. Generally discussion focuses on two salient aspects of these countries about which Americans seem to be deeply suspicious. First, employee relationships are characterized by worker participation in the firm, either by mutual loyalty (Japan) or by structures for worker participation in business decisions (West Germany). Second, there appears to be a greater popular acceptance, and often overt encouragement, of concentrated industries and/or government planning and support for industry. There is a greater acceptance of centralized economic planning and reduced competition in home markets, in contrast to the historical American opposition to these policies.

Employee Relations in Japan

Both Japan and West Germany appear to maintain philosophies and practices of stronger obligations to workers than those that seem to exist in the United States. The Japanese custom of "employment for life" has been widely publicized and has resulted in a normal unemployment rate of less than 3 percent annually over the past decade. In 1980 alone, Japan's number of days lost owing to strikes was one thirtieth the number of strike days that occurred in the United States.[8] The well-being of Japanese employees is held as an objective parallel to, and in some cases above, business profits.

Company paternalism is, of course, only one part of the mutual obligations between employees and employers. For such high regard and commitment Japanese employees developed an intense loyalty to their firms. Indeed they often supplant personal goals and potential aspirations with company goals, a price that might be found to be intolerable to many Americans. Yet the benefits gained by the Japanese economic system appear to be impressive: high labor efficiency, consistently high product quality, minimal labor unrest, and receptivity to innovation and product improvement.

More than any of the specific techniques for maintaining worker solidarity and productivity is the social philosophy that appears to underlie business practices: the Japanese ideology places the highest emphasis on service to general values and purposes, such as human betterment, and the ideology downplays striving for personal achievements in favor of pursuing companywide national missions.[9] Are there lessons that American managers and workers can learn from these Japanese attitudes and values concerning employee relations? One observer of management practices in the United States and Japan finds common characteristics among successful companies in both countries. He labels these characteristics "Type Z" management, which consists of several concepts:

- A corporation's success (and justification) depends on how it deals with customers, communities, competitors, and the world at large;
- Participative decision making is a must;
- A holistic concern for people must be present; and
- Profits are not an end in themselves; management must embrace the values that transcend the financial.[10]

The question remains whether these principles can be, or even whether they should be, widely adopted among American firms.

Union Relations in West Germany

Union-management harmony is generally regarded as a key factor in West Germany's impressive postwar economic success. German labor has consistently assumed a restrained and cooperative attitude toward wage increases and strikes over this period and is widely credited with making a unique contribution to the stability and growth of the German economy. One observer reviews the crucial role of labor in the early success of German postwar policies: "For the economy as a whole, labor's muted and unaggressive policy has been an inestimable advantage. . . . One may even say that at one critical juncture, when the success of the currency reform and of the free market policy in the balance, the day has won largely thanks to labor's restraint."[11]

Today, German labor is noted for its moderate wage demands, for an unwillingness to strike, and for its cooperation with management to plan movement of labor out of heavy industries such as steel and shipbuilding and into more technical sectors.[12] Although about 34 percent of the German labor force is unionized, compared with 20 percent in the United States, strikes are extremely rare and wage demands rarely meet or exceed the level of inflation.[13] Labor's emphasis is on security and stability, indicating a "widespread acceptance of the thesis that only through low inflation and strong savings and investment can an economy remain strong."[14]

A rare exception to organized labor's typically moderate stance in

West Germany occurred in 1984. IG Metal, West Germany's largest union, struck for over six weeks despite stiff resistance to their demands from employers and Chancellor Helmut Kohl's conservative government.[15] IG Metal's basic demand centered around a 35 hour workweek for union members without any decrease in weekly wages. Ultimately the union won a modest wage increase accompanied by a reduced workweek.

This deviation from labor's traditionally cooperative outlook was looked upon quite unfavorably by analysts and the German public. "In a way, the unions have made life much more difficult for themselves by demanding and probably getting too much this round," predicted analyst Norbert Walter.[16] One public opinion poll found 71 percent of the Germans against a reduced workweek.[17] The negative public opinion concerning IG Metal's demands is reflective of the traditional German expectation that labor demands mesh with the nation's best interests. It is interesting to note that IG Metal's 1984 demands came after two years of concessions and higher unemployment levels — both conditions thought to typify recent conditions in the United States.

Generally, benefits of the German economic system are impressive. The per capita income of the German worker surpasses that of his American counterpart, and he is the most highly paid worker in the industrialized world.[18] Job security is great, as unemployment until the 1980s rarely exceeded 5 percent. Over 30 percent of the country's GNP is spent for social services, and the German worker has complete benefits in health, unemployment, disability, strong pension programs, and a variety of other social amenities. In 1979 the average labor contract provided six weeks of vacation a year. Finally, national laws protect the worker against unjust dismissal, and labor compensation and retraining are required in the event of plant closings.

An important element of cooperation between capital and labor in Germany is the institution of worker democracy, or codetermination.[19] All firms employing more than five workers are required to form works councils elected from the laborers. Entirely divorced from the union, the work council consults with management in all operational affairs bearing upon the work force. Consent of the council is required on working conditions, hiring, discipline, terminations, and work allocation. The works council restrains management's autonomy in these areas, but it then facilitates the transmission and implementation of changes.

In addition to the works councils codetermination gives labor substantial representation on the supervisory boards of corporations, generally the equivalent of the American board of directors. This board, which appoints and supervises the management board, must be composed of one-half labor representatives in coal, iron, and steel companies and near-equal representation with management in all other companies of over 2,000 employees. The supervisory boards of stock-issuing companies with less than 2,000 employees are required to have one-third worker representation on the supervisory board.

The economic consequences of worker participation may be a greater degree of industrial peace owing to greater identification of management and labor interests, the presence of mechanisms for providing company information to workers, joint responsibility for implementation of change, and availability of forums for resolutions of differences. Nevertheless, seeking these benefits involves a radical alteration of union and management attitudes toward industrial relations and a reduction in the latitude of pure management discretion. Are there lessons for America in this system, or are American assumptions and values too divergent from this European scheme?

BUSINESS-GOVERNMENT RELATIONS IN JAPAN AND WEST GERMANY

Japan

Japanese society expresses little ambivalence toward economic growth, corporate size, or joint public-private economic cooperation and planning. The Japanese have a national economic mission that is carefully developed and broadly supported, pursued by an activist government through constant interaction, discussion, persuasion, and encouragement.[20] Corporations are thought of as instruments for promoting the public good. Even intellectual circles and government agencies support a probusiness climate in contrast to their U.S. counterparts.

The Japanese are committed to economic growth. National policy (political or social) is judged first by its impact on Japan's balance of payments and trade.[21] The Japanese put their national interests first by fitting their own self-interests into a framework of national needs, goals, aspirations, and values.

Japanese government ministries most concerned with the industrial sector take as their own mission and objectives the economic success of Japanese companies, their international competitiveness, and their constant modernization and improvement.[22] While relations are not always harmonious between public and private leaders, the Japanese system of business-government relations stands out in these regards:

1. A strong desire to identify and work toward common goals, including the willingness of business and government to cooperate with each other;
2. The development of national industrial policy through extensive interaction and formation of consensus among leaders of business, labor, communities, and government;
3. The development of a long-term vision of national and international economics by the government, specifically the Ministry of International Trade and Industry (MITI);

4. Relentless pursuit of this vision by government by creating conditions for strong Japanese companies in the context of international competition; and

5. Specific policies and programs to implement national goals, including determining of company's allowable deductions, including depreciation; securing bank financing; granting necessary permissions, licenses, and permits; promoting mergers and planning the reduction of capacity in declining industries; obtaining and ensuring implementation of new technology, whether foreign or national; and providing subsidies, tariffs, and other protection consistent with the national plan.[23]

This style of business-government relations may not have produced the "Japanese miracle," but it has been a consistent part of Japan's remarkable economic performance. A national economic mission, carefully developed and broadly supported, is pursued by an activist government through constant interaction, discussion, persuasion, and encouragement with a private sector.[24] The results are an economy almost completely in private hands; major industries composed of a few large corporations; and modern, efficient, competitive companies.[25]

Although Japan has often been held up as having the "ideal" business-management relationship, recent studies have presented the possibility that Japanese workers and management are developing outlooks with a "Westernized" focus. Older employees are receiving more pressure from management to consider "voluntary" early retirements. Large companies are developing compensation plans tied to individual performance rather than solely adhering to the traditional seniority-based wage structures. Finally, "decision making by consensus" methodologies pose time lag problems in business arenas where information and technology evolve rapidly, requiring management to make unilateral decisions — more characteristic of the U.S. management system.[26]

The "Westernization" of Japanese business relationships has been attributed to "Western" problems such as increasing unemployment rates, excess middle management, and stronger market competition from lower-wage countries. Yet it may also be that Japan shows indications of surface strains on the system, rather than any deep-rooted problems.

West Germany

In many respects the West German system of business-government interaction is quite different from the Japanese model. Other than macroeconomic policy, the German government does no centralized industrial planning. Free market principles endorsed after World War II of minimal government attention to specific industries and companies are still maintained. On the other hand government ownership of basic industries is more extensive in West Germany than in Japan.

Several similarities between the two countries confront the United States with a reevaluation of policy. First, there is a greater acceptance of large firms and concentrated industries than there is in the United States. Centralized decision making and cooperation with a relatively small business elite is a typical practice. Banks are permitted to take equity positions in corporations, and it is commonplace for large banks to own more than 25 percent of a company through its supervisory board and to influence the plans of the corporation greatly.[27] The resulting development, an unofficial industrial policy, is described in a U.S. House of Representatives staff report:

> Thus through a series of interlocking relationships the banks can exercise a strong influence upon the German economy. In general they have encouraged mergers. Moreover, although the German economy has no planning machinery similar to the French national planning office, the close connections between top bankers and the Ministries of Finance and Economics tend to develop a coordinated view of how German economic policy should develop.[28]

Second, Germany places a high priority on export as vital to economic growth and development, as does Japan. International markets are viewed as the prime context for competition. Germans are said to prefer a "managed home market" of weak competition and higher profits, a situation perhaps only possible within the context of a small business elite. On the other hand export markets are pursued aggressively. It is said that firms like Volkswagen have won such a large part of many foreign markets by the most careful advance planning. They study every conceivable angle of the market and tailor their products and their sales pitches to the particular characteristics of each market. When their trade falls off, they have been willing to absorb losses rather than risk losing connections that they have so laboriously developed.[29]

AMERICAN INDUSTRIAL RELATIONSHIPS

While it may be suggested that West German and Japanese industries are developing characteristics commonly associated with the United States, the reverse may also hold true. Beginning in 1982 and generally holding true through 1984, American labor unions have moderated their wage demands. It is believed that unions and management are beginning to relinquish their previous adversarial stances and are more willing to strive toward satisfaction of mutual goals. In 1982 both GM and Ford offered "lifetime employment" pilot programs to UAW workers. In the boom auto sale year of 1984, the UAW demanded wage increases considered "modest" in that industry sector.

Many other U.S. companies have made efforts to incorporate labor representation on corporate governing boards, institute "quality circles," and otherwise involve employees in decision making with hopes of duplicating the positive work relationships found in West Germany and Japan. Results have been varied, often leading companies to conclude that programs must be more tailored to the U.S. worker in order to achieve consistently positive results.

The appropriate role of the U.S. government in business has been much debated in Congress during the 1980s. Bills have been proposed to allow banks to deal in securities, much like the banking corporations in West Germany are free to do. Other efforts in Congress have centered around the development of import quotas to protect specific industries, trade restrictions to reduce the U.S. trade imbalance, and the creation of a Department of International Trade and Industry.[30] Without difficulty these efforts may readily be likened to some existing programs in Japan.

Yet, to date, there is no overwhelming consensus on an appropriate industrial policy. Those in favor of industrial policy planning believe that the central issue is not the amount of government intervention. Rather they focus the issue on choosing between the formulation of industrial policy on a frequent, ad hoc basis (for example, the Chrysler bailout) versus developing a more coordinated method and more consistent policies. Proponents of a strong industrial policy point to MITI's successes as examples of benefits to be derived from centralized governmental industrial planning. It is suggested by industrial policy sponsors that trade on the international level has become the norm rather than the exception; therefore, the United States can no longer afford to continue its naive ad hoc policy-making efforts.

Persons favoring industrial policy cite numerous examples of "wasted" government resources caused by lack of policy coordination. For example, the government underwrites almost half the R & D efforts in the United States yet has no mechanism for coordinating R & D results.[31]

In fact, there is some evidence that the American public is more receptive to the basic tenets of a formalized industrial policy than they have been in past eras. A 1981 Harris poll showed that a majority of Americans believe economic growth could be enhanced by closer working relationships between business and government to establish goals and priorities and by government encouragement of greater cooperation among business, government, and labor.[32] However, this change in public attitude is tempered by a growing wariness of further government involvement in the economy. While these two outlooks seem contradictory, it has been suggested that Americans are receptive to business-government cooperative partnerships rather than simply increased government intervention in the economy.[33]

Opponents of strong U.S. industrial policy suggest that any centralized governmental industrial planning center will merely serve as a lightening rod for special interest lobbying efforts. According to economic analyst Charles Schultze:

> A federally imposed industrial policy is a solution in search
> of a problem. We have no basic structural deficiency in
> American industry. . . . Imposing an industrial policy is just
> an irrelevant waste.[34]

Other antagonists of industrial policy believe that a Department for International Trade will not perform planning functions as MITI does; they believe, rather, that it will end up as a government lobby for furthering "regressive" protectionist strategies. They also suggest that a formal U.S. industrial policy will slow down the shift of resources to productive industries by allowing allocations to declining industries. Furthermore, money will be wasted on targeted growth industries that may have no commercial future. As Nobel laureate George Stigler points out, "One thing we know about government is that it is not a good entrepreneur."[35]

Industrial policy opponents, while allowing that MITI industrial targeting efforts in earlier decades were quite successful, believe that changes in the world situation do not lend themselves advantageously to MITI's strengths. Nowadays product life cycles are much shorter owing to rapid technological changes; therefore, industries require rapid decision making and increased corporate privacy more than somewhat ponderous assistance from government experts.

The marketplace is the most efficient allocator of resources, according to opponents of formal industrial policy. They propose that industry stands to gain most by more careful observance of the market forces rather than by the institution of government mechanisms, which will only serve to generate distractions or distortions in the market. Furthermore, the U.S. business-government structure does not lend itself to methods used productively in the past by other governments. In the U.S. system industrial policy programs will merely become tools for the politically powerful to get their hands in the till.[36]

DISCUSSION QUESTIONS

1. In light of all the recent changes in the industrial environment, is America able to compete successfully, or does business and/or government need to enact more adaptive measures?
2. If improvements need to be made, what changes between labor and management should occur? What changes in public policy should occur?

3. Evaluate the political feasibility and time requirements of any proposed changes in the current government-business-labor structure.

NOTES

1. "A Drastic New Loss of Competitive Strength," *Business Week,* June 30, 1980, p. 59.
2. Ibid., p. 58.
3. Data from Ibid., p. 60.
4. U.S., Department of Commerce, International Trade Administration, *International Economic Indicators*, September 1984, p. 13.
5. Ibid.
6. "A Drastic New Loss," p. 60.
7. Ibid., p. 65.
8. George Kurian, *The New Book of World Rankings* (New York: Facts on File, 1984), p. 255.
9. Mitz Noda, "Business Management in Japan," *Technology Review*, June-July 1979, pp. 24–26.
10. William Ouchi, *Theory Z* (Reading, Mass.: Addison-Wesley, 1981).
11. Henry G. Wallich, *Mainsprings of the German Revival*, (New Haven, Conn.: Yale University Press, 1955) p. 299.
12. U.S., Congress, Joint Economic Committee, *Monetary Policy, Selective Credit Policy, and Industry Policy in France, Britain, West Germany, and Sweden*, 97th Cong., 1st sess., June 26, 1981, p. 126.
13. Kurian, *The New Book of World Rankings*, p. 243.
14. Joint Economic Committee, *Monetary Policy, Selective Credit Policy, and Industry Policy in France, Britain, West Germany, and Sweden*, p. 127.
15. "Demands for a 35-Hour Week Menace the Economy," *Business Week*, May 28, 1984, p. 46.
16. "An Attempt to Save Face As the Metalworker's Strike Hits Hard," *Business Week,* June 18, 1984, p. 36.
17. Ibid., p. 36.
18. Joint Economic Committee, *Monetary Policy, Selective Credit, and Industry Policy in France, Britain, West Germany, and Sweden*, pp. 127–28.
19. Ibid., pp. 129–30.
20. Edwin O. Reischauer, "The Japanese Way," *Across the Board*, December 1977, pp. 41–42.
21. Peter F. Drucker, "Behind Japan's Success," *Harvard Business Review,* January-February 1981, pp. 83–90.
22. Ezra F. Vogel, *Japan as No. 1: Lessions for America* (Cambridge: Harvard University Press, 1979), pp. 65–84.
23. Ibid.
24. Ibid., p. 84.
25. U.S., Congress, House, *Economic Conditions in the Federal Republic of Ger-*

many. Report Prepared for the Subcommittee on Europe and the Middle East of the Committee on International Relations, 95th Cong., 2d sess., December 29, 1978, p. 32.

26. S. Prakash Sethi, Nobuaki Namiki, and Carl L. Swanson, "The Decline of the Japanese Management System," *California Management Review,* Summer 1984, p. 41.

27. House, *Economic Conditions,* p. 32.

28. Ibid.

29. Ibid. pp. 32–33.

30. Partisanship Dominated Congressional Year, *1983 Congressional Quarterly Almanac,* (Washington, D.C.: Congressional Quarterly Inc., 1984) p. 26.

31. Stuart Eizenstadt, "Industrial Policy: Not If, But How," *Fortune,* January 23, 1984, p. 184.

32. Franklin Strier, "On Economic Planning, Japan and West Germany Have a Better Idea," *Center Magazine,* January-February 1984, p. 40.

33. Ibid.

34. Harry Anderson, "Making Industrial Policy," *Newsweek,* October 24, 1983, p. 99.

35. "Industrial Policy: Is it the Answer?," *Business Week,* July 4, 1983, p. 57.

36. Ibid.

Manifestations of Business-Government Relations in the Mid-1980s
The Case of the U.S. Automotive Industry

AUTO INDUSTRY — 1978–80

General Motors (GM), Ford, Chrysler, and American Motors Corporation (AMC) all enjoyed varying degrees of profit in 1977. An unremarkable statistic by itself, this feat would not be repeated in any of the next six years. By the end of 1978 Chrysler had accumulated a $204.6 million loss.

In 1979 GM and Ford grappled with declining profits, whereas Chrysler racked up a $1.1 billion loss for the year. It had become clear that Chrysler would require some sort of assistance to reverse this increasingly negative income trend. Lee Iacocca, chairman of Chrysler, turned to the U.S. government for support, and the "bailout" of Chrysler was initiated.

The initial conditions for the $1.5 billion government loan guarantee demanded cooperation from everyone — employees, suppliers, and financial institutions.[1] From domestic banks, financial institutions, and other creditors, Chrysler had to find $400 million in new loans that would not be covered by the government guarantees. Congress insisted that suppliers and dealers contribute $180 million by such means as buying stock or extending loans. States and cities that benefited economically as the sites of Chrysler plants were also pulled into the picture; they were to contribute $250 million. Another $300 million was to be raised through a sale of the company's assets. Blue- and white-collar employees had agreed to forego

---

This case is based upon, and in some parts drawn from, Case 2.B of the first edition of this book — "Industrial Policy and the Automotive Industry" — by John D. Aram, Janet Leong, and Carol J. Fritz. Copyright © 1985 Suzanne M. Seifert.

expected wage increases amounting to $203 million. Not satisfied, Congress demanded an additional $259.5 million in Chrysler wage cuts.

In order to receive the government loan guarantee Chrysler was required to submit many decisions to the government's loan board for final approval. By the end of 1980, Chrysler had received $800 million in loans backed by the federal government. In return for providing government support Chrysler gave the government the right to buy company stock for $13 a share.[2]

Chrysler's request for aid and the resultant governmental intervention triggered a heated debate across the country. Some argued that the bailout was necessary, and others argued that it endangered the free enterprise system. The company's most powerful argument for the bailout was the devastating effect that the loss of jobs would have on the economy. At the time of the bailout Chrysler employed 137,000 workers directly and supported another 400,000 on the payrolls of suppliers and dealers. A study conducted by the Department of Transportation concluded that a Chrysler shutdown would cost $1.5 billion in unemployment benefits and erode federal income taxes by $500 million.[3]

Proponents of the bailout quickly pointed out that there has been a long history of federal assistance to troubled industries. The shipbuilding industry has received $5.2 billion in assistance. A special steel loan guarantee program through the Commerce Department has backed $365.2 million in borrowings by five steel companies, and the U.S. Railway Association has $2.1 billion out to railroads.[4]

Opponents of the bailout believed that federal assistance to Chrysler would undermine competition rather than strengthen it. The free enterprise system, they argued, has both winners and losers; and losers should drop out if they cannot compete in the marketplace. Chairman William Proxmire of the Senate Banking Committee said: "For goodness sakes, you can't just have a free enterprise system without failures. Are we going to guarantee businessmen against their own incompetence by eliminating any incentive for avoiding the specter of bankruptcy?"[5]

The auto industry exhibited signs of industrial illness by 1979. Yet it was not until 1980 that GM and Ford registered losses comparable with those of Chrysler's. The U.S. auto industry, in general, lost approximately 5 percent of its market share during 1979. Market share in 1980 was reduced by a similar amount, compounded by a reduction in overall demand for autos.

By most accounts 1980 was a disastrous year for American carmakers. New car sales were down nearly 28 percent as the industry was trying to generate enthusiasm for the next year's models. In 1980 the combined net income for the four major auto producers was a bleak $4,213,525,000 loss.[6] Recession conditions were affecting the country, whereas interest rates reached the 18 to 20 percent range. Close to 300,000 auto employees had been laid off or dismissed, about 1,500 new car dealerships had closed, and imports appeared to be capturing nearly a 30 percent share of the market.[7]

To some, Chrysler's need of a government-backed bailout loan in order to continue operations seemed symbolic of the auto industry's inability to compete under adverse conditions. Even insiders were critical of the automakers' decision-making abilities. "Ford Motor Company resisted new small car designs in the mid 1970's," said Philip Caldwell, Ford chief executive officer and chairman, "and cut spending on future products by about $2 billion."[8] Another Ford executive commented:

> We've generated all this excess baggage, all these ineffi-
> ciencies — this attitude that it doesn't matter what we do
> because the system will carry us. . . . Now it's no longer
> true. . . . It's like a cold shower.[9]

Since the late 1970s, governmental policy toward the auto industry has vacillated between hand holding and handcuffing. In response to industrial pleas a number of government actions had been taken. On June 27, 1980, the *Wall Street Journal* reported:

> The biggest step was to provide federal loan guarantees for
> Chrysler Corp., but there has been action on other fronts.
> The Customs Service increased duties on imported light
> trucks to 25% from 4%. The EPA waived carbon-monoxide
> standards for some 1981-model cars. The administration
> created a joint government-auto research program. And
> Congress will soon ease federal fuel economy standards for
> cars and light trucks.[10]

Government regulations on the auto industry amount to a substantial cost and represent a great source of frustration. Doubtful, however, is the view that government was the root cause of Detroit's problem in the transition to fuel-efficient, small car production. It might be better said that government imposed a set of constraints that limited cash flows, diverted some capital, and distracted executives from the competitive task of strategy development.

AUTO INDUSTRY — 1981

In January 1981 the Chrysler Loan Guarantee Board voted to permit the company to draw another $400 million in federally guaranteed loans, bringing the total government-backed loans to $1.2 billion. Concurrently the board mandated several actions designed to ensure that Chrysler would be a going concern that could survive after 1983 with no need for continued federal help. The terms of the $400 million loan guarantee under the Reagan administration again required the cooperation of bankers, the union, and suppliers:

1. Some 150 lenders of Chrysler, mostly banks, would eliminate the company's $1.1 billion in private debt; more than half of the outstanding loans would be converted to preferred shares, and the remainder would be paid off in 1981 for 30 cents on the dollar.
2. The United Automobile Workers (UAW) would accept $622 in additional wage concessions in exchange for a package of noneconomic gains, including a blue-collar profit-sharing plan.
3. Chrysler's suppliers would agree to $72 million in price cuts.[11]

Iacocca's and the U.S. government's confidence in Chrysler's ability to become profitable was not universally shared. Even after a second quarter profit in 1981 preceeded by two years of losses, industrial soothsayers predicted a gloomy future for Chrysler. Merrill Lynch analyst Harvey Heinbach stated in mid-1981:

> Even if they're [Chrysler] making money, we still don't feel they're making enough to pay off the huge debt they've accumulated and at the same time devote the necessary funds to further develop competitive products.[12]

Direct government involvement in the auto industry extended beyond Chrysler in 1981. Ronald Reagan's promise to "get government off the back of big business" was welcome news to the auto industry, but his adamant "free trader" stance was less popular with carmakers and the UAW in 1981. Both groups were concerned about Japan's increasing market share in the U.S. auto industry and wanted the flood of foreign cars curtailed. Reagan, pressured to respond to the "Japanese auto import threat" yet maintain his image as a free trader, announced that Japan would voluntarily restrain imports.

Beginning in spring 1981, Japan agreed to limit its auto exports to 1.68 million cars annually through spring 1984, when, it was hoped, domestic auto operations would have resolved their problems. The issue of voluntary restraints polarized opinions into free trader and "protectionist" camps. Those arguing the need for voluntary restraints claimed that the auto industry required time to regain strength and temporary restraints were necessary for improvements in U.S. employment figures. Free traders argued that voluntary restraints cause unjustifiable increases in automobile prices. Consumers purchasing higher-priced autos face a significant decrease in disposable income, which ultimately leads to increased unemployment in other industries. Most American industries are forced to maintain a competitive stance or go bankrupt. The auto industry's size, argued free traders, should not allow it to be an exception to the free market philosophy.

AUTO INDUSTRY — 1982

U.S. carmakers were understandably alarmed about their competitive ability by 1982. Three of the four major companies had sustained losses for the two prior years. That 1981 figures showed less red ink than 1980 was only a slight consolation to an industry accustomed to profitability year after year. GM alone posted a profit ($333,000) in 1981. By contrast GM had posted a profit more than ten times as large only three short years before. With these figures in mind GM and Ford readied themselves for the 1982 contract negotiations with the UAW.

Dubbed the "concessions" contract, GM and Ford workers traded their customary wage increases and deferred their cost-of-living adjustments (COLAs) for job security measures and profit-sharing plans. UAW leaders were understandably concerned that 30 percent of the Big Two's UAW members were on layoff. Douglas Fraser, UAW president, stated that the 1982 contract would "stop the hemorrhaging of GM workers' jobs."[13] In summary, the UAW–Ford/GM agreements delineated the following:

- Three quarters of COLAs deferred for 18 months (Ford/GM),
- Four plants reopened (GM),
- Company-funded legal services plan (GM),
- Profit-sharing plans (Ford/GM),
- Pilot "lifetime job guarantee" program (Ford/GM),
- Reduced nonwage benefits available for chronic absentees (GM), and
- No specified wage increases (Ford/GM).[14]

The combined positive effects of the concessions contract, a 3.9 percent inflation rate, and voluntary restraints allowed Chrysler and GM to register profits by the end of 1982. Yet the overall picture was not bright. Changes in production strategy, requiring huge amounts of capital, led to an oversupply of small cars, whereas larger luxury models were in short supply.[15] U.S. new car sales dipped below their previous poor showing in 1981.

The UAW faced an equally dismal picture. U.S. automakers were accelerating their out sourcing (purchase of foreign cars/auto parts). By the end of 1982 the Big Three owned varying portions of foreign auto companies and had numerous other agreements with European and Japanese automakers to supply parts for U.S.-manufactured cars.

The flow of auto-related production orders to foreign companies reduced the need for U.S. autoworkers and drove the UAW to promote a "domestic content" bill in Congress that would require major foreign auto manufacturers, beginning in 1985, to incorporate a certain percentage of American-made parts in their auto exports to the United States.

The specified rate would increase over time and according to the number of units exported by an individual foreign producer. By 1987 any company selling more than 900,000 autos in the United States would be required to reach a 90 percent domestic content level.[16] In 1982 Japanese automakers sold over 1.5 million cars to the United States and averaged 5 percent domestic content. UAW leaders hoped this bill would restore some of the 1 million jobs lost by workers in auto-related industries since 1978.

Opposing the bill were various interest groups including agricultural associations, exporting companies, auto dealerships, longshoremen, Ford, and GM. Reagan also strongly opposed this bill, which he later referred to as a "cruel hoax."[17] Republican representative Bill Frenzyl supported the president's view and proclaimed, "This bill is an exercise in greed. It seeks to protect the jobs of a few, to hurt the jobs of many and to lay the additional costs of job protection on unwilling American consumers."[18] The bill passed in the House of Representatives but was viewed unfavorably in the Senate.

AUTO INDUSTRY — 1983

1983 seemed to be a turning point for the U.S. economy in general and for the auto industry in particular. The Big Three posted a combined 1983 profit of $6.2 billion after three years of losses totaling $4.7 billion. Ford and GM profits were $1.867 and $3.7 billion, respectively. In June 1983 Chrysler paid back $400 million of its federally guaranteed loans. Iacocca announced in July that Chrysler was ready to pay back the remainder of the loan. The debate over the appropriations of public aid to a public enterprise lost some intensity as Chrysler's loan was repaid seven years ahead of schedule.

Ford, GM, and Chrysler had made significant efforts to improve their competitive ability during the early 1980s. Plants had been modernized, inventory controls tightened, labor and management ranks streamlined, suppliers and management held accountable for product quality and competitive pricing, excess production capacity reduced, and cooperation between management and unions emphasized.

The statistics at the end of 1983 were less encouraging for the UAW and employees in auto-related industries. Over 100,000 auto employees remained unemployed in the last quarter of 1983.[19] This attrition in UAW membership can be traced to the effects of out sourcing and reduction in necessary man-hours per car owing to increased automation.

In fact, despite the Big Three's record profits in 1983, auto executives appeared only cautiously optimistic about the future. They claimed that industrial profits were a reflection of improved managerial decisions, reduced interest rates, and stable prices. However, to outsiders the size of auto executive compensation for corporate performance in 1983 seemed to contradict their claims that the fate of the auto industry was, in large part, linked to economic forces outside of management's control.

Philip Caldwell received compensation totaling $1.4 million as a result of Ford's performance in 1983. GM's chairman, Roger Smith, was compensated over $1.49 million for his company's performance.[20] By one business journal's standards Lee Iacocca's compensation totaling $475,000 was considered the "most bang for the buck" in light of his role in Chrysler's financial comeback.

As justification for these figures Caldwell said: "We cannot run a successful company with mediocre people. We have to offer incentives."[21] Bill Brock, U.S. trade representative responsible for negotiating the voluntary import restraint agreement with Japan, did not share this view. In Brock's opinion the executive increases were "unbelievable new management bonuses." He threatened that the bonuses were an indication that import restraints might not be extended past 1985, as protection was no longer needed.[22] UAW leaders, apparently not wishing to add additional heat to the import restraint issue or the upcoming contract negotiations, briefly commented that the executive bonuses were "overly generous."

GOVERNMENT INTERVENTION IN AUTO ISSUES — 1983

The 1985 deadline for import restraints represented a one year extension of the original three year agreement, originally targeted to expire in March 1984. Results of the voluntary restraint agreement were mixed. Both the United States and Japan logged record profits in 1983. Japan exported 30 percent of its cars to the United States yet derived 50 percent of its profit from the American market.[23] According to Brookings Institute analyst Robert Crandall Japanese automakers charged United States buyers 45 percent more for its foreign cars than other important countries were charged.[24]

This in part may explain MITI's (Japan's Ministry of International Trade and Industry) willingness to extend restraints through early 1985 and have not ruled out some form of import limitations in 1985/86. From 1981 to early 1984 the average price of an American car increased 17.4 percent, whereas imported cars were priced 23 percent higher.[25] An estimated $400 was added to car sticker prices — generally attributable to voluntary restraint effects.[26] According to a Wharton Econometrics study, consumers were paying $5 billion extra per year for cars, owing to the voluntary restraints.[27]

Critics and proponents of voluntary restraint measures generally agreed that Detroit used the time period affected by import restraints wisely; however, the two groups offered different explanations for Detroit's motivation. Voluntary restraint supporters claim that automakers acted on their genuine desire to be competitive in the worldwide automobile market.

On the other hand critics suggest that Detroit would not have improved their competitive abilities if they had not initially believed the voluntary restraints to be quite temporary.

Meanwhile, Japanese automakers used the time to further improve their local operations and to expand production capacity in the United States. Honda announced plans to spend $240 million to double its capacity at an Ohio plant, and Nissan was considering adding small-car capacity to its Tennessee plant.[28] Japanese automakers are believed to be expanding locally as a hedge against stronger U.S. protectionist measures.

While Reagan was apparently willing to limit governmental intervention to the negotiation of voluntary restraints, some factions of Congress pressed for additional measures. Industrial policy was one of the major issues debated during 1983/84 in Congress. The Senate developed a bill to create a new Department of International Trade and Industry. This department would oversee various ways to enhance the global competitiveness of targeted critical industries, such as auto manufacturing. This proposal was quite controversial, with free traders claiming that government could ultimately end up determining whether a particular industry was "saved" or "killed." Chrysler's attainment of government-backed loans might be considered a government action that saved an industry. By March 1985 plans for the creation of Department of Trade had generated such strong opposition that President Reagan withdrew his support for the proposed department.

Auto Out Sourcing and Joint Ventures

GM captured automakers' and analysts' attention when it announced that conditions for a joint venture with Toyota were set and production began in December 1984. Each partner was contributing an estimated $150 million in resources. Toyota names the CEO and the companies have equal representation on the board. Each company also shares equally in the supply of car components.[29]

GM expects numerous benefits from this agreement with Toyota: (1) $1 billion savings in new design costs, (2) the aging Chevette model replaced in half the average time at one tenth the average cost, (3) knowledge/expertise in low-cost manufacturing procedures, and (4) "stalling" time till GM is able to build similar cars competitively. Toyota's expectations include a low-risk chance to see if they can build high-quality cars in the United States and a secure entry into the U.S. market, hopefully offsetting any further U.S. protectionist measures.[30]

The joint venture announcement by GM chairman Roger Smith drew sharp criticism from other U.S. automakers. Chrysler characterized the deal as "illegal by anyone's measure," whereas Ford described the deal as "anti-competitive to the core." AMC chairman Paul Tippett added, "Toyota owes this country an automobile plant — and this isn't it."[31] GM predictably claimed to view the deal's impact differently. "I do not foresee any great big earthquake in our industry," stated Smith.[32]

In keeping with Reagan's tolerant attitude toward big business, the joint venture between the world's two largest auto companies to produce a small car in the United States would likely be allowed to go ahead. The Federal Trade Commission (FTC) chose to define "unfair methods of competition" narrowly. FTC officials concluded that the other carmakers' antitrust objections were too speculative to justify an antitrust challenge[33] Chrysler, discontented with the FTC decision, filed suit in a U.S. district court, claiming that GM's joint venture violated antitrust laws.[34]

While decrying the GM-Toyota deal, other U.S. automakers had made, or were contemplating, similar moves. AMC's partnership with Renault included mutual supply of parts and incorporated Renault's new car design.[35] Chrysler obtained 15 percent equity in Japan's Mitsubishi Corporation, and Iacocca later acknowledged joint venture negotiations between the two companies. "We've been discussing it [joint venture] for 10 years, but now we're a little closer to getting together to make a small subcompact."[36] (See Chart 1.)

It is estimated that one third the cost differential between U.S. and Japanese small cars is due to lower Japanese wage ratios. Pooling resources with foreign manufacturers has become an increasingly attractive way for U.S. car producers to narrow the differential. Ford is building a $500 million plant in Hermosillo, Mexico, and expects that plant to produce 130,000 subcompacts by 1987.[37] GM has purchased 50 percent of Korea's Daewoo Corporation's auto operations.[38]

An even greater amount of U.S.–foreign producer out sourcing agreements exist pertaining to the supply of numerous car components. A sample of such agreements include GM's purchase of 121,000 four-cylinder car engines from Brazil, whereas Ford looks to the same country to produce part of its future World Truck. Chrysler has purchased shipments of engines produced by Germany's Volkswagen Corporation.

With present and future out sourcing agreements in mind Detroit kept close tabs on the status of the domestic content bill in Congress. It was approved again in the Democrat-controlled House of Representatives in 1983. The bill faced an uncertain fate in the Republican-dominated Senate, so suporters hoped to introduce the measure in 1984. "Some people who find it easy to say no to this today just might find it harder to say that in an election year," suggested UAW president Owen Bieber.[39]

Japanese automakers shared Detroit's negative feelings about the domestic content bill. They agreed, early in 1983, to extend the voluntary restraints through spring 1985. In the fourth year of import restraints Japan would be allowed to ship 1.85 million autos to the United States — up 170,000 from the original three year agreement. Temporary voluntary restraints allowed Japanese automakers to achieve record profits in 1983 and do not affect their agreements to export car parts. MITI and Japanese automakers hoped this sort of voluntary cooperation would forestall any

CHART 1   *Cooperation between World Auto Manufacturers*

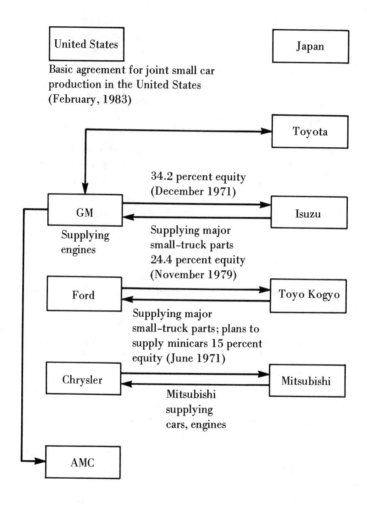

SOURCE: 1984 Ward's Automotive Yearbook, p. 52.

growing momentum for more "permanent" protectionist measures such as increased tariffs, domestic content legislation, or rigid import quotas.

AUTO INDUSTRY — 1984

The auto industry's upbeat 1983 profit reports extended into 1984, leaving little doubt in anyone's mind that the U.S. auto industry can be competitive under certain conditions. So 1983/84 presented the auto industry with a set of quite favorable conditions — not present in the recent past and possibly not duplicable in the near future:

- A recovering economy,
- Interest rates below 15 percent,
- Union concessions,
- Pent-up demand for large cars,
- Drastically reduced new car inventories,
- Low inflation rates, and
- "Artificial" marketplace restraints on foreign competitors.[40]

While it was understood that Detroit was unwilling to jeopardize the possibility of an extension of voluntary restraints through 1986 by appearing too confident, a sincere undercurrent of concern seemed to be present. When questioned in 1984 about Chrysler's position in the marketplace, Iacocca commented, "We live on tenterhooks. Long-term, our problems haven't gone away."[41] Ford acknowledged that its Escort model is no profit maker despite its ranking as a top seller.[42] Meanwhile, GM cautiously predicted that it would produce small cars competitively "sometime in the future." These unenthusiastic comments seem to be in direct contrast with the improvements in productivity statistics cited by the Big Three:

- *Chrysler* — 1981 break-even point of 2.2 million cars reduced to 1.1 million cars.[43]
- *Ford* — 40 percent reduction in break-even point since 1980.[44]
- *GM* — man-hours required per car reduced from 163 in 1981 to 137 in 1984.[45]

U.S. automakers had successively negotiated 1982 contract concessions (representing a potential savings of $2 to $3 million for GM alone), reduced operating costs dramatically, and modernized plants. Yet in 1984 automakers claimed that the Japanese could produce and ship a small car to the United States for $1,500 to $2,000 less than a U.S. automaker could produce the car locally.[46] Iacocca and other auto executives attributed this phenomenon to the undervalued yen and favorable Japanese tax laws, in addition to lower Japanese wage rates. U.S. automakers are left with the uneasy feeling that Japan could duplicate these results with the large-car market in the near future.

1984 Auto Contract Negotiations

The 1984 contract negotiations between the UAW and Ford/GM posed unique and difficult challenges for labor leaders and automakers. Underlying these challenges was the belief that this contract would likely set the precedent for future negotiations between the two parties. Multiple factors compounded the already complex contract negotiations issues:

- Record U.S. automaker profits in 1983 approximating $6.2 billion,
- $6.5 billion in profits for the first six months in 1984,[47]
- Increased automaker involvement in out sourcing,
- Divided UAW rank-and-file opinion on contract priorities,
- Significant decline in number of autoworkers projected by the year 2000, and
- Uncertain "final" date set for the lifting of import restraints.

Owen Bieber, UAW president, faced the difficult task of melding various autoworker's concerns with the concerns of the UAW leaders and appearing at the bargaining table with coherent contract demands. UAW leaders' most pressing concern was to gain job security for its members. A Massachusetts Institute of Technology study recently forecast a 39 percent decline in the number of autoworkers from 1979 to 2000.[48] A sizable wage increase for autoworkers would likely encourage automakers to step up their efforts to produce or purchase foreign cars/auto parts for resale in the United States. Bieber was well aware that every out sourcing agreement made by automakers represented job losses for U.S. autoworkers, ultimately leading to a reduction in UAW bargaining strength.

Some UAW autoworkers shared Bieber's concern. The much-publicized ability of Japan to produce lower-cost, high-quality small cars threatened workers in plants producing U.S. small cars. One Ford Escort assembly worker appeared to sum up the prevalent outlook at his plant: "They'll either have to give us a bigger car to make here, or they'll shut us down. . . . So the big thing is job protection. We shouldn't go overboard on wages."[49]

Unlike workers in small-car plants, large-car assembly workers exhibited a more militant attitude. These workers were quite cognizant of the fact that the 1982 labor concessions helped produce the record auto profits in 1983/84. It is these workers who advocated the "Restore and More in '84" slogan for the 1984 contract talks. One Fisher Body worker claimed, "I'd rather have raises than profit sharing. If they don't make big profits, you don't get anything.[50]

In fact, profit sharing has been no bonanza for autoworkers, even during the 1983 boom sales year. GM and Ford workers received average payments totaling $640 and $440, respectively.[51] Profit-sharing rewards for workers in the highly successful 1984 sales year were estimated to be in the $1,000 to $1,600 range.[52] While these amounts would be acceptable to many U.S. workers, they seem insignificant when compared with the six-digit bonuses awarded to some auto executives in 1983. Other workers saw a high priority for improved pension benefits and a restoration of the nine paid holidays that were eliminated in the 1982 concession contract.

The outcome of the 1984 labor negotiations between the UAW and GM was a contract in which "each side compromised on everything," according to UCLA's (University of California–Los Angeles) Industrial Relations director.[53] The UAW members received 2.25 percent annual pay hikes over three years, payable in lump sums in the second and third years.[54] Lump-sum payments will reduce GM's overtime and unemployment liabilities, and the pay hike was 0.75 percent less than previous increases. The UAW was also able to protect its cost-of-living formula generally.[55]

GM won increased flexibility in the areas of work rules, whereas outsourcing capabilities are only marginally affected. GM pledged to build the Saturn project in the United States and will potentially contribute $1 billion toward a job security fund over a six year period. Payments from the fund go toward supporting or retraining laid-off workers with a minimum of one year seniority.[56] In an effort to eliminate production quality problems associated with substitute assembly workers, GM will pay $50 per quarter to each worker with a perfect attendance record for that period and an extra $100 if perfect attendance is achieved for four consecutive quarters.[57]

While the 1984 compromise contact addressed the top priorities of both bargaining parties, neither side was jubilant. UAW membership, currently hovering around the 350,000 level, was expected to shrink significantly over the three year life of the contract. More than 40,000 workers will qualify for early retirement. An additional 60,000 members might face job loss from other forms of attrition, effects of economic downturns, or plant consolidations.[58] Contract provisions for early retirement incentives and increased pensions serve a twofold purpose: older autoworkers view the contract more favorably, whereas GM gains desired reductions in manpower levels. Meanwhile, automakers are still faced with Japan's estimated $2,000 cost advantage in the small-car market. Although autoworkers viewed the 7 to 8 percent annual wage hikes as modest, Japan's wage costs were expected to rise about 5 percent in 1984.[59]

This wage difference could translate into a larger cost differential in future years. In fact, some auto analysts predicted that if import restraints were lifted in 1985, Japan's share of the U.S. auto market could double from its current 25 percent level to 50 percent. While this opportunity may exist, Japan must also consider the possible repercussions. Data Resources Inc.'s auto analyst John Hammond says, "The Japanese will police themselves pretty heavily to prevent legislated quotas."[60]

Perhaps the U.S. consumer was happiest with the 1984 auto contracts. "There's no obvious reason why GM would have to raise its prices based on this contract," said Hammond. Furthermore, auto contract agreements often set the tone for agreements in related industries. Milan Stone, president of the United Rubber Workers, said he hopes for "a semblance of a tandem relationship with the auto workers" in next spring's rubber negotiations.[61] Lastly, the auto pact lessened consumer fears about runaway inflation triggered by generous union wage increases.

Reagan's Reelection

The reelection of Ronald Reagan was not considered good news by UAW members. During his first term in office and throughout his 1984 campaign, Reagan emphasized his free trader stance.

The enaction of import restraints (ostensibly done on a voluntary basis by Japan but, in reality, the result of U.S.-Japan negotiations) apparently represented an acceptable level of government involvement to the Reagan administration. In fact, the 1984 Republican platform made no significant mention of industrial policy, domestic content issues, or labor policy.

Realizing the short-term effects and long-term implications of out sourcing, the UAW lobbied hard to get protectionist measures passed in Congress. Efforts focused on the domestic content bill. Passage of the domestic content bill would give UAW members "legislated" job security, as domestic and foreign automakers could not introduce "wholly" foreign-made autos into the U.S. market. Reagan spoke out against this bill, while UAW-backed candidate Walter Mondale inserted the following phrase into the Democratic platform:

> It is a sound principle of international trade for foreign automakers which enjoy substantial sales in the United States to invest here and create jobs where their markets are.[62]

Had Mondale been elected president in 1984, further import restraint extensions would have been virtually guaranteed, barring passage of legislation taking even stronger protectionist measures. Reagan's reelection did not offer the same guarantees, but it was generally believed that import restraints would be extended through 1986. When questioned about the possible removal of restraints on Japanese auto imports, Iacocca replied:

> If I were a betting man, I'd have to wager that the U.S. hasn't lost its senses completely. I don't think the quotas will come off, regardless of who is elected President. Some form of restraint will continue. It's in Japan's self-interest.[63]

STRATEGIC POSITIONS WITHIN THE AUTO INDUSTRY

By 1990 GM hopes nonauto operations to contribute at least 10 percent of the company's sales.[64] Some of the company's recent nonauto investments are listed in Exhibit 1. Furthermore, investment in nonauto industries will hopefully smooth out the cyclical nature of the auto industry. GM also intends to follow through with plans to try out unique, high-tech designs for producing a small car — the Saturn project, a project with an estimated $1 billion price tag aimed at eliminating Japan's $2,000 cost advantage in the small-car market.[65]

The Saturn project is "the most clean-sheet-of-paper approach to building a small car GM has ever taken," stated David Cole, director of the University of Michigan's Office for the Study of Automotive Transportation.[66] If the Saturn project lives up to GM's expectations, the anticipated productivity gains from high-tech production methods and less rigid work rules might allow GM to require *fewer* labor hours per car than the Japanese companies.

Apparently questioning the wisdom of GM's overall strategy, Chrysler executive Bennett Bidwell commented, "Roger Smith has more part-

EXHIBIT 1   *GM'S Rush for Partners*

Company	Year	GM Stake (in percent)	GM Investment (in millions of dollars)	Product
Isuzu Motors	1971	34.2%*	56	Pickup trucks, subcompact cars
Suzuki Motor	1981	5*	38	Minicars
Fanuc	1982	50	5	Robots
Toyota Motor	1983	50	100	Subcompact cars
Teknowledge	1984	13*	3	Artificial intelligence
Philip Crosby Associates	1984	10*	4	Quality consulting
Daewoo Group	1984	50	100	Subcompact cars
Electronic Data Systems	1984	100*	2,500	Data processing

*Equity stakes.

Note: Data are from General Motors Corporation.

SOURCE: Business Week, July 16, 1984, p. 50.

ners than Zsa Zsa Gabor."[67] Ford, Chrysler, and AMC have generally confined themselves to overseas auto partnerships and investments in an effort to improve short-term profits and provide a measure of corporate "insurance" against the intense competition expected when the import restraints are lifted. While GM faces the obvious risks associated with corporate ventures into unfamiliar territory, the other three automakers face the everpresent possibility that "domestic content" legislation will finally be approved by both houses of Congress.

As 1984 drew to a close, the Big Three appeared likely to post record profits again and had developed strategies designed to prevent a recurrence of past disastrous years. Inflation and interest rates appeared more stable. Yet no one claimed the battle for competitive ability to be won. When asked in 1984 if the worst days are past for the auto industry, Iacocca responded, "This is a welcome turnaround. I would predict without too much fear that we will do exceptionally well for 3 or 4 more quarters. After that, I'm concerned."[68]

DISCUSSION QUESTIONS

1. Were policies of import quotas and loan guarantees wise? What have been the positive and negative consequences of each of these policies? In other words would we be better off today if we had not had them?
2. What general posture would you now recommend for the government on the following issues:
   - Reducing regulatory restrictions?
   - Extending quotas?
   - Domestic content legislation?
   - Standby loan programs?
3. What conclusions do you feel business leaders, government officials, and union leaders should reach from the recent history of the auto industry?
4. How well do you believe the U.S. auto industry is prepared to compete on a worldwide scale in the long run?
5. Do you think that the U.S. auto industry is more or less affected by government policy than other industries in the United States? How would you characterize business-government relations in another industry with which you are familiar? What should the relationship be in that industry? Why?

NOTES

1. "Santa Calls On Chrysler," *Time*, December 31, 1979, p. 14.
2. "Free and Clean," *Time*, July 25, 1983, p. 55.

3. "Should We Bail Out Chrysler Out?" *Commonweal*, November 9, 1979, p. 613.
4. Fern Schumer, "Chrysler to the Trough," *Forbes*, October 29, 1979, p. 117.
5. "Can Chrysler Be Saved?" *Newsweek*, August 13, 1979, p. 55.
6. "U.S. Auto Industry Operating Results," *1984 Ward's Automotive Yearbook*, p. 177.
7. Reginald Stuart, "The 1981 Cars: Can Detroit Throttle the Imports?" *New York Times*, September 7, 1980, sec. 3, p. 1.
8. "Driving to Rebuild Ford for the Future," *Business Week*, August 4, 1980, p. 70.
9. Ibid.
10. Albert R. Karr and Christopher Conte, "U.S. Now Plans to Aid Ailing Auto Industry, Strive for Cooperation," *Wall Street Journal*, June 27, 1980, p. 17.
11. "Dressing Up a Merger Partner," *Time*, November 12, 1981, p. 51.
12. James C. Jones and Tom Nicholson, "Iacocca's Little Miracle," *Newsweek*, August 3, 1981, p. 67.
13. George Ruben, "Developments in Industrial Relations," *Monthly Labor Review*, May 1982, p. 59.
14. Ibid.
15. Harry A. Stark, "1982: Review/Preview," *1984 Ward's Automotive Yearbook*, p. 10.
16. "Auto Domestic Content," *1983 Congressional Quarterly Almanac*, p. 258.
17. Ibid.
18. Ibid.
19. "U.S. Auto Industry Operating Results," p. 177.
20. "Executive Pay: The Top Earners," *Business Week*, May 7, 1984, p. 96.
21. "Early Warning," *Time*, May 14, 1984, p. 84.
22. David Pauly, "An Embarrassment of Riches," *Newsweek*, May 14, 1984, p. 57.
23. Leslie Wayne, "The Irony and Impact of Auto Quotas," *New York Times*, April 8, 1984, p. F12.
24. Pauly, "An Embarrassment of Riches," p. 53.
25. "Early Warning," p. 48.
26. "Overdrive," *Time*, April 30, 1984, p. 55.
27. Wayne, "The Irony and Impact of Auto Quotas," p. F12.
28. "The All-American Small Car Is Fading," *Business Week*, March 12, 1984, p. 89.
29. "How GM-Toyota Deal Buys Time," *Business Week*, February 28, 1983, p. 32.
30. Ibid., p. 33.
31. "Detroit's Feverish Maneuvering to Sell Small Cars," *Business Week*, January 9, 1984, p. 26.
32. Ibid.

33. "Washington Outlook," *Business Week,* December 19, 1983, p. 129.
34. "A GM-Toyota Plan Goes to Court," *Business Week,* January 30, 1984, p. 32.
35. "Detroit's Feverish Maneuvering to Sell Small Cars," p. 26.
36. "We're a Colony Again: This Time of Japan," *U.S. News & World Report,* April 16, 1984, p. 64.
37. "The All-American Small Car Is Fading," p. 89.
38. Ibid., p. 86.
39. "Auto Domestic Content," p. 258.
40. Harry A. Stark, "1983: Review/Preview," *1984 Ward's Automotive Yearbook,* p. 10.
41. "The All-American Small Car Is Fading," p. 95.
42. "How GM-Toyota Deal Buys Time," p. 32.
43. Wayne, "The Irony and Impact of Auto Quotas," p. F12.
44. Ibid.
45. Ibid.
46. Ibid.
47. "Showdown in Detroit," *Business Week,* September 10, 1984, p. 108.
48. Stephen Talbott, "Auto Negotiators Are Optimistic," *Cleveland Plain Dealer,* September 1, 1984 p. 1.
49. "Showdown in Detroit," p. 108.
50. Ibid.
51. Ibid., p. 110.
52. Ibid.
53. Paul Eisenstein and Mike McNamee, "New Contrast Boosts GM's Ability to Compete," *USA Today,* September 24, 1984, p. 28.
54. Melinda Grenier Guiles and Dale D. Buss, "GM Pact Has Job-Security Gains But Isn't Assured of Ratification," *Wall Street Journal,* September 24, 1984, p. 3.
55. Eisenstein and McNamee, "New Contract Boosts GM's Ability to Compete," p. 28.
56. Guiles and Buss, "GM Pact Has Job-Security Gains But Isn't Assured of Ratification," p. 3.
57. Einstein and McNamee, "New Contract Boosts GM's Ability to Compete," p. 28.
58. Ibid.
59. Steven Flax, "Did GM Give Away the Store?" *Fortune,* October 15, 1984, p. 224.
60. Eisenstein and McNamee, "New Contrast Boosts GM's Ability to Compete," p. 28.
61. "Showdown in Detroit," p. 110.
62. "Politics," *Congressional Quarterly,* June 30, 1984, p. 1573.
63. "We're a Colony Again: This Time of Japan," p. 63.
64. "GM Moves into a New Era," *Business Week,* July 16, 1984, p. 48.
65. Ibid., p. 57.

66. "General Motor's Long-Shot Bid to Beat Japan on Costs," *Business Week,*
    March 12, 1984, p. 91.
67. "GM Moves into a New Era," p. 48.
68. "We're a Colony Again: This Time of Japan," p. 64.

Chapter 3

Developing Public Policy
Processes And Issues

"Too often the Congress has been simply unwilling to make the hard decisions and take the difficult steps." This statement has undoubtedly been applied to the U.S. Congress by someone on nearly every imaginable issue. It is a criticism that might be heard in the context of revamping the social security system, rewriting the Clean Air Act, providing proper incentives for industrial competitiveness, designing equitable tax code revisions, and perusing numerous other policy debates. Such comments express frustrations about the apparent lack of direction and purpose of our national policymakers and communicate what may be a commonly expressed view about a lack of fortitude to deal with the difficult issues of the day.

Does this oft-repeated criticism suggest an inherent weakness in our political system, or does it indicate a long-term strength of our political process? The answer to this question may be important for the future of business-government relations in the United States.

The particular statement quoted above has been attributed to Congressman Jim Wright of Texas in 1975 as he viewed Congress's difficulty in formulating a coherent energy program.[1] While a multitude of national issues could be explored in the context of Wright's statement, energy policy in the 1970s is a useful example of the political context of business-government relations. First, few could argue that Congress and the president did not face an urgent national problem: since late 1973 the country had seen an oil export boycott by the Arab exporting countries, a fourfold increase in the price of imported oil, and a severe recession driven by the increased cost of petroleum. With energy imports amounting to nearly 40 percent of U.S. supplies at middecade, the expectation was great for congressman and for the president to act. National interests were clearly at stake.

Second, the energy problem illustrates the range of fragmented and complex interests involved in business and government relations in the United States. For example, to what extent would the country rely on market pricing to allocate capital to energy production and conservation? However rational economically, the market system encountered the highly political issue of redistributing income: should producing companies benefit from the higher prices arbitrarily introduced by a foreign cartel at the expense of consumers, particularly low-income consumers? Should states richly endowed with oil, gas, and coal profit in relation to energy-poor states or regions? Decisions to control or to decontrol the prices of oil and natural gas struck at the heart of differing group interests about the distribution of income.

The redistribution of income was only one issue inducing a paralyzing political debate among different social interests in the energy crisis. Regulations for environmental quality and for worker safety required additional expenditures of energy; maximizing energy efficiency would require postponing new rules for issues such as industrial air pollution control, nuclear waste disposal, or coal miner safety. The country's energy shortage unquestionably would be aided by greater energy efficiency; could environmental interest groups and workers be required to sacrifice their interests, or would quality-of-life groups be allowed to intensify the energy shortage?

Procurement and subsidy constitute a third way in which governmental response to the energy problem would create relative winners and losers. A requirement to purchase a given quantity of gasohol at prices above market for use in government cars would subsidize midwestern states and private producers of this fuel. A decision to give multibillion dollar loan guarantees to companies for oil shale or tar sand petroleum development would channel public monies to other private firms. Each of these actions has a justification in the name of the public interest; however, each inevitably would favor selective private interests. This fact in itself sparked political controversy.

Energy policy was a major political issue for seven years. What resulted was a series of bills responding to partial aspects of the problem and filled with compromises among producers and consumers, industry and quality-of-life advocates, free market pricing and government controls, and production and conservation incentives. Energy "policy" has been a potpourri of complex pricing schemes, special industry taxes, efficiency regulations, income assistance programs, research grants, and tax incentives. The outcome of the political process well reflects its inputs; diverse and fragmented interests generate a bundle of negotiated solutions, each limited in scope, loosely related in concept, usually uncoordinated, and occasionally conflicting. "It's the best we can hope for," stated one senator in reaction to the 1978 natural gas bill, expressing tired frustration with the struggle among competing interests.[2] His comment may appropriately communicate a realistic level of aspiration for public policy-making in general and may reflect a basic element of the process of public decision making.

This chapter begins with a review of the political insights of the country's Founding Fathers, particularly James Madison, key author of *The Federalist*.[3] Madison articulated a philosophy of government based on countervailing interests, a view that seems to describe today's political process well. Politics has of course grown significantly more complex than envisioned by Madison or as suggested by the brief review of energy policy above. A framework for analysis of public policy questions will be presented that distinguishes between factors involved in the initiation of an issue and factors determining its resolution. The former discusses the roles of ideas, events, and interests in the political process; the latter reviews the parts played by governmental institutions, key personalities, and public opinion. Two examples of policy issues in the 1970s — airline deregulation and oil pricing — are reviewed to illustrate the political process in action.

The descriptions of airline deregulation and oil-pricing policy convey how public policy is formulated through countervailing interests. Some observers of the process, such as economist Lester Thurow, ask whether a more cooperative approach to problem solving is needed to solve major social problems. Borrowing a term from Thurow, we will explore whether the *zero-sum character* of our political process can continue to resolve major issues effectively.[4] For example, increasing savings and investment rates to levels needed for continued economic growth is an issue vital to the business system that needs to transcend traditional party and interest group boundaries. Is it politically conceivable that nonzero-sum policies can be endorsed in a zero-sum political process?

Finally, this chapter seeks to ferret out generalizations for corporate managers from the discussion of political processes. Implications for managers are highlighted in the conclusion.

POLITICAL POWER: WHAT PROTECTION FOR MINORITY FACTIONS?

Sustaining long-term confidence in the American political system and averting debilitating conflict require access to governmental decision making. A group that feels isolated from the process of decision making, or that feels its interests are not adequately accommodated in the outcomes of governmental decisions, represents a risk to the stability and continuity of the society. While the values and interests of social groups may differ widely, confidence of each in the process of decisions is absolutely key to its acceptance of the outcomes as fair.

An excellent example of the disintegrative power of exclusion and widespread charges of unfairness is the American colonists' outrage at the taxation policies of England under King George III. This same demand for fairness dominates the way Americans view governmental processes today. Americans are wary of "special interest" influence on government actions; it is common for leaders of one or another industry to be charged with undue influence on legislation, and probusiness advocates can, on the other hand, be found pointing to the political influence of organized labor.

One critic or another invariably is bemoaning the political power of the elderly, the distortion of national policy by environmental interest groups, or the unfair advantage of minority group members, corporate insiders, or recipients of federal aid.

The single-most important standard by which the American political system must perform is *fairness*. Fairness means access; it means opportunity to be taken seriously; and it means feeling that the ultimate decision, even if it is not the individual's or group's desired outcome, was made for identifiable and defensible reasons. Nothing represents a more direct challenge to a public official than a charge of unfair procedure.

The fairness standard allows the integration of diverse interests in the society and allows adaptation to social changes. What ideas gave insight and guidance to this characteristic of our political process? Let us turn to review political thought at the time the national government was formed in order to identify ways of structuring political debate among competing groups to arrive at national policies.

States Rights versus a Central Government: Will Local Interests or National Interests Predominate?

The center of political life in America after the Revolutionary War resided in each of the thirteen state governments; a Congress of the Confederation existed but with minimal authority of government. Considerable controversy surrounded the question of how consolidated or how autonomous the states should be. Political leaders in some states, New York in particular, advocated the rights of the state over a central government. Sentiment existed among others, though, for a strong central government — undoubtedly, Alexander Hamilton was this position's most vocal and colorful representative.

In 1787 a federal convention was called in Philadelphia to propose modifications to the existing Articles of Confederation, and the delegates proposed a Constitution for a union among the states. The radical nature of this result is indicated in part by the fact that several persons withdrew from the convention, feeling the majority was departing from the original purpose of amending the Articles of Confederation.[5]

In the views of some a central government would allow for a stronger common defense than possible by separate states, and it would better foster development of commerce and industry. On the other hand the citizens of the newly independent states in America had a healthy disrespect for tyranny, and the case for central government would have to be made carefully and convincingly.

Safeguards against the tyrannous use of power in the proposed government were either included in the proposed Constitution or added later. Checks and balances on the exercise of power were incorporated through separating the legislative, judicial, and executive functions of government. A Bill of Rights was added to the Constitution, outlining specific individual rights and their protection from government action. And all powers not explicitly given to the central government were expressly reserved for the states.

New York State was the center of opposition to the proposed Constitution. In order to advance the cause of the Constitution in this key state, Alexander Hamilton, James Madison, and John Jay published a series of letters to the people of New York, later called *The Federalist,* during the year following the Philadelphia convention. Although the significance of these 84 letters in the decision of the New York convention to adopt the Constitution is unknown, they are generally identified as one of the most complete and coherent documents expressing the political thought of the young Republic and the assumptions of political behavior underlying our system of government.

In part these letters dealt with the question of how to ensure that the political process arrives at decisions in the interest of the whole citizenry and not to the benefit of one faction or interest group alone, even if that faction may be a numerical majority. What structure of government will allow all interests or factions to influence the action of government and thus will avert the desire of small groups to fracture and splinter into separate political units? The Federalists saw the possibility to ensure justice and domestic peace in a strong union.

The Wisdom of James Madison

At the time of the Constitutional convention a prevailing view held that the cause of justice could best be served if persons explicitly ensured their own interests by participating directly in governmental decisions. This ideal of "pure" democracy would necessitate relatively small governmental units since physical distance would prohibit direct participation.

In one of the most famous essays of the *The Federalist,* James Madison argued for an alternative means of protecting each social interest. Rather than trying to protect each faction by reducing the size of political units and eliminating diversity, Madison reasoned, oppression is averted by expanding political boundaries and increasing the number and variety of factions. Insert 3.A presents several key passages on the subject of faction from Madison's writing.

Madison's theory of protection from oppression of one domestic interest by another has held up very well, and with the single exception of the Civil War in the United States, the political process based on size and variety of interests has allowed a great diversity of interests to maintain allegiance to the society. The adaptive and integrative characteristics of this system of government are no modest achievements in a fragmented and complex modern world. We now turn to review this system in action.

PROTECTION AGAINST OPPRESSION LIES IN THE SIZE AND DIVERSITY OF FACTIONS

Behind Madison's political analysis resides a fairly disparaging view of humanity. Different opinions form among individuals in any society; and as passions and self-love inevitably attach themselves to opinions, divisions into different interests and parties result. Unless one is willing to destroy the liberty that gives rise to these differences, the main problem becomes one of controlling the effects of self-interest. The following excerpts illustrate his analysis of this situation and his solution to it.

> The latent causes of faction are thus sown in the nature of man; and we see them everywhere. . . . A zeal for different opinions concerning religion, concerning government, and many other points . . . ; an attachment to different leaders ambitiously contending for pre-eminence and power; or to persons of other descriptions whose fortunes have been interesting to the human passions, have, in turn, divided mankind into parties, inflamed them with mutual animosity, and rendered them much more disposed to vex and oppress each other than to co-operate for their common good. . . . But the most common and durable source of factions has been the various and unequal distribution of property. Those who hold and those who are without property have ever formed distinct interests in society. Those who are creditors, and those who are debtors, fall under a like discrimination. A landed interest, a manufacturing interest, a mercantile interest, a moneyed interest, with many lesser interests, grow up of necessity in civilized nations, and divide them into different classes, actuated by different sentiments and views. The regulation of these various and interfering interests forms the principal task of modern legislation, and involves the spirit of party and faction in the necessary and ordinary operations of the government. . . .
>
> A solution to the maintenance of liberty and justice in the society lies in the number and the structure of interested parties; sufficient variety and diversity minimizes the opportunity for oppression. . . .
>
> The smaller the society, the fewer probably will be the distinct parties and interests composing it; the fewer the distinct parties and interests, the more frequently will a ma-

Insert 3.A   continued

jority be found of the same party; and the smaller the
number of individuals composing a majority, and the
smaller the compass within which they are placed, the most
easily will they concert and execute their plans of
oppression. . . .

Extend the sphere, and you take in a greater variety of
parties and interests; you make it less probable that a majority of the whole will have a common motive to invade
the rights of other citizens; or if such a common motive
exists, it will be more difficult for all who feel it to discover
their own strength, and to act in unison with each other.
Besides other impediments, it may be remarked that,
where there is a consciousness of unjust or dishonest purposes, communication is always checked by distrust in proportion to the number whose concurrence is necessary.

SOURCE: Alexander Hamilton, James Madison, and John Jay. "The Size
and Variety of the Union as a Check on Faction," in *The Federalist,* ed. Benjamin Fletcher Wright (Cambridge, Mass.: Belknap Press of Harvard University Press, 1961), pp. 131–35.

PUBLIC POLICY VERSUS GOVERNMENTAL ACTION IN THE UNITED STATES

If the term *public policy* connotes a relatively stable, enduring, and comprehensive set of principles or guidelines for governmental decision making,
it may be more appropriate to speak of governmental *actions* rather than
policies. Few issues in the United States are resolved definitively and remain
unchallenged or unchanged. Public policy is a series of temporary responses to issues and situations — each step partial, incomplete, and open
to challenge and renegotiation. Given the diversity of political forces and
the shifting and fragmented nature of issues and interests, "policy" in the
sense of a predictable governmental response to a known set of circumstances may rarely exist. The system may constantly strive to develop stable
policies, but political processes invariably limit the scope and range of decisions to a less-than-comprehensive set of actions.

Since government actions establish the context or the rules of the
game for corporations that may threaten or support the interests of particular firms or the business system as a whole, contemporary managers have
a stake in understanding the broad contours of the process of governmental actions. The next two sections review some of the salient characteristics
of this process: first, how policy issues originate and second, how policy
outcomes are determined.

How Policy Issues Originate

Events

Fig. 3.1 illustrates three interdependent factors present in any public sector policy debate. First, policy issues can be stimulated by events: the action of the Organization of Petroleum Exporting Countries (OPEC) in 1973 in the Arab oil embargo was an event that initiated a series of problems in the United States for governmental response. The imminent failure of a large corporation such as a Chrysler Corporation or a Continental Illinois bank is another event that threatens some group interest or challenges a centrally held idea. An action-initiating event may be virtually any type of situation: realization that American industry is failing to compete effectively in the international arena, discovery of the toxic effect of a certain industrial chemical, failure of a nuclear plant, or a racial riot. Whether or not these events lead to governmental action depends on a series of other factors. Each event, however, serves to initiate a debate on the proper course of governmental action.

Ideas

The turf of policy debate involves completing ideas and values. A large oil spill, for example, surfaces conflicting values of environmental protection and economic efficiency. Debate about a series of bank failures or the ex-posé of a major violation of insider trading rules invariably occurs in terms of general ideas — the role of market discipline in financial services, the place of fairness in the functioning of capital markets, or the assumptions and rationale of government intervention. Efficiency versus fairness, free-

FIGURE 3.1   *Factors Involved in the Initiation of Public Policy Issues*

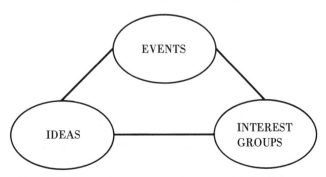

dom versus equity — these constitute central values at the core of political debate. Events are triggers that activate long-standing ideologies.

Interest Groups

A third element of policy debate is the formation of like-minded persons into formal or quasi-formal groups. Common interests may be based on similar values or related to anticipated gains or losses for the persons involved. The gasohol producers of the country, the UAW, or the major steel companies may initiate policy issues by formally appealing for tariffs or quotas on foreign goods affecting their industries. Similarly, interest groups appear on a constant vigil to protect their interests against policy initiatives posed by others.

The last several decades have witnessed a significant rise in so-called public interest groups — private membership organizations developed to mobilize public opinion and exert influence on behalf of special causes such as consumerism, environmental quality, nuclear freeze, and social and civil rights. Many protest demonstrations consist of a group of persons drawing public attention to an unacceptable situation for them. The force and drama of a protest may initiate a political reaction and thus serve as an event in its own right.

Some interest groups are oriented toward intellectual influence — their members advocate a general ideological position such as "supply-side economics" or "more responsive government." Organizations such as the American Enterprise Institute or the Brookings Institution provide a forum for the development and expression of ideologies, particularly in economic policy.

So events, ideas, and interest groups are the ingredients of public policy debates. A controversial and unresolved situation — an issue — may originate from any of these sources, and the ensuing controversy may focus primarily on one or another dimension. Each is, however, vital to the recipe of public issue politics that surrounds and frequently affects the business system.

How Policy Outcomes Are Determined

As events, ideas, and interest groups initiate issue debates and influence the course of the conflict, another set of factors comes into play to determine policy outcomes. The institutions of government — the Congress, the executive agencies, the independent commissions, and the courts — exert major influence on the framing of issues and the shaping of solutions; flows of public sentiment guide and limit the course of events; and the personalities or styles of public officials dramatically alter policy outcomes. Fig. 3.2 presents a scheme of the interrelation between these additional factors in the resolution of public issues. After a brief review of each of

FIGURE 3.2 *Factors in the Initiation and Resolution of Public Policy Issues*

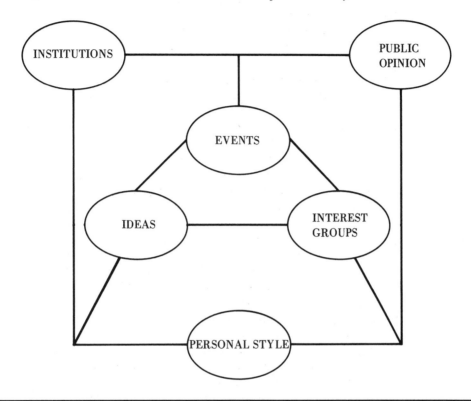

these factors, we examine two public policy issues, airline deregulation and oil pricing, to illustrate the various forces in action.

Institutions

In addition to the President, Congress is one of the highly visible institutions of government. Beyond passing statutes, the powers of Congress are exercised through fiscal appropriation and authorization measures, confirmation of major presidential appointments by the Senate, oversight of all aspects of government activity through standing committees, and special investigative powers.

The centers of power in Congress are numerous, extending from the influential committee structure in each house to political party organizations to affiliations such as the Black Caucus, the Midwest Political Coalition, and other interests that cut across party, Senate or House. The official committee structure of Congress alone is a bewildering array of interacting interests and overlapping jurisdictions allowing an issue to be examined from all angles and exposed to all possible interest groups.

While eminently democratic, the structure of decision making may have the drawback of long delays and loss of central direction.

Political organization outside of Congress may explain as much about the actions of congressmen as does its internal structure, since each legislator has affiliations with, and loyalties to, a complex array of organizations and individuals in a home political district, special interest organizations, and particular elements of the federal bureaucracy. In earlier times political parties exercised considerable control over the voting behavior of individual congressmen. Today, however, a rather broad diffusion of the sources of influence on legislators and the creation of separate and independent bases of power appear to have diminished the role of central political parties. Certainly individual members of Congress have always played powerful roles and continue to do so. But fragmentation and decentralization of power are hallmarks of modern congressional politics.

The bureaucracy, consisting of the executive agencies and independent commissions, is a crucial determinant of public policy outcomes. Agencies, charged with interpreting and implementing legislative mandates, often find themselves at the center of controversy involving Congress, the courts, the Office of the President and other executive agencies, the press, groups having direct interests in the subject of regulation, and public interest groups representing direct or indirect interests in the subject. Agencies attempt to thread their way through this morass of interests and organizations, often buffeted and occasionally discredited in the process. Many regulatory rules, such as the mandatory use of air bag restraints in automobiles or the leasing of previously preserved government wilderness areas for mining, become mired in conflict for years or even decades.

The legislative mandate for regulatory agencies is often general and ambiguous, and thus the range of discretion for implementation is substantial. However, the correspondence between an agency and any one of its external power centers is not direct, and because different groups outside of the agency are often in conflict many agencies experience considerable autonomy.

Many public issues involve conflicts in the rights of differing parties that invariably are turned into legal challenges. The courts thus play a crucial role in extending or limiting the bounds of a debate. A legal ruling, for example, that natural gas wellhead prices fall under the jurisdiction of the Federal Power Commission influenced government involvement in natural resources pricing. Similarly, the courts have defined the priority of affirmative action programs in relation to job seniority in promotion and in layoff decisions. They have stated the bounds of cost-benefit analysis in health and safety regulation, influenced the rules for corporate free speech, defined freedom from unjust dismissal, defined the meaning of monopoly and anticompetitive behavior, and established the basis of personal claims from product injury. No issue of public significance remains untouched by the court system. Legal decision making rarely puts an issue at rest, but it does significantly structure the debate and refocus the efforts of contesting parties. While usually not definitive, the role of the legal system is certainly pervasive.

Public Opinion

Public opinion also influences policy outcomes. If the public is not convinced that $200 billion deficits represent undue risks to the future of society, or that there is a serious problem with the production and conservation of energy in the country, or that the social security system cannot survive under its present structure, then no coherent, long-term solutions will be adopted for these problems. Until public doubts and suspicions about the safety of nuclear energy and the disposal of its radioactive waste materials are resolved, the future for that industry may be dismal. Unless the sense of crisis is sufficiently great or the consensus for change is sufficiently strong, the broad and decentralized process of political participation and decision making guarantees that actions will be incremental, piecemeal, and subject to unending negotiation.

This system of policy-making has the advantage of not moving decisively in one direction or another until broad public support is evident. Its possible drawback may be that a true crisis will not be recognized when one exists and that the delays needed for a national response will be highly costly. Our political system is structured to sacrifice expediency in favor of inclusion. The ultimate adaptability of the system relies on the Madisonian premise that splintering of interests is a greater threat than inability to arrive at a solution to a perceived problem expeditiously.

Personal Style

Finally, leadership weighs heavily in the determination of policy outcomes. A leader, especially the president in the American political system, can appear as a partisan advocate of particular interests or ideas or can appear to stand above the fray in the role of statesman. Presidents can seem decisive or weak, confused or confident and assured, active or reactive, trustworthy or suspicious, intelligent or inept. An effective style lends credibility and power to mold public opinion and to bend the workings of institutions to personal views and public goals. Weak leaders create a vacuum in the political process, which is readily filled by the myriad of interests, organizations, and conflicting ideals. The quality of presidential leadership is perhaps the single greatest opportunity within the system to achieve a definition of mission and to have power exercised in consistent support of concrete directions.

We now turn to examine these ideas in the context of two public policy issues in the 1970s: airline deregulation and oil-pricing policy.

DEVELOPING PUBLIC POLICY: AIRLINE DEREGULATION

Deregulation of the airline industry in the late 1970s provides a case of decisive change in business-government relations. An industry whose pricing and competitive structure had been tightly controlled by government for over 35 years was, in the relatively short space of 3 years, placed in the sphere of market competition with the unprecented proviso that in another 5 years the Civil Aeronautics Board (CAB) would close its doors completely. What political factors were involved in this dramatic departure from past practice? How did ideas, events, interests, institutions, personalities, and public attitudes intersect to cause a dramatic reversal of government policy toward the airline industry?

Issue Initiation

The setting for this sharp reversal of public policy lies in the difference between the climate of ideas and public sentiment present in the late 1930s when the CAB was created and the early 1970s when the wisdom of airline regulation was increasingly challenged. The airline industry in the 1930s was small and highly dependent on contracts with the federal government to carry mail between cities. In 1938 industry revenues amounted to just over $40 million, of which almost 37 percent were mail contracts.[6] From 1935 through 1938 the industry was also quite unprofitable — partly owing to the system of granting mail contracts by the government — having lost nearly $6 million over the four year span.[7]

The public importance of having a reliable means of carrying the mail by air, the apparent risk to industry stability from "destructive competition," the enthusiastic support of government control by industry firms, and the established precedent for price and entry regulation for railroads and motor carriers in the Interstate Commerce Commission were factors that led Congress to pass the Civil Aeronautics Act with little second thought. As one analyst has stated:

> These arguments reflected the nation's widespread ambivalence toward competition in the wake of the depression. Having experienced a disastrous breakdown of the free market — a breakdown highlighted by severe deflation of prices — the nation was leery of relying on unrestrained competition to spur firms to satisfy the public's needs. It was especially nervous about industries which provided essential public services — for example, transportation, communications systems, and electricity.[8]

By the 1970s the experience of the industry had changed significantly and so had the ideas invoked to evaluate its performance. By 1978 the mail subsidy program represented a paltry 3 percent of the industry's $22.3 billion revenues. Uncertainties about the stability of the industry were now resolved. Moreover, the absence of a single major airline bankruptcy might lead experts to question whether innovation was being sacrificed for stability.

Perhaps the most compelling arguments for change, however, derived from the analysis of the economic inefficiency of price and entry controls. Studies showed dramatic differences in airfares between unregulated intrastate routes and similar routes under interstate control by the CAB. An unregulated flight between Los Angeles and Sacramento in 1975, for example, was virtually identical in mileage, flight time, and passengers per year to a regulated interstate flight between Boston and Washington, D.C. Yet the interstate flight cost $41.67, whereas the fare within California cost only $20.47.[9]

Consistently lower prices for comparable intrastate routes led economists as early as the 1950s to challenge the efficiency of continued airline regulation. Moreover, not only were facts available to question the impact of government control, but on a theoretical level, the nature of the industry did not appear to be a natural monopoly and to lend itself to economic regulation. Several general criteria for evaluating the structure of an industry are presented in Insert 3.B in the context of the airline industry.

Economic justification for deregulation of the airline industry had been thoroughly developed by the late 1960s. It remained for a series of events, however, to draw political attention to the industry and to activate personal and institutional processes that might reverse the long-standing nature of business-government relations in this industry.

Between 1969 and 1975 the country and the industry experienced a number of economic changes; after a period of prosperity in the late 1960s and a time of rapid growth and commitment to major new capital equipment by the industry, the country entered a recession. The early 1970s were marked by high unemployment and high inflation — stagflation — and in the fall of 1973 the Arab oil embargo began soon to be followed by shortages and dramatic price increases.

The CAB's response to this economic environment and the difficul-

---

Insert 3.B

THE AIRLINE INDUSTRY: A NATURAL MONOPOLY OR A CASE OF MISPLACED REGULATION?

When is economic regulation appropriate? What are the characteristics of a "natural monopoly" for which governmental regulation is generally accepted as more appropriate? Several important factors to consider are (1) whether the cost of providing the service declines significantly as the amount of service increases, (2) whether there are significant natural bar-

Insert 3.B   continued

riers to entry by competitors, (3) whether there is relatively stable demand across the ups and downs of the business cycle, and (4) whether the costs of operation among producers in the industry are relatively similar and uniform. Reviewing each of these factors in the context of the airline industry suggests its particular structure lends itself more to a competitive structure than to a natural monopoly.

A distinctive characteristic of this industry is that small carriers can compete effectively on individual routes with much larger companies. Thus the costs of maintaining a limited route system or of serving a limited geographic area are not necessarily higher than costs associated with a large and complex service system. Economies of scale are not strongly present in the industry — increases in the volume of service are not proportionately matched by decreases in the unit cost of service. In this sense the industry is not as much a natural monopoly as, say, the electrical power generation industry.

In addition, barriers to entry are relatively low. Although the capital equipment — aircrafts — are expensive, entry is facilitated by the ability to lease airplanes. Moreover, the mobility of an aircraft makes entry into new routes feasible for existing carriers.

Demand for services in power generation is relatively stable across the business cycle. Air travel traffic, on the other hand, is much more sensitive to changes in disposable income and thus fluctuates more widely over time. Where demand shifts downward, the industry needs to be able to react by reducing prices and attempting to expand volume. The economic upswing, then, allows prices to firm or to increase, capital to build, expansion and innovation to occur, or service to improve. Inappropriate regulation of a naturally competitive industry will lead to wide fluctuations in industry profits, as was the case under airline regulation.

Finally, the cost of service in this industry varies by distance, time of day, season, type of service and equipment, the carrier's network of routes, and other factors. Such a differentiated and complex underlying cost structure also argues against regulation; industry performance is more aided by allowing companies to develop specialized strategies that give unique cost and service advantages than to attempt to impose common standards on the industry.

All in all, when viewed according to several concepts of economic reasoning, it appears the decision to regulate this industry as a natural monopoly was ill conceived.

SOURCE: Stephen G. Breyer and Leonard R. Stein, "Airline Deregulation: The Anatomy of Reform," in Robert W. Poole, Jr., ed., *Instead of Regulation: Alternatives to Federal Regulatory Agencies* (Lexington, Mass.: Lexington Books, 1982), pp. 8–10.

ties of the industry appeared to favor strongly the interests of the major regulated carriers at the expense of air travelers and the public at large. A series of unabashed proindustry actions drew strong dissent on the part of industry observers and gave new credibility to the criticisms established in prior years.

In response to a turbulent economy, the CAB tightened controls on competition in the industry.[10] A moratorium on new routes, including route proposals by low-fare carriers, was established. Several major carriers were permitted to meet and negotiate capacity-limitation agreements. Scheduling and price competition were systematically reduced. Airfares were permitted to rise rapidly, increasing more than 20 percent in 1973 alone. The ability of charter airlines, the greatest source of low-fare travel, was substantially limited.

On top of these official actions highly favorable to the industry, a stir was created when the press reported that the chairman of the CAB had taken a trip to Burmuda with all expenses paid by an aircraft manufacturer and several airlines. In the summer of 1974 when Senator Edward Kennedy, chairman of the Senate Subcommittee on Administrative Practice and Procedure, announced that he would hold oversight hearing on the CAB in early 1975, the issue of airline deregulation suddenly moved out of the economic journals and into the arena of politics.

The role of interest groups in the emergence of this public policy issue is less visible than the place of the ideas and events mentioned above. The most direct and tangible interests involved — job security and higher wages for airline company employees, low risk for airline stockholders, and greater security from default for airline lenders — were those protected by the regulation of the CAB. The initiative for a change of public policy had to arise outside of the existing structure of interests, and it was not feasible for those aided by change, namely air travelers, to organize themselves as a political force. This fact may have permitted a latent issue to lie dormant for a period of years until an unwitting series of actions by the CAB struck a spark on the fertile intellectual ground of economic analysis of the industry.

Determining the Outcome

The Kennedy hearings provided a public forum for drawing together previously disparate and relatively unknown criticisms of the anticompetitive behavior of the CAB. The strength of this information served to build political support for change, and coverage of the hearings in the press served to educate the public about the impact of this regulatory system. While airline deregulation was never an issue affecting the public as directly as long lines at service stations during gas shortages, public opinion was at least not opposed to what came to be anticipated as the benefits of deregulation. The only interests outside the major carriers potentially threatened by deregulation were smaller locations that might potentially lose service. Such considerations were, however, outweighed by the advantages to more populated cities, which were likely to receive better service and lower fares. Moreover, commuter service to smaller locations was argued to increase to fill unmet needs. A fairness standard, by which public opinion would be likely to swing, did not present an obstacle to the deregulation efforts.

Leadership for change was provided by an unusual combination of political forces. On the one hand a liberal Senator Kennedy found the existing pattern of regulation to be highly proindustry and to hold little regard for the welfare of industry customers. On the other hand a conservative President Gerald Ford saw the suppression market forces by the government as a significant source of price inflexibility. Deregulation in general became part of his politically oriented program to reduce inflation in the United States, and he threw his support to the withdrawal of government from the airline industry in particular. Backing for deregulation continued at the presidential level throughout the 1970s, as President Jimmy Carter also featured dismantling of price and entry regulation in his economic program.

The full program of deregulation at the CAB did not, of course, occur in one step. The Kennedy hearings were followed by a self-review of the agency endorsing a stance of greater industry freedom. A series of agency rulings tested and defined the resolve of the agency, and several strong administrators, most notably Alfred Kahn, were required to realize fully the potential for essentially putting the agency out of business.

The case of airline industry deregulation is composed of a unique blend of ideas, events, and interests in its origins, and of institutions, personalities, and public attitudes in its resolution. This particular case is perhaps unusual in the absence of organized interests in its origin and in the rapidity and decisiveness of public policy change, once the issue was opened. We now turn to a case of drawn-out and indecisive public debate: the energy crisis and the effort to formulate oil-pricing policy in the 1970s.

POLITICS, OIL PRICES, AND THE PUBLIC INTEREST

The price of petroleum has never been far from the consciousness of the country's elected, and many of its appointed, officials. But when the cost of energy quadrupled in the early 1970s, a sense of crisis became a reality for the American people, and the government's role, competence, and impact in influencing oil prices became a highly debated issue of public policy. A variety of objections — some ideological, others anchored in the enhancement of economic interests — blocked the effort to allow market processes to establish price levels, allocate resources, and determine investment risks. However, neither did the government meet with success in attempting to "manage" prices and allocations through schemes of public control. It is as if public policy were partially paralyzed in choosing a strategy for the national energy problem; the absence of a clear sense of direction meant that energy policy in this country has been disjointed, partial, and incremental.

Initiation of a Policy Issue

Oil did not first emerge as a public policy issue with the Arab embargo in 1973; the history of the petroleum industry has been intertwined with governmental action from the very beginning of this country's widespread use of oil as an energy source. The events of the early 1970s did, however, place the industry on the forefront of the congressional agenda and gave it visibility as an issue in presidential politics. The government's response to the energy crisis of the 1970s was inevitably conditioned by the long history of relations among the government, the oil industry, and the public. As there is rarely a distinct point at which an issue begins or ends, our inquiry starts with a brief historical review of the role of public policy in the industry.

The oil industry has long had an ambivalent relationships with the American public. The industry played a vital part of war efforts in this century with industry and government joining together in service of national goals. On the other hand the industry has been the object of suspicion and distrust by the public. The industry itself has been subjected to chaotic forces involving rapid increases in domestic supply, cutthroat pricing, and unpredictable foreign supplies.

Market dominance was the first major public policy issue focused on the oil industry. By 1900 John D. Rockefeller's oil cartel controlled 87 percent of crude oil supplies, 82 percent of refining capacity, and 85 percent of retail kerosene, fuel oil, and gasoline.[11] Criticisms of Standard Oil's market power as well as the Rockefeller competitive tactics were rampant in the press, within state governments, and at the Federal Trade Commission's forerunner, the Bureau of Corporations. Although new oil discoveries not controlled by Rockefeller had strengthened competition in the industry by 1911 when the Supreme Court decided against the company in the government's monopoly suit, the industry's early history was marked by a divisive, if not alien, relationship with the public.

The government looked at the oil industry differently during World War I, as modern warfare created a national dependence on petroleum. To provide an integrated and coordinated supply of oil to the war effort, President Woodrow Wilson created a National War Service Committee, largely composed of members of the major corporations and representatives from trade associations of smaller producers. This committee, transformed after the war into a private organization called the American Petroleum Institute, was attacked for profiteering and monopolistic practices and putting the private interests of its members ahead of the national welfare.[12] Of course any public suspicion of misdealing was reinforced in 1922 when it was discovered that oil reserves on government land in the West called Teapot Dome were secretly and cheaply leased to private interest in exchange for bribes. Teapot Dome is a symbol today of the industry's early history and provides background for public attitudes toward the energy shortages of the 1970s.

Both state and national governments have also been directly involved in regulating the petroleum industry in the last half century. Contrary to some official predictions in the early part of this century, new domestic discoveries of oil kept pace with a growing demand stimulated primarily by an expanding auto industry and increasing use of oil as a major source of industrial energy. However, within this general growing supply of oil existed considerable instability as old sources were exhausted or as new fields were discovered. Existing rules of ownership encouraged feverish and wasteful exploitation of new finds and led to wide price fluctuations. By one report a major pool found in 1929 near Oklahoma City had 3,600 wells producing by 1931 and had dropped the price as low as ten cents a barrel.[13] The 1920s were marked by boom-and-bust cycles of production and profit, violence between conflicting private interests, and calls for public authorities to rationalize prices and production.

Governmental response was forthcoming, although a stable pattern of public control over the industry was not developed easily.[14] Public commissions in Texas and Oklahoma had attempted to ration production, but new discoveries continually undercut state efforts as excess production could be shipped out of state for sale. The industry and the states looked to the federal government to regulate interstate sale of oil, and in the heart of the depression President Franklin Delano Roosevelt included a plan for governing oil prices and allocation in his National Industrial Recovery Act.

Roosevelt's early efforts to aid the industry were blocked as the regulation of excess oil was found unconstitutional by the Supreme Court in 1935, and federal authority over oil production and prices was outlawed when the whole act was later invalidated. Legislative avenues were not exhausted, however, as a new law provided for federal authority over excess production was passed and Congress approved a formal multistate agreement to coordinate production with demand. This system continued until the late 1960s when demand so outstripped domestic supply that quotas became obsolete.

Significant supplies of foreign oil has been another long-term trend since 1930 that has influenced business-government relations in this industry. World War II and its subsequent economic recovery created a rapidly growing demand for oil. Allocations of world markets among the major international producers failed to limit entry as new countries, largely in northern Africa, opened their own enterprises. By 1953 imported oil constituted more than 12 percent of U.S. supplies, and political pressures by domestic producers mounted to limit foreign supplies. In addition concern was expressed that national security interests were threatened by too great a dependence on foreign oil. In 1955 Congress gave the president authority to limit an imported product if national security were threatened, and in 1959 President Dwight D. Eisenhower implemented mandatory quotas that constituted a major element of the nation's oil policy until 1973. Of course, limiting a major source of supply maintained oil prices.

From 1971 to 1973 President Richard Nixon imposed various price controls on the economy in general and on oil in particular. Resulting major allocation distortions and shortages of gasoline and heating oil led him to remove the long-standing quotas on foreign oil in order to increase supplies. Then, as the country tried to cope with the actions of the Arab producers and the Organization of Petroleum Exporting Countries (OPEC), price controls on oil became a major political issue. As he abolished import quotas, President Nixon increased the existing import fee on foreign oil, which had also been initiated in the early 1930s to protect the domestic oil industry and to encourage development of the domestic refining industry.

The forms of government aid to the oil industry since the 1930s mentioned above — attempts to legislate direct federal control of oil prices and production, endorsement of production coordination among the states, and import quotas and import fees on foreign oil — convey a deep involvement of public sector actions in the workings of the industry. Yet these responses to the dynamics of the industry do not comprise an exhaustive set of industry benefits derived from public policy in recent history. The industry also gained economic benefit from favorable treatment of certain tax policies, namely, depletion allowances, intangible cost deductions, and foreign tax credits. Insert 3.C outlines specific aspects of these tax provisions as they applied to and financially assisted the oil industry.

The oil embargo and sudden increase in the price of oil in 1973 surfaced a complex set of ideas about how to respond to the crisis as well as activated numerous interests that would stand to gain or lose from the direction of public policy. As one views the political struggle over oil price policy in the 1970s, several observations arise from this brief review of the history of the relationship between government and the oil industry. First, the active presence of economic interest groups in debates on oil pricing began long before the question of decontrol in 1973. Since the early 1930s the country had a policy — or at least a series of relatively consistent actions — on oil prices that was highly favorable to the industry. Owing to the rapid rise of prices, the visibility of consumer interests increased, and conflict among different interests was heightened. Also, proindustry ideas shifted somewhat; less was heard of the need for governmental action to stabilize the industry in order to allow it to meet national needs, and more was heard about the need to free it from government price controls in order to allow the market to allocate energy resources efficiently.

Finally, the historical roles of the Congress, presidents, and the courts are evident from this brief review. The oil shocks of 1973 and afterward presented them with new and stressful challenges and conflicts to resolve; oil policy and oil politics, however, was not new ground to any of them.

TAX BREAKS ENJOYED BY THE OIL INDUSTRY: 1926 TO THE MID-1970s [QUOTATION]

PERCENTAGE DEPLETION

Congress in 1926 enacted percentage depletion to establish a rule-of-thumb measure for depletion (depreciation) in the value of a well as its oil or gas is pumped out. Investment in the resource was considered to be a capital investment. The depletion allowance was set at 27½ percent as a compromise between the Senate's 25 percent and the House's 30 percent. Because the deduction was set at an arbitrary percentage of production, the allowance bore no relation to actual costs and permitted tax-free recovery that in some cases vastly exceeded the amount invested in the property. Producers were allowed to deduct 27½ percent of gross income from taxable income, with a limit on the deduction equal to 50 percent of taxable income. . . .

Not until 1969 was any dent made in the special privilege accorded the oil and gas industry. The 1969 Tax Reform Act cut the oil and gas depletion allowance to 22 percent.

Skyrocketing oil prices and widespread animosity toward the industry in 1973–74 renewed attacks on the depletion allowance. Voting for the first time on the question since 1926, the House in 1975 went on record against the allowance, 248–163. The final agreement phased in a lowered allowance for independents, leaving it at a permanent level of 15 percent by 1984 for the first 1,000 barrels of oil production and the first 6 million cubic feet of gas production. Other producers lost the allowance as of January 1, 1975.

INTANGIBLE COSTS

The deduction for intangible costs related to oil and gas production was introduced to the tax code through a series of administrative rulings by the Treasury Department. Congress gave its approval to the practice of rapid write-offs of drilling costs when it passed the Revenue Act of 1954.

The deduction allowed the owner to take an immediate tax deduction for "intangible" expenses — expenditures on

Insert 3.C   continued

labor, fuel, power, materials, supplies and tools — associated with drilling and preparing an oil or gas well for pumping. The deduction was not available for "tangible" costs such as expenditures for pipe, tanks and pumps used in an oil or gas rig.

For most construction projects, intangible costs could be deducted, but they had to be spread over the number of years that the building would be used. For intangible drilling costs, in contrast, a full deduction could be taken in the year the expenditures were made.

FOREIGN TAX CREDITS

Under existing law, corporations can take a tax credit against their U.S. corporation income taxes for taxes paid to foreign governments in nations where their overseas operations are located. In other words, a U.S.-based corporation could cut the taxes it owed the U.S. government by subtracting the amount of taxes it paid to foreign governments on income from overseas operations.

The practice was sanctioned by the government in the 1950s as an indirect means of providing U.S. aid to the oil-producing countries, particularly Saudi Arabia. By labeling as "taxes" most of the charges assessed foreign companies operating on their land, the producing states cooperated with the U.S. government to increase their total take — but at the expense of the U.S. Treasury instead of the oil companies.

President Jimmy Carter in April 1979 asked Congress to tighten the foreign tax credit, but the proposal never moved beyond the hearings stage.

SOURCE: Congressional Quarterly, Inc., *Energy Policy,* 2d ed., (Washington, D.C.: Congressional Quarterly, Inc., 1981), p. 37. Used with permission.

Resolution of the Oil-Pricing Issue

Seven years were required after the shocks of 1973 to arrive at a political solution to the issue of oil pricing. The long and laborious process of political decision making in this case can be attributed to several factors. First, great uncertainty existed about the facts of the energy crisis. Would OPEC cohesion and control prevail? What energy supplies did the United States really have? Could the petroleum industry be trusted? Could the government be trusted? What was the potential for energy from alternative fuels? The crisis caught America unprepared; political certainty, confidence in our institutions, and reliable information were all in short supply.

Second, an intangible factor that might be called *culture* was a barrier to adaptation. Americans were reluctant to see their situation differently and to respond constructively. Not only the daily life-styles of more than 200 million people but a large and complex industrial system had been built on the assumption of cheap and abundant energy. A massive shift in perceptions, habits, and behavior patterns was required, and Americans naturally would be skeptical about the need for change. A predictable response would be to blame outside forces, to deny the need for change, and to hold on to the belief that the situation would correct itself.

Perhaps most important, the problem of oil pricing placed a politically sensitive issue of fairness directly onto the desk of the President and onto the agenda of Congress. Allowing the domestic price of oil to rise to existing world levels, a logical action in the interest of economic efficiency, would be costly to low- and middle-income Americans. The elderly and the poor would suffer disproportionately. Many of our social policies aimed to redistribute income from those with relatively more to those with relatively less; a market-based policy on oil pricing would represent an unprecedented action of "reverse redistribution."

In addition, oil pricing cut directly into regional politics in the United States. Market pricing would favor oil-producing states in the South and the West at the expense of the industrial states primarily in the Northeast. The only viable alternative to allowing distributional effects to result from market processes was to include a principle of geographical fairness in the price of oil through public administration.

Even as public officials were struggling with these difficult issues, forces initiating the energy situation were not static. Late in the 1970s OPEC again increased the price of crude oil, and events in Iran and Afghanistan reinforced the potential instability of the Middle East and America's extreme dependence on foreign oil. The idea that government controls could limit the price of oil and provide protection from OPEC slowly became discredited, as price increases resulted from higher import costs and partial decontrol. Gradually the ultimate value of decontrol in gaining downward pressure on prices gained intellectual support.

Interest group organizations were ever-present participants in the political process. Representatives of consumer, labor, and especially environmental groups held strong and vocal positions on decontrol. On the other side the industry was also deeply involved in energy politics. The number of energy-related political action organizations grew from 12 in 1974 to 128 in 1978, a tenfold increase, whereas the number of political action committees (PACs) overall increased less than three times over these same years.[15] Spending by energy PACs increased from $183,000 in 1974 to $1.9 million in 1978.[16] Oil pricing was one of the bundle of issues in the area of energy that had all the earmarkings of a major political contest.

Against this background of public confusion, technological uncertainty, and tough political issues, the institutions of government — particularly the Congress, the presidency, and the agencies — functioned. The following are several observations drawn from a particularly useful appraisal of the process of energy policy development written by political scientist Walter Rosenbaum.[17] They give a suggestion of the complexity and fragmentation of governmental action.

First, congressional authority over energy matters is not only divided between the House and the Senate but among numerous interests and committees within each chamber. Rosenbaum reports that in the 96th Congress in the late 1970s over 38 committees in the House and some 10 committees and several dozen subcommittees in the Senate held jurisdiction over energy matters. Political maneuvering and rivalry between chambers and committees added to the fragmentation of the process, congressional staff agencies such as the General Accounting Office and the Office of Technology Assessment bid for influence on the course of policy, and ad hoc groups within the Congress such as the Solar Coalition and the Senate Coal Caucus sought to advance particular causes.[18] Such facts simply state the structure of congressional decision making; the interests and outlooks of individual legislators that became expressed in these settings are primarily responsive to the often parochial interests of nearly 600 small and diverse geographic units. "In the end," contends Rosenbaum, "the interests of vastly divergent constitutencies and their claims on Congress, invigorated by periodic elections, gravely inhibit the search for a national consensus on energy policy."[19]

The structure of federal governmental agencies reflects the widespread and uncoordinated actions of the Congress in responding to public issues. Rosenbaum lists 47 separate commissions, agencies, or offices whose spheres of action bear on energy in some significant respect. Of course, conflict is built into the missions and priorities of these agencies, and each is not only protective of its policy claim but often expansionary. Policy trade-offs between energy efficiency and environment quality, between energy production and conservation, between sources of fuel, between industries, between regions, and between economic classes become manifest in interagency warfare. Rosenbaum observed that the executive branch dissolves into a mosaic of disparate bureaucratic interests, each an institutional entity, zealous in an intricate game of alliance and competition with other actors in and outside the administration.[20] A listing and explanation of several common tactics of bureaucratic infighting are presented in Insert 3.D.

While the American Presidents of the 1970s may be first remembered for actions other than their responses to the energy crisis — such as the Watergate affair and Nixon's eventual resignation from office, or the Iranian hostage episode during Carter's administration — the struggle to formulate a defensible energy policy was a continuing, frustrating, and in some cases, damaging element of presidential politics. The predominant task of devising an energy policy fell to Presidents Ford and Carter, and in many respects, the divergence of political interests on energy and the intractability of the issues presented a problem greater than either man. Each was under great political pressure to devise a plan, to show a direction, to act constructively. Yet each was confronted with a divided Congress and a confused public, and each faced a seemingly irreconcilable conflict between the economic justification of decontrolling prices and the difficulty of allowing billions to flow from consumers to producers. The history of energy policy in the mid- to late 1970s is aptly described by the phrase *muddling through*.

While the country debated legislative proposals for gasoline taxes and conservative measures, price controls on oil constituted the real battleground of policy. Over several years the country experimented with a complex and cumbersome structure of prices, involving different prices for new oil, old oil, and new new oil, and attempts to allocate equity among holders of domestic oil and importers through a centralized system called *entitlements*. Gradually the unworkability of price controls became evident, the power of OPEC endured, and no magic solutions to save the American people appeared. The mood of the country shifted, and compromise became feasible. By late decade President Carter was able to strike an accord with Congress permitting full decontrol of oil prices over time with the provision for a "windfall profits" tax on oil company revenues.

Insert 3.D

GAMES AGENCIES PLAY [QUOTATION]

Turfing. An agency's "turf" is its legislative authority, programs, budget, and general mission. Agencies zealously protect their turf, which they suspect is constantly imperiled since one agency's turf may look like opportunity to another. Turf fighting is therefore endemic to bureaucracy.

Look Out for the Clientele. An agency's clientele are the organized interests that have a special concern for its programs. Agencies seek cordial, politically productive relations with their clientele. Agencies often anticipate clientele needs, mobilize these interest groups for political action, and educate their clientele on matters affecting them.

Imperialism.   Agencies desire not only to survive but to prosper. It is typical of agency behavior to seek expansion of its authority, additional programs, and increased public visibility. Imperialism can arise from noble as well as base intentions, sometimes disguised as "protecting the public interest."

Proxy Wars.   Competing clientele groups often mobilize their bureaucratic patrons who, in effect, become proxies for the private group contenders. A common proxy war on the energy front involves policy conflicts between the Department of Energy (responsive to the energy producers) and the Environmental Protection Agency (alert to environmental interests).

Get Help from the Hill.   Agencies constantly form alliances, often shifting, with their friends in Congress on Capital Hill — senators, representatives, committee staffers, and others — and in the White House where they enjoy privileged access. Consequently, major conflicts within bureaucracy seldom end without drawing presidential and congressional sympathizers into the fray.

Waffling.   Agencies "waffle" when they make ambiguous, inconsistent, or contradictory decisions while they ponder what they really want to do about a problem. Waffling often indicates genuine confusion within an agency; sometimes it reflects an inability to make a clear decision. But it is often calculated confusion, meant to keep options open and an agency uncommitted on policy issues.

The Power of Inertia.   Agencies can exercise their power to shape policy by not implementing certain aspects of a program or by refusing to take initiative to change programs. This power often is wielded in disguise, as passive obstruction of policy, when an agency insists it lacks sufficient data to make a decision. Inertia sometimes does arise out of a genuine need to study an issue further. Thus, it is often difficult to determine when inertia is a demonstration of responsibility or an evasion of it.

SOURCE: Walter A. Rosenbaum, *Energy, Politics and Policy* (Washington, D.C.: Congressional Quarterly Press, 1981), p. 87. Used with permission.

Government institutions, presidents, and public opinion were inescapably tied together in the search for a resolution of the oil-pricing issue. In this case the difficulty of achieving early agreement meant that considerable time would have to pass and new experience would have to be gained before positions would soften and compromise would become possible. Oil-pricing policy and airline deregulation provide a contrast in the relative difficulty or ease with which two public issues in the same decade and involving many of the same actors can be resolved.

AIRLINE DEREGULATION AND OIL PRICING FROM A MADISONIAN VIEWPOINT

The "national interest" is an elusive concept. What group does not tend to see its specific cause as coinciding with the national interest? And what proposal for policy change is not garbed in the rhetoric of the national welfare? One need not impute cynicism into the motives of varying interests to accept the validity of their perceptions; group interests are usually embedded in strongly held values and in beliefs about right and wrong. Groups themselves may not be able to tell where more abstract beliefs about a particular policy end and its more direct benefits begin.

The instances of public policy reviewed above — airline deregulation and oil pricing — illustrate the Madisonian premise that our political system should allow participation of a wide range of interests in order to safeguard the society from the domination of any one group. In each case policy changes were made: deregulation of the airline industry, now widely accepted as an intelligent action, is an unprecedented example of how nearly 30 years of public policy was reversed in a relatively short period of time. Of course, this change created uncertainty, risk, and potential loss for those previously protected; no change fails to disrupt the status quo. The point is that private interests were unable to capture public policy indefinitely; the political system responded to the weight of prochange ideas, events, and interests.

Similarly, in the question of oil pricing, an even more sweeping and complex issue, a direction did emerge from the political process that allowed the country to reconcile opposing values and interests. The time was long and the solution may not have been ideal for any specific interest, but the process did work: all parties had their say, none was able to dictate its preferences to the others, and cohesion of the political system was maintained.

Although the political system appeared to work in these two instances, efficiency in arriving at a policy was not its greatest virtue. Airline deregulation was realized some 20 years after economists began challenging the assumptions of regulation. While free market pricing principles are now in place in the petroleum industry, it took price increases dictated by an international cartel to change the industry's view about the government's role in the oil industry. The historically favored position of the industry in public policy could certainly be argued to have distorted market behavior. Finally, although the country arrived at what appears to be a stable oil-pricing policy, seven years' discussion of the issue was a costly debate.

The Madisonian political system favors inclusion and accommodation of interests over speed and rapidity of solution. It is structured to arrive at public policies that hold divergent interests together by allowing any issue to be reopened and renegotiated at any time and by acting incrementally — never at the extreme, always through compromise. As in the case of oil pricing in the 1970s, accumulation of experience with price controls and time for public attitudes to change were necessary for later compromises that were not feasible in an earlier period. Thus expediency of solution was sacrificed in the interest of not alienating any particular group.

EQUITY VERSUS EFFICIENCY: A CENTRAL ISSUE OF PUBLIC POLICY

Equity and efficiency constituted the heart of the debate on oil price decontrol during the 1970s, and the trade-off between these values represents the core issue in many public policy issues. Markets are efficient, and our chances for a long-run rising standard of living are most enhanced by economic efficiency. Furthermore, markets are decentralized and private; they offer our best safeguard against the centralization of political power that can accompany the centralization of economic power in the public sector.

At the same time, markets let the chips fall where they may. The outcomes of market processes create winners and losers in the economic race, and considerable disparities in wealth and income become a fact of the society. The degree of disparity tolerated where basic egalitarian values are present becomes a public issue, and the intersection of politics and economics becomes an important issue for decision. The late economist Arthur Okun states the nature of this conflict in an essay subtitled "The Big Tradeoff":

> American society proclaims the worth of every human being. All citizens are guaranteed equal justice and equal political rights. Everyone has a pledge of speedy response from the fire department and access to national monuments. As American citizens, we are all members of the same club.
>
> Yet at the same time, our institutions say "find a job or go hungry," "succeed or suffer," . . . They award prizes that allow the big winners to feed their pets better than the losers can feed their children.
>
> Such is the double standard of a capitalist democracy, professing and pursuing an egalitarian political and social

system and simultaneously generating gaping disparities in
economic well-being. . . . The contrasts among American
families in living standards and in material wealth reflect a
system of rewards and penalties that is intended to encourage effort and channel it into socially productive activity.
To the extent that the system succeeds, it generates an efficient economy. But that pursuit of efficiency necessarily
creates inequalities. And hence society faces a tradeoff between equality and efficiency.[21]

A case in point serves to illustrate this issue. The elderly are among the
lower-income groups in the society; not only do they have greater health
needs, but they are often less well prepared to meet them financially. Advances in medical science and health care have created a new class of Americans — persons living into their eighties and nineties, which is the fastest-
growing age group in America.[22] The *Wall Street Journal* reported the following figures from the Census Bureau:

> In 1940, only 365,000 Americans were 85 or over, a mere
> 0.3% of the total population. By 1982, the number had
> zoomed to 2.5 million, or 1.1% of the population. By the
> end of this century, . . . the bureau predicts, this oldest old
> group will top 5.1 million, almost 2% of all Americans. By
> 2050, after the postwar babyboomers have all reached the
> highest age brackets, more than 16 million men and
> women will be 85 or over, some 5.2% of the population.[23]

The cost of services, which few would be inclined to deny to this oldest age
group, will escalate proportionately. About 23 percent of those over 85 are
institutionalized compared with only 6 percent of those aged 75 to 84.
Moreover, 40 percent of those over 85 years require help of one or more
persons in daily living. [24] One economist estimates government payments
and services on behalf of persons over 80 was $51 billion in 1984 and will
rise to over $85 billion in 1984 dollars by the year 2000, with no increase
in benefits.[25]

Not only has the structure of the economy changed since the days
of James Madison and the early political philosophers of this country, but
the structure of society is also changing. The "graying of America" is one
trend that has strong implications for our concepts of equity and profound
consequences for our political processes and the role of government in the
economy.

Massachusetts Institute of Technology economist Lester Thurow has
described modern dilemmas such as equity-efficiency trade-offs as "zero-
sum games."[26] All proposals arising from various interest groups have one
common element: they make someone richer by making someone else
poorer. Thus one dollar less in food stamps or housing subsidy for the poor

means one additional dollar remains in the pocket of a high-income individual; greater support for Medicare, Medicaid, or social security translates to higher taxes for those who earn relatively more. There is no way around it: redistribution of income harms capital formation, and increasing the portion of national income in investment means lowering the relative income of the poor. The effects of every transaction sum to zero: $+2$ for one person is necessarily matched by two -1's elsewhere.

Any zero-sum problem is an issue of making short-run trade-offs between conflicting values. Of course, a long-run solution to the question of income distribution might involve expanding the size of the pie through economic growth for everyone to have a bigger slice. However, this solution still begs the question of which groups will sacrifice present income to provide the investment necessary for stimulating economic growth.

The most critical and difficult issue the country may now face is how to increase the productivity and performance of its economy, namely, long-term growth in real income per worker. What is necessary to achieve this goal? One experienced leader in both business and government, Peter Peterson, states the priorities as "to draw down the federal deficit, to promote savings and long-term investment in new plants, in technology, in worker retraining and scientific education and training, and to bring a new view of negotiating to our international economic affairs."[27]

What obstacles exist to possibly prevent these actions? Here the problems of zero-sum dynamics may be felt most strongly: the American society has come to be a consumption, not an investment, society, and the public attitudes and group interests vested in maintaining this orientation are strong. The politics of the aged mentioned above is only one example; the same reasoning applies to holders of federal civil service and military pensions, for example.

Is this problem susceptible to the paralysis of a zero-sum problem, or will it only need time and experience, like the energy crisis, to emerge toward a solution? Will the Madisonian premise of multiple countervailing interests and the American tradition of incremental and fragmented policy response win the day in creating an adequate environment for a healthy economy and provide equity for the social needs of its citizens? Or are we in a new era because of shifts in the basic structure of society where our policies of the past have created vested interests that reduce our ability to balance consumption with investment? Peterson, for one, expresses a pessimistic view of our ability to change easily. A major crisis is the one factor that may be sufficiently strong to submerge narrow interests and to forge a national consensus for change:

> We are a crisis-activitated society. What we may need is an external event, in financial markets, for example, like a big stock market drop and a significant rise in interest rates, which would provide a window of opportunity to create a national consensus behind tough-minded policies. A key

reason the Japanese have been able to achieve as much investment as they have is that they had a post–World War II national consensus behind the development policies the government pursued. In much the same way, the Germans had a consensus behind the idea that superinflation should never be tolerated again, as it was in the 1920s. We may need a crisis to create a bipartisan consensus of the majority of people on the general need to reduce spending, increase investment, change the tax system, put more into human and physical capital.[28]

A CONCLUDING COMMENT: LESSONS FOR AMERICAN MANAGERS

There can be no doubt that the economic issues decided in the political sphere have a direct bearing on the environment of business in the United States. Businesspersons cannot be indifferent to how public policy issues arise and how outcomes are determined; the extent to which private interests can capture public policy or to which we are now playing a zero-sum game on the major issue of economic growth will have serious negative consequences for business, including managers and all other employees. Answers to these uncertainties will not be found quickly or easily. However, it is the role of managers, as well as leaders in other institutions, to identify and phrase the issues, to be familiar with their origins, and to participate in the process of finding solutions.

Another conclusion for corporate managers emerges from this analysis. Even though zero-sum relationships among social and economic interests may not be completely determined, the presence of winners and losers from public actions is sufficiently common to lend credibility to this paradigm as a way of approaching problems involving differing interests. Without waiting to decide whether incrementalism will adequately solve our national problems, it may be well for business leaders to find public policies that develop win-win reward structures. For example, it has been recommended that automatic adjustments in income transfer programs like social security and federal pensions be tied to an index of economic well-being, such as increases in the average national wage rate or even increases in national income per worker. This type of plan would seek to tie the interests of recipients of income programs to increases in the size of the economic pie — increased national wealth will be shared by all interests, and the welfare of diverse parties will increase only if and when national wealth increases.

Of course, the above proposal asks some other group namely, recipients of income transfers, to make short-term sacrifices that will benefit the economy in general and business in particular. Are there such aggregate incentive structures that apply equally well to the business sector? Would it not create a win-win situation if reductions in corporate tax rates or in the taxation of dividends were tied to our ability to reduce tariff protection? There may be various ways in which business benefits can be tied to actions that create advantages for the society as a whole. It may be in everyone's interest to heighten the search for win-win incentives in public policy.

Finally, the nonzero-sum model might be usefully applied by managers to institutional relationships internal to the firm. Corporate relationships with employees, customers, suppliers, and even shareholders can be treated as either zero-sum or nonzero-sum processes. At a general level each of these constituencies and the firm share common interests — neither can be fully successful unless the other is fully successful. On the other hand short-term interactions can often be adversative and win-lose. The task of institutional management, to which we return in a later section of this book, addresses both the more abstract understanding of how interests can be understood in these relationships and what concrete management practices and policies are available to manage them. On the social level of political economy as well as the business level of private management, the nonzero-sum concept may be useful for managers' attention.

DISCUSSION QUESTIONS

1. Review the development of a public policy issue with which you are familiar. Examine its origins and explore how its course has been influenced by institutions, public opinion, and leaders.
2. Compare the process of airline deregulation and oil-pricing policy discussed in this chapter. What conclusions can you draw about the efficiency and effectiveness of public policy development?
3. Do you share Thurow's analysis that political process in the United States is zero-sum? Can you imagine an alternative that would work in the United States? In your view can our policy-making process adequately cope with growing demands for social services and parallel needs to reinvest rather than redistribute national income?

NOTES

1. Congressional Quarterly, Inc., *Energy Policy,* 2d ed. (Washington, D.C.: Congressional Quarterly, Inc., 1981), p. 2.
2. Ibid., p. 3.
3. Alexander Hamilton, James Madison, and John Jay, *The Federalist,* ed. Benjamin Fletcher Wright (Cambridge, Mass.: The Belknap Press of Harvard University Press, 1961).
4. Lester C. Thurow, *The Zero-Sum Society: Distribution and the Possibilities for Economic Change* (New York: Basic Books, 1980).
5. Benjamin Fletcher Wright, ed., *The Federalist,* p. 1.

6. Bradley Behrman, "Civil Aeronautics Board," in *The Politics of Regulation*, ed. James Q. Wilson (New York: Basic Books, 1980), p. 79.

7. Ibid., p. 82.

8. Ibid., p. 81.

9. Stephen G. Breyer and Leonard R. Stein, "Airline Deregulation: The Anatomy of Reform," in *Instead of Regulation: Alternatives to Federal Regulatory Agencies,* ed. Robert W. Poole, Jr. (Lexington, Mass.: Lexington Books, 1981), p. 18.

10. Behrman, "Civil Aeronautics Board," pp. 97–101.

11. David Howard Davis, *Energy Politics,* 2d ed. (New York: St. Martin's Press, 1978), p. 49.

12. Ibid., pp. 52–54.

13. Ibid., p. 57.

14. Congressional Quarterly, Inc., *Energy Policy,* pp. 28–31.

15. Ibid., p. 124.

16. Ibid., p. 125.

17. Walter A. Rosenbaum, *Energy, Politics and Public Policy* (Washington, D.C.: Congressional Quarterly Press, 1981, pp. 61–95.

18. Ibid., pp. 72–73.

19. Ibid., pp. 77.

20. Ibid., p. 85.

21. Arthur M. Okun, *Equality and Efficiency: The Big Tradeoff* (Washington, D.C.: Brookings Institution, 1975), p. 1.

22. "The Oldest Old: Ever More Americans Live Into 80s and 90s, Causing Big Problems," *Wall Street Journal,* July 30, 1984, p. 1.

23. Ibid., p. 1.

24. National Institutes of Health Guide for Grants and Contracts, *Announcement* 13 (Washington, D.C.: November 9, 1984), : 29.

25. "The Oldest Old," p. 1.

26. Thurow, *The Zero-Sum Society.*

27. Douglas N. Dickson and Geraldine E. Willigan, "The Person Prescription: An Interview with Peter G. Peterson, *Harvard Business Review,* May-June 1984, p. 69.

28. Ibid., p. 73.

Jeffrey S. Coomes
John D. Aram

Case 3.A

The Political Economy of Social Security
A Study of Incremental Policy-Making

The launching of congressional budget planning early in 1985 sounded like a familiar script. Congressional leaders confidently talked about across-the-board reductions in governmental spending programs in order to reduce annual deficits projected to run over $200 billion annually for the next several years. President Ronald Reagan put his support behind efforts to reduce social spending, and on the politically sensitive topic of social security, the President said he would not oppose postponements or reductions in social security benefits if overwhelming support was indicated in Congress.

Development of the budget is a lesson in the politics of public policy. Initial aspirations about trimming spending quickly ran into political reality as committee hearings commenced, lobbies were activated, and political coalitions sought to limit serious consideration of cuts in their particular areas. A key element to success appeared to be whether all areas of the budget would absorb a portion of the cuts toward the broader objective of national economic well-being, and a rough approximation of equity would be maintained. If, however, some interests could successfully avoid significant reductions, others could claim inequitable treatment and strengthen their cases against reductions to their particular budget items.

The case for across-the-board, and therefore significant, reductions in government expenditures in the coming years apparently began to weaken as defense-related interests appeared to prevail in placing defense expenditures outside the budget reductions being proposed. Defense Secretary Casper Weinberger, spokesman for defense expenditures, appeared to be the first of many identifiable interest group representatives to avoid or considerably limit the projected damage to their claims on government expenditures.

The social security program was logically a prime target for reductions. A projected $202 billion in fiscal 1986, the program would constitute 21 percent of the federal budget and would be one of the budget's largest single program items. Republican leaders in the Senate suggested a one year freeze in benefit increases to social security recipients by suspending automatic cost-of-living increases. The program was so large that by 1986 such an action would save an estimated $6 billion in the next year alone.[1] Congressional leaders were fully aware, however, that achieving this reduction in social security depended on arriving at a total reduction package of at least $50 billion, including defense cuts.

This plan failed to take hold in the first round of jockeying on the budget during the early months of 1985. Program reductions in defense were successfully removed from the discussion, and reductions in social security expenditures seem to be proposed less frequently and less seriously. By early March Senator Pete Domenici, Republican chairman of the Senate Budget Committee, conceded that the effort to develop a deficit-reduction package by leaders of that party in the Senate had failed.[2] This well-timed announcement appeared to muster pro–deficit reduction forces, since within the next ten days the Senate Budget Committee reported out $50 billion in spending cuts, including freezes on both defense and social security increases.[3] Clearing the Senate Committee, however, was only the first step, as the political game would now broaden and become more complex on the floor of the Senate.

Reducing social security costs is not a new topic on the agenda of Congress; it has preoccupied Congress several times in the last several decades as the system teetered on the brink of insolvency only to be rescued by eleventh hour increases in taxes or reductions in benefits. Nor are budget politics the only context for understanding the political economy of social security; over the long term the program is influenced by the changing demographic characteristics of the nation. The purpose of this case is to examine the interaction of politics and economics in the social security program — today and in its uncertain future.

OVERVIEW

In March 1983 Congress enacted a series of amendments to the Social Security Act designed to guarantee the fiscal integrity of social security well into the twenty-first century.[4] These amendments were designed to save the system from bankruptcy. For 36 million beneficiaries the amendments came just in time: by July 1 of that year the social security trust fund would have been bankrupt.[5]

Although the President's Commission on Social Security Reform added a new ingredient to social security legislation — bipartisanism — the 1983 amendments epitomized a long-standing strategy toward social security reform: incrementalism. Rather than initiate wide-scale reform, Congress chose to make relatively minor revisions that would accommodate interest groups and temper periodic political pressure.

The fact that social security was recently revised, fine-tuned, and otherwise "improved" is not new. Revisions in 1950, 1956, 1965, and 1972 altered the system and expanded coverage to meet current financial obligations and societal expectations. The threat of bankruptcy in 1983 was not unknown to the program; it faced a similar crisis in 1977. In that year Congress enacted the country's largest peacetime tax increase, designed to raise $227 billion in ten years. This action was also supposed to promote fiscal responsibility and safety for the system well into the next century.[6] Yet by 1980 a new round of revisions and changes were needed to ensure solvency of the system.

Congress has struggled with this balancing act since social security was created in 1935. The first financing plan presented to Congress in the mid-1930s projected deficits in the social security trust fund by the 1970s. A compromise suggested by the Roosevelt administration attempted to avert the long-term crisis by increasing the initial tax rate by 100 percent, from 1 percent to 2 percent. Still, long-term problems appeared.[7] The issue has always revolved around long-term financial solvency versus increasing benefits in the short term to meet current needs and expectations. Through the years social security has been changed several times, usually to expand coverage or to increase benefit payments. These changes have institutionalized early retirement for men and women, disability insurance, and automatic cost-of-living adjustments for retirees.

However, changing demographics and a volatile economy have led these changes and improvements to threaten the system's financial viability. The 1977 amendments raised taxes enormously to pay for social security, and the 1983 amendments accelerated the revised taxes on wage earners.[8] It appears that the impact of previous incremental improvements in benefits has placed more pressure on the system than it may be able to withstand.

Maintaining the balance between solvency and expected benefits has not been easy. Today the graying of America and a concomitant decrease in the number of younger workers threaten to place new strains on an already burdened social security system. A lower birthrate has led to the development of a considerably older population with fewer workers available to support an increasing number of retirees. Part of the increase in social security taxes reflects this changing demographic picture.[9] Because social security is essentially a pay-as-you-go system where current workers provide support for current retirees, it is natural that taxes for current workers will increase as fewer employees support a greater number of beneficiaries.[10] These demographic changes threaten to create conflict between older Americans and younger Americans who have just entered or who are just about to enter the work force.

Older Americans have come to rely on social security as a means of support and appear to be willing to fight politically for it. Yet younger workers may tire of the financial burden that social security places on their life-styles and their earnings. It is possible that the final outcome of the social security dilemma rests with the manner in which the two groups *approach* its resolution. The following are several more specific dimensions of this potential social conflict.

AN OLDER, POLITICALLY MORE POWERFUL AMERICA

America is becoming an older society. One survey reported that individuals age 65 and older account for over 11 percent of the nation's population.[11] Another survey reinforced this notion of increasing political strength by reporting that of the active American electorate, 38 percent receive social security benefits.[12]

The elderly are also politically vocal. Margaret Kuhn of the Gray Panthers made the following statement before the House Ways and Means Committee hearings on social security:

> Gray Panthers believe that social security is a contract between the American people and their elected government to provide every citizen with the dignity of financial independence.[13]

Kuhn argued that social security is a right, much like the freedom of speech.[14] By maintaining that social security is a right, groups like the Gray Panthers and other senior citizens' groups attempt to alter the objective of social security. As originally designed, social security was supposed to help "ward off destitution,"[15] not to promote or guarantee financial independence. Viewing the program as a means of financial independence places additional pressures and constraints on legislators who determine the benefits and taxes associated with the program. In this light, enacting changes that substantially curtail or lessen benefits could be politically risky.

The 1982 congressional elections are a good illustration of the potential political power of the elderly. In 1981 and 1982 President Reagan attempted to address the problems of social security and the growing budget deficit. Part of the President's 1981 reform proposal called for "sharp and rapid cuts in early retirement benefits."[16] In early 1982 Republicans proposed reducing the federal deficit by $40 billion with increased social security taxes or decreased benefits.[17] Both proposals were defeated. Many argue that these maneuvers contributed to the loss of 26 House seats for the Republicans in 1982.[18]

If social security is viewed as a right, it is not surprising that elderly political groups are flexing their political muscles and translating increasing numerical strength into political victories. Congressman Claude Pepper, an 83-year-old Democrat from Florida in 1984, was a strong advocate of social security and other senior citizen issues. During the furor over social security reform in the 1980s, Pepper was a prominent and vocal participant in the debate. For instance, after the first two proposals by Republicans to alter social security in 1981 and 1982 were overwhelmingly defeated, Pepper personally traveled "to 26 states to campaign for Democratic candidates and against the GOP's record on the issue."[19] Some 60 of his candidates were elected.[20]

During the midst of the 1984 presidential election Ronald Reagan acknowledged that he was aware of this group's political strength. In August Reagan asked "Congress to enact a special cost-of-living adjustment for social security before the November election."[21] Cost-of-living adjustments are tied to increases in the Consumer Price Index (CPI) of greater than 3 percent, according to the 1972 social security amendments. Reagan's bid for this portion of the electorate was an interesting diversion, since at that time the projected CPI increase was around 2.8 percent, below the required 3 percent. The President's gambit to strengthen his support among older Americans was expected to cost $5 billion in 1985 and to increase interest expense on the deficit by "$500 million annually."[22]

Social security has gradually become incorporated into the political system of American society. Retirees, for whatever reason, have come to view social security as a matter of principle. Attempts to alter the system are viewed as tampering with basic rights. As a result social security appears to have become an untouchable entitlement program. The Republican's loss of 26 House seats in 1982 and President Reagan's cost-of-living adjustment provision in 1984 illustrate the emerging political strength of this sector of the electorate.

A SMALLER, YOUNGER WORK FORCE

The costs of social security continue to escalate, placing a greater burden on a younger and smaller work force. The so-called young worker is not as politically active as his graying counterpart. However, the increasing burden on the current worker may instigate some political reaction.

When social security was established in 1935, there were approximately forty-two workers for every potential recipient in the system. Yet that rate has been decreasing since 1940 to its current three-to-one ratio.[23] As the number of beneficiaries increases and the number of workers decreases, the way to maintain the level of benefits promised is to raise the tax assessed equally to employers and employees to support the program. James Dale Davidson of the National Taxpayers' Union summed up this burden in a report to Congress:

> There is little in the Commission's report to comfort taxpayers, particularly young taxpayers. For the young work-

ers entering careers now, tax rates may reach 25 percent to
33 percent of payroll in order to pay benefits being
promised.[24]

Davidson's projection of even higher tax increases is probably related to
the grim statistic that by the early twenty-first century there will be only
two workers available to support every retiree.[25]

The burden to all workers comes in the form of the social security
tax, a rate that has been increasing steadily during the last decade. For
example, with the current tax rate of 7.05 percent that a worker pays on
his first $39,000 in earnings, the worker contributes roughly $2,750 in social security taxes. By 1990 the same worker will pay 7.65 percent of his
first $40,700.[26]

If social security is viewed as an investment, there is little likelihood
that the current worker will receive a good return on his or her investment,
that is, his or her contribution to the system. In fact, an individual will get
far less in benefits than he or she paid in taxes.[27] One study reports that
"individuals and couples between the ages of 24 and 34 can expect to pay
more in social security taxes than they receive in benefits."[28] The authors
report that in this case new social security wealth — the difference between
what one pays in and what one receives — is negative.[29] Assuming this
scenario is more pronounced in the coming years, will the younger worker
be willing to contribute to pay into the system?

Some observers are concerned that challenges to the viability of social security have already surfaced. In her testimony before Congress,
Kuhn warned of "dangerous divisions . . . arising between the old and the
young.[30] As a greater economic burden for existing workers to carry the
system becomes apparent, younger workers may seriously question the
system.

A POTENTIAL DECREASE IN PARTICIPATION

Coupled with the increasing cost of social security to current workers is the
increasing availability of private pensions, not widely available during the
depression.[31] A 1984 report by the Social Security Administration reported
that between 1970 and 1982 the number of new beneficiaries that also received pensions increased from 25 percent to 40 percent for married couples, from 42 percent to 53 percent for men, and from 12 percent to 24
percent for women.[32] Another study demonstrated that the trend in the
American workplace is toward more pension coverage. This study found
that in 1979, 48 percent of the population was covered by some form of
pension plan.[33]

The 1983 amendments include a tax on benefits for individuals who make over $25,000 and for couples who make over $32,000.[34] Two-income families can expect to generate more-than-comfortable pensions. Added to social security, these benefits could be taxed at a fairly high rate of 50 percent.[35] Are current workers prepared to pay into social security and then have their benefits taxed?

Individuals may object to mandatory participation in the public program and demand the opportunity to substitute private plans to ensure their old-age income needs. Such a development, should it occur, would shrink the number of contributing participants in the system even more and accelerate future fiscal crises for the program.

TENUOUS ECONOMIC FORECASTING

Compounding the demographic pressure on social security, economic assumptions used to formulate the 1983 amendments may be inaccurate. Tenuous economic projections and a growing concern about the impact of social security taxation on economic growth create long-term problems that an incremental political process tends to postpone or ignore.

The actuarial estimates of the short-term and long-term trends for social security were based upon an annual growth rate of 3 percent and an annual unemployment rate of 5 percent.[36] However, actual economic performances during the last ten years have not approached these estimates. Annual growth has averaged 2 percent, and annual unemployed has averaged closer to 6 percent than 5 percent.[37] Economic performance in 1984, for instance, was questionable — inflation-adjusted growth was 2.9 percent and unemployment was 7.5 percent.[38]

The fiscal soundness of social security, then, rests with economic performance. If the economy can perform at levels close to those projected, short-term solvency of social security can be relatively assured. However, the 1970s demonstrated how fickle the economy can be. If the economy does not perform at these levels, the reserve fund may not accumulate the funds required to cushion the system.

In addition, there are the added strains on the younger worker. Inaccurate projections that do not meet economic performance could require additional tax levies to further guarantee the solvency of the system. Financial projections are subject to wide error, and some analysts believe the program will rest on tenuous footing until the beginning of the twenty-first century. According to one report:

> The long-run projections still are guesses, and the experience of the 1970s has surely taught us that much can go wrong with the economy. If anything does go wrong, [social security] is not especially well-equipped to cope with it.[39]

THE IMPACT ON CAPITAL ACCUMULATION

There is an emerging body of work that suggests that social security — through the taxes it requires — has a negative impact on savings.[40] Social security is designed as a current consumption program, a pay-as-you-go or intergenerational program whose taxes are used to pay current beneficiaries. Essentially, the function of social security is to transfer income to the elderly from current wage and salary earners. Pay-as-you-go means that the money is transferred and, to a great extent, spent and not saved. The overall impact on the economy is to lessen the pool of funds available for investment.

Savings play a major role in the economy. Income transfers leave fewer dollars available to persons having higher rates of savings; therefore, capital needed for the expansion of the economy is more expensive. It is generally thought that capital formation for new equipment, plant modernization, and product development leads to economic growth benefiting everyone in terms of an improved standard of living.[41]

Following typical neoclassical economic models, an increase in taxes will lead to a decrease in savings. In the context of social security, as an individual's income is taxed at a higher rate for the purpose of creating retirement income, that individual taxpayer has less money available for savings. Some studies have demonstrated "that the net impact of social security reduces aggregate private savings."[42] In addition, other studies indicate that where individuals assume more responsibility for their income security in old age, such as early retirement, they save more.[43]

FUNDED PENSION: A FEASIBLE SOLUTION?

While the piecemeal fashion of patching up social security alleviates current societal pressures, it has not alleviated underlying threats to its solvency. Changing demographics and increasing costs of the pay-as-you-go social security system appear to have been unresolved.

One possible approach is to create a funded pension program that permits investment and provides for old-age support. Pension funds are growing and are covering more and more workers. Could not Congress recast the entire system into a funded pension program?

A funded system could prove to be more equitable, since each person would receive what he or she had contributed. For participants who do not make enough money or cannot contribute, the government could create special assistance programs. One of the supporting pieces of legislation for the 1935 Social Security Act called for an old-age assistance program, essentially an income transfer program for the elderly who were not covered by social security.[44] In 1972 Congress created Supplemental Security Income (SSI) for social security recipients who needed additional assistance.[45] Similar programs could be created to meet any shortfall in pensions, whether funded in the private or the public sectors.

The major drawback to developing a funded system lies in the cost of making a transition from pay-as-you-go to a funded program. The government would need several trillion to generate one year's interest to cover the cost of current social security obligations.[46] To create a fund, workers would essentially be double taxed "once to pay the benefits of current retirees and again to contribute to the fund that would pay their own retirement in the future."[47]

SUMMARY

An incremental approach to the integrity of social security has postponed the program's day of reckoning. Incrementalism, however, becomes increasingly costly as general economic benefits are reduced through increased income transfers. Moreover, broadened coverage of private pension plans and taxation of benefits may increasingly lead to challenges to the fairness of the system.

The longer the system goes with piecemeal and patchwork remedies, the more costly and therefore the more difficult it will be to change its underlying premises. In fact, it may presently be too expensive to change to a more logical program of funded pensions. The central issue is whether the power of the elderly will be used to channel an increasing proportion of society's wealth to itself. If so, this special interest group's armlock on the economy may lead to long-term losses for all groups, and an incremental political process — initially designed to prevent this outcome — will have failed. The country may be on a course that is too late to change and for which previously reliable processes of political decision making may be ineffective.

DISCUSSION QUESTIONS

1. Evaluate the following assumptions discussed in the case:
    a. The social security program will pose an increasingly intolerable burden on the economy.
    b. The elderly compose a politically powerful interest group whose interests will be increasingly difficult to compromise.
    c. A political process that results in incremental, not radical, changes in public policy may not be capable of moderating the demands of the elderly on the economy.
   Identify counterpoints to these assumptions where contrary evidence exists.

2. Evaluate the likelihood of a series of financial crises in social security financing in the coming decades.
3. Develop your own scenario for the future of the social security program, including economic and equity considerations.

NOTES

1. "Income Security: COLA Freeze," *National Journal,* February 16, 1985, p. 399.
2. Jeffery H. Birnbaum, "Domenici Concedes Defeat in Efforts by GOP Senators in Plan to Cut Deficit," *Wall Street Journal,* March 5, 1985, p. 64.
3. Jeffery H. Birnbaum, "Senate Panel's Deficit-Cutting Plan Gets Lukewarm Welcome from Dole, Others," *Wall Street Journal,* March 15, 1985, p. 2.
4. Alicia Munnel, "The Current State of Social Security Financing," *New England Economic Review,* May-June 1983, p. 62.
5. Timothy B. Clark "Congress Avoiding Political Abyss by Approving Social Security Changes," *National Journal,* March 19, 1983, p. 611.
6. Robert W. Merry, "The Social Security Hot Potato," *Policy Review,* Spring 1984, p. 64.
7. Arthur J. Altmeyer, *The Formative Years of Social Security* (Madison: University of Wisconsin Press, 1966), p. 34.
8. Munnell, "Current State," p.64.
9. Ibid., p. 49
10. Ibid., pp. 49–52.
11. David L. Baumer and Robert L. Clark, "The Effects of Alternative Strategies for Social Security Reform," *Texas Business Review,* July-August 1982, p. 193.
12. "The Untouchable," *Wall Street Journal,* editorial January 16, 1985, p. 28.
13. Margaret Kuhn, *Hearings before the Subcommittee on Social Security of the Committee on Ways and Means,* U.S., Congress, House, 98th Cong. 1 sess., February 4, 7, 8, 1983, p. 225.
14. Ibid.
15. Jason Bergers, ed. *Saving Social Security* (New York: H. W. Wilson, 1982), p. 10.
16. Clark, "Congress Avoiding Political Abyss," p. 614.
17. Ibid., p. 614.
18. Ibid.
19. Ibid.
20. Ibid.
21. "Reagan's Risky Gambit on Social Security," *Business Week,* August 6, 1984, p. 21.
22. Ibid.

23. Munnell, "Current State," p. 50.

24. James Dale Davidson, *Hearings before the Subcommittee*, p. 470.

25. Munnell, "Current State," p. 50.

26. Congressional Quarterly, Inc., *Social Security and Retirement*, (Washington, D.C.: Congressional Quarterly, Inc., 1983), p.14.

27. Martin S. Feldstein and Anthony Pellechio, "Social Security Wealth: The Impact of Alternative Inflation Adjustments," *Financing Social Security*, ed. Colin D. Campbell (Washington, D.C.: American Enterprise Institute for Public Policy Research, 1979), p. 101.

28. Ibid., p. 100.

29. Ibid., p. 101.

30. Kuhn, *Hearings before the Subcommittee*, p. 226.

31. Congressional Quarterly, Inc., *Social Security and Retirement*, p. 114.

32. "More Retirees Have Pensions, Social Security Study Shows," *Plain Dealer*, (Cleveland: Ohio) December 2, 1984, p. 12A.

33. Congressional Quarterly, Inc., *Social Security and Retirement*, p. 139.

34. Munnell, "Current State," p. 53.

35. Ibid.

36. Doug Bandow, "The Faulty Foundations of Social Security," *Wall Street Journal*, April 25, 1983, p. 30.

37. Ibid.

38. Delinda Karle, "Crystal Balls Shine . . .", *Plain Dealer*, (Cleveland: Ohio) January 21, 1985, p. 2E.

39. Lindley H. Clark, Jr., "Social Security Isn't as Secure as It's Cracked Up to Be," *Wall Street Journal*, December 18, 1984, p. 33.

40. Martin S. Feldstein, "Social Security," *The Crisis in Social Security*, ed., Michael J. Boskin (San Francisco: Institute for Contemporary Studies, 1978), p. 21.

41. Willis L. Peterson, *Principles of Economics: Macro* (Homewood, Ill.: Richard D. Irwin, 1980), p. 70.

42. William C. Hsiao, "Indexing Social Security: What to Do," in *Financing Social Security*, ed. Colin D. Campbell (Washington, D.C.: American Enterprise Institute for Public Policy Research, 1979), p. 35.

43. Joseph A. Pechman, "The Social Security System: An Overview," *The Crisis in Social Security*, ed., Michael J. Boskin (San Francisco: Institute For Contemporary Studies, 1978), p. 37.

44. Congressional Quarterly, Inc., *Social Security and Retirement*, p. 14.

45. Ibid., p. 21.

46. June A. O'Neill, "Future Financing of the System," in *Financing Social Security*, ed. Colin D. Campbell (Washington, D.C.: American Enterprise Institute For Public Policy Research, 1979), p. 185.

47. Ibid.

Government Policy in Economic and Social Regulation

Because society is dynamic, each generation inevitably confronts fresh challenges to the task of organizing social and economic affairs. Gradual but powerful changes alter the structure of the economy, spawn new expectations for the business system, and lead to revision of past relations between the private and the public sectors.

The fields known today as economic and social regulation have arisen in response to fundamental, largely unanticipated changes in society and the industrial system. A growing difference in the relative size of large and small firms was one consequence of rapid economic growth in the latter half of the nineteenth century. In addition, the presence of one or several large firms in a single industry affected the dynamics of competition in that industry. Because the number of competitors, the structure of industries, and the competitive practices used between competitors were thought to have consequences for the welfare of society in general, these aspects of the economy fell subject to an area of public policy generally referred to as *industry regulation and antitrust law.*

Similarly, by the early twentieth century a new awareness arose concerning the unintended impact of a few business activities on the general populace. Initially the effects on consumers of some practices and products in the food and drug industries were questioned and found to need improvement. Again, government policy was largely accepted as the instrument by which needed change in business practices could be assured.

Examples of health and safety concerns early in this century were harbingers of numerous current issues of health, safety, and environmental quality and of heightened levels of technological sophistication and social awareness. Social regulation has emerged in this century as a major and controversial dimension of business-government relations.

The three chapters of this section address the origins and major issues in these fields of economic and social regulation. We depart on this review with a discussion of antitrust and trade policy in Chapter 4. The background of the antitrust laws is briefly presented, legal landmarks are reviewed, and current issues and ambiguities in the application of antitrust laws are discussed.

Chapters 5 and 6 address some of the salient issues involving social regulation in the United States. Chapter 5 focuses primarily on the debate about the appropriate level of health, safety, and environmental regulation. Emphasis is placed on understanding cost and benefit arguments both at the general level of the economy and at the level of specific regulations.

Chapter 6 reviews systems for influencing business practices other than direct command and control policies: information disclosure, tort liability, and market-based incentives for pollution reduction, for example. The potential and limitations of alternative influence strategies are discussed.

Chapter 4

Antitrust and Trade Regulation

Business-Government Relations in the Areas of Competition, Concentration, and Conglomerates

The present structure of the U.S. economy was formed in the period between the end of the Civil War and the early 1900s. In this period, marked by an average annual economic growth of nearly 7 percent between 1870 and 1910, relatively small industries developed the size and scope necessary for industrialization. However, this expansion of total production was augmented by changes in the structure of the manufacturing sector. In virtually all areas critical to economic growth — steel, machinery, transportation, oil, food processing — widespread business consolidations, mergers, and combinations occurred. In place of numerous small producers in many different locales, many industries were transformed into a fewer number of larger and more integrated producers.

While internal expansion was a source of firm growth, the primary means of growth was merger. For example, the latter third of the nineteenth century saw a two-thirds drop in the number of steel producers, whereas the volume of industry production increased ten times. Over this same approximate period, the number of shipbuilding firms decreased 50 percent, whereas industry output doubled.[1] These are not isolated instances; many industries experienced consolidation and greater concentration. One historical analysis documents this process:

> By 1901 . . . nearly one-third of the value added in manufacturing was accounted for by industries with concentration ratios[*] of 50 percent or higher. For certain industries

---

*The *concentration ratio* is the percentage of industry sales accounted for by a small group, in this case four, of the largest producers in the industry.

the 1901 figures show ratios as high as 78.8 (steel), 71.0 (paper and allied products), and 57.3 (transportation equipment).[2]

Economic causes for the emergence of this industrial structure are fairly clear: (1) the potential volume from nationwide markets gave cost advantages to larger firms; (2) combination of numerous small manufacturers into a large production system improved efficiency in planning, management, and capacity utilization; and (3) expansion backward into the supplying industry or forward into the buying industry reduced unit costs, lowered customer prices, and allowed greater profits for reinvestment.

Major industrialists themselves assigned the cause of concentration to the destructive nature of competition, according to a report on this subject submitted to the U.S. Congress in 1900. Reporting the testimony of many leading industrialists, the study stated that "among the causes which have led to the formation of industrial combinations, . . . competition, so vigorous that profits of nearly all competing establishments were destroyed, is to be given first place."[3] In addition, a freely competitive economy provided opportunity for amassing tremendous personal wealth, a process aided by the construction of industrial empires under the control of a single person or family.

The transformation from fragmented to more concentrated industries was not smooth and harmonious. It was often marked by severe and occasionally ruthless competitive tactics such as the undercutting of competitors' prices to drive them out of business. At the same time, collusion and combinations between competitors often substituted for cutthroat competition. Market control was frequently gained through the creation of "trusts" in which stockholders of competing firms would exchange their shares for certificates in a common corporation, or trust. The management of the trust could then coordinate pricing and production volume of former competitors to maximize profits. By 1900 such combinations or similar arrangements existed in the petroleum, sugar, whiskey, tobacco, steel, silver mining, and copper industries, as well as in many others. One exhaustive compilation of trusts published in 1904 listed seven "greater industrial trusts" that controlled over 1,500 plants and had a capitalization of $2.7 billion and identified another 298 "lesser industrial trusts" with control of nearly 3,500 plants and capitalization of $4 billion.[4]

Industrial consolidation had a number of economic and political consequences. Often, smaller producers were unable to survive for lack of efficiency or the predatory pricing of larger firms. Small competitors often failed. In addition, it meant that the economic power of some groups, such as farmers, who were geographically dispersed would be weakened. Industry consolidation into firms of national scope also threatened the stability and survival of smaller, independent wholesalers and retailers. Perhaps most important, the rapid consolidation of visible industries rekindled Jeffersonian skepticism and fear of centralized economic power.

Unrestricted corporate growth and industry dominance, marked by questionable tactics of competition and economic dislocations, generated public hostility toward large and monopolistic corporations. Economic historians have identified converging sources of opposition to the emergence of monopolistic combinations and trusts:

> During the post–Civil War period, the opposition to government-granted monopoly was transferred to private monopolies created by mergers and combinations. This feeling against restraints of trade and private monopoly was intensified by the unfavorable situation of a number of politically powerful groups. Farm organizations, especially, were outspoken in their condemnation of monopoly and big business. The bargaining position of labor left the working man particularly susceptible to arguments advocating regulation or abolition of monopoly. The spread of large-scale enterprise in most industries was also at the expense of small businessmen who felt, with some justice, that they had been ruined by the ruthless, competitive tactics of large corporations. Finally, the impoverished condition of the southern states left the people of that area with a bitter prejudice against Yankee industrialism which was easily transferred to the giant corporations.[5]

Destructive competition, business collusion, and public distrust of increasing corporate size and economic centralization influenced public policy in several ways. First, the government became involved in stabilizing the railroad industry through the Interstate Commerce Commission (ICC) in 1887. Small shippers, generally facing higher costs than large shippers, welcomed government involvement; persons and businesses paying higher rates because their routes were less heavily used supported regulatory control of rates; and the railroads themselves saw government control as a means of relief from cutthroat and debilitating price wars within the industry. Although the ICC lacked any significant power to regulate rates in its early years, the commission was strengthened by subsequent legislation and played a strong role in industry regulation until recent times.

Second, in passing the Sherman Act in 1890, the first national antitrust legislation, Congress embarked on a long and circuitous path of national policy toward industry structure and methods of competition. The Sherman Act prohibited monopolies and the intent to monopolize; it was followed in 1914 with legislation aimed at limiting mergers and outlawing specific anticompetitive trade practices. Relatively few pieces of legislation compose the framework of public policy toward the structure of industries and standards for competitive behavior among firms.

Preserving economic competition and stability through industry regulation and antitrust laws has proved to be an elusive and difficult task. Government economic regulation, attempting to reduce destructive competition and protect the interests of small producers, today is judged to add significant inefficiencies of its own. Antitrust legislation, despite good intentions, has seemed unable to deal with the diverse and complex nature of industries. Simple and universal rules for preserving competition and for limiting concentration have largely escaped definition, leaving the field of antitrust full of confusion and contradiction.

Society continues to be skeptical of industries composed of a few producers, to criticize mergers of multibillion dollar companies lacking an apparent economic justification, and to question the social and political impact of increased corporate size and industry concentration. The role of public policy in economic structure and competition, prone to conflicting expectations and values, continues to be a major focus of business-government relations.

Policy issues in the area of economic concentration and competition are generally divided into problems of industry *structure* (monopoly and oligopoly) and problems of firm *behavior* (price fixing and other trade practices). The first two sections of this chapter address questions of structure, a third section examines the impact of various marketing and trade practices on interfirm competition, and a final section concerns conglomerate mergers, an area failing to conform neatly to either structural or behavioral definitions but a topic of national attention.

MONOPOLY POWER AND GOVERNMENT REGULATION

Early History

Governmental regulation of business had an irregular history in the last third of the nineteenth century. In the 1870s the states and the railroads had fought strenuously over the issue of rate regulation. In 1877 the Supreme Court, in *Munn* v. *Illinois,* reaffirmed state powers to regulate railroad and warehouse rates for agricultural products. However, other efforts to control anticompetitive actions often failed owing to the interstate nature of key industries such as transportation, and state action languished. The idea of national regulation of railway rates arose as early as the 1860s and survived a series of ups and downs until the Interstate Commerce Commission Act was passed in 1887. However, in the struggle between the industry and the ICC that followed this legislation, the Supreme Court virtually stripped the ICC of any power, leaving it only to recommend rates and routes to the companies. It was more than 20 years later when, assisted by the support of President Theodore Roosevelt, the ICC's regulatory powers were strengthened and the commission took the form that would serve as a model of business-government relations in the communications, trucking, airline, and electric and nuclear power industries.

Antitrust regulation similarly faced an uneven early history. State prohibitions against monopoly and restraint of trade were increasingly popular in the late 1800s but were hampered by the fact that most trusts and combinations were interstate and therefore inaccessible to individual state action. This situation again led to the mobilization of antitrust forces at the national level and the passage of the Sherman Antitrust Act of 1890. Although this act passed the Senate with only a single dissenting vote, there were wide differences of opinion concerning its validity, and few government cases were initiated.

The Supreme Court gave a mixed interpretation to the Sherman Act. When the sugar trust, which controlled 98 percent of sugar refining in the United States, was challenged under this law in 1895, the Court ruled that manufacturing is not commerce and declined to break up the monopoly.[6] On the other hand, in several other decisions the Supreme Court did find overt price or market-sharing agreements among competitors to be in restraint of trade and therefore illegal (see Insert 4.A). For example, in 1897 the Court found that rate agreements among 18 railroads were illegal restraints of trade,[7] and in 1899 it ruled that a market-sharing agreement among member companies of the association of steel pipe manufacturers was illegal.[8]

In its early years the Sherman Act's prohibition against restraint of trade was used more effectively against price fixing and collusion among firms than its strictures against monopoly were used to dissolve combinations of firms. In fact, the late 1890s was one of the great periods of industrial consolidation in U.S. history. All of the seven "great" trusts listed by Moody in 1904 were formed during or after 1899, and the vast majority of lesser trusts were formed after the Sherman Act was enacted in 1890.

Teddy Roosevelt's presidency, which began in 1900, marked a new approach to antitrust. Roosevelt believed that giant corporations and combinations were natural and largely beneficial organizations; in his view there were such things as "good" monopolies. Roosevelt preferred regulation by federal chartering and requiring firms to make public disclosures similar to company annual reports of today. As Congress rejected such supervisory legislation, Roosevelt was left with the existing tool of the Sherman Act to regulate large firms. Reinforced with his appointment of several liberal justices, the Supreme Court embarked upon a new view of the Sherman Act that viewed trusts as good or as bad. Within this concept the Standard Oil Company was broken up when the Court found it to be acting "unreasonably" in restraint of trade.[9] On the other hand, U.S. Steel was challenged but was found to have acted "reasonably," although no one questioned whether it was a virtual monopoly.[10] In other words size and economic power were not illegal per se, according to the Court; monopolists' actions needed to be judged against a "rule of reason." The tension

Insert 4.A

KEY PROVISIONS OF THE SHERMAN ACT

Sections 1 and 2 are the basis for litigation under the Sherman Act. The central clauses are simple and straightforward prohibitions against restraint of trade and monopolies:

> Sec. 1. Every contract, combination in the form of trust or otherwise, or conspiracy, in restraint of trade or commerce among the several States, or with foreign nations, is hereby declared illegal.
>
> Sec. 2. Every person who shall monopolize, or attempt to monopolize, or combine or conspire with any other person or persons, to monopolize any part of the trade or commerce among the several States, or with foreign nations, shall be deemed guilty. . . .

In the original legislation, violations were misdemeanors with a maximum fine of $50,000 and/or one year of imprisonment. In 1974 Congress amended the penalties for price fixing to become a felony, and fines were increased to $100,000 for individuals and $1 million for corporations per count, and the maximum jail sentence was changed to three years.

SOURCE: 26 Stat. 209.

between legislative and judicial attempts to define per se illegal firm behavior and the practical necessity to judge the reasonableness of corporate actions constitute a consistent tension in the field of antitrust development.

Enacted from popular discontent, weakly enforced for a dozen years, and subject to differing interpretations of *interstate commerce* and *reasonable monopolies*, the early history of the Sherman Act illustrates the country's ambivalent response to industrial concentration. Congress's failure to define *monopoly* and *restraint of trade* in 1890 led to fluctuating interpretations in government policy.

Emergent Problems of Measurement and Interpretation of *Monopoly*

Concepts of monopoly proved no easier for the judicial system. Judges have also been unable to establish hard and fast principles for the interpretation of antitrust laws. An example of a classic issue in nearly any monopoly case is the appropriate definition of the *relevant market*. If a market is defined narrowly, a single firm appears to be more dominant than if the market is defined broadly. For example, if the manufacture of jogging shoes is defined as a separate market, a single manufacturer will usually have a larger market share than if the relevant market is defined as athletic footwear, running accessories, or even sports apparel. In a legal action the government or other plaintiff argues for a narrow market definition in which the company being sued may have a significant portion, and the defendant's lawyers usually make a case for a broad market definition, in which the firm is likely to be a minor actor.

In a famous case involving DuPont Corporation, the government argued that the relevant product market was cellophane, of which DuPont's 75 percent share would appear to be a monopoly. The company thought the relevant market was "flexible wrapping materials." By this definition DuPont had only an 18 percent market share — hardly a monopoly.

How is one to decide? The judge in the DuPont case utilized the concept of cross-elasticity of demand: if two products served the same users and were interchangeable, they were in the same market; if a price change in cellophane materially affected the demand for other wrapping materials, the broader market definition would apply.

But this rule is not simple either. How much of a price rise for cellophane would be necessary for a 10 percent increase in demand for other materials for the broader market definition to apply? This question has not been generally answered by the judicial history of the Sherman Act.

Another case of alleged monopoly involved the product ReaLemon, processed lemon juice. If processed lemon juice is a separate market, Borden's ReaLemon had nearly 89 percent of market sales in 1974. If processed lemon juice and fresh lemons are in the same market, ReaLemon held a 9 percent share.[11] Processed lemon juice has unique characteristics, including convenience, low perishability, and price, and it is located in a different area of the grocery store than are fresh lemons. Do these characteristics make it sufficiently different from fresh lemons to be a separate market? An administrative law judge concluded that the product characteristics of reconstituted lemon juice placed it in a separate market in which it had monopoly power. This opinion was supported on appeal to the Federal Trade Commissioners, and Borden was required to cease various pricing policies seen to discourage entry and growth of competitors.[12]

The complexity of markets, product lines, and services defies consistent and general definitions; case-by-case analysis may introduce inconsistencies, conflicts, and ambiguities into the law. It is possible to seize upon the existing product-market focus of a successful company and to say this is "the market" without a consistent and universal frame of reference for market definition. Interpretation of *monopoly power* is thus fraught with judgmental problems, and the unique character of many markets has led to few hard and fast precedents or to consistent applications of antimonopoly laws.

Industrial Development and Market Power

One reason why antitrust law may be susceptible to inconsistent application is inherent in the process of economic development. Classical economic theory largely assumes that *competition* means price competition, whereas in modern industry competition is only partly based on price. In fact, from the standpoint of corporate strategy, a company's interests are to establish a market niche, a competitive strength, or an image that allows it to operate successfully without the head-on, overt pressure of strong price competition. Companies seek to establish buffered market positions, or refuges, due to technological superiority, manufacturing expertise, market power, or a unique image that serves as protection from strenuous price competition and affords above-average opportunities for profit.

Here is a partial listing of competitive factors that can buffer a company from the impact of price competition:

- An economy of scale resulting in low unit costs,
- Product differentiation,
- A widely recognized trademark associated with product quality,
- Technological superiority and/or patent protection,
- A high market share and the more rapid lowering of units costs owing to accumulated experience,
- Control of access to distribution channels,
- Heavy consumer advertising,
- Vertical integration,
- Oligopolistic industry structure and price leadership, and
- Government regulation of industry pricing and of market entry by new competitors.

The desire for a buffer is a positive instinct that is an incentive for product improvement, identifying and meeting consumer needs, reaping benefits of technological innovation, inventing means of lowering production costs, and increasing customer convenience. All these, in addition to direct price competition, are important and legitimate competitive tactics within industries.

As an industry matures and its rate of growth slows, narrowing of the number of competitors occurs. Some companies succeed in industry competition, and others fail; some competitive strategies take hold and offer profitable market niches, and others fall by the wayside or the companies are absorbed by other firms. Over time, existing market shares, economies of production, proprietary technology, distribution networks, or capital investment can act as "barriers" to new or potential competitors. A stable, concentrated industry structure may be conducive to price leadership rather than price competition, and incentives for innovation and customer responsiveness may not be as great in a stable industry as they were in an earlier, more dynamic phase of industry growth.

On the other hand, incentives for improvement may arise outside the specific industry. Firms failing to live up to their potential may face a threat of takeover by companies seeking diversification, or the ability of foreign competitors to penetrate American markets may provide incentives to maintain market and technological competitiveness. Also, data on high market share companies do not suggest a general picture of lethargy and lack of progress. Overall, large companies holding high market shares are marked by higher-than-average prices, but they also tend to have higher-than-average product quality and tend to spend proportionately more for research and development.[13]

The process of industrial development is more complex than the world envisioned by Sherman Act prohibitions against monopoly and the intent to monopolize. Recognizing this condition while interpreting the act has led the courts to some novel doctrines. For example, in 1945 circuit court judge Learned Hand concluded that Alcoa had established control of 90 percent of the aluminum market.[14] But, as shown in Insert 4.B, he acknowledged that the company may have arrived at this position from "superior skill, foresight and industry."

In other words Justice Hand apparently recognized that industry competition over time may narrow the number of competitors, and the more successful firms may arrive at positions of market power not owing to monopolistic intent but simply as a consequence of superior performance. By allowing market dominance to occur as a natural result of industry maturity, the "thrust upon" defense appears an effort to reconcile the prohibitions of the act with the realities of dynamic competition. Not surprisingly, this defense has been used, but not fully tested, in subsequent litigation.

Judge Hand's opinion, as shown in the second paragraph of the insert, had another unusual twist: while he raised the "thrust upon" defense, he also ruled that it did not apply in Alcoa's case. To him, Alcoa's anticipation and planning for sales increases were apparently more devious than "superior skill, foresight and industry." His effort to reconcile the ideal of competition with the fact of industry concentration appears, finally, to introduce more confusion than clarification.

"Competition has always contained the seeds of its own potential destruction," writes Betty Bock, director of antitrust research at the Conference Board, a business research association, "since successful competition carried to the extreme may leave only one firm in an industry."[15] This dynamic nature of industrial development has placed the ability to determine consistently what is good and what is bad about industrial concentration out of our reach.

In summary the Sherman Act was not a deterrent to the vast movement of industrial consolidation at the turn of the century. In fact, it may have stimulated merger activity by limiting overt price fixing and weakly attacking monopoly power. On the other hand the Sherman Act was not an entirely hollow document, as it established and continues to define im-

Insert 4.B

JUDGE LEARNED HAND AND THE ALCOA DECISION OF 1945 [QUOTATION]

It does not follow because "Alcoa" had such a monopoly, that it "monopolized" the ingot market: it may have not achieved monopoly; monopoly may have been thrust upon it. . . . persons may unwittingly find themselves in possession of a monopoly, automatically so to say: that is, without having intended either to put an end to existing competition, or to prevent competition from arising when none had existed; they may become monopolists by force of accident. . . . A market may, for example, be so limited that it is impossible to produce at all and meet the cost of production except by a plant large enough to supply the whole demand. Or there may be changes in taste or in cost which drive out all but one purveyor. A single producer may be the survivor out of a group of active competitors, merely by virtue of his superior skill, foresight and industry. . . . The successful competitor, having been urged to compete, must not be turned upon when he wins. . . .

It would completely misconstrue "Alcoa's" position in 1940 to hold that it was the passive beneficiary of a monopoly, following upon an involuntary elimination of competitors by automatically operative economic forces. . . . [I]t sought to strengthen its position by unlawful practices. . . . There were at least one or two abortive attempts to enter the industry, but "Alcoa" effectively anticipated and forestalled all competition, and succeeded in holding the field alone. True, it stimulated demand and opened new uses for the metal, but not without making sure that it could supply what it had evoked. . . . It was not inevitable that it should always anticipate increases in the demand for ingot and be prepared to supply them. Nothing compelled it to keep doubling and redoubling its capacity before others entered the field. It insists that it never excluded competitors; but we can think of no more effective exclusion than progressively to embrace each new opportunity as it opened, and to face every newcomer with new capacity already geared into a great organization, having the advantage of experience, trade connections and the elite of personnel.

SOURCE: United States v. Aluminum Co. of America, 148 F. 2nd 416 (1945).

portant boundaries for business behavior. First, it provided a basis for out-lawing blatant and excessive forms of collusion, such as price fixing and market sharing among competitors; and second, it placed limits, although not strict ones, on the establishment of very powerful monopolies. The latter was done inconsistently, owing to difficulties in operationally defining monopolies and difficulties in coming to terms with natural market evolution toward concentration. However, limits on the freedom to monopolize were established, if only by the potential threat of prosecution.

MERGERS AND INDUSTRY STRUCTURES

At the time Woodrow Wilson was elected to the presidency in 1912, several weaknesses of the Sherman Act were widely apparent. First, the act could operate only after a monopolistic position had been obtained. Mergers, a common means to achieve market power, could not be prevented because of the likely reduction of competition; rather, the government or a private party had the more difficult task of challenging an established firm after the merger had taken place. Second, specific practices of unfair competition were not identified, and the government or private plaintiff was forced to show restraint of trade in every case involving a practice such as price discrimination. President Woodrow Wilson gave leadership to public and congressional desires to strengthen the antitrust laws, and in 1914 Congress enacted two pieces of legislation to remedy these weaknesses in the Sherman Act: the Clayton Act and the Federal Trade Commission Act.

The Clayton Act pertains both to areas of industry structure and to firm behavior. It prohibits mergers that *may lessen* competition to anticipate and forestall increases in concentration or monopoly power. The Clayton Act also outlaws anti–competitive market practices such as price discrimination. Issues pertaining to the structure of industries are addressed in this section, and Clayton Act applications to firm behavior are discussed in the following section. (See Insert 4.C.)

Impact of Market Structure on Prices, Profits, and Innovation

Justification of the Sherman and Clayton acts rests upon the belief that decentralized markets are more economically efficient and conducive to higher rates of technological advancement than are more concentrated industries *because of stronger competition*. Since antitrust policy rests on this assumption, it may be well to review how empirically defensible it actually is.

A strong case against industry concentration involves analysis of prices charged to consumers under differing industry structures. Several studies have addressed this relationship by comparing price levels of commodities such as retail gasoline, consumer loan credit, or food across regions varying in the structure of the local retail industry. Thus, if the retail

Insert 4.C

KEY PROVISIONS OF THE CLAYTON ACT

The following sections are the critical provisions of the Clayton Act (as amended) against mergers and against price discrimination and exclusive dealing:

> Sec. 7. [mergers] That no corporation engaged in commerce shall acquire, directly or indirectly, the whole or any part of the stock or other share capital [or] . . . the whole or any part of the assets of another corporation engaged also in commerce, where in any line of commerce in any section of the country, the effect of such acquisition may be substantially to lessen competition, or to tend to create a monopoly.

> Sec. 2. (a) [price discrimination] That it shall be unlawful for any person engaged in commerce . . . to discriminate in price between different purchasers of commodities of like grade and quality . . . where the effect of such discrimination may be substantially to lessen competition or tend to create a monopoly in any line of commerce. . . .

> Sec. 3. [exclusive dealing] That it shall be unlawful for any person engaged in commerce, in the course of such commerce, to lease or make a sale . . . of goods, wares, merchandise, machinery, supplies or other commodities . . . on the condition, agreement or understanding that the lessee or purchaser thereof shall not use or deal in the goods, wares, merchandise, machinery, supplies, or other commodities of a competitor or competitors of the lessor or seller, where the effect . . . may be to substantially lessen competition or tend to create a monopoly in any line of commerce.

SOURCE: 69 Stat. 282.

gasoline industry in the Minneapolis–St. Paul area is substantially more concentrated than is this industry in Salt Lake City, are prices in the former higher than the latter, as would be predicted by antitrust policy?

Evidence on this question supports policy to preserve decentralized industries. For example, a study of gasoline prices in 22 cities showed that price levels were positively correlated with local market concentration, although a given level of competition had more impact on prices within the unbranded segment than among the premium, branded sellers.[16] Another study of local banking found that a wide range of local banking rates and services — interest rates on deposits, checking account service charges, checking account overdraft charges, business hours, and interest rates on new car loans — were significantly more favorable to customers in cities where the banking industry was less concentrated.[17] The authors of this study concluded that bank performance can be significantly reduced by actions that increase concentration in banking markets.

Insert 4.D reproduces a finding from a comprehensive study of food

---

Insert 4.D

STRUCTURE-PRICE RELATIONSHIP IN FOOD RETAILING

In the mid-1970s the Joint Economic Committee undertook an analysis of the relationship between profit and price levels in the U.S. food retailing industry. The table below presents the estimated costs of a grocery basket consisting of 100 items, based on studies of food prices in 32 metropolitan areas varying according to the degree of industry concentration.

Two measures of seller concentration are related to food prices. The first, four-firm concentration ratio, was the percentage of total area sales accounted for by the top four firms in the metropolitan area. The second, relative firm market share, indicates the percentage of the top four firms' sales held by a single company.

Estimated Costs of Grocery Baskets for Different Combinations of Relative Market Share and Four Firm Concentration, October 1971 (In Dollars)

Relative Firm Market Share	Four-Firm Concentration Ratio			
	40	50	60	70
10	90.95	—	—	—
25	91.65	92.54	94.34	96.48
40	93.16	94.05	95.85	97.99
55	94.18	95.07	96.87	99.01

Thus prices appear to increase as a function of both industry concentration and the market power of the leading firm within the top four companies. The estimated cost difference between the least and most concentrated market structures is 8.9 percent.

SOURCE: U.S., Congress, Joint Economic Committee, *The Profit and Price Performance of Leading Food Chains, 1970–74,* 95th Cong., 1st sess., April 12, 1977, p. 66.

retailing between 1970 and 1974. One readily perceives the same result here: estimates of food prices directly correlate with increases in seller concentration. While local retail services may not have the same threat of substitute products as national industries, they would seem to be vulnerable to the entrance of new competitors and thus to be reasonable tests of structure-price relationships in nationwide industries. It is hard to dispute the presence of a relationship between concentration and prices, although one might argue that price differences between concentrated and unconcentrated industries are not great.

Market concentration and profit levels also seem to be related. Profit-to-sales ratios for firms in the most concentrated categories of the food-retailing study (four-firm concentration of 70, single firm relative market share of 55), for example, are estimated to be ten times higher than profit-to-sales for firms in the least concentrated category (four-firm concentration ratio of 40 and single firm relative market share of 10.)[18] In general the relationship of profits and structure is complicated by whether significant barriers to entry exist — large economies of scale, high product differentiation, or proprietary technology, for example. Generally, concentration is strongly correlated with high profit rates where barriers to entry are high: in "high barrier" industries, a 1 percent increase in after-tax return on stockholders' equity is associated with each ten-point increase in the concentration ratio.[19] Although disagreements on measurement and research methodology in this area are legion, these general results appear widely accepted. A respected scholar of the field, economist F. M. Scherer, attempts to state precisely the status of the issue:

> One could quibble at length about the results of these and the many other studies attempting to relate some index of profitability to concentration, entry barriers, and other variables. To do so would be to lose track of the main message in the jumble of distracting noise. Despite sometimes formidable mismeasurement, there is a rather robust tendency for a positive association to emerge between seller concentration and profitability.[20]

The relationship between concentration and technological progressiveness appears less straightforward than the associations between (1) prices and profits and (2) market structure. Research largely indicates that very small firms in atomistic industries often have neither the long life nor the sufficient resources needed for technical advancement. On the other hand, strong monopolistic structures lack the competitive threat that is an incentive to stay on the forefront of technology. According to Scherer, interpretation of available knowledge on this issue suggests an inverted U-shaped curve in which technological innovativeness is maximized within moderate market concentration. In several studies this optimal point proved to be at 50 to 55 percent of the market held by the four largest producers.[21] If this

FIGURE 4.1   *Hypothesized Relationship of Innovation to Market Structure*

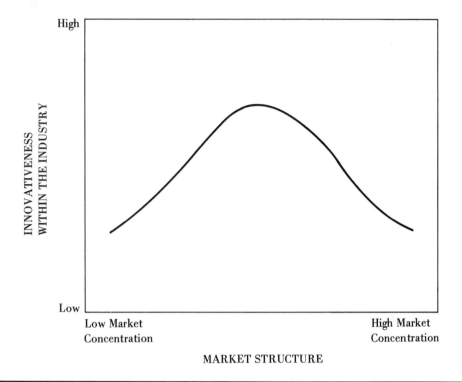

result is valid, some degree of market concentration is beneficial to industry progressiveness. (See Fig. 4.1).

The Dilemma of the Clayton Act: Preserving Competitors or Preserving Competition?

Similar to the Sherman Act's prohibition of existing monopolies, Section 7's intention to prevent anticompetitive mergers has proved difficult to implement. First of all, merger cases contain the same difficulties of the relevant market determination as monopoly cases; the product market may be argued to be broad or narrow, depending on one's perspective. In monopoly cases the geographical market is inevitably nationwide, but in merger situations the language of the Clayton Act invites varying judicial interpretations. The act states that competition should not be lessened "in any section of the country"; whether this means regional, statewide, or even local is left open to question.

From a literal perspective *any* merger among firms in the same industry reduces the number of competitors and therefore reduces competition. On a deeper level the combination of two small producers might actually increase the level of competition; where other producers are larger, a merger among firms with complementary strengths might enhance overall industry competition, or the acquisition of a failing company by a financially strong firm might strengthen the industry. To say that any merger will reduce competition may protect competitors more than competition; but to say that each situation "depends" may again fail to provide consistent policy.

A famous 1961 merger case in which the acquisition of Kinney Company by Brown Shoe Company was successfully challenged by the government highlights these issues.[22] Brown Shoe was the third and Kinney the eighth largest retailer in an industry that was growing more concentrated, although still well dispersed across a number of competitors in different geographical locations of the country. If the merger had been allowed, the four largest retail firms would have accounted for only 23 percent of all shoes sold, although this figure had been rising over the previous 15 years. The two companies, if combined, would have had more than 20 percent of the market in women's shoes in 32 cities, more than 20 percent of the market for children's shoes in 32 cities, and more than 40 percent of the men's shoe market in 6 cities. In 118 cities the combined firms would have had more than a 5 percent share in at least one line, and they would have had more than a 5 percent share in all three lines of shoes in 47 cities.

In viewing this case the Court made the following judgments about the relevant market:

1. Men's, women's, and children's shoes were each independent markets since there could be no substitution of products between customer groupings. The Court also found important distinctions with respect to separate production facilities, prices and price sensitivity, and specialized vendors. These factors supported the view that the products did not compete with each other.

2. The geographic market consisted of all areas having a city of 10,000 people or more in which Brown and Kinney both retailed shoes. In this unusual definition the geographical market did not need to be a single contiguous area and was limited to cities where Brown and Kinney were both presently competing.

The Supreme Court upheld the lower court's decision that this merger violated Section 7 of the Clayton Act. The Court found that the merger lessened competition both (1) by foreclosing opportunities for other manufacturers to market shoes through Kinney's retail outlets, reducing competition in the supplier-buyer relationship, and (2) by accelerating the trend toward concentration among competitors in shoe retailing.

In addition to the Court's logic in defining products and geographic markets, the case is noteworthy for the Court's interpretation of the legislative intent of the amended Clayton Act. This point of view, presented below, expresses an ideological distrust of large sellers and concentrated industries and a preference for a decentralized, atomistic industry structure with more numerous small sellers. In this case the social philosophy of antitrust was able to override arguments for economic efficiency:

> It is competition, not competitors, which the Act protects. But we cannot fail to recognize Congress's desire to promote competition through the protection of viable, small, locally owned businesses. Congress appreciated that occasional higher costs and prices might result from the maintenance of fragmented industries and markets. It resolved these competing considerations in favor of decentralization. We must give effect to that decision. Other factors to be considered in evaluating the probable effects of a merger ... lend additional support ... to the conclusion that this merger may substantially lessen competition. One such factor is the history of tendency toward concentration in the industry. . . . We cannot avoid the mandate of Congress that tendencies toward concentration in industry are to be curbed in their incipiency, particularly when those tendencies are being accelerated through giant steps striding across a hundred cities at a time. In the light of trends in this industry we agree ... that this is an appropriate place at which to call a halt.[23]

This view has been a major theme of government policy toward business for most of this century. It is shown not only in the Brown Shoe case but in a number of other court decisions in which an ideological rationale was used to preserve a larger number of smaller competitors.[24] This judicial predisposition was reinforced by an aggressive stance on the part of the Justice Department in challenging mergers among competitors in the same industry (horizontal mergers).

Since the mid-1970s the judicial system has turned away from emphasizing the impact of a merger on the number of competitors and accepted the examination of a merger's impact on competition;[25] in some cases the Court has decided greater concentration does not lessen competition and may even enhance it. This position obviously weakens universal rules and forces a case-by-case analysis of the specific situations. Yet this position may be more consistent with economic realities.

The legislative and judicial history of the Clayton Act creates a major deterrent to mergers among large firms competing in the same geographical and product markets. At the same time, the law is applied more flexibly in relation to combinations between competitors or among buying and supplying firms where a substantial lessening of competition is not definitive.

As we will see in a later section on conglomerate mergers, the antitrust law is a very weak deterrent to mergers among noncompeting firms.

INDUSTRY REGULATION AND DEREGULATION: RECENT HISTORY AND IMPACTS

Just as the courts have moved toward a closer review of the likely impact of a merger on industry competition, legislators have reassessed the logic and rationale for economic regulation under the structure of the independent regulatory commissions. By the mid-1900s the model of railroad regulation had been applied to other national service industries, including communications, electric power, air and sea transportation, and nuclear power. In addition, long-considered public regulation of the banking system was created in 1913 with the establishment of the Federal Reserve System. In the 1970s the climate of opinion reversed this historical trend; economic efficiency and the operation of free markets have been emphasized by removing governmental controls on firms in these industries.

History

The airline industry was the first major participant in the recent governmental movement toward the deregulation of industries considered vital to the nation's well-being. Eagerly signed into law by Carter in 1978, S. 2493 cleared the way for the airlines to begin to operate more autonomously. Apparently sailing through both houses of Congress with wide margins of approval, the bill had in fact aroused strong negative sentiments among airline industry representatives and airline labor unions. Both groups claimed that passage of this legislation would result in service cuts and job losses.[26]

Two years later Congress approved bills leading to the deregulation of the trucking and railroad industries. Described as a "sound and very strong bill" by Senate Commerce Committee chairman Howard W. Cannon, the trucking deregulation bill S. 2245 also passed easily in the House and Senate.[27] Once again, the industry's major participants denounced deregulation attempts. Regulated carriers, represented by the American Trucking Association, and the International Brotherhood of Teamsters claimed S. 2245 would wreak havoc within the industry; the result would be excessive competition, bankrupt trucking firms, and job losses.[28]

Significant railroad deregulation legislation, also passed in 1980, shared many commonalities with the other industry deregulation laws outlined in Insert 4.E. Railroad deregulation, represented by S. 1946, "emphasized the elimination of needless regulation and greater reliance of the

Insert 4.E

KEY TRANSPORTATION INDUSTRY DEREGULATION PROVISIONS

AIRLINE DEREGULATION ACT — 1978

- The Civil Aeronautics Board (CAB) was directed to place "maximum reliance" on competition within the industry, preserve service to small communities, and prevent anticompetitive practices.
- The CAB was ordered to authorize new services that were "consistent with public convenience and necessity."
- Carriers were permitted to lower rates 50 percent below or 5 percent above the "standard industry fare."
- The CAB was to be abolished on January 1, 1985, unless Congress acted to extend CAB existence.

MOTOR CARRIER ACT — 1980

- The Interstate Commerce Commission (ICC) was directed to set national policy to promote competitive and efficient trucking service.
- Carriers' previous antitrust immunity was disallowed when setting rates for single-line hauls.
- Carriers may raise or lower rates by 10 percent, within certain restrictions.
- Operating permits were to be issued to any potential carrier considered "fit, willing and able" to provide service.

STAGGERS RAIL ACT — 1980

- National policy was set to minimize regulation and to allow, to the extent possible, competition.
- The ICC was only allowed to determine "rate reasonableness" under "limited competition" conditions.
- The ICC was allowed to exempt carriers from regulations if the rules were not necessary to carry out national policy or to protect shippers from market abuse.

SOURCE: "Congress Clears Airline Deregulation Bill," *1978 Congressional Quarterly Almanac,* pp. 496–503; "Congress Clears Trucking Deregulation Bill," *1980 Congressional Quarterly Almanac,* pp. 242–47; "Bill Deregulating Railroads Approved," *1980 Congressional Quarterly Almanac,* pp. 248–55.

marketplace where there is effective competition," according to Senator Cannon.[29] Unlike major airline and trucking companies, the American Association of Railroads supported deregulation; railroad owners believed that increased autonomy within the industry would provide a satisfactory rail network and reduce the number of railroad bankruptcies. Major railroad consumers, typically shippers, withdrew strong opposition to S. 1946 after some provisions were added that shippers felt addressed their concern that railroads would charge excessive rates in captive market areas.[30]

Impact

Isolating the initial impact of deregulation on industries such as airlines, trucking, and railroads proved difficult during the early 1980s: deregulation and a recessionary economy occurred almost simultaneously. However, by the mid-1980s the removal of many prohibitions against free pricing and entry of competitors into the newly deregulated industries has had some significant effects on those industries.

While each industry responded somewhat differently, all three groups found themselves in an environment that would only allow for the survival of the very fittest. To adapt successfully to their new, minimally regulated environment, established trucking, airline, and railroad companies began grappling with new strategies designed to cope with increasing intraindustry mergers, numerous nonunion and lower-cost competitors, and violent price wars.

New competitors flocked into the airline and trucking industries. From 1973 to 1978 no new airlines were created; the next six years saw the established airlines facing tough competition from 22 newly created national and regional airlines.[31] Furthermore, the new airlines were typically nonunion and more inclined to share profits with employees rather than pay the higher wage rates commanded by union employees.

In the trucking industry an even more dramatic expansion of the industry was taking place. Over the initial four year deregulation span, 10,000 new carriers entered the market — representing a 40 percent increase within the industry. Once again, the new entrants were typically nonunion and the International Brotherhood of Teamsters reported that from 1981 to 1983 union member layoffs had risen 9.8 percent.[32] Insert 4.F describes additional effects of deregulation in the trucking industry. By contrast, an increasing number of mergers between established companies occurred in the railroad industry. In 1980 Chessie Systems and the Seaboard Coastline merged into the CSX system. Fearing for their financial survival, some other railroads followed suit within the next few years.

In all three industries the largest and most efficient industry leaders are expected to be financial winners and survive quite handily under deregulated conditions. Large airlines have successfully negotiated more

Insert 4.F

TRUCKING DEREGULATION: TRAVELING AN UNCHARTED COURSE

Trucking began its life as a *regulated* industry in 1935. During that time period the industry was facing low entry costs and a decline in freight to be hauled — a combination that threatened to throw many trucking companies into economic ruin. Government action was deemed necessary to keep the industry rolling in the face of the 1930s economic depression. Later, in 1948, the Reed-Bulwinkle Act further differentiated the trucking industry from unregulated industries by allowing regulated truckers to set rates collectively and remain immune to antitrust charges — subject to ICC approval. Major trucking companies and the International Brotherhood of Teamsters found regulation a comfortable way of life, whereas shippers and independent truckers clamored for changes in the existing laws.

The American Trucking Association (ATA) successfully preserved the status quo within the industry till 1980. "Anything the ATA wanted, it got," claimed Chester Stranzek, a former ATA member. Over strong objections within the industry, Congress enacted the Motor Carrier Act in 1980. The bill included the following provisions: (1) truckers had greater freedom to determine prices; (2) antitrust immunity for some collective rate making was ended; and (3) barriers to entry in the industry were lowered. To date, the impact of trucking deregulation has led to the following dispersed results; winners and losers abound.

- Rates charged for average truckloads have fallen 25 percent from 1978 to 1983.
- 85,000 to 107,000 Teamsters were laid off as of April 1983.
- The number of carriers in operation rose from 18,100 in 1980 to 25,342 by June 1983.
- The rates on *partial* loads has increased 15 percent a year since 1981.
- The ten largest carriers increased their market share from 40.7 percent to 48.5 percent from 1980 to 1982.
- "Entry into the industry" applications approved by the ICC rose from a rate of 69.8 percent in 1976 to 95.4 percent in the first year of deregulation.
- From 1980 through mid-1984 more than 350 known bankruptcies occurred within the trucking industry.

Large trucking companies, strong and successful in regulated times, have grown larger — whereas the reverse has held true for the previously powerful International Brotherhood of Teamsters Union. Union leaders' proposals to allow a lower-cost, two-tiered wage system, in an effort to facilitate the rehiring of laid-off workers, was soundly rejected by union members in October 1983. A frequent and vocal advocate of deregulation, the

Insert 4.F   continued

Reagan administration garnered the support of the Teamsters Union in the 1984 election year by forestalling any demands for further trucking deregulation during that year. Meanwhile, the Department of Transportation obviously interpreted the trucking deregulation statistics positively and proposed further deregulation measures for 1985.

SOURCE: Agis Salpukas, "Trucking's Great Shakeout," *New York Times,* December 13, 1983, p. D1; James C. Miller III, "First Report Card on Trucking," *Wall Street Journal,* March 8, 1982, p. 26; Daniel Machalaba, "Skidding Lobby," *Wall Street Journal,* February 21, 1984, p. 1; "Congress Clears Trucking Deregulation Bill," *1980 Congressional Quarterly Almanac,* p. 242.

competitive union contracts and initiated more efficient routing systems. Major railroads have entered into cooperative agreements with the trucking industry — effectively capitalizing on the strengths of both industries. The largest trucking companies have spent millions to upgrade their fleets since deregulation was initiated and now offer customized services to shippers that are designed to improve the efficiency and timeliness of their freight operations.[33] Successfully restructuring their operations, the largest trucking companies reported increases of up to 120 percent in their 1983 earnings.[34]

To become more competitive, some airlines and trucking companies, such as Frontier Airlines and Consolidated Freightways, created nonunion companies that would compete, to some degree, with their unionized operations. Both airline and trucking unions have decried this strategy. However, others involved in these industries have praised the competitive efforts of the three groups. According to the National Industrial Transportation League, America's largest shipping organization, "deregulation has benefitted all partners in our national transportation system — shippers, carriers and consumers."[35]

The success stories of deregulation are numerous; however, some consumer, worker, and industry segments have experienced significant losses attributable to decreased government involvement. Since the first major deregulation efforts in the airline industry were set into motion in 1978, the deregulation casualty list has continued to grow. Railroads, no longer bound by joint rate rules, are able to raise their freight rates substantially if they operate in an area unchallenged by competition; this situation has led rail shippers to demand reregulation of the industry.[36] Some lightly populated areas of the country, which have proved unprofitable to service, have been left earthbound by the airlines — who reduced their routes into many small, isolated cities. Numerous medium-sized trucking companies, reasonably profitable prior to deregulation, were squeezed out of business during the price wars following the 1980 Motor Carrier Act. In response to these, and other, unintended side effects of deregulation, some unions, consumer groups, and industry coalitions have begun lobbying for reregulation of the three industries.

Meanwhile, other industries, such as banking and communications, have experienced some governmental deregulation, and efforts in this area are expected to accelerate over the next few years. In 1982 Congress allowed banks to set their own interest rate ceilings on most short-term deposits, and the use of automated tellers has allowed banks to offer de facto interstate banking services, without running afoul of the law.[37] Companies without banking charters have been permitted to purchase banks, and there is movement afoot to keep the deregulation momentum going in this industry. The Treasury Department has suggested that banks be allowed to offer a complete line of financial services and has requested that Congress reduce the Federal Reserve's power to regulate the entry of bank holding companies into other fields.

On the communications front the Federal Communications Commission (FCC) has led the battle for deregulation. Among other deregulation efforts, the FCC has encouraged Congress to (1) eliminate the need for broadcast stations to renew their licenses every five years, (2) increase the number of radio and television stations that a company may own in a given area, and (3) abolish federal rules pertaining to the manner in which stations must conduct public affairs programming.[38] In areas that do not require congressional legislation, the FCC has moved decisively to reduce government involvement. Already requirements for childrens' programming have been lessened, and the commission has eliminated previous guidelines that specified the minimum amount of air time that a radio station must dedicate to news and public affairs.[39]

Larger members of both groups, able to view deregulation impacts in other industries, typically support decreased government involvement in their affairs, and supporters of such legislation claim that if the government does not act quickly, the banking industry will effectively deregulate itself through existing loopholes in the law. Smaller industry participants, with limited financial resources, fear they may be squeezed out in a manner experienced by the midsized trucking firms after deregulation took hold in that industry; thus these groups argue that deregulation will decrease, not increase, competition within the banking and communications industries over the long run.

CLAYTON ACT PROHIBITIONS AGAINST FIRM BEHAVIOR OR CONDUCT

The sections of the Sherman and Clayton acts discussed above deal with the existence of monopolies or mergers among firms that may tend to reduce competition or to create a monopoly. These criteria of market *structure* seek to control the degree of market dominance by a single firm or a few competitors. Another approach taken by the antitrust laws has been to control the anticompetitive *behavior* or marketing practices of firms. Section 1 of the Sherman Act, prohibiting restraints of trade, was the first piece of legislation to take this tack and has been used to outlaw price-fixing and market-sharing agreements as discussed earlier. Key sections of the Clayton Act in this area are Section 2, which prohibits price discrimination that lessens competition, and Section 3, which outlaws exclusive dealing and arrangements that tie the sale of one product to the purchase of another (see Insert 4.C). While these prohibitions have straightforward and noble intentions, their application to practical situations is often as ambiguous as restrictions on monopolies and mergers. Let us look more closely at these specific concepts and their applications.[40]

Price Fixing

Price fixing is perhaps the practice most consistently and unwaveringly prohibited by judicial interpretation of the antitrust laws. Beginning in the early history of the Sherman Act with its ruling against rate agreements in the railway industry and supported by subsequent judicial decisions, there has been an absolute prohibition placed on price agreements among competitors. Price fixing is termed a *per se violation*, meaning that no extenuating circumstances can alter the illegality of a price agreement. In contrast to concepts of market structure — which face complicating factors of reasonableness, market definition, and superior foresight and skill — price fixing has remained a strong and relatively enforceable concept.

However, the term *relatively* must be applied to the enforceability of price fixing as well as to other antitrust doctrines. As long as overt actions — meetings, phone calls, memos — among competitors can be related to a common pricing system, few difficulties arise in application of the per se rule. However, overt acts may not be apparent, and more subtle forms of cooperation may exist; coordination may be tacit rather than explicit, and price signaling among major competitors in concentrated industries is eminently feasible. Trade associations often distribute cost and pricing information to member firms that can be the basis of tacit price coordination. In these cases no explicit proof of collusion may be available; but there may be signs of action in concert, namely, parallel prices. As a result even price-fixing concepts are not absolute.

Price Discrimination

Charges of price discrimination have been a primary source of support for trade regulation throughout recent history. In prohibiting discriminatory pricing the Clayton Act sought to protect the smaller regional producer from the predatory tactics of a larger multiregional competitor. It is illegal for a larger seller to price his or her product lower in one region than another to drive a smaller local seller out of business and thus gain control of a regional market. The Robinson-Patman Act, which supplements the Clayton Act in this area, makes it illegal for producers to give rebates and discounts only to large retailers and not to small retailers.

The intention to protect the smaller seller is clear from these acts; but the reason for price differences between regions for a large seller, or the reason for lower prices to large buyers, may not be so obvious. First, lower prices in one region may reflect lower costs of production due to differences in location, greater plant efficiencies, or larger product volume. Second, price differences within a firm across regions may reflect differing types of competition in local markets. But perhaps most important, price differentials may increase competition by allowing local market entry and penetration of a strong, multiregional seller. Consequently, price discrimination has not been a per se application, and few universal rules of conduct exist in this area.

Exclusive Dealing, Territorial Allocations, and Tying Agreements

Often, manufacturers want to place restrictions on retailers who carry their products. A producer may wish to prohibit retailers from carrying products of competitors, an arrangement called *exclusive dealing*. Moreover, a manufacturer may seek to create exclusive sales territories so that its products do not compete with each other. Another manufacturer may make the purchase of one product, such as salt, dependent on the purchase of another product, such as salt dispensing machines. This, a product tying agreement, obviously limits the retailer's freedom of purchase of salt dispensing machines. Conflicts over tying agreements easily arise among manufacturers and their franchisees: the image and reputation of a fast-food chain is protected by requiring purchase of product ingredients, but required purchase of kitchen equipment may not be necessary to protect the manufacturer's product.

The effects of these arrangements on competition must be evaluated case by case. Exclusive dealing reduces competition between products within a single retail establishment but does not reduce competition in the general region and may *increase* competition by providing price and supply stability to smaller retailers. Similarly, creating exclusive territories for dealers is another practice occasionally used by manufacturers of consumer products. In this case the manufacturer restricts each dealer or franchisee to a given territory to prevent competition among dealers carrying the same brand of product. This practice may have a twofold impact on competition — it may reduce *intrabrand* competition but increase competition *between* brands. Tying contracts may reduce competition for the tied product (salt machines or food ingredients) but may increase competition for the tying product (salt and fast foods). If the tied product is essential to the quality of the first product (a difficult judgment at times), the tying relationship is probably more, rather than less, competitive.

These points illustrate how aspects of firm behavior might be either procompetitive or anticompetitive, depending on the context and situation. These factors have prevented the existence of any hard and fast rules; while antitrust doctrines express a valid intent, their influence is not simple or straightforward.

THE FEDERAL TRADE COMMISSION ACT

In order not to impose an overly restrictive and burdensome interference with business by attempting to define all unfair practices, the Congress in 1914 passed a companion measure to the Clayton Act that provided an unrestricted prohibition against "unfair methods of competition," a phrase that has been interpreted to give the FTC power to attack violations covered by other antitrust laws. However, this act also outlaws "deceptive acts and practices," thus providing authority to attack firms' actions that may not lessen competition but that may be deceptive to consumers. The Federal Trade Commission Act has been amended specifically to outlaw false advertising.

Moreover, the FTC was given power to order that a company "cease and desist" from a particular practice subject to judicial review. This power gives the FTC potentially greater regulatory control of business practices. In the mid-1970s this power was extended to apply to industries in addition to individual firms alone, thus granting the FTC power to stop industry-wide practices without challenging each specific firm.

The agency was severely criticized in the late 1960s by both Ralph Nader and the American Bar Association for timidity and ineffectiveness in fulfilling its public mandate of consumer protection.[41] The 1970s saw a revitalization of the agency, including an aggressive attack on misleading or false advertising; the granting of permission to advertise for professional groups such as lawyers, dentists, and doctors; and the development of novel concepts such as "shared monopoly" for attacking oligopolistic industry structures. Of particular importance the FTC was given the authority to develop trade regulation rules (TRRs), providing the commission with a powerful tool to use in its efforts to eliminate unfair and deceptive trade practices. The authority to write TRRs allowed the FTC to change the mode of operation, pertaining to trade, for entire industries. The commission found itself involved in controversial issues of children's advertising, regulation of standards for used-car sales, requirements for funeral home information disclosures, the private use of widely established trademarks such as Formica, and the fairness of business practices used in professional golf shop sales, restaurant menus, and hearing aid dealers. These businesses are not traditional, concentrated manufacturing industries; rather, they are service industries, largely composed of small, independent, and local businesses. The FTC adopted a strong consumer protection orientation, as opposed to the more traditional approach that attempts to preserve competition.

The recent history of the FTC has been volatile. The focus of the commission in the 1980s has been in three highly controversial areas — unfair or deceptive acts, regulation of professionals, and agricultural cooperatives. In each area the FTC has met strong opposition and powerful political lobbies. In part, pressure from these organized lobbies persuaded Congress to occasionally veto rules made by the commission. However, a 1982 Supreme Court ruling forbade, as unconstitutional, the use of congressional vetoes in this manner.

FTC action in the area of "unfair or deceptive practices" has concentrated on the regulation of advertising. According to congressional legislation in 1950, false advertising has to be misleading in a "material" respect. Materiality is to be judged on the basis of representations or suggestions made about the product by statement, word, design, device, or sound and whether these representations either fail to reveal facts about the product or fail to reveal consequences that may result from the use of the product under prescribed conditions or under customary conditions of product use.[42] Advertisers have objected to the FTC's use of TRRs to curtail advertising, which it believes to be false or unfair. Critics of the FTC claim that the agency has gone beyond traditional boundaries of advertising regulation and is embarking "upon experiments in social legislation."[43] In particular, advertisers objected to the proposed TRR that would restrict the manner in which cereals with a high sugar content could be promoted on children's television shows.

As a result of FTC activism in this arena, moderates, such as former FTC chairman James Miller, have called for Congress to enact legislation requiring the FTC to show consumer injury before a formal complaint could be issued.[44] Supporters of the FTC's active role suggest that legislation of this type would reduce the desirable level of protection currently being provided to consumers.

A second highly controversial thrust of the FTC concerns the regulation of professionals in various fields, including law and medicine. The American Bar Association (ABA) and the American Medical Association (AMA) have both lobbied for an amendment that would place them outside the FTC's jurisdiction on issues pertaining to consumer protection. Arguing for exemption, the ABA claimed that its members' activities are already well monitored; the AMA also presented this argument while adding that its professionals are members of non-profit, "learned" societies rather than businesses.[45]

The agency remains convinced that, in fact, these professions require regulation, as their own self-monitoring mechanisms have not effectively eliminated price fixing, boycotts, and other conspiracies to restrain competition.[46] To these ends the FTC has endeavored to curtail advertisements for medical services that may not adequately outline the medical risk involved, eliminate restrictions placed on professions by states and professional organizations that may not serve a useful purpose, and promote competitive practices within these professions.[47]

Interested in extending its efforts in a third controversial area, the FTC has sought authority to monitor agricultural cooperatives' activities, which it believes may run afoul of antitrust laws. Partially immune from antitrust laws, farmers who belong to agricultural cooperatives may *collectively* process, prepare, handle, and market their products.[48] FTC officials argue that the "exempted" status was created to assist the small farmer, yet it is producers such as Sunkist and Dairymen Inc. that are major beneficiaries in this case.

Currently the FTC is generally barred from examining the affairs of agricultural cooperatives, and it has been left up to the Department of Agriculture to protect consumer interests. In support of the FTC's claim that agricultural cooperatives should not be "an exception to the antitrust rule," the agency has underlined the Department of Agriculture's lack of regulatory activity in this area; the department has not challenged mergers between cooperatives nor prices affected by cooperative activity in 60 years.[49]

The commission's expanding involvement in politically sensitive areas combined with the 1982 Supreme Court ruling has led some congressional members to call for an alternative legal method for monitoring FTC rulings. By late 1984 alternative methods had been proposed for congressional consideration, although no proposal had attracted sufficient political support.

CONGLOMERATE MERGERS AND CORPORATE SIZE

The overriding purpose of antitrust policy is the maintenance of economic efficiency through preservation of competitive markets. Efficient allocation of resources and incentives for innovation are the predominant justifications for either structural or behavioral antitrust concepts.

At the same time, the social and political roots of antitrust have been important historical influences on government policy and remain so today. It is recalled that nonagrarian activities such as manufacturing and banking were opposed by Thomas Jefferson in the eighteenth century; his ideal of self-reliant individualism had no place for centralized economic functions. In the mid-1800s agrarian populism expressed itself in the person of Andrew Jackson, who was a symbol of opposition to the wealthy and economic elite. In 1832 Jackson vetoed a bill for the Second United States Bank stating, "It is easy to conceive that great evils to our country and its institutions might flow from such a concentration of power in the hands of a few men irresponsible to the people."[50]

Opposition to business concentration and corporate size on social grounds has been a consistent theme of the twentieth century as well. The massive congressional study in 1900 by the U.S. Industrial Commission acknowledged fears about the threat of the widespread emergence of large trusts to personal initiative, social progress, and community stability.[51] Securities regulation in the 1930s was stimulated by awareness of the absence of accountability of large publicly held corporations and their role in the collapse of financial markets in 1929.

Finally, the late 1960s saw a surge in the number of conglomerate firms, companies diversifying into unrelated business areas by acquisition of other firms. While not an obvious threat to market competition, nor representing an increase in concentration within specific industries, the growth in sizable acquisitions by conglomerate firms was paralleled by an apparent increase in the percentage of national output controlled by large corporations. In 1979 the implications of this movement were the subject of Senate hearings on a bill, S. 600, to limit corporate acquisitions on the basis of size alone.

Led by Senators Edward Kennedy and Howard Metzenbaum, S. 600 proposed to restrict large corporate mergers unless a positive impact on competition could be shown. Specifically, the bill had the following provisions: (1) to prohibit acquisitions in which each company had sales or assets exceeding $2 billion; (2) to outlaw acquisitions in which each company had sales or assets exceeding $350 million unless the acquisition would result in the substantial enhancement of competition, would result in substantial efficiencies, or would result in a divestiture equivalent to the smaller of the two companies; and (3) to prohibit acquisitions in which one party has $350 million in sales or assets and the other 20 percent of a $100 million market, also subject to the same defenses allowed under (2).[52] Testifying at hearings on this bill, Michael Pertschuk, chairman of the FTC, expressed a view that seemed an echo of Andrew Jackson's statement nearly 150 years earlier: "As a Nation, we do not now and never have trusted excessive concentrations of social, political or economic power. We distrust excessive concentrations of power over production, over natural resources, over the lives of employees and communities, and over political institutions."[53]

While these values are sufficiently strong to push the challenge to large firms to the forefront of public discussion, the evidence on the point is neither sufficiently plentiful nor clear to lead to the enactment of new antitrust policy controlling corporate size alone. Consequently an uneasy and unresolved tension appears to be maintained between (1) the proponents of such legislation, who see no economic advantages of conglomerates and worry about their negative social and political effects, and (2) the opponents of such legislation, who see no explicit social and political drawbacks and believe in the importance of allowing economic forces to find their own way. These issues merit closer examination.

Major Trends

The first great period of merger activity was between 1899 and 1901 when companies in mining and manufacturing valued at more than $26 billion in 1972 prices were acquired. However, as discussed earlier, these were largely combinations among competitors in the same markets, or horizontal mergers, which are largely prohibited today by the amended Clayton acts. The second intensive period of corporate mergers was between 1966 and 1969. In 1968 alone, for example, the value of acquired firms in mining and manufacturing reached above $15 billion in 1972 prices.[54] This latter movement was composed primarily of acquisitions of firms unrelated to the acquirer's primary business. This was diversification involving "pure" conglomerate mergers.

In the late 1970s and early 1980s another increase in large mergers appeared to be taking shape as the acquisition of large firms by already large firms, often in other industries, became a relatively common occurrence.

Shell Oil Company's acquisition of Belridge Oil Company in 1979, with a $3.65 billion price tag, represented a quantum leap in the cost of companies being acquired up to that point. In a matter of two years, however, the size of that transaction would pale beside the $6.6 billion surrendered by U.S. Steel Corporation in order to acquire Marathon Oil Company and the $8.8 billion paid by E. I. DuPont de Nemours for Conoco Inc. In 1979 the Shell Oil/Belridge Oil deal was over two-and-a-half times the size of the next largest acquisition, yet by 1984 this deal would not qualify as one of the top three acquisitions of the year. Table 4.1 identifies the seven largest acquisitions occurring during 1984.

Fig. 4.2 illustrates recent trends in merger activity that contribute to public concern of economic concentration. While the number of net mergers (acquisitions minus divestitures) had been going down until 1981, the number of sizable acquisitions or mergers among already large corporations has been on the steady increase.

What effect do corporate consolidations have upon the economy as a whole? The most common index is to view the percentage of total nonfinancial assets or the percentage of value added that is accounted for by the largest 100 or 200 firms in the economy. If these percentages are increasing, then more and more of the economy is controlled by relatively few corporations and individuals. Table 4.2 presents data on aggregate concentration of value added between 1947 and 1976. This figure shows a slow but steady increase in aggregate concentration of value added between 1947 and 1976. Although there might be disputes over the true rate of increasing concentration, there is little doubt of a general tendency toward greater concentration in the manufacturing sector.

Observers differ in analyzing the importance of this phenomenon. For example, the noted economist F. M. Scherer made the following anal-

TABLE 4.1   *Largest Corporate Acquisitions/Divestitures, 1984*

Acquirer	Acquired	Price (billions of dollars)
Chevron Corporation	Gulf Corporation	13.4
Texaco Incorporated	Getty Oil Company	10.12
Mobil Corporation	Superior Oil Company	5.7
Kiewit-Murdoch Investment Corporation	Continental Group Incorporated	2.75
Beatrice Companies	Esmark Incorporated	2.71
General Motors Corporation	Electronic Data Systems Corporation	2.6
Broken Hill Proprietary Co.	General Electric (Utah Int'l Unit)	2.4

Note: The Broken Hill/General Electric deal represents the sole divestiture transaction.

SOURCE: Tim Metz, "Debate over Mergers Intensifies Amid Record Surge of Transactions." *Wall Street Journal,* January 2, 1985, p. 6B.

ysis before the Senate Subcommittee on Antitrust, Monopoly and Business Rights in 1979:

> Had all the companies acquired between 1948 and 1975 survived as viable independent enterprises instead of being acquired, the number of U.S. manufacturing and mining corporations with assets of $10 million or more at the end of 1975 would have been approximately 5,900 rather than the 3,946 actually in existence. Certainly this means that mergers have led to a substantial diminution of the number of independent centers of business decision-making initiative.
>
> Decisions that were once made in the smaller towns and cities are now shifted to a relatively few industrial agglomerations. Decision-making claims on new investments and major technological innovations are longer and more complex. Control over capital . . . is more concentrated.[55]

On the other hand, J. Fred Weston claims that aggregate concentration is largely due to the influence of six of the largest and most capital-intensive industries in the economy: motor vehicles, chemicals, petroleum extraction

FIGURE 4.2   *Big Deals versus Overall Trend, 1975–81*

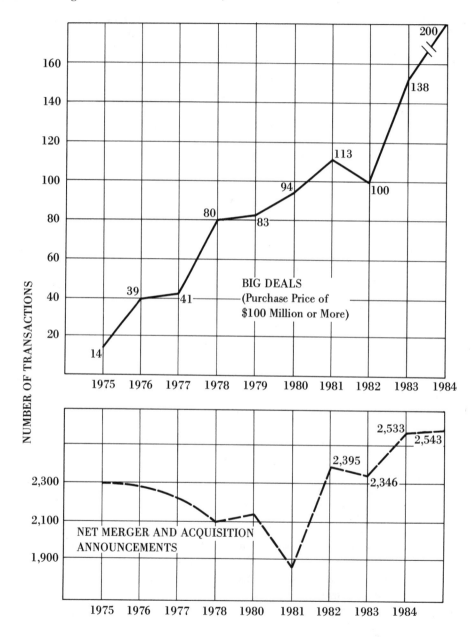

SOURCE: W. T. Grimm & Co., Chicago, Illinois.

TABLE 4.2 *Share of Total Value Added By Manufacture Accounted for by the 50, 100, and 200 Largest Manufacturing Companies for Selected Years* (In Percent)

Year	50 Largest	100 Largest	200 Largest
1947	17	23	30
1954	23	30	37
1958	23	30	38
1962	24	32	40
1963	25	33	41
1966	25	33	42
1967	25	33	42
1970	24	33	43
1972	24.5	33.1	43.1
1976	24.5	33.5	44

SOURCE: U.S., Congress, Senate, Subcommittee on Antitrust, Monopoly and Business Rights of the Committee on the Judiciary, *Mergers and Economic Concentration,* 96th Cong., 1st Sess., 1979, pt. 1, p. 85.

and refining, steel, electrical products and equipment, and aerospace.[56] The firms in these industries produce 30 percent of value added in the U.S. economy and account for 35 of the 50 largest industrial firms. Aggregate concentration, therefore, is not due to merger activity among large firms but is instead a function of a few inherently large and capital-intensive industries that represent a high percentage of total manufacturing. From these observations Weston draws the following conclusion:

> No merger law is going to change the share of total value added accounted for by these big industries unless it makes them more inefficient and they lose relative share that way. But the underlying technological and economic considerations that make six industries 30 percent of manufacturing are not going to be fundamentally affected by the merger law. . . . The underlying technology of a developed economy produces high aggregate concentration regardless of merger policy.[57]

Economic Effects

Unfortunately, efforts to understand the economic effects of mergers have been inconclusive and are unlikely to turn the tide of opinion either in favor of or against conglomerate acquisitions. In fact, it seems the empirical work in this area is so diverse and contradictory that nearly any stand can be taken. For example, defenders of corporate freedom to merge and acquire point to studies of stock values of firms before and after particular acquisitions. Some studies consistently show that stockholders of acquired companies receive gains in the value of their stock ranging from 14 to 20 percent, a finding consistent with the theory that the function of acquisitions is to discover and reprice undervalued assets.[58]

Studies of the impact of acquisitions on the market value of the acquiring company's stock show a more mixed, but not unfavorable, picture. On the whole shareholders of the acquiring firm can be expected to do as well as and perhaps better than they were doing prior to the acquisition — as stated by one proponent of corporate mergers:

> Studies also suggest that the shareholders of the acquiring companies benefit. Some studies show them receiving statistically significant positive abnormal returns even though their companies have announced that they intend to pay a substantial premium over market price for the share of another company. Other studies show them receiving normal returns.[59]

Opponents of the conglomerate movement point to a different set of studies that suggest shareholders of conglomerate companies at best do equally well as shareholders of nonconglomerates and often do more poorly. These studies focus on the market values of merger-intensive firms instead of analyzing the impact of acquisitions, regardless of the nature of the acquiring firm. Various studies have shown that conglomerates often buy firms that are more profitable than themselves, thus improving their own profitability, rather than buy and improve "failing" firms,[60] that overall conglomerate financial performance is lower than the returns of the average of the firm's home-base industries,[61] and that acquisitive conglomerates had a lower return to stock market investors, 10.6 percent below the return to nonconglomerate investors over the ten year period from 1967 to 1977.[62] Concluding a summary of these and other studies, Scherer states that

> conglomerate mergers do little or nothing on average to enhance industrial efficiency, and if anything, their tendency during the past decade leans on the side of an adverse net efficiency impact. . . . If a single sweeping generalization must be rendered, they are a deadly serious but preponderantly sterile managerial ego game.[63]

Overall, the economic aspects of corporate acquisitions resist simple conclusions. Consolidations can have the positive effects of improving the utilization of poorly managed assets and of allowing firms to diversify and strengthen themselves. These results benefit investors, consumers, employees, and communities, for they involve improving corporate efficiency and strengthening competitive ability. Increased size may bring vital economies of production, distribution, and technological innovation. At the same time, acquisitions do not necessarily imply such positive outcomes and may result in negative effects. The evidence concerning conglomerate performance is not at all favorable, and there is real question whether any economy-of-scale benefits are obtained in combinations of multimillion- and - billion-dollar corporations.

The economic question boils down to whether one stresses the absence of proven *positive* effects and is restrictive toward mergers, or whether one emphasizes the absence of proven *negative* effects and is permissive. At present, forces of opinion appear sufficiently well balanced to create a virtual standoff in antitrust public policy. Seeing that a clear policy direction on corporate size and large acquisitions is not forthcoming from economic analysis, we must turn to evidence on the political consequences of aggregate economic concentration.

Political Effects of Corporate Size

Opponents of large corporations and conglomerate-type acquisitions have traditionally feared a concentration of economic and political power in the hands of a few. Although this view will always be an ideological position, empirical evidence on the question of large business influence on government has recently begun to develop. For example, one pair of investigators examined the impact of corporate size, industry size and concentration, profitability, and geographical dispersion on public policy issues such as corporate tax avoidance rates and state motor fuel excise tax rates.[64] Based on these studies, the authors draw the following conclusions: (1) larger firm size yields greater political power, (2) larger industries with more producers are less successful politically, and (3) businesses in industries vulnerable to governmental intervention owing to high concentration or profitability are less inclined to be politically active on the issue of tax reductions. It should also be noted that even statistically significant results about economic variables and firm size may not explain much about variance in public policy. In the study just mentioned, for example, only 16 percent of the variation in public policies across states was accounted for by five variables measuring economic structure and firm size.

Various studies address questions of business structure and political involvement using different industries, measuring different variables, and finding different results. Although this field of research is so young that few results have been tested and reaffirmed by subsequent studies, certain trends do appear to emerge. Reviewing the extent of present knowledge led scholar Edwin Epstein to establish the working model presented in Figure 4.3.[65]

This model shows firm size and industry concentration, as *one* set of dimensions influencing industry political efforts. And even then, research about the political effects of concentration produces inconsistent results: some studies suggest that concentrated industries carry more political "weight," whereas others indicate that industries of larger numbers of smaller and more dispersed firms aid political causes.[66] Epstein's own work on political action committees (PACs) in the 1978 congressional elections also fails to arrive at alarming conclusions with respect to the impact of corporate size. There was a strong tendency for the larger of the *Fortune* 1,000 companies to form PACs. For example, 56 percent of the top *Fortune* 500 industrial companies had active PACs in the 1980 election campaign, compared with only 13 percent for the second 500 largest industrials. Although the number of corporate PACs in this group of companies had increased nearly 50 percent since 1978, only 35 percent of the total 1,000 had active PACs in 1980.[67]

Present information does not support the view of a close relationship among firm size, industry concentration, and political activity. However, available studies represent scarce and largely primitive efforts to tackle a highly complex question. Additional information should be forthcoming and should shed more light on this controversial topic.

FIGURE 4.3   *Model of Key Industry Factors Influencing Political Involvement*

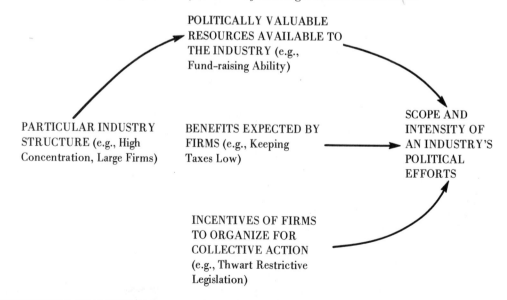

Technological, Organizational, and Social Effects

Finally, the conglomerate movement faces other challenges; the acquisition movement creates a barrier to technological progress, removes the locus of economic decision making from local interests and community needs, and disrupts personal careers and effective managerial teams. These charges are equally or more difficult to define and measure than the other alleged effects of the conglomerate movement and industry concentration, and, consequently, they largely remain in the realm of subjective experience and ideological perspectives.

One vocal spokesperson on the adverse effects of many corporate acquisitions, and particularly of forced takeovers, is William C. Norris, chairman of the board and chief executive officer of Control Data Corporation.[68] Reflecting on a wide range of experiences in a career with high-technology, enterpreneurial businesses, Norris sees serious, harmful effects resulting from many mergers and acquisitions. First, he finds unnecessary and wasteful disruption of employees' careers and community involvements. Responsibilities, aspirations, and rewards to managers of the acquired firm are often adversely affected; many employees sense their jobs may be eliminated or transferred in the transaction. Community ties must often be severed, and business involvement in the local community can be expected to decline. A study conducted in Wisconsin supports this point: the impact of takeovers of local companies was found to depress the local economy.

> In three out of four cases, the acquired company severed its ties with local banks, local accountants, and local attorneys. It often cut off local suppliers and advertising agencies to consolidate accounts with the new parent, and it frequently reduced financial contributions to community activities. . . . Most of the companies, after being acquired, saw their own growth rates drop — which further accelerated the economic decline.[69]

Norris particularly bemoans the negative effect acquisitions have on the technological capability of the acquired firm. According to his experience, a decline in innovativeness is felt, first, through the dampening effect of a large bureaucracy on the entrepreneurial climate of a smaller company and, second, through the loss of creative employees and subsequent disruption of the entrepreneurial team owing to the innovation-stifling atmosphere of the larger company.

Norris observes that these negative effects on the acquired company are not compensated by potential innovation in the acquiring company because resources are placed into acquisitions rather than into internal product and process development:

As corporations rush to put their spare cash into acquisitions, R & D and new plants suffer. Furthermore, because of rising costs of R & D, the increased risk of launching new products (both because of rising costs and because many of the easier things have already been done), and relentless stockholder pressure to increase earnings, the emphasis today in most large corporations is on further improvement of existing products and reducing labor content and materials cost. The development of new products and services suffers in this kind of atmosphere. The bureaucracy of many large organizations today perceives the development of new products and services as unnecessarily risky. Hence, they are resisted and the merger route is taken to increase earnings.[70]

Norris is not opposed to all mergers and acquisitions — only to those not justified by complementary products and services or by financial difficulties of the acquired firm. In addition, he feels a careful weighing of non-financial factors in the acquisition proposal should be made and allowed to override financial considerations. This view has been formalized by shareholder approval of a policy on social justice that mandates evaluation of social impact in any proposed acquisition by Control Data. Whether all Norris's perceptions turn out to be valid, his views and the formal policies adopted by Control Data represent a conscientious and responsible effort to develop a functional corporate response to an important and controversial policy issue.

JOINT RESEARCH VENTURES

Finally, the federal government has not remained insensitive to the costs and risks associated with corporate R & D. Prior to the passage of S. 1846, joint research efforts were considered illegal if they ran contrary to a "rule of reason" test in a court of law. Acknowledgedly vague, the test intended to prevent agreements or ventures between companies that would serve to provide the involved corporations with an unjustifiable competitive advantage.[71] A triplication of damages incurred by firms in competition with the antitrust violators has been the financial penalty required by law in antitrust lawsuits.

In the wake of rapidly evolving international technological advances, this piece of antitrust legislation has been closely scrutinized as to its effect on American competitiveness in the world market. Many companies have claimed that the vagueness of the law, combined with the severity of the penalty, has effectively discouraged them from entering into noncollusive, joint research efforts. Furthermore, according to some industry leaders, the presence of such a restrictive antitrust measure forces each firm to "reinvent the wheel" in order to gain technological advances; inter-company research efforts would allow American companies to compete on an international level in a more cost-effective manner.

Apparently in agreement with the negative industry analysis pertaining to the impact of antitrust laws on R & D, Congress has relaxed certain antitrust provisions relative to joint corporate research endeavors. Revisions in U.S. antitrust law now allow companies to engage in joint research without having to risk a triple damages assessment against them. Only actual damages will be charged against the companies if their joint research ventures are found to be in violation of antitrust laws and they have registered their research program with the attorney general and the FTC. Furthermore, Congress has ordered the courts to consider "the effects of competition in properly defined, relevant markets and development markets" when ruling on antitrust lawsuits that stem from joint research efforts. The inclusion of this provision allows the courts to weigh the potential for increased competition arising from joint research with the potential anticompetitive effects of such a corporate partnership. A staunch supporter of relaxed antitrust laws, the Justice Department's antitrust chief, William F. Baxter claimed, "Success is pro-competitive, not anti-competitive."[72]

BUSINESS AND GOVERNMENT RELATIONS IN THE CONTEXT OF ANTITRUST POLICY: A CONCLUDING COMMENT

As the process of industrialization in the United States gained momentum at the end of the nineteenth century, a new era of business-government relations emerged. Rather simplistic concepts of decentralized laissez-faire capitalism were inadequate to explain widespread processes of debilitating competition, collusion among competitors, and the emergence of market-dominating trusts. Acceptance of economic regulation of the railroads and enactment of the Sherman, Clayton, and Federal Trade Commission acts were early efforts to constrain competition where it seemed detrimental, to prevent collusive and unfair practices, and to prohibit large firms from possessing monopolistic market power.

These laws were methods of groping to identify public policies that maintained allegiance to ideals of competitive markets while allowing for the obvious economic benefits of large-scale production, distribution, and organization. The economic changes and governmental responses of the day created the earliest interface of direct government supervision of the business sector and initiated a continuing stream of policy issues in business-government relations.

This chapter has reviewed two constant tensions in this field. The first is the conflict between the ideals and the realities of economic markets. Theoretical models of market decentralization, economic efficiency, technological progress, fair competition, and consumer welfare are relatively easy to state in the abstract but relatively difficult to apply to specific circumstances. The realities of economies of scale, the ability of firms to develop buffered competitive positions, the presence of "superior foresight, skill, and industry," and the ambiguous effect of many business practices on competition prevent a straightforward application of abstract notions about competition and concentration. As a result the antitrust laws represent a patchwork of noble efforts to operationalize competitive ideals, which are effective guidelines to corporate behavior only in limited circumstances.

A second tension lies within the social and political implications of the maturation and concentration of economic markets. From the earliest period and throughout recent history, large companies have been challenged on the ideological grounds of political dangers inherent in concentrations of economic wealth and of the adverse effects on local communities of economic decision making by distant business units. These concerns arise from values and beliefs that cannot be fully disproved nor fully validated. In the context of conglomerate mergers today, the battleground of policy consists of a contest between two ideological streams that were capable of being unified in an earlier stage of economic development but that conflict in a more advanced stage. The first strand is the preference for economic decentralization, local control, and small scale; the second is the desire for minimal government role in economic affairs and the relatively free rein of market forces where no social objective is obviously threatened. Both positions stem from the traditional American ethic of individualism, which is perhaps the reason that antitrust policy has never been, nor will likely be, a simple and stable dimension of business-government relations.

DISCUSSION QUESTIONS

1. What relevant historical events led to the Sherman Act? What are the major provisions of the act? What are the difficulties of applying the Sherman Act to potentially monopolistic situations?
2. What economic effects might be anticipated from concentrated or non-concentrated industries? Do the Sherman and Clayton acts create aids or obstacles to industry concentration?
3. What aspects of firm behavior fall under the realm of trade regulation? Why has governmental regulation in this area proved particularly vexing?
4. What corporate policy issues arise with respect to conglomerate mergers? Do you support the intent and/or the specifics of S. 600? Why or why not?

NOTES

1. Gilbert C. Fite and Jim E. Reese, *An Economic History of the United States* (Boston: Houghton Mifflin, 1973), p. 349.

2. Harry N. Scheiber, Harold G. Batter, and Harold Underwood Faulkner, *American Economic History* (New York: Harper & Row, 1976), p. 235.

3. U.S. Industrial Commission, *Preliminary Report on Trusts and Industrial Combinations*, vol. 1 (Washington, D.C.: Government Printing Office, 1900), p. 9.

4. John Moody, *The Truth about the Trusts: A Prescription and Analysis of the American Trust Movement* (New York: Moody, 1904), pp. 453–67.

5. Fite and Reese, *An Economic History*, p. 411.

6. *United States v. E. C. Knight Co.*, 156 U.S. 1 (1895).

7. *United States v. Trans-Missouri Freight Association*, 166 U.S. 290 (1897).

8. *Addyston Pipe and Steel Company v. United States*, 175 U.S. 211 (1899).

9. *Standard Oil Company of New Jersey v. United States*, 221 U.S. 417 (1920).

10. *United States v. United States Steel Corporation*, 251 U.S. 417 (1920).

11. Betty Bock, "The Great Lemon Juice 'Monopoly': A Cautionary Tale," *Across the Board*, July 1977, pp. 11–16.

12. Federal Trade Commission, "Complaints and Orders, 1976–1979," ¶21,490. *Trade Regulation Reporter* (Chicago: Commerce Clearing House, 1980).

13. Sidney Schoeffler, Robert D. Buzzell, and Donald F. Heamy, "Impact of Strategic Planning on Profit Performance," *Harvard Business Review*, March–April 1974, pp. 141–42.

14. *United States v. Aluminum Co. of America*, 148 F. 2nd 416 (1945).

15. Betty Bock, "Overview," in *Articulating the Tensions: Social, Political, and Economic Components of Competition*, Information Bulletin no. 29, printed document, Conference Board, 1977, p. 2.

16. Howard P. Marvel, "Competition and Price Levels in the Retail Gasoline Market, *Review of Economics and Statistics* 60 (May 1978): 252–58.

17. Arnold A. Heggestad and John J. Mingo, "Prices, Non-Prices, and Concentration in Commercial Banking," *Journal of Money, Credit, and Banking* 8 (February 1976): 107–17.

18. U.S., Congress, Joint Economic Committee, *The Profit and Price Performance of Leading Food Chains, 1970–74*, 95th Cong., 1st sess., April 12, 1977, p. 56.

19. F. M. Scherer, *Industrial Market Structure and Economic Performance*, 2d ed. (Chicago: Rand McNally, 1980), p. 277.

20. Ibid., pp. 278–79.

21. Ibid., pp. 433–38.

22. *Brown Shoe Co., Inc. v. United States*, 370 U.S. 294 (1962).

23. Ibid., pp. 344–46.

24. For a discussion of this issue, see Thomas W. Dunfee and Frank F.

Gibson, *Modern Business Law: An Introduction to Government and Business* (Columbus, Ohio: Grid, 1977), pp. 87–94.

25. See ibid., pp. 95–99.
26. "Congress Clears Airline Deregulation Bill," *1980 CQ Almanac*, p. 498.
27. "Congress Clears Trucking Deregulation Bill," *1980 CQ Almanac*, p. 242.
28. Ibid., p. 243.
29. "Bill Deregulating Railroads Approved," *1980 CQ Almanac*, p. 248.
30. Ibid.
31. "The Friendly Skies of Deregulation," *Inc.*, February 1984, p. 33.
32. Agis Salpukas, "Trucking's Great Shakeout," *New York Times*, December 13, 1984, p. D1.
33. Pat Wechsler, "Trucking: A Case Study," *Dun's Business Month*, May 1984, p. 48.
34. Ibid.
35. "Industry Groups Speak Out for Deregulation," *Dun's Business Month*, January 1984, p. 97.
36. Reginald Stuart, "To Regulate, to Deregulate, or, Now, to Reregulate," *New York Times*, October 29, 1984, p. A16.
37. Susan Lee, "Bank Deregulation: The Force Is With Us," *Wall Street Journal*, July 11, 1983, p. 18.
38. Jeanne Saddler, "Push to Deregulate Broadcasting Delights Industry, Angers Others," *Wall Street Journal*, April 16, 1984, p. 31.
39. Ibid.
40. See Dunfee and Gibson, *Modern Business Law*, chap. 5, for a useful discussion of these issues.
41. For a discussion of these reports, see Philip Heymann "A Failing Agency: The Federal Trade Commission" (Kennedy School of Government, case publication series C14–76–119, 1976), pp. 76–119.
42. 15 USC 55.
43. Bruce Mulock, "Federal Trade Commission: Reauthorization Issues," Issue Brief, *Congressional Research Service*, September 26, 1984, p. 8.
44. Ibid.
45. Ibid., p. 4.
46. Ibid., p. 5.
47. Ibid.
48. Ibid., p. 6.
49. Ibid.
50. Andrew Jackson, "Veto Message (10 July 1832)," in *American Economic Policy since 1789,* ed. William Letwin (Chicago: Aldine, 1961), p. 120.
51. U.S. Industrial Commission, *Preliminary Report*, p. 31.
52. U.S., Senate, *Hearings before the Subcommittee on Antitrust, Monopoly and Business Rights of the Committee on the Judiciary,* 96th Cong., 1st sess. on S.R. 600, "The Small and Independent Business Protection Act of 1979," pt. 1, pp. 641–44.
53. Michael Pertschuk, in ibid., pt. 1, p. 14.

54. F. M. Scherer, in ibid., pt. 2, p. 135.

55. Scherer, in ibid., pt. 2, p. 137.

56. J. Fred Weston, in ibid., pt. 1, pp. 536–80.

57. Weston, in ibid., pt. 1, pp. 539–41.

58. George J. Benston, *Conglomerate Mergers: Causes, Consequences, and Remedies* (Washington, D.C.: American Enterprise Institute for Public Policy Research, 1980), p. 44.

59. Ibid.

60. J. Fred Weston and S. K. Mansinghka, "Tests of the Efficiency Performance of Conglomerate Firms," *Journal of Finance*, September 1971, pp. 919–36.

61. Thomas F. Hogarty, "The Profitability of Corporate Mergers," *Journal of Business*, July 1970, pp. 317–27.

62. Harry H. Lynch, "Financial Performance of Conglomerates" (Boston: Harvard Business School Division of Research, 1971), abstruact, p. 3.

63. Scherer, *Hearings*, pt. 2, p. 142.

64. Lester M. Salamon and John T. Siegfried, "Economic Power and Political Influence: The Impact of Industry Structure on Public Policy," *American Political Science Review* 71 (1977):1026.

65. Edwin M. Epstein, "Firm Size and Structure, Market Power and Business Political Influence: A Review of the Literature," in *The Economics of Firm Size, Market Structure and Social Performance*, ed. John J. Siegfried (Washington, D.C.: Bureau of Economics, Federal Trade Commission, July 1980), p. 252.

66. Ibid., pp. 244–48.

67. Data provided by Edwin M. Epstein compiled from *FEC Report on Financial Activity, 1977–78*, Interim Report no. 4 (May 1979); *FEC Report on Financial Activity, 1979–80*, Interim Report no. 9 (October 1980); and *Fortune* Directories, May 7, 1979, June 18, 1979, July 16, 1979, May 4, 1981, June 15, 1981, and July 13, 1981.

68. William C. Norris, "Irresponsible Mergers & Acquisitions" (Unpublished paper, March 4, 1980).

69. U.S. White House Commission on Small Business, *America's Small Business Economy: Agenda for Action,* Report to the President (Washington, D.C.: Government Printing Office, April 1980), p. 17.

70. Norris, "Irresponsible Mergers & Acquisitions," p. 9.

71. Robert D. Hershey, "Stiff Antitrust Laws Called Rein on U.S.," *New York Times*, August 1, 1983, p. D2.

72. Ibid.

Case 4.A   John F. Cady

The U.S. Soft Drink Industry
Territorial Allocations

In late August 1976, Sidney P. Mudd, president of the National Soft Drink Association, the national organization representing soft drink bottlers, was considering what recommendations he should make to his member companies concerning their efforts to maintain exclusive territorial arrangements for the distribution of soft drinks.

In particular, he wondered if he should recommend that the soft drink bottlers and franchise firms abandon their costly five-year effort to keep these arrangements and recommend that they consider implementing some alternative soft drink distribution system.

BACKGROUND

Mudd remembered clearly the shock that was felt in the industry in mid-January 1971 when the Federal Trade Commission (FTC) announced its intention to issue complaints against seven soft drink franchise firms. The seven firms — Crush International, Dr Pepper, the Coca-Cola Co., PepsiCo Inc., the Seven-Up Co., the Royal Crown Cola Co., and National Industries (Cott Corp.) — had been notified that the FTC has "reason to believe" that the antitrust laws of the United States (specifically Section 5 of the Federal Trade Commission Act)* had been violated.

The complaints were formally issued on July 15, 1971. Some time later an eighth company, the Canada Dry Corp., was served with a similar complaint. These complaints alleged that the eight companies had hindered or eliminated competition in the soft drink industry by restricting soft

---

*Section 5(a)(1) of the Federal Trade Commission Act (15 USC 45) states: "Unfair methods of competition in commerce, and unfair or deceptive acts or practices in commerce, are hereby declared unlawful."

---

drink bottlers to sales in exclusive designated geographical territories. (Appendix to Case 11.A presents the legal arguments presented by the FTC against the eight soft drink companies.)

Because none of the eight companies had signed consent decrees (which state that the company has done nothing illegal but will not undertake the conduct outlined in the complaint in the future), it was generally believed that five to seven years would be required for hearings, trials, and appeals before the matter would be legally settled.

As it turned out, by 1976 that time estimate appeared quite conservative. In October 1975, an administrative law judge had ruled in favor of the companies and their system of exclusive territories. The FTC had appealed that decision, and the final judicial outcome was uncertain.

Between the 1971 FTC complaints and the current appeal the industry had also presented its case to Congress through hearings before the House of Representatives Subcommittee on Monopolies and Commercial Law. The purpose of the hearings was to determine whether the soft drink industry territorial allocations should be granted a specific antitrust exemption. The first hearings were held in 1972, and a second set of hearings were held in June and July of 1976. The arguments presented by the industry favoring the granting of an exemption and the arguments presented against granting the exemption had followed closely the arguments presented at the original trial.

Mudd believed that no one could accurately predict the outcome of the court appeal or the antitrust exemption request. Still, he was unsure as to what course of action to recommend to the members of the National Soft Drink Association.

THE SOFT DRINK MARKET

In 1974 the U.S. soft drink market was estimated to be $8.9 billion in manufacturers' sales. By 1976 sales figures translated into a per capita consumption rate of 547 cans or bottles of soft drinks per year. Per capita consumption was growing at an annual rate of 7 percent.

Until the early 1970s coffee had been the most popular beverage in the United States. Coffee's status as the most popular beverage was replaced in 1971 when soft drinks comprised 26 percent of the total commercial beverage market. Virtually all of the increase in per capita soft drink consumption had come at the expense of alternative beverages, since overall per capital commercial liquid consumption had remained stable over the past 50 years.

Soft drink consumption patterns showed sharp seasonal and climatic effects. For example, one study found that soft drinks were purchased with weekly frequency by 77 percent of all families during the summer contrasted with only 48 percent in the winter. Per capita soft drink consumption was heavier in the South than anywhere else in the United States.

Consumer tastes and a willingness to try new products had a strong impact on consumption patterns. On a national basis, cola had been the most popular soft drink flavor since 1920, when it replaced ginger ale. Since 1947 cola drinks accounted for an average of 60 to 65 percent of beverages sold, and these were followed in preference by lemon-lime, orange, ginger ale, and root beer drinks.

Industry sources credited the emergence of low-calorie soft drinks with the conversion of new soft drink consumers from nonconsumers. One source explained, "Before the introduction of low-calorie soft drinks, consumers voiced two primary reasons for avoiding soft drinks — caloric content and restricted diet. With the advent of the dietetic drinks, these two barriers no longer existed." Saccharin-based dietetic soft drinks, which replaced cyclamate-based drinks in 1969, accounted for 10 percent of the total soft drink market in 1970. Dietetic soft drink sales were increasing at a rate of 12 percent per year.

New categories of soft drinks such as "isotonic" (Gatorade) and "thirst quenching" (Mountain Dew, Fresca, Kick) had also stimulated soft drink consumption.

By 1971 soft drinks were available in over 99 percent of the more than 200,000 retail food outlets in the United States. In addition, soft drinks were available in almost every restaurant, service station, sports stadium, tavern, hotel, and motel. It was estimated that the number of retail outlets distributing soft drinks in the mid-1970s were over 1 million. In addition, soft drinks were available in over 1.4 million vending machines; fountain-dispensed soft drinks were sold in over 100,000 retail outlets.

In addition to the availability of soft drinks generally, there had been a dramatic increase in the number of package sizes and types on the market. In 1975 soft drinks were available in 32 different sizes ranging from 6 to 64 ounces, in returnable and nonreturnable bottles. Soft drinks were also packaged in 12 and 16 ounce cans.

THE SOFT DRINK INDUSTRY

The soft drink industry was divided into two primary producing segments: (1) national, regional, and local franchised soft drink brands and (2) controlled-label soft drinks.

Franchised Soft Drink Brands

The bottling of flavored soft drinks began in the United States in the latter half of the nineteenth century. Prior to that time, syrup had been used almost exclusively as a base for soft drinks served at soda fountains for immediate consumption. During this period a growing number of extract or syrup manufacturers were attracted into the industry. These companies developed and introduced many new proprietary flavors, including Hires, Vernor's, Clicquot Club, Dr Pepper, Coca-Cola, and Pepsi-Cola.

Many of these proprietary companies soon began to franchise the right to bottle their common law trademarked products. In 1899 the Coca-Cola Company granted an exclusive trademark license to J. B. Whitehead and B. F. Thomas to produce and sell bottled Coca-Cola in most states. Whitehead and Thomas were to be both processors and sellers of bottled Coca-Cola, manufactured from Coca-Cola syrup under a trademark license, rather than simply distributors of a finished product. Ancillary to the trademark licensing agreement, Coca-Cola specified an exclusive geographic territory in which only Whitehead and Thomas could sell soft drinks under the Coca-Cola trademark. Because of the large size of its territory, the company created by Whitehead and Thomas, in turn, franchised hundreds of independent local bottlers to produce and sell bottled Coca-Cola in exclusive geographic territories within that part of the country covered by the original Whitehead and Thomas license.

Pepsi-Cola in 1908, Dr Pepper in 1926, and other proprietary syrup companies soon followed Coca-Cola in franchising independent bottlers to produce and sell their respective trademarked soft drinks in exclusive geographic territories. These ancillary territorial restrains were deemed essential by the industry at this time to develop a nationwide system for manufacturing and marketing their packaged products. The system of territorial restrictions was believed to be a stimulus to induce local independent businessmen to provide the capital necessary to finance the venture. Not only did trademark owners need local businessmen to build plants and purchase equipment and bottling supplies, they needed their goodwill in the community to establish a demand for and promote the new national soft drink brands as they attempted to compete with local products.

To provide the necessary inducement for local entrepreneurs to supply the capital required and make the necessary effort to promote consumer acceptance of new soft drink products, soft drink franchisors routinely included exclusive territorial provisions in trademark licenses. These restrictions encouraged greater development of promotional efforts since exclusive licensees knew that neither their licensors or other licensees could obtain a "free ride" on their marketing efforts. They had also made possible the licensor's maintenance of quality control, thereby ensuring uniform application of his common law trademark, and facilitated the franchisor's production planning by enabling greater accuracy in calculating the forthcoming demand for syrup in a territory. The restrictions had also reduced the selling cost of the product by avoiding duplication of sales effort in a territory and encouraged the franchised bottler to develop the potential of his territory to the fullest, thereby maximizing sales of the franchised product.

By 1972 there were over 50 syrup companies who had franchised local bottlers; 36 of these syrup companies had nationwide distribution through the franchised bottlers.

The franchise company manufactured and sold syrups or flavoring concentrates to the bottlers. Franchise companies also underwrote most of the advertising and promotion expenditures made in connection with their trademarked products; provided advice and technical assistance on production, quality control, management, and sales problems; and engaged in development and test marketing of new products and containers.

The bottlers were the manufacturers and distributors of packaged soft drinks produced from the franchisor's syrup or concentrate and manufactured according to his standards and specifications. The franchised bottler decided on the plant and equipment to be used, the volume of production by size and type of container and product mix, as well as the price to be charged and the manner in which market penetration could be maximized and the widest possible distribution of soft drinks secured throughout the franchise territory.

Various strategies had developed among syrup and concentrate manufacturers in response to the continuing controversy over territorial restrictions in bottling. Coca-Cola, the largest of the manufacturers, had formed a Bottler Consolidation Department, which was designed to oversee and administer a program to encourage the consolidation of its current bottlers. In recent years small bottlers had been acquired by larger bottlers (including some owned by Coca-Cola), and this trend was expected to continue. J. Lucien Smith, president of Coca-Cola, stated that shifts in population concentration, improved transportation, changes in communications systems, changing tastes, and economies of scale had all tended to reduce the number of bottling plants and increase the size of some territories.

Since Coca-Cola had the first territories established for soft drink bottling, these territories tended to be geographically smaller and, hence, less economical than those territories developed by more recent entrants into the market. It had been noted by several industry analysts that Coca-Cola suffered competitively, on occasion, as a result of inefficient-sized bottler operations.

An alternative strategy had been for the syrup and concentrate manufacturers to integrate forward into bottling. PepsiCo, Inc., which was the second largest manufacturer of syrup and concentrate, operated bottling facilities serving New York City, Boston, Milwaukee, and the state of Michigan. Industry sources estimated that Pepsi-Co-owned bottling facilities served over 46 million people in the United States in 1975. Other syrup and concentrate manufacturers also had integrated into bottling, but none covered such a substantial portion of the population as did PepsiCo bottlers.

Controlled-Label Soft Drinks

The development of the contract canner in the 1960s added a new dimension to competition in the soft drink industry — the controlled label.

Controlled-label soft drinks, which were in-house products marketed under the proprietary brand names of soft drink retailers such as 7-Eleven Cola (7-Eleven), Yukon Club Cola (A&P), and Check Cola (Winn Dixie), had proliferated and accounted for around 15 percent of store soft drink sales by the early 1970s.

Shelf space was allocated generously to controlled-label soft drinks, and the vigorous point-of-sale promotion and local advertising devoted to these products had contributed to their substantial gains in the past. Most industry observers expected controlled-label soft drinks to increase their competitive pressure on the other producer segments of the market.

ANALYSIS BY THE FEDERAL TRADE COMMISSION

The cases brought by the FTC against the eight major soft drink firms all relied on the same basic economic analysis.

Alan Ward, director of the Bureau of Competition, and H. Michael Mann, director of the Bureau of Economics had stated the position of the FTC, publicly, several times including before various committees of the House of Representatives.

The analysis by the FTC staff showed that the principal effect of territorial restrictions in the soft drink industry was the elimination of all intrabrand competition by preventing bottlers of the same brands from competing with each other for the same customers. Where interbrand competition was as weak as in the soft drink industry, the analysis concluded, elimination of intrabrand competition has severe anticompetitive effects.

The alleged lessening of competition in the soft drink industry resulting from territorial restrictions was estimated by the FTC to cost consumers over $250 million per year in higher prices.

The FTC did not rely on the effect of the territorial restrictions on consumers as its sole argument, however. Also included in their analysis was the effect of the restrictions on small business. The FTC staff argued that the soft drink industry territorial restrictions had encouraged small bottlers to leave the industry by confining their operations to uneconomically small areas, thereby preventing them from growing to efficient size.

The FTC staff did emphasize that their cases against the eight soft drink firms did not challenge the lawfulness of syrup manufacturers restricting a bottler to a particular manufacturing location or the right of a syrup manufacturer to select its bottlers.

Summarized, the case presented by the FTC against the soft drink firms emphasized six major points:

1. Elimination of territorial restrictions would result in lower soft drink prices. Consumers would save $50 million a year for each percentage point the average price of soft drinks drops. Since prices of the same

brand of soft drink within the same market area varied by much more than 5 percent, consumers might save over $250 million annually.

The FTC analysis indicated that if territorial restrictions were removed, food wholesalers and retailers would be free to shop around to purchase soft drinks from the bottler of a particular brand who offered the lowest price and/or best service. As a consequence, soft drink prices and service would be improved. Competition at the distribution level would ensure that the food wholesalers and retailers would seek purchases from the lowest price bottler and pass on much of the savings to consumers.

2. Price competition among brands in the soft drink industry was extremely weak. Interbrand competition was inadequate for the following reasons.

   a. 42 percent of the bottlers of the brands of the eight top syrup manufacturers (whose brands accounted for over 80 percent of the total soft drink sales) were multibrand bottlers. For example, Coca-Cola Bottling Co. of New York marketed both Coca-Cola and Dr Pepper.

   b. Strong consumer preference for particular brands, developed by intensive advertising, had further restricted the effectiveness of interbrand competition.

   c. The concentration level among local bottlers was extremely high. In a typical market area, four bottlers controlled 70 percent of the market. As a general proposition, the higher the degree of concentration, the lower the degree of competition and the higher the price level.

3. Territorial restrictions resulted in high local concentration levels, which lessened competition and led to higher prices. A reduction in concentration levels by increasing the number of bottlers competing in a market area would benefit consumers in the form of lower prices.

4. The soft drink bottling industry had increasingly become dominated by large bottling companies, and the perpetuation of territorial restrictions would further increase the domination by a few large firms. And 40 (out of 2,300) individual bottling companies accounted for over one third of total soft drink sales. In addition, a very small number of bottlers of Coca-Cola, Pepsi-Cola, and Seven-Up served the majority of the population (Exhibit 1).

   In recent years many bottling franchises had been purchased by large conglomerate firms. By virtue of their acquisitions, several conglomerates including Westinghouse Electric, Beatrice Foods, Illinois Central Industries, General Tire and Rubber, Borden, Wometco Enterprises, and General Cinema had become some of the largest bottlers in the country.

5. Territorial restrictions had hastened the demise of small bottlers by limiting them to territories too small to support an efficient-sized plant. This was due, according to the FTC, to the great changes in transpor-

EXHIBIT 1   *Dominance of Soft Drink Bottling by Large Plants—Growth Patterns for 1967–71*

Plant Size by Annual Sales Volume	1967[a]		1968[b]		1969[c]		1970[d]		1971[e]	
	Number of Plants	Percentage of Total Sales	Number of Plants	Percentage of Total Sales	Number of Plants	Percentage of Total Sales	Number of Plants	Percentage of Total Sales	Number of Plants	Percentage of Total Sales
Over $2,000,000	161	52.1	173	54.0	228	61.7	446	64.3	463	68.9
$1,000,000 to $2,000,000	289	10.0	289	14.6	309	12.9	230	10.0	230	8.8
$500,000 to $1,000,000	537	15.0	548	13.8	494	10.3	579	12.5	563	10.8
$300,000 to $500,000	549	9.4	596	7.9	566	5.9	533	5.7	496	4.8
$100,000 to $300,000	1,252	5.4	1,107	6.4	996	6.2	827	5.3	767	4.4
Under $100,000	763	2.1	701	1.7	601	1.3	416	1.0	396	0.8
Unclassified volume	99	—	87	—	75	—	75	—	75	—
Total	3,650		3,501		3,269		3,106		2,990	

[a]"Soft Drinks," January 1968, p. 24.
[b]"Soft Drinks," January 1969, p. 35.
[c]"Soft Drinks," January 1970, p. 23.
[d]"Soft Drinks," January 1971, p. 35.
[e]"Soft Drinks," January 1972, p. 23.

tation and distribution systems that had taken place since territory boundaries were established. Under the system of territorial restrictions, the number of bottling companies had declined from 5,200 to 2,300 between 1945 and 1970. This was due to small inefficient bottlers selling to larger nearby bottlers who subsequently liquidated the assets of the acquired firm and served the additional territory from their existing plants. Ending territorial restrictions would not save all bottlers, but more would ultimately survive without the restrictions, since elimination of restrictions would enable some small bottlers to grow to a more efficient size (Exhibit 2).

6. Territorial restrictions had prevented bottlers, retailers, and consumers from obtaining the cost savings that central warehousing may offer. It was noted by the FTC that central warehousing was a method of distribution used by food retailer cooperatives, food wholesalers, and food chains for the majority of food products sold in food stores. The FTC believed that bottlers, wholesalers, and retailers should be free to choose whatever distribution system suited their needs rather than having a system imposed on them by the syrup manufacturers.

THE INDUSTRY RESPONDS

The analysis by the FTC staff of the competitive effects of territorial restrictions in the soft drink industry drew heavy criticism from most firms and prompted a rebuttal to the allegations by the National Soft Drink Association. This rebuttal challenged the factual and derived conclusions developed by the FTC.

The association maintained that industry prices were not excessive; on a per ounce basis branded soft drinks in returnable packages, despite inflation, were being sold at the same price as they were at the turn of the century.

According to the association, over and above the competition that existed between soft drinks and other beverages, there was pervasive interbrand competition in the soft drink industry itself, and such competition has increased annually.

Nationally, 75 companies marketed over 180 trademarked brands, and regionally and locally produced brands provided substantial competition. An expanding market for soft drinks had produced several new entrants into the national market over the last decade, including Fairmost Foods, Inc., and Shasta (division of Consolidated Foods), as well as a host of private labels, and expanded distribution of specialty mixers such as Schweppes mixes. The growth of the contract canner and bottler in recent years had also led to a rapid proliferation of controlled-label soft drinks marketed by food chains, grocery cooperatives and wholesalers, convenience store groups, drug store chains, and others. There has also been an increasing tendency by nationally franchised companies such as Dr Pepper,

EXHIBIT 2 *Areas of the Country Served by the Ten Largest Coca-Cola, Pepsi-Cola, and 7-Up Bottlers*

	1970 Population
Coca-Cola Bottlers	
Coca-Cola Co.	28,059,793
Coca-Cola Bottling Co. of New York, Inc.	21,082,460
Associated Coca-Cola Co., Inc.	12,203,103
Coca-Cola Bottling Co. of Los Angeles	11,256,398
Houston Coca-Cola Bottling Co.	7,246,468
James E. Crass Coca-Cola Bottling Plants, Inc.	5,306,326
Atlanta Coca-Cola Bottling Co.	3,892,458
Coca-Cola Bottling Corp., Cincinnati, Ohio	3,728,577
Coca-Cola Co. of Miami, Inc.	2,839,075
Coca-Cola Bottling Midwest, Inc.	2,536,780
Pepsi-Cola Bottlers	
PepsiCo, Inc.	37,524,621
Pepsi-Cola General Bottlers, Inc.	14,373,219
Rheingold Corp.	10,717,867
General Cinema Corp.	10,375,627
Allegheny Beverage Corp.	5,031,511
MEI Corp.	4,431,131
Pepcom Industries, Inc.	3,638,957
Pepsi-Cola Bottling Co. of Washington, D.C., Inc.	2,835,713
RKO General, Inc.	2,369,556
American Pepsi-Cola Bottlers, Inc. (formerly All-American Beverages, Inc.)	1,095,688
7-Up Bottlers	
Westinghouse Electric Corp.	15,936,749
Joliet 7-Up Bottling Co.	15,502,593
Joyce Products Co.	14,862,033
7-Up Bottling Co. of Philadelphia	9,241,363
JFW Enterprises, Inc.	4,085,740
7-Up Bottling of St. Louis	3,921,840
General Cinema Corp.	3,807,477
Midrock Corp. Beverage Division	3,167,416
Mid-Continent Industries, Inc.	2,634,541
7-Up Co. of Kansas City, Mo.	2,289,669
Population of Total United States	203,235,298

SOURCE: 1970 census of population and territories of bottlers.

Canada Dry, and Crush International to enter local markets in which they had not previously distributed their products. (See Exhibit 3 for a listing of the soft drink products available in a single metropolitan area in June 1976.)

EXHIBIT 3 *Soft Drink Brands Available in the Washington, D.C., Market Area — June 1976*

	Package Types and Sizes
Regular cola soft drink brands currently in market	
Coca-Cola	6½R, 16R, 10NR, 16NR, 12C
Pepsi-Cola	16R, 10NR, 16NR, 28NR, 12C
Royal-Crown Cola	16R, 16NR, 32NR, 64NR, 12C
Canada Dry Jamaica Cola	18NR, 64NR
Rock Creek Cola	16NR, 28NR
Shasta Cola	64NR, 12C
Bala Club Cola (Acme)	28NR, 64NR
Ideal Cola (Acme)	12C
Blair House Cola	28NR
Shasta Cherry Cola	12C
Yukon Club Cola (A&P)	28NR, 64NR, 12C
7-Eleven Cola	28NR, 12C
Pantry Pride Cola	16NR, 64NR, 12C
C & C Cola	64NR, 12C
Co-op Cola (Consumer's Co-op)	28NR
Dart Cola (Dart Drug)	28NR, 64NR, 21C
Richfood Cola (Memco)	12NR, 28NR, 64NR
Frank's Cola	16NR, 28NR, 12C
People's Cola	28NR, 12C
Drug Fair	28NR, 64NR, 12C
Grand Union Cola	48NR, 64NR, 12C
Giant Cola	28NR, 64NR, 12C
Glee Cola	12C
Cragmont Cola (Safeway)	16NR, 28NR, 64NR, 12C
Dixi Cola	13C
Diet cola soft drink brands currently in market	
Tab	16R, 10NR, 16NR, 12C
Diet Pepsi	16NR, 28NR, 12C
Diet-Rite Cola	16R, 16NR, 32NR, 64NR, 12C

EXHIBIT 3 *continued*

Sugar Free RC Cola	16NR, 32NR, 12C
Rock Creek Trim Cola	16NR, 28NR
Shasta Diet Cola	33.8 (1 liter) NR, 64NR, 12C
Faygo Diet Cola	12C
Bala Club Diet Cola (Acme)	16NR
Yukon Club Diet Cola (A&P)	28NR
Cott Diet Cola	16NR
Pantry Pride Diet Cola	28NR
No Cal Diet Cola	16NR
Weight Watchers Diet Cola	12C
Hoffman's Diet Cola	16NR
Frank's Diet Cola	16NR
Grand Union Diet Cola	28NR, 12C
Giant Diet Cola (Giant Food)	16NR
Cragmont Diet Cola (Safeway)	16NR, 28NR, 64NR, 12C

Full line flavors and mixers
  Schweppes (mixers and flavors)
  Nehi (mixers and flavors)
  Crass (mixers and flavors)
  Canada Dry (mixers and flavors)
  No Cal Diet Flavors
  Rock Creek (mixers and flavors)
  Blair House (mixers and flavors)
  Shasta Diet Flavors
  Faygo Diet Flavors
  Cragmont Flavors (Safeway)
  Cragmont Diet Flavors
  Bala Club Flavors (Acme)
  Ideal Flavors (Acme)
  Frank's Flavors
  Weight Watchers Flavors
  Co-op Flavors
  7-Eleven Flavors
  Tru-Ade Flavors
  Dixie Flavors
  Pantry Pride Flavors
  Shasta Flavors
  Faygo Flavors
  Cott Diet Flavors
  Yukon Club Flavors
  Hoffman Flavors
  Dart Flavors (Dart Drug)

Individual flavors and brands
  Hawaiian Punch
  Welch's Grape Soda
  Canada Dry Tahitian Treat
  Sugar Free Canada Dry Ginger Ale
  Wink
  Fresca
  Sprite
  7-Up
  Diet 7-Up
  Dr Pepper
  Diet Dr Pepper
  Nu Grape
  Lipton Tea
  Nestea
  Mountain Dew
  Cherry Smash
  Frostie Root Beer
  Dad's Root Beer
  A&W Root Beer
  Hires Root Beer
  Sugar Free Dad's Root Beer
  Sugar Free Hire's Root Beer
  A&W Diet Root Beer
  Yoo Hoo Chocolate
  Brownie Chocolate

EXHIBIT 3   *continued*

Richfood Flavors (Memco)
People's Flavors
Drug Fair Flavors
Grand Union Flavors
Glee Flavors
Giant Flavors

R = Returnable
NR = Nonreturnable
C = Can
#'s = Ounces

Although the association noted that there was high concentration among bottlers in some local markets, such concentration was natural since over 60 percent of all bottling plants were located in cities with populations under 50,000, and such populations were insufficient to support large numbers of firms. Therefore, industry spokesmen maintained that concentration was neither abnormal nor anticompetitive. Moreover, because new firms were entering the industry, concentration of industry sales among a few leading brands was decreasing, while profits among national brand bottlers were declining.

In support of their contention that concentration was declining, the association cited an FTC staff report — "The Structure of Food Manufacturing." This report noted that the soft drink industry four firm concentration ratio had declined from 88 percent in 1954 to 75 percent in 1963 and 71.5 percent in 1970. In addition, the market shares of the leading soft drink companies had been quite unstable. Seven-Up lost 50 percent of its market share from 1960 to 1970 from 12 percent to 6 percent. Canada Dry had fallen from 8.7 percent in 1960 to 3.3 percent in 1970. Even the market leader, Coca-Cola, had lost market share, declining from 53 percent of the market in 1940 to around 40 percent by 1970.

In local markets competition was viewed as similarly intense. One reason for the intensity of local competition was the growth of small franchisors such as Dr Pepper. Many of these producers used the bottlers of the major firms in the industry to gain market access. In 1970, 457 of the 840 domestic bottlers of Coca-Cola bottled soft drinks of one or more additional franchise companies. In the case of Dr Pepper, which was bottled by over 125 of Coca-Cola's bottlers, market share had increased from 2.2 percent (32.5 million cases) in 1960 to 3.5 percent (153.7 million cases) in 1970. Other small franchisors such as Ma's Old Fashioned, No Cal Corp.,

Schweppes, and Vernor's Inc. had successfully expanded using the same technique.

The association concluded that the multibrand franchise had functioned as a device by which lesser-known brands could penetrate the market quickly. Thus, the range of consumer choice at retail was broadened. The association also noted that if a bottler handled several brands and thereby increased his sales, the additional sales generated by supplemental brands would increase a bottler's utilization of plant capacity, raise efficiency, lower costs, and hold down prices charged retailers for soft drinks.

A second stimulus to local competition was the growth of contract canners and controlled labels. The growth of the contract canners had enabled many retail organizations, who either did not wish to or were not able to integrate backward into production of soft drinks, to establish their own controlled label. In 1958 only four of the top 40 food chains produced their own soft drinks. By 1968 more than 30 of the nation's largest food chains sold controlled-label soft drinks. Between 1962 and 1967 controlled-label soft drinks increased their share of store sales from 4.5 percent to 15 percent.

The association maintained that entry barriers were obviously not high in the soft drink industry since in the past ten years scores of firms had attempted to enter the industry. Firms attempting to enter included Del Monte, Beech Nut, Howard Johnson's, General Mills, Nestle, Sunkist, Shasta, and Faygo. Although some of these firms failed in their attempt to enter the industry, there had been some notable successes.

One such success was Shasta. Since 1960 when Consolidated Foods acquired Shasta Water Company, Shasta had developed into a 27-flavor line of diet and nondiet soft drinks. The firm, in 1972, marketed in 44 states and sold 68.7 million cases or 1.6 percent of the market in 1970.

New forms of competition had also developed. Howard Johnson's produced and sold its own brand of cola in all Howard Johnson's restaurants. Allegheny Beverage Corporation, a vending machine firm, had installed almost 17,000 Valu Vend soft drink machines in 1971 and had proclaimed its intent to "blanket the nation with Valu Vend vending machines."

The association contended that the combination of new entrants on the national level, the growth of contract canners and bottlers, the increasing sales of controlled labels, and the entry into untapped local markets had made the soft drink industry highly competitive.

The effect of all of these competitive pressures, noted the association, was competitively low profits. In 1969 the average net operating income before taxes for bottlers was 7.7 percent of sales, and for small bottlers, only 3.85 percent. In that same year, for companies on the *Fortune* 500 list, the net-operating-income-before-taxes-to-sales ratio was over 9 percent. The average rate of return on corporate assets for soft drink bottlers had fallen substantially from an average of 18 percent in 1939 to slightly over 6 percent in 1954.

In response to the FTC staff charge that the bottling industry was made up primarily of franchise company-owned plants, publicly held multiplant corporations, and conglomerates, the association presented figures showing that 93 percent of the bottling plants in the United States in 1971 were privately held. Of these plants 1,765 (61.3 percent) were located in cities with populations less than 50,000. Only 100 bottling plants were franchise company owned; 65 were owned by publicly held corporations and only 60 bottling plants were owned by conglomerates. Conglomerate-owned plants accounted for less than 4 percent of total soft drink production in 1972.

In addition to refutation of the FTC allegations, the association provided a study concluding that removal of the exclusive territorial restrictions would result in a lessening of competition, higher retail prices, and a demise of small bottlers.

These conclusions resulted from an analysis demonstrating that the industry would come to consist entirely of three elements: the present major brand-owning companies; a few very large franchised bottling companies that would be large enough to negotiate favorable contractual terms with the brand-owning companies; and the large food retailing companies who would expand through backward integration into soft drink bottling, either of national brands or of their own branded products. The study estimated that smaller bottlers and minor brands would disappear and that many smaller retail outlets now served by these bottlers would find themselves either without service altogether or faced with such unfavorable terms that they would be unable to distribute soft drinks.

Mudd pondered the alternative recommendations that he might make to member firms. He could recommend that the industry maintain its efforts in the courts to keep the current system of territorial restrictions. He could also recommend that additional resources be devoted to the attempt to gain an antitrust exemption through the Congress. In addition to these actions, Mudd also knew that the association could assist members if strategies such as those employed by Coca-Cola and PepsiCo became prevalent among manufacturers. He did not know, however, what effect widespread bottler consolidation or vertical integration would have on the industry.

Mudd had heard considerable discussion among legal experts that the current appeal by the FTC was likely to be successful. If the soft drink industry lost this appeal, he did not know if the Supreme Court would hear an appeal by the industry.

The attempt to gain an antitrust exemption seemed equally unpredictable. The leadership of the House of Representatives was wary of granting antitrust exemptions in the post-Watergate, post–oil embargo years. The 1976 congressional repeal of resale price maintenance laws also indicated a legislative attitude of concern about consumer, rather than producer, welfare.

DISCUSSION QUESTIONS

1. Why did the FTC feel that territorial allocations in the soft drink industry lessen competition? How strong is the legal precedent for this view?
2. On what basis did the industry argue that the elimination of territorial allocations would lessen competition?
3. Which of these arguments do you find more convincing? If you were a court judge deciding on the FTC appeal, how would you decide the case, and why?

APPENDIX TO CASE 4.A: THE U.S. SOFT DRINK INDUSTRY TERRITORIAL ALLOCATIONS

Legal Arguments Presented by the FTC against the Eight Soft Drink Companies

TERRITORIAL RESTRICTIONS CONSTITUTE A *PER SE* VIOLATION OF SECTION 5 OF THE FEDERAL TRADE COMMISSION ACT

Territorial restrictions of the same nature as those challenged in the soft drink proceedings have been declared by the Supreme Court to be illegal *per se* under the antitrust laws. In *United States* v. *Arnold Schwinn & Co.*, 388 U.S. 365, 379 (1967), a case which involved Schwinn's imposition of territorial restrictions on the distributors of its bicycles, the Court held

"Under the Sherman Act it is unreasonable without more for a manufacturer to seek to restrict and confine areas of persons with whom an article may be traded after the manufacturer has parted with dominion over it. *White Motor* [v. *United States*, 372 U.S. 253 (1963); *Dr. Miles* [*Medical Co.* v. *John D. Park & Sons Co.*, 220 U.S. 379 (1911)]. Such restraints are so obviously destructive of competition that their mere existence is enough. If the manufacturer parts with dominion over his product or transfers risk of loss to another, he may not reserve control over its destiny or the condition of its resale."

Recently, in an unanimous opinion the Supreme Court reaffirmed this doctrine in *Federal Trade Commission* v. *Sperry & Hutchinson Co.* — U.S. — (1972). In summary, the Supreme Court has held that once a manufacturer has sold its products, it cannot under the Sherman Act lawfully restrict the territories in which, or the persons to whom, the products may be sold. Since violations of the Sherman Act are also violations of Section 5 of the Federal Trade Commission Act, (15 U.S.C. §45), under the holding of *Federal Trade Commission* v. *Cement Institute*, 333 U.S. 683, 693 (1948), this doctrine applies to the Commission's soft drink proceedings which were brought under Section 5 of the Federal Trade Commission Act.

Several lower court decisions, with but one exception, have construed *Schwinn* to hold that territorial restrictions are *per se* illegal: *Janel Sales Corp.* v. *Lanvin Perfumes, Inc.* 396, F. 2nd 398, 406 (2nd Cir. 1968), *cert. denied,* 393 U.S. 938 (1968); *Hensley Equipment Co.* v. *Esco Corp.,* 383 F. 2nd 252, 263 (5th Cir. 1967); *Interphoto Corp.* v. *Minolta Corp.,* 295 F. Supp. 711, 720 (affirming the temporary restraining order requiring shipments of products outside of the area in which the dealer had been restricted), 417 F. 2nd 621 (2nd Cir. 1969); *Sherman* v. *Weber Dental Mfg.,* 285 F. Supp. 114, 116 (E.D. Pa. 1968); *Chapiewsky* v. *G. Heilman Brewing Co.,* 1969 Trade cases ¶ 72, 712 (W.D. Wis. 1969); *Fagan* v. *Sunbeam Lighting Co., Inc., Eastern,* 303 F. Suppl. 356, 361 (S.D. III. 1969); *United States* v. *Glaxo Group Ltd.,* 302 F. Supp. 1, 8–11 (D.D.C. 1969), (further proceeding) 5 CCH Trade Reg. Rep. ¶ 73, 190 (D.D.C. 1970).

The sole exception is *Tripoli Co.* v. *Wella Corp.,* 425 F. 2nd 932 (3rd Cir. 1970), *cert. denied,* 400 U.S. 821 (1970), which concerned restrictions on the sale of products with potentially hazardous effects on consumers' health, to persons other than state-licensed barbers and beauticians. Clearly, there are no potentially hazardous products involved in these proceedings. Indeed, few food products exist which are less dangerous than soft drinks. Rather, involved here is a restriction on the area in which independent bottlers can resell their products. Moreover, *Tripoli* appears inconsistent with the holding in *Ethyl Gasoline Corp.* v. *United States,* 309 U.S. 436, 450 (1940), which involved restrictions on the resale of a gasoline additive to particular purchasers. These restrictions were found by the Court to be unlawful.

TERRITORIAL RESTRICTIONS CONSTITUTE AN ILLEGAL HORIZONTAL MARKET DIVISION

In addition to the illegality of the vertical market division, an unlawful horizontal market division exists between those syrup manufacturers having wholly owned bottling operations* and their bottlers which also is *per se* illegal. The market division allegation in these matters is based upon the fact that the independent bottlers, licensed by the syrup manufacturers, operating near areas in which the syrup manufacturers have wholly owned bottling operations, are potential competitors of the syrup manufacturers' bottling operations. This potential competition is snuffed out by the terri-

---

*The Coca-Cola Co., PepsiCo Inc., Royal Crown Cola Co., Dr Pepper Co., Cott Inc. and Canada Dry Corp. have wholly owned bottling or canning operations. Seven-Up and Crush International, Ltd. do not.

torial restriction provisions in the bottlers' contracts with the syrup manufacturers, which prohibit their bottlers from selling outside their assigned territories. By agreeing that they will not compete outside of the territories allocated to them by the syrup manufacturers, the independent bottlers and the syrup manufacturers' wholly owned bottling operations avoid competition with each other. Thus, the bottlers' contracts constitute a division of markets between competitors, *i.e.*, between the independent bottlers and the syrup manufacturers' wholly owned bottling operations. In view of the substantial sales of soft drinks by the syrup manufacturers, these proceedings constitute significant market division cases, regardless of their not-to-be-slighted vertical aspects.

Market division agreements between competitors have been illegal *per se* since *United States* v. *Addyston Pipe & Steel Co.*, 175 U.S. 211 (1899). This principle was recently reaffirmed in *Burke* v. *Ford*, 389 U.S. 320 (1967). See *United States* v. *Penn-Olin Chemical Co.*, 378 U.S. 138 (1964). The use of trademark licensing to divide markets by competitors has been condemned by the Supreme Court as being illegal *per se* to the same extent as market division accomplished through other means. *Serta Associates, Inc.* v. *United States*, 393 U.S. 534 (1969), (*per curiam*); *United States* v. *Sealy, Inc.*, 388 U.S. 350 (1967); *Timken Roller Bearing Co.* v. *United States*, 341, U.S. 593 (1951).

The *Attorney General's Committee to Study the Antitrust Laws*, 26 (1955), has stated that agreements among competitors to divide markets have no purpose other than the elimination of competition. As the Supreme Court noted in *Burke* v. *Ford*, "When competition is reduced, prices increase and unit sales decrease." 389 U.S. 320, 322 (1967). Thus, the effect of market-allocation agreements is similar to price-fixing agreements in that both types of agreements adversely affect price and both are considered *per se* illegal under the antitrust laws.

The recent decision of *United States* v. *Topco Associates, Inc.*, 1970 Trade Cases ¶ 73, 388 (N.D. Ill. 1970), argued before the Supreme Court, 40 U.S.L.W. 3246, (November 23, 1971), raises the question of whether all horizontal market division agreements are *per se* illegal. *Topco* involved a member-owned marketing organization which is a common purchasing agent of private label food and nonfood products for 25 medium-sized supermarkets. Challenged were the provisions of the membership agreements which specified the areas in which Topco members could sell Topco-label products. Also in contention were the provisions of the agreements which required members to obtain permission to expand the sales of Topco products into another member's territory. The Court held that the *per se* illegality of market division agreements did not apply to this arrangement and applied a rule of reason approach to it. It held that the territorial restrictions enabled Topco members "to compete more effectively with national chains whose private label brands are sold exclusively through their own outlets," *Id.*, at ¶ 89,562, and were therefore lawful. Oral argument in *Topco* was held before the Supreme Court on November 16, 1971, at which time the Solicitor General urged that the restrictions be held *per se* illegal. 40 U.S.L.W. 3245 (November 23, 1971).

However, even if the lower court's decision in *Topco* is affirmed by the Supreme Court, it would not affect this proceeding. The rationale of the lower court's opinion in *Topco* is that restrictions imposed by medium-sized firms are lawful as they permit these firms to compete more effectively with large national firms. As is apparent, the facts in these soft drink proceedings are significantly different from those in *Topco*. These proceedings involve the largest firms in the soft drink industry. Thus, even if *Topco* is not reversed by the Supreme Court, its holding would be inapplicable to this proceeding.

Respondents assert that the territorial restriction system is an effective method of marketing their products. A similar argument was made in *Schwinn*. In rejecting this argument and instead finding illegal *per se* Schwinn's restrictions on the areas in which its retailers and wholesalers could sell, the Court observed, "But this argument, appealing as it is, is not enough to avoid the Sherman Act proscription, because in a sense, every restrictive practice is designed to augment the profit and competitive position of its participants. Price fixing does so, for example, and so may *well-calculated division of territories*." (388 U.S. at 375) (Emphasis added.)

A similar argument of justification was rejected in *United States* v. *Masonite*, 316 U.S. 265 (1942). Although this was a price-fixing case, the *Attorney General's Committee to Study the Antitrust Laws*, discussed *supra*, points out the similarity of the two practices. The court in *Masonite* stated

"Since there was price-fixing, the fact that there were business reasons which made the arrangements desirable to the appellees, the fact that the effect of the combination may have been to increase the distribution of hardboard, without increase of price to the consumer, or even to promote competition between dealers, or the fact that from other points of view the arrangements might be deemed to have desirable consequences would be no more legal justification for price-fixing than were the 'competitive evils' in the *Socony-Vacuum* case." (316 U.S. at 276).

Parties to market division agreements have also argued that such an agreement is necessary to protect the members of the agreement from ruinous competition. In 1898, this argument was first rejected in *Addyston Pipe & Steel*, 85 Fed. 271, 219 (1898), aff'd., 175 U.S. 211 (1899). There the court held that

"***however great the necessity for curbing themselves by joint agreement from committing financial suicide by ill-advised competition, [the agreement] was void at common law***"

Thus, the Court has emphasized that with respect to vertical territorial restrictions and horizontal market division, the only relevant consideration in determining their lawfulness is to ascertain whether the restrictions exist. If they do exist, then they are declared unlawful without any inquiry into their competitive effect.

Conglomerate Mergers and the Public Interest
Exxon's Acquisition of Reliance Electric

In May 1979 Exxon Corporation announced it was making a tender offer to shareholders of Reliance Electric Company valued at $1.17 billion. The business press, though caught by surprise, reacted immediately, acclaiming the move as "one of the boldest, most brilliant corporate maneuvers in recent years — but also one that could turn into a political disaster for Exxon and its fellow oil companies." It was generally felt among observers that "in winning the battle Exxon was in danger of losing the war."[1] The following reasons were cited to support this view:

- With price controls on oil to be lifted gradually through 1981, President Carter had proposed a "windfall-profits" excise tax to recapture a good part of the expected added oil revenues. Some congressmen had been pushing for even higher taxes than the President wanted. The Exxon move gave the high-tax faction an immediate talking point since it was felt that Exxon did not need the money for exploration.
- The Reliance takeover also could give added support to Senator Kennedy's bill to bar oil companies from making acquisitions valued at more than $100 million, to force oil companies to reinvest their profits in energy-producing projects.
- Exxon's status as the largest industrial company in the world made it a natural target for critics of the oil industry. The oil company's revenues were even larger than the gross national product of wealthy Saudi Arabia.

This case reviews the nature of each company and describes an invention claimed by Exxon as the motivation for its acquisition of Reliance. A basic question in this case is whether the acquisition serves the public interest.

THE ACQUIRER: EXXON CORPORATION

In 1978 Exxon was the nation's second-largest industrial corporation, with sales of $64.9 billion. It also was the largest oil company in the world. Operating in the United States and in nearly 100 other countries, its principal business was energy, as it was involved in exploration for and production of crude oil and natural gas, manufacture of petroleum products, and the transportation and sale of crude oil, natural gas, and petroleum products. In addition, Exxon had interests in the exploration, mining, and selling of coal and uranium and the fabrication of nuclear fuel, and it manufactured and marketed petrochemicals.[2]

Exxon Enterprises was a company division formed in 1964 to develop new nonoil divisions. Since then, this division had developed and marketed office equipment, including telecopiers and word processors. Despite the efforts of the corporation, profits had been minuscule; in 1978 Exxon's nonpetroleum units contributed less than 1 percent of revenues.

Owing to increases in worldwide oil prices, Exxon accumulated an "embarrassment of riches" — in 1978 the company's cash flow (net income plus depreciation and depletion) amounted to nearly $4 billion. Still, the oil industry did have problems, indicated by the fact that Exxon was stripped of much of its foreign oil in 1974. The Organization of Petroleum Exporting Countries (OPEC) was selling more and more of its oil on the world spot market to the highest bidder, which often was not Exxon. In addition, exploration for oil had been costly and disappointing. Since 1973 Exxon spent $4.2 billion in exploration and production, yet during the same time, its reserves of crude oil had fallen 20 percent.[3]

Exxon apparently concluded its situation called for intensification of the strategy to diversify. The company was reported to want to pump large amounts of its bountiful assets into nonoil businesses, preferably by acquisitions: its major problem was to find "a new game comparable to oil."[4]

Most of Exxon's strategy had resulted in energy-related diversification as it successfully diversified in at least three different energy areas:

- In 1970 it produced its first coal. Since then, it has amassed one of the largest coal reserves in the world: over 9 billion tons.
- It has mined uranium since before 1970.
- Exxon is the world's largest nuclear fuel fabricator.

It appeared Exxon would need to diversify into and/or develop nonoil divisions to prosper in the long run. Yet this strategy was threatened when Senator Edward Kennedy introduced legislation in August 1979 that prohibited the top 16 oil companies from acquiring control of any other company with more than $100 million in assets unless the acquisition would "enhance competition" or "promote energy extrapolation, extraction, production or conversion." Proponents of this "antioil" bill believed oil companies should grow internally through the creation of new assets, and they were attempting to force the oil companies to invest their profits in the expansion of domestic energy supplies, instead of buying nonenergy assets.

Critics of the bill made several points. Since the bill would force large oil companies to reinvest their profits in petroleum exploration and production, it would probably have the following effects:

- It would reduce the access of oil companies to essential sources of financing, thereby reducing the resources available to continue the search for new energy reserves.
- It would force the companies to be more conservative in their exploration programs at a time when declining domestic petroleum reserves require greater risk taking. Furthermore, it would impair the ability of American companies to participate with other companies in investments abroad, thus reducing their access to vital foreign energy supplies.

As it turned out, the bill passed the Senate Judiciary Committee by a narrow margin and was later defeated on the Senate floor.

THE ACQUIRED: RELIANCE ELECTRIC COMPANY

At the end of 1978 Reliance Electric was nearly a billion dollar corporation engaged in developing, manufacturing, marketing, and servicing a broad line of industrial equipment. Earnings after taxes in 1978 were $64.6 million on sales of $966 million.[5] The largest part of Reliance's business was derived from its electrical group in the design and manufacture of electrical motor drives and from control products and systems used primarily in manufacturing and mining. The company also had a mechanical group producing products to transfer power from the shaft of a motor to various types of machinery used by industry. Smaller components of the business were electronic and mechanical weighing, measurements, and process control equipment and a line of specialized hardware for the telecommunications industry.

Reliance was a fast growing and profitable company. Since 1973 net sales had increased 82 percent, net earnings were up 145 percent, and fully diluted earnings per share had risen 132 percent. It had also been an acquisition-minded company: in 1978 Reliance had completed a $345 million acquisition, and in March of 1979 it consumated another purchase that added about $500 million to its level of sales.

In the electrical equipment industry Reliance was a major producer but not the largest. For example, the motor segment of this industry was a $4 billion a year business — General Electric held the largest share with 20 percent, Westinghouse Electric was second with 11 percent, and Reliance was third with its 10 percent share. The fourth-place firm was Emerson Electric with 7.5 percent of the market.

One outstanding fact of the proposed acquisition was the amount of the actual tender offer. Exxon had offered $72.50 a share for Reliance's stock when the shares were trading for $34.50. Reliance stock, in fact, had never traded above $41 a share. The size of the increment, according to a Wall Street report, dumbfounded even Reliance's financial advisers, who had been expecting that Exxon would not go above $60 a share.[6]

Charles Ames, president and chief executive officer of Reliance, said in testimony before the Senate Antitrust Committee that he personally would prefer that Reliance remain independent but that from the standpoint of the company's shareholders and investors, he could not oppose Exxon's bid.[7] In fact, Reliance's board of directors neither endorsed nor opposed the offer but expressed the opinion that the price was fair, leaving it to the stockholders on whether to tender their shares. More than 95 percent of them did.

THE ALTERNATING CURRENT SYNTHESIZER

Exxon had made a public statement that the reason for the takeover was to use Reliance's manufacturing and marketing expertise in connection with the rapid development and marketing of Exxon's new variable voltage and variable power processing technology. Howard C. Kauffmann, president of Exxon, had demonstrated the "new" technology at a press conference on May 18, 1979.[8] He had displayed a mysterious-looking, silver-colored metal box, which was hooked up for demonstration purposes to an electric fan, whose blades speeded up or slowed down on command from the box. He had declared that the application of the device to electric motors of all sizes ultimately could produce energy savings equivalent to a million barrels of oil a day or 100 million tons of coal a year.

The alternating current synthesizer (ACS) device modifies the form of electric current used to run a motor so that the motor may be operated at any speed. The slower the motor runs, the less power it uses. In contrast, most standard electric motors operate at a constant speed, usually geared to the maximum load expected. Output from the machines the motor is driving is controlled by gears, valves, dampers, and other mechanical devices while the motor is running at full speed. Though Exxon conceded that the ACS technology was not brand new (eight or ten companies including Reliance had such systems on the market), they pointed out that the existing approaches to increased motor efficiency had not taken off as yet. A general manager of Westinghouse's process equipment division had said that until recently energy costs had not been high enough to justify the initial cost of the ACS. He had added that an ACS system includes "several cabinets full of electronics" and could cost 30 percent to 40 percent more than a standard single speed AC motor with simple controls. He also said that a crossover point was imminent at which it would be worthwhile to invest more initially to save electricity.[9]

Of the ACS segment of the market, Reliance had a leading 20 percent market share. Exxon's primary interest in taking the company over had apparently been the acquisition of this particular segment of Reliance's business. It was understood in the market that Exxon was anxious to acquire this business to help market a "major" advance in ACS technology. Industry sources said that there seemed to be at least three broad areas of application for the ACS technology:

- It could be used in many industrial applications where full speed and power are not required all the time, such as fans, pumps, and compressors.
- The system could be used in certain industrial processing, such as steel rolling or paper making, where variable speed is essential. At present, that equipment is usually powered by DC motors and drive systems, which are efficient at full speed but lose efficiency rapidly when they are slowed down. The AC system would save more electricity because it was more efficient at lower speeds.
- The system could be used in equipment that now employs internal combustion engines, including oil field pumps, compressors, lift-trucks, and conveyors, where motors are already making headway against engines. A few years from now it could be used in electric trucks, buses, and automobiles. The sources add that the variable speed and energy efficiency are ideal for these applications. And as gasoline and diesel fuel continued to get scarcer and more expensive, electric power probably would take over more and more jobs from engines.[10]

Public leaders, especially Senator Howard Metzenbaum of Ohio, had reacted to Kauffmann's claim by saying that if the claim were true, the acquisition was in the public interest; however, if there was reason to believe that Exxon was taking advantage of the energy crisis to sell the American people on one of the largest cash acquisitions in history, Exxon should not be allowed to proceed.[11] Many business leaders had stated that Kauffmann's "energy-saving" claim was unsubstantiated and should be treated as such.

THE FEDERAL TRADE COMMISSION AND THE ACQUISITION

At the end of May 1979 the FTC moved to block the takeover, arguing that it violated federal antitrust law. The legal action against the merger was taken under Section 7 of the Clayton Act, which was initially passed in 1914. The amended version of this section read:

> No corporation may acquire . . . the stock . . . or assets of another corporation . . . where in any line of commerce in any section of the country, the effect . . . may be substantially to lessen competition, or to tend to create a monopoly.

The FTC had contended that Exxon was on the verge of entering the motor drives industry on its own and that its subsequent decision to acquire Reliance lessened competition by removing Exxon itself as a potential competitor in the industry. Part of the evidence crucial to the FTC's case was the indication that Exxon took steps in late 1978 or early 1979 to move toward market entry for electronic variable-speed drives through internal expansion.[12] For example, the corporation hired Korn-Ferry International, an executive search firm, to recruit managers for an ACS operation. Exxon also talked with parts suppliers, installed a computerized management information system, and produced an ad brochure. If the FTC could prove Exxon planned to enter the industry on its own, it would have a much stronger antitrust case than if Exxon had decided initially that internal expansion was not feasible. A major question in the FTC proceedings was how difficult it was for a company that was not in the motor industry to get into it. If it could be proved that there were no barriers, the FTC could support its charge that the acquisition lessens competition. Testifying before the Senate antitrust subcommittee in June, Charles Ames, President of Reliance, stated that setting up production to enter the electric motor industry would not take very long, but getting acceptance of a product in the marketplace could take years.[13]

An internal Exxon memo, written on October 28, 1978, commented that an acquisition "provides an excellent base for competing broadly in major segments of [the] electrical equipment industry."[14] Another memo written November 10, 1978, suggested the only way to "satisfy objectives of market penetration" was through a major acquisition.[15] The FTC accused Exxon of putting up a smokescreen in the form of a new product to diversify into the capital goods business successfully.

Jo Graves, senior vice-president of Exxon Enterprises, Inc., explained the company could have made a profit if it entered the electrical motor industry on its own and, probably, would have had a higher return on investment than a purchase. However, internal expansion did not meet the company's "business development" objectives because the division would have been too small. The electric motor industry was mature, with no new entrants in the last two decades. Exxon had decided it did not want to develop successful small businesses. Instead, they appeared to want acceptable, yet lesser returns on a larger business.

Some congressmen had suggested that a way to resolve the problem could be a licensing arrangement whereby Exxon would lease the technology to companies in the electric motor industry. The FTC, however, argued that such licensing would not cure what it contends were anticompetitive effects of the merger. The FTC claimed to have a solid basis from which they could argue that licensing would not help, since a recent study by Booz, Allen, and Hamilton had shown that "very little" licensing of novel technology is done.[16] The study, a survey of licensing in the U.S. electric industry, shows that joint ventures and acquisitions are the preferred methods of introducing technology. The study, done for Exxon, also concluded that the financial requirements necessary to develop Exxon's new technology "are beyond the resources of many of the potential licensees and present significant business risks that will limit the eagerness of major firms to commit these resources."

Joint venture arrangements are often used to introduce novel technology, especially when small technology-based companies wish to introduce some major product innovation. The small company technological innovators often go into joint ventures with a large partner corporation that supplies the marketing power and often the capital. Some landmark studies had shown that as much as 74 percent of technological innovations originate in small corporations. Among the inventions of small companies are air-conditioning, Bakelite, the automatic transmission, and stereophonic sound systems. The societal implications of the alternative strategies available to Exxon had not been examined, but it was evident that these implications would largely determine whether the takeover would be allowed.

Exxon managers were initially quite optimistic that antitrust action would not be successful, citing the following cases for their optimism:

- *FTC* v. *Atlantic Richfield Co.* The FTC contended that ARCO could have entered the market on its own instead of purchasing Anaconda Co. The FTC lost. 1976.
- *FTC* v. *Black & Decker.* The FTC opposed acquisition of McCulloch Corporation on the same grounds. The FTC's case was dismissed. 1976.
- *FTC* v. *BOC International Ltd.* Federal court overturned an FTC order that BOC sell its interest in Airco Inc. 1978.[17]

On the other hand, there had also been some instances where mergers had been disallowed on the grounds of "probable" anticompetitive effects. The best known example was Proctor & Gamble's (P & G's) acquisition of the assets of Clorox Chemical Company in 1957, which parallels the Exxon-Reliance case.[18] In P & G's case the merger was neither horizontal, vertical, nor conglomerate but rather a product-extension merger. Similarly, Exxon's move might be categorized as an "industry-extension" merger. The core question in both cases is whether the merger substantially lessens competition. The answer requires an analysis of the present and a forecast of the future, competitive environment of the industry.

While any acquisition eliminates the potential competition of the acquiring firm, the acquisition of a small firm by a large firm outside the industry may increase competition in the industry by providing capital, technology, and management to a smaller, weaker competitor. Clorox commanded a 49 percent market share in liquid household bleach, and with Purex, the other major producer, accounted for 65 percent of the market. Clearly, the liquid bleach industry was highly concentrated. In 1967 the Court concluded that the P & G acquisition would tend to decrease competition and was unlawful; P & G was ordered to divest Clorox. The thinking of the Court appeared to be that no social value would result from a merger of two financially strong firms, each with a strong market share. The presence of financially "deep pockets" in each merger partner would tend to lessen, rather than strengthen, competition. In contrast to P & G, when Exxon moved to acquire Reliance, there were several electric motor firms in the industry, and none of them had better than a 30 percent market share. Also, Exxon's action was different from P & G's attempted acquisition of Clorox since Reliance was the third largest firm in its industry, while P & G boldly moved against the largest firm in the liquid bleach industry. On the other hand, Reliance was considered to be the leading firm in the variable-speed-drive industry, the apparent reason for Exxon's acquisition bid.

Another case where the FTC blocked a merger on similar grounds involved Bendix Corporation's attempted acquisition of Fram Corporation, a leading producer of various kinds of filters, including automotive and aerospace filters.[19] A U.S. Court of Appeals established that the probability of Bendix's entry into the market was clear and the only question was the form such entry would have taken. It was established that Bendix had three choices: (1) to expand internally, (2) to make a toehold acquisition looking toward expansion on that base, or (3) to merge with a leading firm. It was felt that the first two would have promoted competition, whereas the third would not. The court concluded that Bendix was the most likely of a limited number of possible entrants capable of making a significant entry by acquisition and expansion of a smaller firm. Consequently, the elimination of that potential entrant and competitor is highly significant for its effect upon competition.

STATUS AS OF YEAR'S END — 1979

The FTC charged that the Exxon-Reliance merger would create "a dangerous probability" of the combined companies dominating the electronic variable-speed-drive industry. The agency also said that such dominance would discourage other marketers of similar products. It also claimed to have evidence that at one point Exxon was planning to enter the market on its own. Federal District Judge Harold Greene issued a ten-day restraining order at the request of the FTC on July 30, 1979. However, he did not provide any clues as to whether the FTC would get a decisive longer-term injunction against the takeover that it was seeking. In his opinion, Judge Green said that a major task of the judge hearing the FTC's injunction request would be to balance the merger's market implications against any energy benefits. "Where public interest lies in that regard . . . could and should significantly influence the outcome of the proceeding," he said.[20]

To protect Reliance shareholders from a drop in their stock's price in case divestiture were ordered, the FTC directed Exxon to hold Reliance as a separate entity. This resulted in Exxon's purchase price of $1.17 billion being frozen indefinitely. As litigation dragged on from July to September 1979, Reliance's stockholders sued Exxon for consummation of the purchase, claiming they were being deprived of about $2.5 million per week in interest income that could have been earned on the purchase price. At the end of October 1979 the U.S. district court allowed Exxon to buy Reliance's stock if it kept the drives business separate. The FTC claimed the ruling was a "total victory." Litigation on the antitrust lawsuit appeared unlikely to be resolved for several years.[21]

POSTSCRIPT

Several difficulties arose after the acquisition.[22] First was an acquisition made by Reliance of Federal Pacific Company shortly before the Exxon offer had turned up problems. Federal Pacific had allegedly falsified tests on a major product, a circuit breaker, and this fact was not discovered by Reliance until after Federal Pacific had been acquired. Withdrawing this product from the market gave Reliance a fourth-quarter loss of $36 million. Owing to this loss, Reliance contributed only $4 million to Exxon's consolidated profits of $5.56 billion. However, even if Reliance had not run into a problem with the circuit breaker recall in the fourth quarter of 1980 and had earned an expected $40 million, the return to Exxon shareholders from the purchase of Reliance would have been only 3.4 percent.

Second, on March 22, 1981, Exxon was reported to have abandoned the ACS device as early as November 1980 and was said to be working on an alternative design.[23] Apparently, the laboratory model Exxon had developed ran into problems in adapting to a variety of manufacturing conditions involving overload protection, heat buildup, part durability, and interference with other factory devices. The key problem in Exxon's appraisal of the invention appeared to be the company's lack of manufacturing experience.

Exxon officials were reported to feel that the acquisition ended up saving the corporation a good deal of money. Exclusive of salaries for the project personnel, the company spent only $15 million on the ACS project, or less than Exxon's average net profit for every single day of 1980. In fact, the failure of the invention, argued Exxon officials, actually demonstrated how much the corporation needed the motor manufacturer.

DISCUSSION QUESTIONS

1. Evaluate Exxon's acquisition of Reliance Electric from the standpoint of Reliance's stockholders and from the standpoint of the stockholders of Exxon.
2. How would you interpret the *public interest* in this acquisition? Does the public interest dictate the FTC should accept or challenge the acquisition?
3. What general posture would you recommend for the government in relation to conglomerate mergers?

NOTES

1. "Exxon's Takeover Bid Is Called a Bold Strike But Is Politically Risky," *Wall Street Journal*, June 12, 1979, pp. 1, 31.
2. Exxon Corporation, *1978 Annual Report* (New York: Exxon Corporation, 1979).
3. "Exxon: Searching for Another Game That Equals Oil in Size," *Business Week*, July 16, 1979, p. 80.
4. Ibid.
5. Reliance Electric Company, *1978 Annual Report* (Cleveland, Ohio: Reliance Electric Company, 1979).
6. "Exxon's Takeover Bid," p. 1.
7. "Exxon's Need to Buy Reliance to Enter Field Is Scrutinized," *Wall Street Journal*, June 27, 1979, p. 13.
8. "Exxon's Takeover Bid," p. 31.
9. Ibid.
10. Ibid.
11. Ibid.
12. "FTC Will Try to Convince Court Exxon Was About to Become Rival of Reliance," *Wall Street Journal*, August 10, 1979, p. 4.
13. "Exxon's Need to Buy," p. 13.
14. "FTC Will Try to Convince," p. 4.
15. Ibid.
16. "Licensing by Exxon Wouldn't End FTC's Opposition to Merger with Reliance Unit," *Wall Street Journal*, August 21, 1979, p. 3.
17. "FTC Staff Opposes Exxon's Acquisition of Reliance Electric on Antitrust Ground," *Wall Street Journal*, July 27, 1979, p. 3.
18. *Federal Trade Commission* v. *Proctor & Gamble Company*, 386 U.S. 568 (1966).

19. *Bendix Corporation* v. *Federal Trade Commission,* 450 F. 2nd 534 (1971).
20. "Exxon Purchase of Ohio Concern Blocked by Court," *Wall Street Journal,* July 30, 1979, p. 6.
21. "Exxon Must Keep Reliance's Drives Unit Separate Pending End of FTC Challenge," *Wall Street Journal,* October 29, 1979, p. 8.
22. "What Exxon Learned about Motors," *New York Times,* March 22, 1981, pp. F1, 15.
23. Ibid., F1.

Chapter 5

Health, Safety, and Environmental Quality
Changing Expectations and Modern Controversies

At the turn of the century the perceived threats of corporate size, market power, and the social impact of industrialization began to generate pressures for controlling the consequences of economic growth. The relatively passive role of government began to change in the late nineteenth century: the first regulatory commission, the Interstate Commerce Commission (ICC) was formed in 1887; antitrust legislation was enacted in 1890 and again in 1914; and the Pure Food and Drug Act, an early and unprecedented governmental action in consumer protection, was passed in 1906.

In retrospect these developments foreshadowed a governmental activism that would gain momentum during the twentieth century. The first great wave of public restraint on the private sector was seen in the 1930s, and the second occurred in the 1960s and 1970s. Determining the proper role of government in influencing social consequences of economic development has become a major public policy problem, a strongly contested issue in business-government relations.

Perhaps the more recent confrontations of business and society were inevitable in an advanced industrial economy with a technologically dependent populace. Concern was fostered by alarming books such as Rachel Carson's *Silent Spring* and Ralph Nader's *Unsafe at Any Speed;* threats to public well-being such as repeated oil spills, DC-10 crashes, and the Three Mile Island accident caused further anxiety. Thus, over the past two decades a security-oriented reform movement developed, and a great increase in public regulation of business resulted.

The consequences of these developments are important. First, corporations have changed: plants, production processes, and products have been modified to comply with standards for product and workplace safety and environmental protection; demand is growing for new professionals in occupational health, toxicology, environmental engineering, product safety, and quality control; new organizational systems and management practices have been developed. Second, the number of government administrative agencies engaged in setting and enforcing standards mandated by numerous pieces of social legislation has been growing. Misdirected, contradictory, or overly ambitious examples of this regulatory effort have become highly visible to the public, lessening confidence in governmental intervention as a solution to social ills. Finally, the cost of a higher level and broader scope of protection has gradually seeped into the American awareness, raising questions about the limits of protection, its benefits in relation to its costs, and alternative approaches to influencing business behavior.

This chapter addresses the difficulties of making public policy in the areas of health, safety, and environment — fields currently of major significance to business operations. Our inquiry begins with a brief definition of *social regulation* and moves to consideration of social regulation's pervasiveness and consequences. This leads to large, yet elusive, issues, such as the formation of public perceptions toward risk, the role of science and the media in making public policies, and the difficulty of estimating costs and benefits of proposed protective measures.

Although the present chapter focuses on problems of public influence of business behavior within the existing rule-oriented regulatory framework, this is only one type of public policy, only one available means of regulating corporations. Other public strategies and institutional mechanisms for influencing business actions in the areas of health, safety, and environment — such as market-based incentives, the legal system through liability suits, and internal corporate policies and practices — will be discussed in the next chapter.

THE REGULATORY SYSTEM

Public regulation of private enterprise is vast, pervasive, and fragmented. (See Insert 5.A.) The Congressional Quarterly *Federal Regulatory Directory* listed 83 federal regulatory agencies in 1983/84.[1] Most systems for organizing this subject distinguish between "older" economic regulation and "newer" social regulation. The former is characterized by independent commissions — such as the ICC, the Federal Communications Commission, and the Federal Maritime Commission — which were set up to control the conditions of competition (entry of new competitors, service distribution, and pricing) of entire industries. These agencies are the focus of the recent "deregulation" movement, a topic addressed in Chapter 4.

A second major regulatory thrust seeks to control the human and social consequences of competitive economic activity. These agencies have specific constituency groups — workers, investors, consumers, users of the environment, employees with pensions, prospective employees — whose economic or social interests are the object of protection. These programs are the focus of regulatory reform to control the proliferation of rules and to introduce economic impact considerations into rule making. Issues of business-government relations dealing with health, safety, and environmental quality are the subjects of this chapter.

The scope of social regulatory programs is staggering. Programs exist in agencies as diverse as the Treasury Department, the Department of Agriculture, and of course, the Departments of Labor and of Health and Human Services. The following is a list of the most visible and controversial agencies with a mandate for social regulation:

- The Food and Drug Administration (FDA) was created to protect the public from health hazards present in food, cosmetics, and drugs. The authority of this agency extends to product testing, standard setting, licensing products, conducting research, and disseminating information on products in these areas. It is involved in numerous issues concerning the marketing of ethical drugs and the use of additives in foods.
- The Highway Traffic and Safety Administration (NHTSA) is involved in developing safety standards for vehicles sold in the United States and establishing mileage efficiency for vehicles. Passenger restraint systems and bumper collision requirements are two disputed topics in this field.
- The Environmental Protection Agency (EPA) has a broad mandate to improve and maintain environmental quality involving air and water quality, toxic substances, preservation of natural resources, and many other aspects of the physical environment. Auto emission controls, hazardous waste disposal, and industrial air and water emission standards are several of the more visible issues it must consider.
- The Occupational Safety and Health Administration (OSHA) is charged with encouraging employers and employees to reduce hazards and occupational illnesses in the workplace. It has standard-setting au-

---

Insert 5.A

ORGANIZATION OF GOVERNMENT REGULATION

The table below presents by year of establishment and by organizational structure 13 agencies listed in the *Federal Regulatory Directory* of 1983 as "major" regulatory agencies. Several patterns are apparent in this listing: (1) an early reliance on industry-type economic regulation and particularly the use of the independent regulatory commission, (2) the substantial number of major agencies created between 1933 and 1938 and the beginning of a reliance on executive branch regulatory agencies in this period, (3) the virtual absence of major new regulatory agencies between 1940 and 1965, (4) the absence of new industry regulation since the early 1970s, and (5) an increasing frequency of issue-oriented and executive branch agencies since the mid-1960s.

Insert 5.A   continued

	Independent Commission		Executive Branch
Year	Industry Specific	Issue Specific	
1887	Interstate Commerce Commission		
1913	Federal Reserve System		
1914		Federal Trade Commission	
1920	Federal Energy Regulatory Commission (formerly the Federal Power Commission)		
1933	Federal Deposit Insurance Corporation		
1934	Securities and Exchange Commission		
	Federal Communications Commission		
1935		National Labor Relations Board	
1938			Food and Drug Administration
1965		Equal Employment Opportunity Commission	
1970			Environmental Protection Agency
			Occupational Safety and Health Administration
1972		Consumer Product Safety Commission	

SOURCE: *Federal Regulatory Directory 1983–84* (Washington, D.C.: Congressional Quarterly Inc., 1983), pp. 82–426.

thority and can establish record-keeping requirements as well as educational and monitoring programs. Measures of worker protection, equipment changes for safety, and allowable chemical emissions in the workplace are subjects on which controversy has been generated in reaction to OSHA policies.

The Consumer Product Safety Commission (CPSC) seeks to protect the health and well-being of consumers chiefly by promulgating standards of product safety and banning products from the marketplace.

- The Federal Trade Commission (FTC) seeks consumer protection through ensuring free and fair business competition, protecting the public from false advertising, and exposing deception in product packaging and labeling. In addition, this agency is concerned with business practices that tend to lessen competition or lead to monopoly.

These agencies represent a large part of the total effort to regulate health, safety, and environmental quality; but there exist many additional areas of governmental action — control of conditions of lending, protection of women and minorities against discrimination, aircraft safety, and protection of employee pension rights, to name a few. The powers of these agencies and their approaches to influencing private action vary widely. In addition, the costs of complying with their rules and public support for their actions differ. Let us examine some specific issues.

THE REGULATORY IMPERATIVE

The Impact of Technology

There are numerous reasons for a late twentieth century surge in public sentiment for safety and health protection. One obvious source is the advanced level of technology. Diethylstilbestrol, acrylonitrile, mercaptans, trichloroethylene — these ominous sounding names are not part of the average person's experience. One cannot rely on his or her own sense to evaluate their potential harm or benefit to oneself or to society. The inaccessibility and uncertainty of the world of synthetic chemicals and other high technology seem inherently threatening. One's involuntary dependence on the use of unknown and distrusted chemicals understandably is a strong source of protectionist feeling.

Changes in Social Structure and Values

Other sources of the health and safety movement are reflections of changes in society. Increases in population longevity have led to occupational diseases, more prevalent in later life, becoming a more visible threat to society. Also, a more economically advanced society may place greater emphasis on aesthetics as opposed to survival values and may be led to greater appreciation of "quality" as opposed to "quantity." Greater relative fulfillment of material goals may lead the society to see quality of life as a frontier and health and safety as rights rather than aspirations.

Health, safety, and environment can also represent important values in the expression of individualism — a political rather than an economic expression of individualism based on humanitarian and technological, not market, values. Sociologist Nathan Glazer comments:

> Two faces of individualism: the more rugged economic and institutional individualism of the United States, hampered and hobbled by a new kind of individualism devoted to self-realization, to the protection of the environment, to suspicion of big business and big organization. . . . Principally, the first kind has contributed to the most marked characteristic of the modern United States, its enormous productivity, while the second clearly places some limits on how this productivity may be realized. Both kinds are suspicious of government, but both are willing to enlist it.[2]

The new individualism is not supplanting the old; but it will not be denied a position of coexistence, and it can act to hinder the old. At the very least it calls attention to what has become a world of complex and interdependent values. Insert 5.B describes several studies identifying health risks to society from advanced technology.

Government as Insurer of Individual Rights

The Jeffersonian heritage of humane and social values has, at different times in U.S. history, provided a counterweight to the unbridled expression of economic values. Exposure of conditions threatening to health and safety has traditionally aroused public opinion and led to corrective legislative action. Attention and publicity concerning public health, safety, or environmental problems are the driving forces for governmental action.

Insert 5.B

TECHNOLOGY AND SOCIETY: COPING WITH THE PRESENCE AND RISKS OF TOXIC SUBSTANCES

Disclosures about the suspected health effects of technology-based manufacturing processes often appear to run far ahead of our preparedness to understand, let alone to shape, complex interactions between technology and society. Several disturbing incidents suggesting a close tie between industrial use of chemical technology and significant health risks came to light as the nation embarked on the last half of the decade of the eighties. These incidents may foreshadow an increasingly difficult and perplexing

Insert 5.B   continued

problem for business, society, and government. Examples include the following:

- A government study identified 250,000 workers as having higher-than-normal risks of developing cancer owing to exposure to toxic substances on the job. This figure includes 59,000 foundry workers exposed primarily to coal tar and metal fumes, 50,000 miners exposed to uranium and silica dust, and tens of thousands of chemical workers exposed to formaldehyde, asbestos, pesticides, dyes and solvents, and other toxic chemicals in the workplace. A detailed study of workers exposed to one carcinogenic substance indicated that 74 percent did not even know the chemical was harmful.
- In 1981 a leak was discovered in the underground toxic storage tank of Fairchild Camera & Instrument Corporation, a major high-technology company making semiconductors. Unfortunately the tank was located only 2,000 feet from a well providing drinking water to the local community. Tests conducted by the California Department of Health Services after the leak was identified found concentrations of toxins in the water as high as 800 times the state's recommended level. A study released in early 1985 of health problems in the community found a 2.4 times higher rate of miscarriages and a 3 times higher rate of birth defects compared with a similar nearby community. One federal study of storage tank failures in Silicon Valley identified 300 leaks of dangerous chemicals potentially threatening to underground water supplies.
- A great deal of attention was placed on the safety of Union Carbide's methyl isocyanate plant in Institute, West Virginia, during the aftermath of the major leakage from a similar plant in Bhopal, India. On January 24, 1985, it was reported that the West Virginia plant had had 28 methyl isocyanate leaks over a four year period, one of which consisted of 840 pounds. The methyl isocyanate incident appeared to indicate a general absence of knowledge about toxic air pollutants and their control. Only a few of many potentially hazardous gases were being regulated, and the means of dealing with other chemicals to increase public safety effectively and efficiently was by no means clear.

SOURCE: Cathy Trost, "Higher Disease Risk Seen for 250,000 Exposed to Toxins in Job, Data Show," *Wall Street Journal,* January 24, 1985, p. 8; "Union Carbide U.S. Plant Had Gas Leaks, EPA Says," *Wall Street Journal,* January 24, 1985, p. 8; Michael W. Miller, "Study Says Birth Defects More Frequent in Areas Polluted by Technology Firms," *Wall Street Journal,* January 17, 1985, p. 8; Robert E. Taylor, "Union Carbide Internal Report Warned of Hazards at U.S. Plant, Waxman Says," *Wall Street Journal,* January 25, 1985, p. 2.

The logic of protection is readily perceived, and the humanitarian argument for public action is often compelling.

Consider, for example, some of the findings of the House Committee Report that led to the enactment of the Occupational Safety and Health Act of 1970:

- Over 14,500 American workers die each year as a result of their jobs;
- Over 2 million workers are disabled annually through job-related accidents; and
- Over $1.5 billion is wasted in lost wages each year owing to occupational accidents and diseases, and the cost to the gross national product is over $8 billion per year.[3]

In these circumstances legislators might find inaction irresponsible. Leaving aside the choice of policy tools, a democratic government would appear to be compelled to regulation in the perceived public interest.

Each new piece of regulatory legislation results from an awareness of the magnitude of a specific problem and the apparent lack of reason or justification for senseless suffering. In this process little thought may be given to the cost of regulating as opposed to the cost of not regulating, to the probability or improbability for success in correcting by regulation, to the possibility that the problem may be self-correcting via other mechanisms, or to the need for flexible design of regulatory requirements. These are often long-term and uncertain questions in a situation that appears to call for immediate and concrete action.

In the early 1970s information concerning hazardous household products frequently surfaced. In the early 1970s, for example, the Public Health Service estimated that 700,000 children were injured by toys each year; the Department of Health, Education and Welfare estimated that 3,000 to 5,000 deaths and 150,000 to 250,000 injuries each year resulted from burns due to flammable garments and indoor furnishings; and the FDA said safety hazards in baby cribs had killed 133 infants in a three year period.[4] Reform-minded individuals have identified a myriad of concerns: auto safety, air quality, product safety, ethical drugs, worker health, fairness in advertising, noise, hazardous substances, acid rain, food additives, contaminated water, and many many others. Once society, or a significant segment of it, begins to attend to risk reduction and quality improvement, the potential products, manufacturing processes, and sources of pollution that may become targets of regulation are practically infinite.

THE GROWING BY-PRODUCTS OF REGULATION

Just as society has grown vocal in identifying risks inherent in present economic activity and in calling for the public regulation of these effects, observers of the unintended consequences of regulation have also become numerous and forceful in their views. These individuals point out that the impact of protective regulation goes far beyond risk reduction; the costs of protection appear to be greater and more numerous than initially thought. It has become painfully apparent that protection is not a free good — that someone either (1) pays a direct or indirect cost or (2) foregoes a benefit otherwise attained. Let us examine each of these mechanisms in more detail.

Economic Costs of Regulation

It is easy to see that social regulation directs economic resources into "non-productive" areas of the economy. For example, pollution control equipment rather than more efficient production technology is purchased, engineering effort is taken away from product development and devoted to safety features, and administrative time is given to planning for workplace safety as opposed to market development. One widely publicized study of costs, conducted for the Business Roundtable, an association of presidents of large corporations, compiled costs of compliance in 1977 with six major government programs by 48 large corporations.[5] Private costs to the companies of complying with environmental protection, equal employment opportunity, occupational safety and health, energy, pension rights, and fair trade practice regulations amounted to $2.6 billion. Incremental capital costs for the companies in the sample amounted to 3.3 percent of all capital expenditures in 1977. Twenty percent of administrative, research, and development outlays by all companies resulted from regulation, and mandated costs were equivalent to more than a 1 percent price increase for these companies. Because about 77 percent of the costs of compliance were due to regulations of the EPA, the impact on manufacturing companies in the sample was even greater; incremental compliance costs were nearly 23 percent of their after-tax income.

Even though they are gross estimates, these figures tend to show the amount of capital not otherwise available for possible reinvestment in plant modernization, new product development, or business expansion. The figures also illustrate pressures on smaller businesses, affecting their survival capacity and their rate of small business growth.

Perhaps the most comprehensive and widely publicized attacks on the costs of government regulation have come from the Center for the Study of American Business, led by Murray Weidenbaum, former chairman of the Council of Economic Advisors of the Reagan administration.[6] Weidenbaum's cost estimates are computed by multiplying the government's known administrative costs of regulatory activity by a factor of 20 to calculate the cost of private compliance with the regulations. The multiplier of 20 is taken from 1976 estimates of the relationship between administrative and compliance costs. Calculated by this method, the cost of compliance to business was $97.9 billion in 1979, based on agency administrative costs of $4.8 billion.[7] Weidenbaum concludes this is an excessive cost for social regulation.

A widely used indicator of the growth of government regulation is the size of the *Federal Register*, the official reference for all proposed and final rules. In 1960 the *Register* was 9,562 pages long; by 1980 it had increased nearly eight times and contained 74,120 pages. In 1980, 40 federal agencies alone issued nearly 8,000 new regulations.[8] These regulations collectively represent significant costs of compliance.

Weidenbaum and others point out that the costs of government regulation are not all direct. Beyond the out-of-pocket expense of compliance with agency rules are large numbers of hidden expenses such as the administrative and clerical time spent on processing necessary paperwork and the additional staff specialists required for control of safety and health in processes and products and supervision of pollution emissions. A recent government study placed the cost of the paperwork burden, including personal taxes, for individuals and corporations at 1.3 billion hours annually. Costed at $10 per hour, this would be an annual expense of over $10 billion.[9]

Social regulation is also charged with depressing the level of technological innovation in the economy and the rate of increase in worker productivity. These factors dramatically affect economic growth, expansion of employment, and reduction of the inflation rate. Economist Paul MacAvoy estimates that if social regulation reduces the gross national product by 0.5 percent per year, after a decade the economy is operating a full 6 to 7 percent below its capacity.[10]

A detailed study of the causes of changes in productivity conducted by Edward Denison for the Brookings Institution in 1979 covered two periods: 1948–73, when productivity (measured as national income per person employed) increased 2.6 percent a year, and 1973–76, when it declined an average of −0.6 percent — a period-to-period difference of 3.2 percentage point.[11] Denison tried to ascertain the role social regulation played in creating the substantial difference between the two periods. The study empirically measured the amounts of labor and capital employed for pollution abatement and protection of employee safety and health, a factor termed *the legal and human environment*. This factor was judged to explain 12.5 percent of the difference in productivity between the two periods, a significant but not dramatic figure.

Critics of social regulation also point to the fragmented effects of rules and their conflict with other national goals. Environmental protection often appears to conflict with energy independence; for example, the development of synthetic fuels is likely to have a large environmental impact. Oil drilling, overland transport of oil and gas, construction of port facilities, refinery location, and waste disposal threaten the natural state of the environment and, to some degree, disrupt its natural processes. Pollution control on cars constitutes energy-demanding protection of the environment, which has many parallels in pollution controls in industrial operations for environmental reasons.

The regulation of sulfur dioxide from coal-burning electric utilities in Ohio is a poignant example of how environmental, energy, and economic factors become intertwined.[12] Ohio, which burns more coal than any other state, uses 70 percent of its coal consumption for electricity generation. Ohio coal supplies 65 percent of the state's need, but this coal has a high sulfur content and generally does not meet EPA standards for sulfur dioxide emissions. Ohio utilities have two broad options: purchase and use out-of-state coal, which has a lower sulfur content, or install scrubbers to clean the emissions from Ohio coal. The first alternative has the advantage of a lower rise in the cost of electricity — approximately a 3 to 12 percent increase on residential consumers' bills. However, this alternative also has the disadvantage of reducing Ohio production of coal and putting up to 15,000 miners out of work. The use of scrubbers would lead to a 10 to 28 percent rise in the cost of electricity to residential consumers.

Benefits that Regulation Eliminates

While protecting individuals who may be victims of unrestrained corporate actions, social regulation has the unwelcome by-product of eliminating benefits to those who would be better off in the absence of regulation. The economic case against regulation argues the existence of this indirect effect: the cost of regulation is found in people without jobs who would have had them, in consumers paying higher prices who would have had lower prices, and in communities having a lower tax base that would have had a higher one. This analysis pits one person's health and safety against another's economic well-being.

As is illustrated in Insert 5.C, the conflict over benefits can be expressed strictly in terms of effects on health as well; the prohibition of a given drug protects individuals for whom the drug may have negative effects but withholds benefits from persons who would use it without negative results. The presence of a regulatory bias of protecting individuals "at risk" is suggested by a comment attributed to former FDA commissioner Alexander Schmidt: "In all our history, we are unable to find one instance where a Congressional hearing investigated the failure of the FDA to approve a new drug."[13] Reflecting on the apparent built-in pressure from Congress for the FDA to disapprove new drugs, David Weimer of the University of Rochester states:

> Victims of harmful side effects or their survivors make dramatic witnesses who can help attract media coverage; those who suffer because some drug that would have been beneficial to them that has not been approved by the FDA often do not even know they have been harmed. Person-

Insert 5.C

POLICY DILEMMAS AND POLITICAL CONSERVATISM IN NEW DRUG APPROVALS

The problem of weighing benefits and risks in policy affecting new drug approvals is illustrated by the case of the drug Triazure.

Triazure was developed in the late 1960s as a treatment for psoriasis, a severe and extremely painful, although nonfatal, skin disease that was reported to affect some 2 to 8 million Americans in the mid-1970s. Existing treatments of surface cream applications were often ineffective, and the only known effective drug, methotrexate, was a known carcinogen that could produce severe bone marrow depression, liver injury, and death.

In premarketing clinical studies Triazure was shown to be a very effective agent against psoriasis, although it was also associated with blood clotting or thromboembolism in 2.5 to 4 percent of the 566 patients using it. It had also resulted in three deaths. Unfortunately, sufficiently rigorous studies had not been done to determine if the clotting problems were associated with the psoriasis or with Triazure.

In early 1974 the FDA faced a decision of whether to (1) approve the drug for commercialization, (2) disapprove it pending further rigorous studies of its possible side effects, or (3) approve it subject to strong warnings aimed to protect susceptible patients and subject to stringent postmarketing research by the manufacturer.

The first alternative would serve to optimize the benefits to the relatively larger group of individuals who would be positively aided by the drug in their disease. The second would protect and seek to minimize risk to the smaller subgroup of individuals with psoriasis who would be at risk by taking the drug. (This policy choice might also present a hardship to the small drug company involved, which claimed it did not have the resources for an extended investigation.) The third alternative would try to take a position between these two alternatives, making the drug available to treat the disease while minimizing the risk to a small group.

The subsequent events are instructive. The FDA chose the third alternative and general marketing began, along with controlled experimental treatment. Within the first year eight cases of severe and unusual blood clotting were reported among the 500 to 1,000 users of the drug. The FDA acted swiftly to withdraw the drug from the market, especially in light of the recent development of a new and much safer treatment for psoriasis. Shortly thereafter, the whole matter was reviewed at a congressional hearing, and the FDA was challenged on the "propriety and legality" of its approval of the drug.

SOURCE: U.S., Congress, House, *Hearing before a Subcommittee of the Committee on Government Operations,* "FDA's Regulation of the Drug 'Triazure,'" 94th Cong., 2d sess., October 27, 1976.

alized suffering is much more newsworthy than statistical suffering.[14]

Charles Schultze, former chairman of the Council of Economic Advisors, offers a theory of why policy decisions have tended to protect those who would pay a cost rather than those who would receive a benefit.[15] He believes political decisions in the United States are subjected to the maxim "Do no direct harm," which derives from early American distrust of central government and the felt need to protect individuals from intrusion and interference by government. As the role of government has shifted in this century to protect the individual from health and safety risks inherent in industrialization and technology, government may have lost sight of the benefits from the economic development. Owing to the historical principle of protecting individuals from harm, immediate and visible risks may outweigh more distant and less visible benefits in public policy formulation.

REJOINDER TO THE COSTS-OF-SOCIAL-REGULATION ARGUMENT

Opponents of health and safety regulation have built a strong case against the unintended consequences of government programs, but they are not arguments sufficiently overwhelming to end debate. Costs-of-compliance studies typically do not account for health and safety expenditures in the absence of regulation, nor do they address which of the mandated investments actually lead to productivity improvements. Econometric studies of the incremental costs and incremental benefits make different assumptions of compliance than Denison's study and show a net stimulus to economic growth from the employment and investment required by health, safety, and environmental quality rules.[16] Other studies look in painstaking detail into the impact on costs and productivity of specific regulations on particular firms and seek to aggregate effects of regulation onto a national scale. Rarely do such firm- and industry-specific studies show more than minor effects on firm productivity or on gross national product.[17] Also, the inflationary impact of regulation rarely includes analysis of social costs not incurred — oil spills that did not happen, insurance claims that were not filed, or property that was not damaged — as a result of agency programs. For example, it has been estimated that by preventing a single lost day of one manufacturing worker due to a work-related accident, a typical company saves $14,000.[18] Finally, typical economic indexes of growth fail to take into account growth in the "quality of life," which people also value — and the survival of natural beauty, reduced noise, and rare animal species.

As the field of social regulation has begun to mature and the controversies surrounding it have become more sophisticated, several trends appear. First, the controversies are at the margins, rather than at the core, of regulation. Current questions are whether new drug requirements can be more flexible, which specific lands should be preserved or explored for natural resources and minerals, or whether emission standards of a particular chemical should be reduced from 10 parts per million (ppm) to 1 ppm. This issue is not whether social regulation will be or will not be but rather how strict or how loose it will be for the next period of time.

Second, the present climate of countervailing arguments concerning safety, health, and quality leads us to look more deeply at the concept of risk. We need to understand how attitudes toward risks and risk reduction are formed and to determine what levels of risk can be accepted as a matter of public policy.

Finally, the debate on social regulation has moved solidly into the arena of cost-and-benefit quantification. Ideological and personal arguments for government policy more and more appear to be insufficient bases for decision making. This implies that multiple impacts, side effects, and longer-term considerations of regulation will increasingly be considered. This is probably a useful movement but not one automatically or even easily satisfied. The next two sections of this chapter review some of the issues involved in public attitudes toward risk and the difficulty of formulating national policies toward risk, and various dimensions of the cost-benefit controversy.

RISKS AND THE PUBLIC EYE

The problem of assessing risks inherent in the use of technology or in the conduct of various personal activities lies at the heart of public policy formulation in the area of health and safety regulation. As risks increase, greater benefits might be expected from their control and reduction; and consequently, greater costs can be anticipated as risks are reduced. Unfortunately, perception of and knowledge about risk are not clear-cut and precise. Because public policies and the utility of decision-making instruments such as cost-benefit analysis are tied to assumptions about risks, our exploration of the issue begins here.

Public Perceptions of Risk

Recent studies of the perception of risk in familiar activities and technologies by experts and the public have uncovered some interesting facts.[19] First, people can correctly distinguish between high- and low-risk events. For example, in judging the perceived riskiness of 30 activities, people identified smoking, handguns, alcoholic beverages, and motor vehicles as the most frequent sources of death, and smallpox vaccinations, spray cans, pesticides, and skiing as among the least risky sources of dying. However, compared with the actual statistical frequencies of these events, individuals generally overestimated low-risk items and vastly underestimated the high-risk items. For example, motor vehicle fatalities, which are actually about 50,000 per year, were estimated by the public at closer to 300 per year. Interestingly, this judgmental error applied to a panel of experts as well, although not to the same extent; the "experts" judged motor vehicle fatalities at just under 10,000 per year.

Another important observation from these studies is that the public's assessment of risk is not directly related to perception of frequency of fatalities. For example, nuclear power was rated by the public very high as a risk but very low by the same people in terms of actual estimated fatalities. It appears that the perception of risk is influenced by a lot more than one's view of the probability of death from a particular source. The study described above included the following factors as heightening intuitive risk perception: involuntariness; the uncertainty, newness, and unfamiliarity of the risk; inability to control the risk; catastrophic nature; and likelihood of fatality. The greater presence of these factors in the case of nuclear power over electric power, for example, explains why nuclear power was perceived as more risky than electric power, even though the study participants believed actual fatalities from nuclear power were much lower than from electric power. The involuntary, catastrophic nature of many high-technology fields (toxic chemicals, recombinant DNA, nuclear energy) is undoubtedly a strong source of the controversies that often surround them.

Another important factor in risk assessment appears to be the expected benefits from a given action.[20] As would be expected, acceptability of a risk increases with greater benefits. The existence of pleasure or benefit is probably why many people undertake risky activities, such as smoking or driving, which they already perceive to be among the highest levels of risk. Of course, part of the problem is that "benefits" to some, say from smoking, are not benefits to others who may be forced to share some of the risk from smoke. Insert 5.D draws attention to the presence of risk in everyday activities and cleverly illustrates the extent to which risk might be considered in activities normally taken for granted.

The Role of the Expert

This discussion has emphasized the role that intuitive and subjective factors appear to play in public perceptions of risk. Even though perceptions might be argued to be irrational when riskiness is not related to actual fatalities, risk perceptions must be treated as facts by business since people do act upon their perceptions, rational or not.

In addition, the discussion has suggested that risk perceptions of identified "experts" may not always correspond to actual risks. While experts' perceptions of risk are tied more closely to their estimates of fatalities than are the public's perceptions of risk, experts have been shown to underestimate vastly the absolute frequency of various fatalities.

However, the limits of science further reduce the reliability of expert

Insert 5.D

DECISIONS, DECISIONS, DECISIONS [QUOTATION]

The moment I climb out of bed I start taking risks. As I drowsily turn on the light I feel a slight tingle; my house is old with wiring and there is a small risk of electrocution. Every year 500 people are electrocuted in the United States. I take a shower, and as I reach for the soap, I wonder about the many chemicals it contains. Are they all good for the skin, as the advertisements claim? My clothes have been cleaned with the best bleaching detergent. Most bleaching agents contain a chemical that fluoresces slightly in the sunlight to enhance the whiteness. Does this make bleaches carcinogenic?

I ponder this risk as I walk down to breakfast, taking care not to fall upon the stairs. Falls kill 16,000 people per year — mostly in domestic accidents. Shall I drink coffee or tea with my breakfast? Both contain caffeine, a well-known stimulant which may be carcinogenic. I have a sweet tooth; do I use sugar which makes me fat and gives me heart disease, or saccharin which we now know causes cancer? It is better to abstain.

After breakfast I make a sandwich for lunch. My son likes peanut butter. But improperly stored peanuts can develop a mold which produces a potent carcinogen — aflatoxin. In Africa and Southeast Asia, where aflatoxin appears more frequently, it has been blamed for numerous cases of liver cancer. In our (less natural) society storage facilities are better, so the risk is less — but it is not zero.

I prefer meat. But Americans, like other prosperous people, eat too much meat. It is not certain, but a meat-heavy diet probably contributes to cancer of the colon.

I live seven miles from work and can commute by car, by bicycle, or by bus. Which has the lowest risk? To travel by bicycle would keep my weight down, and bicycle riding does not cause pollution — but statistics show that it is more likely to involve me in an accident. And since a bicyclist is unprotected, fatal accidents are also frequent on a bicycle. A car would be safer, but a bus is safest. I am happy that I no longer have to choose between a horse and a canoe; both are more dangerous (per mile) than a bicycle. . . .

Insert 5.D   continued

Just as I go to bed I take a glass of beer. Alcohol causes cirrhosis of the liver and has been associated with oral and other cancers. However, the relaxing effect of the beer will reduce my stress and permit a good night's sleep. This will prolong my life and is worth the risk.

The beer is in a green glass bottle which contains chromium, a small amount of which enters the beer. Chromium is a known carcinogen when ingested in moderate quantities, but it must not be avoided altogether because it is essential to life in small concentrations. How much chromium should I take to minimize the risk? Is the amount in the beer too much? Should I drink the beer from a plastic bottle? A plastic bottle suitable for beer has just been banned because a trace of the chemical from which the plastic was made could dissolve in the contents, and there is a suspicion that the chemical is carcinogenic.

I ponder this decision as I put on my pajamas. Are the pajamas inflammable? There is always a small risk of fire starting while I am in bed. Is the risk of being burnt in a fire greater or smaller than the risk of cancer caused by a flame retardant such as TRIS?

I remember the truism "more people die in bed than anywhere else," so at least I'm in the right place.

SOURCE: Richard Wilson, "Analyzing the Daily Risks of Life," *Technology Review* 81 (February 1979):41–42, 46. Used with permission.

opinions. In many health and safety areas, hard knowledge of causes and effects is simply not obtainable. Scientific results — of the carcinogenicity of different chemicals, for example — are partial, fragmented, and often unreliable, if not contradictory. Long-term risks and interactions with other conditions are unknown, and generalizing from animal testing to human behavior can be a dubious endeavor. Insert 5.E describes various sources of scientific uncertainty associated with the effects of acid rain.

Another issue in the role of the expert is the apparent difficulty of separating facts from values, or objective science from subjective preference. Apart from the problem that apparently equally good science may yield conflicting results, there may also arise a problem of personal values overriding scientific objectivity. The point is not that scientists should remove themselves from the policy questions but whether a conscious effort

Insert 5.E

SCIENTIFIC UNCERTAINTY IN POLLUTION EFFECTS: THE DILEMMAS OF ACID RAIN

About 27 million tons of sulfur dioxide are emitted each year from electric utilities and other coal-burning power plants in the United States. Most of this pollution originates in the Great Lakes region and the Midwest; owing to clean air regulations, though, high stacks have been installed on most coal-burning facilities and emissions are currently pushed into the atmosphere and dispersed widely. Air currents eventually deposit about one half of the sulfur dioxide emissions onto the eastern third of the country and another sixth in Canada.

Controversy about "acid rain" centers on the question of sulfur dioxide pollution. Various studies have concluded that this pollutant increases the acidity of precipitation in certain regions of New York and New England, dramatically altering the pH or acid content of the soil. Acidification, it has been argued, is causing alarming damage through forest retardation, deterioration of aquatic systems, corrosion, and health effects.

Beyond heated public discussion of acid rain and various proposals for regulation of sulfur dioxide emissions, little scientific evidence of the presence of acid rain or its effects is at hand. The following are several reported sources of scientific uncertainty:

* In order to affect the acid-alkaline balance on earth, sulfur dioxide must first be oxidized to a sulfate ion, dissolve in water, and wash to the ground. Where sulfur dioxide comes down and in what form depends on a variety of atmospheric conditions as well as the presence of oxidizing agents; consequently it is highly uncertain. Reductions in sulfate on the ground can not be presumed to follow linearly from reductions in sulfur dioxide emissions.
* Sources of emissions for deposits of sulfate in a given locale are currently unknown. It is not possible to tell specifically where concentrations of acid rain originate.
* Local geological conditions may have as much or more impact on soil than sulfate deposits from the rain. Forests generally increase soil acidity, so replacing farmland with forests and reducing the number of forest fires aggravate acidity. Also, a greater portion of conifers relative to deciduous trees increases acid runoff and, according to the New York Department of Environmental Conservation, the number of conifers has increased by 70 percent in this century, whereas the amount of farmland has dropped in half. Moreover, high alkaline content of some soils and bedrocks serves to neutralize acid deposits from precipitation, whereas more acidic natural conditions are aggravated by acid rain.

Insert 5.E   continued

Weak knowledge about the sources of acidity is complicated by the absence of experimental results that establish causes and effects between acid rain and either ecology or human health. However suspicious acid rain may be, few direct links have been reliably established. Each hypothesized effect seems to generate other causal explanations of the same result, none of which are readily or easily resolved.

Should the government legislate costly regulation with little certainty about the nature of the problem or the likelihood that its action will change the situation? Or should the government postpone action until better knowledge is available, thereby risking extensive harm to ecological systems and human health? These are conundrums of which policy controversies are made.

SOURCE: Peter Huber, "The *I-Ching* of Acid Rain," *Regulation*, September-December 1984, p. 15.

is made to segment facts from values in the process of considering policy questions.

This point is discussed by John G. Kemeny in his personal conclusions as participant and chairperson of the president's commission on the accident at Three Mile Island. Kemeny, a mathematician, philosopher of science, and president of Dartmouth College, expressed grave concerns about the process of social decision making on issues of sophisticated technology. Among his observations were instances of scientists lacking the ability to separate personal views from technical knowledge:

> In the course of our commission's work, we again and again ran into cases where emotions influenced the judgments of even very distinguished scientists. This was most disturbing to me, and I was reminded of that famous incident when Galileo was forced to recant some of his great discoveries because they ran counter to religious beliefs. Today the problem is not with religion per se, but I kept running into scientists whose beliefs border on the religious and even occasionally on the fanatical.... These people distort their own scientific judgments and hurt their reputations by stating things with assurance that they know, deep down, could only be assigned small probabilities. They become advocates instead of unbiased advisors. This is incompatible with the fundamental nature of science and it creates an atmosphere in which there is a serious mistrust of experts: even when the hard evidence is

overwhelming, if the issue is sufficiently emotional you can always get an expert to dispute it and thereby help throw all of science into national disrepute.[21]

The Role of the Media

Unquestionably, newspapers, radio, and television play a major role in the reporting of events and in the formation of public perceptions. Because many aspects of technology are uncertain and possibly hazardous, and because irresponsibility in the private or the public sector is "news," the media aggressively pursues and covers potentially threatening incidents. This stance is a public service; it provides a useful external source of disclosure of corporate and governmental officials. At the same time, it can be abused, especially when the situation is complex, technical, and not fully understood. A disservice to the public can be done by the media's tendency to simplify unfairly or to draw premature conclusions. When this occurs, the difficulty of formulating public policy is magnified in a situation that may already be subject to emotionally based perceptions and to incomplete or conflicting scientific evidence.

There is no easy answer for what constitutes fair reporting. By definition, in controversial topics each side is bound to feel the opposition has been given too much credibility and one's own view has been given too little. Insert 5.F presents statements of two recent critics of press coverage on scientific matters. In the first an official of the Chemical Manufacturers Association calls for more "balance" in media reporting; the second is Kemeny speaking about the press coverage of the Three Mile Island study commission and arguing against too "balanced" a story. Instead, the press is advised to make an independent determination of credibility. It appears the press cannot win.

Insert 5.F

WHEREIN LIES THE MEDIA'S RESPONSIBILITY?

What is fair and unfair treatment in the hands of the mass media? Who is to judge what is balanced or biased reporting? Can adversaries ever be expected to agree on answers to these questions?

Fair coverage appears to be forever in the eye of the beholder. Consider the following two statements: the first, made by a representative of the chemical industry, calls for more balanced reporting; the second, by the

Insert 5.F   continued

chairperson of the National Commission for Study of the Three Mile Island accident, warns against too great an effort by the media to balance a story:

> This fair city, Washington, D.C., must surely be the one place on earth where sound travels faster than light. Here is a circus of curved mirrors and distorted images, of lights and shadows, of leaks and red herrings — where it daily becomes more difficult to separate fact from fiction. It is hardly strange, then, that reporters often get snared into transmitting to the nation some weird illusions and delusions — or, worse, of being used as pawns in a power game by people seeking to get something out of government.
>
> What we in the chemical business would like to see is a press getting to the real facts behind problems, then reporting them in realistic perspective — so that the public and government can react rationally to situations in terms of their real dimensions and not as mountains built up out of molehills, or vice versa. In essence, we expect no more from the press than the same kind of balanced coverage of our industry that reporters themselves would expect if someone else were reporting on them.
>
> ---
>
> I saved for last what troubles me most about the media: their treatment of scientific subjects. They love controversy. And that is probably good for the American people when it is a question of political elections, when it's a matter of covering Democrats and Republicans or liberals and conservatives and giving them equal space. But this produces a strange effect when reporting scientific stories, because the two sides to every scientific "controversy" do not necessarily deserve equal space. I left Washington fully expecting to read the following story someday in one of our morning papers: "Three scientists by the names of Galileo, Newton, and Einstein have concluded that the earth is round. However, the *New York Times* has learned authoritatively that Professor Joe Doe has conclusive evidence that the earth is flat." And then the article will go on, perfectly unbiased, giving equal space to both sides of the issue.

SOURCE: James N. Sites, "Chemophobia, Politics and Distorted Images," *Vital Speeches of the Day,* December 15, 1980, p. 154; John G. Kemeny, "Saving American Democracy: The Lessons of Three Mile Island," *Technology Review* 83 (June–July 1980):72. Used with permission.

COST-BENEFIT

The existence of general arguments for and against environmental, health, and safety protection and the difficulties of accurate risk assessment discussed in the previous sections of this chapter have pointed to the need for a more concrete and systematic tool of analysis to assist in judging the advisability of specific regulatory actions. The most discussed and debated concept for these purposes appears to be cost-benefit analysis; therefore, we now turn to examine its potential in this area. We shall see that this technique, as all technology, is not a panacea; rather its utility depends upon the uses to which it is applied.

Cost Assumptions

At first blush the compilation of costs incurred from a regulatory action is straightforward — some would say more easily expressed and quantified than benefits. The direct costs of reducing benzene emissions in the industrial workplace from 10 ppm to 1 ppm are easily defined. The cost of new equipment, the interest rate, and the recurring and nonrecurring operating costs can be estimated reasonably well and used to calculate a per year cost of compliance.

However, this type of estimating is open to various charges: (1) it fails to account for the realization of economies of scale in the production of control technology, (2) it ignores the existence of the "learning curve" in which equipment and operating costs decline owing to discoveries of cost-savings methods based on experience, and (3) it fails to incorporate the reduced costs and increased benefits from new technology that may be developed to achieve compliance.[22] Advocates of these views are fond of pointing to the regulation of vinyl chloride where predicted costs of compliance ran as high as $90 billion and actual costs were later thought to be in the range of $34 million.[23]

Benefit Assumptions

The difficulties inherent in benefit estimation appear many times more evasive than assessing costs, although attempts can be made as illustrated in Insert 5.G. A principal problem inherent to benefit estimation is that of placing a value on human experience — either the value of a life saved or the reduced pain, suffering, and human travail resulting from a protective regulation. While the issue of valuing human life may be a callous undertaking, the need to formulate public policy forces the issue. If there are some limits on which everyone could agree — for example, no more than half the gross national product should be spent to save a life — then the issue is finding the actual acceptable limit of expenditures to save a life.

Insert 5.G

WHAT PRICE AN OCEAN BOTTOM WORM?

Not only are benefits to humans grist for cost-benefit formulas, but values of natural ecology and wildlife also fall subject to benefit assessment.

An example involves the debate over preservation of the nation's wetlands (swamps, bogs, marshes and other soggy sod) versus utilization of the land for industrial, commercial, or residential development. Recently, the U.S. Army Corp of Engineers has learned how wetlands act as natural sponges in holding back floodwaters, and is utilizing them instead of building dams and cutting channels. Another value, still not completely understood, is the neutralizing impact of wetlands on chemical spills. Furthermore, it appears wetlands soak up nitrates, phosphates and toxic metals and could help mitigate the impact of acid rain and pesticides.

Methods of valuing wetland areas are far from certain. Costs of replacement by flood control and water treatment facilities are evident, but also income from hunting and recreation, and market values might also be considered. One economist asserts that the "embodied energy" of wetlands creates a worth, on the average, of $4,000 an acre per year.

These figures omit the important value of hunted and non-hunted wildlife as well. Parties in legal suits involving the damage of wetlands or the possible conversion of the lands to human use are increasingly having to place dollar values on animal species. Fiddler crabs, seaworms, whistler swans, blue herons, and wood ducks may all receive market equivalent values. The going price? Six cents for a single ocean bottom worm and $31 for a hunted wood duck.

SOURCE: Clayton Jones, "Price-Tagging America's Wetlands Could Help Fend off the Bulldozers," *Christian Science Monitor,* December 23, 1980, p. 3. Used with permission.

Many modes have been proposed; a number of efforts have been addressed. Consider as examples the following methods of valuing a life:

- An early approach to placing a value on an individual's life was called the "foregone earnings" method. This is an idea based upon the discounted cash flow technique. It calculates the present value of estimated future earnings that are foregone due to premature death. In addition, estimated medical costs and other associated expenses are often included.
- A newer method has arisen that is termed "willingness to pay." The value of life is estimated from questions people are asked about how much they would be willing to pay to reduce the probability of their death by a certain small amount. Results of these studies yield values anywhere between $50,000 and $8 million per life saved.
- A third method is based on the analysis of wage premiums for dangerous jobs or hazardous occupations. For example, if a group of workers is paid a wage increment of $3 million for jobs that have two deaths per year above the expected frequency, they have valued each life at $1.5 million. Studies of this type have yielded values between $300,000 and $3.5 million.[24]

Overall, various systematic reviews of the empirical and theoretical literature attempting to assess the value of a human life appear confident in identifying for public policy consideration the range of $170,000 to $3 million per life.

Each of the methods described above makes some assumptions that may not be widely shared. For example, each approach evaluates life worth or asks the individual to evaluate it within the individual's existing economic level. The results will naturally show a higher value on the life of the person with more income, wealth, and earning potential. Use of economic level as a determinant of benefit assessment and its resulting inequities may not be a defensible basis for public policy formulation.

Second, questionnaire or wage differential information may not be a reliable predictor of human behavior. People may place a much greater value on life or health after an injury, illness, or death than before it. In this sense these estimating approaches may undervalue risk reduction ultimately expected by society. Given the many ambiguities inherent in studies of this type, such wide ranges of value-of-life estimates are not surprising.

Cost-Effectiveness Analysis

Given the difficulties of estimating benefits and of placing confidence in cost-benefit ratios, a simpler, more reliable, yet comparative approach is attractive. One alternative that may have substantial utility is the analysis of the cost-per-additional-life-saved, or cost-effectiveness, approach. In this method it is only necessary to calculate the cost of a policy option and to estimate the additional lives saved from it. For example, one author reports (1) a study from France that indicated $30,000 was being spent per life saved through road accident prevention and $1 million per life saved through aviation accident prevention and (2) a study from England showing costs of $10,000 and $20 million to save lives of agricultural workers and apartment dwellers, respectively.[25]

John Graham and James Vaupel present an analysis of 57 policy options in the United States from this perspective.[26] They reviewed studies of the costs and benefits of various health, safety, and environmental proposals including mandatory air bags, the 55 miles per hour speed limit, mandatory smoke detectors, clean air standards, alcohol safety programs, and chemical emissions in the workplace. Table 5.1 below, summarizing their findings, indicates, first, the large number of policy proposals showing a cost per life saved as negative or zero and, second, the wide range of cost-effectiveness programs. The single least cost-effective option reviewed was estimated to cost over $169 million per life saved.

The authors observe that a general ability to differentiate among the values of public policies does not depend on an exact measurement of costs and benefits, nor is quantification necessarily biased against social regulation. Over 80 percent of the policies reviewed in this study would fall within generally accepted ranges of most studies of the upper value of a human life ($170,000 to $3 million) and might, therefore, be deemed cost effective.

Of course, this measure of policy impact has drawbacks by focusing only on lives or life-years saved. It either ignores many other benefits of protective regulation, such as decreased pain and suffering and reduced insurance payments and medical costs, or it gets caught up trying to translate these different impacts into equivalencies for lives saved. Like any

TABLE 5.1   *Cost Distribution of 57 Policy Alternatives*

Cost	Per Life Saved	Per Years of Life Saved
< $0	13	13
> $0 and $100,000	16	31
> $100,000 and $700,000	12	8
> $700,000 and $10 million	11	4
> $10 million	5	1

SOURCE: John D. Graham and James W. Vaupel, "The Value of a Life: What Difference Does It Make?" (Paper presented at the Association for Public Policy Analysis and Management, Boston, Massachusetts, October 24–25, 1980), pp. 9–13.

other method in this complicated area, cost-effectiveness analysis is a beginning point, not the endpoint, of discussion.

Economic Analysis and Political Processes

Any tool of decision making, such as cost-benefit or cost-effectiveness analysis, may fall subject to personal predispositions.[27] On the one hand, advocates of health and safety regulation may feel that cost-benefit analysis would be an unfortunate screen for public officials to hide behind, a means of circumventing the "hard" decisions of how to protect worker health. By reducing the questions to narrow quantitative considerations, officials might be absolved from taking full complexity and multiple criteria into account. Use of cost-benefit analysis might be an attempt to reorient public policy toward an ideological point of view that minimizes values of health and safety and that subverts the intent of the enabling legislation.

On the other hand, opponents of more regulation may say that the only question is whether decisions will be based on hard analysis or on "intuition." Persons of this persuasion also argue that objections to explicit and systematic analysis usually derive from the proregulatory values and ideologies of public officials rather than from difficulties inherent in the analysis.

At the heart of this debate often lies the mandate of a specific piece of legislation. In some cases, such as environmental protection, Congress dictated a "balancing" of environmental and economic factors, leaving the relative weights placed on these elements to administrative regulation. In other statutes, such as the consumer product safety or the occupational health and safety acts, Congress made no explicit requirement to consider economic issues. These pieces of legislation, though, invariably require the empowered agency to act "reasonably" and "practically," and interpretation of what is *practical* lends itself to differing opinions about the role of economic criteria in regulation. In the final analysis the extent of regulation is largely a social and political, not an administrative or judicial, judgment.

THE ENVIRONMENT OF BUSINESS: A CONCLUDING COMMENT

The aspect of the business environment addressed in this chapter is a complex and elusive dimension of business-government relations. Undeniably there has been a movement toward individual protection from the by-products and unanticipated consequences of industrialization and technology. At the same time, there are numerous unforeseen, and perhaps still unknown, costs of regulation. Unfortunately no conclusive knowledge about relating aggregate benefits and costs of social regulation exists.

The task of policy formulation becomes no less difficult in considering regulation project by project or policy by policy. Limited and primitive methods for evaluating actions are available for making decisions having deep personal consequences for a few individuals and far-reaching economic effects on many people. Neither result can be ignored.

To this uncertainty in evaluation one must add an apparent high degree of subjectivity in personal attitudes toward risk, an incomplete state of knowledge about cause and effect relationships in science, and honest disagreement among experts about the implications of technical knowledge. One is not surprised at the piecemeal, fragmented, and often contradictory nature of public policy toward business regulation. In this complex array of forces the media is called upon to educate the public, although ways of doing this are often open to challenge.

While some may question whether our system of democracy is suited to making policy in this degree of uncertainty and technical knowledge, the problems lie more in the difficulty of the issues to be solved than in a defective decision-making process. There is no doubt that considerable muddling through will be required, but the alternative of a "tyranny" of experts is certainly no more appealing.

One implication for these issues is that every effort should be made to balance health, safety, and environment with economics in the original drafting of legislation, for the balancing becomes no less difficult in administrative or judicial processes. Another constructive approach may be to exercise greater restraint: restraint on the part of government and specific interest organizations to pursue protection without regard to its cost or effectiveness, restraint on the part of the public to be better informed for making deliberate judgments about risks, and restraint on the part of corporate managers to recognize that attitudes toward risks are necessarily subjective and that the economic function and future of the firm are inextricably bound to health, safety, and environmental values. A norm of restraint plus a concerted effort to study, analyze, disseminate, and debate information in the widest possible context should allow the most socially desirable direction to emerge.

DISCUSSION QUESTIONS

1. Review the debate on health, safety, and environmental protection. What are the reasons for growth in governmental social regulation? What are the major consequences of the government's actions?
2. Develop an argument on the side of this question different from the position you typically assume. Be prepared to argue this different point of view in class.
3. What roles do you feel experts and the media presently play in the formation of social policy toward health and safety risks? Do you feel changes in these roles are warranted?
4. Can questions of human health and safety be reduced to quantitative analysis? Should they be? Why or why not?

NOTES

1. *Federal Regulatory Directory 1983–84* (Washington, D.C.: Congressional Quarterly Inc., 1983), pp. 82–455.
2. Nathan Glazer, "Individualism and Equality in the United States," in *On the Making of Americans: Essays in Honor of David Riesman*, ed. Herbert J. Gans, Nathan Glazer, Joseph R. Gusfield, and Christopher Jencks (Philadelphia: University of Pennsylvania Press, 1979), p. 132.
3. U.S., Congress, House, *Occupational Safety and Health Act Report*, 91st Cong., 2d sess. H. Rept. 91–1291, p. 14.
4. Lester A. Sobel, ed., *Consumer Protection* (New York: Facts on File, 1976), pp. 103–12.
5. Arthur Anderson & Co., *Cost of Government Regulation Study: A Study of the Direct Incremental Cost Incurred by 48 Companies in Complying with the Regulations of Six Federal Agencies in 1977* (New York: Business Roundtable, 1979), pp. 14–16.
6. Murray L. Weidenbaum, *Business, Government, and the Public* (Englewood Cliffs, N.J.: Prentice-Hall, 1977); and idem, *The Future of Business Regulation* (New York: AMACOM, 1980).
7. Weidenbaum, *The Future*, p. 23.
8. Congressional Quarterly, "Reagan, Congress Planning Regulatory Machinery Repair," *Weekly Report* 39 (1981): 409.
9. Clyde H. Farnsworth, "Burden of Federal Paperwork: A Billion Citizen Hours a Year," *New York Times*, January 18, 1981, p. 1.
10. Paul W. MacAvoy, "The Existing Condition of Regulation and Regulatory Reform," in *Regulating Business: The Search for an Optimum* (San Francisco: San Francisco Institute for Contemporary Studies, 1978), p. 5.
11. Edward F. Dension, *Accounting for Slower Economic Growth: The United States in the 1970s* (Washington, D.C.: Brookings Institution, 1979), pp. 1–6.
12. "Sulfurous Struggle: Ohio Utilities, Coal Industry Battle EPA Over Clear-Air Bill and Who Must Pay It," *Wall Street Journal*, February 15, 1979, p. 46.
13. David Leo Weimer, "The Regulation of Therapeutic Drugs by the FDA: History, Criticisms, and Alternatives" (Discussion Paper no. 800F, University of Rochester, May 1980), p. 33.
14. Ibid., p. 33.
15. Charles L. Schultze, *The Public Use of Private Interest* (Washington, D.C.: Brookings Institution, 1977), pp. 70–72.
16. Council on Environmental Quality, *Environmental Quality*, Tenth Annual Report of the Council on Environmental Quality (Washington, D.C.: U.S. Government Printing Office, 1979), chap. 12, pp. 639–82.
17. W. Curtiss Priest, "Methodology for a Microeconomic Case Study of Productivity and Regulation: The Asbestos Industry" (Paper presented

at the Association for Public Policy Analysis and Management, Washington, D.C., October 24, 1981), p. 27.

18. Peter J. Sheridan, "What Are Accidents Really Costing You?" *Occupational Hazards*, March 1979, pp. 41–43.

19. Paul Slovic, Baruch Fischhoff, and Sarah Lichenstein, "Rating the Risks," *Environment* 21 (1979): 14.

20. Chauncey Starr and Chriss Whipple, "Risks of Risk Decisions," *Science* 208 (June 1980): 1114–19.

21. John G. Kemeny, "Saving American Democracy: The Lessons of Three Mile Island," *Technology Review* 83 (June-July 1980): 65–75.

22. Nicholas A. Ashford, "The Limits of Cost-Benefit Analysis in Regulatory Decisions," in John Mendeloff, "Reducing Occupational Health Risks: Uncertain Effects and Unstated Benefits," *Technology Review* 82 (May 1980): 70–72.

23. Samuel E. Epstein, "Cancer, Inflation, and the Failure to Regulate," *Technology Review* 82 (December-January 1980): 42–53.

24. These issues and figures are drawn from John D. Graham and James W. Vaupel, "The Value of a Life: What Difference Does it Make?" (Paper presented at the Association for Public Policy Analysis and Management Conference, Boston, Massachusetts, October 24–25, 1980), p. 1.

25. David Okrent, "Comment on Societal Risk," *Science* 208 (April 25, 1980): 372–75.

26. Graham and Vaupel, "The Value of a Life," pp. 9–13.

27. Mendeloff, "Reducing Occupational Health Risks," pp. 73–74.

Laetrile
A Question of Social Justice

The Food and Drug Administration (FDA) has often found itself at the focal point of public attention; sometimes it has been the recipient of loud and vigorous praise, as when it was hailed as the public's remedy against the sale of dangerous meat products. Sometimes it has been bitterly criticized, as when it attempted to remove saccharin, an artificial sweetener, from the market. The FDA had taken its action on saccharin after numerous tests indicated that the sweetener contributed to the development of cancer when given to rats in extremely large doses. But it could hardly have anticipated the hostile reaction that followed from weight-watchers who used saccharin and manufacturers who sold it.

By the summer of 1977 the FDA was facing a tough battle with forces of public opinion. By that time it was clear that the FDA's official stand on the controversial cancer cure Laetrile was meeting with stiff opposition. Not only did hundreds of thousands of cancer suffers believe they should be able to take Laetrile, but a number of state legislatures had already expressed their disagreement with the FDA by passing laws that legalized Laetrile in their respective states. It was a problem that was slipping beyond the simple issue of Laetrile's medical effectiveness; now people were charging that the FDA's ban on Laetrile was a denial of a fundamental right to free choice, as guaranteed by the U.S. Constitution.

Indeed, pressure was beginning to mount for a public trial of Laetrile, where the drug would be administered to humans instead of rats, to respond to the Laetrile advocates' challenge that only human tests could establish the effectiveness of Laetrile. Even Dr. Franz Ingelfinger, respected editor of the *New England Journal of Medicine,* who himself was a cancer sufferer, was beginning to suggest publicly that a human test of Laetrile would do more to bury Laetrile than any public criticism from the FDA.[1]

Copyright © 1981 Thomas Donaldson. Used by permission. Recent developments and study questions have been added by Carol J. Fritz.

BACKGROUND ON THE DRUG LAETRILE

Laetrile has a long and improbable history. Essentially a drug that is obtained by concentrating the extract from apricot pits, Laetrile was not discovered in any ordinary way. It was discovered during the 1920s in San Francisco by a physician who had hoped to discover a special ingredient that would improve the taste of bootleg whiskey.[2] But instead of discovering the secret to smooth whiskey, Ernest Krebs happened instead upon a strong apricot extract that seemed to have positive effects in the curing of cancer; or, at least, it seemed to retard the growth of tumors in the rats with which the doctor experimented. Unfortunately the extract did not appear to have the same remarkable effect on cancer in humans, and Krebs abandoned his project.

It remained for Ernst Krebs, Jr., the son of Ernest Krebs and himself a medical school dropout, to attempt to isolate the active ingredient in his father's apricot mixture. In 1944 he announced that he had succeeded in identifying and isolating the all-important cancer-curing element. He then proceeded to name that ingredient "Laetrile."[3] There remains, however, a strong doubt among professional chemists as to whether such a drug even exists. Following Kreb's own recipe, laboratory researchers have been unable to isolate anything other than the substance amygdalin, which chemists have known about for a long time and which has never been known to have any medical use.[4] Interestingly enough, however, proponents of Laetrile use the terms *Laetrile* and *amygdalin* interchangeably, recognizing no significant difference between the two substances.

Krebs, Jr., himself, offers the most articulate version of how the drug presumably works. Laetrile contains, among other things, the poison cyanide, which works together with an enzyme found in many cancer cells called *betaglucosidase*. According to Krebs, the curative powers of Laetrile are simple to understand: the cyanide that it releases attacks the cancer tumor, while not affecting the ordinary, noncancerous cells. The normal cells are spared from the effect of the cyanide because they contain an enzyme called *rhodanese*, which detoxifies cyanide when present in moderate amounts.[5]

More and more, defenders of Laetrile are extending the claims of the drug's benefits to include not only positive effects against already established cancers but also preventative powers against possible or future cancers. Thus, in many quarters of the pro-Laetrile movement, supporters are urging normal, healthy people to either take Laetrile pills or to eat foods that supposedly contain high amounts of the drug — for example, carrots, lima beans, and beets. The movement to defend Laetrile has now become an established part of the regime of some health food devotees, and it is included along with organically grown food and goat's milk in their list of necessary health food substances.[6]

Apart from its possible cancer-curing benefits, Laetrile has a special advantage over conventional methods of cancer treatment: it is extraordinarily cheap. With the median cancer cure in 1973 standing at $19,000, Laetrile's price is almost insignificant in comparison: about $10 per injection and $1 per pill.[7]

DETERMINING THE EFFECTIVENESS OF LAETRILE: EARLY REPORTS

In announcing that Laetrile is the "most tested of all cancer cures," the FDA stated that every one of the scientific tests conducted using animals, five studies by the National Cancer Institute alone, has shown that Laetrile has no effect against cancer whatsoever.[8] In addition to the strong opposition of the FDA, most other official medical organizations have proclaimed the drug's worthlessness: Laetrile's use is officially opposed by the American Medical Association (AMA), and spokespeople from the National Cancer Institute, the American Cancer Society, and the Sloan-Kettering Institute all denounce the effectiveness of Laetrile as a cancer cure.

But some individual sufferers of cancer are willing to claim fantastic effects for the drug. For example, Hugh Wildermuth (age 59), a farmer from Akron, Indiana, was diagnosed as having muscle cancer and given a year or less to live by his doctors. Even after seven weeks of cobalt radiation therapy, and after taking large doses of a conventional drug, actinomycin D, Wildermuth was regarded as an incurable case by his doctors. Instead of abandoning hope, however, Wildermuth traveled from Indiana to Tijuana, Mexico, where a group of rebel physicians operate a number of Laetrile clinics. At the Clinica del Mar, Wildermuth received three grams of Laetrile each day through injections and, later, was placed on a "maintenance" program in which he ingested Laetrile pills. Three years later, Wildermuth's lymph nodes were shrunken, and he claimed not to be suffering from cancer at all. Doctors, however, doubt that Wildermuth's cancer was cured, assuming it was actually cured, by means of the Laetrile treatment. More likely, they suggest, is that the traditional treatment that he underwent before his trip to Tijuana was really responsible for the recovery.[9]

Unfortunately, professional researchers and doctors are not convinced by the personal testimonials of Laetrile users. Doctors generally claim that the case histories of fantastic cures leave out important information. Surprisingly enough, one of the pieces of information that researchers often complain is missing is evidence that the person actually had cancer in the first place.

In the absence of concrete information from users, most doctors are inclined to accept the results of laboratory experimentation. A variety of scientific tests have been conducted by well-respected researchers that conclude that Laetrile is ineffective against cancer. The only apparent counterexample to this trend occurred during the early 1970s when researcher

Kanematsu Sugiura, at Manhattan's famed memorial Sloan-Kettering Institute, used Laetrile in mice that had breast cancer. In the mice given Laetrile only 21 percent showed spreading of the tumor to the lungs, whereas in those given salt solution, 90 percent did show signs of spreading. As might be expected, the pro-Laetrile faction has taken this test as representing important supporting evidence for their tests.

But in June 1977, Sugiura's original study was disavowed by Sloan-Kettering. Claiming that his original experiment was not "blind," in the sense that he both knew that mice were receiving Laetrile and attempted to determine the existence of cancer with the naked eye (a very risky business), Sloan-Kettering requested a repeat of the original experiment. Indeed they requested not only a single repeat but a double one, and this time Sugiura could find no significant difference between the spread of cancer in the two test groups. Although Sugiura still believes that Laetrile can be effective against cancer, the Sloan-Kettering Institute has stated publically that "Laetrile was found to possess neither preventive . . . nor anti-metastatic, nor curative anti-cancer activity."[10] Lewis Thomas, the distinguished president of Sloan-Kettering, was more abrasive. He said, "These are bad times for reason all around. Suddenly all of the major ills are being coped with by acupuncture. If it's not acupuncture, it is apricot pits."[11]

In an attempt to check more closely on the claims of individual Laetrile users, the FDA invited Ernesto Contreras, a former Mexican army doctor who now runs perhaps the largest Laetrile clinic, Clinica del Mar, to submit a number of cases of his own choosing for inspection by medical authorities. Contreras responded to this request by presenting 12 cases that presumably represented Laetrile cures. But the findings of the FDA were not encouraging. Of the 12 cases, the FDA says 6 had died, 3 could not be traced, and the remaining 3 all had been exposed to traditional treatment and therapy, including extensive surgery, radiation treatment, and the use of conventional drugs.[12]

THE SALE AND PRODUCTION OF LAETRILE

Laetrile is now produced in at least ten factories around the world, most of which were started by a special foundation headed by Andrew McNaughton, which is at least nominally dedicated to the exploration of scientific concepts. McNaughton has himself been active in the Laetrile controversy since 1956, and it was he who started one of the largest and most profitable Laetrile clinics in Mexico, the Clinica Cydel, located in Tijuana. McNaughton's past history is not perfectly spotless: he was earlier convicted of fraud in a Canadian mining venture and was accused by the U.S. Securities and Exchange Commission of making untrue statements in a Laetrile stock venture.[13] At the Clinica Cydel and the Clinica del Mar, it was estimated for 1977 that 7,000 patients would be tested and treated as a part of the Laetrile program, at an average weekly cost of $350.00 The manufacture of Laetrile for sale and distribution is also a profitable business. Most of the Laetrile imported to the United States is produced at the Cyto Pharma de Mexica in Tijuana. Frankly admitting that they are in business to make a profit, the owners claim to look forward to an expanded U.S. market. Their factory is already apparently quite profitable, however, and operates 24 hours a day, while processing over six tons of apricot seeds a month.[14]

Many businesspeople in the United States have expressed interest in manufacturing Laetrile within the continental United States. The market appears ready and growing, and consumers would be happy to avoid the almost 700 percent markup that is now given to blackmarket Laetrile entering the United States. Unfortunately for potential U.S. manufacturers, there appears to be little way of avoiding the FDA ban. Even if individual states legalized the manufacture and sale of Laetrile — which appears to be a definite possibility — the FDA still has control over all interstate traffic. Since most states do not produce apricots in the amounts necessary to manufacture Laetrile, this means that importing the requisite apricot pits would constitute a federal legal infraction. Already some U.S. manufacturers of Laetrile, attempting to operate undercover, have been raided and closed down.

THE FDA'S POSITION: MOUNTING OPPOSITION

While admitting that Laetrile may not be damaging in itself, the FDA maintains that its use tends to make people seek remedies that are worthless in place of remedies that hold out some chance of success. This is undoubtedly the argument that the FDA tends to emphasize more than any other. The syndrome that occurs, it argues, involves a patient being informed that he has cancer and told that he must undergo painful, expensive, and possibly unsuccessful traditional methods of treatment. Shocked and afraid, the patient is emotionally ready to believe almost anyone who promises to relieve him of his disease in a cheap, painless manner. Having been persuaded by the promoters of Laetrile, the patient then stops pursuing traditional treatment in favor of a Laetrile cure. Unfortunately, the FDA argues, the cancer does not wait for the patient to be treated unsuccessfully by Laetrile — thus the patient is actually victimized by the very remedy he counted upon to save his life. The FDA claims to know of cases of women with cervical cancer, which has a high rate of cure (about 65 percent), who have refused surgery in favor of Laetrile — and have died. Eugenia Chapman, Illinois state representative, has put the case succinctly by saying, "Persons victimized by cancer should not be victimized twice." And Dr. De Vita of the National Cancer Institute has remarked: "Hardly a day goes by now that I don't hear of a case of a patient dying after leaving accepted treatment and taking Laetrile."

On the other hand, the proponents of Laetrile argue that it is not a question of whether Laetrile works: instead it is an issue of freedom of choice. To deny a person the freedom to choose his own means of treatment, Laetrile defenders argue, is akin to denying him freedom of speech or freedom of worship. How, defenders ask, can the FDA allow the American public to consume unlimited amounts of cigarettes, the use of which has been demonstrated to cause cancer, while denying people the right to use Laetrile? The position of the FDA, it is said, almost approaches the kind of Big Brotherism that is incompatible with a democratic government.

Since the thalidomide crisis of the early 1960s, the FDA has been required by law to license only substances that are both safe and effective. Because of its view that Laetrile is worthless as a cure for cancer, the FDA has taken a strong stand against its use and has organized teams of expert witnesses to testify against Laetrile at public hearings.

The opposition to the FDA's position of Laetrile was increasing so rapidly by 1977 that it appeared to be seriously challenging the authority of the agency. By June of 1977 seven states — Alaska, Arizona, Florida, Indiana, Nevada, Texas, and Washington — had all legalized Laetrile in one form or another. Some states had legalized both its sale and manufacture, whereas others had simply legalized its use under specified conditions. Also by the summer of 1977, it appeared that three more states would soon be joining the original seven, and legislation was pending in more than a dozen. In October of 1976 the Tenth Circuit U.S. Court of Appeals in Denver ruled that the FDA's record on Laetrile was "grossly inadequate" and refused to overturn lower court rulings that allowed patients to buy and transport Laetrile.[15] In addition, the court forced the FDA to listen to testimony from individual Laetrile users and to hold public hearings on the general subject of the drug's use. Even the *New York Times* had asked, in a column dedicated to the discussion of Laetrile, "Shouldn't people be allowed to choose their own placebo, for better or worse?" And Federal District Judge Luther Bohanon of Oklahoma City ruled that it was legal for certain terminally ill cancer patients to import the drug Laetrile from Mexico.

More significantly from the standpoint of the FDA, there was a strong and mounting pressure by the summer of 1977 to test the drug publicly through a controlled and well-supervised program that used humans instead of laboratory animals. Franz Ingelfinger, editor of the *New England Journal of Medicine*, argued that a public trial would do more to get rid of Laetrile than any official debunking. As he put it, "Forbidden fruits are mighty tasty, especially to those who hope that a bite will be life-giving."[16] Laetrile users and proponents strongly supported human tests, especially since they thought that Laetrile was more effective on humans than on rats.

RECENT DEVELOPMENTS

In July 1980 the National Cancer Institute (NCI) sponsored a clinical trial of Laetrile on humans at four medical centers in the United States. Preliminary results, from data coordinated at the Mayo Clinic, were made public on April 30, 1981, and showed no substantive benefit from Laetrile.[17]

The study treatment was developed in accordance with the writings of Laetrile practitioners, and several practitioners served as consultants. In addition to Laetrile, a program of "metabolic therapy" was used that included enzymes, vitamins, and minerals and a diet restricted in meat, animal products, refined flour, refined sugar, and alcohol. Thus treatment was in keeping with current practice.[18]

Subjects were cancer patients with a broad spectrum of measurable tumors for which no other treatment had been effective, or for which no proven treatment existed. All subjects gave their informed consent. Cyanide levels in the blood were monitored, and in one case treatment was stopped when the level became dangerously high.[19]

Of the 156 patients for whom data have been reported, 90 percent showed progression of the disease within three months of the start of the Laetrile treatment, with 50 percent showing such evidence within one month; 50 percent died within five months; and only 20 percent still were alive at the end of eight months. One patient showed a partial reduction in tumor size that lasted for ten weeks, after which the tumor grew despite continued Laetrile therapy. Although 19 percent of those who had felt the effects of the disease prior to the Laetrile treatment claimed that they felt better at some point during the study, only 5 percent of those still in the study during the tenth week claimed any improvement. Results were consistent with those expected with a placebo or inactive medication.[20]

Although this study indicates that Laetrile does not seem to be effective in treating cancer, the fundamental question of freedom of choice, or of the extent to which the FDA should regulate one's medical treatment in a life-threatening situation, remains unanswered.

During the late 1970s, a new dimension was added. Diana and Gerald Green had moved to Massachusetts with their 21-month-old son Chad, so that the boy could be treated for leukemia at Massachusetts General Hospital. Dr. John Truman used chemotherapy treatments to keep the leukemia in a state of remission, first by injection and later by pills to be taken at home. When leukemia reappeared in blood tests, it was learned that the parents had not given the chemotherapy pills but had substituted Laetrile.[21]

When the parents refused to have chemotherapy reinstated, the matter was taken to court where Truman testified that without chemotherapy the boy would die. Upon this basis the court made Chad a ward of the state for medical purposes only, leaving the boy in the custody of his parents. Chemotherapy began again, at state expense, and the boy improved.

Treatment with Laetrile was denied because of its incompatibility with chemotherapy.[22]

The parents fled to Mexico with three-year-old Chad so that he could be treated at the clinic of Dr. Ernesto Contreras with a regimen of Laetrile, vitamins, health pills, and chemotherapy. Because of the incompatibility previously mentioned, signs of cyanide poisoning appeared in Chad, and Massachusetts Attorney General Francis X. Bellotti obtained a court order demanding the return of the boy. Kidnapping charges had been considered but were not made.[23]

The Greens, who were receiving financial support from the National Health Foundation, described by *Time* as a right wing California group that also opposed fluoridation of water, and from private citizens who felt that the state had no business in this matter, refused to bring the child back to Massachusetts.[24]

Chad Green died in Mexico nine months after being taken there. Unfortunately, no autopsy was performed. Therefore, it cannot be known with certainty whether the boy died from the normal progression of cancer or from a buildup of cyanide from Laetrile, or from some other cause.

When the parents of the dead child returned to Massachusetts, they faced civil and criminal contempt changes in Plymouth, Massachusetts. Former Assistant Attorney General Jonathan Brant told the court that with chemotherapy Chad might still be alive. The Greens apologized to the court and asked for forgiveness. Judge Francis Keating found the Greens guilty but gave no sentence, stating, "Any further punishment beyond what had already been endured would certainly be unfair."[25]

This case received wide publicity. For some it represented a violation of freedom of choice in selecting medical treatment. For others it became a rallying point in efforts to keep Laetrile from being sold in the United States.

Another widely publicized case involved actor Steve McQueen. The world first learned of his fight against mesothelioma, a rare and deadly form of cancer that affects the tissues lining the chest and abdomen, in October 1980 when his voice, labored and rasping, was heard on Mexican radio praising the nonspecific metabolic therapy he was receiving at the Plaza Santa Maria General Hospital in Baja California (Mexico). "Congratulations," he said, "and thank you for helping to save my life."[26] This radio broadcast later was used on U.S. television with pictures of McQueen's two-bedroom cabana at the hospital, but without pictures of McQueen, whose features were said to have changed because of the disease.

McQueen was under a treatment devised by former Texas dentist William Donald Kelley that included Laetrile, vitamins, minerals, and a diet with large amounts of raw vegetables and little fish or chicken or meat.[27] Thus the regimen was similar to the diet and supplements tested by the NCI study.

November 1, McQueen left Mexico and returned to his ranch in

Santa Paula, California. A *New York Times* report said that it was unclear whether he would return to the clinic.[28]

On November 7, 1980, McQueen underwent surgery in Juarez, Mexico, during which Dr. Cesar Santos removed a five-pound tumor from the abdomen, stating afterward that somebody should have operated on him immediately after the tumor was discovered. Although Santos felt that McQueen did not have much time to live, he decided to remove the tumor to relieve the pain from its pressure.[29]

McQueen died November 7, at age 50, from heart failure following the surgery. This was three months after he had gone to Mexico for Laetrile and metabolic therapy.[30]

One wonders whether McQueen would have chosen different treatment if the results of the NCI tests of Laetrile and the metabolic diet, being conducted at that time, had been known, or if he would have taken this treatment anyway, knowing that the alternative was drugs and high-voltage radiation with almost certain death within a year.

DISCUSSION QUESTIONS

1. Should an individual, given currently available information on the effectiveness of a form of therapy, have the right to exercise freedom of choice in accepting or rejecting it? Should a distinction be made between the choice of therapy for a child (such as Chad Green) and for a consenting adult (such as actor Steve McQueen)? Should the nature of the disorder — that is, life-threatening or not — make a difference?
2. What should be the role of a regulatory agency such as the FDA: to provide information for intelligent decision making or to regulate the availability of treatment? Would you answer differently if the treatment under question was merely ineffective, or if lack of safety were uncovered?
3. What role should the court system and Congress play in deciding medically related issues? Are there other organizations that should be involved?

NOTES

1. "Damn the Doctors — and Washington," *Time,* June 20, 1977, p. 54.
2. "Laetrile: Should It Be Banned?" *Newsweek,* June 27, 1977, p. 50.
3. Ibid.
4. Ibid.
5. Ibid.
6. "Banned Cancer Drug Gains in Some States," *New York Times,* April 17, 1977, p. 28.

7. "Victories for Laetrile's Lobby," *Time*, May 22, 1977, p. 97.

8. "Banned Cancer Drug," *New York Times*, p. 28.

9. "Laetrile: Should It Be Banned?" p. 52.

10. Ibid., p. 56.

11. "Victories for Laetrile's Lobby," p. 97.

12. "Laetrile: Should It Be Banned?" p. 52.

13. Ibid., p. 51.

14. Ibid.

15. "F.D.A. To Hear Testimony on Cancer Drug Laetrile," *New York Times*, February 18, 1977, p. 16.

16. "Damn the Doctors — Washington," p. 54.

17. National Institutes of Health, National Cancer Institute, *Clinical Study of Laetrile in Cancer Patients, Investigators' Report: A Summary* (Press Release, April 30, 1981).

18. Ibid.

19. Ibid.

20. Ibid.

21. "A Battle over Cancer Care," *Time*, February 12, 1979, p. 25.

22. Ibid.

23. Ibid.

24. Ibid.

25. "Ample Penalty: Defiance of Court Is Excused," *Time*, December 22, 1980, p. 74.

26. M. Clark and R. Henkoff, "Strange Sort of Therapy," *Newsweek*, October 20, 1980, pp. 65–66.

27. Ibid.

28. "McQueen Leaves Clinic," *New York Times*, November 1, 1980, p. 50.

29. "Steve McQueen, 50, Is Dead of a Heart Attack after Surgery for Cancer," *New York Times*, November 4, 1980, p. 21.

30. Ibid.

John D. Aram
Lawrence R. A. Esser

Case 5.B

Carcinogens and the Courts
OSHA's Losing Battle for
the Benzene Standard

Between 1954 and 1964 six people who had worked at a Goodyear Tire and Rubber Company pliofilm plant in Ohio died of leukemia, a form of cancer in which there exists an excess of white blood cells. The pliofilm plants manufactured a food wrapping using a process that involved a chemical called *benzene*. As benzene was known to be toxic, the level in the air was controlled to keep down benzene poisoning by inhalation.

In the 1940s this level was kept below 100 parts per million (ppm) of air, and in the late forties, the level was reduced to 25 ppm. Seemingly, such small levels of the chemical were quite safe. To be sure, workers at these facilities were given blood counts — those who showed any problems were removed from operations involving benzene until their blood was normal.

In 1977 an Occupational Safety and Health Administration (OSHA) researcher completed a study of the leukemia deaths in the pliofilm plants. According to his study, the deaths could be linked to the levels of benzene in the plants. Benzene had previously been tied to leukemia, but only at levels of about 100 ppm. His was the first study to find leukemia at levels below 100 ppm, and possibly lower than 10 ppm. As a result of this report, the standard, already at 10 ppm, was dropped to 1 ppm by OSHA as an emergency measure until a permanent standard could be instituted.

This move set off perhaps the greatest controversy over a regulation that has been seen by OSHA, an already controversial regulatory agency. The standard was challenged by industry as unsubstantiated and unreasonably expensive, considering no tangible benefits could be offered.

The chemical benzene, the center of this controversy, is described by the *Merck Index* as a "clear, colorless, highly flammable liquid, characteristic odor."[1] It was discovered in 1825 and comes primarily from two sources: as a by-product of gasoline refining and from coke-oven emissions in the steel-making process. Among the many uses listed are chemical synthesis, insecticides, lacquers, rotogravure printing, and rubber production.[2] Benzene is also found in the air around gasoline refineries and stations, as it is used as an octane booster replacing lead.

The toxicity of benzene at high concentrations is well known. At levels greater than 20,000 ppm, the central nervous system is affected, leading to respiratory paralysis and death. At levels in the 250 to 500 ppm range, loss of appetite, fatigue, and headaches can occur. Both inhalation and skin contact can result in benzene poisoning, although inhalation poses the greater risk.

At levels below 100 ppm benzene's action is more subtle yet no less dangerous. The chemical, through the body's metabolism, can affect DNA molecules in the bone marrow and injure tissue that forms blood.[3] This leads to various forms of blood abnormalities, including leukemia; thus benzene is classified as a carcinogen. Leukemia is most likely to develop when one has been exposed to the chemical for five years or longer.[4]

The link between benzene and leukemia dates back to 1928 when French physicians posited the theory that the two were connected, and in the 1940s the relation between benzene and blood disorders was established and standards were set to safeguard workers in Massachusetts.[5] As more evidence of this connection became available, the standard was lowered. In 1969 a 10 ppm exposure limit over eight hours, with brief periods of higher exposure, was accepted by the American National Standards Institute.[6] In 1971 this standard was endorsed and accepted by newly formed (1970) OSHA. Again in 1974, the standard was deemed safe by the National Institute of Occupational Safety and Health (NIOSH), the National Academy of Science, and the International Workshop on the Toxicology of Benzene, all prestigious institutions.[7]

The level of benzene and the exposure of workers can be controlled in the workplace by a number of methods including localized ventilation, regular testing of the atmosphere, monthly blood counts, use of respirators, and the rotation of personnel to keep exposure to a minimum.[8] At the 10 ppm level the cost of such caution had been borne by industry without, in the view of business, excessive expense. When OSHA set the 1 ppm standard, the cost of this sudden and strict measure upset benzene users and producers. For the first time, OSHA was seriously challenged in a regulatory attempt.

OSHA was established by the Occupational Safety and Health Act in 1970 as part of the Labor Department. Labor groups, such as the AFL-CIO, had lobbied for the act for two years, seeking a reduction in occupational injury, illness, and death.[9] The act itself aims "to assure so far as possible every working man and woman in the nation safe and healthful working conditions and to preserve our human resources."[10] In addition to the administration, the NIOSH, a research agency, was formed as a division of the Department of Health, Education and Welfare (now Health and Human Services). The administration is authorized to perform a number of duties: carrying out experimentation and research in occupational health problems, establishing programs to encourage safety and health practices, providing an enforcement program by which inspectors are allowed to enter private workplaces and issue citations to employers having unsafe working conditions, setting and enforcing standards (including emergency temporary standards), collecting statistics, carrying out informational programs, and extending grants to states to aid their occupational safety and health programs.[11]

The secretary of labor is authorized to "set mandatory occupational safety and health standards applicable to businesses affecting interstate commerce."[12] This includes emergency standards. The secretary is likewise empowered to revoke standards should they be demonstrably unnecessary.

The definition of a *standard* and the secretary's authority to set standards have generated much of the controversy. Specifically, Section 3(8) of the act defines an occupational safety and health standard as follows:

> A standard requires conditions, or the adoption or use of one or more practices, means, methods, operations, or processes, *reasonably necessary* or appropriate to provide safe or healthful employment and places of employment. [Emphasis added][13]

Further, Section 6(b)(5) specifies how the secretary is to deal with toxicity standards:

> The Secretary . . . shall set the standard which most adequately assures, *to the extent feasible*, on the basis of *the best available evidence*, that no employee will suffer *material* impairment of health or functional capacity. [Emphasis added][14]

In establishing the standard the secretary must consider the latest scientific evidence as well as the feasibility of the standard.

It should be pointed out that words such as *reasonably, feasible,* and *material* were included in the act because of Congress's fear that requiring standards that protected workers from "any" impairment of health would render the act simply unworkable. It was argued by one senator that such requirements would make standards impossible to attain; not only is it unrealistic to expect a riskless workplace, but the costs of attempting to do so would ruin many businesses.[15] While Congress chose not to impose absolute health and safety standards, the terminology written into the act was still to become a major source of confusion regarding the 1 ppm standard.

THE BENZENE STANDARD

The 1 ppm standard had its origin in an Emergency Temporary Standard (ETS) announced by Secretary of Labor Ray Marshall in early May 1977 and effective May 21, 1977. The secretary claimed that "overwhelming evidence" of a connection between benzene and leukemia necessitated swift action.[16] He mentioned studies that showed the fatal effects of high levels of benzene and the health threat of lower standards, already at 10 ppm.

The reaction to the ETS by industry was mixed and showed little concern that the standard would seriously affect the companies involved. Dow Chemical, for example, commented that the ETS was "very stringent" but not at all impossible to meet.[17] At the same time, it defended the 10 ppm standard as safe.[18] Monsanto felt that while the cost of new monitoring equipment was a consideration, the greatest difficulty would be in the required training programs to explain the benzene hazard to employees.[19] Exxon Chemical Company said that the 10 ppm standard was "adequate" and did not see any reason for the ETS.[20]

The evidence referred to by the secretary of labor was the study done on the Goodyear pliofilm workers. This research was conducted by an investigator, Peter D. Infante, of NIOSH in early 1977. His study showed that workers exposed to levels below 100 ppm and possibly even below 15 ppm contracted leukemia at a rate five times greater than normal. These results were seen as especially important by OSHA because the workers had been exposed only to benzene and not to any other solvents.[21]

Because of the postulated link to leukemia at low levels, the 1 ppm benzene exposure was selected by OSHA as "the lowest possible level capable of being achieved given present technological and analytical expertise." Further, OSHA believed that 1 ppm was probably safe.[22]

According to the act, an ETS must be published in the *Federal Register* before a proposed permanent standard can be promulgated. Interested parties can file objections to the rule and request a hearing within 30 days after an ETS has been announced. The American Petroleum Institute (API) challenged the promulgation of a permanent standard by OSHA and hearings were scheduled for July 12, 1977. In the meantime the ETS was suspended by court injunctions at the request of industry groups.

The Infante study was heavily criticized in the hearings. The Manufacturing Chemists Association (MCA) presented several witnesses who challenged Infante's results. Aside from the fact that none of the NIOSH researchers, including Infante, were physicians, Dr. Robert Olson pointed out that the benzene levels in the pliofilm plants were only required to be 100 ppm and it was therefore unlikely that these workers were exposed to levels lower than that.[23]

Another MCA representative, Dr. Irving Tabershaw, felt that the levels were in fact much higher than 100 ppm. He further proposed that the pliofilm leukemia cases were a "cluster," apparently common in leukemia cases. He noted that no other cases of leukemia had been found in the plants since 1961.[24]

Dr. Steven Lamm presented testimony challenging risk levels derived from the Infante study. Looking at the Infante data and another study, he equalized the conditions and found that the two predicted similar results: assuming that workers already exposed were inhaling an average of 3 ppm, the drop to 1 ppm would result in one less case of leukemia every 15 to 35 years. Lamm refigured risk levels at 3 ppm, then extrapolated to 1 ppm, arguing that the Infante data in fact predicted no more excess cases than normal.[25] Finally, an industrial hygienist testified that benzene detectors used in the 1940s "would not accurately measure anything in the zero to 50 ppm range."[26]

OSHA representatives at the hearing took the general position that although the standard would be strict and costly, it would be possible for industry to meet. Further, it argued that because *no* safe level had been found for benzene, it had to be dropped as low as possible.

For the first time a set of detailed costs was presented by Arthur D. Little, Inc., consultants hired by OSHA. Briefly, the initial investment for all affected companies in air monitoring, engineering controls, gathering of medical data, and protective equipment would be $267.3 million. Operating costs would be $124 million in the first year and $74.4 million annually thereafter. The effect on price was estimated to be small, approximately a 1 percent increase in the producers' price for benzene.[27]

THE ADMINISTRATIVE DECISION AND ENSUING LEGAL ACTION

Following such public hearings, the secretary can either go ahead and publish the standard or decide that the standard, based on testimony, is unnecessary. Secretary of Labor Ray Marshall chose the former and published the permanent standard in February of 1978. This was challenged by the API and the National Petroleum Refiners Association who filed a petition in the Fifth District Court of the United States in New Orleans challenging the validity of the standard.[28] Industry's main complaint against the benzene limit was the high cost involved in meeting 1 ppm while lacking any quantifiable benefit. Representatives pointed out that no substantial evidence had been put forth that established a link between 10 ppm and leukemia. In light of this, they saw no reason to be subjected to such stringent controls. OSHA, as well as the Industrial Union Department of the AFL-CIO, defended the standard on the assumption that "benefits from the reduction 'may be appreciable.'"[29] OSHA's view was based on its earlier contention that because no safe level had been found for benzene, "exposure to lower levels . . . would be safer than exposure to higher levels."[30]

Just before the court case in New Orleans in June 1978, a study conducted by a former Dow Chemical researcher, Dante Picciano, provided data that linked benzene with leukemia at levels below 10 ppm. "Picciano relied on an average exposure figure for each worker [at a Texas Dow Plant] that was based on a series of measurements taken over the previous two years — all of them involving less than 10 ppm." He concluded that even at low levels "benzene had led to the high incidence of [damaged chromosomes in blood cells]."[31] This study was not included in the New Orleans case because it had not been part of the earlier OSHA hearings.

In October 1978 the New Orleans court decided against the 1 ppm standard on the grounds that the lack of any quantified benefit rendered impossible any assessment of a cost-benefit relation.[32] OSHA's argument of "no safe level" was rejected, and its contention that only the feasibility (absence of serious financial difficulty) of the standard needed to be shown was discarded.

OSHA's only recourse at this point was to request that the Supreme Court review the circuit court's decision. In a memorandum written to request a reversal of this decision, Secretary of Labor Ray Marshall noted that the act required no cost-benefit analysis of the secretary: "The [act] does *not* require the Secretary to establish that the costs of particular reductions in exposures to toxic substances are justified by quantifiable benefits."[33]

During late 1978 and 1979 briefs were prepared to support or oppose the granting of a review by the Supreme Court. Supporting briefs were sent by the secretary of labor, the Industrial Union Department (AFL-CIO), and also the American Iron and Steel Institute, which, while opposing the standard, felt that a Supreme Court review was necessary to review the case properly.

The position of OSHA, the secretary of labor, and the AFL-CIO might best be summed up by a statement in a brief filed by the AFL-CIO:

> The [New Orleans] court said that the Secretary "must regulate on the basis of what is known rather than what is unknown." . . . So he must. But, as Socrates taught long ago, the highest knowledge is knowing the limits of our own knowledge. That knowledge has special force when, as here, the inquiry is at "the frontiers of scientific knowledge." . . . The Secretary's instant determination was based not, as the [New Orleans] court of appeals would have it, on arbitrary assumptions, but in precise accord with . . . Section 6(b)5, on the best scientific knowledge available. . . .
>
> . . . . It remains the duty of the Secretary to act to protect the workingman . . . even in circumstances where existing methodology or research is deficient.[34]

Opposition to the granting of Supreme Court review came from the API, the MCA, the Chemical Specialties Manufacturers, the Rubber Manufacturers Association, the E.I. DuPont de Nemours and Co., the Adhesive and Sealant Council, and the Republic Steel Corporation. In an opposition brief these groups defended the New Orleans court's decision as "perfectly sensible."[35] Citing the lack of evidence to show that low-level exposures are linked to leukemia, they argued that the court had correctly defined OSHA's responsibility in establishing the standard:

> Before lowering the permissible exposure level from 10 to 1 ppm, OSHA must develop "rough but educated" estimates of the risks from exposures below 10 ppm and utilize such estimates to show "a reasonable relationship" between the "one-half billion dollar" costs and the lowered risks [that is, health benefits] attributable to reducing exposure to 1 ppm.[36]

In short, industry was mainly arguing against the limit on the basis of a lack of cost-benefit analysis, as they had done successfully in the New Orleans Fifth Circuit Court of Appeals.

The positions of the parties were clear: OSHA, as represented by Ray Marshall and the AFL-CIO, supported the standard on what they felt was the best evidence available and argued that cost-benefit analysis was irrelevant. The respondents held that cost-benefit analysis should be the basis of the decision on whether to implement the standard. In February 1979 the Supreme Court agreed to review the case.

SUPREME COURT DECISION

On July 2, 1980, the Supreme Court announced a decision to uphold the lower court's ruling against the 1 ppm limit, but not for the same reasons. As the *Wall Street Journal* reported, "The decision wasn't the clear-cut victory business groups and opponents of government regulation had sought. Five of the nine justices wrote opinions on the case, diminishing its force as a precedent."[37]

In the majority opinion, written by Justice Stevens, the Fifth Circuit Court's decision was reviewed and divided into two parts: (A) "that OSHA had exceeded its standard-setting authority because it had not shown that the new benzene exposure limit was 'reasonably necessary or appropriate to provide safe or healthful employment' as required by Section 3(8)"[38] and (B) "because Section 6(b)(5) does 'not give OSHA the unbridled discretion to adopt standards designed to create absolutely risk-free workplaces regardless of costs.'"[39]

The majority of the Court agreed that the secretary must show that a health risk is significant as in part (A). The Court did not feel that a cost-benefit analysis as mentioned in part (B) was relevant to the decision unless a significant risk at lower levels was found. Nor did it address the question of the secretary's responsibility to make feasibility analyses on new standards. It simply addressed the fact that OSHA had failed to show clearly the risk involved in not setting the standard to 1 ppm as it was required to do by Section 3(8) of the act.

Among the concurring views, Justice Powell paid particular attention to the cost-benefit issue. First, he stressed that a health risk must be significant before large expenditures are to be considered. Not only has OSHA failed to carry its burden of proof, but also, he concluded, "the statute . . . requires the agency to determine that the economic effects of its standard bear a reasonable relationship to the expected benefits."[40] A standard is unreasonable if the expenditures for adherence are "wholly disproportionate to the expected health and safety benefits."[41]

The dissenting opinion was written by Justice Marshall. His first point was that the Supreme Court had no authority to interfere with the act: "Under our jurisprudence, it is presumed that ill-considered or unwise legislation will be corrected through the democratic process," not through judicial review.[42]

Second, Marshall stated that the case at hand had as its "critical problem . . . scientific uncertainty."[43] Because the risk could not be quantified and might be great in the future without the 1 ppm standard, the American worker could be left exposed to the cancer danger. In this regard he agreed directly with OSHA, which held that the standard was necessary because existing evidence showed *no* safe level.

Third, Marshall attacked the majority opinions as "arrogant" and "unfair." They "remind the members of this court that they were not appointed to undertake independent review of adequately supported scientific findings made by a technically expert agency."[44] The justices, Marshall argued, were taking it upon themselves to decide on technical issues in which they had no expertise.

Finally, the dissenters argued that the secretary had acted properly by carefully gathering evidence and hearing testimony. In spite of scientific uncertainty, "he gave 'careful consideration' to the question of whether the admittedly substantial costs were justified in light of the hazards of benzene exposure. He concluded that those costs were necessary in order to promote the purposes of the act."[45] Marshall interpreted the act as requiring the secretary to impose strict regulations even when the evidence was uncertain.

THE BENZENE DECISION: IMPLICATIONS AND ISSUES

This Supreme Court decision marked the first major restraint ever imposed on OSHA in its regulatory action. The difficulty lay in providing clear and quantifiable substantiation of the need for the 1 ppm limit. Beyond this lay the issue of cost-benefit: when and how should the benefits of a standard outweigh its costs? At issue also was the mandate of OSHA:

exactly what was OSHA's obligation to consider risks and benefits? Finally, what role should the courts play in the settling of such issues? Could they be relied upon to assess objectively a situation involving technicalities with which they might well be unfamiliar? Each of these issues had an important role in the benzene standard dispute.

Substantiation of Benefits

The first issue centered on the definition of a *significant* health risk. To one person *significant* might mean one excess case of leukemia every year, whereas to another, it might mean one excess incident every 30 years. Both interpretations have validity. When *significant* becomes attached to human health and life, the issue becomes difficult to decide.

OSHA was heavily criticized for not presenting a clearer idea of the risk involved in the 10 ppm level. Estimates of this risk had been made and offered to OSHA in the form of benefit assessments. In fact, these had been considered in the 1977 hearings, but because of the difficulties and uncertainties involved in such estimates, they were not used as quantitative "proof" of the need for the 1 ppm level. OSHA repeatedly argued that the risks were unknown and therefore the level should be kept as low as feasible. Because of the lack of even an "educated guess" in this direction, the Supreme Court found itself unable to accept the standard.

Justice Powell felt that OSHA should define the meaning of *significant*. "It is the agency's responsibility to determine . . . what it considers to be a 'significant' risk."[46] Once this was done, OSHA could, with the support of science, institute a standard even if the probability of harm could not be absolutely proven. Again, because OSHA had made no clear step in this direction, the Court ruled against the standard.

The question of significant risk, if decided by OSHA, then becomes a question of "acceptable risk." How much risk is tolerable? How is such a level to be set? As one judge, David Bazelon, wrote in *Science*, "The question, then, is not whether we will have risk at all, but how much risk, and from what source."[47] This issue was left open by the Supreme Court decision.

Cost-Benefit Analysis

The problem of cost-benefit, although addressed by the Fifth Circuit Court, was postponed for later cases by the Supreme Court. Originally, Arthur D. Little presented the costs as a $267 million capital investment, with $123 million first-year operating costs and yearly costs after that of $74 million. OSHA refigured the costs on the premise that after initial installation of engineering controls the 1 ppm level would be reached in most plants, thus lowering the need for much of the monitoring equipment and physical examinations and lowering annual operating costs to $34 million.[48]

Generally, these figures were accepted by industry and by the courts, and it was agreed that such investment would achieve the 1 ppm standard. What industry and the New Orleans court did not accept was spending of this amount of money when benefits were not clear. Training programs, engineering controls, air monitoring equipment, respirators, and administration would all have to be paid for by the company.

Although there seems to be little difficult in calculating costs for regulation, the assessment of benefits was a particularly difficult issue in the benzene case. One writer remarked, "American laws do not given explicit directions for considering risk-benefit factors and economic arguments usually are contested with the implicit assertion that health has a supreme value whose economic costs need not, should not, be considered."[49]

This attitude is reflected in the act, which gives no instruction on whether cost-benefit analysis should be used. The words *reasonably necessary* and *feasible* were not taken by OSHA to mean that the benefit should be related to the cost but simply that the costs should be able to be borne by industry without serious financial difficulty. Thus, if any benefit could be shown, the cost was more or less irrelevant under these conditions.

The Supreme Court seemed divided not over costs but over benefits. In general, the concurring justices felt that because no clear evidence of risk was presented, OSHA had no basis on which to impose such high costs on industry. The dissenters argued that the costs had been shown to be affordable by industry and that the existence of any benefits justified these costs. In the overall decision this question was also left open, as the Court declined to rule on the basis of cost-benefit.

A significant problem in benefit assessment is attaching some level of risk to a human life and putting some value on that life. Essentially it boils down to the question, What value is to be placed on life or health?

OSHA's Mandate

Both court decisions raised the question of the authority of the Secretary of Labor and OSHA: exactly what were they required to do by the act, and what were they allowed to do? The main source of controversy regarding regulatory authority was the act's wording; because it was ambiguous and guidelines for requiring benefits were lacking, the Secretary had to rely on his own interpretation, believing that as long as the procedures outlined in the document were duly followed, his authority would not be questioned. For these reasons the act itself was criticized.

There is more than just a legal authority question involved — a problem of when and how the regulator should make a decision regarding a standard was also present. Clearly the act was meant to protect workers. But anyone faced with uncertainty, especially regarding health or life, is in a dilemma: if a decision is made to regulate, the regulator may face challenges to the standard and to his or her authority. If the regulator decides not to regulate, the individual must live with the possibility that others are being exposed to preventable risk. An official of the Environmental Protection Agency stated it this way:

> Unfortunately, regulators don't have the luxury of putting off decisions until certainty arrives. Enormous scientific uncertainty surrounds the potential risks and benefits of most chemicals, yet these benefits and risks exist. Therefore, a regulator's every action — or inaction — represents a decision of some kind. Whatever way they decide, regulators run the risk of making the wrong decisions in the midst of pervasive uncertainty.[50]

The Role of Courts in Scientific Issues

Another issue in this controversy is the ability of the courts to intervene in technical cases. Justice Marshall attacked his colleagues for supposing that they could rule on technical issues. In fact, all of the justices agreed that it was not the Court's duty to decide on a standard: "Congress, the governmental body best suited and most obligated to make the choice confronting us in this case, has improperly delegated that choice to the [secretary] and, derivatively, to this Court."[51]

It is difficult to assess whether the courts in this case were looking for clear, quantified data or for estimates. Generally they sought a guideline that would unequivocally establish a particular standard as right or as wrong. Because OSHA could not, or did not, provide such a guideline, the courts found it impossible to make any judgment as to costs or benefits.

If the Congress, the secretary of labor, and technical experts are all unable to establish a guideline, should the courts examine the quantitative side of the problem? As another judge noted, "Judges have little or no training to understand and resolve problems on the frontiers of nuclear physics, toxicology, hydrology, and a myriad of specialities. . . . These cases often present questions that experts have grappled with for years, without coming to any consensus."[52]

ISSUES FOR MANAGEMENT

Because of the involvement of industry in controversial issues such as benzene, it must be asked what role management plays: How can business people deal with problems having complex technical effects? What position should industry take on these issues?

As industry proceeds with chemicals, high technology, and greater involvement with science, it takes the risk that sooner or later this involvement will raise questions of safety with which neither government agencies, the judiciary, nor legislatures can deal effectively. In addition, the public may not be well equipped to make decisions on scientific issues: "The most important element of our government, the voter, simply cannot be expected to understand the scientific predicate of many issues he must face at the polls."[53]

Concerns about safety and health may turn to hostility if business and science become too far removed from public understanding and trust in the interests of profit and research. If scientists and business leaders were to suspect risks involved in certain industrial processes, but fail to investigate or disclose them because of additional costs involved, the credibility and autonomy of business might be seriously eroded.

Given such a complex situation, what alternatives might be considered? Should business establish guidelines for investigation and disclosure of risk information? Can the adversary relationship between government and industry be improved on these issues?

DISCUSSION QUESTIONS

1. What are the key aspects of OSHA's legislative mandate? Is this proper regulatory guidance in the area of worker health and safety protection or are changes in this mandate warranted?
2. Evaluate the Supreme Court's benzene decision in the light of OSHA's mandate and the available evidence on benzene. Make clear your agreement or disagreement with the majority view of the Court.
3. Suppose OSHA had shown a significant health risk at 10 ppm. Should the cost of achieving a 1 ppm level be taken into consideration in evaluating the legality of the standard?
4. The issue of scientific uncertainty might be said to lie at the heart of the benzene case. What implication of this uncertainty do you see for business, regulatory agencies, and the courts?

NOTES

1. *Merck Index,* ed. Martha Windholz, 9th ed. (Rahway, N.J.: Merck & Co., Inc., edition, 1976), p. 138.
2. E. R. Plunkett, *Handbook of Industrial Toxicology* (New York: Chemical Publishing, 1976), p. 51.
3. Ibid.
4. Ibid., p. 52.
5. "Industrial Union Department, AFL-CIO v. American Petroleum Institute," *Occupational Safety & Health Reporter* (Washington, D.C.: Bureau of National Affairs), no. 17 (July 17, 1980), pp. 1588–89.

6. Ibid., p. 1588.
7. U.S. Sup. Ct. Records & Briefs, *Industrial Union Department* v. *American Petroleum Institute,* Docket no. 78–911, Opposition Brief, pp. 78.
8. Plunkett, *Handbook,* p. 52.
9. "Protecting People on the Job: ABC's of a Controversial Law," *U.S. News & World Report,* cited in *Contemporary Problems in Personnel,* ed. W. Clay Hamner and F. L. Schmidt (Chicago: St. Clair Press, 1979), p. 479.
10. "The Occupational Safety and Health Act of 1970," *Labor Relations Expediter* (Washington, D.C.: Bureau of National Affairs, 1970), p. 6201.
11. Ibid., pp. 6201–25.
12. Ibid., p. 6201.
13. Ibid., p. 6202.
14. Ibid., pp. 6204–5.
15. Senator Peter Dominick quoted in *Industrial Union Department* v. *American Petroleum Institute,* pp. 1612–13.
16. "Benzene Emergency Standard Set by OSHA," *Chemical & Engineering News,* May 9, 1977, p. 4.
17. Ibid.
18. "OSHA Issues Stiff Benzene-Exposure Standards," *Oil and Gas Journal,* May 9, 1977, p. 29.
19. "Benzene Emergency Standard," p. 4.
20. "OSHA Issues," p. 29.
21. "Benzene Emergency Standard," p. 4.
22. Ibid.
23. "MCA Opposes Longer Benzene Exposure Limits," *Chemical & Engineering News,* August 8, 1977, p. 7.
24. Ibid.
25. U.S. Sup. Ct. Records & Briefs, Affidavit of Dr. Steven H. Lamm, p. 33.
26. "Industry's Challenge on Benzene," *Business Week,* August 22, 1977, p. 30.
27. "OSHA Pushes Stiffer Benzene Exposure Rules," *Chemical & Engineering News,* August 1, 1977, p. 12.
28. "U.S. Benzene Rules Challenged in Court By Two Oil Groups," *Wall Street Journal,* February 6, 1978, p. 4.
29. "Court Overturns OSHA Benzene Standard," *Chemical & Engineering News,* October 16, 1978, p. 8.
30. Ibid.
31. "Research that Clouds the Benzene Issue," *Business Week,* June 26, 1978, p. 43.
32. "Court Overturns," p. 8.
33. U.S. Sup. Ct. Records & Briefs, Memorandum of Secretary of Labor Ray Marshall, p. 40.
34. Reply Brief (AFL-CIO), in ibid., p. 17.
35. Oppositions Brief (APA et al.), in ibid., p. 3.
36. Ibid., pp. 3–4.

37. "Regulations Limiting Worker Exposure to Benzene Are Voided By High Court," *Wall Street Journal,* July 3, 1980, p. 4.
38. *Industrial Union Department* v. *American Petroleum Institute,* p. 1587.
39. Ibid.
40. Ibid., p. 1608.
41. Ibid.
42. Ibid., p. 1617.
43. Ibid.
44. Ibid., p. 1619.
45. Ibid., p. 1623.
46. Ibid., p. 1603.
47. D. L. Bazelon, "Risk and Responsibility," *Science* 205 (July 20, 1979): 277.
48. *Industrial Union Department* v. *American Petroleum Institute,* p. 1593.
49. Gio Batta Gori, "The Regulation of Carcinogenic Hazards," *Science* 208 (April 18, 1980):256.
50. S. D. Jellinek, "On the Inevitability of Being Wrong," *Technology Review,* August-September 1980, p. 8.
51. *Industrial Union Department* v. *American Petroleum Institute,* p. 1610.
52. Bazelon, "Risk and Responsibility," p. 278.
53. Ibid.

Chapter 6

Alternatives to Rule-Oriented Regulation of Business
The Role of Market Forces in Health, Safety, and Environmental Protection

Debate over government social regulation of business often overshadows the influence of market forces and other decentralized, flexible mechanisms on business behavior. In fact, it might be argued that the best discipline on business is the free market — in buying products, or selecting places of employment, individuals ultimately determine a firm's survival or failure. A business cannot market dangerous or defective products or maintain unsafe working conditions for very long before its reputation is damaged, its products fail to sell, and its quality workers defect to other firms. Many would argue that the competitive forces of the marketplace are the most effective regulator of poor business practices.

Business critics may charge that market forces are an imperfect discipline on business and, at best, offer indirect, long-term protection of consumer and worker interests. To this point market advocates argue that where the market is imperfect and may lead to injury, for example, individuals can take legal action to recover damages. The courts provide a forum in which rights of consumers, workers, and the public are defined and resolved in relation to business. The field of product liability law, for example, is particularly well developed. Furthermore, the common law system is a method of conflict resolution that circumvents centralized governmental control and costly, uniform rules for all business situations. When market operations are inadequate, it is argued, the law of torts provides a useful method of settling disputes between private parties.

Even if the common law of torts does not adequately provide recourse to problems such as pollution — instances when a health hazard can rarely be traced to a specific company — proponents of the market reply that if government must become involved, there are more flexible and efficient ways than employing standardized rules to correct problems. If it comes to regulation, this viewpoint emphasizes policies that utilize market incentives to correct pollution and other problems. Centralized and standardized rules are considered less effective than regulatory systems that complement market forces and capitalize on business's natural motive to find efficient solutions to problems.

Consumer choice, court action, and market-based government regulation constitute significant factors in the business environment and must be considered important dimensions of the relationship of business to the public and to government. Although they may not receive the same publicity as the cost-benefit debate or as reports on the cost of federal paperwork, they have long-term importance to business.

This chapter examines individual choice, tort law in the context of product liability, and market-based regulatory strategies as external influences on business decision making. Particular emphasis is placed upon the role of market forces as a discipline on management. A final section of the chapter explores the general impact that health, safety, and environmental issues have had on corporate planning and identifies several planning systems that may successfully incorporate these external values into day-to-day organizational decision making.

CONTRIBUTIONS OF MARKET CONCEPTS TO INDIVIDUAL PROTECTION

Competition strongly influences business actions; without competition, business has no natural incentive to adapt to external values. When firms must compete for consumers and employees, they will naturally be sensitive to the wishes and wants of these groups. But where environmental resources such as clean air and water exist independent of competition and no cost is associated with their use, business has no incentive to conserve them. Consequently, pure market concepts inherently lend themselves more to situations involving choice, competition, and market pricing than to those involving universal and "free" materials such as clean air and water.

If workers and consumers know about health and safety risks *and* if they act on this knowledge, competition for labor and customers forces companies to internalize these values. On the other hand, if information is incomplete or individuals are unable, for whatever reason, to act on their information, business does not receive correct market signals of the importance of health and safety factors, and competitive forces may inadequately protect workers and consumers. How well natural market forces protect consuming groups and employees is the subject of the following sections.

Dynamics of Consumer Markets

Consumer choice plays an indispensable role in the market concept of firm adaptation. The withdrawal of patronage, or even the threat of it, forces firms to anticipate changes in consumer attitudes and to explore areas of unmet consumer needs. Economist Albert O. Hirschman states the classical view of the consumer's role and the power the consumer holds over the firm:

> The consumer who, dissatisfied with the product of one firm, shifts to that of another, uses the market to defend his welfare or to improve his position, and he also sets in motion market forces which may induce recovery on the part of the firm that has declined in comparative performance. This is the sort of mechanism economics thrives on. It is neat — one either exits or one does not; it is impersonal — any face-to-face confrontation between consumer and firm . . . is avoided and success and failure of the organization are communicated to it by a set of statistics; and it is indirect — any recovery on the part of the declining firm comes by courtesy of the Invisible Hand, as an unintended by-product of the customer's decision to shift.[1]

There are, however, several practical difficulties with complete reliance on this concept of firm adaptation. First, substitutes or alternative products may not be readily available to a dissatisfied consumer. Second, as in the case of a few persons having life-threatening reactions to a particular drug, only a small group of consumers — too small to represent a significant market force — may be negatively affected by a product. Third, the consumer may not have the knowledge, capacity, or time to obtain fully adequate information for making purchase decisions in all relevant areas. The individual may have, in effect, an "information processing problem."[2]

There are several reasons why reliance on personal knowledge is becoming more difficult in the area of consumer purchasing.[3] High levels of affluence and economic growth have led to a greater range of products and services with which to be familiar, as well as proportionately more income spent on consumption. More specifically, though, advanced technology creates products having features that lie outside one's sphere of experience or perception. Rapid technological change makes existing information about products more quickly obsolete. These factors frustrate many individuals attempting to gather and absorb relevant information for their consumer decisions. Insert 6.A illustrates the relative disadvantage of the consumer in purchase decisions compared with the industrial buyer.

The consumer, however, is not totally alone in the purchase decision. The product itself, sales personnel, consumer information publications

Insert 6.A

INDUSTRIAL VERSUS CONSUMER PURCHASING

As a rule industrial buying involves a substantially larger volume of purchase than does consumer buying. This fact leads to the following implications, which generally indicate that self-protection is more feasible in industrial buying situations.

- Industrial buying warrants the dedication of many more resources to the search process. A 5 percent reduction of price on a purchase of several hundred thousand dollars is more worthwhile seeking than is a similar reduction on a purchase of several dollars.
- Companies often have the presence of experts in manufacturing, engineering, or purchasing to aid in nearly any purchase decision. They tend to rely on specialists rather than on an individual with a broad range of expertise.
- Larger purchases place a higher value on experimentation, trials, or pretesting prior to purchase. This is seldom feasible for an individual.
- Many large companies can set specifications for a unique product and call for competitive bids. The consumer at large faces a choice among existing products.
- A large user can make reliable internal comparisons between products. Consumers rarely have this opportunity.

In short, the problem of information processing seems to lie with the consumer alone, owing to these significant strengths of the industrial buyer. Whereas industrial markets are composed of professionalism on both sides, a full-time professional seller faces a part-time amateur buyer in consumer markets.

SOURCE: Richard H. Holton, "Advancing the Backward Art of Spending Money," in *Regulating Business: The Search for an Optimum* (San Francisco: Institute for Contemporary Studies, 1978), pp. 126–30.

such as *Consumer Reports,* acquaintances, and one's own experience are sources of product information. These are useful but may suffer from lack of objectivity in advice giving, or they may lack specific experience relevant to the individual's purchase decision. One's own experience with the product also appears a useful guide when purchases are frequent, performance characteristics are self-evident, the rate of technological change is slow, and the terms of sale are stable.[4]

Information Disclosure: Remedy or Ruse?

Aimed at the major problem of information access, disclosure regulation is designed to reinforce the market principle of individual choice and to afford greater consumer protection. Such regulations in recent years allow consumers to make informed choices. The consumer area has seen the enactment of various "truths" legislation: truth in labeling, truth in packaging, truth in lending. Moreover, controversies have arisen about worker access to job-related information, such as the health risks associated with various jobs and the worker's right to know the results of his or her medical evaluations.

Yet more product information may be of limited practical value to consumers. A survey of public attitudes toward consumer issues conducted by the Louis Harris organization and the Marketing Science Institute found that a full 80 percent of a representative population sample agreed that "many safety problems which people have with products arise because they don't read the instructions properly."[5] In contrast, 52 percent of the same sample felt that product safety problems arise because instructions are inadequate.

In addition, disclosure regulations may only slightly lighten the heavy hand of government. Disclosure rules may lead to presentation of information that is not particularly used by or helpful to consumers, adding to the cost of services or products and perhaps detracting from their appeal and obscuring actual differences. Disclosure regulation imposes significant administrative costs on companies and introduces another point of public control and inspection.

One Harvard University lecturer has suggested that utilization of information disclosure, in lieu of direct regulation, is most effective when the costs of disclosure are relatively less expensive, consumers are able to adapt the information provided to their individual situations, the information is presented in an educational manner, and the information can be absorbed quickly by consumers.[6] According to these guidelines, a product label listing a number of specific "DO NOT USE . . ." warnings would be less effective than a label that explained briefly what harmful side effects might be triggered by inappropriate use of the product.

A particularly heated controversy has surrounded the question of persuasive versus informational advertising. Public concern over advertising is illustrated by the fact that the Harris survey of attitudes showed 46 percent of the public felt "most" or all television advertising was "seriously misleading." Another 39 percent felt "some" was misleading.[7] Advertising in newspapers and magazines fared somewhat better: 28 percent responded that most or all was seriously misleading, and 50 percent felt only "some" was seriously misleading.

Advertising is both a source of information and an attempt to persuade the consumer. It relies upon a privilege granted to the seller to present its best case to the consumer; at the same time, the seller may be tempted to exaggerate the product qualities in a variety of ways or to use emotional associations and symbols that the buyer may not consciously recognize. Consideration of advertising presents additional complexities to the formation of public policy toward business. On the one hand, advertising may enhance freedom of choice by disseminating product information and stimulating competition; on the other, it may create artificial product differences and mislead the consumer.

Industry generally claims that people are aided by advertising in making purchase decisions. Opponents charge that much advertising is false, misleading, and deceptive and that product claims should be permitted if supported by objective and independent evidence. They believe there should be "truth" in advertising. The Federal Trade Commission (FTC) is charged with the responsibility to restrict "false and deceptive" advertising; one of its proposed guidelines would require advertising to be informational and all unique claims to be backed by reliable and valid documentation. Some of the arguments against and for this proposal are outlined in the following:

Cons:

*   Developing conclusive documentation may be prohibitively costly for some unique products;
*   A barrier to market entry may be created for a new and small producer with a distinctive product but limited financial resources to allocate toward extensive documentation;
*   Companies using advertising as a major competitive tool would be penalized; this would hold particularly true in consumer-oriented markets where corporate strategies involve strong promotion and advertising; and
*   Attempts to require test results for product claims may lead to a morass of legalistic debates on issues such as how closely test results must be replicable, how well testing conditions must simulate actual consumer use, how an expert is defined, and so on.

Pros:

*   Strict standards for advertising claims will safeguard consumer interests, allowing them to base buying decisions on full and accurate information;
*   Incentives for product R & D may be strengthened, enhancing product competition on the bases of price, quality, and service; and
*   Truth in advertising should promote an honest consumer-producer relationship and develop a positive business image in the public eye.

Labor Market Processes

How well do markets function where workers must exercise choice in their own interests? The same threat of breaking relations with the firm observed in consumer choice applies to employee relations as well — departure is an alternative for an individual who wants to better his or her situation, and it may also induce actions by the firm to recover from decline. However, relying on employee departure as a problem signal may be poor practice since a firm's more specialized or competent employees often have greater job mobility and are more likely to leave when dissatisfied. Albert Hirschman suggests also that availability of substitutes or replacements may mask the true decline of the firm's employee relations.[8]

Upon scrutinizing the efficiency of labor markets in the American economy, labor economist Lloyd Reynolds has identified several sources of market imperfections — observable phenomena that would not result under the perfect operation of supply and demand for labor.[9] For example, under perfect competition for labor one would not see unemployment at peaks of the business cycle, or different wages paid for the same work in the same locality, or increases in money wages when there is unemployment. Why do such apparent market imperfections exist? Among the reasons for these abnormalities are two particularly relevant conditions: labor market information is inadequate, and labor mobility is limited.

Both workers and employers have only incomplete information. Attempts to increase information and expand choices are costly in terms of both time and money. Therefore, both prospective employees and employers continue to make employment decisions on partial information.

With respect to labor mobility, Reynolds makes the parallel point that nonwage "investments" by employees and by employers must be taken into account in explaining a lower degree of labor mobility than would be predicted by wage differences alone. Movement of labor from low-paying to higher-paying jobs and from region to region would be greater if employers and employees considered only wages. In addition to whether other workers are available at a lower wage, employers consider the costs of recruiting, hiring, and training good workers. Similarly, employees, having gone through sometimes arduous learning and training periods, have a personal investment in a job that weighs against changing to another job with higher pay. Seniority, location, and personal acquaintances are additional investments on the part of the employee that may be lost in a job change.

One can apply these ideas to information and mobility in the context of the health and safety characteristics of a job. Information may not be known by managers or by scientists — let alone by the workers involved. Information about the health risks of a job opening in another company is at least as difficult, and often more difficult, to obtain. Judging whether a wage premium compensates for possible increased risk is nearly impossible. Similarly, to the extent employee "investments" exist, the individual is less likely to move to an equivalent job that may carry less health and safety risk. These factors appear to present substantial impediments to the functioning of labor markets as protection for worker health and safety.

The foregoing discussions suggest the advantages and disadvantages of a market-based approach to consumer and worker protection. Market forces over time undoubtedly do influence business standards for con-sumer and employee relations and induce corrective action in specific firms. At the same time, they are incomplete, partial, and imperfect mech-anisms. The concepts of free labor and product markets that originated in the eighteenth and nineteenth centuries were born to an economy very different from what we know today: low differentiation of products and little job specialization, local and largely personalized systems of product distribution, highly relevant personal experience in purchasing decisions, and low technology in manufacture. Moreover, threats to health and per-sonal well-being were much different than they are today. Perhaps more important, whatever risks were perceived were largely accepted as a normal aspect of living. Today, broad confidence in personal choice and market-based solutions appears to require the following: (1) easy access to infor-mation about health and safety aspects of jobs and products, (2) sufficient expertise and time for individuals to assess and independently evaluate this information, (3) only minimal costs associated with job changing or product switching, (4) the presence of unusually large wage premiums for risky jobs, and (5) existence of markets for higher-priced but lower-risk prod-ucts. These strenuous conditions, not easily met in today's labor and prod-uct markets, explain why health and safety issues continue as problem areas in business-government relations.

COURT-BASED DECISION MAKING AS INDIVIDUAL PROTECTION: CONCEPTS AND TRENDS IN PRODUCT LIABILITY

Through the courts, government plays an adjudicative role in disputes be-tween the firm and private parties (consumers, employees, members of the public) — an influence on business outside of the visible rule-making role of government. In place of rules the courts rely on a vast body of prior cases. This body of earlier cases, or precedent, provides close continuity to the past and yet allows flexibility for the courts to interpret rights and re-sponsibilities between parties in the light of changing social and economic circumstances.

The law of redress of injuries to persons and private parties is termed *tort law,* and it resides within the judicial system administered by the states. The law of torts offers the advantage of decentralized evolution of the law and rulings close to local circumstances. On the other hand, it also allows substantial diversity and often leads to a lack of uniformity be-tween states. To a national firm operating in many states, diversity can be a source of confusion.

Tort law applies to a variety of situations involving the firm. Workers can sue a firm for violation of their rights as accepted in the body of the common law of torts in their state. In addition, workers and members of the public appear to be gaining increasing rights in the courts to compensation on health and safety questions.

One area of well-developed, court-based law pertains to the rights of consumers to sue a manufacturer for injury resulting from use of its products. This long-standing area of common law significantly affects business decision making. Because the courts appear to be placing stricter liabilities on business, this field of law will be reviewed in greater depth.

Product-related injuries do occur; they involve loss of income, mental or emotional stress, irreparable body damage, and perhaps even death. The field of product liability attempts to define principles for allocating responsibility for personal injuries and for determining financial compensation. The question is: Should consumers absorb major responsibility for injuries because of our belief in ultimate self-reliance in the choice of products and care in their use, or should public policy (through court action) redistribute responsibility for injury to corporations to spread the cost of reducing or insuring risk more widely across society?

Throughout this century the movement in court-based common law has been to redistribute risk and financial consequences from product injury away from individuals who have suffered injury and toward manufacturers of products. The courts increasingly hold business responsible for the marketing of nondefective, safe products, a trend that places new restraints on business decisions. Three major doctrines mark the evolution of judicial decision making concerning product liability: negligence, *res ipsa loquitur,* and strict liability.[10]

Negligence and the Manufacturer's Duty of Care

Under traditional concepts a reasonable person acting without intent to injure and without negligence was not at fault and could not be held liable for another's injury. The burden of proof was on the injured person to show negligence in the design or manufacture of a product that caused an injury. Major elements of the plaintiff's burden of proof were to show that the manufacturer had a duty of care in relation to the product user and that this duty was in fact violated. *Duty of care* means that the manufacturer should take the actions of a reasonably prudent person to avoid injury to another.

Res Ipsa Loquitur

If the system of negligence worked well where products were simple and the buyer-seller relationship was largely direct, it was bound to run into problems when confronted by more complicated distribution systems, larger manufacturing organizations to which the plaintiff did not have access, and more sophisticated products and services. The courts came to recognize the difficulty to the plaintiff of proving a valid claim under these circumstances and began to utilize a new doctrine called *res ipsa loquitur* ("the thing speaks for itself") when the plaintiff appeared to be disadvantaged by inaccessibility of information. For example, if an unopened soda bottle suddenly explodes in the hand of a waitress, causing injury, the defect in the product is obvious. Under this doctrine the courts have decided that the manufacturer has primary access to and control over the product's production and distribution and is in the best situation to prevent accidents. The waitress must still show the manufacturer had a duty of care toward her, but she is released of the obligation to prove that the manufacturer breached or violated this duty. Instead, under *res ipsa loquitur* the burden of proof shifts to the manufacturer to show it was not negligent in its duty of care to the product user. In other words the producer can defend itself by showing reasonable efforts to avoid product defects.

Strict Liability

A further development in product liability holds the manufacturer liable for injury caused by a defective product regardless of the reasonable measures that may have been taken to prevent defects. This concept, called *strict liability,* applies when both parties are innocent, and it places all responsibility for injury with the manufacturer. The strict liability doctrine is used when a person involved in a hazardous activity, such as blasting or keeping wild animals, causes injury to another without being negligent. The court's inclination to hold the initiator of the activity responsible has now been applied to the relationship between business and consumers.

The doctrine of strict business liability for product injuries first appeared in a minority view in *Escola* v. *Coca-Cola,* a California case in 1944.[11] Although expressing a minority view in this case, one judge stated that business is best suited to reduce the risks of defective products and therefore should, as a matter of public policy, be held strictly liable for product-related injuries.

> Even if there is no negligence . . . public policy demands that responsibility be fixed whenever it will most effectively reduce the hazard to life and health inherent in defective products that reach the market. . . . It is to the public interest to discourage the marketing of products having defects that are a menace to the public. If such products nevertheless find their way into the market, it is to the public interest to place the responsibility for whatever injury they may cause upon the manufacturer, who, even if he is not negligent in the manufacture of the product, is responsible for its reaching the market.[12]

In 1963 these beliefs became the majority court opinion in *Greenman* v. *Yuba Power Products, Inc.,* 59 Cal. 2nd S7, 377 897 (1963), which involved a home power tool manufactured by Yuba. In this case the injured plaintiff, Mr. Greenman, was able to prove the tool was defective when a block of wood he was working on flew out of the machine, injuring his head. The court ruled that negligence on the part of Yuba was not relevant to the case; Yuba was held liable for injury caused by its product simply because it proved to have a defect in its ordinary intended use.[13] Yuba is generally considered a landmark case that has profoundly influenced other court-based product liability cases. Today a plaintiff generally needs to prove only that a product was defective in its ordinary use; manufacturers cannot use absence of negligence as a defense. In adopting a strict liability doctrine, the courts have attempted to allocate risk to provide maximum incentives for firms to produce and market safe products.

By adopting this view the courts have placed additional restraints on business. Whether the seller could not have foreseen a particular injury or whether the plaintiff obviously knew of a danger inherent in the product has been judged as irrelevant to the firm's liability. That a manufacturer changed a product after it caused an injury may be used to show the original product had a design defect. In addition, a question arises as to whether the courts will continue to require that the product be used for its intended purpose when causing an injury. For example, one court is reported to have found a perfume company liable for injury when a boy's neck was burned as his friend tried to scent a lighted candle by pouring perfume over it.[14] The later decision questions whether an injury must be due to a defect in the product. In a recent departure from traditional limits of product liability claims, the California Supreme Court (Insert 6.B) declared that a plaintiff is not required to identify the particular manufacturer of a product that caused injury to recover damages. Instead, producer liabilities were assigned on the basis of market share at the time of the product's use.

These developments in product liability suggest a dramatic change in the environment of business. Previously, manufacturer negligence had to be proved by the injured party. Later under *res ipsa loquitur,* the manufacturer had to show it was not negligent. Now, negligence is rarely an issue in product liability since the strict liability doctrine places responsibility on the manufacturer for injuries arising from product defects. A manufacturer may become liable for injuries from any use or misuse of the product or for injuries where the product may not even have been produced by the defendant company.

Predictably, these changes have caused heated debate on the need for federal legislation to rationalize the product liability situation. Wisconsin Senator Bob Kasten has introduced a legislative proposal that would substitute the standard of *reasonable prudence* for the current strict liability standard in instances where the quality of a product's design is under ques-

Insert 6.B

THE CONTINUING REVOLUTION IN PRODUCT LIABILITY

Regardless of the increasing degree to which manufacturers are held responsible for injuries or illnesses caused by their products, it has still been a tenet of product liability cases that the plaintiff be able to identify the specific manufacturer of the product that caused injury. A court case in California, which the U.S. Supreme Court declined to review, reverses this long-standing doctrine and "has rocked the legal community."

The case involves DES, a hormone drug prescribed in the 1950s by doctors in order to prevent miscarriage. Later the drug was discovered by scientists to be associated with cancer in the daughters of some women who had taken it during pregnancy. In response to these findings, the FDA banned the drug.

In the mid-70s a woman whose mother had taken the drug 26 years before was found to have a tumor in her bladder. Because of the long lapse of time, this plaintiff was unable to show which specific company manufactured the drug taken by her mother. Nevertheless she sued the five manufacturers of the drug who controlled most of the market at the time, and the California Supreme Court held that her inability to identify the single producer should not stand in the way of her legitimate claim. The court cited a previous case in which two hunters were held responsible for shooting a third hunter, when it was not clear which bullet hit him, because it was obvious that one of the two had.

Legal experts expressed some difference of opinion about the meaning of the Supreme Court's decision not to review the case, but most were unanimous in assigning major significance to this departure from prior case law. The ruling appeared to open the courts to numerous related claims, as well as to raise some difficult questions about relevant market definitions and required shares. There are already reported to be thousands of DES cases in the courts, and it is certain that this California decision will affect cases dealing with analogous circumstances.

SOURCE: "Product-Liability Law Is in Flux as Attorneys Test a Radical Doctrine," *Wall Street Journal,* December 30, 1980, pp. 1, 4.

tion or the manufacturer did not expressly note a flaw in its product.[15] It would be the responsibility of the consumer to prove that a firm did not demonstrate *reasonableness* or *prudence* when it designed a particular product for the market. Under the proposed bill a firm may be shown to be unreasonable or imprudent if it is demonstrated in court (1) that the firm actually knew the product was "unreasonably dangerous" or (2) that a reasonably prudent firm would have known that use of the product exposed the consumer to an unreasonable level of risk.[16]

Hailed as enlightened product liability legislation by some, Senator Kasten's proposal would require judges rather than juries to decide an appropriate level of damages to be awarded the plaintiff and allow lawsuits only for two years after a product was known to have caused an injury to the plaintiff. Additionally, companies would be prohibited from holding a manufacturer liable for a defect in a capital good after a 25 year period had elapsed.[17] Underlying the above product liability qualifications is the belief, on the part of some congressional members, that existing product liability standards are inequitable and inflict an unnecessary hardship on manufacturers.

Product Liability: How Effective a Control?

The power of individual consumers to recover damages for product injury has been significantly enhanced by the historical development in product liability; court-based law now appears to play a significant role as a decentralized and private system of consumer protection. Increased responsibility placed on manufacturers should exert a force for heightened managerial attention to factors that may cause consumer injury. There are specific actions that firms can take in response to their emerging responsibilities in product liability. First, they can take extreme care in the development of products from the standpoint of user safety and seek to market products safe in design. Second, management can stress the importance of strong and reliable quality control, so that products designed to be safe are actually safe when produced. Finally, management can take steps to warn users of any dangers that are not open and obvious by providing instructions on use and warnings to consumers.

"Risk" insurance is seen by some as a possible means for avoiding the problems arising from litigation and as a substitute for command-and-control regulation in certain situations. Implementation of this alternative would require companies producing, transporting, testing, or being otherwise involved with products/services that pose potentially hazardous risks to consumers or the environment to obtain insurance protection commensurate with the level of risk associated with their product or service. Insert 6.C outlines some potential benefits and difficulties arising from the substitution of insurance for traditional regulation or litigation.

The threat of litigation alone may be a powerful preventive force on the behavior of manufacturers. To the extent that internal practices of product design and manufacturing control are strengthened and improved to avoid litigation, the system of product liability acts as an effective private system of social control in consumer interests. Following the $125 million verdict against Ford Motor Company concerning a flawed Pinto gas tank, a governmental task force determined that producers stepped up their ef-

Insert 6.C

RISK INSURANCE: ONE METHOD FOR INTEGRATING GOALS OF SAFETY AND CREATIVE CORPORATE RISK TAKING

"Risk" insurance has been considered a possible alternative to direct regulation and product liability litigation under certain conditions. In effect, requiring a company to insure its risky products or services forces the firm to assign a monetary value to any potentially hazardous operation in which it might wish to become involved and guarantee that compensation is available to those harmed by corporate risk taking. Such a requirement, in theory, would not stifle desirable corporate risk taking as direct regulation might but would allow a means for companies to engage in risky endeavors at a cost. As the insurer, not the firm, would potentially bear the responsibility for compensation should the product or service cause harm, insurance would likely be refused to an irresponsible company or for an extremely hazardous endeavor. Otherwise, the risk of the endeavor would be reflected in the size of the insurance payment.

Risk insurance is a well-established practice in some areas. Health, automobile, and life insurers all incorporate multiple risk factors into their insurance. However, the ability of risk insurance to eliminate undesirable risk taking while allowing companies to engage in some potentially risky, yet beneficial, endeavors rests on a number of assumptions:

- The degree of risk can be accurately determined, measured, and quantified by the insurer and the firm incurring the risk;
- The appropriate level of "risk" responsibility can be individually assigned in situations where a number of different companies are involved at different stages of the risky endeavor;
- Insurers will not underestimate their potential liabilities in an effort to obtain large premiums from companies involved in extremely hazardous activities;
- Some level of risk in the insured company's endeavor is acceptable to the public;
- The insurer is capable of underwriting all the costs associated with the occurrence of an accident;
- The insurance rate premiums are substantial enough to deter companies from undertaking undesirably risky endeavors; and
- Companies unwilling or unable to obtain insurance will refrain from embarking on a risky endeavor in the absence of direct regulation.

While risk insurance as an alternative to command-and-control regulation has proved successful in some areas, the potential problems of this alternative multiply rapidly when implementation of this concept is envisioned on a broad scale. Many of the possible problems arising from corporate

Insert 6.C continued

risk taking are not well defined, much less quantified. For example, it is very difficult to assess the risks associated with the unintended release of newly developed, toxic chemicals into the atmosphere, and appropriate compensation for damage caused by chemical exposure may be even harder to define. Therefore, this alternative may be most attractive in situations where the risks have been fairly well established and the cost associated with undesirable risk taking (expensive insurance premiums) is perceived by companies as less desirable than the possible benefits to be derived from the risky endeavor. Additionally, insurance, in lieu of regulation, may provide a solution for situations in which the risk increases dramatically in relation to the number of firms involved in a particular activity. Firms with poor safety records would find it difficult to pay higher risk premiums and remain competitive with more conscientious firms.

SOURCE: Joseph Ferreira, Jr., "Promoting Safety through Insurance," in *Social Regulation,* ed. Eugene Bardach and Robert A. Kagan (San Francisco, Calif.: Institute for Contemporary Studies, 1982), 12:267–88.

---

forts to control product quality and improve product designs; it was believed that avoidance of similar costly product liability litigation was one of the producers' prime motivators.[18]

In addition to multimillion dollar settlements, courts have demonstrated a willingness to increase the size of awards to plaintiffs in more typical product liability lawsuits, and product users have become more willing to initiate the litigation process. Product liability lawsuits appeared in court ten times more often in the 1970s as compared with the 1960s; the average product liability award in the mid-1970s totaled $221,000.[19]

However, to the extent that particular businesses react to product liability exposure by insuring risks without initiating, or being required by the insurer to initiate, risk reduction measures, the result will simply be escalation in the cost of liability insurance and in the price of the products. Medical doctors, fearful of costly malpractice suits, have opted to order exhaustive medical testing for patients — in many cases, raising the costs of medical care without noticeably improving the quality of health care provided. One study concluded that in 1975 alone the costs of these "defensive" medical practices raised the U.S. health care bill by $2.3 billion.[20]

It is also true that legal action serves to claim compensation for the injured party only after an injury. While the threat of injury claims can be a reforming and preventive force, its impact may often be uneven, long-term, and ultimately uncertain. Especially where a person has been killed by an unsafe product, no amount of compensation helps *that* person. In addition, in legal action individuals assume the burden of initiating a suit; therefore, lack of money or knowledge may prevent their benefiting from the existence of legal rights. Moreover, reliance on litigation may create an incentive for suits to be filed that have no realistic claim for compensation. Encouraging long-shot chances for favorable decisions contributes nothing beyond manufacturer harassment. Reliance on legal action as a primary device of consumer protection has major drawbacks for both consumers and producers.

MARKET-BASED INCENTIVES IN ENVIRONMENTAL PROTECTION

Environmental quality does not lend itself to market pricing, as do consumer wants and labor supply; nor is there a well-developed body of business liability in common law for environmental protection. Yet, if no costs are associated with polluting the air and the water, with spoiling the natural setting, or with unsafe disposal of toxic wastes, the environment will be consumed freely, even to the point of exhaustion.

For these reasons it is not surprising that environmental protection has been a major focus of regulatory effort and rule making in recent years. Lacking other mechanisms to influence private actions, the public sector has resorted to a high level of command-and-control regulation. It is also not surprising that advocates for business have tried to introduce more flexibility and efficiency into the government's regulatory approach by seeking market-based policies for environmental protection.

The goal of public policy in environmental protection is to assign external social costs of deterioration to the private parties that generate pollution. The public sector seeks to ensure that producers take account of the actual value society places on clean air, a natural environment, healthy water resources, recreation, and so forth. In other words public policy confronts the problem of designing a system that incorporates the external costs of corporate action into the decisions of the firm.

Deficiencies of Rule-Oriented Regulation

Criticisms of most social regulatory programs are numerous and frequent: they have a missionary zeal for a single cause that ignores costs they impose, they conflict with and subvert other national objectives, and they harass and handicap business. But do they achieve the objective of internalizing external costs?

Generally, one would have to conclude that external costs are internalized, although the means are coercive and may create as many problems as they solve. Some additional costs to producers are passed on to consumers in the form of higher prices and to the public in the form of higher taxes to support regulatory agencies. Attempting to achieve social goals of health, safety, and environmental quality results in everyone bearing some of the cost.

One of the more serious challenges to regulation by standardized rules is inefficiency; the same pollution standards are imposed on all producers regardless of their volume of pollution, their manufacturing processes, or their costs of pollution control. Greater pollution reduction for the least amount of dollars invested might be gained by greatly reducing emissions from many low-volume polluters whose operations can be cheaply modified than by moderately reducing pollution from a few high-volume polluters who would face huge investment costs. If interindustry differences in the cost of controlling a particular pollutant vary significantly, then uniform standards for all polluters are bound to be inefficient: industries with lower costs of control will be asked to reduce pollution less than the most efficient level, and industries with higher control costs will be forced to reduce pollution more than overall efficiency dictates.

The main public policy issue is flexibility: Is it possible to design a more cost-efficient system of regulation and thereby get more improvement in environmental quality for the same cost or to obtain the same level of protection at less cost? The following descriptions are two experimental attempts to answer this question.

Pollution Charges

Pollution charges are one proposed means of internalizing the social costs of pollution.[21] Under this policy, fees are charged to polluters; those producing more pollution or more dangerous pollutants pay higher fees. The incentive to control pollution stems from the producer's motivation to reduce assigned fees.

Why is this system considered a cost-efficient method of pollution control? If charges can be assigned on the basis of firms' relative costs of pollution control, it is possible to place the highest fees on firms that can achieve greatest cleanup for the lowest expenditure. Thus the environmental benefits of a given investment for pollution control are maximized. This policy contrasts with a rule-oriented system requiring all firms to implement the same control technology or to achieve the same level of emissions.

While attractive theoretically, the pollution charge approach has several difficulties.[22] First, the charge system raises the question of the goal of the policy: Is the goal to achieve a short-term standard with the least social investment, or is the goal to achieve the lowest cost per pound of emission controlled? A second difficulty is that use of pollution charges requires knowledge of individual firms' cost control. Gaining and maintaining detailed information of this type across a range of pollutants would constitute a tremendous bureaucratic endeavor. Third, establishing actual charge schedules would involve considerable guesswork. If the charges were too low to motivate cleanup, they might be hard to raise; if they were too high, they would be inefficient. Fourth, it may not be seen as fair to place the burden of pollution control on a few firms simply because they have lower control costs. These problems indicate that distributing the costs of improvement involves equity judgments that are more political than economic decisions, and pollution charges may not be politically popular or feasible.

Marketable Rights to Pollute: Bubbles, Offsets, and Banking Pollution Reductions

What would happen if the government established an acceptable level of pollution for a given pollutant in a given area, printed certificates or rights to emit this pollutant in small amounts, and held an auction in which the rights were sold to the highest bidders? In concept, at least, those firms for whom cleanup was very expensive would bid up the price beyond the willingness to pay of firms for whom cleanup was cheaper. Firms not owning rights would be faced with installing controls to reduce their pollution, and firms possessing the rights could go ahead and pollute. Society would be well-off since acceptable levels of pollution would be achieved, and reduction would be obtained by reducing pollution where the costs of control were least. No detailed knowledge of costs by the private sector would be necessary, and firm-by-firm pollution rules would be eliminated.

Because of its greater simplicity, variations of this concept are being utilized and tested on a limited basis. The first of these is the widely touted "bubble" concept, in which emission standards are applied to an imaginary bubble placed over a large plant rather than to every single smokestack or source of air pollution in the facility. Thus the plant is able to trade more pollution from one stack against less from another, which encourages the firm to reduce pollution at the points where it is cheapest. In a sense this constitutes a system of marketable pollution rights underneath an umbrella — some sources are given rights to pollute when others must drastically reduce emissions. It encourages cost efficiency because the firm is encouraged to meet the overall standard in its least-cost manner. Since December of 1979 the Environmental Protection Agency (EPA) has allowed firms to apply this concept in control of airborne emissions. By mid-1984 approximately 200 bubbles, in 27 states, were either on corporate drawing boards or had been implemented. The EPA has projected that corporate savings from proposed or actual bubbles, as of 1984, totaled over $702 million.[23]

Another variation of this concept has been developed by the EPA to permit the economic development of areas that are not in compliance with air quality standards. For example, suppose air quality in Nashville is already poorer than public standards permit and a large industrial firm that would add 5 percent more air pollution wishes to locate there. In the interest of economic development, the community wishes to have the plant, but it also desires not to worsen air quality. Under a policy of "offsets" the new firm in Nashville may persuade existing firms to reduce their pollution until air quality is better or equal to what it was before the new plant opened. [Thus existing facilities may act to offset the added pollution by a new plant.] In addition, the new firm may be permitted to pay for the cost of pollution reduction in existing firms if these reductions are less expensive than further reducing its own pollution.

Similar to the bubble concept, this practice allows standards to be applied to a large geographical area instead of being applied merely to individual sources (see Insert 6.D). It also allows some firms to pollute more — to have rights to pollute — and others less, and it sets up market-oriented decision mechanisms that tend to allocate the costs of incremental pollution reduction to firms having the lowest costs of cleanup. In addition, since 1979 firms have been allowed to "bank" pollution reductions for possible future sale — a system that for the first time may offer an incentive for firms to reduce emissions below a specified level. By October 1981, over 1,500 offset transactions had been identified by the EPA, with prices for some pollutants running as high as $1,000 per ton. Some 20 states had incorporated some level of banking provisions in their state implementation programs.[24]

Insert 6.D

BENEFITS FROM FLEXIBLE REGULATION

Growing interests in flexible regulation are illustrated by the following examples of companies experimenting with "bubbles" and "offsets."

Applications of the bubble concept:

- A study done for duPont concluded that the "bubble" concept could apply to 35 of the company's 100-plus domestic plants. In 1980 dollars, pollution control costs were estimated to be reduced to $55 million from $136 million owing to the different control strategy. One plant in Deepwater, New Jersey, now eliminates 80 percent of hydrocarbon emissions for $20 million a year; use of the bubble concept would permit capturing 89 percent of these emissions at a cost of $5 million.
- The 3M company may find a solution to its problem of hydrocarbon emissions in its Bristol, Pennsylvania, plant by combining technology and flexible regulation. Replacing a hydrocarbon solvent with a new solventless process on the coating of surfaces of several of its pressure-sensitive tapes, the company may make smokestack equipment unnecessary on three of its four production lines. The products to which the new solventless process do not apply will need one smokestack, which owing to a bubble over the entire plant, is unlikely to need a control.

Insert 6.D   continued

Applications of the "offset" policy

- In order to allow General Motors Corporation to build a plant in Oklahoma City without placing the area out of compliance for air quality, sources of pollution from other companies had to be found. In this case four oil companies donated hydrocarbon offsets of more than 5,000 tons per year by shutting down storage tanks or equipping them with floating roofs or vapor-recovery systems.
- In New Braunfels, Texas, General Portland Cement Co. wanted to install a coal-fired preheater in its cement plant, a process that would add 950 tons of particulate pollution a year. In order to gain an offset, General Portland was able to pay for installing bag filters on the rock crushers of another company in the same area. This action reduced particulate emissions by over 1,000 tons per year, allowing the new preheater to be installed.

SOURCE: Donald E. Veraska, "EPA the Regulatory Innovator," *Chemical Business,* July 18, 1980, pp. 41–46.

What is the ultimate potential of market-based incentives as a regulatory strategy? The experiments reported above are encouraging and may gain a greater role in environmental policy. It is clear, however, that only limited experiments have taken place to date within a large and extensive system of command-and-control regulation. Market-oriented schemes have noteworthy advantages, but they are unlikely to settle all issues. For example, they do not resolve critical issues of establishing the acceptable levels of emissions or eliminating inequities in the distribution of pollution reduction. Furthermore, the social acceptability of paying for a license to pollute may be doubtful. As these issues gain clarification through political processes, the ultimate role of economic incentives in environmental policy will become clearer.

While it is not a market-based approach, another regulatory policy that attempts to address the difficulties of equitable pollution regulation in a flexible manner has been termed *tiered regulation*. Discussed in Insert 6.E, tiered regulation illustrates one method for overcoming some of the problems associated with inflexible regulatory policy.

MANAGEMENT AND ORGANIZATIONAL IMPLICATIONS OF HEALTH AND SAFETY ISSUES

Discussions of the last two chapters have examined the problems of health, safety, and environmental policy from a variety of perspectives. The last

Insert 6.E

TIERED REGULATIONS: AN ANSWER TO REGULATORY WOES?

Applying uniform regulatory standards to particular industries holds an obvious attraction due to its basic simplicity. Moreover, applying one regulatory standard across the board to each and every company within an industry may arguably be the "fairest" way to accomplish regulatory goals. However, others have argued persuasively that "tiered" regulations may actually serve societal goals more effectively in many instances.

Under the "tiered" concept, companies, industrial activities, substances, etc., may be classified by a regulatory agency and regulated differently. One common classification used pertains to the age of a facility. For example, older power plants are required to comply with less stringent pollution regulations than new power plants. One rationale for the tiering of air pollution regulations within this industry touches a very sensitive economic nerve. Older power plants were not physically designed to accommodate the newest anti-pollution equipment and would be forced to shut down; leading to increased unemployment in the surrounding communities.

In other instances tiered regulations have been applied to different industrial activities. After determining that workers in the textile industry faced the risk of contracting brown lung disease caused by exposure to cotton dust, OSHA enacted regulations to reduce the workers' exposure. However, it was also determined contraction of brown lung disease varied by job task. Application of a single strict regulation across job categories — regardless of the job's "risk" level — would cost the industry $808 million annually. Ultimately cotton dust exposure was regulated by job category; causing textile workers to be exposed to different levels of dust but to equal levels of health risk. Application of tiered regulations in this instance cost the cotton makers one-fourth the amount associated with a uniform standard.

These examples suggest that tiered regulations may be the panacea for all of society's regulatory woes. A logical question arises as to why tiered regulation is not used more frequently by government agencies. Outlined below are some of the *disincentives* associated with tiered regulatory systems:

- Prohibitive data collection costs faced by new agencies attempting to predetermine the costs/benefits of various levels of regulation;
- Implementation of tiered regulations requires a higher level of agency expertise and a larger agency staff; both are scarce resources in light of limited agency budgets;
- Lack of a "natural" constituency lobbying for tiered regulations in certain situations;

Insert 6.E   continued

- There is the increased likelihood of litigation initiated by companies objecting to their classification;
- Easily determinable or appropriate classifications are lacking (the availability of medical records reduced the potentially subjective measurement of brown lung "risk"); and
- Legislatively imposed time constraints limit agencies to *prompt* rather than *effective* regulatory action.

Therefore, it may be logically concluded that tiered regulations will remain underused to the extent that these disincentives outweigh any political incentives to implement such a regulatory policy. In the previous examples it seems quite likely that the cotton industry brought considerable pressure to bear on government to reduce their regulatory compliance costs, and government has always been concerned with maintaining or increasing employment levels within local communities.

SOURCE: Timothy J. Sullivan, "Tailoring Government Response to Diversity," in *Social Regulation: Strategies for Reform*, ed. Eugene Bardach and Robert A. Kagan (San Francisco, Calif.: Institute for Contemporary Studies, 1982) 5:119–38.

chapter reviewed the nature and growth of government regulation, public attitudes that have generated governmental involvement, and the unintended consequences of rules for health and safety protection. This chapter has addressed policy alternatives other than "command and control" to influence business behavior. The search has been for a more flexible means to increase the freedom of both those who want greater personal choice *and* those who want freedom from controllable injury and illness.

One dominant fact must be pointed out in this process of analysis: regardless of the specific debates and controversies, health, safety, and environmental quality constitute a substantial, institutionalized, and ongoing dimension of the business environment. While the exact role of government may be under dispute, the existence of a new and tightly drawn destiny between business and society is not in doubt.

Identifying flexible, cost-effective, and market-oriented public policies are important problems for business and government. Yet, regardless of the changing features of public policy, business must still manage effectively in an environment that is radically different from the past. New concepts of management and organization involve reorienting the corporation to this external environment. These notions are not primarily addressed to whether scrubbers should be installed or whether the product safety staff should be strengthened. Rather, the concepts involve a broader approach of how to organize and manage planning and decision making where external health, safety, and environmental factors are significant constraints and pose unanticipated problems in conducting normal business activities. The following are several examples and descriptions of concepts and practices that appear to be aimed at meeting this adaptive requirement.

REGULAR CONDUCT OF BUSINESS ACTIVITY

External restraints on business presently represent a "whole new ball game" for corporate management. A good example is the scope of environmental requirements pertaining to new plant construction. In 1979 John Quarles, a former EPA administrator, conducted a survey of federal regulatory approvals necessary for the siting and construction of new industrial plants or expansions of existing plants.[25] The regulations, spawned from six major pieces of environmental legislation, were not only numerous and complicated, but Quarles argues that the degree of uncertainty and delay cumulatively introduced by these regulations has created an entirely new and unfamiliar setting for management decision making. Quarles states that "the experience of companies in obtaining necessary approvals to commence construction on new projects in even the recent past may be entirely misleading as to the proposals for obtaining similar approval on future projects."[26]

In other words, in this and perhaps other areas of corporate action, the past is not a good indication of the future. New management practices and attitudes may be necessary just to be able to make the same investments that were made in earlier periods. The most obvious impact is the increased lead time — a minimum of two or three years for new plant construction to begin — and the requirement this places on the firm for more advanced planning. In addition, new information about environmental impacts is required in advance of construction: care must be taken to avoid violation of one regulation while modifying plans to accommodate another, and approvals granted early must not be allowed to expire before all approvals are obtained. The whole process adds time constraints and demands on the planning capabilities of the firm.

A second major problem is the high degree of uncertainty introduced by an approval process that may ultimately result in canceling a project after years of effort and millions of dollars in costs. New or expanded plant decisions now face a greater degree of ambiguity and risk, especially in their early stages. Plant capacity modification may be necessary, or plant location reevaluated. Management is required to obtain and incorporate environmental information into the functions of research and development, financial planning, and corporate and business planning itself. As Quarles points out, the mastery of the uncertainties and ambiguities in the new environment of management demand a broader input from nontraditional sources of information:

> Top management should recognize that *additional elements are now needed for effective decision-making* and management. New inputs are required to provide a full foundation for critical decisions. These cover the wide range of pertinent environmental, regulatory, and technological factors. Monitoring of legal and regulatory trends must be conducted to spot future problems. Similarly the local political climate must be constantly re-evaluated. Finally, decisions to construct new facilities cannot be relied upon as an answer to corporate needs until final regulatory approvals have been obtained, and contingency plans for alternative facilities must be maintained.[27]

Society greatly needs the products, productive efficiencies, and jobs that are created by new plant construction and existing plant expansion. At the same time, society has developed regulatory obstacles that create substantial delays, uncertainties, and difficulties to such industrial development. In a sense the public has thrown a challenge at corporate management to pursue economic development at a new threshold of awareness and respect for the interdependence of economics and environment. This challenge may strain the management and organizing capacities of individuals and corporations; at a minimum it calls for the development of skills for managing additional complexity and uncertainty. The new managerial environment in many health, safety, and environmental areas demands a faster rate of learning and a higher level of professionalism just to maintain existing levels of economic activity.

Anticipatory Management

Besides "staying even" with the imposing regulatory environment, some companies are attempting to anticipate development, not in legislative and regulatory affairs alone but in the moods and expectations of society that may become translated into crises of business and society and potentially into public policy. Two significant examples are the Environmental Policy Staff at Monsanto Company and the Office of Consumer Affairs at Western Union Telegraph Company.

First, as a result of a decision by the Food and Drug Administration to reverse an earlier approval of Monsanto's plastic bottle, Cycle-Safe, the company instituted a system of developing and managing a strategy for the company's impact on its environment (see Insert 6.F).[28] This system consists of a network of industrial hygienists, epidemiologists, physicians, toxicologists, and environmental engineers — more than 800 people mostly reporting to the line managers throughout the corporation. The system also includes a mandatory technical and environmental review of every project above $5 million, a team of analytical scientists to scrutinize the company's

Insert 6.F

MONSANTO'S CYCLE-SAFE BOTTLE: A FAILURE THAT SUCCEEDED

In the late 1960s one of the Monsanto's research capabilities was in the area of developing low permeability polymers, plastic materials that would not absorb or transmit liquids. Based upon their work in this area of chemistry, the company saw the opportunity to develop and introduce the first plastic soft drink container in the United States. The product was designed to be refillable and thus contribute to environmental improvement by reducing the need for disposal. In the course of this product's development the company pursued an open relationship with external groups, namely, the FDA and environmentalists, and did extensive chemical testing and research on analytical technique itself. In June of 1975 the Cycle-Safe bottle was introduced into the marketplace.

Less than two years later the bottle was dead. The FDA had received a study showing carcinogenic effects of a long-term rat feeding program using the same polymer — acrylonitrile — as used in the Cycle-Safe bottle. The FDA, apparently under pressure from environmentalist and health groups, reversed itself and banned the chemical from use in food packaging.

Several lessons for Monsanto are reported from this incident:

1. Planning for the product with respect to external forces took place with close attention to preventing environmental hazard. Less emphasis was placed on health risks that were not as much in the public eye at the time. In other words the company failed to anticipate an emerging issue and wrongly projected the existing environment into the future.
2. Similarly, the experience taught the company that scientific techniques are also a moving target. Advances in the methods of toxicology and analysis were made over the life of the project so that new data emerged after the company had screened the project for health effects and after FDA approval. An officer of the company states that "extensions of state-of-the-art scientific techniques must be taken into consideration over the course of a long project life. As analytical methods continue to improve, more . . . problem chemicals will be detected in previously acceptable products."
3. The inherent ambiguity of this additional information is another lesson from the case. While much more data may be available, there is anything but a consensus about what they mean for human health. Finding trace chemicals in daily products tells nothing about human risks and hazards. Yet within this ambiguity, managers, legislators, regulators, and other interested parties must find a rational way of making decisions.

Insert 6.F   continued

4. Because of this experience the company organized to bring to a focal
    point interactions with governmental bodies, scientific developments in
    analytical technology, and product safety testing. This body, an Envi-
    ronmental Policy Staff, seeks to incorporate long-range environmental
    planning into doing business. Through this staff and other mecha-
    nisms, the company is attempting to realize a systems approach to in-
    novation that includes social, cultural, intellectual, managerial, and po-
    litical components. If this concept can be realized, then the Cycle-Safe
    bottle was truly a success.

SOURCE: Monte C. Throdahl, "When Planning Isn't Enough — The
Story of the Cycle-Safe Bottle" (Presentation to the 1980 Annual Meeting
of the Industrial Research Institute, Tarpan Springs, Florida, May 6, 1980).

---

chemicals for even trace amounts of dangerous substances, and a formalized three-tiered testing procedure for the health and safety of new products. The purpose of this commitment of personnel and resources is
threefold:

1. To develop a surprise-free understanding of environmental issues that
    impact, or will impact, on the corporation;
2. To be able to deal effectively and efficiently with crisis where there is
    failure to anticipate; and
3. To improve communication of responsible corporate actions to em-
    ployees as well as the external public.[29]

A senior vice-president of the company refers to this system as an attempt
to institutionalize self-policing or internal "whistleblowing" in the company.
The idea is to gain as much information as possible about the wider ramifications of products and processes to foresee risks and control all facets of
the company's actions. Monsanto wants to be able to change materials,
redesign processes, and terminate or initiate projects based on all relevant
information at an early stage. It is seeking to internalize health, safety, and
environmental values into management decision making. This additional
effort and cost might be expected to be well returned in greater flexibility
— few costly decisions reversed by outside pressures for other than economic reasons and perhaps the identification of social needs and corresponding products that would not otherwise be seen.

     At stake in this thinking at Monsanto is the role of the corporation
in society. It is a view that respects the legitimacy of health and safety values
as corporate responsibilities, and it is a private, market-based response to

an interdependent society. The broad rationale for the company's movement in this direction is the following:

> In a world that daily is becoming smaller, wiser and more interdependent, no segment of society can operate independently of the others.
>
> Citizenship is as essential to a corporation's future as bottom line profits. Therefore, it is to our benefit to encourage citizenship not from the outside, not from the board room, but actively and knowingly from every level and every location of the corporation.[30]

Monsanto appears to be elevating environmental responsiveness to a level of corporate policy and systematic practices that embody a concept or philosophy of management and society.

Another company that is reportedly undertaking a similar development in the area of consumer responsiveness is the Western Union Telegraph Company.[31] According to Vice-President for Consumer Affairs Mary Gardiner Jones, the company similarly aims "to increase the ultimate success of the company by heightening the management sensitivity and responsiveness to consumer needs and expectations and to ensure that the practices and policies of the corporation respond to the needs and expectations of the consuming public."[32]

This objective is pursued in several ways at Western Union. First, there is an attempt to get valid and reliable information about consumer needs and levels of satisfaction into the decision-making processes of the corporation. This is being done by systematizing consumer complaints coming to the corporation, conducting regular and special surveys of the attitudes and needs of customers, employees, and complainants, and researching the performance of the company's complaint handling system. In addition, the office conducts audits of the degree of consumer satisfaction with new services and programs, evaluating reactions to advertising, credit, guarantees, and various promotional practices. It institutes corrective action programs of employee education and development in consumer relations and implementation of organizational procedures for handling customer problems (see Insert 6.G). It may involve consumer education programs as well. Finally, the office aspires to make management more directly and intensely aware of the realities of the consumer movement and of the values of consumerists. Through consumer-executive encounter sessions or participation of consumer representatives in the early stages of company decisions, the goal is to find a way to join external consumer interests with internal decision making.

For what benefits would these activities be undertaken? The potential payoffs are flexibility gained from an understanding of the broader

Insert 6.G

CONDITIONS FOR SUCCESS OF AN OFFICE OF CONSUMER AFFAIRS

Consumer affairs can signify a wide variety of activities ranging from complaint handling and public relations to a policy and planning function that is integral to the company's decision making. This latter role is the aspiration of the consumer affairs unit at Western Union; its director, Mary Gardiner Jones, outlines the key elements for success in such an office.

1. The office should report directly to the president or executive vice-president and have its own budget-initiating authority. Top-level support is vital for developing and implementing priorities and for getting the work of consumer affairs understood and accepted by the entire organization.
2. A corollary to positioning the office is having access to information: knowing about projects at an early stage; having input into policies that bear upon consumers (as most do in some form); and having contracts and forums for identifying problems and educating managers. Access to information clearly depends on top-level support, but also requires an ability to maintain good relations with relevant departments and managers.
3. The influence of consumer affairs also depends on the ability to quantify information. The impact of new products or procedures on consumer relations, the relationship of customer satisfaction or dissatisfaction to sales, and the expected benefits from service changes are areas in which documentation and quantification are needed for management decisions. The consumer affairs specialist can serve to make explicit the short-term expense and revenue versus the long-term benefits of consumer satisfaction of various actions.
4. **Getting the greatest advantage from a consumer affairs effort involves developing performance standards for service quality and customer satisfaction that are incorporated into the performance measurement system of all managers. The difficulty of formulating a valid, meaningful, and long-term performance system is substantial, and the challenge of meaningful integration into management appraisal is great. However, this level of acceptance indicates a company's desire to make consumer relations an integral, rather than a tangential, element of its business concept.**

SOURCE: Mary Gardiner Jones, "The Consumer Affairs Office: Essential Elements in Corporate Policy and Planning," *California Management Review* 20 (Summer 1978): 70–77. Used with permission.

ramifications of a product or service and the ability to avoid costly delays, reversals, and acrimonious relations with outside groups. Drawing upon surveys of consumer and business attitudes, Mary Gardiner Jones argues for integrating management awareness with the consumer environment:

> The free enterprise system is not in question, as some believe. What consumers are saying is that they do not trust business. Corporate managers must understand this, as it is critical to their attitudes toward the consumer movement and all that the consumer movement is telling business about how it is performing in the marketplace.[33]

A CONCLUDING COMMENT: RESPONSES TO HEALTH AND SAFETY PROBLEMS

This chapter has attempted to draw out some of the wider interactions between business and the health, safety, and environmental movements. Governmental policy, involving both implementation of legislation through regulation and policies written into case law through the judicial system, has become a major external force on business decisions. The discussion of government regulation in this chapter has focused on the search for market-related means of influencing business behavior. The role of choice and exit was discussed and disclosure regulation was reviewed; product liability was examined as a private system of incentives for safer design of products and stronger controls in manufacturing; and pollution changes and marketable rights were described as market-based approaches to environmental protection.

The issue of consumer protection appears to derive, in part, from an inability of individuals to gather and process relevant information about products and services. It is little wonder that business-government relationships have changed if, in reality, economic and technological advancements challenge individuals' capabilities and confidence to act in their own best interests. Possible solutions to this problem deserve long and deep rethinking.

The last section of this chapter focused the discussion on corporate management where policies and actions of several companies seek to integrate external concerns with internal decision making. Even after all is said and done about the role of government, science, the media, the courts, cost-benefit, effluent charges and marketable rights, consumer freedom, disclosure regulation, advertising, and product liability, a question about the role of corporate policy remains: To what extent can corporations act to incorporate external values in their decision-making processes? Examples from Monsanto and Western Union are experimental responses that address the general level of guiding and directing the corporation. They describe practical, goal-seeking, action-oriented systems that aim to enhance the corporation's success in a new environmental context.

These particular policies and practices may succeed, fail, or be modified in various ways. Their significance lies in the effort and intention of these companies and their managers to explore and experiment with means for internalizing external values and costs in the interests of both firm and society. These efforts compose an important, private, and decentralized approach to resolving the same problems to which a spate of laws, regulations, and court actions are responding. Any review of the effect of health, safety, and environmental values on business must include a discussion of the role and potential impact of corporate policies.

DISCUSSION QUESTIONS

1. What is your appraisal of the effectiveness of market forces in protecting the health and safety of consumers and industrial workers?
2. What is the nature of the evolution of product liability law, and what are the implications of this evolution for corporations and managers? How effective, in your opinion, is tort law as a mechanism of control over corporate health and safety practices?
3. What is the logic of market-based schemes of pollution control? What are the difficulties of these systems? Which alternatives strike you as most feasible?
4. How useful is the idea of "anticipatory management" for corporations? What might be obstacles to success for systems such as those of Monsanto or Western Union? How effective do you consider corporate policy and planning systems in broad-scale consumer and environmental protection?

NOTES

1. Albert O. Hirschman, *Exit, Voice, and Loyalty: Responses to Decline in Firms, Organizations, and States* (Cambridge: Harvard University Press, 1970), pp. 15–16.
2. Richard H. Holton, "Advancing the Backward Act of Spending Money," in *Regulating Business: The Search for an Optimum* (San Francisco: Institute for Contemporary Studies, 1978), 125–56.
3. This discussion is drawn from ibid., especially pp. 133–39.
4. Ibid., p. 136.
5. Louis Harris and Associates, Inc. and Marketing Science Institute, *Consumerism at the Crossroads: A National Opinion Research Survey of Public Activist, Business and Regulatory Attitudes toward the Consumer Movement* (Stevens Point, Wisc.: Sentry Insurance Co., 1977), p. 9.

6. Michael O'Hare, "Information Strategies as Regulatory Surrogates," in *Social Regulation,* ed. Eugene Bardach and Robert A. Kagan (San Francisco, Calif.: Institute for Contemporary Studies, 1982), 10:222, 236.

7. Harris and Associates, Inc. and Marketing Science Institute, *Consumerism at the Crossroads,* p. 12.

8. Hirschman, *Exit, Voice, and Loyalty,* p. 26.

9. Lloyd G. Reynolds, *Labor Economics and Labor Relations,* 7th ed. (Englewood Cliffs, N.J.: Prentice-Hall, 1978), p. 110.

10. This discussion is based upon a case written by Professor Robert Dickie, "Managing the Product Liability Situation (A)," School of Management, Boston University, BU 739–050, 1978.

11. *Gladys Escola* v. *Coca-Cola Bottling Co. of Fresno,* 24 Cal. 2d 453.

12. Ibid., at 462.

13. Dickie, "Managing the Product Liability Situation (A)," pp. 5–7.

14. "The Devils in the Product Liability Laws," *Business Week,* February 12, 1979, pp. 72–78.

15. Jacqueline Calmes. "Product Liability Bill Involves Arcane Terms," *1984 Congressional Quarterly,* December 8, 1984, p. 3068.

16. Ibid.

17. Ibid.

18. Eugene Bardach and Robert A. Kagan, "Liability Law and Social Regulation," in *Social Regulation,* ed. Eugene Bardach and Robert A. Kagan (San Francisco, Calif.: Institute for Contemporary Studies, 1982), 11:253.

19. Ibid., p. 252.

20. Ibid., p. 254.

21. See, for example, Charles L. Schultze, *The Public Use of Private Interest* (Washington, D.C.: Brookings Institution, 1977); or Allen V. Kneese and Charles L. Schultze, *Pollution, Prices and Public Policy* (Washington, D.C.: Brookings Institution, 1975).

22. See *Environmental Quality,* Tenth Annual Report of the Council on Environmental Quality (Washington, D.C.: U.S. Government Printing Office, December 1979), chap. 12, pp. 639–82.

23. U.S., Environmental Protection Agency, *Emissions Trading: Status Report,* May 10, 1984, p. 1.

24. U.S., Environmental Protection Agency, *Emission Reduction Banking and Trading: Status Report,* October 1, 1981, pp. 1–2.

25. John Quarles, "Federal Regulation of New Industrial Plants," *Environmental Reporter* 10 (May 4, 1979): 1–51.

26. Ibid., p. 45.

27. Ibid., p. 46.

28. This discussion is drawn from Monte G. Throdahl, "Blowing Your Own Whistle — A Corporate Perspective" (Remarks to AAAS Annual Meeting, San Francisco, January 4, 1980), pp. 1–8.

29. Ibid., p. 3.

30. Ibid., p. 8.
31. Mary Gardiner Jones, "The Consumer Affairs Office, Essential Element in Corporate Policy and Planning," *California Management Review* 20 (Summer 1978): 63–73.
32. Ibid., p. 63.
33. Ibid., p. 69.

Product Performance and Warranties
Consumer and Producer Obligations

It was January 16, 1981, when Gary Husel, a traveling service representative for the National Motor Company in the Indianapolis District Office, found a letter in his mailbox from a Mr. and Mrs. Schmidt, asking for assistance in getting their 1976 Lifestyle van repaired. The letter claimed that the vehicle had a problem with the carrier bearing. (The carrier bearing holds together the two-piece driveshaft that is typical of this type of vehicle.) According to the letter, the carrier bearing had failed, allowing the driveshafts to separate, leaving the vehicle inoperable. The letter also claimed that this problem had occurred numerous times while the vehicle was under warranty. Husel thought nothing surprising about the letter other than that the owners claimed the problem had occurred while the vehicle was under warranty. Being the person responsible for customer relations in the part of the state the Schmidts were from and the fact that good company policy required an investigation into any problem supposedly similar to a problem that occurred while a vehicle was under warranty, Husel placed the letter along with about a dozen others into his owner-relations folder for further action. Normally Husel would have taken a complaint letter on a five-year-old vehicle and had his assistant send a "Sorry, we cannot assist you in this matter" letter.

Within a few days Husel called the Schmidts to find out additional information about the problem. He spoke with Mrs. Schmidt, and she claimed that the vehicle had never worked properly for very long because of continued carrier bearing problems and that the bearing had failed again. She also said that National Motor had paid for all the repairs and the National dealer in DeMotte, Indiana, had been the one working on them. Husel asked her if they had any repair orders as verification of the prior work being completed. Mrs. Schmidt said National and the dealer had all the paperwork. Before hanging up, Husel said he wanted to check his office records and the dealer's records for verification of a prior problem and he would then recontact her to tell her his findings. If he could verify prior problems as she claimed, he would make arrangements for the vehicle to be inspected to determine if the current problem was related. If it was related, he would then decide what, if anything, National would do toward paying for the needed repair.

Following the conversation with Mrs. Schmidt, Husel went to his office files to look for past correspondence relating to the Schmidts. The current files containing information from 1981, 1980, and 1979 held nothing. Husel then searched the older files in the storage room and found a copy of a complaint form National uses to record phone conversations between customers and National employees. This particular form was dated February 5, 1978, and was between Mrs. Schmidt and a Miss Davis, a National employee. The form revealed that the van currently had 12,891 miles on it, was purchased June 17, 1976, and had been into a dealer at least five times over the last year and a half for carrier bearing problems that started shortly after the vehicle was purchased. On the bottom of the form was a space provided for the service representative to write in his or her comments and actions. On this form was stated: "10–5–78, Problem Resolved — Customer Happy. A. Brown." Attached to the form was a questionnaire sent from the home office in Detroit after the phone call complaint form was turned in by the service representative asking numerous questions about the handling of the reported problem. One question of interest asked: "Was the problem you reported to us resolved to your satisfaction?" It was answered: "No."

By the end of January 1981, Husel had made a visit to the National dealer in DeMotte, Indiana. While there he asked the service and parts managers if they recalled the Schmidts' vehicle and the problems they encountered with it. Surprisingly, both people who had always appeared sharp and as having good memories to Husel could remember nothing of the vehicle or the customers. Husel assumed they had forgotten the incident because it had occurred over two years ago. Fortunately, within a minute the owner arrived and Husel asked him if he recalled the vehicle and the customers. Immediately the dealer recalled the situation. He said that he did not sell the vehicle — the closed dealer in Roselawn, Indiana, had — and that the service representative at the time, Miss Brown, had asked him to have his people work on the vehicle because the selling dealer could not repair it properly. The dealer also said that when his people worked on it, it was already out of warranty. They worked on it a couple of times, and once the Schmidts last picked it up, he assumed it must have been fixed because he never heard from them again.

Husel then asked for copies of the repair orders. As in the situation in his office, 1978 records were in storage. Husel and the service manager went into the storeroom, searched the files, and could find nothing. Husel had no access to the repair orders of the closed dealer and was disappointed not to find any here to substantiate prior work. Even without repair orders he felt the dealer's statement and the complaint form he found were enough evidence to prove that the problem had occurred under warranty and that if the same problem occurred again, he had better authorize a repair to keep out of trouble with the law. Indiana's interpretation of the law did not require an extension of a written warranty for the time a vehicle was inoperable as some states did, but past experience told Husel that Indiana courts generally take the opinion that a component of a vehicle had better give at least one full year or more of problem-free service. The "or more" depended on the frequency of the problem and the expected cost of repair. Husel knew it was well over one year since the vehicle had been repaired last, but it apparently had failed numerous times and he figured he should play it safe by having National pay for the repair.

Husel called the Schmidts thinking he had good news to tell them as long as the current problem turned out to be the same as the old one. When he spoke with Mrs. Schmidt and told her what National was going to do, he recalled that she did not sound the least bit happy. First of all, she said that she could not bring the vehicle to the dealer for an inspection because it was not driveable, which Husel said would be no problem. He would drive out with someone and inspect it. Second, Mrs. Schmidt wanted to know if National was going to reimburse them for the car they had to rent for the last two years. Astonished, Husel said: "What do you mean 'reimburse you for two years of a rental car'?" Mrs. Schmidt then proceeded to tell him that the vehicle had been inoperable for over two years. It had been broken since a few weeks after they last had it in at the DeMotte dealer in October 1978, and they had to rent a car for transportation. Never having heard anything so incredible, Husel asked why they had waited two years to contact National or the dealer about the problem. Husel recalled never getting an answer to this question — just silence.

Husel became irritated and told Mrs. Schmidt that he thought National's offer to fix the vehicle was extremely fair considering that the vehicle was over five years old, that it had been sitting for two years with no action on their part, and that rental assistance was out of the question. Mrs. Schmidt then asked if his decision was final. After confirming that it was, she said, "I'll see you in court." Then she hung up.

Following this conversation, Husel wrote a short report describing the events up through his conversation with Mrs. Schmidt and then discussed the matter with his two supervisors. His supervisors agreed that the offer to repair the vehicle was fair and that the rental request absurd, and the issue was dropped.

In June 1981 the office Husel worked out of received a court summons from Indiana State Court, Valparaiso, Indiana, charging National Motor Company in breach of warranty for failure to abide by the requirements of the Magnuson-Moss Warranty Act.[1] It was filed by Mr. and Mrs. Robert Schmidt and asked for $20,000. Included in the $20,000 was the price of the van, financing charges, insurance, and legal fees. Trial was set for early May 1982.

In September 1981 Mr. Robert DeBerg, a Valparaiso attorney hired by National to defend them in the case, contacted Husel to set up a time to discuss the situation and make a joint inspection of the Schmidts' vehicle, which he had already cleared with the Schmidts' attorney.

When they met, Husel told DeBerg all the events as described so far, DeBerg asking questions as they proceeded. When the questioning was over, they went to Schmidt's house, met the Schmidts, and proceeded to look at the vehicle. The vehicle looked as if it had been sitting a long time: flat tires, cobwebs all over it, bird excrement everywhere, and very dirty. Crawling underneath the vehicle, Husel identified the broken carrier bearing, pointing it out to DeBerg. When asked by DeBerg if they had driven the vehicle lately, Mr. Schmidt said the vehicle had been sitting in that exact spot for almost three years. Husel noticed the mileage at 14,628, not much more than the 12,891 reported to National in February 1978. DeBerg also asked the Schmidts why they had not made any further attempts to get the vehicle fixed until January 1981. Mr. Schmidt said they had fooled around with the van for over two years after they bought it and could never get it fixed properly. They had called National in Detroit for assistance and spoken to a Miss Davis, had met a Miss Brown from National out of Indianapolis, and had had it to two dealers and never had the problem resolved. Finally, he said they did not know what else to do, so they just parked it. In late 1980 they were convinced by a friend to see an attorney about the problem, and that started the whole process.

Following this inspection, Husel did not hear anything about the case until early April 1982, when DeBerg called him requesting that they meet again and prepare for the trial. When they met a few weeks later, DeBerg asked a few questions and said he had asked National's legal staff in Detroit to settle the case out of court. He told them National would lose the trial because numerous attempts had been made at fixing the vehicle, starting shortly after it was purchased, and it was still disabled, an issue that was in direct violation of federal warranty law. DeBerg felt that if National offered to settle now, they could bargain for a lower settlement, save legal fees, and avoid the bad publicity. He went on to say that the trial would be by jury, always sympathetic to a consumer complaint, and the issue was basically "explosive." This opinion also emanated from one of the partners of his law firm who told him to "get rid of the case." Husel was surprised to hear these statements from the attorney who was supposedly going to defend his corporation. Husel felt the company would win the case because the customers had made an absurd demand for two years of rental assistance after making no attempt to get the vehicle fixed during that time. Besides, the vehicle was almost six years old now.

Following the conversation with DeBerg, Husel discussed the pending trial with the two supervisors and told them of his recent conversation with DeBerg. The supervisors were aware of DeBerg's request for an outside settlement, and he had tried recruiting them to push his position with the Detroit legal staff. Both supervisors agreed with Husel that National would win the case, and they were not going to make an attempt to influence the legal staff. The supervisors and Husel called the legal staff in Detroit, and had a four-way conversation with Ms. Henderson — she was the person in charge of handling the case there. Ms. Henderson pointed out that the management did not like the warranty law and wanted no precedents set from its successful application. When the conversation ended, all agreed that National would win the case because the customers did nothing for over two years and then demanded rental assistance, both grounds for dismissal.

DISCUSSION QUESTIONS

1. Review the facts of the case as presented. Would you advocate, as Gary Husel did, that National pursue the case in court?
2. As a corporate executive, what action would you support? Why?
3. How would you be inclined to decide this case as a juror? What would be your primary considerations?
4. Finally, how would you speculate that the jury decided the case?

NOTE

1. The Magnuson-Moss Warranty–Federal Trade Commission Act was passed into law January 4, 1975. In terms of warranties, this act:
   a. requires manufacturers who issue written warranties on products costing more than $10 to label each warranty as "full" if it meets federal minimum standards or "limited" if it fails to meet those standards.
   b. sets federal minimum standards requiring that full warranties: commit the firm issuing the warranty to repair any defect within a reasonable time frame and without charge; allow the consumer to choose a refund or replacement without charge if a defect is not corrected by a reasonable number of attempts; allow a consumer to file suit in state or federal courts for damages from failure to comply with a warranty and to recover court costs if he won.

   It should be noted that automobile warranties are termed *limited* because certain repairs are considered maintenance and the tires are warranted by the tire manufacturer. In the court case described in this case, the court determined that the warranty involved would still be subject to treatment as a "full" warranty because the item of concern, the carrier bearing, would be included in a full warranty if the vehicle had one. Also, the intent of the law was not to let manufacturers off the hook by classifying all their warranties as limited, thus excluding themselves from federal regulations.

John D. Aram
Lawrence R. A. Esser
Suzanne M. Seifert

Case 6.B

EPA and the Bubble
Flexible Regulation or
Air Quality Giveaway?

At a large steel plant in the Midwest, an environmental engineer and a representative from the U.S. Environmental Protection Agency (EPA) stood surveying the area around the works. What they saw were not dusty car-filled parking lots and truck lanes. Rather, they watched tanker trucks spraying water on areas that had not been paved over, vacuum trucks sucking up grit from the ground, and huge piles of raw materials being wetted down by spraying systems. Earlier that morning the EPA official had seen all 6,000 workers in the plant bussed in from parking lots on the outer bounds of the plant property.

The agency representative was not startled by these activities. She knew that they had been developed over a few years by the engineer standing next to her, and she had been present when he gave presentations to the EPA describing the innovative plan to control "fugitive emission," the dust particles carried into the atmosphere by winds that blew over the parking lots, roads, and material stockpiles around the building. The engineer had long suspected that a portion of the high level of "particulates" in the air around steel mills came not from process (production) emissions but from windblown particles. To combat this problem he had developed a systematic approach to keeping the dust down.

For some time the engineer had tried to convince the EPA to allow him to let some of the process emissions from smokestacks increase in return for the reduction in the outside emissions. Finally, a 1979 EPA policy allowed such trade-offs to be made, and the engineer could seek official approval of his system for controlling air pollution.[1]

The scene described here is hypothetical only in detail. There is such a plant in the Midwest — Armco Steel in Middletown, Ohio — and there is an environmental engineer, named John Barker, who developed and tested the process in Middletown. Barker's system began receiving much attention in late 1980 from the business press because it was developed within the company, not by a regulatory agency. It was an application of a concept that developed in the 1970s known as the "bubble concept" of air pollution control.

EPA AND CONVENTIONAL CONTROLS

The EPA, a regulatory body formed in 1970 to consolidate the many federal programs concerned with the environment, is in charge of enforcing the Clean Air Act, passed in the same year.[2] In the years that the agency had enforced air pollution standards, it followed the act by focusing on emissions from "industrial point sources," for example, a kiln in a cement plant. When a standard for the amount of pollution (usually in tons per year) was set, companies were required to install collectors (for particulates or granules) or "scrubbers" (for vaporous pollution, usually some chemical) to maintain the standard.

The agency is directed by the Clean Air Act to "set specific and rigorous limits on the amounts of pollutants that may be emitted from any 'new source' of air pollution."[3] This new source performance standard, or NSPS, is intended to force firms to use the best available technology to reduce emissions from any new source. If a plant is expanded with new stacks, these stacks are subject to the NSPS, and the firm must pay for the technology to meet this standard.

This forcing of technology, from an environmental viewpoint, is an important advantage of the NSPS. With new and better systems for controlling air pollution comes the added benefit of lower emissions each time a source is added to a plant. If a new plant with many sources is built, all its point sources have to be equipped with the best available systems, giving an incentive for pollution control manufacturers to improve their products constantly.

Another advantage of requiring the NSPS to be met by the best equipment is the greater ease of monitoring compliance with EPA standards. The agency knows that equipment installed on the new source is controlling emissions properly. As long as the company maintains the equipment, the EPA does not have to monitor all sources constantly for compliance.[4]

However, one drawback of concentrating on point sources and specifying equipment is the possibility of overlooking other sources of pollution — for example, the dust emissions at Armco's mill. Also, focusing only on point source emissions leaves little or no room for antipollution innovation on the company's part; there is no incentive for a firm to come up with alternatives for controlling pollution when all methods are prescribed.

Probably the primary disadvantage of point source regulations is their high cost to the firm — the estimated $20 million cost to Armco to install conventional controls is one example. There is no flexibility in determining least-cost methods of control; the standards for each source are set and the firm must comply. Unfortunately, the expense may be greater for some firms than others. A small company with one facility that wants to add a process involving a new smokestack may find its expansion proportionately more expensive than would a larger company.

These disadvantages, along with the general feeling among businessmen that the government was overregulating and intruding too much into the private sector, were used to pressure the EPA to revise its regulatory strategy and to allow more innovation and flexibility for management in deciding how to meet standards. The trend in the late 1970s was away from direct controls and toward more market-oriented means of curbing pollution. The basic idea is "modifying . . . the incentive pattern" for "a society that relies on private enterprise and market incentives to carry out most productive activity."[5]

THE BUBBLE CONCEPT

The bubble concept, rather than concentrating on a single smokestack, treats a whole plant with all its smokestacks as a source. Envision three stacks — 1, 2, and 3 — all on the same plant. Stack 3 is the least costly to modify to maintain the standards, whereas stacks 1 and 2 are much more expensive to modify for compliance. Under the bubble policy the plant would be required to meet an overall standard for the three stacks. To do this in the least-cost way, the firm will greatly modify stack 3 and modify 1 and 2 to a much lesser extent. Under former regulations all three would have been modified, with 1 and 2 much more expensive to control than 3.[6]

The new policy simply treats the entire plant as if it were under a bubble that could emit only a certain amount of pollutant. Within the bubble the company will identify and reduce pollution sources that can be controlled for lower costs and thus create an optimal mix of controls where overall emissions will not exceed the standard for the bubble.

The fact that the concept will save Armco money is verified by both Armco and the EPA. The dust control project initially cost about $4 million. To install the proper equipment in the plant under usual EPA regulations would cost about $20 million. Thus a new savings of $16 million is achieved by substituting the dust control system for conventional filters. Armco has estimated that implementing this plan at its other plants would yield initial savings as high as $42 million.[7] In this case not only would savings result, but more than six times as many tons of particulates would be kept out of the atmosphere than under traditional requirements (4,000 tons versus 652 tons).[8]

In addition, the agency has developed the idea of multiplant bubbles:

Multi-plant bubbles can consist of a few adjacent sources or extend to an area-wide bubble over many different firms. They would let participating firms get more control from other member firms whose control costs are lowest or whose impact on air quality is highest. These firms would share overall costs equally, cutting each participant's current cost burden and combining equity with efficiency.[9]

In conjunction with this idea, the EPA has devised a way for firms to "bank" pollution reductions below standard and sell them off to other firms. For example, suppose that Firm I and Firm II are under a multiplant bubble agreement. Firm I has one smokestack that is so cheap and so easy to control that it has managed to keep that stack at 200 tons *below* the clean air standard. On the other hand, Firm II has one stack, very expensive to modify, that is emitting 200 tons *over* the limit. Rather than modify its stack at high cost, Firm II can ask Firm I to apply its reduction to Firm II so that the emissions of the two plants balance. Firm II pays Firm I for this offset or trade, a solution far less costly than refitting the Firm II stack. At the same time, the overall standard is being met to the satisfaction of the EPA.[10]

These systems seek to provide incentives for firms to reduce their emissions where they can do so cheaply. Further, application of the bubble concept promotes cooperation between firms and encourages an optimal mix of controls among the plants in the multiplant bubble. On the other hand, the multiplant bubble may lead to a problem regarding unfair competitive practices. It is conceivable that several firms in an area might exclude others from sharing in the regional bubble, subjecting them to higher costs of control. Similarly, two firms in the competitive market that have plants close to each other might agree to a multiplant bubble to lower costs for both, thus putting themselves ahead of other firms in the market unable to take advantage of such savings.

A major advantage to industry is that a firm's engineers can work on innovative mixes of control, looking for new sources of pollution and new methods of control. While all experimentation must be done within the framework of state and EPA laws, it affords management a degree of flexibility that older methods did not allow and represents a more conciliatory orientation than the governmental appraoch in the late 1960s and the 1970s. The EPA has pointed out that this restraint of regulatory power may produce greater cooperation between affected firms and the agency.[11]

The bubble policy, despite its appeal, is not without problems. One limitation is the slower development of improved pollution control technology if *new* sources are allowed to come under the plant bubble. In a 1978 case, *ASARCO* v. *Environmental Protection Agency*, it was pointed out that "the new source performance standards are designed to enhance air quality, while applying the bubble concept would allow operators to avoid installing the best pollution control technology on an altered facility as long as the emissions in the entire plant do not increase."[12] If the NSPSs are not applicable to these new sources, then there is little incentive for equipment manufacturers to develop continually better controls to meet a market for the "best pollution control technology."[13]

Another potential problem arises when the EPA has to monitor a whole plant rather than single point sources for air quality. It is much easier to place monitors (or check controls) in each stack when they all have the same standard. Each stack may have a different standard with the bubble, thus making the job of tracking compliance more complex. This problem may be exacerbated with multiplant bubbles.

Another major disadvantage is that the process of obtaining approval for a bubble plan, even with streamlining attempts by the EPA, is somewhat slow and involved. Not only must an applicant go to the EPA; he or she must also apply to the state in which the plant is located to make sure that state standards (which may be more strict than federal) are being met. Because this takes so long, as of 1981, the EPA proposed that this be consolidated into a joint state-EPA review.[14] Such a proposal would alleviate problems experienced by firms such as 3M, for which a spokesman has stated, "The real problem is the 'long, drawn out, and tedious' process EPA has for implementing the bubble policy. He claims that the application procedure alone is a 'deterrent' to any company contemplating a bubble."[15]

The agency has acknowledged one other problem with the plan — the fear that once firms set their optimal mix and control previously disregarded sources of pollution, they may become vulnerable to tighter control on these methods and sources. That is, the EPA would use revealed locations and means by which greater pollution control is possible to tighten standards in the future. Such an action by the EPA would constitute a disincentive for plants to search out innovative pollution control methods, the more companies find the more places the EPA might impose regulations.

RECENT HISTORY OF THE BUBBLE IDEA: THE NSPS CONTROVERSY

The agency had resisted the idea of the bubble when it was first proposed in 1972. At the time it had two main objections to the idea: (1) it would make emissions standards extremely difficult to enforce, and (2) it would reward operators using few controls by requiring only that standards be maintained at present levels.[16] Because of pressure from industry and the Department of Commerce, the EPA proposed new regulations that would define a source as a plant rather than just a point source. At the time, it still required that any new smokestacks or emission points be subject to the NSPS and therefore to the requirement of utilizing the best available technology.[17]

This action reflected a turning point in the agency's attitude toward regulation. In the first few years of its existence, it was more aggressive in its stance toward industry. Its policy was "fair but firm":

> Our program has placed emphasis on thorough prepara-
> tion and consideration of all facts pertinent to a case . . .
> combined with an unflinching readiness to take whatever
> enforcement action that might be required to deter recal-
> citrance or foot-dragging and to compel needed abatement
> efforts.[18]

By 1981 the controlled trading concept, including the bubble policy, had been implemented for several years on a preliminary basis; the EPA stated the following reform objectives:

> — to achieve our environmental objectives most efficiently
>   by finding *least cost solutions* to environmental problems;
> — to develop *incentives for business to innovate* in the design
>   of more effective control systems and less polluting
>   (more conserving) production processes;
> — to administer our program with the *least possible hassle* to
>   ourselves and those with whom we work.[19]

The inauguration in 1981 of a new president sympathetic to industry indicated that such changes would be supported by the government. In early 1981 Vice-President George Bush, as head of the newly formed Presidential Task Force on Regulatory Relief, proposed that the EPA policy be amended to include *new* smokestacks under the bubble, as well as existing facilities.[20]

There was still one large group that was fighting the EPA's policy changes, especially the recommendation that new point sources be included under the bubble. This group consisted of environmentalist organizations such as the Sierra Club, the Natural Resources Defense Council, and Friends of the Earth. These groups had substantial public support and political influence in Washington and were often involved in public hearings and lawsuits concerning new pollution laws.

The Sierra Club has challenged the inclusion of new point sources under the bubble in the 1978 ASARCO case. The organization pointed out that such a provision would allow operators to avoid the NSPS regulations and thereby "postpone the time when the best technology must be employed."[21] Further, the Clean Air Act specifically stated the goal to *enhance* air quality, not just *maintain* it. The new policy, argued Sierra Club, circumvented this goal in the interests of industry. The Court agreed with the Sierra Club and ordered the EPA to keep the new sources subject to NSPSs.

During the Carter administration regulations remained unchanged, and any new source had to be fitted with the best available equipment.

When the Reagan administration assumed office in 1981, the idea of including new stacks under the bubble was proposed, and environmental groups again pointed out the inconsistency of this policy with the objectives of the Clean Air Act. As one environmentalist said, "This reflects the Reagan Administration's general philosophy on the Clean Air Act which is sympathetic to business complaints but not very sympathetic to the Act's objective — healthier air."[22]

Further, the environmentalists argued that relaxing regulations on air pollution would lead to further "rollbacks" in controls under the guise of economic incentives for industry. The director of the Sierra Club in Washington responded to the proposal, "They [Reagan and EPA] will attempt to gut pollution control laws . . . for the economic benefit of industry."[23] Such laws include control of air and water pollution as well as constraints on the use of industry protected lands.

The agency pointed out the problem of disincentives to modernization created by adherence to point source control methods. The main thrust behind the new administration's proposal was that point source controls inhibit business expansion and impose costs on industry, resulting in inefficiencies. The incentives provided by including new sources under the bubble would encourage improvement and construction of facilities.

This proposal occurred when the EPA was trying to change its orientation toward business from an adversary to a cooperative attitude. Relaxing requirements on industry for granting of approval of a bubble was an example, and the new source proposal fit within such reforms. The EPA maintained that air quality would not be hurt by such actions, but it did not reply to the environmentalists' charge that air quality would not improve.

POSTSCRIPT — 1985

By early 1985 EPA's progress toward flexibility and industry cooperation had been reinforced. For example, to address the slow and involved process of approving individual bubbles, the EPA dramatically increased the agency's bubble staff and technical assistance budget.[24] Next the agency began permitting states to write "generic" rules, allowing them to obtain advance approval for bubbles rather than having every bubble effort approved by the EPA on an individual basis. Generic rules have reduced the bubble's resource drain on state agencies and regional EPA centers while affording industry a reasonable assurance that a well-designed bubble plant — meeting state qualifications — would not be blocked by the EPA.[25]

One other significant problem existed with the EPA's controlled-trading concept: the fear of many firms that once they set their optimal pollution level mix and controlled previously disregarded sources of pollution, they would become vulnerable to more stringent agency regulations — that is, the EPA would use revealed locations and means by which greater pollution control is possible to tighten future standards.[26] Such an action by the EPA would constitute a disincentive for plants to search out innovative pollution control methods. In October 1980 the EPA tackled this problem head-on; bubble applicants were permitted to use an application procedure that allowed them to identify currently undetected ways in which they polluted, yet protected them from self-incrimination.[27]

Increased governmental and industrial interest in controlled-trading programs led to the implementation of three EPA-approved formal emission banking systems by October 1984; numerous other banking systems were nearing the implementation stage by that time. Some 37 bubbles, directly approved by the EPA, have saved firms millions of dollars when compared with the compliance costs of traditional regulatory methods.[28]

By the early 1980s controlled-trading success stories began attracting the attention of corporate leaders promoting the EPA's newly emerging image as a regulatory agency with a cooperative orientation toward business. As of fall 1981, a number of corporations could cite substantial financial savings directly attributable to the EPA's acceptance of the controlled-trading concept.[29]

Achieving significant cost savings while actually improving the air quality in many areas has heightened interest in applying controlled-trading concepts to other areas of pollution regulation. Both water pollution and mobile source pollutants (motor transportation) are being evaluated as to their compatibility with the EPA's three new programs.[30]

Change has also occurred with respect to the inclusion or exclusion of new sources of pollution at plants covered by a bubble or proposing to be covered by a bubble. Following the ASARCO decision, the EPA promulgated a bubble policy in 1980 that distinguished between areas meeting air pollution control standards and those not attaining established standards. This "dual" system permitted new sources of pollution from a plant to come within that plant's existing or proposed bubble. If, however, the area surrounding the plant was not attaining established pollution goals, the NSPS requirements would be in force for the plant, and additional pollution would have to meet the best available technology standard. The latter was true even if increases in emissions from one source in the plant were completely offset by reductions elsewhere in the same plant. The key factor in the EPA's policy was the fact that the geographic area was out of attainment. Since NSPSs were intended to improve, rather than just maintain, air quality, the EPA declared that the plant bubble concept was not applicable.

This interpretation of the EPA's policy was challenged by the Natural Resources Defense Council (NRDC) as a violation of the Clean Air Act Amendments of 1977.[31] Congress required the EPA to regulate each source of pollution but did not state whether a source could be a whole plant or whether a source meant each component of pollution within a plant. The NRDC charged that the act required the EPA to treat any source of air pollution emitting over 100 tons of pollution a year as a stationary source and therefore as outside of the bubble concept.

The task of the Supreme Court, then, was to decide whether a narrow or broad definition of *source* should be used. After examining the legislative history of the act, prior court rulings, and the arguments of the contestants, the Court decided that the EPA should have flexibility to define the "source" of pollution differently in differing contexts. In the words of the majority opinion:

> An initial agency interpretation is not instantly carved in stone. On the contrary . . . the agency, to engage in informed rule making, must consider varying interpretations and the wisdom of its policy on a continuing basis.[32]

Thus the Court affirmed the EPA's policy of including new sources under the bubble in some circumstances and not in others and gave the agency latitude to determine some trade-offs between environment and economics as matters of administrative policy. How this sphere of discretion would be used by the EPA and whether its application would be as controversial in the future as it was in the recent past were matters to be determined.

DISCUSSION QUESTIONS

1. What are the main reasons in favor of including new pollution sources under the bubble concept? What are the main arguments against this policy?
2. What criteria should be used to decide whether to include new pollution sources in the bubble concept or to maintain the NSPSs outside of the bubble?
3. Evaluate the Supreme Court's decision against the National Resources Defense Council. Do you support or not support this decision? Explain.
4. The EPA is reported to be replacing adversative relations with accommodation toward the industrial sector. What are the potential gains and risks involved in its new approach? What style of business-government relations do you favor in the area of environmental protection?

NOTES

1. "Will John Barker's Bubble Burst?" *Industry Week*, September 29, 1980, pp. 63–65.
2. The Urban Institute, "Balancing the Objectives of Clean Air and Economic Growth: Regulated Markets in Emission Reductions" (Washington, D.C.: National Bureau of Standards, unpublished report ETIP-79–62, June 1979), p. 3.
3. *ASARCO Inc.* v. *Environmental Protection Agency*, 8 ELR 20166.
4. U.S., Environmental Protection Agency, "Checklist of Regulatory Alternatives" (Unpublished report, July 1980), p. 1.

5. C. S. Schultz, *The Public Use of Private Interest* (Washington, D.C.: Brookings Institution, 1977), p. 13.

6. U.S., Environmental Protection Agency, "Emission Reduction Banking," Emission Reduction and Trading Publication no. BA-115, November, 1980, p. 11.

7. "Clean-Air Fight: Plain Dust Is the Key to Pollution 'Bubble' at Armco Steelworks," *Wall Street Journal,* October 1, 1980, p. 1.

8. "EPA Plans to Clear Its 'Bubble' Proposal for Armco, Inc. Plant," *Wall Street Journal,* October 21, 1980, p. 8.

9. U.S., Environmental Protection Agency, "Regulatory Reform at EPA, Controlled Trading, Innovation & Permitting," (Unpublished paper, December 1980), p. 1.

10. Environmental Protection Agency, "Emission Reduction Banking," p. 12.

11. Environmental Protection Agency, "Checklist of Regulatory Alternatives," p. 8.

12. *ASARCO* v. *EPA,* 8 ELR 20164.

13. *ASARCO* v. *EPA,* 8 ELR 20169.

14. U.S., Environmental Protection Agency, "The Controlled Trader," *EPA* 1(February 1981):1.

15. "3M May Be the First to Get Under the Bubble," *Chemical Week,* September 3, 1980, p. 47.

16. *ASARCO* v. *EPA,* 8 ELR 20166.

17. *ASARCO* v. *EPA,* 8 ELR 20169.

18. U.S., Environmental Protection Agency, "The First 2 Years: A Review of EPA's Enforcement" (Unpublished report, February 1973), p. 2.

19. Environmental Protection Agency, "Regulatory Reform," p. 1.

20. "Reagan vs. Environmentalists: First Puff of Smoke in Clean Air Battle," *Christian Science Monitor,* March 10, 1981, p. 1.

21. *ASARCO* v. *EPA,* 8 ELR 20169.

22. Richard Ayres, National Resource Defense Council, quoted in "Reagan vs. Environmentalists," p. 12.

23. Brock Evans quoted in ibid., p. 12.

24. Michael H. Levin, "Implementing the 'Bubble' Policy," in *Social Regulation,* ed. Eugene Bardach and Robert A. Kagan (San Francisco, Calif.: Institute for Contemporary Studies, 1982), 3:82.

25. Ibid.

26. Ibid., p. 91.

27. Ibid., p. 82.

28. U.S., Environmental Protection Agency, *Emissions Trading: Status Report,* October 1, 1984, p. 1.

29. Levin, "Implementing the 'Bubble' Policy," pp. 85–86.

30. Ibid., p. 87.

31. 52 USLW 4845.

32. 52 USLW 4852.

How Moral Men Make Immoral Decisions

"We feel that 1972 can be one of Chevrolet's great years. . . . Most of the improvements this year are to engines and chassis components aimed at giving a customer a better car for the money. . . . I want to reiterate our pledge that the 1972 Chevrolets will be the best in Chevrolet history. . . . We recognize that providing good dealer service is the surest way to keep quality built Chevrolets for 1972 in top quality condition. . . . This is the lineup of cars for every type of buyer that we offer for 1972. Cars that are the best built in Chevrolet history. . . ."

The words seemed to fall out of my mouth like stones from an open hand. Effortlessly. Almost meaninglessly. It was August 31, 1971. I was power-gliding through the National Press Preview of 1972 Chevrolet cars and trucks at the Raleigh House, a mock-Tudor restaurant-banquet hall complex in suburban Detroit. The audience was filled with reporters from all over the country. In their midst was a plentiful sprinkling of Chevrolet managers. The new product presentation and question-answer session went smoothly, and I was stepping down from the podium and receiving the usual handshakes and compliments from some of the sales guys and a few of the members of the press when a strange feeling hit me:

"My God! I've been through all this before."

It was a strange feeling because somehow I was detached from it all. Looking down on myself in the banquet hall surrounded by executives, newsmen, and glittering Chevrolets. And I was questioning why I was there and what I was doing. The answers were not satisfactory.

"This whole show is nothing but a replay of last year's show, and the year before that, and the year before that. The speech I just gave was the same speech I gave last year, written by the same guy in public relations about the same superficial product improvements as previous years. And

J. Patrick Wright, "How Moral Men Make Immoral Decisions," chapter 4 from *On a Clear Day You Can See General Motors*. Copyright © 1979 Wright Enterprises. Adaptation reprinted by permission.

the same questions were being asked by the same newsmen I've seen for years. Almost nothing has changed."

I looked around the room for a brief moment searching for something, anything, that could show me that there was real meaning in the exercises we were going through, that the national press conference and the tens of similar dealer product announcements I conducted across the country were something more than just new product sales hypes. But I found nothing.

Instead, I got the empty feeling that "what I am doing here may be nothing more than perpetuating a gigantic fraud," and a fraud on the American consumer by promising him something new but giving him only surface alterations — "tortured sheet metal" as former chairman Frederic G. Donner used to say — or a couple of extra horsepower and an annual price increase. A fraud on the American economy, because I always had a vague suspicion that the annual model change may be good for the auto business in the short term but that it wasn't good for the economy and the country. Couldn't the money we spent on annual, superficial styling changes be better spent in reducing prices or in improving service and reliability? Or seeking solutions to the sociological problems that our products were creating in areas of pollution, energy consumption, safety, and congestion?

And a fraud on our own company because, when General Motors began to grow on the principle of annual model changes and the promotion of something new and different, cars were almost all alike with the same basic color — black. There was room for cosmetic changes as well as substantial advancement in technology with new and better engines, more sophisticated transmissions, improved performance, and comfort characteristics.

But now there was nothing new and revolutionary in car development, and there hadn't been for years. As a company, we were kidding ourselves that these slight annual alterations were innovative. They were not. We were living off the gullibility of the consumer combined with the fantastic growth of the American economy in the 1960s. Salting away billions of dollars of profits in the process and telling ourselves we were great managers because of these profits. This bubble was surely going to break, I thought. The consumer is going to get wise to us, and when he does we will have to fight for a long time to get back into his favor.

It seemed to me, and still does, that the system of American business often produces wrong, immoral, and irresponsible decisions, even though the personal morality of the people running the businesses is often above reproach. The system has a different morality as a group than the people do as individuals, which permits it to produce ineffective or dangerous products willfully, deal dictatorially and often unfairly with suppliers, pay bribes for business, abrogate the rights of employees by demanding blind loyalty to management, or tamper with the democratic process of government through illegal political contributions.

I am not a psychologist, so I can't offer a professional opinion on what happens to the freedom of individual minds when they are blended into the group management thought process of business. But my private analysis is this: Morality has to do with people. If an action is viewed primarily from the perspective of its effect on people, it is put into the moral realm.

Business in America, however, is impersonal. This is particularly true of large American multinational corporations. They are viewed by their employees and publics as faceless. They have no personality. The ultimate measure of success and failure of these businesses is not their effect on people but rather their earnings per share of stock. If earnings are high, the business is considered good. If they are low or in the red ink, it is considered a failure. The first question to greet any business proposal is: How will it affect profits? People do not enter the equation of a business decision except to the extent that the effect on them will hurt or enhance earnings per share. In such a completely impersonal context, business decisions of questionable personal morality are easily justified. The unwavering devotion to the bottom line brings this about, and the American public until now has been more than willing to accept this. When someone is forced into early retirement in a management power play or a supplier is cheated out of a sale by under-the-table dealings, the public reaction is generally, "Oh, well. That's business." And management's reaction is often, "It's what's on the bottom line that counts." A person who shoots and kills another is sentenced to life in prison. A businessman who makes a defective product that kills people may get a nominal fine or a verbal slap on the hands, if he is ever brought to trial at all.

The impersonal process of business decision making is reinforced by a sort of mob psychology that results from group management and the support of a specific system of management. Watergate certainly proved what can happen when blind devotion to a system or a process of thought moves unchecked. Members of the Nixon administration never raised any real questions about the morality of the break-in and the coverup. The only concern was for the expedient method to save the system. So, too, in business. Too often the only questions asked are: What is the expedient thing to do to save the system? How can we increase profits per share?

Never once while I was in General Motors (GM) management did I hear substantial social concern raised about the impact of our business on America, its consumers, or the economy. When we should have been planning switches to smaller, more fuel-efficient, lighter cars in the late 1960s in response to a growing demand in the marketplace, GM management refused because "we make more money on big cars." It mattered not that the customers wanted the smaller cars or that a national balance-of-payments deficit was being built in large part because of the burgeoning sales of foreign cars in the American market.

Refusal to enter the small car market when the profits were better on bigger cars, despite the needs of the public and the national economy, was not an isolated case of corporate insensitivity. It was typical. And what disturbed me is that it was indicative of fundamental problems with the system.

GM certainly was no more irresponsible than many American businesses. But the fact that the "prototype" of the well-run American business engaged in questionable business practices and delivered decisions that I felt were sometimes illegal, immoral, or irresponsible is an indictment of the American business system.

Earlier in my career, I accepted these decisions at GM without question. But as I was exposed to more facets of the business, I came to a realization of the responsibilities we had in managing a giant corporation and making a product that substantially affected people and national commerce. It bothered me how cavalierly these responsibilities were often regarded.

The whole Corvair case is a first-class example of a basically irresponsible and immoral business decision that was made by men of generally high personal moral standards. When Nader's book threatened the Corvair's sales and profits, he became an enemy of the system. Instead of trying to attack his credentials or the factual basis of his arguments, the company sought to attack him personally. This move failed, but, in the process, GM's blundering "made" Ralph Nader.

When the fact that GM hired detectives to follow and discredit Nader was exposed, the system was once again threatened. Top management, instead of questioning the system that would permit such an horrendous mistake as tailing Nader, simply sought to preserve the system by sacrificing the heads of several executives who were blamed for the incident. Were the atmosphere at GM not one emphasizing profits and preservation of the system above all else, I am sure the acts against Nader would never had have been perpetrated.

Those who were fired no doubt thought they were loyal employees. And, ironically, had they succeeded in devastating the image of Ralph Nader, they would have been corporate heroes and rewarded substantially. I find it difficult to believe that knowledge of these activities did not reach into the upper reaches of GM's management. But, assuming that it didn't, top management should have been held responsible for permitting the conditions to exist that would spawn such actions. If top management takes credit for a company's successes, it must also bear the brunt of the responsibility for its failures.

Furthermore, the Corvair was unsafe as it was originally designed. It was conceived along the lines of the foreign-built Porsche. These cars were powered by engines placed in the rear and supported by an independent, swing-axle suspension system. In the Corvair's case, the engine was all-aluminum and air-cooled (compared to the standard water-cooled iron engines). This, plus the rear placement of the engine, made the car new and somewhat different to the American public.

However, there are several bad engineering characteristics inherent in rear-engine cars that use a swing-axle suspension. In turns at high speeds they tend to become directionally unstable and, therefore, difficult to control. The rear of the car lifts or "jacks" and the rear wheels tend to tuck under the car, which encourages the car to flip over. In the high-performance Corvair, the car conveyed a false sense of control to the driver, when in fact he may have been very close to losing control of the vehicle. The result of these characteristics can be fatal.

These problems with the Corvair were well documented inside GM's engineering staff long before the Corvair ever was offered for sale. Frank Winchell, now vice-president of engineering, but then an engineer at Chevy, flipped over one of the first prototypes on the GM test track in Milford, Michigan. Others followed.

The questionable safety of the car caused a massive internal fight among GM's engineers over whether the car should be built with another form of suspension. On one side of the argument was Chevrolet's then general manager, Ed Cole, an engineer and product innovator. He and some of his engineering colleagues were enthralled with the idea of building the first modern, rear-engine American car. And I am convinced they felt the safety risks of the swing-axle suspension were minimal. On the other side was a wide assortment of top-flight engineers, including Charles Chayne, then vice-president of engineering; Von D. Polhemus, engineer in charge of chassis development on GM's engineering staff; and others.

These men collectively and individually made vigorous attempts inside GM to keep the Corvair as designed, out of production or to change the suspension system to make the car safer. One top corporate engineer told me that he showed his test results to Cole, but by then, he said, "Cole's mind was made up."

Albert Roller, who worked for me in Pontiac's advanced engineering section, tested the car and pleaded with me not to use it at Pontiac. Roller had been an engineer with Mercedes-Benz before joining GM, and he said that Mercedes had tested similarly designed rear-engine, swing-axle cars and had found them far too unsafe to build.

At the very least, then, within GM in the late 1950s, serious questions were raised about the Corvair's safety. At the very most, there was a mountain of documented evidence that the car should not be built as it was then designed.

However, Cole was a strong product voice and a top salesman in company affairs. In addition, the car, as he proposed it, would cost less to build than the same car with a conventional rear suspension. Management not only went along with Cole, it also told the dissenters in effect to "stop these objections. Get on the team, or you can find someplace else to work." The ill-fated Corvair was launched in the fall of 1959.

The results were disastrous. I don't think any car before or since produced as gruesome a record on the highway as the Corvair. It was designed and promoted to appeal to the spirit and flair of young people. It was sold in part as a sports car. Young Corvair owners, therefore, were trying to bend their cars around curves at high speeds and were killing themselves in alarming numbers.

It was only a couple of years or so before GM's legal department was inundated with lawsuits over the car. And the fatal swath that this car cut through the automobile industry touched the lives of many GM executives, employees, and dealers in an ironic and tragic twist of fate.

The son of Cal Werner, general manager of the Cadillac division, was killed in a Corvair. Werner was absolutely convinced that the design defect in the car was responsible. He said so many times. The son of Cy Osborne, an executive vice-president in the 1960s, was critically injured in a Corvair and suffered irreparable brain damage. Bunkie Knudsen's niece was brutally injured in a Corvair. And the son of an Indianapolis Chevrolet dealer also was killed in the car. Ernie Kovacs, my favorite comedian, was killed in a Corvair.

While the car was being developed at Chevrolet, we at Pontiac were spending $1.3 million on a project to adapt the Corvair to our division. The corporation had given us the go-ahead to work with the car to give it a Pontiac flavor. Our target for introduction was the fall of 1960, a year after Chevy introduced the car.

As we worked on the project, I became absolutely convinced by Chayne, Polhemus, and Roller that the car was unsafe. So I conducted a three-month campaign, with Knudsen's support, to keep the car out of the Pontiac lineup. Fortunately, Buick and Oldsmobile at the time were tooling up their own compact cars, the Special and F-85, respectively, which featured conventional front-engine designs.

We talked the corporation into letting Pontiac switch from a Corvair derivative to a version of the Buick-Oldsmobile car. We called it the Tempest and introduced it in the fall of 1960 with a four-cylinder engine as standard equipment and a V-8 engine as an option.

When Knudsen took over the reins of Chevrolet in 1961, he insisted that he be given corporate authorization to install a stabilizing bar in the rear to counteract the natural tendencies of the Corvair to flip off the road. The cost of the change would be about $15 a car. But his request was refused by the Fourteenth Floor as "too expensive."

Bunkie was livid. As I understand it, he went to the executive committee and told the top officers of the corporation that if they didn't reappraise his request and give him permission to make the Corvair safe, he was going to resign from GM. This threat and the fear of the bad publicity that surely would result from Knudsen's resignation forced management's hand. They relented. Bunkie put a stabilizing bar on the Corvair in the 1964 models. The next year a completely new and safer independent suspension designed by Frank Winchell was put on the Corvair. And it became one of the safest cars on the road. But the damage done to the car's reputation by then was irreparable. Corvair sales began to decline precipitously after the waves of unfavorable publicity following Nader's book and the many lawsuits being filed across the country. Production of the Corvair was halted in 1969, four years after it was made a safe and viable car.

To date, millions of dollars have been spent in legal expenses and out-of-court settlements in compensation for those killed or maimed in the Corvair. The corporation steadfastly defends the car's safety, despite the internal engineering records that indicated it was not safe and the ghastly toll in deaths and injury it recorded.

There wasn't a man in top GM management who had anything to do with the Corvair who would purposely build a car that he knew would hurt or kill people. But, as part of a management team pushing for increased sales and profits, each gave his individual approval in a group to decisions that produced the car in the face of the serious doubts that were raised about its safety and then later sought to squelch information that might prove the car's deficiencies.

The corporation became almost paranoid about the leaking of inside information we had on the car. In April of 1971, 19 boxes of microfilmed Corvair owner complaints, which had been ordered destroyed by upper management, turned up in the possession of two surburban Detroit junk dealers. When the Fourteenth Floor found this out, it went into panic and we at Chevrolet were ordered to buy the microfilm back and have it destroyed.

I refused, saying that a public company had no right to destroy documents of its business and GM's furtive purchase would surely surface. Besides, the $20,000 asking price was outright blackmail.

When some consumer groups showed an interest in getting the films, the customer relations department was ordered to buy the file, which it did. To prevent similar slipups in the future, the corporation tightened its scrapping procedures.

Chevrolet products were involved in the largest product recall in automotive history when, in 1971 the corporation called back 6.7 million 1965–69 Chevrolet cars to repair defective motor mounts. The rubber mounts, which anchor the engine to the car, were breaking apart and causing the engine to lunge out of place. This action often locked the accelerator into an open position of about 25 miles per hour. Cars were smashing up all across the country when panicky drivers couldn't stop them or jumped out of them in fright. The defect need never have been.

At Pontiac, when I was chief engineer, we developed a safety-interlock motor mount, which we put on our 1965 car line. It was developed because we discovered that the mounts we were using were defective. We made our findings and the design of the new motor mount available to the rest of the car divisions. None of them opted for it.

However, reports started drifting in from the field in 1966 that the Chevrolet mounts were breaking apart after extensive use. The division did nothing. Dealers replaced the mounts and charged the customers for the parts and labor.

When I got to Chevrolet in 1969, the reports about the motor mount failures were reaching crisis proportions. When a motor mount failure was blamed for a fatal accident involving an elderly woman in Florida, I asked Kyes, my boss, to let me quietly recall all the cars with these problem mounts and repair them, at GM's expense. He refused on the ground that it would cost too much money. By 1971, however, the motor mount trouble was becoming widely known outside of the corporation because unsatisfied owners were complaining to local newspapers, the National Highway Traffic Safety Administration, and several consumer groups.

The pressure began to build on GM to recall the cars with these mounts. Soon GM began to repair these cars at company expense, but it refused to recall all the cars, preferring to wait until the mounts broke in use before doing anything. Bob Irvin, of the Detroit *News,* who was receiving huge numbers of complaints, began to write almost daily stories about the mount trouble and GM's steadfast refusal to recall all the cars.

The fires of discontent were further fanned when Ed Cole, who was opposing the recall internally, was asked by a reporter why GM continued to refuse to recall the cars. He replied that the mounts were not a problem and that anyone who "can't manage a car at 25 miles per hour shouldn't be driving." It was an unfortunately callous remark, for which I am sure Cole was later sorry. But he became more rigid in his stance against a recall campaign. So I wrote a memo to my immediate boss in 1971, Tom Murphy, and it said in part:

> At this point in time, it seems to me that we have no alternative (but to recall the Chevrolets). Certainly if GM can spend over $200,000,000 a year on advertising, the $30 or $40,000,000 this campaign would cost is not a valid reason for delaying. Certainly, it would be worth the cost to stop the negative publicity, even if management cannot agree to campaign these cars on moral grounds.

Murphy received the memo and returned it to me, refusing to accept it.

Finally, about a month or so later, under the weight of government, consumer group, and newspaper pressure, GM recalled the 6.7 million cars with defective engine mounts. The price was about $40 million to recall the cars and wire the engines to the car so that they wouldn't slip out of place when the mounts broke.

But the cost was much greater in the incredibly bad publicity GM received because of its unwillingness to admit its responsibility for the defect and to repair the cars on its own. It was really a case of the corporation taking an attitude of "the owners be damned" when it came to spending the money it needed to fix the engine mount problem.

The motor mount affair reflected a general corporate attitude toward the consumer movement, an attitude shared by some American businesses in a wide variety of industries. The reason that consumer advocates, such as Ralph Nader, have emerged as public champions, and that city, state, and national governments have set up offices to look after consumer affairs, is that the people have legitimate beefs about the quality and safety of the products they are buying. If almost everybody who bought products were happy with them, there would be no Naders at the local, state, or national level. And even if there were, their cries would fall on deaf ears.

Car service is an example of an area of wide consumer displeasure today. At best, automotive service is poor. Car owners are suspicious of their dealers' service. More and more people are turning to the corner gasoline station mechanic for service, even though the nearby dealer is supposedly the specialist at fixing their car. The reason is that the auto companies, especially GM, have never committed themselves to improving the serviceability of the dealership.

A car dealer is judged by how many new cars he pushes out of the showroom doors in the front and not how he services them in the back. Dealers are graded primarily on their sales results, because this puts money into the corporate bank account and profit on the financial sheet. A big-volume dealer with a poor service operation is handled very gingerly by the manufacturer. Unfortunately, he often gets better treatment from the company than the dedicated, conscientious dealer with lower volume who invests heavily in a proper service facility.

The relationship between the company and its retail dealer body is a study in paradox. The corporation depends on its dealers to market its cars and trucks. Without the dealer body, GM or its competitors could not stay in business. Dealers and their businesses represent about half the total investment in GM.

The local Chevrolet or Buick dealer often is the only personal contact a customer has with GM. His perceptions of GM and its car divisions come from the way he is treated at the retail sales level. Such interlocking needs between the dealers and the company would seem to dictate a close and friendly relationship between the two.

In some cases, most often with high-volume dealers, this is the case. More often, behind the smiles, handshakes, and backslapping of dealer-company sales meetings, there is an adversary relationship that is contrary to the practical dictates of business. Dealers often don't trust the company and vice versa.

The tone for an adversary relationship between company and dealers has been set, I think, by shoddy treatment of the dealer body. While GM owes its very existence today to its dealers, the manner in which GM has manipulated and browbeaten them falls into the area of questionable ethics.

When I got to Chevrolet, the dealer body as a whole was very distrustful of divisional and corporate management because it had been left with a string of broken promises about new product developments and the exclusivity of its markets. In one instance, Bob Lund, Chevy's general sales manager, and I were asked to attend a Fourteenth Floor meeting to report on how Chevrolet dealers would react if Pontiac dealers were given a version of the compact Nova. At the time, our dealers were selling every Nova they could get into their dealerships. They also had been promised by corporate management that they would have this compact car market all to themselves among GM's divisions.

Before the meeting "upstairs," I was called into a small top management conference by Kyes and told that if I opposed a decision to give a Nova derivative to Pontiac, the small-car program I was pushing (the K-car project) would be taken from Chevrolet. Nevertheless, in the meeting I opposed the move, along with Lund, on the ground that our dealers couldn't get enough Novas as it was and that we had to keep our promise of exclusivity to them.

Lund and I were wasting our breath; the corporation gave Pontiac a version of the Nova called the Ventura. As it turned out, Pontiac dealers had trouble selling their compact cars, while Chevrolet dealers lost sales that they practically had in the bag. They were livid at the double-talk they had been given by the Fourteenth Floor. And my small-car program was never approved.

This was not an isolated case. The dealers are often bounced around at the whim of corporate management. And it is a wonder that car dealers have not formed an organization like the National Football League Players Association to represent their consolidated interests before the manufacturer. In the past, when GM effected a price cut to meet its competition or improve the sales of a particular car line, the cut often came out of the dealer's markup.

In other words, hypothetically assuming that GM announced a 4 percent price reduction on a $3,000 car, this would be a drop of $120 on the sticker price of the car. The public would praise the corporation's move, but what it wouldn't know was that the price of that car to the dealer from the company hadn't changed one bit. The company had lowered the manufacturer's suggested retail price by $120 by narrowing the profit spread between that price and the price of the car to the dealer. If the spread was 21 percent, it fell to 17 percent. The price reduction came out of the dealer's potential profit.

The company often leans on its dealers to maintain or increase its own profit levels, with little regard to the dealer's business climate. After the Arab oil embargo there was a sharp drop in big car sales. GM's big car divisions watched their business drop 50 percent or more. The plight was the same for the dealers, yet GM continued to force big cars on dealers with no relaxation in the payment schedules.

A practice that I opposed in GM was the constant pressuring of dealers to buy their service and after-market parts from the General Motors Parts Division (GMPD), when they could get some of the same parts cheaper from the warehouse distributors of the AC Spark Plug and Delco Product divisions.

Nevertheless, to keep GMPD viable, pressure was constantly applied to the dealers to buy parts from GMPD at a higher price. When GMPD held a big sales push, a car division sales or service representative would be given a quota of, say, 25,000 spark plugs to sell.

He'd walk into a GM car dealer and say, "Your quota is 1,000 spark plugs." If the dealer balked, he was badgered and browbeaten by the sales representatives of his own car division to meet his quota. In the end a balking dealer knew that the company held the upper hand because it could get even in many different ways, one of which was to slow up deliveries to him of hot-selling cars. Sometimes, large-volume dealers who were important to the corporation could fend off this pressure without fear of reprisal. But, more often than not, dealers had to knuckle under and buy the parts from GMPD at a higher price than they could get elsewhere.

In a somewhat different situation, there was a Chevy dealer in Florida who was the low bidder on the sale of a large fleet of cars. To win the bid he had to price the cars very close to his own cost. So, to save about $35 a car, his bid included Motorola radios instead of the GM-built Delco units. This $35 represented most of the profit for him per car. When the dealer ordered the cars from Chevrolet, sans Delco radios, the company representative contacted him and made it clear that unless he bought Delco radios for the cars, his order would be delayed three to four months. Such a delay would bring the cars to the dealer much later than the delivery date promised to the fleet customer. The Florida dealer was forced to buy Delco radios, and he made very little profit on the sale of these cars, while GM made thousands of dollars on the Delco radios alone. Later, I ran into a divisional guy who was gleeful in his replay of this case, crowing about how he forced this dealer to take company radios.

In many respects I felt that the dealers had carried the division and the corporation through rough sales periods. Chevy's dealers kept the division afloat during the mid-1960s. Our thanks for their help was to put the squeeze on them constantly for every last nickel of corporate profit. Our policies with dealers were shoddy. What we were doing was often a blatant violation of our own precepts of free enterprise.

When we were called down before congressional hearings to explain our side of the growing problem of governmental control of the industry, a frequent defense of our business was that we needed to preserve the free enterprise system. "In a free market, the customer is the winner. And the true principles of business prevail because the customer decides which businesses are successful and which are not," the corporation would tell any willing ear.

Yet, within our corporate walls we engaged in business practices that were not only monopolistic but sometimes were downright violations of the free enterprise system. We stifled competition. Our dealers weren't always free to run their business as they saw fit. We were forcing them at times to buy our parts and products at inflated prices.

We certainly could not tolerate the use of inferior parts by our dealers in repairing GM vehicles. But we sure as hell shouldn't have forced them to pay higher prices for our own parts than they could get elsewhere in the company. And, in situations where they had the choice of choosing our products, such as Delco radios or a competitor's product of similar quality, we should have had to sell the dealers on the merits of the GM product over the competition. That is what free enterprise is all about. We shouldn't have forced our dealers to take the GM product. If GM was buying a product from one company, it would buy it the cheapest way. That is just good business. Therefore, it felt what we were doing with our dealers was immoral and probably illegal.

So I told the Chevrolet sales executives, who were our dealer contact people, that we were never again going to force our dealers to pay more for a product they could get cheaper elsewhere. That was an order. There would be no more intimidation of Chevrolet dealers by the field sales force about buying spark plugs from GMPD. Our dealers could get GM parts where they got the best price.

Word quickly got to the Fourteenth Floor about this directive (I think it took less than an hour). I got a call that Mr. Kyes wanted to see me in his office immediately. When I got there, he was red-faced and mad. He launched a 15-minute, blistering attack on me as a person, citizen, employee, and businessman. I was verbally raked up one end of executive row and down the other. I thought he was going to fire me on the spot. His diatribe ended on a typically low note:

"You don't know how business is done. You're a goddamn amateur, DeLorean."

"That's just the way I feel. You don't solve the problem of an unequal discount structure on our parts by intimidating the dealers into paying a higher price. What you should do is look for a way to fix the problem," I responded.

I left his office. My order stuck. Chevrolet people stopped pressuring our dealers to take parts from GMPD.

Suppliers often feel the brunt of corporate power, pressure, and influence. A GM decision to stop buying one part from a particular company can send that firm into bankruptcy. GM and its auto company cohorts hold the power of life and death over many of their suppliers. In most cases that power is exercised responsibly. In some cases it is not.

During the development and introduction of the subcompact Vega, a problem arose in controlling emissions on the engine with two-barrel carburetors. We asked GM's Rochester Products Division to help us work on this problem. Its executive refused. We had to add a $25 air pump to these engines to burn exhaust gases more effectively. It was a costly and unsatisfactory remedy to the problem.

Holly Carburetor Co., an independent supplier, however, gladly worked with us on the problem. It developed a different type of two-barrel carburetor that promoted better combustion of the fuel in the engine. We were able to meet the pollution standards with this new carburetor. We could get rid of the expensive air pump and improve engine performance. This saved Chevrolet about $3 million per year.

Now, development of such a new product by an outside supplier carries with it an implicit gentleman's promise by the company that the supplier will get some of the business. Suppliers sometimes do not take patents on such work, or if they do, they give their client free access to the design. In this case, when Rochester Products Division found out about the Holly breakthrough, it got panicky that it was going to lose the Vega business. The corporate management came to Rochester's aid and threw out Holly as a possible supplier on the carburetor it designed and gave the job to Rochester. Chevrolet's director of purchasing, George Ford, a tremendous man of sound integrity, brought the problem to my attention. We fought our way to the top of the corporation. Holly was finally allowed to keep a little piece of the business.

The morality of such arbitrary action compelled me to write a memo to my superior, Tom Murphy, after the Holly incident in August of 1971, and send a copy to Ed Cole. It said in part:

> Obviously, Holly will never help us again — and Rochester will never again heed one of our threats to go outside — so that the next time the $3,000,000 a year (cost savings) will go down the drain. Needless to say, the impact on our technical and purchasing people has been great — because we have made them a party to a questionable, shabby business practice against their will.
>
> I have instructed our people to stop getting outside quotations in competition with Allied Division, since it is unfair to ask a firm to spend time and money preparing a quote when they have no chance at the business. I should point out that outside quotes have enabled Chevrolet and GM to reduce our product costs by over $30,000,000 per year over the past two years.
>
> In my opinion, this decision was shortsighted — and is one of the main reasons that General Motors has not led in a significant technical innovation since the automatic transmission. Power steering, reheat air conditioning, power brakes, power windows, disc brakes, the alternator and the two-way tail gate all originated with our competitors.

The memo concluded:

> To my mind, a supplier who makes a significant contribution earns some business — to use our suppliers otherwise

is immoral. To use the size and might of General Motors
in this way borders on illegality and invites antitrust action.

I never got a reply to this memo, but my dwindling stock as a team player
fell a few extra points.

DISCUSSION QUESTIONS

1. In your own view, what is John DeLorean's complaint with General
   Motor's management? Do his examples carry credibility with you — do
   they indicate a serious weakness in General Motors and/or other large
   industrial firms?
2. Assuming DeLorean's charges are not trivial, what is the solution to the
   problems he identifies? What are your recommendations to
   management?
3. What is necessary for your recommendations to be implemented on a
   broad scale? What is the likelihood this will occur?

Institutional Management
Governing the Corporation

Who controls the corporation? Is private power exercised in a way that leads to the public interest? Do corporations have a responsibility to society above and beyond an economic function? These questions, commonly heard in discussions about the role of corporations in society, do not challenge the private enterprise system as the source of society's wealth; they do suggest, however, issues that arise frequently about how this role is implemented and its broader social and political implications.

A basic premise of the American economic system is that social goods are created through private economic pursuits. To the extent the system is perceived to allow personal financial gains without corresponding social benefits, the control and credibility of the corporation are open to attack. The issues of corporate governance address the structure of decision making that seek to minimize divergence of interests among individuals, firms, and the wider society.

Corporate ethics concerns the values implicit or explicit in a decision, and the values embedded in a decision are, naturally, influenced by the structure and process of the decision-making process. Consequently the study of corporate governance is — an analysis of top management decision making — a major approach to the analysis of ethics in management.

This section takes three specific approaches to the questions of governance. The first chapter, Chapter 7, examines governance from the standpoint of the corporate board of directors. Public policy toward the board and the board's private management lie at the heart of any discussion about corporate control today.

Chapter 8 expands the discussion of decision making and managerial accountability to review the roles of professionals — primarily accountants and lawyers — in the modern corporation. Many demands on managerial knowledge, skill, and practice will be found in directing the professional activities in the firm.

In recent years many firms have experienced new, productive ways of broadening governance process to include employees more fully, and employee-employer relationships remain an important focus of public policy and corporate development. Relations between the firm and employees constitute the material of Chapter 9, the third and final chapter in this section.

Chapter 7

The Corporate Board of Directors

Relationships to Management, Investors, and the Public

The assumption of individuals as primarily pursuing their self-interests is an essential premise of capitalism: it allows economic competition and results in the overall welfare of society. Similarly, pursuit of narrow personal interests is central to the democratic political process. We have seen earlier that setting "ambition against ambition" in politics has provided enduring protection against the centralization of power in the United States.

While faith is placed in the individual as a source of economic energy and political involvement, American society has also realized the need for institutions to guard against unrestrained self-interest and self-aggrandizement. In other words a system of social control is necessary to cope with the possibility or the actuality of a breakdown in self-control.

American traditions have been inventive in allowing personal choice while protecting the public from misuse of liberty. Foremost among these American traditions is a strong reliance on mechanisms that seek to segment functions and responsibilities. Segmentation of responsibilities is primary to the concept of the separate legislative, judicial, and executive branches of government. Segmentation of functions is designed to prevent the occurrence, or even the temptation, of self-serving decisions that might arise from combining functions and centralizing power. Moreover, requirements for public hearings, access to public records, and the freedom of an independent press represent forms of social control against the extension of self-interest into power aggrandizement in the public sector. Distrust of secrecy and consistent effort to democratize our institutions are safeguards against the excesses of individualism.

One benefit of clear demarcation of the public from the private sector is also rooted in the notion of checks and balances. A strong private sector serves as a check on the threat of loss of liberty from centralized public decision making, and a strong federal government has, in part, grown in response to a need to check the perceived excesses of private pursuits. Similarly, corporations have their own internal checks and balances structures; labor organizations, the separation of the controller's office from line management, and the requirement for an outside financial audit are all forms of control on management's actions.

Finally, watchdog roles are created within institutions to ensure that execution of tasks conforms to the intent and policy of the organization; the army's inspector general serves a control function with the investigatory and punitive power over the army's line organization; the General Accounting Office (GAO) of the federal government investigates and reports undesirable deviations of programs from their intended purposes; departments of internal auditing in corporations conduct operational and financial audits and play an influential role.

The American creed of faith in the individual is balanced by a healthy skepticism of selfish motives and fear of centralization. Skepticism and fear generate sensitivity to conflicts of interest and self-dealing. One of the hallmarks of the individualist ethic is a predisposition to challenge authority — a challenge that represents long-run insurance on the maintenance of individual freedom.

SOCIAL CONTROL AND THE MODERN CORPORATION

The American fear of unbridled power influences attitudes about the growing size and complexity of modern corporations. Public control over business activities was present in mercantile capitalism through widespread government sponsorship of commercial activity, but such direct governmental control of corporations is an unattractive prospect today. Furthermore, control exercised through direct personal contact possible in a small-scale economy is not even remotely feasible in today's huge and complex world. The invisibility of business decision making to the outsider, the inaccessibility to information, and the psychological distance between the average citizen and corporate leaders are largely functions of the largeness and diffused character of the business sector. Given the common presence of multimillion dollar, multiproduct, multinational corporations, it simply is not obvious who is responsible for specific actions or how and why particular decisions are made. Granting even the best of intentions to managers, large corporations are naturally subject to traditional American fears and suspicion of concentrated power.

Boards of Directors

The corporate board of directors is a creature of the corporation's bylaws that are specified by the laws of the state in which the firm is incorporated.

State laws establish only the most general standards for the role of the board; it is typical for directors simply to be charged with "the management of the affairs of the corporation." Few conditions are placed on the size, the composition, or the frequency of meetings. The board of most privately held corporations consists of the owner-manager, family, and trusted associates. When a corporation issues stock to the public, purchasers of large amounts of stock often take board positions. In addition, it is not unusual to find major creditors, attorneys, and CEOs of other companies as directors. By and large, individuals are invited to participate as directors at the pleasure of the firm's chief executive, who is often also chairman of the board. The shareholders' and directors' roles in nominating new board members and the wisdom of combining the roles of the board chairman and CEO are controversial issues discussed in a later section.

Boards also have great latitude in their degree of activity and participation in the affairs of the corporation. Minimally, corporate boards are usually required by state statute to meet once a year to declare any dividends and to hire, compensate, and replace the CEO. Of course, most boards are substantially more involved in establishing the direction and evaluating the performance of the corporation than suggested by these minimal functions, although questions remain about the extent to which director involvement is possible and whether the board is an effective mechanism for ensuring competent and responsible management.

Management versus Shareholder Control

In a highly competitive and decentralized economy dominated by relatively small firms, questions of corporate governance would seldom arise. Firm owners manage their enterprises and act in concert with their own personal interests. The absence of other parties participating in ownership drastically simplifies the process of governing the firm. When firms are small and the results of their actions are localized, there is no significant group of people — workers, citizens, customers — dependent on a single business, and claims of external "stakeholders" are uncommon.

However, increases in size, scope, and public ownership of the modern corporation change this, as a separation develops between corporate ownership and managerial control. Now, owners often number in the hundreds of thousands or millions, they are widely dispersed, and they rarely take a direct interest in management actions. Rather, they are interested primarily in the return on, and valuation of, their investments. The corporation now faces a question of whether management, which has actual control of the corporation, has incentives, rewards, and goals consistent with shareholder interests and whether the corporate board is prepared to exercise adequate control if management fails to serve shareholder interests.

In addition, the scale and visibility of publicly held corporations have increased, and constituencies other than stockholders are well organized, vocal, and able to pursue their claims and press their expectations for corporate action. Nontraditional and ill-defined, but strong, claims on corporate action complicate the process of corporate governance. A gradual evolution of the corporation and its environment has, particularly in the last decade, focused public scrutiny and concern on the ultimate governing unit, the corporate board.

Wide attention to the separation of management and control was first stimulated by the classic study of Adolf Berle and Gardiner Means in 1933 entitled *The Modern Corporation and Private Property*.[1] Through close analysis of available information on ownership of the 200 largest corporations at the time, these authors classified companies according to the degree of owner versus management control. Their study concluded that 44 percent of the companies were under management control (no single individual, family, or association of business interests held more than 20 percent of the company's stock) owing to the wide dispersal of stock ownership. Moreover, an additional 21 percent of the companies were in management control through the use of legal devices such as holding companies. The implications of this information for Berle and Means is presented as an excerpt from their book in Insert 7.A.

The Berle and Means study was one of the first to direct attention to the emergence of the "corporate system" and to show how aggregate concentrations of wealth, large corporate size, and separation of ownership from control created a fundamentally new economic structure. Since this ground-breaking study, a number of authors have researched various facets of corporate ownership. One later study, replicating the Berle and Means approach, found that the degree of management control had widened in large corporations: approximately 75 percent of the largest 500 nonfinancial corporations in 1963 were judged to be under management control.[2]

Other researchers have attempted to explain control by dominant minorities or by investment institutions, but the inevitable debate on statistical methods has not eliminated the problem of how to establish management accountability to the individual investor in the large publicly held corporation.[3]

More than an empirical study of large corporate ownership, Berle and Means' work confronted the ability of traditional laissez-faire economic concepts to explain the new economic structure. A number of questions were raised in this work about the applicability of classical ideas of competition, individual initiative, and private enterprise in the new corporate context.

An even more current issue is the widespread ownership of our publicly held companies by professionally managed investment funds. By one estimate, at least one third of the equity of U.S. publicly owned companies is held by pension and mutual funds, and for many big companies, funds own closer to 50 percent of the company.[4] Managers of these funds are trustees for their fund investors, and they are obliged to seek the highest

Insert 7.A

IMPACT OF THE MODERN CORPORATION [QUOTATION]

Whereas the organization of feudal economic life rested upon an elaborate system of binding customs, the organization under the system of private enterprise has rested upon the self-interest of the property owner — a self-interest held in check only by competition and the conditions of supply and demand. Such self-interest has long been regarded as the best guarantee of economic efficiency. It has been assumed that, if the individual is protected in the right both to use his own property as he sees fit and to receive the full fruits of its use, his desire for personal gain, for profits, can be relied upon as an effective incentive to his efficient use of any industrial property he may possess.

In the quasi-public corporation, such an assumption no longer holds. . . . it is no longer the individual himself who uses his wealth. Those in control of that wealth, and therefore in a position to secure industrial efficiency and produce profits, are no longer, as owners, entitled to the bulk of such profits. Those who control the destinies of the typical modern corporation own so insignificant a fraction of the company's stock that the returns from running the corporation profitability accrue to them in only a very minor degree. The stockholders, on the other hand, to whom the profits of the corporation go, cannot be motivated by those profits to a more efficient use of the property, since they have surrendered all disposition of it to those in control of the enterprise. The explosion of the atom of property destroys the basis of the old assumption that the quest for profits will spur the owner of industrial property to its effective use. It consequently challenges the fundamental economic principle of individual initiative to industrial enterprise.

SOURCE: Adolf A. Berle, Jr., and Gardiner C. Means, *The Modern Corporation and Private Property* (New York: Macmillan, 1933), pp. 8–9. Copyright 1932 by Macmillan Publishing Co., Inc., renewed 1960 by Adolf A. Berle, Jr., and Gardiner C. Means. Used by permission.

immediate return for their investors even if that does not necessarily coincide with the apparent long-term interest of the company in which they have invested. This structure of ownership is thought by some to pressure managers into a short-term profit orientation. Discussing the shift of voting power in the corporation from owners to fiduciaries, Peter Drucker states:

> The classicial defense of ownership has always been that the "owner" has an abiding, long-term interest in the welfare of his property and that, therefore, his decisions are

more likely than those of anyone else to balance and optimize the interests of all who have a stake in the enterprise:
those of the owner, to be sure, but also those of employees,
creditors, suppliers, customers, the economy and society in
general.

The owner's self-interest, argued the Roman lawyers
2,000 years ago when they developed the legal concept we
now call "property," was most nearly compatible with the
true interest of the enterprise. But the new legal "owners"
of our publicly owned businesses are forbidden as fiduciaries even to consider the interest of the enterprise. . . .
And how do we reconcile the justified interest of beneficiaries who need to be "investors" rather than "owners," and
whose priorities therefore are quite properly liquidity and
the fast buck, with the welfare of society's wealth- and job-
producing asset: the going concern, the enterprise?[5]

Issues of ownership, control, accountability, and decision making
criteria at the highest corporate levels have repeatedly arisen in this century
as many firms have increased in size, public ownership, social influence,
and visibility. Owing to an inevitable interdependence between the public
and private interests, corporate performance and the structure of executive
decision making have come under close scrutiny at various times in our
recent history. The remainder of this chapter continues with a review of
the context for the Securities and Exchange legislation of the 1930s. Several incidents giving rise to public concerns about corporate control since
the mid-1960s are discussed, and public and private responses to these issues are presented, including recent regulation such as the Shareholder
Communication Rules of 1978. A final section addresses the topic of corporate social integration, arguing that only apparent conflict exists between
the concepts of profit maximization and social responsibility — both perspectives can be incorporated in what might be termed a *value-creating* relationship between directors and managers.

MANAGEMENT AND SHAREHOLDER INTERESTS

Before the Securities and Exchange Legislation

The issue of the compatibility of owner and manager interests radically
changed in 1933 and 1934, the years of the enactment of the Securities and
Exchange legislation. Deceptive and misleading sales efforts for corporate
securities, self-dealing by corporate managers, and outright fraud in securities transactions were problems that worried Berle and Means and were
targets of government regulation in securities legislation. Stockholders had
come to play largely passive roles in corporate control, and managers' ma-

jor incentives could easily be personal, rather than corporate, earnings. It became clear that there were no mechanisms to prevent managers from overriding the interests of stockholders to maximize their private gain. For example, Berle and Means present a case in which managers holding 60 percent of the stock of a corporation might be tempted to sell a piece of their personally held property to the corporation at a million dollars above its fair market value. The loss the managers would suffer as majority owners of the corporation would be more than compensated for by their million dollar private gain on the transaction. The 40 percent minority stockholders would be the actual losers. As the managers' ownership of the corporation decreases and both profits and losses to the company occur less and less to them, the opportunities of profiting at the expense of the corporation appear to be more directly to their benefit.[6]

Also of concern in this period were instances of clear profiteering from a privileged position of management: benefiting from the diversion of profits between parent and subsidiary or between classes of stock, using "insider information" in market operations, or manipulating markets through misleading information. The "pyramiding" of holding companies within holding companies, the widespread stock manipulations, the exposure of rampant financial conflicts of interests, and most of all, the damage to the small investor, which were all parts of the great market crash of 1929, set the stage for the securities regulation of the early 1930s.

What was to prevent abuse of power in the absence of direct stockholder control of corporations? If owners would not, or could not, assert control, it was nearly inevitable that government would establish a countervailing influence, as it did with the enactment of the Securities Act of 1933 and the Securities Exchange Act of 1934.

The Securities and Exchange Acts

Together these acts constitute the backbone of governmental influence on the offering of corporate securities to the public and on the operation of capital markets and professional securities dealers. On a broad level the securities laws require the registration of public offerings of corporations, including specification of information to be provided and determination of required signatures of corporate officers verifying the completeness and accuracy of the information. The laws establish liabilities for presenting false information to the public in the sale of securities, and they define and outlaw practices of price manipulation and other deceptive devices. In addition to defining standards of conduct and establishing legal accountability for deception and fraud, the 1933 act contained a provision for a mandatory annual audit of the issuers' financial statements by an independent public accountant, a requirement that has been much scrutinized in recent years. (Implications of this requirement will be reviewed in the following chapter.) Finally, the securities legislation established the Securities and Exchange Commission (SEC) as an independent regulatory agency to administer the laws.

The reporting requirements of the SEC are numerous: they involve reporting of detailed information in the prospectus and registration statements for public offerings of securities, information inclusion in proxy solicitations, and rules for reporting director and officer trading in the company stock. In short the SEC seeks to protect investor interests by requiring companies to provide information that is directly relevant to investor decisions.

Disclosure regulation is an indirect influence: it permits private action and decision while serving the purpose of yielding complete and accurate financial information. It aims to influence the premises and intentions of corporate action, the process of decision making, rather than the outcomes of decision making. The requirement of disclosure with the threat of litigation for false or misleading statements encourages involvement of legal counsel, board participation, and strong development of internal accounting systems.

The disclosure requirements of the securities laws, and thus of the SEC, are based upon the philosophy that public accountability is a powerful control on behavior. A business executive once remarked that he addressed ethical elements of decisions by asking himself if he would mind having his decision printed on the front page of the next day's paper; the possibility of public knowledge greatly influences personal behavior. William Gladstone, an English statesman, stated this view in saying, "Publicity breeds responsibility." In interpreting the Securities Act of 1933 Felix Frankfurter agreed: "The blackmailer lives in darkness. Public financing must live in the light of day."[7]

TRADITIONAL CHECKS ON CORPORATE POWER

The Last 20 Years

A number of disturbing corporate actions in the 1960s and early 1970s illustrated the apparent inadequacies of corporate control. One of the more prominent examples was the visible board failure of Penn Central with its quiescent and submissive board, unwittingly controlled and steered by management into financial disaster. Penn Central's 1970 bankruptcy caused a wave of stockholder and creditor suits that challenged the boards' abdication of management responsibility. One Penn Central director later described the board's role:

> At each Penn Central directors' meeting, which only lasted an hour and a half, we were presented with long lists of relatively small capital expenditures to approve. We were shown sketchy financial reports which were rarely discussed in any detail. The reports were not designed to be

revealing, and we were asked not to take them away from the meeting. And we always had an oral report by the CEO promising better results next month which never came true.[8]

The SEC, upon conducting a detailed investigation into the collapse of Penn Central, was more direct:

Management's efforts involved misrepresentations as to the affairs, prospects, financial results, and value of assets of the Penn Central complex. The misrepresentations were made in many forms of communications to the investing public and stockholder.[9]

Various safeguard mechanisms had failed in the case of Penn Central; not only the board's control over management but also the outside audit and the oversight of the Interstate Commerce Commission (ICC) had failed to expose and correct a worsening financial situation. Other instances of management misrepresentation came to light in the 1960s and 1970s. In 1969 false financial statements of the National Student Marketing Corporation were disclosed; and in the early 1970s the public was exposed to financial misrepresentations from Stirling Homex and extensive fraud at Equity Funding. The pattern of isolated, but similar, events in these years raised fresh questions about the checks and balances system of corporate control in relation to management discretion and decisions.

As the tangled web of relationships and financial dealings of the Watergate investigation unraveled in the mid-1970s, additional deficiencies in the responsibilities of the board of directors came into public focus. Many companies had, through executives, made substantial illegal political contributions or had been deeply involved in foreign bribes and payoffs. Numerous companies voluntarily disclosed illegal political payments and large overseas bribes to avoid SEC prosecution. At least one corporation disclosed the diversion of some $13 million of corporate funds to a hidden slush fund over a 13-year period, and by the end of 1977, U.S. companies had disclosed hundreds of millions of dollars in questionable payments.[10]

In various cases these actions involved "off-the-books" transactions and showed the degree management could act autonomously without answering either to the stockholders directly or to their board representatives. More than the absolute sums of money, or the instances of the use of poor judgment, the absence of management accountability was the startling fact and the cause for reexamination of the corporate governance process.

New Issues in the 1980s

A fresh set of challenges to managerial accountability, largely arising in the area of mergers and acquisitions, came to the fore in the early 1980s. Several practices drew public criticism in a heightened wave of corporate take-over attempts. The first was the policy of granting management contracts to company executives, ensuring them substantial financial payments in the event the company was acquired. An outcry against these contracts, called *golden parachutes,* reached a crescendo in the complex takeover battle between Bendix, Martin Marietta, Allied, and United Technologies. In the course of the fight between Bendix and Martin Marietta, William Agee, instigator of the conflict and CEO of Bendix, secured a $4 million golden parachute from the Bendix board. Eight days after Bendix was acquired by Allied Corporation, Agee exercised his right to this tidy sum by resigning from Allied. In fact, 16 Bendix executives, 28 persons at Martin Marietta, 2 officials at Allied, and 64 executives at United Technologies were covered by golden parachutes.[11]

Golden parachutes have been criticized as providing financial benefit for management at the expense of the company's shareholders. Corporations are usually acquired when their assets are judged to be under-performing and shareholder values are judged to be undervalued. Why, opponents of golden parachutes ask, should management receive a reward or a bonus for having done a poor job? Why should corporate assets be transferred to poor-performing managers? In response, advocates of golden parachutes respond that a management contract reduces financial uncertainty for managers at the time of a likely acquisition attempt by another company, allowing the executives of the target company to be objective and to act in their shareholders' interests. Yes, critics respond, but this is supposedly what they were being paid to do in the first place; why do they need the security of a lucrative contract to carry out an assumed responsibility?

Another recent development in the area of corporate takeovers is called *greenmail.* In this case a private investor or group of investors usually buys between 10 and 25 percent of the stock of a publicly-held corporation. The investor group then requests a position on the corporate board or threatens to make a tender offer for control of the corporation. Greenmail occurs when the firm's present management agrees to buy the raider's shares at a handsome profit and at a price significantly higher than other shareholders can obtain if they were to sell their stock. In taking such an action management and the board are usually seen to be seeking to avert a takeover battle and potential loss of their management positions.

Is the use of greenmail to fend off a takeover artist in shareholders' interests? Critics argue that it is inequitable for corporations to buy large blocks of their own stock at a premium price from one shareholder and not another, and that this practice may simply be another way of protecting a weak management at the expense of all shareholders. Insert 7.B describes a study conducted at the SEC which lends substantiation to their charges.

Counterarguments to the skeptics' questions are provided in defense. Golden parachutes, for example, add to the cost of a proposed takeover and ensure the strength of the acquiring company's intentions. Green-

---

Insert 7.B

GREENMAIL: HOW DO SHAREHOLDERS FAIR?

By 1984 the trend toward greenmail payments to corporate raiders appeared to be accelerating. Between 1979 and the end of 1983 about $5.5 billion dollars was paid by firms to select groups of shareholders to purchase their common stock. Over $3.5 billion of this total occurred in 1983 alone.

The repurchase of common stock was less important than the fact that the companies usually paid a considerable premium to a few stockholders that was not available to all the company's owners. In 1983 such greenmail payments represented a premium of more than $600 million above the market price of the stock, and for the four-year period this premium was more than $1 billion dollars.

What is the impact of greenmail transactions on the stock holdings of the other shareholders of these companies? Do they fare well or poorly? Or is the value of their stock uninfluenced by these dealings? A study of this question was conducted by the Office of the Chief Economist of the SEC.

The study evaluated 89 cases of greenmail using statistical techniques that establish changes in stock prices (and thus in shareholder wealth) relative to the movements of the market as a whole. Major conclusions from this study were:

* All shareholders of the targeted companies experienced initial increases in wealth upon the release of public information that a shareholder or group of shareholders acting in concert had established ownership of more than 3 percent of the firm's stock. Shareholders received an average return of 9.7 percent owing to the announcement of an outside group or individual purchase of a large block of stock. It would appear that interest in the company of an outside group leads to speculation that all shareholders will benefit.
* Stock prices drop considerably on the average, however, as it becomes evident that a tender offer would not be made. The initial appreciation of the stock is more than offset by its later depreciation. The average return to shareholders of all the companies studied due to the whole incident — initial announcement and announcement of greenmail payments — was a negative 3.7 percent.
* An additional analysis was conducted where it appeared that the dissident stockholder group was contesting control of the corporation. This situation would represent the greatest threat to the employment security of the existing management, since a successful effort to gain control would invariably be followed by a change of management. Losses to shareholders in these situations were even more dramatic —

Insert 7.B   continued

the loss in stock value due to the greenmail payment averaged 6 percent.

The author of this study concluded that greenmail payments support the welfare of managers and are not in the interests of shareholders: "It becomes possible, therefore, for incumbent management to offer a relatively more lucrative payment to the dissident block-holder, even if the best interests of all shareholders are served by a change of control." The solution to this problem proposed by the SEC is relatively simple — require shareholder approval of any stock repurchase agreements — although by mid-1985 this proposal remained under discussion in Congress.

SOURCE: Office of the Chief Economist, Securities and Exchange Commission, *The Impact of Targeted Share Repurchases (Greenmail) on Stock Prices* (Washington, D.C.: Securities and Exchange Commission, September 11, 1984).

mail is simply a variation in the sophisticated game of finance; every transaction involves a winner and a loser, and if one is not prepared to accept the risk of losing against more able players, that person should get out of the game.

Another controversial issue of managerial accountability is *insider trading.* The SEC has interpreted the prohibition of the Securities and Exchange Act against fraudulent and deceptive action by corporate officers and directors to include the public trading of the company's stock based on material nonpublic information. In other words it is illegal for corporate officials to profit from knowledge available to them by virtue of their inside position in the firm. In practice this means that insiders cannot sell the company stock for a six-month period after purchase, they cannot sell the company stock short, and they must register all trades with the SEC as public information within 30 days of the trade.

The reasoning behind these regulations is the protection of the investing public. Our capital markets are based on the premise that public goods are created through processes of private gain; private gains having no apparent benefit for the economy or society as a whole are vulnerable to challenge. Why, it might be asked, should corporate insiders stand to benefit financially in the trading of company stock simply by virtue of their position of insiders? Is this role consistent with the concept of directors as trustees and managers as administrators of the shareholders' interests?

Insider trading is argued to promote capital market efficiency by providing information on the true state of a company to the market through knowledge of insider trades. This information allows for the adjustment of stock prices at the earliest point and thus aids increased efficiency of the trading system. Moreover, investors do not appear to require any greater premium for the greater risk associated with companies in which insiders trade actively versus those in which they do not.[12] If no greater risk is perceived, where is the harm to outsiders? And if no harm to outsiders can be demonstrated, why regulate insider trading?

Golden parachutes, greenmail, and insider trading each constitute a controversial issue bearing upon shareholder-director-management relationships. In some cases the government has acted to curb such practices. The Deficit Reduction Act of 1984, for example, included a 20 percent "excise tax" on recipients of golden parachutes that were approved after a tender offer, and this law removed the deductibility of the cost of the parachute to the corporation. In addition, in 1984 Congress increased the penalty for illegal insider trading to treble damages, thereby strengthening the SEC's influence on this practice.

These issues of managerial accountability in the early 1980s are variations on earlier challenges to the system of corporate ownership and control. The validity of specific questions on greenmail and insider trading will necessarily await the development of more information and the emergence of a public consensus. At a more general level, however, they do indicate a continuing tension concerning managerial accountability and corporate legitimacy, which remain imperfectly resolved questions in our economy. We turn now to review three traditional checks and balances in the lights of the challenges to corporate governance in the last several decades: the economic marketplace, the legal framework of officer and director liability, and the board's responsibility to maintain management oversight.

The Marketplace

There is no question that the forces of economic competition and free movement of capital exert a powerful discipline on the performance of corporate managers. Consistently poor earnings performance and low returns on capital generally do lead to replacement of deficient managers. Moreover, the threat of a takeover or acquisition of a poorly performing company by a strong performer is realistic; new owners are very likely to replace a weak management to increase the performance of assets. Thus the market can act as a discipline on a poorly performing corporate management.

How thoroughly, however, does this mechanism function? Directors may take years to assign responsibility for poor economic performance and replace management, while the damage to the corporation's financial position may be severe. Or, as in the case of Penn Central and others, directors may never be presented with a true picture of the financial condition of the corporation or be able to dispose of management. Also, while acquisition by another firm is always a possibility, it remains uncertain and unpredictable as a control process. Further, some corporations have altered their charters, or bylaws, to make takeover attempts by other corporations more difficult. One official observer of these trends, ex-SEC chairman Harold Williams, states, "Charter amendments requiring super majorities to alter corporate bylaws, the staggering of director terms of office, and similar devices serve to insulate management from the possibility of ouster by an outsider — regardless of the performance of management or the price the outsider is willing to pay."[13]

How, then, can the small investor be adequately protected against inept or fraudulent management performance? The most common method offered to stockholders is to sell their stock, which, combined with few buyers, spells a decline in stock price. This alternative of selling is what economist Albert Hirschman calls the "exit" option — to leave or withdraw from affiliation with the company.[14] Entrance and exit decisions for owners define the domain of the economist and can exert a powerful force for reform, but they may be only part of the total picture. The public would probably not expect the small stockholder, simply for being small, to bear the brunt of financial loss without some opportunity to participate in and influence corporate affairs. Thus the option to exit, while useful and common, may not be a completely acceptable answer. The alternative of internal participation and influence, namely governance, also needs to be taken into account.

The point is not to discredit the discipline of market forces; they are real, and they are indispensable to a private economic system. At the same time, they may not be completely sufficient forces — particularly in concentrated industries and in the context of large corporations, exactly the situations where the issue of accountability of power has its greatest force.

Legal Obligations of Management

The legal establishment of director and officer responsibilities to the investing public was one dimension of the Securities and Exchange legislation of the 1930s. The securities legislation ensures that a substantial amount of information will be available to investors and establishes management accountability for its accuracy. In general, directors and officers are liable for losses suffered by investors who rely on misleading or inaccurate information, for director negligence in performance of duties, or for the stock market profits of insiders who take advantage of their privileges and advanced knowledge of developments important to the company.

While officers, directors, and stockholders are protected from personally meeting the financial obligations of the corporation by the limited liability provision of incorporation laws, officers and directors are personally liable for violation of the securities laws. Directors are not, in other words, protected by the corporate shell for violation of the securities laws or for other illegal actions such as price-fixing. One corporate legal expert summarizes the antifraud rule of the securities legislation:

> Rule 10b-5 provides that it shall be unlawful for any person: (a) to employ any device, scheme, or artifice to defraud, (b) to make any untrue statement of a material fact necessary in order to make the statements made, in light of the circumstances under which they were made, not misleading, or (c) to engage in any act, practice, or course of business which operates or would operate as a fraud or deceit upon any person, in connection with the purchase or sale of any security. The rule applies to any person and to any security, whether registered or not and whether debt or equity.[15]

The existence of personal liability leads to the question of what standards of performance are applied to directors. When has a director been negligent in ensuring the accuracy of information? How careful does one have to be? If the directors' judgment turns out to be unwise and the corporation loses a substantial amount of money, do the directors have an acceptable defense?

Two tests have been applied to define the limits of director care and negligence. The first of these, incorporated in most state laws, is the *reasonable director standard:* the standard of care to which directors are bound is that which "ordinarily prudent and diligent men would exercise under similar circumstances."[16] The second rule, somewhat stricter, is relied upon more by the courts and written into the federal securities laws as Section 11 of the 1933 act. This has been termed a *reasonable person standard,* which requires a director to conduct a reasonable investigation "required of a prudent man in the management of his own property."[17] Insert 7.C describes one court case in which directors were found liable for not exercising their duty of due care in signing a false registration statement.

Insert 7.C

A DIRECTOR'S RESPONSIBILITY OF DUE DILIGENCE

A landmark case in defining director responsibility for due care, or due diligence, concerned a construction company named Barchris. This company, facing financial distress, decided to raise needed capital by issuing new securities. Not long after selling the securities, the company went into bankruptcy. As the actual financial condition of the firm came to light, the firm was sued by the purchasers of the securities who claimed the information given in the securities registration statement and the prospectus to potential buyers was false and misleading. The court ruled that, in fact, assets were substantially overstated and liabilities were understated; and

Insert 7.C   continued

the court held management, lawyers, underwriters, auditors, and directors liable for this misrepresentation.

A special question pertained to the defense of two outside directors who had joined the Barchris board just at the time the registration statement was filed with the Securities and Exchange Commission. Neither director conducted an independent investigation of the accuracy of the prospectus, although they had inquired into the general condition of the company before joining the board and relied upon other directors and the accountants to attest to the statement's accuracy.

Establishing the obligations of these directors, the judge of the U.S. District Court of New York stated what has come to be a judicial precedent for director diligence:

> Section 11 imposes liability in the first instance upon a director, no matter how new he is. He is presumed to know his responsibility when he becomes a director. He can escape liability only by using that reasonable care to investigate the facts which a prudent man would employ in the management of his own property. In my opinion, a prudent man would not act in an important matter without any knowledge of the relevant facts, in sole reliance upon representations of persons who are comparative strangers and upon general information which does not purport to cover the particular case. To say that such minimal conduct measures up to the statutory standards would, to all intents and purposes, absolve new directors from responsibility merely because they are new. This is not a sensible construction of Section 11, when one bears in mind its fundamental purpose of requiring full and truthful disclosure for the protection of investors.

SOURCE: Escott v. *Barchris Construction Corporation,* 283 F. Supp. 643 (1968).

These are difficult standards to apply — in fact, one legal observer, Larry Soderquist, states that the latitude of these standards makes it impossible "to distill from the case law a set of specific rules to govern the conduct of directors."[18] Moreover, a director is usually able to mount a strong self-defense on the grounds of the reasonable director or the reasonable person standards. This defense lies in the demonstration that the director conducted a reasonable investigation of the material and had reason to believe, and in fact did believe, in the accuracy of the information.

A related defense against negligence is termed the *business judgment rule,* which says that directors are not liable for business decisions that failed or worked out poorly. In other words placement of capital is a choice the investor makes and a risk he or she bears. In general the courts have ruled that a director can be absolved of errors by acting in good faith and without a corrupt motive.[19] As a final resort corporations commonly pay for directors' and officers' insurance covering them against suits involving business judgments. It is important to note, though, that insurance cannot be provided for actions that involve breaking the law.

Naturally, the Penn Central, Equity Funding, and similar fiascos were followed by a rash of stockholder lawsuits. Yet these examples illustrate that legal action is essentially recuperative to the damaged parties. Not only is it lengthy and costly, but it generally fails to influence policy in a forward sense or to guide management in desired directions. Litigation is certainly both a deterrent to negligence and a mechanism in which investors may recoup losses in the event of improper conduct; but litigation seems less reliable as a channel for ensuring high levels of responsibility to shareholders.

For these reasons it would be hard to argue that judicial rules have provided a check on anything other than gross director misconduct or negligence. Soderquist states the courts generally hold "directors liable for active mismanagement, fraud, of self-dealing, while rarely imposing liability for an alleged failure to direct," and he reports another legal expert's appraisal of director liability law in which negligence in the absence of self-dealing was found to be "a search for a very small number of needles in a very large haystack."[20]

On the other hand the law may be broadening; increasingly directors are subject to *reason to know* standards that call for a more active and aggressive fulfillment of obligations. There is some indication that director liability is being expanded to include management integrity in addition to the safeguarding of the firm's assets, and there may be a broadening of director due care responsibilities beyond the purchase and sale of securities to areas such as compliance with environmental and consumer protection laws.[21] However, these developments are not as yet sufficiently clear and widespread to redefine the effect of legal checks on director responsibility.

Boards of Director Oversight

If failures of corporate control in the 1950s and 1970s indicated deficiencies in economic and legal checks on management power, they particularly highlighted the inconsistent and often weak role of corporate boards. Events of these years lead to a growing realization of the discrepancy between the level of ideal director diligence and responsibility and the actual functions of many boards of publicly held corporations.

Studies conducted of large corporation boards in this period documented the submissive role of many directors to corporate management.

Insert 7.D, an excerpt from a study of boards by Myles Mace of the Harvard Business School, indicates that board functions were found to be largely advisory, failed to exercise strong discipline for management, and were subject to a conflictual relationship with the firm's CEO. It was widely observed that few companies had meaningful board audit committees, procedures for director nominations by shareholders, or a board majority of directors without some economic or familial tie to present management. One chief executive, commenting on these points, said, "Directors are far more likely to identify with and protect the interest of the chief executive, who in fact selects them, than the interests of the stockholders, who technically elect them and to whom they are legally responsible."[22] Similarly, former chairman of the SEC, Harold Williams, commented on the very natural and benign human tendency of selecting directors disinclined to criticize management. When this tendency occurs, "management tends to invite on the board people who are compatible, if not indebted, to the corporate chief executive officer and the management."[23] Furthermore, the common practice of having inside (management) directors is fraught with obstacles to independent and objective views: "Corporate employees as directors depend on the chief executive, not only for their tenure on the board, but for their promotions and salaries, and are therefore disinclined to challenge him on management recommendations."[24]

Viewing the corporate board as a traditionally weak but also potentially strong mechanism of institutional accountability, the SEC has implemented a series of rules intended to reform and strengthen corporate boards. Within its philosophy of disclosure, and after a long series of public hearings and corporate testimony, in 1978 the SEC announced a new set of regulations entitled "Shareholder Communications Rules."

1978 SHAREHOLDER COMMUNICATIONS RULES

Revelations of management misrepresentations and financial indiscretion and acknowledgment that boards have failed to serve as a meaningful check and balance have led to public scrutiny of corporate governance and

Insert 7.D

OBSERVATIONS OF BOARD FUNCTIONING [QUOTATION]

In companies where the president and members of the board of directors own only a few shares of stock, it was found that most boards do provide a source of advice and counsel to the president. Those interviewed — company presidents as well as outside directors — perceived the role

Insert 7.D   continued

of outside directors to be largely advisory and not decision-making.

Also it was found that in most companies the boards of directors serve as some sort of discipline for the management — the president as well as those in subordinate positions. Company presidents and their associates know that periodically they are required to appear before the board of directors and to account for their stewardship of the company's operations since the last reporting date. Even though the president is usually quite sure that board members will not ask discerning or penetrating questions, the requirement of a periodic appearance before a board of professional peers does cause the executives to review their operating results, to identify problems, and to give explanations.

It was found also that most boards of directors exercise a decision-making power only in the event of a crisis such as the sudden death or disability of the president, or recognition by the board that the management performance is so unsatisfactory that a change must be made in the presidency.

It was found that boards of directors of most companies do not do an effective job in evaluating, appraising, and measuring the company president until the financial and other results are so dismal that some remedial action is forced upon the board. Any board has a difficult job in measuring the performance of a president. Criteria are rarely defined for his evaluation. The president's instinct is to attribute poor results to factors over which he has no control. The inclination of friendly directors is to go along with these apparently plausible explanations. Control of the data made available to the board which provides a basis for evaluation of the president is in the president's own hands, and board members rarely have sufficient interest and time to really understand the critical elements in the operations of the company.

SOURCE: Myles L. Mace, *Directors: Myth and Reality* (Boston: Division of Research, Graduate School of Business Administration, Harvard University, 1971). Used with permission.

calls for reform. Although significant, a relatively few number of laws may distract us from numerous but less visible situations in which management acted with a high sense of responsibility or in which a corporate board served as an effective mechanism of corporate direction and control. Still, the instances of deficient action and control appear to be sufficiently numerous and varied, and the logic of expanded board disclosure appeared to be sufficiently powerful to activate the countervailing powers of the public sector.

The SEC took the dominant role in this reform, and the final rulings reflect its basic strategy of disclosure regulation. After much public testimony and debate, new requirements for information to be included in proxy statements were released.[25]

Director Accountability: Surfacing Affiliations

A major thrust of the SEC ruling is to make public any director's economic or personal relationship to the firm. The intent of the communication ruling is to highlight the relationships of directors to the firm, making their affiliations known to the investing public. The philosophy of this regulation is the logic of disclosure: publicity increases responsibility because any affiliation that cannot be defended in the light of day is unlikely to be in the corporation's interest and therefore is likely to be changed.

What responsibilities are sought, and what corporate conduct is the object of this influence? To the extent a director has a major affiliation with the company as a family member, supplier, customer, investment banker, or other relationship, factors other than the overall welfare of the corporation may influence the decisions of the director. The director's loyalties may be divided between the interests of the corporation as an entity and narrower personal interests. As a family member or former employee, the director may have a social or personal relationship with the CEO that may influence the director's behavior. While a major customer or supplier or investment banker may not have a personal conflict of interest, he or she may also simply approach the affairs of the corporation from a narrower perspective than would otherwise be the case. Inhibitions on free and objective action may arise for the "inside director," who, as a manager, is subordinate to the CEO and yet who, as a director, is charged with reviewing and evaluating the CEO's performance. A similar problem may arise for a CEO who is both an employee of the board and its chairperson. The commission asserted the view that

> the interests of shareholders are best served by a board of directors which is able to exercise independent judgement, ask probing questions of management and bring to the company a broader perspective than that of management.[26]

The desired attitude is independence — developing perceptions and arriving at judgments from the single standpoint of overall corporate interests. The SEC recognized that independence is a state of mind more than an identifiable relationship: the nonexistence of a particular relationship does not guarantee an independent state of mind any more than an affiliation automatically inhibits it. However, the commission felt that the "nature and scope of a director's relationship with the issuer and its management certainly bears upon his independence, and . . . information respecting such relationships should be provided to shareholders when they exercise their franchise."[27]

Specifically, corporations are required to provide the following information for all board nominees and directors:

- any employment relationship to the corporation in the last five years;
- familial relationship to any of the corporation's executive officers;
- more than 1 percent ownership in a company that (1) purchases from the corporation goods or services that are more than 1 percent of the corporation's gross revenues, (2) holds more than 1 percent of the corporation's debt, or (3) represents sales to the corporation in excess of 1 percent of the director's firm's gross revenues;
- association with the corporation's law firm within the last two years; or
- association with an investment banking firm providing services to the corporation.

It is also important to note that no prohibitions are established against management or inside directors. The view that inside directors have a significant and vital contribution to board affairs is widely accepted. The question is more one of balance between unaffiliated and affiliated directors. The Shareholder Communications Rules emphasize the responsibility of a firm's directors to be aware of potential director conflicts of interest and to appraise the composition and performance of the board in the light of the purpose and objectives of the company.

In addition to requiring disclosure of directors' affiliations, the commission requires provision of information on board organization and functioning. First, the corporation's proxy statement must state whether the board has standing audit, nominating, and compensation committees. The functions and members of each of these committees must be identified, and the number of meetings of the full board in the last year must be stated. Finally, directors failing to attend fewer than 75 percent of the total board meetings plus the total meetings of committees of which they are members must be named.

The intent seems to be to cast "the light of day" onto board composition, with the belief that disclosure will not be an impediment to responsible boards and that it will be a constructive force for the reform of poorly organized and weak boards. Certainly the information required is not neutral — to disclose that such basic committees do not exist, have no functions, are controlled by only a few persons, or fail to achieve good attendance would be unfavorable publicity. Of course, a big difference may exist between bare compliance and meaningful functioning.

Additional Opportunity for Shareholder Participation

The SEC moved in several ways to strengthen opportunities for stockholder participation in director nominations. First, corporations having nominating committees need to state whether shareholder nominees will be considered for election, and if so, the procedures for stockholder nominations must be described. Second, if shareholders are presenting one or more candidates for director election, and if the management intends to issue a statement in opposition, the SEC has established procedures to protect the dissident stockholders from what they consider to be materially false or misleading statements. Management must, within a specified time, submit to the stockholder proponents the opposition statement, and the proponents have a limited time to provide the commission with their objections. The commission, then, makes a final judgment on what may be presented in the corporation's proxy statement.

Additional requirements were declared in 1979 to facilitate further the process of shareholder participation in the election of directors. A key element of these rules gives shareholders the opportunity to vote on nominees individually, rather than as a slate.[28]

The impact of these rules may perhaps be little more than to encourage stockholders who are already predisposed toward participation to pursue their involvement. More than this, however, these steps may indicate the SEC's commitment to the opportunity for greater corporate democracy through shareholder participation, an issue that is likely to reappear in the future.

Strengthening the Hand of the Dissident Director

Resignation is always an option for a discontented director; and according to the study by Myles Mace, it is the most common form of resolving serious disagreement between a director and management. The Shareholder Communications Rules provide a director who resigns or declines to stand for reelection with the right to have a summary of any disagreement with management on matters of operations or policies published by management. Management, as well, is offered the opportunity for a brief rejoinder. Public disclosure of the substance of the disagreement is solely the option of the resigning director.

The impact of this rule may also be relatively invisible to the public. Directors' options to go public may strengthen their hands in the course of debate prior to resignation, and this may, infact, be the desired result from the standpoint of the SEC.

CORPORATE SOCIAL INTEGRATION

Concepts of Social Responsibility and Corporate Ethics

Few would disagree that the role of the corporate board is to enhance the economic value of the firm — a function that reinforces the role of directors as trustees of the owners' financial interests. However, beyond this specific and widely accepted principle, great confusion enters discussion about the role of the firm and of its board of directors.

The corporation is fundamentally an economic institution, and neither the firm's nor society's interests are served by diverting its attention and resources away from this purpose. This point of view is perhaps best expressed by economist Milton Friedman's memorable phase: "The social responsibility of business is to increase its profits."[29]

Yet the last several decades have been marked by a growing awareness of social and political dimensions of business decision making, an awareness evident in the rise of consumer, environmental, civic, and other interest or stakeholder groups that often press for corporate action on particular issues. It may be impossible in a sophisticated, media-oriented, and democratic society — one inherently skeptical of bigness — to ignore extraeconomic implications of corporate decisions.

Debate about the role of the firm ebbs and flows in American society. There can be little question of the interdependence of economic pursuits with wider social values and political processes, and there appears to be no reluctance in society's willingness to scrutinize and attempt to influence corporate actions. Still it is not clear what responsibilities corporations hold for the wider consequences of their actions. The legal duties of directors to manage the firm are specified, if only generally; the ethical or social duties of directors remain in a large, gray area of discretion.

Another way of focusing this issue is to examine the meaning of *public* in the phrase *publicly-held corporation*. In a literal sense *public* means that shares of ownership are offered to any member of society. On the other hand *public* can be defined more broadly to account for various social, political, and ethical ramifications of corporate action. "Corporation affairs are still too widely deemed private affairs," wrote Felix Frankfurter in the early 1930s, "and the desire about them, intrusions into private business. . . . When a corporation seeks funds from the public it becomes in every true sense a public corporation . . . its bankers and managers themselves become public functionaries."[30] Many persons might be willing to agree that the character of the country's largest and most visible firms implies something more than the literal interpretation of this term. Yet its exact meaning remains elusive.

Arguing that the separation of ownership from control in the modern firm reduces the profit-maximizing motive, Berle and Means state that a "variety of claims by various groups in the community" will supplement the economic criterion of corporate decision making. This analysis, however, leaves open the question of identifying which claims are legitimate and which may not be. Also, if a claim is believed to be legitimate, should there be any limits on that group's claim on corporate assets?

One response to this predicament is to place the responsibility for determining proper corporate actions, that is, for creating an appropriate balance among competing claims, on the board itself. Thus without specifying exact standards of behavior for all firms and all circumstances — without seeking and imposing external ethical standards — responses can be forged on a firm-by-firm basis. The board's responsibility, from this vantage point, is to ensure that the firm has its own ethical position — a consistent set of principles of conduct or criteria to guide individual and group action.

One method by which to establish such a position is the systematic analysis of the firm's transactions and interactions with important groups in its environment. As described in Insert 7.E, analysis of relevant "stakeholders" in the firm can make explicit the expectations of different groups and can encourage planned managerial responses.

One might call the above view an "institutional" approach to resolving the more philosophical debate about the social responsibility of business. In short this point of view states that no general solution will be identified — that the best solution is to structure institutions appropriately and let each create and abide by its own ethic of social responsibility. This approach has the advantage of relying on a process — board decision making — rather than waiting for wide agreement on the general issue, the attainment of which appears an unlikely prospect.

A general recommendation consistent with this approach was given by the Business Roundtable's Policy Committee's report entitled *The Role and Composition of the Board of Directors of the Large Publicly Owned Corporation*.[31] A committee of representative managers of America's large corporations stated that the corporate board should ensure the long-run interests of owners by considering the impact of corporate activities on the society

Insert 7.E

STAKEHOLDERS AND STRATEGIES IN THE CORPORATE BOARDROOM

While the importance of corporate sensitivity to external groups is widely recognized, relations with key groups are typically managed on an ad hoc, case-by-case basis. *Stakeholder analysis* refers to a more comprehensive, systematic framework for analyzing a firm's relationship with its external constituents. R. Edward Freeman, author of a book on stakeholder management, shows how the process of managing relations with groups not traditionally considered within strategic planning frameworks, such as environmentalists or government agencies, should be part of strategic management. Stakeholder analysis is a consistent way of identifying, analyzing, and responding to critical interdependencies. It represents an active, integrated approach to achieving corporate purpose.

Each group or individual who either affects or is affected by the achievement of the firm's mission has a "stake" in corporate decisions and actions. Freeman describes a systematic means of identifying these stakes, and he outlines a managerial process for setting priorities among them. An important outcome from this analysis is determination of the timing and degree of participation of stakeholders in decision making in the firm. Among Freeman's key questions for managers arising from his framework are:

1. Who are our stakeholders? What are our assumptions about critical groups or individuals?
2. How do stakeholders affect each division, business, and function, and its plans?
3. Have we allocated resources to deal with our stakeholders?

The role of stakeholders in determining the identity of the firm is never more clear than when legitimate, competing ownership interests exist. Freeman examines several incidents where seriously divided boards of directors competed for corporate control — a struggle for managerial control at Beatrice Foods and Fairchild Industries' attempts to acquire Bunker-Ramo. Analysis of the competing groups and their claims illustrates how the very definition of the corporation depends on its relation to the outcome of the owner conflict. Freeman argues that a similar analysis can and should be undertaken to identify strategic directions in normal, although less dramatic, circumstances.

The stakeholder concept is suggested to be useful in coordinating the work of directors and is proposed to lead to more effective boards. As the highest level of corporate officials, directors are responsible for the integration of the institution with all constituents that have an interest in the firm's survival. The methodology of stakeholder analysis may provide a needed framework for fulfilling director responsibilities and roles.

SOURCE: R. Edward Freeman, *Strategic Management: A Stakeholder Approach* (Marshfield, Mass: Pitman, 1984).

and on the interests of groups not immediately identified with the corporation.

A more specific statement to this effect is given by Kenneth Andrews of the Harvard Business School, who has written widely on the modern role of corporate boards. Andrews states:

> It is the function of a unique strategy ... to identify those profit-detracting and responsibility-enhancing activities that a company should engage in, namely those most closely related to its mission. It is much more appropriate for a paper company, obviously, to pay attention to the effluent polluting its streams than to the support of the arts, as much as the arts need support. The range of causes in the world that require attention and could benefit from both corporate management competence and from its money are utterly endless. It is, I would submit, the function of a board to determine those noneconomic activities in which it should engage. These activities flow from the social cost of the economic commitments and from the values and aspirations of the people who have some view of the level of corporate citizenship to which their corporation should aspire.[32]

In the final analysis this point of view assumes there are direct trade-offs between profit and responsibility and that the role of the board is to manage the trade-offs consistent with corporate strategy.

If there is a drawback to this perspective, it may be that the knowledge, tools, and skills for developing a true corporate ethical posture are no more available on the level of the firm than they are in general. Directors may be no more successful at achieving social and economic integration than anyone else.

While the "institutional" approach has some merit, there appears to be little evidence that it has in fact allowed movement on the issue of corporate social integration. The same criticisms are made of firms, the same charges are leveled at the private business system, and the same problems of managerial accountability reoccur. Neither the profit maximization nor the social responsibility schools of thought have resolved the issue of the role of the firm, and the institutional approach at best allows for frequent vacillation and an uneasy truce between these opposing points of view.

Creating Integration through Corporate Culture

Thomas Peters, coauthor of the best-seller *In Search of Excellence*,[33] reports the CEO of Scandanavian Air System (SAS) as saying that the airline's 10 million passengers a year each have contact with an average of five SAS employees.[34] The essence of corporate strategy at SAS, says the CEO, Jan Carlzon, lies in "fifty million moments of truth a year."[35] In other words the strategy of the firm does not reside in the abstract and distant plans of the officers, corporate planners, or directors; rather, the strategy lies in the millions of specific actions undertaken by each person in the firm in his or her daily work.

How might one describe the daily actions of employees in a firm that takes the philosophy of profit maximization seriously? What would guide their conduct? One view is that they would act in each transaction with suppliers, customers, other employees, and dealers in a way that (1) seeks to achieve corporate goals in the immediate transaction and (2) increases the likelihood of another successful transaction with the other party in the future. In short, a profit maximizing firm would attempt to ensure that nonzero-sum transactions occur in every minute contact, every "moment of truth" for the firm.

What, on the other hand, would describe the daily actions of employees in a firm that truly takes the philosophy of social responsibility seriously? It would be hard to argue any differently from the above — that every transaction occurring in the firm in relation to internal and external constituencies has nonzero-sum qualities. That is, the goals of each party to the transaction are treated as valid and positive-sum outcomes that increase the likelihood of successful transactions in the future.

The CEO of another company — a successful silicon valley firm — was asked by Peters to identify the best marketing person in the firm. The CEO responded that this person was not even a member of the marketing department. "The best marketing person in this firm," responded the CEO, "is that man or woman on the loading dock who decides *not* to *drop* the box into the back of the truck."[36] Does the profit maximization or the social responsibility motive best explain the behavior of the loading dock employee? The action of this employee contains both what is wanted by the company and what is wanted by the customer. Where these philosophies may appear conflicting and irreconcilable at a philosophical level, they are highly compatible in terms of specific actions. Governance may consist more of developing and inculcating a culture of shared norms and values that have consequences in daily actions than efforts to arrive at agreement about fundamentally vague and abstract principles.

The Board's Role in Developing a Corporate Culture

The corporate board plays several roles in integrating social responsibility and profit maximization through a system in which a firm's "fifty million moments of truth a year" approach positive-sum transactions as closely as possible. Transactions between the management and the board — the information and issues that directors are asked to consider and the quality of the discussion about them — reflect win-win, win-lose, or lose-lose relationships. If directors are passive and/or the CEO is defensive, the possibility for divergence between shareholder and management interests is increased. Where interests or points of view may diverge, the commitment of both parties to full information and to an integrative solution must be present. From the standpoint of shareholders, transactions between management and directors are filled with many hundreds of individual moments of truth.

The quality of interactions at the top of the organization — in this case between management and directors — is likely to be an indicator of the quality of the firm's interactions with its other constituents, such as dealers, customers, suppliers, and employees. The likelihood of a positive-sum action system developing with other groups is low when it is essentially absent between directors and management. The board plays an important role as a practical test of the broader corporate action system.

A positive-sum action system at the board level has also been termed a *value-creating orientation*. A value-creating board is composed of director and CEO orientations that allow utilization of the complete resources of directors and of management to realize the economic potential of the firm. This board is well organized and exercises control over management. As directors are confident that management is honest and open with the board, they can use board procedures and information to serve the common interests of management and the board. Fig. 7.1 presents a framework in which to think about several "pure" types of boards based on different CEO and director orientations. It also identifies the dominant means of change within each type toward a more value-creating board.

THE BOARD'S ROLE IN MANAGERIAL CAPITALISM: A CONCLUDING COMMENT

The aspirations and requirements of a popular democracy in mature capitalism become expressed in expectations for public accountability of large corporations. The focus of this chapter has been on the corporate board of directors as one mechanism for establishing such accountability. The point of worrying about director affiliations, the work of board committees, and shareholder nominations procedures is to understand the issues and mechanisms for creating management accountability and to ensure corporate credibility and legitimacy. The general issue is whether the corporate board will guide the corporation to adapt and respond to its complex environment and, in turn, build and sustain public confidence. Although not dictated by the assignment of property rights and not enforceable in a court of law, the nature of business and society interdependence compels attention, experimentation, and effort to gain experience with the board concept of corporate accountability. The degree to which this task is pursued successfully may also carry important implications for future business-government relations. If the effort at internal reform fails to proceed, pro-

FIGURE 7.1 *Types of Corporate Boards and Strategies for Change Toward a Value-Creating Board*

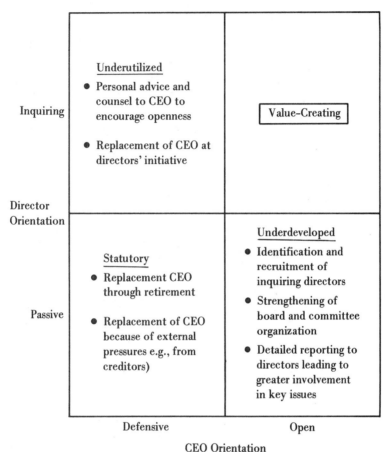

SOURCE: John D. Aram and Scott S. Cowen, *Information for Corporate Directors: The Role of the Board in the Process of Management* (New York: National Association of Accountants, 1983) p. 33.

posals for federal chartering of corporations and governmentally mandated board composition and organization may gain momentum.

This point of view toward concepts of corporate accountability at the board is by no means universally accepted. The concept of the private economic enterprise is anchored in the strict assignment of property rights and in a clearly defined, operational, and proven concept of the limited role of the firm in a market economy. While this view of the firm should continue to provide the backbone of the economic structure of society, the visible and dominant role of the modern corporation may also lead to changes in the role of the corporate board. Taking into consideration the separation of ownership and control, the vast scale of the modern corporation, and the intertwining of social, political, ethical, and economic values in modern society, the corporate board will increasingly be seen as a body with tasks and functions distinct from those of management. The board is the pivotal ingredient for reconciling multiple interests in the long-term interest of the corporation and for exercising appropriate direction and control over management. The establishment of effective corporate governance through the corporate board holds the promise of integrating the firm and its constituencies in a private and decentralized manner and of maintaining the firm in the historical sense of a private enterprise. Such processes of governance also capture the broad meaning of *ethical behavior* in corporate decision making; explicit attention to multiple values and criteria in decisions and finding means for integrative or win-win outcomes constitutes the essence of ethical behavior.

Management, then, will need to perceive the broader role of the board and to act to encourage and strengthen the board's performance in this role. Management control of the board may be a convenient position to assume, but it may also be a detriment to the long-run interests of the corporation. Managers increasingly need to assume a broad view of corporate governance and make certain that the structure of corporate decision making fulfills a high standard of accountability and value creation that will ensure long-run corporate survival.

DISCUSSION QUESTIONS

1. How would you explain the emergence of corporate governance as an issue for corporations in this century?
2. How is the corporate board of directors part of a system of institutional checks and balances? How would you weigh its role in relation to other checks and balances?
3. What is the disclosure philosophy of the SEC? Do you believe that such a philosophy of public policy toward business can be effective? In what areas of corporate actions would you expect it to be most and least effective?
4. What promise does reform of the corporate board hold for business-society integration? What obstacles does it face?

NOTES

1. Adolf A. Berle, Jr., and Gardiner C. Means, *The Modern Corporation and Private Property* (New York: Macmillan, 1933), p. 94.

2. Robert J. Larner, *Management Control and the Large Corporation* (New York: Dunellen, 1970), pp. 9–24.

3. Phillip I. Blumberg, *The Megacorporation in American Society* (Englewood Cliffs, N.J.: Prentice-Hall, 1975), pp. 84–130.

4. Peter F. Drucker, "Taming the Corporate Takeover," *Wall Street Journal,* October 30, 1984, p. 30.

5. Ibid.

6. Berle and Means, *The Modern Corporation,* p. 122.

7. Felix Frankfurter, "The Federal Securities Act II," *Fortune,* August 1933, p. 53.

8. Louis W. Cabot, "On an Effective Board," *Harvard Business Review,* September-October 1976, p. 41.

9. Securities and Exchange Commission, Accounting Series Release no. 173, "In the Matter of Peat, Marwick, Mitchell & Co.," *Federal Securities Law Reporter* ¶72, 195, July 1, 1975.

10. U.S., Congress, Senate, Committee on Banking, Housing, and Urban Affairs, *Report of the Securities and Exchange Commission on Questionable and Illegal Corporate Payments and Practices,* 94th Cong., 2d sess., May 1976, Exhibit A, pp. 1–9.

11. Philip L. Cochran and Steven L. Wartick, "Golden Parachutes: A Closer Look," *California Management Review* 26 (Summer 1984):111.

12. Mark J. Moran, "Insider Trading in the Stock Market: An Empirical Test of the Damage to Outsiders" (Working Paper no. 89, Center for the Study of American Business, July 1984).

13. Harold M. Williams, "Corporate Accountability and Corporate Power" (Paper presented at Carnegie-Mellon University, Pittsburgh, October 1979), p. 4.

14. Albert O. Hirschman, *Exit, Voice, and Loyalty: Responses to Decline in Forms, Organizations, and States* (Cambridge: Harvard University Press, 1970), p. 4.

15. Richard A. Stohr, "Legal Responsibilities, Liabilities and Protection of Directors," in *Corporate Directorship Practices* ed. Jeremy Bacon and James K. Brown (New York: Conference Board, 1975), p. 81.

16. Larry D. Soderquist, "Toward a More Effective Corporate Board: Reexamining Roles of Outside Directors," *Securities Law Review* 10 (1978): 243–65.

17. 15 U.S.C., Section 77k(c).

18. Soderquist, "Toward a More Effective Corporate Board," p. 248.

19. Stohr, "Legal Responsibilities," p. 76.

20. Soderquist, "Toward a More Effective Corporate Board," p. 150.

21. Hurd Baruch, "The Foreign Corrupt Practices Act," *Harvard Business Review,* January-February 1979, p. 33; Stohr, "Legal Responsibilities," p. 81.

22. Ben W. Heineman, "What Does and Doesn't Go On in the Boardroom," *Fortune,* February 1972, p. 157.

23. Williams, "Corporate Accountability," p. 7.

24. Ibid.
25. Securities and Exchange Commission, Release no. 34–15384, "Shareholder Communications: Shareholder Participation in the Corporate Electoral Process and Corporate Governance Generally, Final Rules," *Federal Securities Law Reporter* ¶81, 766, December 6, 1978.
26. Ibid., p. 58523.
27. Ibid., p. 58524.
28. Securities and Exchange Commission, Release no. 16356, "Shareholder Communications, Shareholder Participation in the Corporate Electoral Process and Corporate Governance Generally," *Federal Securities Law Reporter,* ¶82, 358, November 21, 1979.
29. Milton Friedman, "The Social Responsibility of Business Is to Increase Its Profits," *New York Times Magazine,* September 13, 1970, pp. 122–26.
30. Frankfurter, "The Federal Securities Act II," p. 111.
31. Business Roundtable, Policy Committee, *The Role and Composition of the Board of Directors of the Large Publicly Owned Corporation* (New York: Business Roundtable, January 1978).
32. Kenneth R. Andrews, "Difficulties in Overseeing Ethical Policy," *California Management Review* 26 (Summer 1984):136.
33. Thomas J. Peters and Robert H. Waterman, Jr., *In Search of Excellence: Lessons from America's Best-Run Companies* (New York: Harper & Row Publishers, 1982).
34. Thomas J. Peters, "Strategy Follows Structure: Developing Distinctive Skills," *California Management Review* 26 (Spring 1984):111–25.
35. Ibid., p. 112.
36. Ibid., p. 120.

Viking Air Compressor, Inc.

As he left the president's office George Ames wondered what he ought to do.* His impulse was to resign, but he knew that could be a costly blot on his employment record. Moreover, there was the possibility that he was seeing things in a distorted way, that he might later regret leaving Viking before he really knew all the facts bearing on his position and its future. He decided to wait for another week before making up his mind, and in the meantime he made an appointment with Professor Farnsworth of the Amos Tuck School of Business Administration at Dartmouth College to get his advice. Ames had received his M.B.A. degree from the Tuck School the previous June.†

Viking Air Compressor was founded in Bradley, Connecticut, in 1908 by Nels Larsen, an inventor and engineer who left the Westinghouse Electric Company to start his own organization. Larsen had both a successful design for a new type of air compressor and a talent for management. He led Viking to steadily increasing successes in the air compressor industry.

In 1971 Viking held a steady 25 percent of the air compressor business in the United States, with total annual sales of $180 million. John T. Larsen, grandson of the founder, was chairman of the board and chief executive officer. Three other descendants of the founder were officers of the company, and the rest of the management team had been developed from Viking employees who rose through the ranks. The ownership of Viking was substantially in the Larsen family hands.

In March 1971 Oscar Stewart, vice-president for personnel admin-

---

*Most of the names in this case have been disguised.

†Ames received his A.B. from the University of Michigan in June 1966. He spent three years as an army officer, concluding as a captain in Vietnam, before entering Tuck in September 1969. He was married in June 1971.

---

istration of Viking, visited the Amos Tuck School to talk with M.B.A. candidates interested in a new position to be created in the Viking structure the following June. Stewart explained to Dean Robert Y. Kimball, Tuck's director of placement, that Viking had never hired M.B.A.'s directly from business schools but wanted to experiment in 1971 with this method of bringing fresh ideas and new techniques into the firm.

The corporate officers had decided, according to Stewart, to begin to test the effectiveness of the recruitment of M.B.A.'s by hiring a business school graduate to become director of public affairs, with the assignment of coordinating the relationships between Viking and outside agencies seeking financial contributions from the company.

As Stewart described the job to the students he interviewed at Tuck in March 1971, it would contain such tasks as (1) proposing to the board of directors the best criteria to use in deciding how to make corporate gifts to charitable organizations of all kinds, (b) supplying the chief officers of the company with information about the participation of Viking employees in public service activities, (3) recommending future strategy for Viking in the employment of women and members of minority groups, and (4) serving as secretary to the newly formed Committee on Corporate Responsibility, which consisted of five members of the board of directors.

George Ames accepted the post of director of public affairs at Viking. He had been chosen by Vice-President Stewart as the most promising of the five attractive Tuck applicants for the new position. After a short vacation Ames reported for work on July 1, 1971, and immediately plunged into the difficult task of gathering information about his new assignment. It soon became clear that his primary task would be to work with the board Committee on Corporate Responsibility, mainly to propose new policy guidelines to the board at its September 10 meeting. Stewart said there were two other areas of high priority: the corporation's attitude toward public service of employees and developing criteria for corporate philanthropic giving.

As Vice-President Stewart explained to George in early July, the Committee on Corporate Responsibility was created at the January meeting of the Viking board after unanimous endorsement of the suggestion made by Thomas A. Barr, pastor of the local Congregational Church and one of the four outside members of the 12-man board. Reverend Barr's major support for his recommendation was the observation that the General Motors Corporation had taken a similar step, under some pressure, and that corporate responsibility was an idea whose time had come on the American scene. In response to the question, What will such a committee do? Reverend Barr replied that there need be no hurry in defining the detailed responsibilities of the committee but that there could not possibly be any harm or drawbacks from setting it up as soon as possible. He added that the public relations value of such a gesture should not be underestimated. In establishing the Committee on Corporate Responsibility, the board voted to require the first progress report from the committee in September 1971.

The Committee on Corporate Responsibility met following the February meeting of the board of directors and decided to delay any definite action until an executive secretary could be hired. Vice-President Stewart was asked to keep this post in mind as he interviewed M.B.A. graduates of several of the leading business schools, and so he did.

George Ames met with the chairman of the Committee on Corporate Responsibility at a luncheon on July 21, 1971, arranged by Vice-President Stewart. The committee chairman was Paul Merrow, one of the most respected lawyers in northern Connecticut and the son of one of the first board members of Viking when the company was incorporated in the 1920s. Merrow expressed his pleasure that George Ames was working on the corporate responsibility question and asked him to prepare a report that might be reviewed by the committee just prior to the September board meeting. What he wanted, he explained to Ames, was an analysis of the three or four possible approaches to corporate responsibility that the directors ought to consider. He asked for a listing of the pros and cons of these various approaches. He said that Ames should consider this very much like an assignment in a course at the Tuck School. He would be performing a task that none of the board members had the time or academic background to do, and thus he would substantially improve the decision making of the board of directors.

Merrow concluded the luncheon by saying that he would like Ames to proceed on his own during the summer but that he would be glad to confer with him in early September. Merrow explained that he was leaving the next day for a legal conference in Europe and would be on an extended vacation until September 6. He said that he had "the proxies" of the other committee members and that they would prefer not to get involved in working on the committee tasks until after the September board meeting.

George Ames worked assiduously during August, reading all the articles and books he could find in the area of corporate responsibility, including the background of developments in the General Motors situation. He decided not to talk about this particular assignment with other officers of the company, primarily because of Merrow's injunction that the committee itself would prefer not to engage in substantive talk about the issues until the September board meeting. George feared he would do more harm than good by talking before he knew his subject well.

In early September John Larsen asked George to see him, and the following conversation took place:

John Larsen: I've asked you to see me this morning and tell me what progress you have been making in developing background materials for the work of the Committee on Corporate Responsibility. Mr. Merrow told me he had asked you to do some digging and that you would have a brief report to make at the September 10 meeting of the board. I know Mr. Merrow hoped he would be back from Europe in time to talk with you before the board meeting, but it now appears he will be lucky to make the meeting at all. He expects to arrive in town about noon on the tenth.

George Ames: Mr. Larsen, I appreciate the opportunity I have been given to help Viking by developing recommendations about possible strategies for the company to follow in the area of corporate responsibility. Mr. Merrow told me I ought to develop alternative proposals for recommendations to the board, and I have as recently as yesterday finally been able to narrow the field so that I can make four recommendations with confidence.

I realize the board may prefer to consider them one at a time, at different meetings, but I would like to tell you about all four so that you will know what my report will contain.

I have decided that the most important issue in the area of corporate responsibility is equal-opportunity hiring. I have been able to develop statistics from the personnel records that show that Viking is rather far behind most major national corporations in the percentage of blacks and women now employed, and although I am sure conscientious efforts have been made by all officers to remedy this, I cannot stress too strongly how much of a time bomb the present situation is. There will be wide ramifications if we do not improve our record.

The second item of priority that I see is the development of corporate sanctions for public service activities of employees. I believe the company should grant paid leaves of absence for employees who wish to accept public service posts. At present we have done that only for two vice-presidents who have been in charge of the Northern Connecticut United Fund. In each case the man was lent to the charitable organization for two full weeks. What I have in mind is a much wider program that would grant employees leaves of absence to work in poverty programs in urban ghettos, or in VISTA projects in Connecticut or neighboring states.

It seems to me a third priority is to develop a committee of consumers who will monitor the safety features and other quality items having to do with our products. If we do not do this, we will have Ralph Nader breathing down our necks, as has already happened in the automotive industry and some others.

Finally, I strongly recommend that we close our sales contact in Capetown, South Africa, and establish policies that will avoid our being embarrassed as a corporation by discriminatory or dictatorial policies of foreign governments, which will become critically important political and social issues here in this country.

I feel sure these are great issues of our times, and I hope the board will be willing to debate them at the September 10 meeting. I know I could learn a great deal in my position if such a debate could take place.

Larsen: Young man, I want to congratulate you on how articulately you have told me about some of the things you have learned in the M.B.A. program at the Tuck School. I envy fellows of your generation who go through M.B.A. programs because you get an opportunity to think about policy problems at a much earlier age than my generation ever did. Indeed my only complaint is that the business schools go too far to educate young men to think they know how to run a company long before they have enough real experience to be even a first-line supervisor.

Now I think you have your assignment all backward as secretary to the Committee on Corporate Responsibility, and I will tell you why I think that. The committee hasn't even met yet, and your remarks make it sound as if you have written the final report. Worse than that, it sounds like the final report of the Committee on Corporate Responsibility of the General Motors Company, not Viking. Everybody knows we've done as good a job as we can to hire blacks and women. There just aren't many such people in the work force in our part of Connecticut who could fit our talent standards, and we are going to follow our historical policy of nondiscrimination as we hire the best people to do Viking jobs. We owe it to our stockholders to make a profit, and if we don't do that, we don't have the right to do anything else.

Your remarks on public service activities for our employees are equally off target. The first obligation of our employees is to give a fair day's work for a fair day's pay. All public service activities are extracurricular activities, and that's the way they must be. For us to sponsor public service on company time we would have to discriminate between good and bad activities, and that would get us into partisan politics and preoccupy all of our executive time. How would the company have done if I had been a part-time chief executive officer in the last five years? That is a preposterous idea! At the same time by working harder on my regular job I have been able some evenings and some weekends to work in fund-raising activities for the Boy Scouts, YMCA, and heaven knows how many other charitable organizations. I would expect every employee to do the same and not to expect the corporation to subsidize activities in their roles as private citizens. As far as public service is concerned, live and let live should be our corporate motto. If we encourage public service activities and include them as part of our compensation and promotion system, we will be bogged down in a fantastic collection of information about private lives, which will lead to chaos. Even the most superficial examination of this question should have led you to see the problems with the route your theory took you.

As far as the safety of our products and other demands consumers might make, that's all done through the marketplace, as you will come to understand. If our products were not safe or durable, they wouldn't sell. You could have found this out had you talked with our production and marketing people, as you certainly should have done by now. It's our responsibility to decide after careful market research what the air compressor needs of America are and will be in the future. We don't need a special panel of bleeding hearts to lead us along paths where we are already expert.

As for our selling operations in South Africa, I'm afraid you just don't know what you are talking about. As long as there is no plank of American foreign policy or federal law that tells corporations where they can and where they can't sell their products, American businesses must depend on the free market system. President Nixon is talking about opening the trade doors to mainland China. Do you think for one moment the practices of the Chinese government are any less nefarious in some respects than the practices of the South African government? Of course not. And yet you would probably urge me in your liberal way to establish a selling office in Peking just to go along with the new liberal ideas of our president, and I call that kind of pragmatism ridiculous.

Come to think of it, how could you miss this opportunity to lecture the board on our responsibilities for pollution control and our obligations to get out of the military-industrial complex by canceling all of our air compressor contracts with the federal government!

Young man, you have shown yourself to be a wooly-minded theoretician, and I want to tell you that bluntly now so that you will not think me hypocritical at any later point. I will tell the Committee on Corporate Responsibility that you have not had time to prepare your first briefing of the board of directors, and then I want to have a meeting with you and the chairman of the Corporate Responsibility Committee on Monday morning, September 20.

That's all I have time for now. I'll see you later.

DISCUSSION QUESTIONS

1. Describe the structure and functioning of the board of directors at Viking. Assuming the case data are representative of board operations, is this an effective or an ineffective board? What can you infer about characteristics of an effective board?
2. Viking is controlled by the Larsen family. Under these conditions, what difference does the functioning of the board make?
3. Why did George Ames get into trouble? What could he have done differently?

Consolidated Petroleum Corporation

The board of directors of Consolidated Petroleum Corporation met at the call of its chairman in a special session at the company's New York City headquarters at 10 A.M. on Monday, May 3, 1976. As they entered the boardroom that morning, several directors sensed and commented on the tension in the air. Prior to the appearance of the chairman, outside directors talked quietly together at one end of the room, while inside officer-directors clustered at the other end. Background for the meeting was a number of disturbing developments during the preceding year. One of the developments — the revelation that Consolidated, like some other large business organizations, had made illegal political contributions and possibly had bribed foreign government officials — had led a few months earlier to the creation of a Special Review Committee of outside directors. On April 23 the committee transmitted to the full board a report embodying findings, conclusions, and recommendations, together with a statement of a minority view of one member of the committee.

When the chairman entered the room, the directors took their customary seats around the long oval table. The chairman opened the meeting by saying:

> Gentlemen, I've called you together because this company is facing a crisis — probably the most serious and urgent situation that has arisen in the entire history of the business. I don't think I'll get any argument about that description of our position. I hope you're all prepared to continue this meeting through the rest of this day, and if necessary, into the evening until we decide what we are going to do and how we are going to do it.

Consolidated Petroleum Corporation was, in its principal line of business, an integrated oil company (ranking thirteenth in 1975 sales among U.S. oil companies) engaged in the production, procurement, transportation, refining, and marketing of petroleum and natural gas and products derived therefrom. The company also participated, through wholly owned subsidiaries as well as through joint ventures and minority investments, in the chemical, plastics, and minerals industries and, to a minor extent, in the production and marketing of certain other products and services.

Financial and operating data for Consolidated Petroleum for the years 1971 through 1975 are shown in Exhibits 1 through 3. Sales and earnings on total capital for major U.S. petroleum companies for 1971 through 1975 are shown in Exhibit 4.

For the fiscal year ended December 31, 1975, Consolidated Petroleum reported total revenues of $4.8 billion, the second highest in the company's history, although down 12 percent from 1974. Net income of $210 million was the third highest ever recorded but 34 percent less than in 1974. Earnings per share were $1.08 against $1.64 in 1974.

The following information about the company's current position and developments in 1975 is excerpted from Consolidated's Annual Report and SEC Form 10-K:

1. The company's principal resources were its capability as a finder, producer, refiner, and marketer of petroleum; its reserves of petroleum, coal, and various minerals; its diversification into other industries with strong growth and profit potential; and its healthy financial position.

2. In 1976 Consolidated Petroleum planned to undertake an aggressive program of petroleum exploration and production, with total expenditures at an all-time high of more than $600 million, almost half for projects in the United States.

3. The company's balance sheet showed cash and marketable securities aggregating more than $500 million. A major part of this resource would be committed to reversing the decline in Consolidated's U.S. petroleum production. Included in this program would be vigorous development of oil and gas acreage acquired in the Gulf of Mexico since 1972 when federal offshore lease sales were resumed. Developmental work would also be pushed for the company's discoveries in the North Sea petroleum field and in certain nonpetroleum properties. In addition, a substantial investment would be made in chemical operations to upgrade the value of products and thereby participate in product/markets close to final consumers.

4. The fall in revenues and even greater decline in net income during 1975 were attributed to several developments:

    a. While earnings from U.S. petroleum operations were more than 9 percent higher than in 1974, foreign petroleum profits fell 65 percent. The U.S. gain was caused principally by improved margins on petroleum products that were partially offset by a de-

EXHIBIT 1 *Consolidated Statement of Income and Retained Earnings* (In Millions of Dollars)

	Year Ended December	
	1975	**1974**
Revenues		
Sales and other operating revenues	4,751	5,386
Interest income	55	54
Other revenues	8	25
	4,814	5,465
Deductions		
Purchased crude oil, products, and merchandise	2,192	2,641
Operating expenses	393	445
Exploration and dry hole expenses	95	77
Selling, general, and administrative expenses	366	343
Taxes on income and general taxes	1,268	1,417
Federal Energy Administration entitlements	67	4
Depreciation, depletion, amortization, and retirements	189	183
Interest on long-term financing	34	36
	4,604	5,146
Net income	210	319
Retained earnings at beginning of year		
As previously reported	1,557	1,330
Restatement	(72)	(72)
As restated	1,485	1,258
Cash dividends	(99)	(92)
Retained earnings at end of year	1,596	1,485
Per share data		
Net income	1.08	1.64
Cash dividends	0.51	0.47

cline in U.S. production and an increase in exploration and dry hole costs. The fall-off in foreign earnings was attributed partly to nationalization of company properties in several Middle East and Latin American countries, loss of certain markets to nationalized producer-country sales organizations, and in some countries, high government-mandated costs that reduced normal selling margins. In addition, refining and marketing operations

EXHIBIT 2 *Consolidated Statement of Financial Position*
(In Millions of Dollars)

	Year Ended December	
	1975	1974
Assets		
Current assets		
Cash and marketable securities	551	530
Receivables	707	855
Inventories	343	326
Prepaid expenses and other current assets	41	21
Total current assets	1,642	1,732
Investments in associated companies	73	66
Investments in affiliates and long-term receivables	132	136
Properties	1,871	1,811
Deferred charges	9	6
Total assets	3,727	3,751
Liabilities		
Current liabilities		
Notes payable and current long-term debt	65	56
Accounts payable	527	558
Consumer sales and excise taxes payable	48	36
Liability to plastic partnership	41	—
Accrued U.S. and foreign income taxes	185	253
Accrued rents and royalties	30	60
Other current liabilities	225	256
Total current liabilities	1,121	1,219
Long-term debt	388	441
Deferred production payment proceeds	17	—
Liability to plastic partnership	—	54
Deferred income taxes	111	84
Other long-term liabilities	47	32
Minority interests	106	94
Total liabilities	1,790	1,924
Shareholders' equity		
Capital stock — authorized 90,000,000 shares, without par value: issued 63,573,248 shares stated at	265	265
Paid-in capital	209	209
Retained earnings	1,596	1,486
	2,070	1,960

EXHIBIT 2 *continued*

	Year Ended December	
	1975	**1974**
Less 5,150,192 and 5,170,331 shares, respectively, in treasury, at cost	133	133
Total shareholders' equity	1,937	1,827
Total liabilities and shareholders' equity	3,727	3,751

in Europe suffered from that region's generally stagnant economy during the year.

b. Chemical earnings fell because of sluggish demand in both the United States and abroad.

c. Losses from minerals operations were reduced in 1975, but these activities continued to be unprofitable, as they had been for a number of years.

5. Effective July 1, 1973, the company had entered into a partnership (Unique Plastics Company) under which the company and David Chemicals Corporation owned and operated on a 50-50 basis the plastics business previously conducted by Consolidated Petroleum's Chemical Division. Provision was made for the company's 50 percent share of anticipated future losses in certain commitments of the partnership; the company's share was projected to be $72 million. This entire provision was recorded prior to 1975. Losses realized and charged to this reserve were $29 million and $5 million in the years 1975 and 1974, respectively. The provision for losses reflected continuing and additional anticipated difficulties in achieving a consistent level of control over quality of output in the production of the principal product of the business, a specialty plastic compound of high market potential but extremely erratic behavior under large-scale continuous-flow processing. Consolidated Petroleum's management told its shareholders that it believed that the loss provision remaining after deduction of the recorded losses represented a reasonable estimate of future costs that might be associated with the resolution of production problems.

Consolidated Petroleum's board had undergone one shocking and several seriously disturbing experiences during 1974 and 1975. The shocking experience was the revelation, initially in news reports in the *New York Times* and the *Washington Post* and later in testimony before the Securities and Exchange Commission (SEC) and various congressional committees, that corporate funds had been contributed to political parties and candidates in the United States and several foreign countries, and alleged bribes paid to

EXHIBIT 3   *Major Business Segments (In Millions of Dollars)*

	Total		U.S.		Foreign	
	1975	**1974**	**1975**	**1974**	**1975**	**1974**
Sales and other operating revenues (includes consumer excise taxes)						
Petroleum	4,483	5,095	1,984	2,000	2,499	3,095
Chemicals	244	275	161	168	83	107
Minerals	23	16	23	16	—	—
Other	1	—	1	—	—	—
	4,751	5,386	2,169	2,184	2,582	3,202
Net income (loss)						
Petroleum						
Producing, refining, and marketing operations	295	379	185	158	110	221
Amortization of nonproducing leases and exploration and dry hole expense	(93)	(75)	(47)	(32)	(46)	(43)
	202	304	138	126	64	178
Chemicals	21	24	15	1	6	23
Minerals	(8)	(7)	(5)	(5)	(3)	(2)
Other	(5)	(2)	(5)	(2)	—	—
	210	319	143	120	67	199
Employed capital and net assets (December 31)						
Petroleum	1,965	1,982	1,061	1,172	904	810
Chemicals	242	189	166	117	76	72
Minerals	97	54	63	47	34	7
Other	8	8	8	8	—	—
Corporate	294	299	103	118	191	181
Employed capital	2,606	2,532	1,401	1,462	1,205	1,070
Long-term debt	388	441	215	219	173	222
Other long-term liabilities	281	264	109	121	172	143
Net assets (shareholders' equity)	1,937	1,827	1,077	1,122	860	705

EXHIBIT 4 *Major U.S. Petroleum Companies — 1973–75*

	Sales (Millions of Dollars)			Percentage of Earned Total Capital		
	1975	1974	1973	1975	1974	1973
Exxon	44,864	42,062	25,724	12.8	17.3	15.5
Texaco	24,507	23,255	11,407	8.3	15.1	13.8
Mobil	20,620	18,929	11,390	10.0	13.4	13.0
Standard-California	16,822	17,191	7,762	10.3	13.4	12.8
Gulf	14,268	16,458	8,417	9.8	14.4	12.1
Standard-Indiana	9,955	9,085	5,416	11.6	15.5	10.2
Shell	8,144	7,634	4,884	10.8	14.3	8.8
Continental	7,500	7,041	4,215	12.1	12.2	10.6
Atlantic-Richfield	7,308	6,740	3,983	7.2	10.9	7.3
Occidental	5,346	5,538	3,456	8.8	15.4	6.4
Phillips	5,134	4,981	2,990	11.1	15.5	9.3
Union	5,086	4,419	2,552	9.7	12.0	8.7
Consolidated	4,814	5,465	2,805	9.7	14.3	10.1
Sun	4,389	3,800	2,286	7.9	13.7	9.8
Ashland	3,637	3,216	2,053	11.0	11.3	9.8
Cities Service	3,201	2,806	2,035	6.6	9.9	7.2
Amerada Hess	3,180	3,745	1,896	9.1	14.4	19.6
Getty	2,984	2,742	1,601	12.4	14.3	7.9
Marathon	2,878	2,832	1,579	10.8	14.8	12.2

certain foreign government officials had been recorded as commission payments to agents and other legitimate business expenses. This matter became the subject of an investigation by the SEC when it was revealed that some of the contributions and alleged bribes had been hidden in various operating accounts, while others had been handled through funds that were never incorporated in the company's official accounting records.

Less shocking but clearly disturbing to some outside directors were several other developments that surfaced in 1973, 1974, and 1975:

1. A Federal Trade Commission complaint was issued in July 1973 against several petroleum companies of which Consolidated was one, charging violation of Section 5 of the Federal Trade Commission Act and alleging a combination or agreement to monopolize the business of refining crude oil. This proceeding remained in a relatively early stage of development in 1976.

2. In June 1975 a class action suit was filed by the state of California in the United States District Court for the Northern District of California

alleging violations of federal antitrust laws by a group of petroleum companies including Consolidated. Early in January 1976 this suit was consolidated for purposes of discovery in the United States District Court for the District of Connecticut with class action suits previously filed by the attorney generals of Connecticut and Kansas against a number of petroleum companies including Consolidated, alleging multiple violations of state and federal antitrust laws. These suits sought treble damages in an unspecific amount and injunctive relief including divestiture by the defendants of their oil exploration and production activities.

3. In 1975 a number of United States senators and representatives began vigorously to promote legislation that would dismember vertically integrated petroleum companies, with the stated objective of reducing their market power and monopolistic or quasi-monopolistic practices and promoting more intensive competition within the industry in the interest of consumers.

4. A class action suit was filed in 1974 on behalf of all members of the United Steel Workers in the Federal District Court for the Northern District of Indiana against several large petroleum companies including Consolidated, charging the defendants with violations of the federal antitrust laws and seeking damages in the amount of $750 million before trebling and injunctive relief.

5. Several suits against Consolidated were filed in 1975 in various states, charging violations of federal, state, and local antipollution legislation and regulations.

6. During 1975 a number of derivative actions were filed by shareholders on behalf of the company, later consolidated into a single complaint that alleged that certain directors and officers of the company had violated various sections of the Securities Exchange Act of 1934 and had permitted waste of corporate assets. In general, the complaint charged that since 1960 the defendants were responsible for the unauthorized disbursement of almost $4 million of corporate funds for unlawful political contributions and other similar unlawful purposes in the United States and abroad, and that the disbursements were concealed by means of false entries in the books of the company and its subsidiaries, with the result that reports filed with the SEC and proxy statements disseminated to shareowners during this period were false and misleading. The complaint alleged that the company's independent accountants knew or should have known that such irregularities existed and that they aided in the concealment of such matters by failing to conduct a proper audit or to disclose matters known to them.

7. A number of actions were brought against the company and its officers during 1975 alleging discriminatory or other inequitable employment and promotion policies and practices prejudicial to the rights of members of minority groups and women.

Shaken by these developments, several outside directors proposed that the board establish a Special Review Committee to investigate thoroughly (1) the use of corporate funds for political purposes, (2) other matters that the committee might judge essential in relation to the legality and morality of the behavior of the company officers and managers, and (3) the role of the board in the management of the company. It was proposed that the committee be composed of five outside directors — William Perrine as chairman, Lewis Appleton, David Count, Carl Walden, and Joseph Yost — and authorized to draw upon internal and external staff assistance to the extent required to complete its assignment.

The chairman, supported by the president, objected to this proposal on the following grounds:

1. To the extent that corporate funds had been disbursed for purposes or in a manner contrary to law in the United States or in foreign countries, the actions were not in accord with established company policy, were concealed from and were unknown to senior officers, and were the subject of investigations already in progress under top management direction.
2. Allegations about the illegality of certain of the company's trade practices were without merit and all charges would be successfully rebutted.
3. Established company policies and practices governing environmental pollution and employment conditions were in full compliance with relevant laws and administrative rulings.
4. The Consolidated Board, and in particular its outside members, could not properly and effectively play a larger role in the management of the business, nor would the outside directors be able or willing to invest the substantial additional time required to become more closely involved in ongoing affairs.
5. The appointment of the proposed committee would inevitably be reported in the business press and would be widely interpreted as an expression by outside directors of lack of confidence in operating management, with consequent unfortunate repercussions on the price of the common stock and on the morale of all management personnel.

In the ensuing lively discussion the chairman expressed the view that the appropriate and only viable responsibility of the board was to select the chief executive officer (CEO) to maintain a general familiarity with his performance as evidenced by overall financial results and similar measures, to support his policies and strategies if they produced satisfactory results, and to discharge him and install a successor CEO if his performance was judged unsatisfactory. Several outside directors disagreed with this view as unduly restrictive and unresponsive to newly emerging public pressures for a more active role for corporate boards.

When the chairman discovered the strength of their contrary position, he stated that despite the fact that the outside directors were a minority of the board's membership, he was unwilling to take the issue to a vote that would divide a board that had always found it possible to act unanimously. He therefore agreed to the appointment of the proposed Special Review Committee. He suggested, however, that the committee's mission be restricted to items (1) and (2) of the initial proposal. Several outside directors objected to such a restriction and said that it would be useful to extend the committee's task to include a broad assessment of the board's functions and responsibilities. One of the group observed that he could no longer accept as satisfactory Consolidated's financial performance, which he described as below average for the industry for several years. Another outside director was critical of the company's diversification program and added that the board had never had an opportunity to evaluate that strategy in depth, with detailed staff analysis of alternative investment opportunities, risks, and projected payouts.

After further discussion, which one director characterized as "sharp but not belligerent," the chairman agreed to give the Special Review Committee the proposed broad mission.

In January 1976, before the Special Review Committee had completed its investigation, without either admitting or denying the allegations in the complaint, the company consented to the entry of a Final Judgment of Permanent Injunction, Consent, and Undertaking in the matter of the *Securities and Exchange Commission v. Consolidated Petroleum Company* before the United States District Court for the District of Columbia. The judgment enjoined the use of corporate funds for unlawful political contributions or other unlawful purposes and also enjoined the company from violating Sections 13(a) and 14(a) of the Securities Exchange Act of 1934 and the applicable rules thereunder by filing materially false and misleading annual or other periodic reports or proxy statements that failed properly to reflect such expenditures.

The board of directors of Consolidated Petroleum Company was composed of the following members in 1976:

Edwin Huntington, chairman and chief executive officer, Consolidated Petroleum Company. Employed by the company as a petroleum engineer after graduating from the University of Texas, Huntington rose through technical and management ranks, served in a variety of assignments in the United States and overseas in all parts of the petroleum and gas area, but not in other divisions, was elected president and chief operating officer in 1965 and chairman and chief executive officer in 1968. He was 63 years old in 1976, with two years to serve before mandatory retirement. Huntington was largely responsible for bringing to the board all of the outside directors serving in 1976 except William Perrine and Joseph Yost.

Paul Gallery, president and chief operating officer, Consolidated Petroleum Company. Employed by the company as a geologist after graduating from Colorado School of Mines, Gallery was assigned, after about five years in petroleum exploration, to the refinery function where he worked under Huntington's direction. Thereafter, his career followed Huntington's in the senior man's various assignments. He was Huntington's choice for president when that position was vacated by Huntington's election as chairman of the board. He was 58 in 1976 and was expected to succeed Huntington as chairman in 1978.

Lewis Appleton, chairman of the board, Union Commercial National Bank of New York (one of the six largest banks in the city). An old friend of Huntington's and the head of the company's lead bank, Appleton joined the Consolidated board in 1969. All of his career was spent in commercial banking after graduating from Princeton with a major in economics and the Harvard Business School where he concentrated in banking. First employed by Chase Manhattan in New York, he transferred to Union Commercial in midcareer with a principal responsibility for the development of the bank's national account business with major corporations. He was 63 in 1976.

David Count, president, Atlantic Institute of Technology (AIT), one of the country's leading scientific and engineering schools. Following his doctoral work in organic chemistry at Cornell, he pursued an academic career of increasing distinction in research at Cornell, Columbia, and AIT. He became dean of the faculties at AIT in 1955 and was selected as president by the institute's trustees in 1963. A director of several major corporations, he accepted an invitation from Huntington to join the Consolidated board in 1971. He was 62 in 1976.

Arthur Gallon, senior vice-president, Consolidated Petroleum Company, responsible for the company's petroleum and gas activities. Gallon was employed by Consolidated as a refinery process engineer in 1945 after graduating from Baylor and completing two years of military service. He advanced through management ranks in a variety of U.S. and international assignments. He took command of the petroleum and gas activities on Gallery's promotion to president in 1968 and was elected a director of the company the following year. He was 56 in 1976.

Monroe Howard, senior vice-president, Consolidated Petroleum Company. The chief financial officer of the company, Howard was responsible for the treasury and controller functions. Trained in accounting at the Wharton School, Howard worked for several years for one of the largest public accounting firms, which included Consolidated Petroleum as one of its clients. Having become acquainted with a number of Consolidated's controller and financial staff people as a result of his work on the Consolidated account, Howard was recruited by the company's controller as a principal deputy in 1952; he later served as controller and then treasurer before accepting appointment as senior vice-president in charge of both departments in 1968. He became a director in 1972. He was 61 in 1976.

Walter Johnson, senior vice-president, Consolidated Petroleum Company, in charge of administrative services and planning. A graduate of Williams College and the Columbia Graduate School of Business, Johnson worked for a number of years for a large international management consulting firm, first as a staff associate and then as partner. In the late 1950s he headed a consulting team that studied the administrative and planning process in Consolidated Petroleum. With the acceptance by the client of the team's recommendations for reorganizing and redirecting the company's headquarters staff services and planning activities, Johnson accepted an invitation in 1965 from Huntington's predecessor as chairman to assume responsibility for implementing the reorganization plan. He was named a senior vice-president in 1970 and joined the board in 1972. He was 58 in 1976.

Crosby Kennedy, senior partner, Kennedy, Swift, Rose, & Christianson (one of the larger New York corporate law firms and principal outside counsel for Consolidated Petroleum). A graduate of Harvard College and Harvard Law School, Kennedy joined the firm of which his father was a founder and was continually associated with it thereafter except for service in the navy during World War II. He became senior partner following his father's death in 1970. A longtime friend of Huntington's, he was invited to join the Consolidated board in 1971.

Philip Lewis, chairman, president, and chief executive officer, Inter-Continental Aerospace Corporation. A graduate of West Point and a career military officer, he attained the rank of brigadier general in the air force before electing early retirement to accept a position as vice-president of Inter-Continental. He became that company's chief officer in 1970. Inter-Continental was a high technology company and an important subcontractor on a number of military prime contracts in the aerospace field. General Lewis met Huntington as a fellow member of a yacht club on Long Island's North Shore where they were small-boat racing enthusiasts and competitors. After the acquaintance developed into friendship, General Lewis accepted Huntington's invitation to fill a vacancy created by the retirement of an outside member of the Consolidated board. He was 57 in 1976.

William Perrine, retired from his position as chairman of the board, Whipple Industries (a very large, diversified company with divisions in a number of industries). Perrine was a self-made man who had gone to work at the age of 16 as an apprentice machinist in a small manufacturing company. His hard work, aggressiveness, ambition, and ability to learn from every job experience supported his rise through foreman and factory management ranks until, at the age of 27, he was asked to become general manager of the company when the owning family could no longer provide for its effective administration. He proceeded to buy out the family interest within three years and then carried through a public stock offering and the first of a series of acquisitions and mergers that built the giant organization from which he retired in 1973. Perrine joined the Consolidated board in 1962 and participated in the selection of Huntington to serve as president and then chairman. He was 68 in 1976.

John Rosterman, senior vice-president, Consolidated Petroleum Company, in charge of chemical and mineral activities. A graduate of the University of Michigan Engineering School, Rosterman worked up through management levels from his start as a process engineer in a medium-sized chemicals company. When the company was acquired by Consolidated Petroleum in 1962 as a building block in its plan for developing a petroleum-based chemical business, Rosterman was second in command of the company. Within a few years he was promoted to the top position in Consolidated's chemicals division. In 1968 he was made a senior vice-president in charge of both chemicals and minerals. He joined the board in 1974. He was 60 in 1976.

Thomas Thompson, senior vice-president, Consolidated Petroleum Company, responsible for foreign operations. A graduate of Yale, Thompson entered the Foreign Service of the State Department and served several duty tours in the Middle East where he became acquainted with officers of a number of U.S. petroleum companies. At the age of 40 in 1954 he left the State Department and joined Consolidated as a vice-president responsible for relations with Mideast and North African governments. In 1965 his assignment was broadened to include all foreign operations. He became a director in 1974. He was 62 in 1976.

Carl Walden, a director of several large corporations, formerly managing partner of a major international management consulting company. As a young graduate of the Harvard Business School, Walden helped to found what became over the next 25 years one of the leading consulting organizations — a firm he was largely responsible for developing in its early years and for administering in the following period when its size was substantial and its reputation secure. He retired from the firm at the age of 50 to work as a "professional director," serving on the boards of a number of large companies where his earlier experience with the problems of companies across a broad spectrum of industries and his accumulated knowledge and wisdom might be valuable. He accepted an invitation to join the Consolidated board in 1971. He was 55 in 1976.

Joseph Yost, dean, Graduate School of Business, Colharstan University (one of the country's leading institutions of higher learning). Yost's career included an early period teaching management after acquiring an M.B.A. and Ph.D. at Columbia, a middle period when he served as senior staff officer and assistant to the president of a large manufacturing company, and a third period in which he returned to academia as dean of a major business school. He was brought on the Consolidated Petroleum board by Huntington's predecessor as chairman and was involved in the selection of Huntington as president and later as chairman. He was 64 in 1976.

Carrol Ziegler, senior vice-president, Consolidated Petroleum Company, responsible for technology and research at the corporate level and in the divisions. Ziegler earned his doctorate in molecular biology at MIT and thereafter worked as research administrator in several major corporate research laboratories. He joined Consolidated in the capacity of director of research and technology in 1967, was elected senior vice-president in 1969, and became a director in 1971. He was 50 in 1976.

Consolidated Petroleum's board of directors met six times annually on the first Thursday of every second month. Meetings typically began at 10:00 A.M. and continued through a working lunch. Committees on the board usually scheduled their meetings for the afternoon preceding a regular meeting of the full board, although on occasion they met at other times.

The board had the following standing committees:

1. *Executive.* Empowered to act for the board in emergencies between regularly scheduled board meetings and, from time to time, specifically authorized to act for the board with respect to a defined decision situation.
2. *Finance.* Generally responsible for overseeing the financial condition, trends, prospects, and plans of business.
3. *Budget.* Generally responsible for reviewing proposed annual operating budgets and recommending their adoption by the board.
4. *Executive Compensation.* Concerned with the full range of top management compensation, including salaries, bonus plans, stock option plans, and pension plans.
5. *Audit.* Generally responsible for reviewing with the company's outside auditors the scope, principal procedures, and results of their work, as well as any observations they might contribute about the integrity and adequacy of control systems.

The Executive Committee was composed of the chairman, the president, and one outside director, an assignment rotated annually among outside directors. The Executive Compensation and Audit committees were composed exclusively of outside directors.

Directors received monthly financial and operating reports in considerable detail for the corporation as a whole and also for the operating divisions. These reports were accompanied by analytical material prepared by the corporate finance staff, noting and explaining trends and deviations from standards. Consolidated Petroleum had a formal long-range planning system generally covering a five-year planning horizon with annual review and updating. The updated long-range plan was submitted annually to the board for its review and approval and on these occasions was the subject of verbal explanation. Special reports were made to the board from time to time when a significant decision such as a proposed acquisition was under consideration by management.

The regular bimonthly meetings of the board were conducted in accordance with the discipline of a planned and familiar agenda. At a typical meeting the chairman, after disposing of the minutes of the preceding meeting and other formalities for the record, would open with a general review of operations during the preceding two months and comments on near-term prospects for the business. He would then invite the president to supplement his remarks on the basis of his closer familiarity with specific operating details. At each meeting two or three senior line managers, some board members, and other nonmembers would address the board on performance and prospects in their areas of responsibility. These presentations were carefully prepared, typically with an elaborate supporting array of visual aids, and board members, particularly outside members, had an opportunity to make observations and raise questions. Outside directors usually posed few questions. Such questions as were raised were ordinarily directed at eliciting explanations of developments and prospects in somewhat greater depth than had been offered in the original presentations.

Comments of several outside directors described the character of board meetings and the environment in which the board fulfilled its obligations prior to 1975. One outside director observed: "This is an orderly and gentlemanly group. The inside members clearly know their place in relation to the Chairman, and the outside members generally hold to the view that their principal responsibility is to select competent people to run the company and then support them as long as they bring in acceptable results. That has certainly been the case in this organization as long as I have been a director."

Another outside director described the board as "passive but prudently observant. We have all the information necessary to maintain our appropriate watching brief. We could have more information if we asked for it. We never have the feeling that we might be refused anything we wanted."

A third director observed, "With competent management, there is really very little for outside directors to do except in crisis. Competent management seldom permits a crisis to occur. Even when the Arabs decided to change the whole petroleum ball game in 1973, there was little that any that any outside director of this company could contribute. Management was on top of the situation, kept the board informed about what was happening and what they were doing about it, and none of us knew enough about the business to develop any original ideas or even to suggest significant alternatives to management."

A fourth director said, "I've been on boards where there was acrimonious discussion, political maneuvering, and even aggravating nit-picking. In general, these situations occurred because management was not delivering a satisfactory performance, or because management was divided within its own house, or because an external force — such as a radical technological change that disrupted a major market, or a threatened unfriendly takeover bid — impacted on the business. Or even because one or two outside directors didn't understand their proper role. But we haven't seen any of that here at Consolidated Petroleum."

The report of the Special Review Committee, made available to the full board on April 23, 1976, concluded that during the 1960–75 period a total of approximately $4 million of corporate funds had been used for political contributions and related purposes. The report stated that at least $2 million of this amount was expended by the company in foreign countries, mostly in circumstances that the committee concluded were lawful or as to the legality of which the committee expressed no judgment. The remaining expenditures for political purposes in the United States and in a few foreign countries were characterized by the committee as illegal.

The committee's report also commented on its investigation of knowledge of such contributions both abroad and in the United States on the part of certain of the company's executives. The report noted that all senior executives denied any knowledge of illegal contributions in the United States, and most of them denied any knowledge of contributions, whether legal or illegal, in other countries. Nevertheless, the report concluded that senior officers, even if ignorant of the payments, could not completely disavow responsibility for them and indeed should have taken steps to ensure that such contributions were not made and, if made, were brought to their attention.

With respect to the allegations of bribes given to certain foreign government officials and others, the report concluded that deficiencies in financial reporting and control systems, absence of policy guidance from the corporate-level to country-level operating managers, and the committee's inability to make clear distinctions between legitimate and valuable agents and illegitimate interveners who received payments to which no specific business services could be related combined to render any judgment cloudy. Bribery had probably occurred, the report stated, but its magnitude and pervasiveness could not be determined. It was beyond dispute, however, that Consolidated's management and information systems lacked both qualitative and quantitative standards and controls that would outlaw the use of bribes to advance the interests of the business — particularly in national cultures that traditionally had a relaxed attitude toward bribery —

and identify the prohibited practice if it occurred.

The committee recommended the establishment and implementation of policies and procedures that would preclude unlawful political contributions in the future and proposed changes in internal accounting and reporting procedures that would strengthen information and control systems in this area, including termination of all "off-the-books" funds for any purposes. The committee further recommended that the board consider additional steps to ensure a more rigorous control over the behavior of managers at all levels in their relationships with governmental organizations, political parties, and their personnel. It proposed the creation of a committee of the board on business principles and policies with specific responsibility for formulating a code of ethical behavior applicable to managers at all levels of the company in both U.S. and foreign operations.

The report stated that the committee had not undertaken to appraise the weight of the evidence for the charge that almost $4 million of corporate funds had been expended for unlawful purposes and without proper authorization, and that certain disbursements had been concealed by false accounting entries or otherwise. That was a matter for judicial determination. The committee's great concern was for the future. However, it observed that the committee found no indication that the practice of making such disbursements without authorization or proper recording was recently initiated. It might have been going on for some time. The committee did not address the question of whether outside auditors might reasonably have been expected to uncover such practices. This was an issue for consideration by the board's Audit Committee. To the committee's knowledge, the company's U.S. political contributions had not been washed through a foreign subsidiary.

The report noted that decisions about political contributions had apparently been made in Consolidated's organization one or two levels below the vice-presidential level in both the U.S. and foreign countries. How far up the line such actions were known, or might reasonably be expected to have been known, was not investigated. It clearly appeared, however, that there was no evidence of explicit prohibition of such actions.

In its study the committee had found that the general feeling among Consolidated's managers was that Consolidated's behavior in the questioned areas was not different from that of other companies in the petroleum and other industries, and that the people engaged in the criticized practices were acting in ways they sincerely believed to be in the best interests of the company.

The report also observed that Consolidated's principal outside legal counsel was not engaged in defending directors and officers against the shareholders' complaint. Another law firm was specifically employed by Consolidated for this assignment. Directors' liabilities, if any, arising from this and other suits would be covered, at least in part, by insurance paid for by Consolidated.

The report then turned from the issues of political contributions and bribery to what it described as "fundamental considerations related to the general governance of the company and particularly the role of the Board of Directors." It presented the following principal conclusions:

1. Consolidated's Board has not satisfactorily implemented its responsibility for maintaining effective oversight of the conduct of the business. The outside Directors have not been furnished, nor have they requested, essential information about critical aspects of company policies and practices.

2. Important strategic decisions involving basic changes in the company's business and investment and potential future investment of resources have not been adequately reviewed by the Board at the formative stage, with opportunity to consider options and trade-offs. The normal procedure has been to ask the Board to approve programs that have been fully developed at lower management levels and have been endorsed by senior management.

3. Outside Directors constitute a minority of the total Board and new Directors have generally been selected by the Chief Executive Officer with no more than formal approval by the existing Directors.

4. Inadequate attention has been given by the Board — because of its relatively passive role in the governance of the company — to the company's responsiveness to new societal expectations and demands for corporate policies and practices in such areas as personnel administration and environmental hygiene.

5. The audit responsibility has been fulfilled at no more than a bare minimum level of compliance.

Each of these conclusions was supported by considerable detail of facts and observations compiled by the committee in carrying out its assignment. Discussion of conclusion (2) included extensive criticism of the company's chemicals, plastics, and minerals operations, covering both program commitments and management performance. A major thrust of the criticism was the failure to bring outside directors into a knowledgeable position about these diversifications early in the planning stage and to project long-term programs and alternatives.

The report then presented for board consideration a number of specific recommendations that amounted, in the committee's judgment, to a major change in the membership, structure, and work of Consolidated's board — a change described as "essential for the effective implementation of the Board's responsibilities as defined by the relevant laws and the demands laid upon business by our evolving society." The principal recommendations follow:

1. At the earliest possible date, two additional outside directors should be added to the board, so that outsiders would constitute a majority of the membership.

2. Within three years, the composition of the board should be further changed by the removal from board membership of all inside directors except the chairman, the president, and two other officers designated by the chairman. The removed inside directors should be replaced by new outside directors.

3. The new outside directors referenced in (1) and (2) above should be selected by a special committee of outside directors. The chairman could, if he desired, propose individuals for the committee's consideration and could also indicate to the committee his objection to any prospective board member under consideration by the committee.

4. The specific responsibilties and duties of outside directors should be described in writing and that description, after review and approval by the board, should be incorporated in the board's minutes. The description should include a statement declaring the right of any outside director to request information in any desired detail on any aspect of the company's plans and operations and, at the director's choice, to address the request to the chairman or president or directly to any company officer.

5. A new committee composed of outside directors, designated as the Agenda Committee, should be responsible, in consultation with the chairman, for preparing the agenda for all board meetings.

6. The composition of the Executive Committee should be changed to consist of the chairman and two outside directors, with all outside directors serving, in turn, annual assignments as members of this committee.

7. The board should be involved in Consolidated's formal long-range planning system not, as heretofore, simply as audience giving brief, formal assent to a completed plan but at an earlier stage, with presentation to the board of principal planning options and trade-offs and an opportunity for directors to question line officers about planning assumptions and conclusions and to propose alternatives.

8. The responsibility of the Audit Committee should be broadened to include oversight of the thoroughness and integrity of all management information and control systems and the implementation of corporate policies. Further, the enlarged assignment should be formally described in writing and incorporated in the board's minutes.

9. A new board committee of outside directors, designated the Committee on Public Affairs, should be created, with responsibility for reviewing policies and practices in such socially and politically sensitive areas as

political contributions, environmental hygiene and safety (both within Consolidated facilities and in the communities surrounding facilities), personnel administration, product safety, governmental relationships (at all levels in the United States, federal or local, and in other countries), and relations with various "publics" — customers, suppliers, shareowners, employees, and the like.

This comprehensive program for redesigning the membership, organization, and work of the Consolidated board reflected primarily the ideas of Appleton, Count, and Yost. At the committee's final meeting before concluding its work and submitting its report, these three directors argued:

> The complex and demanding requirements of corporate governance today and tomorrow — with multiple responsibilities to shareowners, employees, and local and national publics — requires a board that is capable of being objective toward and independent of operating management. The membership, structure, and duties of such a board must be clearly defined. Without intervening in the detail of operations, the board must function in a way that facilitates and compels its involvement in the formulation of fundamental corporate goals, policies, and strategies. This philosophy underlies our proposals for Consolidated.

Perrine then stated:

> I am going to join the Messrs. Appleton, Count, and Yost in recommending the full list of our Committee's proposals because I think the company needs strong shoring up and this will be the means to get it. I'm particularly in favor of getting a majority of outsiders on the Board as soon as possible, vigorously policing our ethics program, and moving ahead with a much broader and deeper approach through the Audit Committee. This is only the beginning of things, however, as far as I am concerned.
>
> What we should be primarily concerned with as directors of Consolidated is that the company has not been delivering the kind of bottom-line performance it should be delivering, that it has to do better, and that top operating management must accept that responsibility and deliver on it. If it doesn't, then the board should discharge the management and replace it with more competent people. In short, I think we should appraise management in terms of the results it achieves. And I think the correct measuring stick is the performance recorded by, say, the top three or four

performing companies in the industry. A professional
baseball manager or a professional football coach holds his
job when he produces a winning team, and loses it when
he doesn't. That's an appropriate rule in business, too.

I think we have to be very careful when we start getting
the board involved in long-range planning. We can't afford
to relieve management of any responsibility here. It's their
job to present the plans, and we'll review them. It's our job
then to hold their feet to the fire — above all, the feet of
the chief executive officer and the chief operating officer
— and demand outstanding accomplishments. Then we
will be in the proper position to do what the shareowners
fundamentally expect from the board — to hire the best
managers we can find for the company, pay them appropriately when they perform effectively, and replace them
when they don't. When we discuss our report with the full
board I'm going to say these things to everybody, including
Ed Huntington. But I don't consider this to be in any sense
a minority report, as I understand Carl Walden proposes
to write.

Walden then read aloud to his committee associates his proposed minority
report, as follows:

I am in substantive agreement with many — even most —
of the recommendations of the majority of this Committee.
However, because I am so concerned about the timing of
the various moves and the way the moves are made, I want
to record my opinions in a minority report. I'd like to stimulate full board consideration and discussion of my two key
points.

The first issue is timing. If we who are the independent
directors of Consolidated Petroleum do all of the things
that our Committee has recommended, we are going to be
overwhelmed. I just don't see how we can organize and
serve on so many new committees, lay down intelligently
their detailed functions and responsibilities, dig deeper
into the planning and managerial programs of the company, and simultaneously bring several new outsiders on to
the board. Some things we should start on immediately —
the vigorous enforcement of an ethics policy, a reconstituted and freshly mandated Audit Committee, and the formation of a Nominating Committee, for example. Other
things should evolve, I believe, as we work out longer-term
relationships between the board and management.

This brings me to my second point, which is a matter of overall philosophy. The worst thing that could happen to Consolidated Petroleum right now would be to have a show-down between the senior management group and the board, with the result that one side has to get out. We have not reached this point in either the financial or the operating condition of the company — nor have we in the state of our communications with Mr. Huntington and his top associates. Yet if we, too, dictatorially insist upon an excessively rapid implementation of all our recommendations, we are in grave danger of establishing an adversary relationship between board and management which would have only harmful results.

On the contrary side, I think we have an unusual opportunity here to do something that will be of lasting benefit to the company. I believe we should begin to discuss among ourselves — outside directors, inside directors, and even some other members of senior management — what the role of the board really should be in Consolidated Petroleum. And I mean in the exact circumstances in which this company finds itself. We need to ask ourselves a number of questions, such as, "What information should the board be getting, and when and how should it be presented to us? What kind of benchmarks should be established for management so that we can appropriately measure their performance? And over what period of time?" We have a very delicate balance here — and we're not the only U.S. company in this situation — between guiding and doing, between evaluating and supporting, between the short run and the long run, between management interests and prerogatives and shareowner interests and prerogatives. And I don't want us to rush into a lot of fast decisions without careful and deliberate thought.

Accordingly, I propose that for at least the next year we begin the dialogue that will lead us in orderly fashion to greater trust and understanding between outside directors and operating management. I suggest that we move the board to a monthly meeting schedule, with formal meeting times from 9:30 to at least 12:30. I suggest that we actively seek out new outside directors who can bring us special expertise in areas where the company has acknowledged problems. Above all, let us present a united front to the press and to our shareowners, not criticizing management and ourselves, but openly stating that we are moving professionally and harmoniously toward the development of a company that has set for itself higher goals in all areas and has established logical and rational programs and timetables to achieve those goals.

When Carl Walden had completed reading his proposed minority report, Chairman Perrine said:

> Fine, I think Carl's viewpoint should go to the full board along with the majority report. As far as I'm concerned, however — speaking as one member of this Committee and of the board — the whole situation, and I mean especially the operating situation, demands prompt action; not further time-consuming discussion. I think we have a responsibility to the shareowners and to ourselves to act, to act promptly, and to get results.

DISCUSSION QUESTIONS

1. What are the salient characteristics of Consolidated Petroleum and of its board?
2. Has the Consolidated board been effective? Will the recommendations of the Special Review Committee improve its effectiveness?
3. Is there anything in addition to these recommendations that will be necessary to improve board effectiveness?
4. What is the difference between Perrine's and Walden's approach to the Special Review Committee's report? Which do you support and why?

Chapter 8

Professionalism in the Corporation

Developments in the Roles of Auditors, Lawyers, and Managers

The senior management of a firm has a range of available approaches for relating to the corporation's board of directors. At one extreme it can develop a board of experienced, knowledgeable persons who can assist and advise management in major decisions and plans. When management seeks this board role, it takes pains to inform directors of problems and opportunities in an early stage, provides thorough and detailed information on major operations, calls upon directors for special expertise, and responds seriously and fully to director questions. At the other extreme, management can choose to use the board in a minimal fashion. Directors can be nominated and selected for reasons other than their experience and judgment, they can be presented decisions rather than problems and issues, information can be too general or too detailed for their effective use, and they can be rarely utilized.

The corporate board has undergone changes in recent years and must conform to new requirements for information disclosure. Yet management maintains a wide range of discretion in the role and functioning of the corporate board. Ultimately the social legitimacy of the corporation may depend on the use of this managerial discretion to ensure a credible process of corporate governance.

Management's discretion in the affairs of corporate governance is not limited to the role of the corporate board. There is a series of other individuals whose organizational roles are largely subject to the practices and policies of management — individuals who can also make a major contribution to public confidence in the integrity of management. These individuals — public accountants, internal auditors, and legal counsel — might be called "management professionals." They, like the corporate board, have an important role to play in the internal governance of corporations, and they also are heavily influenced by management's definition of their roles.

A director's special contribution to corporate governance derives from the existence of a fiduciary responsibility to stockholders above and beyond the director's role in assisting and advising management. Similarly, public accountants, lawyers, and internal auditors all have a code of professional ethics or a set of principles independent of management. To the extent managers incorporate these standards into the decisions of the corporation, they are promoting a high level of professionalism in the firm.

The contributions of management professionals can be seen as vital ingredients in the policies and practices of the firm, or as the source of unwanted intereference with managerial prerogatives. Professional managers incorporate ethical standards and social norms into the internal processes of decision making in systematic and organized ways; and they look to public accountants, auditors, and lawyers as major sources of such standards and norms.

This chapter examines corporate policies and practices that reflect a high degree of professionalism in management. The roles of external and internal auditors and of corporate counsel are given primary attention, but not without regard to the related importance of the audit committee of the board and the place of corporate codes of conduct. Above all, the chapter is intended to underscore the impact of the manager's own attitudes, influence, and leadership in the degree of professionalism in the corporation.

Our discussion begins with a focus on the practice of internal financial control in corporations, a concept that immediately relates the roles of managers, directors, public accountants, and internal auditors. *Internal control* is the set of policies and procedures that seeks to ensure the integrity of the corporation's financial reporting system, clearly an area in which the public holds high expectations for corporate performance and thus an area bearing upon corporate legitimacy.

Attention to internal control has been given significant impetus in recent years by the passage of the Foreign Corrupt Practices Act, which mandates corporate performance in the area of internal accounting control. Taking this act as a point of departure, we are led to consider the roles of managers, directors, and professionals in the governance processes of the firm.

THE FOREIGN CORRUPT PRACTICES ACT AND INTERNAL ACCOUNTING CONTROL

Prohibition of "Improper Payments"

To prohibit foreign bribes and questionable payments, Congress in 1977 passed an amendment to the Securities Exchange Act of 1934, which was called the Foreign Corrupt Practices Act. While some degrees of flexibility remain for companies in the form of minor favors or "facilitating payments" to lower-level foreign officials, the Congress wrote a tight statute placing heavy penalties on managers and firms who induce or influence foreign officials in the misuse of their official positions, regardless of the customs or laws of the country or the practices of other international businesses. The law also makes illegal the use of subsidiaries or other arrangements to make payments indirectly.[1]

Although this law was overwhelmingly passed by both houses of Congress, it remains controversial and intensely opposed by some businesspersons. The annual loss of U.S. export income due to the law is thought to be over $1 billion per year,[2] which in 1979 represented about 1 percent of U.S. exports. Some industries appear to be particularly vulnerable to the restrictions of the act. For example, it has been reported that between 1976 and 1979 the United States dropped from first to fifth place in the share of the overseas construction market, placing it behind Japan, Korea, West Germany, and Italy.[3] Other industries, or particular companies, appeared little affected. E. I. Dupont, with over $3 billion in overseas sales in 1978, was reportedly unaffected by the legislation because "its own corporate code of ethics is more rigorous and predated the passage of the U.S. law."[4] Nevertheless, many American companies feel unfairly handicapped in the sphere of international competition, and to many the law appears a futile effort to impose domestic standards of conduct upon public officials around the world, at our own expense.

Provisions for Record Keeping and Internal Accounting Control

While the overseas payments provision is the most immediate, visible, and controversial element of this law, the act also contains several aspects that may, in the long run, be farther-reaching and more profound. Other than the existence of bribes on a broad scale, the falsification of corporate records was a major and shocking result in the unraveling of the Watergate affair. While the prohibition of foreign payments is debated in terms of imposing American standards of morality, loss of export income, and threat to American jobs, the fact of falsification of records and the apparent weaknesses of corporate controls on management's potential misuse of the firm's assets was an issue upon which little debate was possible.

Two provisions of the act address the areas of accurate record keeping and internal accounting control. First, all publicly held companies are required to "make and keep books, records, and accounts, which, in reasonable detail, accurately and fairly reflect the transactions and dispositions of the assets of the issuer."[5] While this statement may seem a rather innocuous and minor requirement for corporations, it provides a major precedent from the standpoint of governmental regulatory powers. Until this point the Securities and Exchange Commission's (SEC's) powers had been limited to questions of the failure of corporations to disclose factors that may materially affect the accuracy of financial statements. Under this law it could often be argued that overseas payments for a multibillion dollar corporation were not large enough to be financially material. Bribes, for example, would have to be enormous to make a reflection on stated earnings.

The record-keeping provision of the Foreign Corrupt Practices Act sets forth a much stricter standard of recording accurately and fairly the disposition of assets of the corporation. One observer states the intent of this requirement was to attack three major deficiencies of record keeping revealed in the overseas payments investigations:

- Records that failed to record improper transactions at all;
- Records that were falsified to disguise aspects of improper transactions that were otherwise recorded correctly; and
- Records that correctly stated the quantitative aspects of transactions but failed to record their "qualitative" aspects.[6]

The result is that a corporation that chooses to make a questionable payment overseas, and to not record it for what it is, qualitatively and quantitatively, can be charged with violating the record-keeping provision of the act. Of course, accurate recording such as "bribe to the minister of trade of country X to obtain countrywide marketing authorization" would be self-incriminating and absurd. The point is that a company can be prosecuted more easily for failing to record the transaction accurately than it can be prosecuted for failing to disclose a material expenditure. Moreover, the record-keeping requirement is not limited to recording of foreign transactions but encompasses all transactions and thus embraces any other questionable or illegal practices such as political contributions, income tax fraud, or self-dealing by insiders.

If the SEC's previous disclosure requirements were intended to set standards for directors and management about the accuracy of financial information released to the public, the record-keeping rule of the act goes beyond information standards to dictate corporate accounting standards. In this sense it reaches more deeply and directly into the internal workings of the organization. It is worthwhile to note that Congress found general disclosure requirements inadequate to induce what was felt to be fully adequate bookkeeping; Congress bypassed the obvious option of strengthening disclosure requirements to include information on overseas payoffs and, instead, acted to require accurate and fair records and accounts.

Another provision of the law bears upon internal accounting control and is also an unprecedented requirement for standards of management practice, as opposed to standards for financial information disclosure. Borrowing directly from the American Institute of Certified Public Accountants' (AICPA's) own statement on auditing practice, Congress declared that publicly-held companies must develop and maintain a system of internal accounting controls in order to provide reasonable assurances that transactions follow management's authorization, transactions are appropriately recorded, access to assets is authorized, and records are reconciled periodically with actual assets. In short, internal control must include management policies and procedures to ensure the integrity of corporate assets by prevention of error, fraud, theft, and misdirection. These are not insignificant issues; one recent report quotes a statement of the congressional Joint Economic Committee that the cost of embezzlement, bribery, stock manipulations, and antitrust violations is $44.6 billion a year, ten times higher than street crimes of robbery, burglary, and larceny.[7]

Congress's standards of internal control are not new or unusual; they were taken directly from the certified public accountants' own professional statements of auditing standards. That they are now legal requirements, under which companies, managers, and directors can be held liable, is new. In other words these standards are no longer voluntary for publicly held corporations.

There has been much debate about the meaning of these requirements. Surprisingly, neither the legislative history of the Foreign Corrupt Practices Act nor the subsequent releases of the SEC pertaining to the act give specific requirements and procedures of good internal accounting control. The difficulty of identifying a universal and complete set of internal controls is so great that companies still do not know what is specifically required of them. While this state of affairs has the clear disadvantage of introducing uncertainty and possible confusion into corporate management, perhaps the silver lining is that the absence of specifics should force company managers to reexamine their firm's activities and their control procedures, encouraging them to arrive at their own custom-designed system for compliance with the intent of the law. In the long run this freedom may not only be more satisfying for managers, but it may also be a more effective means, from a regulative standpoint, of improving internal control.

Maintaining the integrity of the firm's assets is obviously a responsibility of corporate management. Internal control, management's means of ensuring this integrity, is an important management activity because all human systems are subject to fallibilities of error, theft, or actions of individuals that expend corporate resources in ways inconsistent with the corporate direction. (See Insert 8.A.) Specific managers can understand this

Insert 8.A

INTERNAL ACCOUNTING CONTROL: DEFINITIONS AND AMBIGUITIES

Because the accuracy and reliability of a corporation's financial statements depend in part on the firm's internal control — its method of safeguarding

Insert 8.A   continued

assets and of maintaining financial records — assessment of internal accounting control is subject to professional standard setting by public accountants. The American Institute of Certified Public Accountants (AICPA) defines responsibilities and standards for internal control procedures and their evaluation by public accountants.

One of the most basic concepts of accounting control is the segregation of functions — that the initiation and authorization of an activity be separate from the accounting for it. In less technical terms this is the concept that a hungry dog not be put in charge of guarding the bone. The AICPA's *Statement on Auditing Standards No. 1* describes the rationale for segregation of functions in the following terms:

> Incompatible functions for accounting control purposes are those that place any person in a position both to perpetuate and to conceal errors [unintentional mistakes] or irregularities [intentional distortions of financial statements or embezzlement] in the normal course of his duties. Anyone who records transactions or has access to assets ordinarily is in a position to perpetuate errors or irregularities. Accordingly, accounting control necessarily depends largely on the elimination of opportunities for concealment. For example, anyone who records disbursements could omit the recording of a check, either unintentionally or intentionally. If the same person also reconciles the bank account, the failure to record the check could be concealed through an improper reconciliation. This example illustrates the concept that procedures designed to detect errors and irregularities should be performed by persons other than those who are in a position to perpetrate them — i.e., by persons having no incompatible functions.

Accounting control consists of other concepts as well, such as the responsibility of management to establish, supervise, and maintain the firm's system of internal control and the need for personnel of competence and integrity who understand and follow prescribed procedures. However, while the AICPA defines generally applicable concepts of good accounting control, the professional recognizes "the organizational and procedural means of applying them may differ considerably from case to case because of the variety of circumstances involved."

SOURCE: American Institute of Certified Public Accountants, *Statement on Auditing Standards No. 1* (New York: AICPA, 1973), pp. 21–23.

principle well or poorly, they can give internal control its proper emphasis or reduce it to a subordinate role, and they can insist on the development and maintenance of good control procedures or allow procedures to be lax and incomplete. Here professionalism enters management practice; management's attitude, understanding, and intent in maintaining financial integrity are the key elements of internal control in general and of compliance with the Foreign Corrupt Practices Act in particular.

Management and the Creation of a Control Environment

Financial integrity and internal control are not principles that can be implemented by management alone. The process clearly starts with management but involves a number of other parties, including specialists in accounting and the law. Management, however, remains the central agent in establishing the emphasis on control in the corporation — it is the center of leadership for seeing that the complex system of policies, roles, and procedures is functioning effectively. The following comments address management's role more extensively before turning to the roles of other key aspects of effective control, namely, the board audit committee and the corporation's relationship to its external auditors, corporate codes of conduct, and the roles of internal auditors and legal counsel.

Both the SEC and the AICPA greatly emphasize what is termed the *environment* of internal accounting control. This important concept states that broad, intangible factors such as managerial attitudes, organizational structures, clarity of objectives and policies, and personnel quality are equal in significance to more operational accounting procedures. The AICPA argues that accounting control begins with management's effort to establish an "appropriate level of control consciousness." A special committee report of this professional group conveys the intangibility of some control factors and the difficulty of imposing a uniform set of procedures on all companies:

> The committee has found the term *internal accounting control environment* to be a convenient way to describe factors [that have a significant impact on a company's accounting control procedures and techniques.] Some are clearly visible, like a formal corporate conduct policy statement or an internal audit function. Some are intangible, like the competence and integrity of personnel. Some, like organizational structure and the way in which management communicates, enforces, and reinforces policy, vary so widely among companies that they can be contrasted more easily than they can be compared.[8]

The AICPA and the SEC strongly rely on top management and board leadership for establishing a control environment that reaches all company employees. In one sense what is meant is no less than sound managerial actions that are highly desirable as good management practice in general. The AICPA report observes:

> Leadership is formulating and communicating an appropriate atmosphere of control consciousness that must come from the board and top management. That leadership involves creating an appropriate organizational structure, using sound management practices, establishing accountability for performance and requiring adherence to appropriate standards for ethical behavior, including compliance with applicable laws and regulations.[9]

On the one hand, leadership in the area of accounting control is no different than leadership in other areas of management practice; it involves clarifying the organization, building patterns of communication for establishing common direction, setting performance expectations, and closely evaluating results — widely accepted elements of good management practice in all areas of corporate action.

On the other hand, leadership in financial control implies executive attention to the specifics of the internal control system. Good management practice in business planning, organization, and review constitutes a major step toward good accounting control, but managers also need to understand and emphasize the additional specific elements of internal control. Let us turn to examine concrete organizational mechanisms, procedures, and managerial actions that provide leadership and high personnel performance in the area of internal control.

THE BOARD AUDIT COMMITTEE

An audit committee of the corporate board has never been the subject of legislation nor has it been required by the SEC. However, since 1940 it has been increasingly acknowledged by managers, certified public accountants, government officials in the SEC, and legislators to play a crucial role in the effectiveness of corporate control. The audit committee movement actually began in the late 1930s with the SEC's attempt to strengthen the process of the independent audit by recommending a nonofficer committee of the corporate board nominate outside auditors, who would then be elected by stockholders.

As most reform movements the idea of a board audit committee arose out of financial scandal involving a single company; in this case the SEC proposed McKesson and Robbins adopt a nonofficer audit committee of the board as a remedy for a management fraud in which nearly 22 percent of the firm's reported assets were fictitious.[10] In the 1960s and 1970s public doubt about the adequacy of corporate control and the integrity of the existing outside audit process was regenerated by several visible cases of corporate mismanagement and the revelations of questionable payments transactions. By the late 1970s the AICPA had recommended that a permanent board committee of outside directors nominate the independent auditor and review its work, the SEC both officially and unofficially repeatedly endorsed the outside director audit committee, congressional committee reports and hearings stressed this point, and the New York Stock Exchange on June 30, 1978, made the existence of such a committee a condition of listing on the exchange. Finally, the internal controls provision of the Foreign Corrupt Practices Act gave new impetus to this proposal, since it is hard to imagine an effective management control system that does not originate at the board level. Hurd Baruch, special counsel to the SEC from 1969 to 1972, observes that "the SEC may well take the position that the *only* appropriate control over certain activities is the establishment of an audit committee of the board of directors."[11] And, in fact, SEC action in various judicial cases and administrative proceedings since the act has dictated the presence and duties of a board audit committee as a remedy for violations of the act.[12]

Audit Committee Tasks and Roles

Given the near unanimous endorsement of the importance of board audit committees, the issue becomes: What should the committee *do* to fulfill this important function? One experienced practitioner outlines a particularly rigorous schedule of activities, including the review of major accounting decisions, problems, and disclosures; supervision of the timing, scope, and cost of the company's independent audit; and scrutiny of the independent auditor's letter to management and management's response on weaknesses in internal control.[13] The committee's responsibility also involves investigation into any weak areas of operations discovered by the audit and investigation into the "integrity of reported facts and figures, ethical conduct, and appropriate disclosure."[14] Insert 8.B lists some of the responsibilities of the audit committee of a large and well-known firm in the financial services industry. While every audit committee may not engage in every task listed, these activities are a particularly thorough statement of audit committee duties; a broader involvement of a particular committee probably indicates it is more thoroughly discharging its duties.

Implicit in this list of specific activities is the very important function of establishing and maintaining a corporate system of checks and balances — a key function of the committee that should be explicitly recognized. In addition to making agreements with and reviewing the work of management, internal auditors, and outside auditors independently, the audit

Insert 8.B

RESPONSIBILITIES OF A BOARD AUDIT COMMITTEE

Widespread adoption of board audit committees in the last decade have led to questions about their authority, roles, and missions. The following excerpts are taken from a study of the information requirements of directors in general and audit committee members in particular of publicly-held firms. These statements are extracted from the Statement of Authority of the audit committee of a large financial services firm.

Internal Controls

1. To direct members of senior management of the corporation to comply with legislation dealing with accounting or internal controls, with the control requirements of regulatory bodies, with generally accepted accounting principles, and with the corporation's policies governing activities in the areas of sales and marketing.
2. To direct the implementation of a formal program of internal control monitoring and to review its results periodically.
3. To review the reports of independent accountants and internal auditors for significant internal control findings, recommendations, and management action on them.

Internal Auditing

1. To determine, through observation and discussion, that all levels of the internal auditing function are staffed by competent professionals who have adequate training and experience.
2. To determine, through observation, discussion, and review of internal audit plans, that internal auditing gives appropriate recognition to audit areas based on relative risk.
3. To review and approve the annual (tactical) and long-range (strategic) internal audit plans; to evaluate the activities of the internal audit department in comparison with the audit plans; and to review and approve significant or major modifications to previously approved plans.
4. To review significant audit findings and recommendations and management's response to them.
5. To conduct meetings with the director of internal auditing to discuss confidentially, without the members of the corporation's management present, matters which the director might be reluctant to discuss if they were present.

Insert 8.B   continued

Independent Accountant

1. To evaluate, with the assistance and advice of the corporation's executive committee and/or senior management, the professional qualifications, reputation, and, where applicable, past performance of candidates for appointment as the corporation's independent accountant.
2. To recommend to the board and/or to the corporation's executive committee the appointment of the independent accountant.
3. To determine that the independent accountant maintains actual and apparent independence from, and a proper working relationship with, the corporation's management.

Financial Statements

1. To require senior management to present to this committee the annual Form 10K, the annual consolidated financial statements (or any other financial statements deemed appropriate by this committee), and a commentary on those financial statements that focuses on significant items.

Professional Services

1. To review and approve any service (audit or nonaudit) that the corporation's principal independent accountant is to perform.
2. To review and approve any service (audit or nonaudit), with an anticipated cost greater than $25,000, which other independent accountants are to perform.

SOURCE: Reprinted from John D. Aram and Scott S. Cowen, "Inside the Merrill Lynch Audit Committee," *Directors & Boards,* Spring 1984, pp. 30–31. Copyright by the National Association of Accountants. Used by permission.

committee can use its position with each party to evaluate the capability and performance of each of the other parties. This is a function of ensuring the performance of the *system* of roles and relationships within internal control. Responsibilities of the committee that express this system of check and balance management have been stated as

- discussing the quality of work, degree of helpfulness, and fairness of charges of the independent auditors with the internal audit chief and members of management;

- establishing with the independent auditors that no limitation on the scope of the audit was imposed by management;
- asking the independent auditors to assess the effectiveness of the internal audit department and obtaining evaluations of key financial and accounting personnel; and
- making clear to the internal audit chief the duty to have direct contact with the audit committee.[15]

Overseeing of Outside Auditor Independence

While the increasing emphasis on the board audit committee has evolved in recognition of the need for an identified source of corporate control, the "necessity" of the independent audit was required by the Securities Act of 1933. The purpose of the outside audit is to provide investors with an impartial review of the accounting practices and the financial statements of publicly held firms. The audit ensures the reliability of the financial information prepared by management and thereby helps safeguard the assets of the company. The auditor's independence from management pressure in this work is, of course, fundamental to the credibility of such an assurance.

When is "independence" present? The answer to this is more obvious when independence is threatened; several clear, specific standards have evolved over time with respect to the ways in which an individual auditor's judgment might be compromised. For example, the public accountant is prohibited from having *any* direct or indirect material financial interest in the audit client. Neither the accountant nor any of his firm's members can act as promoters, underwriters, voting trustees, directors, officers, or employees of the client firm during the period of an audit engagement. These principles, where the threat to independence is self-evident, have also been extended to familial relationships, client indemnification of auditor for normal professional risks, and payment of contingent fees to the auditor.[16] Independence is considered to be enhanced by the absence of any personal interest — financial, familial, or psychological — that might cause the auditor's judgment to differ from the opinion of an auditor not having the particular interest.

Corporations, in general, audit committees, specifically, and also audit firms have been increasingly forced to focus their attention on external and internal conditions that might impact auditor independence. Heightened competition among audit firms for clients, poor economic conditions, and lucrative management advisory service contracts have all been cited as conditions that potentially reduce an audit firm's independence from its client.

Accounting firms have recently begun facing stiff price competition when vying for audit contracts. In 1983, according to a survey taken by the public accounting industry's newsletter, 36 percent of the companies who changed audit firms that year cited "a break on audit fees" as the reason for the switch.[17] Downward pressure on audit fees has led some observers to claim that outside auditors are "skimping" on their audit efforts. In fact, a commission appointed by the AICPA reportedly found a number of instances where auditors had falsified records of their work.[18] While this may not be directly equated with loss of independence, it does suggest that auditors may be more willing to accept a company's reports at face value in order to reduce the time spent on a particular auditing assignment.

Another inhibitor to auditor independence may also be related to the increased willingness on the part of companies to switch auditors. The public accounting newsletter survey pointed out that 24 percent of the companies that changed auditors in 1983 had received less than an "unqualified" endorsement of their financial statements by an outside auditing firm.[19] Evidently believing that audit firms have traded endorsements of financial statements for renewed audit contracts, Abraham Briloff, accountancy professor at City University of New York, claimed auditors "have not fully recognized their responsibility to insist on the fairest representation of economic reality" but rather auditors have acquiesced to "management desirous of getting the best report card."[20]

Poor national economic conditions, experienced in the early 1980s, have impacted the issue of audit independence in two significant ways. Companies have applied more pressure on outside auditors to accept and endorse "creative accounting" practices by the firm. According to Thomas Kelley, AICPA vice-president, "Twenty-five years ago, managers looked first to certified public accountants for guidance. Now they say, 'Here's how we intend to account for this. Are you going to go along?'"[21] Second, depressed economic conditions tend to increase the number of corporate bankruptcies; in turn this has led to "financial autopsies" that exposed questionable audit practices that otherwise might have gone undetected if bankruptcy had been avoided.

Finally, some believe that an auditing firm's independence is threatened when advisory services are included in a corporation's relationship with its audit firm. Two schools of thought exist on the desirability of allowing the audit firm to perform these dual functions for their clients. A number of auditors have claimed that performing management consulting services actually heightens their ability to conduct a thorough, in-depth audit, as they are more knowledgeable about their client's operations. Addressing this issue, Robert Mednick, chairman of Arthur Anderson's committee on professional standards, suggested, "There's a synergy. Using expertise in [management consulting] really improves the quality of the audit."[22]

Mednick's positive outlook is not universally accepted. Others have suggested that accounting firms have begun to view their audit services as secondary to their more profitable advisory services. Realizing that accounting firms might have difficulty issuing a negative opinion on a firm's financial statement if a lucrative consulting contract were at stake, the SEC encouraged corporate board members to become more sensitive to this potential dilemma. To this end the agency identified and proposed four criteria or factors that board members, especially audit committee members, should take into consideration in decisions about management advisory services. A summarized listing of the criteria and factors are included in the following:

1. *Economic Benefits.* The audit committee should consider whether greater efficiency in nonaudit work arises from the auditor's knowledge of the company. Management and board members need to recognize their responsibilities to shareholders by weighing efficiency against any threat to auditor independence.
2. *Supplanting Management's Role.* If management lacks sufficient competence in the area of consultation, the accountant may be inclined to alter the normal advisory role by participating in the conduct of operations. This situation threatens the capability of the auditor to audit the results of his or her own work.
3. *Avoidance of Self-review.* The auditor may be less perceptive of weakness in an accounting system he or she has designed than he or she would be to weakness in a system designed by another party.
4. *Auditor's Dependence on Management Advisory Services.* Management should regularly evaluate the relationship of the auditor's nonaudit to audit fees.[23]

By January 1982 the SEC had rescinded its statement on auditor's independence and management advisory services and no longer required companies to report the percentage of nonaudit fees paid to public accountants.[24] In the spirit of public deregulation the SEC placed responsibility on audit committees, boards of directors, and managements to maintain the public confidence in the integrity of the process of financial reporting.

The issue of auditor independence did not completely escape the public limelight after 1982; instead it has taken on broader dimensions. Courts, accounting firms, corporations, and the AICPA have found themselves embroiled in debates over two critical questions concerning the audit responsibilities of the public accounting firm. First, for whom does the audit firm perform the audit function — solely for the client firm or also for users of the firm's financial statements, such as the investing public and creditors of the client firm? Second, which of the these parties should have the rights of redress if an audit firm is allegedly negligent in its audit report on a company's financial statement? Insert 8.C outlines the debate on these two questions.

Insert 8.C

AICPA WARNS "INCREASING OUTSIDE AUDITORS' ACCOUNTABILITY MAY DECREASE QUALITY OF AUDIT"

A court in the state of New York recently held that a major accounting firm's alleged negligence in performing its audit responsibilities leaves the accounting firm liable to "any class of persons whose reliance on the audit is forseeable." Prior court decisions have typically limited the audit firm's liability to the company that hired the audit firm. Only in cases of fraud on the part of the accounting firm would the audit firm be accountable to shareholders, creditors, or even suppliers.

In defense of this change of position the New York court held that the development of accounting rules/standards and the passage of federal securities laws are "revolutionary developments" indicating an audit firm is now answerable to large factions of the general public if an audit is found to be negligent.

A recent legal brief submitted by the AICPA to a New York appelate court acknowledged that changes have occurred in the accounting profession but argued that none have been so "revolutionary" to alter the fundamental nature of the accountants' relationship to the public. The AICPA argued that accounting firms' liability for negligence should be limited to the audited corporation — as has been the established precedent since the 1930s. In support of its position the AICPA outlined a number of undesirable circumstances, problems, and ramifications that might result from allowing the public to hold the accounting firm liable for audit negligence:

- Accountants would conceivably be liable for indeterminate financial settlements for indefinite periods of time to unknown numbers of persons.
- To make accountants' liability for negligence equivalent to their liability for fraud is to create a gross imbalance between the nature of the wrong and the scope of liability.
- Liability actions typically arise when the audited company fails to meet its financial obligations. Therefore, while potential investors may sue the accounting firm for recovery of losses, the accounting firm cannot likely force the company to share in any compensation payments.
- It is unfair to impose the risk of "limitless liability" upon auditors, as negligence does not typically enrich them, nor are they knowingly performing their tasks in a negligent manner.
- As auditor liability insurance costs increase, audit firms must raise their prices, placing a disproportionately large financial burden on small businesses.
- There is a significant risk that audit firm insurance will become un-

available because of the inability of a firm's insurer to assess the scope of potential claims.

- Excessively cautious opinions would be issued by auditors on the accuracy of a company's financial statements. Investors and creditors would get very little use out of an auditor's opinion as auditors would be compelled to issue "qualified" opinions in order to reduce their exposure to liability lawsuits.

While the above arguments may be compelling and persuasive on the surface, the Supreme Court has implied that the AICPA's concerns are tangential to the central issue facing audit firms. In a 1984 decision Chief Justice Warren Burger emphasized the auditor's obligation to society. According to Burger, "By certifying the public reports that collectively depict a corporation's financial status, the independent auditor assumes a public responsibility transcending any employment relationship with the client." Apparently the Supreme Court believed that other concerns — such as the AICPA's — are of secondary importance or would not materialize if auditors were adequately performing their duties. Meanwhile, supporters of increased auditor accountability have underscored the Supreme Court decision with a basic and pointed question: What useful purpose does an audit opinion serve, if not to alert the public to questionable corporate accounting practices?

SOURCE: State of New York, Court of Appeals, "Brief of American Institute of Certified Public Accountants as *Amicus Curiae*"; *Credit Alliance and Leasing Corporation* v. *Arthur Anderson & Co.*, Index No. 21064/81, December 21, 1984; Lee Berton, "Investors Call CPA's to Account," *Wall Street Journal*, January 28, 1984, p. 26.

CORPORATE CODES OF CONDUCT

The code of conduct represents another area of corporate policy receiving renewed attention owing to its potential role in good internal control. As suggested earlier in the report of the AICPA, a code of conduct is one visible means of demonstrating the intention to comply with the Foreign Corrupt Practices Act. Conduct policy is a forward-looking, anticipatory action, and in this sense, it might be considered to be preventive. While there is very little uniformity in the content of corporate codes of conduct, the number of companies having some conduct statement is relatively high. One questionnaire study of 611 companies reported that 77 percent had a formal code.[25] This result was strongly correlated with company size, as only 40 percent of companies with revenues under $60 million reported having such codes and 97 percent of the category of largest companies, revenues above \$4 billion, reported their presence. This result seems to verify a usefulness to large corporations of conduct policies beyond the intent of the Foreign Corrupt Practices Act. In this context the author of the study notes the value of such codes:

> The immense size of many corporations, along with decentralized and geographically dispersed operations, has created senior management concerns over how to build a shared management philosophy, and insure predictable and appropriate behavior in ambiguous circumstances and in situations where corporate and personal motives may not be congruent. The code of conduct has been a tool in this effort.[26]

An intensive content analysis of 30 codes in this study indicated that conflict-of-interest policies were the single most common element; 73 percent of the codes contained conflict-of-interest components, although only about half of these detailed types of conflict-of-interest situations; other common items concerned political contributions, use of inside information, payments to government officials and political parties, gifts, favors, and entertainment, and unrecorded or falsely recorded funds or transactions.

It is obvious that a code of conduct, by itself, is neither necessarily meaningful nor trivial. Again, its role and impact probably depend heavily on underlying management attitudes, and perhaps most indicative of management's attitude is the administration of the code. Questions of administration center on the code's distribution, its identification of violations, the explictness of procedures for suspected violation, and the enforcement of its penalties. In addition to the breadth and detail of the code, these factors will determine its impact on internal control and its utility to top management.

Codes of conduct are in an early stage of development as a management tool of direction and control. Yet the imperatives of large diversified corporations, as well as the emerging interpretation of good internal control, suggest a heightening of its importance. It is likely that we are presently seeing only the beginnings of conduct policies as a well-developed, organizationwide, and visible element of managerial practice.

CORPORATE PROFESSIONAL ROLES

Internal Auditing

The careful design of financial control — proper segmentation of functions, systems of authorization and recording of transactions, and so forth — has not only been a long-standing practice of good management but actually is now a requirement of the Foreign Corrupt Practices Act. Owing to the importance of good financial control, it was probably inevitable that management would wish to have an appraisal of the corporation's control practices that was independent of the treasurer, controller, and operational managers who plan and supervise the control systems. This function, of course, is a key aspect of the role of internal corporate auditing. In fact the existence of internal auditors is now so taken for granted that the function was discussed earlier in relation to the board audit committee without explicitly recognizing its relatively recent growth in status and significance to corporate management.

A study published in 1984 demonstrates the relative growth of internal auditing personnel. A survey of 330 directors of internal auditing from a cross section of U.S. industry indicated that the rate of growth in internal audit positions in the responding companies had increased 52.6 percent between 1974 and 1984, substantially faster than the overall 10.1 percent growth rate of the companies' employees over this same period.[27]

The work of internal auditing appears to be so central to implementation of the requirements of the Foreign Corrupt Practices Act that the act has been jokingly referred to as the "Internal Auditor Full-Employment Act of 1977."[28] This legislation is bound to have a major and sustained impact on the role of internal professional auditors in corporations. "The FCPA has provided us with the mechanisms for getting the message to operating management that they are responsible for internal control," says one controller. Summarizing the feelings of other financial executives, in general, he states, "We now have the 'club' we need to get the job done."[29]

What do internal auditors do? The work of internal control is generally divided into two segments. First, the function of *accounting control* pertains to checking the accuracy and reliability of accounting data and thus ensuring that assets are properly valued on the firm's financial statements. A second function, called *administrative control,* evaluates whether managerial or operational policies are properly followed in the organization. Thus an internal auditor's work may lead to an appraisal of electronic data processing (EDP) security; to an assessment of employee screening, training, and compensation procedures; to an evaluation of whether capital expenditure decisions are implemented following management's instructions; or to a review and recommendations for improved inventory reconciliation methods. The authors of the 1984 survey of internal auditing propose the following definition for this profession:

> Internal auditing, which is ultimately responsible to the owners of the enterprise, is a service to senior management and other enterprise interests that includes (1) monitoring management controls; (2) anticipating, identifying, and assessing risks to enterprise assets and activities; (3) investigating actual and potential lapses of control and incidents

of risk; and (4) making recommendations for improvement of control, the response to risk, and the attainment of enterprise objectives.[30]

Naturally, a large proportion of the work of internal auditors is dedicated to assessing the adequacy of financial and accounting controls. Insert 8.D

Insert 8.D

ACTIVITIES AND PROJECTED CHANGES IN AUDIT EFFORTS

	Allocation of Time (percent)	
	Now	**In Five Years**
Detection of errors and irregularities. This activity is directed at the prevention or timely discovery of errors and irregularities in the processing or recording of transactions	20	15
Monitoring management control. Management control strives to obtain compliance with the applicable rules and procedures established by company policy.	27	26
Performance evaluation. This activity assesses the efficiency or the effectiveness with which company goals are attained.	14	19
Monitoring internal accounting control. Internal accounting control strives to ensure that published financial statements present fairly the financial position and results of operations of the company in accordance with generally accepted accounting practice or other appropriate standards and that assets are appropriately safeguarded.	32	28
Decision-making review. This activity evaluates the effectiveness of management's operating and financial decisions.	7	12
	100	100

SOURCE: Robert K. Mautz, Peter Tiessen, and Robert H. Colson, *Internal Auditing: Directions and Opportunities* (Altamonte Springs, Fl.: Institute of Internal Auditors Research Foundation, 1984), p. 60. Used with permission.

describes the major activities of internal audits and reports the opinions of a sample of directors of internal auditing on how these activities are likely to change by 1989.

Ambiguities in the Reporting Relationships of Internal Auditors

A specific issue about internal auditing pertains to the proper organizational location of the function. Companies should follow the well-accepted principle that auditing be independent of the activities it audits. However, if an audit staff performs both operational and financial audits, and if even the CEO's and board chairman's expense accounts are getting greater scrutiny, then where could this independent function be located? Former SEC chairperson Harold Williams recognized this dilemma in a statement on the organization of internal control:

> Internal auditors are, by the very nature of their work, placed in a somewhat schizophrenic position. It is essential that the internal auditor maintain independence in relation to the activities subject to audit. The realities of corporate operations, however, also dictate that the internal auditor serve management in fulfilling its particular responsibilities. This dual role will at times put the internal auditor under conflicting pressures.[31]

These tensions may have no easy resolution, for as one observer has said, "Coping with role conflicts is, after all, the essence of the art of corporate governance."[32]

Recognition of conflicting pressures and the importance of internal auditing to corporate governance are perhaps a couple of reasons why directors of internal auditing have become increasingly tied to the audit committee of the board of directors in recent years. A full 80 percent of the respondents to the 1984 survey of internal auditing directors stated they were responsible to the audit committee of the board for audit-reporting purposes. Although this did not imply they were solely responsible to the audit committee, it represents a significant shift in the visibility and potential influence of internal auditing.

However dramatic has been the rise in visibility of this function, the role is not without continuing ambiguities. For example, although 80 percent of the directors of internal auditing surveyed stated responsibility to the audit committee for audit reporting, only 7 percent stated responsibility to this committee for salary and promotion purposes. The firm's chief financial officer and its CEO were the two most frequently mentioned positions for internal audit reporting for pay and promotion. While reaffirming their belief that many internal auditors would place the company's interests ahead of their personal careers, the authors of this study did state some reservation about the difference between reporting for auditing purposes and reporting for salary and promotion. They stated, "On the other hand, there may be instances where career considerations may impair judgment, resulting in a situation that is not in the best interest of the company."[33]

This reservation appeared to be given substance in participant responses to another question in the survey. Table 8.1 presents information from this survey in response to the question "Which of the following matters *would* you take directly to the Audit Committee?" The data of this table suggest considerable reluctance to consider taking an auditing issue to the audit committee that may challenge a decision or reflect poorly on the performance of the firm's senior management. As such, this survey information suggests unresolved ambiguities in the reporting relationships of internal auditors and may indicate that further clarification is needed in the development of their roles.

Corporate Counsel

Having discussed the roles of board members, internal auditors, and independent auditors in the process of institutional governance, this overview now turns to a final and critical element — that of legal counsel. A relative latecomer in the examination of governance problems, a reappraisal of the role of corporate counsel may be gaining momentum.

We have seen that the substance of governance issues is the attempt to minimize the conflict between dual loyalties: that the predominance of board members is not placed in a position to evaluate the performance of their own boss, that internal auditing is independent of the activity it audits, that public accountants have no interests that might influence their judgments in the performance of the outside audit. The potential for divided loyalty of an inside corporate lawyer is also present: on the one hand, this person is hired by, is subordinate to, and works for an executive officer of the corporation, usually the CEO. On the other hand, the attorney's Code of Professional Responsibility states that counsel's responsibility is to the corporation as a whole, technically called the "entity": "The corporation lawyer owes his allegiance to the entity and not to a stockholder, director, officer, employee, representative, or other persons connected with this entity."[34] While there is no inevitable conflict of these two roles, there is potential conflict, which, on occasion, surfaces into public view. Take, for example, the following situations in which the interest of the entity is not clear:

- A lawsuit in which shareholders are suing management in the name of the corporation for mismanagement or theft of corporate assets creates a difficult situation for the corporate counsel: an attorney obviously cannot advise management, who is his (her) employer, and also advise the corporation under these circumstances.

TABLE 8.1   *Percentage of Actions that Would be Taken to the Audit Committee by Directors of Internal Auditing*

	Total Number	Percentage Yes	Percentage No
1. Significant misuse of corporate assets by a corporate officer.	278	76	24
2. Noncompliance with capital-budgeting requirements by the vice-president of manufacturing.	252	5	95
3. A shortage in the cash receipts from a substantial branch office that the controller acknowledges but contends is not of sufficient importance to bring to the attention of the audit committee.	111	41	59
4. Information that leads you to believe that the chief financial officer is pressuring the controller to make some accounting changes in order to increase earnings.	156	58	42
5. Failure by your superior to fund three new internal audit positions that you as director of internal audit feel are essential.	134	49	51
6. Reduction by your superior of funds available for internal audit training.	72	26	74

SOURCE: Robert K. Mautz, Peter Tiessen, and Robert H. Colson, *Internal Auditing: Directions and Opportunities* (Altamonte Springs, Fl.: Institute of Internal Auditors Research Foundation, 1984), pp. 76–77. Used with permission.

- Counsel can be called upon to aid the management of the employing corporation in defending against an unfriendly takeover attempt by another company. Are the "entity's" or stockholders' interests necessarily parallel to management's in this case? Would stockholders be better off taking a mediocre offer to sell their shares, or would they be better off continuing with the present lackluster but consistent management?

- What principles should guide a corporate attorney who questions the legal or moral implications of an action of management? Can the attorney address the problem in a way that does not create an adversative relationship between attorney and employer, and also does not force the attorney to pay personally the cost of the conflict by losing his or her job?[35]

Corporate power and control lie at the heart of each of these situations in which the interests of the entity are ambiguous, and while these role conflicts have been discussed in the context of inside counsel, they are potentially present for outside counsel as well.

The most vexing and elusive of the attorney's ethical dilemmas appears to be the potential conflict of organizational loyalty with a superior and professional responsibility to the corporation, a tension described by Victor Palmieri in Insert 8.E. What options exist for an attorney who feels management has taken an illegal or questionable action or has failed to present complete information or an accurate reflection of the risks inherent in a given action?

There appear to be two developing efforts to address this situation: one a professional response, the other a matter of corporate policy. The first is the American Bar Association's proposed revision of its Code of Professional Responsibilities.[36] This proposed code explicitly states an obligatory hierarchy of actions for an attorney who discovers a corporate action that is "legally improper and likely to result in significant harm to the organization." The first step is to request an internal review with the board of directors or the shareholders. If action is not forthcoming at this level and the violation of law is likely to result in "irreparable injury to a person having ownership or membership rights in the organization," the attorney has a further obligation to notify the injured person or make a public disclosure. These are controversial, and as yet unapproved, proposals within the American Bar Association, but they indicate the profession's efforts to grapple with institutional issues of the day.

A second way to deal with potential role conflicts of legal counsel is the approach of corporate policy development. In this case management thinks through the potential for conflicts of interest in relation to the long-term interests of the organization and establishes guidelines or policies for counsel to follow if a conflict should arise. Insert 8.F from Connecticut General is an example of the forward planning of the management-counsel relationship in the event of a significant divergence of views. Although this statement is not a guarantee to the corporation of constructive action by counsel — the personal risks remain high — it is an anticipatory effort to develop a path for counsel out of an ethical dilemma, should one arise. It represents a statement of intent on how the legal role should be managed from the standpoint of the long-run institutional interest of having an effective executive system with proper checks and balances.

Insert 8.E

INDEPENDENCE IN THE LAWYER'S ROLE [QUOTATION]

The biggest problem, in my judgment, is the corporate lawyer's traditional conception of his own role. Until a crisis arises, the lawyer who sits with the board typically sees himself as the chief executive's counsel. He is usually selected by the CEO and serves, if not at his pleasure, at a level of compensation and tenure that is highly dependent on the CEO's pleasure.

Therefore, the lawyer tends to relate to the chief executive as the client and to deal with the board as an especially important constituency of management which, like other constituencies, has to be managed. This perspective, consciously or unconsciously, governs the participation in all interactions between the board and management. . . .

In effect, the lawyer serves as counsel for both the management and the board, and his advice to each should be the same. Despite the fact that he usually reports to the chief executive and often develops a close personal relationship with him, to be effective he must remain independent in respect to the performance of his legal function.

SOURCE: Victor Palmieri, "The Lawyer's Role: An Argument for Change," *Harvard Business Review,* November-December 1978, p. 34. Reprinted by permission of the *Harvard Business Review.* Copyright © 1978 by the President and Fellows of Harvard College; all rights reserved.

Insert 8.F

AN ANTICIPATORY SOLUTION TO POTENTIAL CONFLICT OF INTEREST FOR LEGAL COUNSEL AT CONNECTICUT GENERAL [QUOTATION]

If, as the corporation's chief legal officer, you either (a) disagree with my decision to overrule a professional opinion of yours on a matter where you consider the impact to

Insert 8.F   continued

be important to the welfare of the organization, and (b) on which I have chosen not to report to the directors that such a difference of view exists, or (c) feel that a piece of information I have chosen not to give the board is material and should be given to them, it shall be your responsibility to bring the matter promptly to the attention of the board to make your views known.

In either instance, I instruct you to talk to me first, so that we can determine whether it is simply a case of misunderstanding between us which we can deal with as such. If that is not the case and you do not persuade me to change my position, you will then make your report on the matter to the chairman of the board, or in his absence, the chairman of the audit committee. I desire to accompany you to make my own views known at the same time. You must not, however, allow such a desire on my part to keep you from making your report with or without me.

While I have described this suggestion to you as springing from my obligation to the board, I also see it as serving me well in another way; by ensuring that I have the support of our chief legal officer in a given important decision unless you have promptly made it clear that I do not.

A note from the chairman accompanied this letter to the general counsel:

> This is to inform you that if you bring such an issue to me and I find that I do not share your view of it, I will, nevertheless, arrange an audience with you of the full board if you so request. Having been given that facility, you have the responsibility to use it, if, in your judgment, it is in the best interest of the corporation for you to do so.

SOURCE: Editor's Comments in "From the Boardroom," *Harvard Business Review,* November-December 1978, p. 44. (Excerpt from the letter of the president of Connecticut General Insurance Co. to the general counsel [included in the Board of Director's Manual].) Reprinted by permission of the *Harvard Business Review.* Copyright © 1978 by the President and Fellows of Harvard College; all rights reserved.

IN SUMMARY: MANAGERIAL PROFESSIONALISM AND CORPORATE GOVERNANCE

Dealing with divergent interests is not a new problem for corporate management. Managers are familiar with opposing interests and conflict between marketing and research, production and engineering, and staff and line and are aware of divisional rivalries in the corporation. Fortunately most of these conflicts within the organization are subsumed under the superordinate goal of corporate economic performance, and knowledge in the field of management for integrating these interests is quite well advanced.

Issues involving corporate legitimacy and professionalism in management, however, present different and more unfamiliar problems to managers. Goals and interests appear to be more complex and more divergent; they have ethical overtones, and they cannot automatically be assumed to fall under a common superordinate goal. Conflicts between personal interests and corporate interests often involve values other than solely corporate economic performance. Experience and knowledge in dealing with these issues are not well developed, and pressure from outside the corporation for improving management of this complex range of interests has increased in recent decades.

This chapter has reviewed the roles of a number of corporate officeholders whose presence creates complex situations for managers. Members of the board audit committee, external auditors and internal auditors, and lawyers all maintain a professional or fiduciary responsibility in addition to their responsibility to serve management. By virtue of their offices, persons in these roles have points of view and responsibilities that operational managers do not necessarily hold and that are important to the overall governance of the corporation and to its credibility and legitimacy in society.

However, they are also roles over which management has considerable discretion, and they can be structured to be played effectively or ineffectively. The roles and responsibilities of persons in these positions can be used to guide and control the corporation in the interests of stockholders, managers, and society; or they can be interpreted as insignificant and irrelevant or as infringements on managerial autonomy. The difference constitutes the degree of professionalism in management.

What are critical abilities for coping with the relatively unfamiliar problems of corporate governance? First would seem to be an understanding of the origins of the call for corporate accountability and a belief in the corporate and public benefits of developing stronger accountability. The increased size and scale of many companies today and their visible social, economic, and political consequences present new problems of accountability not faced in either the early American system of governmental sponsorship of business nor the late nineteenth century American version of laissez-faire economics. Because the characteristics of society and business are today significantly different from these periods, new solutions to the issue of accountability are imperative.

A second management implication can be abstracted to this point: the governance of corporations requires managers to appreciate how decisions may be influenced by oversights, distortions, or dysfunctional biases due to the existence of personal interests of decision makers other than the long-run goals of the corporation. A variety of terms — *independence, objectivity, conflicts of interest* — are used to express dimensions of accountability. In the final analysis a manager's understanding of when the decision process may run the risk of being compromised by narrow and personal interests is the issue at stake in corporate governance.

Executives need to be able to determine whether directors, managers, and specialists interact effectively or whether role ambiguities, overlaps, or conflicts lead to defective policy formulation and decison making. The skill of governance requires an ability to develop a configuration of roles and relationships that places long-term interests in the mainstream of corporate decision making and that serves as a system of checks and balances in the interest of the institution. This capacity recognizes the logic and utility of structures, policies, and procedures in organizing the corporate control function and in anticipating and minimizing ethical dilemmas.

Finally, the corporate leader needs action skills for developing an effective governance system. Roles need to be defined and redefined explicitly, the changing nature of director and specialist responsibilities needs to be understood and aided, and actual or potential conflicts of interest need to be surfaced, confronted, and resolved. This is rarely popular or easy work. The absence of a crisis makes it easier to allow ambiguities and conflicts to drift, to tolerate inactive board members, or to be insensitive to the role of management professionals in corporations. This skill requires the belief that raising potentially unpopular issues — ones often experienced as personal threats — and insisting on necessary changes are worth the long-run payoff for all parties.

Corporate leadership is in transition from a stage in which a strict economic function predominates to a stage of institutional leadership in which accountability, governance, and societal functions play significant roles. For the manager the difference is between being a decision maker and being the architect of a broader decision-making structure in which the manager plays a significant, but not exclusive, role. It requires acute awareness that corporate decision making needs to be independent of any particular personal or political purpose. These qualities of institutional leadership should work to preserve the private system of economic organization that America knows and appears to want.

DISCUSSION QUESTIONS

1. What is your understanding of internal control? Who does it involve? What management practices does good control require?

2. In your view, what are the possible sources of threat to the independence of a firm's external auditors? How great a threat are these factors? What can management do to minimize threats to auditor independence?

3. What do the roles of board members, external auditors, internal auditors, and corporate counsel have in common? What are the lessons for management of these common elements?

NOTES

1. Hurd Baruch, "The Foreign Corrupt Practices Act of 1977," *Harvard Business Review*, January-February 1979, p. 46.

2. "Justice Department Aide Outlines Policy of 'Review' for Firms' Payments Abroad," *Wall Street Journal*, November 9, 1979, p. 10.

3. "U.S. Firms Say '77 Ban on Foreign Payoffs Hurts Overseas Sales," *Wall Street Journal*, August 2, 1979, pp. 1, 9.

4. Ibid., p. 9.

5. 15 U.S., Congress, Section 78dd — 1,2. PL 95–213, [1979 Supp.]

6. Baruch, "The Foreign Corrupt Practices Act," pp. 33–34.

7. Henry W. Tulloch and W. Scott Bauman, *The Management of Business Conduct* (Charlottesville: Center for the Study of Applied Ethics, The Colgate Darden Graduate School of Business Administration, University of Virginia, 1981), p. 3.

8. American Institute of Certified Public Accountants, Inc., *Report of the Special Advisory Committee on Internal Accounting Control* (New York: AICPA, 1979), p. 12.

9. Ibid., pp. 12–13.

10. Securities and Exchange Commission, Accounting Series Release no. 19, "In the Matter of McKesson and Robbins, Inc.," *Federal Securities Law Reporter*, ¶72,020, December 5, 1940.

11. Baruch, "The Foreign Corrupt Practices Act," p. 38.

12. George J. Siedel III, "Legal Dimension of Internal Accounting Control and the Foreign Corrupt Practices Act," in *Internal Control in U.S. Corporations: The State of the Art*, ed. Robert K. Mautz, Walter G. Kell, Michael W. Maher, Alan G. Merten, Raymond R. Reilly, Dennis G. Severance, and Bernard J. White (New York: Financial Executives Research Foundation, 1980), pp. 405–34.

13. Ralph F. Lewis, "What Should Audit Committees Do?" *Harvard Business Review*, May-June 1978, p. 22.

14. Ibid., p. 174.

15. Ibid., p. 26.

16. Public Oversight Board Report, *Scope of Services by CPA Firms* (New York: American Institute of Certified Public Accountants, Inc., 1979), pp. 29–30.

17. Gary Klott. "Auditors Feel the Heat of a New Scrutiny." *New York Times*, May 13, 1984, p. F26.

18. Ibid.

19. Ibid.

20. Clemens P. Work, "Now It's 'Cooked Books' That Draw SEC Fire." *U.S. News & World Report,* September 3, 1984, p. 71.

21. Ibid.

22. Klott, "Auditors Feel the Heat of a New Scrutiny," p. F26.

23. Securities and Exchange Commission, Accounting Series Release no. 264, "Scope of Services by Independent Accountants," *Federal Securities Law Reporter,* ¶72,286, June 14, 1979.

24. Securities and Exchange Commission, Accounting Series Release no. 296, "Relationships between Registrants and Independent Accountants," *Federal Securities Law Reporter,* ¶72,318, August 20, 1981; idem, Accounting Series Release no. 304, "Relationships between Registrants and Independent Accountants," *Federal Securities Law Reporter,* ¶72,326, January 28, 1982.

25. Bernard J. White, "Corporate Codes of Conduct: A Mechanism of Internal Control," *Internal Control,* in Mautz et al., pp. 381–90.

26. Ibid., pp. 381–82.

27. Robert K. Mautz, Peter Tiessen, and Robert H. Colson, *Internal Auditing: Directions and Opportunities* (Altamonte Springs, Fla.: Institute of Internal Auditors Research Foundation, 1984).

28. "Internal Auditors Find Themselves Loved As Rules Stiffen for 'Clean' Sets of Books," *Wall Street Journal,* January 15, 1980, p. 40.

29. Michael Mayer and Bernard J. White, "Manager's Journal: Corruption Control," *Wall Street Journal,* August 25, 1980, p. 14.

30. Mautz et al., *Internal Auditing,* p. 32.

31. Harold M. Williams, "Current Problems in Financial Reporting and Internal Controls," *Internal Auditor,* October 1979, p. 41.

32. Victor Palmieri, "The Lawyer's Role: An Argument for Change," *Harvard Business Review,* November-December 1978, p. 38.

33. Mautz et al., *Internal Auditing,* p. 73.

34. Palmieri, "The Lawyer's Role," p. 34.

35. Ronald D. Rotunda, "Law, Lawyers, and Managers," in *The Ethics of Corporate Conduct,* ed. Clarence Walton (Englewood Cliffs, N.J.: Prentice-Hall, 1977), pp. 127–45.

36. Stephen Soloman, "The Corporate Lawyer's Dilemma," *Fortune,* November 5, 1979, pp. 138–40.

American Steel Corporation and the Foreign Corrupt Practices Act

William McNally, comptroller of the American Steel Corporation, had just come from an executive committee meeting that was called to discuss the Foreign Corrupt Practices Act of 1977. During the meeting Richard Maloy from the law department had outlined the legal implications of the act, and in particular, the provisions of the accounting section that not only covered multinational corporations but domestic ones as well. American Steel Corporation, a large domestic steel producer, conducted limited business abroad, and as the meeting unfolded, it became apparent that the corporation officers were not fully satisfied that their responsibilities under the act were being fulfilled. Because of the far-reaching implications of the act, William McNally had been appointed to chair a committee to investigate the corporation's current accounting practices as they applied to the act and to make recommendations to the executive committee in two months.

It is against this background that McNally began to formulate his strategy and investigations. The first two sections of this case provide important information on the American Steel Corporation and the Foreign Corrupt Practices Act of 1977. The following sections present McNally's activities and observations over the two-month period prior to his meeting with the executive board.

AMERICAN STEEL CORPORATION

The American Steel Corporation, one of the nation's oldest and most respected steel firms, was currently undergoing an expansion program that would fully integrate their operations from the mining of raw materials to the sale of finished products. This expansion effort was expected to make American Steel more competitive with the giants of the steel industry. It was well known within the industry that dependence on outside suppliers for raw materials placed the purchasing firm in a vulnerable position in terms of price and local labor strikes, which often occurred at the mines. For these reasons American Steel had recently purchased an iron ore mining facility in Venezuela and a 50 percent interest in two coal mines in West Virginia.

David Becker, William McNally's assistant, had been instrumental in the negotiations that led to these acquisitions. He was responsible for providing the necessary financial analysis on the mines and for reviewing American's own financial position in the market.

The American Steel Corporation operated five large, domestic steel mills. Each mill had the capability to convert raw materials into molten iron through their blast furnaces and then further process the iron into steel through open-hearth and basic oxygen furnaces. The steel was formed into finished products such as plates, sheet, tin mill products, structural products, and pipe. Sales were made directly to the customer and through the corporation's numerous warehouses. There were no sales offices outside of the continental United States, and foreign sales were made only as a courtesy to established U.S. customers. At the time of McNally's investigation, over 75,000 employees worked for American Steel, which, last year had sales of over $3.5 billion. The formal organization of American Steel is along bureaucratic lines with fixed rules and an ordered hierarchy.

The corporation had established a sophisticated standard cost accounting system. This system enabled the plants and headquarters to identify problem areas that were in need of attention. The standard cost was integrated into a general accounting system at each plant and facility location and then compiled for the entire corporation at headquarters. Each plant's operations and methods were standardized as much as possible to make the financial reporting data comparable. For example, the recording of yields from ingot to finished product involved many intermediate steps. The accounting for the steel at each stage of conversion would therefore be uniform from plant to plant. The newly acquired mining operations, however, had not been required to adopt the standard cost system but, instead, continued with the same accounting methods that existed before the acquisitions.

THE FOREIGN CORRUPT PRACTICES ACT OF 1977

The Foreign Corrupt Practices Act of 1977 was passed as an outgrowth of the Watergate congressional hearings, which revealed a pattern of secret and illegal domestic political contributions by U.S. corporations. Further investigation by the Securities and Exchange Commission (SEC), prior to the passage of the act, revealed the existence of slush funds that were used to make secret payments, not only in the United States but around the world. The act, which was signed into law and became effective on December 19, 1977, consists of two separate provisions. The first requires that accurate books and records be maintained and that a system of internal accounting controls be established. The second prohibits the direct or indirect payment of bribes to foreign officials or political parties.

The accounting sections of the act, as amended on February 15, 1979, require that all firms registered with the SEC establish records that reflect the transactions of each company in reasonable detail and, in addition, maintain internal accounting control systems to ensure compliance with the act. The law specifically states that registered companies shall under Section 13 (b):

> (A) make and keep records, books, and accounts, which, in reasonable detail, accurately and fairly reflect the transactions and dispositions of the assets of the issuer; and
>
> (B) devise and maintain a system of internal accounting controls sufficient to provide reasonable assurances that —
>> (i) transactions are executed in accordance with management's general or specific authorization;
>> (ii) transactions are recorded as necessary (I) to permit preparation of financial statements in conformity with generally accepted accounting principles or any other criteria applicable to such statements, and (II) to maintain accountability for assets;
>> (iii) access to assets is permitted only in accordance with management's general or specific authorization; and
>> (iv) the recorded accountability for assets is compared with the existing assets at reasonable intervals and appropriate action is taken with respect to any differences.[1]

The accounting provisions as stated were intended to eliminate bookkeeping devices designed to conceal questionable or illegal payments but are not limited to payments of foreign officials. Therefore, the accounting section of the act applies not only to multinational corporations but also to wholly domestic ones as well. With respect to internal accounting controls, the Senate committee noted "that management must exercise judgment in determining the steps to be taken and the cost incurred, in giving assurance that the objectives expressed [by the accounting provisions of the act] will be achieved. Here, standards of reasonableness must apply."[2]

Finally, under the Foreign Corrupt Practices Act any person who willfully violates any provision of the act can be fined up to $10,000 or imprisoned for up to five years, or both.

Legal responsibility for insuring compliance with the act with respect to the accounting section is assigned to the financial vice-president, comptroller, treasurer, tax director, and internal auditor.

The second section of the act prohibiting foreign corrupt practices applies to all companies, not just those registered with the SEC as outlined in the Accounting Section. This section of the act is broken down into five distinct parts: (1) the use of an instrument of interstate commerce (such as the telephone or the mails) in furtherance of (2) a payment of, or even an offer to pay, "anything of value," directly or indirectly (3) to any foreign official with discretionary authority or to any foreign political party or foreign political candidate (4) if the purposes of the payment is the "corrupt" one of getting the recipient to act (or to refrain from acting) (5) in such a way as to assist the company in obtaining or retaining business for or with or directing business to any person.[3] Congress, however, was careful to distinguish between bribes to government officials and government employees. Whereas it could be conceivable to corrupt an official with a small sum of money, it would not be considered a violation to make "grease" or "facilitating" payments to a government employee to expedite the normal flow of work. Under the second section of the act, an unprecedented maximum fine of up to $1 million can be imposed on the company involved.

Responsibility for insuring compliance with the act with respect to foreign bribery includes not only those mentioned under the Accounting Section but executives in the areas of foreign sales and operations as well.

Finally, in all cases where a charge is brought against a company for violation of the Foreign Corrupt Practices Act, the chief executive officer and the chief operating officer can expect their own conduct and knowledge to be investigated.

CASE FINDINGS

After an in-depth briefing by the legal department on the requirements of the Foreign Corrupt Practices Act, William McNally concluded that his emphasis should be concentrated on the internal accounting controls specified in the act. One area of control that seemed particularly troublesome was the fact that American Steel did not have a formalized internal audit staff to spot-check the different accounting areas. Instead, the company relied upon each manager to set up his own system of internal audits and, further, depended on a certified public accountant's annual audit of the corporation to detect any irregularities.

As an initial step each manager of accounting at the plants, mines, and headquarters was directed to prepare a listing of their internal accounting controls within two weeks. The listings were to include such items as receiving practices, inventory controls, truck and shipment controls, payroll, and account analysis. The list that would be received from each of the managers along with their comments was intended to provide a base against which a control standard with specific requirements would be developed.

The result of the survey revealed that inconsistencies in the specific handling of financial transactions existed throughout the corporation's plants. McNally found that one plant had the same person ordering, receiving, and verifying receipt of material, while another plant had each of these functions separated. Another finding was that the clerk responsible for making up the plant payroll also made up his own. The list of discrepancies in the plants was extensive and varied.

Of greatest concern to McNally was the obvious lack of controls at the newly acquired mines. It appeared that a system of internal controls was never stressed under prior management, and since the acquisitions there had been no program established to separate accounting functions. In addition the operating managers of the West Virginia coal mines, who held a 50 percent interest in the operation, were becoming increasingly reluctant to divulge all of their financial information to headquarters. Financial information received from Venezuela was inconsistent and thought to be caused by differences in accepted accounting methods between the United States and Venezuela. As a result William McNally decided to send a task force headed by David Becker to Venezuela to investigate the mine's present accounting procedures. The task force was expected to report back to McNally within one month.

As the more effective control standards were being developed for implementation, it became apparent that numerous exceptions had to be made for accounting at the two mining facilities. As a result William McNally decided to visit the West Virginia coal mines personally to examine their accounting system. McNally received a cool welcome by the operating managers, making communications difficult and strained. The mine's chief accountant, who had worked for the managing owners for 23 years, unwillingly revealed only the information that he was asked to furnish, volunteering no further information. Two major concerns began to surface during McNally's analysis at the mines: (1) while inventories were taken on stockpiles of coal, there was no record that they were being reconciled; and (2) a single vendor was awarded the contracts for hauling, crushing, and sundry disposal. These functions performed by the vendor constituted the major portion of the mine's outside service contracts. McNally observed that control was lax, with no formal procedure for admitting or releasing vendors' trucks from the mine. In addition there was no apparent control on the ordering of material. When a mine foreman needed material, a request was made to accounting, where the order was filled without any higher approval. When questioned about this practice, the operating managers explained that the mines operated as a "big family" and that material ordering had never been abused. They stressed that it was this trust among employees that had made the mine so successful. William McNally remained at the mine for one week, observing numerous abuses relating to internal control. On his return to headquarters, William McNally asked that a complete investigation be done on the vendor who had been awarded the outside service contracts at the mine.

In the meantime McNally was becoming increasingly anxious to learn about the financial analyses that David Becker had conducted on the mines. Because Becker's presentation had swung the decision in favor of purchasing these facilities, McNally could not help but wonder if, in the enthusiasm of these acquisitions, a less-than-thorough financial analysis might have been done on the iron ore and the coal mines.

As the project for the development of the control standards progressed, it became clear that two sets of standards would have to be developed — one for the plants and another for the mines. One reason for this dual development was the fact that the plants were highly mechanized as a result of the computations necessary in the standard cost system and, therefore, had direct access to the computers at headquarters. The mines, however, still submitted all of their information by courier and teletype.

Three weeks after David Becker had left for Venezuela, reports began to come back to headquarters concerning the status of the iron ore mining operation. The accounting as it related to the mining operations was not seen as troublesome and with slight modifications could be brought into compliance with headquarter's accounting policies. The operating personnel, along with the transferred Americans, enjoyed a good working relationship and understood the goals and objectives of the American Steel Corporation. There was, however, one major problem that David Becker had not originally discovered. It had been customary for management at the mine to make facilitating payments to low-level Venezuelan customs officials to expedite customs procedures. Recently, however, the commissioner of customs had called upon mine officials and informed them that the export duty rate was to be increased threefold unless American Steel could "persuade" the commissioner to reverse his stand on this proposed increase. The price of persuasion was $100,000, which the mine officials paid without alleged knowledge of the parent company.

Shortly thereafter, William McNally received the report he had requested on the outside vendor at the West Virginia coal mines. The vendor was the brother-in-law of one of the operating managers and had been consistently awarded the service contracts for many years.

With the executive committee meeting two weeks away, McNally is pondering his recommendations to the executive committee. He is now fully aware that he is out of compliance with the Foreign Corrupt Practices Act, particularly with respect to the accounting requirements of the act. He is aware that the board of directors is pleased that vertical integration has finally taken place and that they are determined to make the mines into a profitable part of the steel-making process. Nevertheless, the foreign payment to the Venezuelan customs commissioner and the situation with the mines in West Virginia could possibly make the American Steel Corporation liable for a large fine, incurring the loss of community respect as well. The matter of the best method to disclose the foreign bribe, as required by

SEC filings, has also proved to be an uncomfortable question. In addition to these problems, William McNally is not certain that he has devised a self-perpetuating system of internal accounting controls through the development of control standards. He is aware of the intent of the Foreign Corrupt Practices Act, which was to ensure that adequate control systems were installed and maintained "sufficient to provide reasonable assurances" that the specified objectives of the act would be met. He wonders if there might be some better way to ensure increased financial control and compliance with the act.

DISCUSSION QUESTIONS

1. Review the problems of internal control at American Steel's manufacturing plants and at their newly acquired coal mines. Be prepared to state why these incidents are violations of good accounting control and develop your recommendations to the executive committee on how they should be remedied.

2. What plan of action would you recommend to McNally about the payment to the Venezuelan commissioner of customs? Does the fact that this payment was unknown to officials of American Steel mitigate its seriousness in your mind? What instructions would you recommend American Steel give to Venezuelan mine officials for handling similar situations in the future?

3. Consider long-term politics that American Steel might adopt to avoid the development of problems such as those uncovered by William McNally.

NOTES

1. 15 U.S.C., Section 78 (q) (b) (2).
2. U.S., Congress, Senate, Committee on Banking, Housing, and Urban Affairs, *Foreign Corrupt Practices and Domestic and Foreign Investment Improved Disclosure Acts of 1977*, 95th Cong., 1st sess., S. Rept. 114, July 7–8, 1977, p. 8.
3. Hurd Baruch, "The Foreign Corrupt Practices Act," *Harvard Business Review*, January-February 1979, pp. 44, 46.

Crisis in Conscience at Quasar

A Provocative Case of Ethics at Quasar Stellar Company Underscores a Difficult Management Problem

FOREWORD

This case history, based directly on an actual situation, emphasizes the complex and arduous problem of ethics — business and personal — facing managers today. Undoubtedly, ethical conduct has always been a problem of some proportion, but in today's competitive business environment perhaps it is even more so. The case raises the issue of the correct course of action for managers who are confronted with accepting questionable conduct of their superiors by being expected either to agree to it or to close their eyes to it.

Mr. Fendrock is Vice President of Avion Electronics, Inc. in Paramus, New Jersey. His experience includes directing operations for Avion, which specializes in military electronics and sophisticated electronic systems for NASA's space program involving the Gemini and Apollo craft; consulting in the United States and in Europe; and doing advanced studies in the management sciences at Stevens Institute of Technology.

The increasingly competitive business environment has resulted in a condition in which many managers are being subjected to tests of conscience for which they are ill prepared — indeed, for which there may be no preparation. It has become increasingly difficult for them to act their individual parts well, and still retain free and clear consciences.

The thesis of this article is that modern-day managers are often faced with situations where they are required to commit themselves, either openly or tacitly, to an action they may not agree with. They may be participating, willingly or unwillingly, in activities that are morally and ethically cloudy; questionable from a business point of view; and perhaps, of doubtful legality.

The subject here is not the case of an act that is patently illegal; or where the responsibility is specific and detailed; or where the facts are clear-cut and defined. Rather, the issue under scrutiny involves unclear, undefined areas of activity where, by association, an individual is involved in a course of action that he *believes* — not necessarily *knows* — is wrong.

THE CASE SETTING

Universal Nucleonics Company, the parent company for a number of wholly owned subsidiaries, suddenly found itself in the embarrassing position of having to report that its earnings for the year would be substantially lower than had been announced at the end of the previous quarter. Shortly thereafter, a statement appeared in the "Who's News" section of the *Wall Street Journal* reporting that Quasar Stellar Company, one of Universal's subsidiaries, had a new president and a new vice-president of finance (replacing the former controller).

As time went on, the financial community learned that Universal had discovered that one of its subsidiaries had been withholding the truth, purposely distorting the facts, or otherwise misrepresenting the situation at hand in its monthly reports to corporate headquarters. By the time Universal had realized the actual condition of Quasar's financial situation, it was too late to correct it without affecting the reported year-end earnings of the parent company.

The two individuals most directly concerned at Quasar — John Kane, president, and Hugh Kay, controller — had both "resigned." It was generally agreed by the board of directors that there would be no public announcement as to the reasons for the resignations. Privately, however, the director stated flatly that out-and-out fraud was involved; another, more in tune with the times, said that the situation was directly attributable to the pressures to make good and the tendency to have a positive outlook on the outcome of all individual company problems.

Corporate headquarters was vitally interested in finding out why, given the organizational structure at Quasar, no feedback had been received independently of the president-controller monthly statement; whether any of the other executives were involved in the reports either knowingly or unknowingly, willingly or unwillingly; and finally, what steps could be taken to prevent a recurrence of the situation in the future.

Fact-Finding Team

To resolve these questions, Universal's executive committee decided that a direct approach should be taken. The executive vice-president and the vice-president of industrial relations for the corporation would conduct a series of interviews with the Quasar Stellar personnel who might have been involved. Both men were well qualified to appraise the situation. Jim Bowden, the executive vice-president, was both an operating and a financial man, having spent a number of years in each area. Hubert Clover, vice-president of industrial relations, was a former professor of industrial psychology at one of the leading business schools.

It was further agreed that each executive would interview different men, compare notes, and then speak with each other's interviewees if the situation so warranted. After studying the organization chart (see Chart 1), and the company's "Manual of Responsibilities," they decided it would be best to talk with Peter Loomis, vice-president–marketing; George Kessler, vice-president–manufacturing; and William Heller, vice-president–engineering.

LOOMIS'S SESSION

The scene opens in a small conference room at Quasar Stellar Company. The first man to be interviewed is Peter Loomis, vice-president–marketing, who is known to be outspoken, demanding, and intensely loyal. Loomis is greeted by Hubert Clover.

Clover: Pete, as you know, the purpose of our chat is to see if we can learn something from this unfortunate episode that can help to prevent such an occurrence in the future. I would like to get your version of what has happened and any suggestions you may be able to offer as to what can be done to help our planning.

Loomis *(defensively):* Well, Hubert, you know I thought very highly of John. I'm certain you are aware that he hired me for this job. I don't mind admitting that I think the decision to fire him was unwarranted and ill advised.

Clover: If there is one thing I am certain of, Pete, it is that there is no question of your loyalty to John. I hope that won't bias your outlook. As for John's resignation, perhaps the best I can say is that on the basis of all facts available, the board decided this was the only logical course of action. And if . . .

Loomis *(interrupting):* Let me set the record straight on two points. My loyalty to John was based on respect for his abilities — not on personal grounds. And I'm not disagreeing with you, either on the basis of the facts available at the time or on those turned up by the investigation, that the action was not warranted. But I also feel that there was too hasty a collec-

CHART 1   *Organization Chart of Quasar Stellar Company*

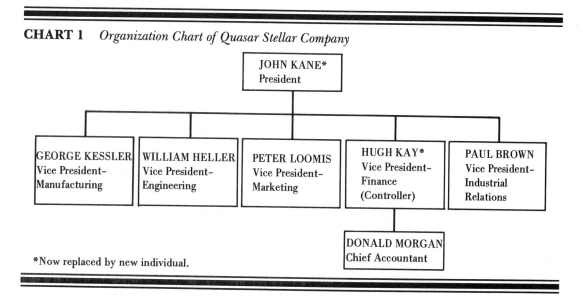

*Now replaced by new individual.

tion of facts and an overreaction resulting in his dismissal. What I'm saying is that had a more thorough and penetrating investigation been made, the conclusions would probably have been different.

Clover (*attempting to lead the interview back*):   I understand your point, Pete, but what are some of the additional facts that you think could have influenced the decision differently?

Loomis: You are most likely aware that the failure to receive the Apollo and LEM contracts had significant effects on the overall picture. But when John informally notified headquarters that our chances of receiving these two jobs were less than 50–50, he was told he was just being pessimistic. It was quite evident to him that the board of directors felt these were two prestige jobs that we simply had to get. The trouble was that while we dissipated our efforts on trying to land these low-probability programs, a half-dozen other less known, but perhaps more lucrative, opportunities slipped by.

Clover: You say John told headquarters about this. Have you any idea why the so-so probabilities and the alternatives were not openly presented and discussed at the appropriate company board meeting?

Loomis: To be frank, the 50–50 chance was an after-the-fact estimate. When the decision was made to pursue the two jobs, because of the pressure from headquarters and knowing what the work could mean to Quasar, I was undoubtedly too optimistic myself. A staff meeting was held in which the two marketing efforts were reviewed in detail.

Clover: Who attended that meeting?

Loomis: As I recall, there was George Kessler, Bill Heller, Hugh Kay, John, and myself.

Clover: Was it unanimously agreed that you should go after the two contracts?

Loomis *(shaking his head):* Oh, no! Bill felt very strongly that we should. He thought that the engineering department could gain a heck of a lot by being involved — state-of-the-art stuff. George was against the effort. He argued that production would be severely affected, because these projects would require such a long-term engineering effort before production could start. He wanted more immediate work that would occupy his work force. Hugh was with George. Not only was he worried about overhead and profits, but he had a "gut feeling" that our chances were less than what I forecast. He was right, of course. John was in favor of pursuing the contracts only if we had about a 75% chance of capturing each. John tossed the ball to me when he asked what our chances of getting the jobs were. At the time, I indicated that while I couldn't stick my neck out to 75%, I was willing to guess it would be much closer to 75% than to, say, 50% or even 60%. Considering the attitude at headquarters, the stakes, and my projection, we finally decided to go after both.

Clover: Are you saying that you didn't really feel that your chances were as close to 75% as you indicated?

Loomis: I believe they weren't. But that isn't to say that I didn't feel they could or should have been.

Clover: How long had you been with the company when this meeting took place, Pete?

Loomis: Just about nine months. I'm quite sure I know the reason for your question. Actually, I was not as familiar with the company as I should have been to express so strong an opinion on such an important matter.

Clover: Obviously, you showed a good deal of enthusiasm . . .

Loomis *(interrupting again):* And, I'm afraid you'll have to agree, naiveté. Remember, however, that this is — or at least was — a gung-ho operation. I was anxious to earn my spurs. Those contracts would have put us on the map and made Quasar and Universal household words.

Clover: I can certainly understand your decision to go after the big fish, but, once you found that you were out of fishing water, why was headquarters not kept informed of the deteriorating market picture? Wouldn't that have been the logical thing to do?

Loomis: Logical, yes, but hardly practical. In retrospect, that is probably what we should have done, but let's go back six months. That's when our fears of a drop in production began to inject themselves. Hugh's warnings about profitability were proving to be only too accurate, and there was nothing that could be pulled in at the last minute to bridge the gap.

Clover: Yes, but you must have known very early that your odds were way off.

Loomis *(after a pause):* Well, perhaps I did not emphasize that fact strongly enough. I assure you, however, that both George and Hugh did, since their operations were directly and indirectly involved.

Clover *(bothered by Loomis's evasiveness):* How, then, was the decision reached not to inform headquarters of this situation? Didn't it bother you to think that there might be adverse effects on employment?

Loomis: Once the decision was made to go after the two projects, any reversal could only result in a loss of face and prestige. Like the gambler at the roulette wheel, we plunged deeper — with about the same odds — and lost. I must confess that I had my moments of doubt about our course of action. It was quite clear that people could get hurt, but that, too, is all part of the game. Frankly, at no time did it occur to me that I had a greater responsibility than the one I had to John. Perhaps this is wrong, but I have always felt that I owe more loyalty to my supervisor than to the company. And besides, I'm not certain to what degree personal morality should enter into business decisions.

Clover: Pete, let me ask you one final question. What do you think we might do to prevent this sort of thing from happening again in the future?

Loomis: Frankly, I feel that headquarters should give us more independence. For example, if headquarters had not exerted pressure on us to pursue these two contracts, we might have followed a different course. To me, what happened was that headquarters decided on a set course of action, passed the word down, and then — when it became impossible for us to follow through — they looked for scapegoats. Both John and Hugh were sacrificed because of poor headquarters policy.

Clover *(rising):* Thanks for a frank and open presentation of your thoughts on the situation, Pete. By the way, Jim Bowden may or may not wish to speak with you, depending on how things go in general. In any event, we'll let you know later. Once again, thanks for your ideas.

Loomis: Thanks for asking. I honestly thought this might just be allowed to die on the vine without anyone looking deeper into it.

Follow-Up Questions

Hubert Clover brooded over his interview with Loomis, scanning his notes in a manner that suggested more sorrow and disappointment than thought. He then decided to summarize his observations and to recommend that Bowden not interview Loomis. But, after reviewing the results of Clover's conversation, Bowden concluded that there was one more thing he wanted resolved: Why had not Loomis, in routine fashion, been put in a position to send a report back to headquarters that would have been at variance with the official statement? Later that afternoon, the two men got together. After exchanging the usual pleasantries and engaging in small talk related to the previous interview, Bowden asked the specific question he had in mind.

Bowden: The one thing that puzzles me, Pete, is why you were not able to transmit your misgivings about the possibility of receiving the two contracts directly to the corporate vice-president of marketing.

Loomis: Your question, Jim, implies that I was *unable* to do this. Actually, it was always possible, but I was not *required* to do it. However, I was expected to give my observations to John and to support him in any decision he made as to how the information was to be handled.

Bowden: Your answer implies to me that you were fully aware that two distorted monthly reports were sent to corporate headquarters. Am I correct in this assumption?

Loomis: From what I have said to both you and Jim, there is no doubt that your conclusion is correct. And, to be honest, I was completely aware of the distortions in the reports. I can only repeat what I said earlier this afternoon to Hubert: my loyalty is to my supervisor, and I always support him in his use of information in any way he sees fit.

KESSLER'S INTERROGATION

The next man to be interviewed was George Kessler, vice-president–manufacturing, who was an old-timer by Quasar standards, having been at Quasar for 15 years. He was known for his outspokenness, integrity, and forcefulness. Clover and Bowden decided that Bowden should conduct the interview with Kessler because there existed a somewhat close relationship between them. As a former operations man, Bowden had taken a direct interest in manufacturing, and he had developed a healthy respect for Kessler. Bowden greeted Kessler, and the two exchanged a few pleasantries.

Bowden: I guess we could keep up the chitchat all day, George, but I'm afraid we've got to get down to business. A fellow in your position must have seen what was coming — how in hell could you let it happen?

Kessler: I would rather continue reminiscing about old times than get into this. To answer your question, Jim, I saw what was coming; but to turn the question back to you, how could I possibly have prevented it?

Bowden: All right, George, you couldn't have stopped it. Really, what I am asking is this: Seeing what was happening, wasn't there something you could have done to raise the storm signals?

Kessler: You know me well enough to realize that I am not one of the gung-ho types. While I had tremendous respect for John's ability to analyze a situation, I always suspected that he had a streak of the gambler in him. Let's face it; if he had pulled those two jobs out of the hat, he would have been Universal's brightest star.

Bowden: Getting back to the point, George, wasn't there some way for you to signal headquarters of what was happening?

Kessler *(frowning)*:   You insist on pursuing this point, don't you? Jim, you know as well as I do that I answered directly to John. I'm not going to beat a dead horse; but, without going into details, I think I expressed my views strongly on the approach we were taking. Certainly, I was concerned about a number of things . . . the number of old-time employees who were going to take a beating if this thing fizzled, as it did; what might actually happen to the company overall; and what I owed to myself as well as to John. Taking all these points into consideration, I did what I thought was morally and managerially right, and I don't say that lightly. In expressing my doubts so forcefully, perhaps I did a disservice to everyone I tried to help.

Bowden: In what way do you think you performed a disservice?

Kessler: In short order, I found myself outside of the actual development of the monthly reports. The result was that any influence I might have exerted in determining what information was to be generated for headquarters was cancelled out.

Bowden *(nodding):* I appreciate your dilemma, George, and I also respect the position you took. But don't you feel that there might have been some way to get this back to our office?

Kessler: In weighing my responsibility to the company, corporate headquarters, employees, self, and supervisor, I may possibly have erred in following too narrow a path. It seemed to me at the time, and I feel the same way even now, that with the organization structure we have, my only approach was to try to change things through the existing framework. My efforts failed. Perhaps I should have been more adventurous and requested — demanded, if you will — an audience with you fellows. But I am certain that if a similar situation arose again, I still would not do this.

Bowden: Then let me ask you what you think can be done to prevent this from happening in the future.

Kessler: To me, there must be an approach that will allow for greater communication between headquarters and the company office. Perhaps the answer lies in having an executive committee sign the monthly report; or possibly having each committee member prepare a short concurrence or dissent report of his own, after the pattern of the Supreme Court; or even a more direct approach of having each manager give an independent report to his respective staff contact at corporate headquarters. The fact is, so long as we have a characteristic line and staff organizational structure, we can only follow the channels of communication that the chief executive officer decides on. No self-respecting manager would consider surreptitiously reporting behind his superior's back.

Bowden *(rising and extending a handshake):* George, thanks for your observations. I like your suggestion of a concurrence or disagreement by an executive committee. I hope the next time we have a little get-together it can be under more pleasant circumstances.

HELLER'S INTERVIEW

To some extent, the interview had merely reinforced Bowden's estimation of Kessler. However, he couldn't help but feel a sense of frustration that a man of Kessler's caliber did not find a way to communicate his misgivings to those who could have done something about the developing Quasar problem.

After reading Bowden's notes, Clover concluded there was no need for him to talk with Kessler. Instead, he decided to carry on with the next interview. The final man singled out was William Heller, vice-president–engineering, an intense, serious-minded, pipe-smoking engineer whose forte was considered to be research and development, not administrative work. He too was a long-term employee, having been with Quasar over ten years. Clover met him at the door of the conference room and, with a wave of his hand, motioned Heller to a chair.

Clover: I suppose the idea of sitting down to discuss this problem is not the most appealing thing to you, Bill. I hope it won't be as painful as realizing that an R & D project is going sour.

Heller: Since your call a few minutes ago was not completely unexpected, I prepared for this by fixing myself an extra tightly packed pipe of tobacco. It will give me more time to think about your questions.

Clover: What can you contribute to our understanding of the things that happened here, and do you have any suggestions as to how they might be prevented in the future?

Heller: I wonder if you could narrow your question somewhat. Exactly what would you like me to address myself to?

Clover: The specific problem, Bill, is this. Do you have an idea why Quasar's deteriorating condition was not reported back to headquarters? Of greatest interest, of course, is the overall condition of the plant operation, but the decline in engineering activity is something you can probably elaborate on in detail. Any light you can shed will be useful.

Heller: While you have become more specific, I still have a wide-open field. Probably I should first outline what happened to engineering, and from this we might then be able to work into the bigger picture. How does that appeal to you?

Heller: About a year ago, it became obvious that our engineering activity, including both research and development and general engineering, was going to decline. The decision was made that a joint effort with marketing would be undertaken. After a series of meetings, it was decided to pursue actively and aggressively two relatively large contracts.

Clover: Those would be the Apollo and LEM contracts. *(Heller nods assent.)* When you say it was decided that those two contracts would be pursued, what did this imply?

Heller: It meant that a radically new — for us — course of action was decided on. Always in the past we had operated as a subcontractor to primes on large systems. However, John and Pete took the stand that we were in a position to enter the system area itself. Frankly, while I had initial skepticism about this approach, John portrayed the picture in optimistic terms. He was convinced that the contracts would be awarded more on the basis of marketing activity than on the engineering proposal, and he was equally confident that Pete's personal contacts would help us in capturing this work. Apparently John knew, or he felt he knew, that Pete had influence with the right people where those two contracts were involved. Thus, while in the past we had been merely keeping our fingers in the pie and hoping to get a piece of the action, it was decided at that point we would go the whole hog after them.

Clover: And you agreed with this approach?

Heller: As I indicated, initially I was skeptical. Our organization is simply not capable of coping with proposals of this size. However, after John and Pete argued their case so persuasively, I was fully in favor of the decision. Actually, I knew it involved a lot of risk, but Quasar stood to benefit greatly if it worked out, and so I went along with them on it.

Clover: What did you think the chances were of getting those contracts, Bill?

Heller (*pausing to light his pipe*): To me, our chances were less than those expressed by Pete, who, as I recall, said he figured them to be closer to 75% than to 60% or so. Frankly, I would have guessed 60% to be the upper limit on our chances for each contract. However, even at that, it seemed like a good risk because, if we had captured but one of them, engineering would have benefited greatly.

Clover: And how about the rest of the plant operations?

Heller: Here, unfortunately, I was shortsighted. While the engineering activity would benefit, in retrospect the company as a whole could conceivably lose if only one or, perhaps, even if both contracts were awarded to Quasar. I might add that this point was brought out strongly by George and Hugh. To offset this argument, however, it was pointed out that while a temporary downturn might occur, in about two years Quasar would be hard-pressed to satisfy the requirements for the projects. In addition, Quasar would become so well known that interim work would be easy to come by.

Clover: Might it not also have worked to Quasar's disadvantage? How can you assume that other companies would be willing to give you work, knowing that it would be short term and that you certainly would give attention to your own contracts once it was time to begin production?

Heller: Yes, it was an optimistic outlook and probably very shortsighted from a total company point of view.

Clover: Even assuming that the decision was a good one when made, why didn't someone recognize it was the wrong course before the entire operation went sour?

Heller (*puffing on his pipe for a moment*): Now you are in an area that is too deep for me. Once it was decided on to pursue those contracts, my group concentrated its efforts on the technical proposal. We are extremely thin in this area. Therefore, our R & D activity was almost totally devoted to the proposal. Let me add that for approximately a 3-month period, 10- to 12-hour days and 7-day weeks were common for my staff.

Clover: But this very activity reduced your effectiveness on current work, did it not, and resulted in costly overruns and delays on contracts already in the house?

Heller: Unfortunately, yes, but that was not totally unexpected. We attemped to minimize the overruns and delays, but some were certainly inevitable. Since we were trying to maintain our staff, a lot of the added cost went into overhead and project charges as we stockpiled personnel during the initial period when the decline began to manifest iself. Of course, we had to face facts later and let some people go when it became apparent that the plans were not working out.

Clover: At that point, why didn't the company reverse itself, abandon its course, and go after some short-term subcontract work? And why didn't you get back to headquarters with your problem?

Heller: At that point, both John and Pete felt retreat would be impossible. Frankly, I supported them against my better judgment, both because I could see no way to change their attitude, and because I had an obligation to do my utmost in attempting to rectify the situation. Now, then, your other question as to why headquarters was not informed is difficult for me to answer. What can I say?

Clover: I would like a frank comment on this point, Bill.

Heller (*knocking the ashes from his pipe*):   Both John and Pete stood high in my book. I don't pretend to be a business manager; rather, I am an engineering manager. The tangibles of engineering are something I grasp and manipulate readily, but the intangibles of business are quite another thing. In retrospect, it's easy to criticize past decisions, but I respect the decisions that were made then. I personally felt there was an obligation to the parent company, but even though I disagreed with the principle of not reporting the situation to headquarters, I accepted it as a business decision.

Clover: Then you were aware, were you not, that the reports sent to headquarters distorted conditions at Quasar to such an extent that the status of projects was inaccurately reported, actual and projected earnings were blatantly inflated, and the entire status of the operation was totally misrepresented? How could you have accepted such a situation?

Heller: If only I could answer you in a manner that might express my feelings at the time. Was I aware of what was going on? Yes, of course, I was. But I didn't *want* to know about it. I will go so far now as to say that I tried *not to know* what was being done. Realistically, once I accepted the basic decision to ride the thing out, I felt stuck with the consequences. There was nothing, as I saw it, that I could do to alter the course taken.

Clover: Bill, did you have any opportunity to bring this to the attention of headquarters?

Heller: Formally, no, of course not. No mechanism existed, or perhaps should ever exist, for circumventing top management. On a few occasions I might have had the opportunity to mention to the corporate vice-president of engineering what was happening, but I certainly would not do that.

Clover (*shaking his head slowly*):   I think you will agree such a situation should never be allowed to exist. Can you offer any suggestions as to how information of such importance to the welfare of both the company and the corporation could be made available to top management without violating any precepts — actual or imaginary?

Heller: I have given considerable thought to this point. I honestly feel that what gets reported back to headquarters can only reflect what the president sees fit. I would hit the ceiling if I found out one of my project managers was reporting directly or indirectly to the president. By the same token, the president shouldn't have to guard against insurgency in his ranks. The corporation might use an internal audit team composed of knowledgeable personnel to make frequent checks on various phases of the operation. Apart from that, I've no suggestion.

Clover: Bill, your pipe's been cold and empty long enough. Thanks for your comments. Hopefully, we won't need another one of these sessions with you.

MORGAN'S OPINIONS

Clover discussed his report with Bowden, and they agreed that another interview with Heller was unnecessary. Then they went over the results of all three interviews in depth. When they had finished, they decided to pursue two additional questions from two other specific areas: (a) Why did the accounting people not find a way to report to headquarters? (b) What was the quality of the morale of the personnel during this period?

Accordingly, Donald Morgan, chief accountant, and Paul Brown, vice-president–industrial relations, were invited to sit down with Bowden and Clover, respectively, in two simultaneous sessions. Since both corporate fact finders felt that too much briefing might tend to "lead" the interviews and stifle response, they agreed that the only statement they would make at the start would be to the effect that efforts were being made to prevent a repetition of the Quasar situation in the future.

Bowden: Don, you certainly are aware of the upheaval here at Quasar, and I suspect you know pretty well the reason for it.

Morgan: Yes, I have a good idea of what's what.

Bowden: I wonder if you would care to express your opinions on two specific points. First, why was it not possible to have the information fed back to corporate headquarters once the deteriorating situation began and, second, what might be done to prevent what happened from taking place again?

Morgan: As standard company policy on reports, we generate our financial statements from whatever information is given to us. Our statements, in turn, are sent to the controller's office, and he does what he sees fit with them. Should we receive instructions from his office to reorganize, let's say, or otherwise manipulate the reports there is very little we can do but follow instructions. This is particularly true when matters of judgment are involved. Let me give you a for-instance: if a project is reported as being behind schedule by the program manager and after review by the controller's office it is decided that it is not all that far behind, naturally adjustments are made. Or, say, an expected contract has not yet been received, but management decides to open up a project number anyway and begins accepting charges in anticipation of receiving the job; this, too, is done. So far as I can see, this is nothing more than exercising management prerogative. I will summarize my position by saying that I do pretty much what I am told. Sometimes I may not like it, but my job is not to set policy or to question decisions. Rather, it is to follow instructions.

BROWN'S OBSERVATION

At that point, Bowden decided that he had heard enough and abruptly ended the interview. Meanwhile, Clover was undertaking his interview with Paul Brown.

Clover: Paul, can you give any insight into the state of morale during the period when Quasar was apparently falsifying reports to the home office and after it became apparent that a serious problem existed?
Brown: For a while, everybody acted as if they were on "pot"; everyone was filled with high expectations. To be sure, there were a couple of exceptions. But, in rapid fashion, things began to settle down and disillusionment set in. Many people sensed that there was trouble ahead and that nothing was being done. After a month or two, the exodus began, and, as you know, it still hasn't ceased. I know that some of the managers tried their best to hang onto their key people, but as usual it was just this caliber of individual who could read the writing on the wall and got out while the getting was good. I'm equally certain that a number of the other top people would have left except for loyalty to the company and their fellow employees, their years of company service and/or other factors. My only other observation on this is that I hope our new president and controller have been selected more for solid, long-range accomplishments than for flashy, short-term results.

The interviews having been concluded, Clover and Bowden are now faced with drafting a series of recommendations on the individuals interviewed and the steps to be taken by Universal Corporation.

DISCUSSION QUESTIONS

1. What ethical choices did Loomis, Kessler, and Heller each find themselves facing? How did each respond to John Kane's actions? How did each resolve his personal dilemma?

2. Identify and evaluate several methods of improving *formal* internal control at Universal that would minimize the likelihood of falsification of the subsidiary to the corporate offices.
3. Identify and evaluate several methods of improving *informal* internal control for example, leadership, professional attitudes, group decision making, that would minimize the likelihood of falsification.

Chapter 9

Governance in the Workplace
The Integration of Employer and Employee Interests

Concepts and practices discussed in the two previous chapters relate to two important managerial functions: fulfilling obligations of trusteeship to stockholders and generating public confidence and credibility in the corporation. The promise of corporate governance is the integration of a wide range of social and economic interests into corporate policy; its process involves the establishment of clear lines of managerial accountability and the redistribution of some decision-making power to corporate boards and to management professionals in the firm.

In addition to investors, employees are a second group of direct corporate participants whose stake in the distribution of power is immediate and personal. The following developments illustrate employee power in the firm:

- the legitimation of unions and collective bargaining in the 1930s was a clear reorganization of power relationships between laborers and management;
- recent legislative protection for individual employee's claims for non-discriminatory personnel practices and for a healthy and safe work environment has imposed standards and restrictions on managerial power;
- current movements that increase the level of employee participation in work decisions and employee ownership of firms are governance and control issues; and
- efforts to secure greater civil liberties in the workplace — freedom of speech, privacy, and association — call for redefining the limits of managerial power and developing mechanisms of supervisory accountability.

Beyond a doubt, familiar problems of control and of governance exist in both employee and investor relations to the corporation.

The presence of a control dimension in employer-employee relationships is based on several characteristics of modern organizations. First, most employment organizations are structured as hierarchies in which senior positions inherently carry more authority than lower or more junior positions. An uneven distribution of power is an inevitable and necessary element of hierarchy. Yet its presence may give rise to various questions: Is the distribution of power commensurate with responsibility? Does it result in "fair" rewards to upper and lower members? Are there checks on the misuse of power in the employment relationship? The fact that not all levels or groups of participants may agree on answers to these questions creates conflict and stress in corporations. Vital issues of governance — how the varied interests of different parties can be integrated — arise.

A second cause of control as a universal organizational characteristic is firm size. As some corporations grow to include hundreds of thousands of members, directing and controlling human activities becomes extremely complex. Control procedures, such as budgets and standard operating procedures, may risk leading to standardization and depersonalization. Other control procedures such as close supervision may risk leading to arbitrariness and inequity between persons. Large organizations often take on the characteristics of private governments: they develop and administer rules, make equity decisions among members, and adjudicate internal disputes and conflicts. The large size of many employing organizations not only creates conditions for group or class interests to emerge but also generates challenges to rules and decisions made by managers. The nature and complexity of control engendered in large corporations compel attention to processes of organizational governance.

This chapter reviews several governance mechanisms in the employer-employee relationship. Some of these, such as collective bargaining, are the source of much experience and knowledge about the integration of worker and corporation interests. Others, such as employee-owned firms or organizational "due process," are newer and less institutionalized concepts in workplace governance. In both cases attention will be devoted to exploring the nature of these mechanisms and their positive and negative effects on corporate governance.

We begin with a brief review of the labor movement and the emergence of collective bargaining as an institutional process, turn to quality of work life (QWL) projects and employee ownership as forms of worker participation, and end with a discussion of the movement toward employee rights in corporations and the potential for fair hearing and appeal systems in organizations. Business-government relationships in the interactions between employers and employees will be examined where they are influential.

THE LABOR MOVEMENT

There is no single, universal justification for the existence of labor unions. Rationales for collective labor action vary from a need to overcome the dehumanizing aspects of the workplace to a need to redress the imbalance of power between the workman and the manager in a modern industrial economy.[1] If, as Karl Marx argued, industrialization implies the separation of workers from the "means of production" and the development of militant class interests,[2] then bargaining with unions may reduce worker alienation from the firm by creating mutual dependence and integration of labor and management interests. According to one authority on the labor movement in American industrial development, a powerful logic of the union movement was that "establishment and practice of collective bargaining [would] substantially reduce the economic strife bequeathed by industrialization. Instead of class battle, collective bargaining [offered] negotiation and the exploration of mutual interest and purposes."[3] The institutionalization of labor power and the necessity for good faith bargaining between union and employer created an explicit interdependency that, while often full of strife and conflict, increased labor's stake in the survival of the market system and, to that great extent, was integrative. This development of industrial history merits review.

Industrial Relations in the Age of Enterprise

The labor movement is a clear example of how the growth of America's industrial system created new challenges to its own premises and success. The emergence of a large, relatively homogeneous work force gave rise to explicit recognition of common interests by working people and to a powerful call for institutionalized protection of the collective interests of laborers. The accompanying statement by Milton Derber in Insert 9.A summarizes the general social and economic developments involved in changing the structure of the late nineteenth century labor force.

Earlier discussion of the evolution of ideology in business-government relations highlighted judicial conservatism in the late nineteenth and early twentieth centuries. In fact the Court's decision to strike down a New York law limiting the work hours of bakers for reasons of health in *Lochner* v. *New York State*, discussed in Chapter 2, shows the prevailing view of the period: an aversion against permitting government to intervene in the employer-employee contract. The Court's additional reluctance to view collective labor action as legitimate is explained by Wellington in a historical analysis of the law and the labor movement:

> The court's concern for the employer appeals for its acceptance to the value society places on private property

Insert 9.A

FORCES ACTING ON THE ROLE OF LABOR UPON ENTERING THE TWENTIETH CENTURY [QUOTATION]

Rapid change has been a characteristic of life in the United States throughout most of its history, but no period surpassed the last third of the nineteenth century in this respect. From the standpoint of industrial government, hardly a single relevant environmental factor failed to undergo drastic transformation. A newly industrializing nation with about a 35 million population became the industrial and economic giant of the world with a population of about 75 million. A society of small owner-operated workshops and factories dependent on the skilled artisan evolved into a system of mass production utilizing large numbers of unskilled laborers and dominated by huge trusts under the control of finance capitalists. . . .

By the end of the century, marked inequalities scarred the scene. Big city slums teemed with impoverished families in the midst of unparalleled national affluence. The distinctions between the wealthy and the poor were intensified, not only by spreading income levels but by growing differences in standards of dress, housing, education, culture, and recreation. The sudden vast influx of non-English-speaking immigrants from continental Europe added to class stratification. It is no wonder that the social-psychological climate of the period, following on the heels of the traumatic experience of a convulsive Civil War, was a hurly-burly of protest and conflict, of trying to recapture the past or leap into a utopian future, of reformism and radicalism, of uncertainty and experimentalism, of rapid and frequent shift from one position to another.

SOURCE: Milton Derber, *The American Idea of Industrial Democracy, 1865–1965* (Urbana: University of Illinois Press, 1970), pp. 29–30. Copyright 1970 by the Board of Trustees of the University of Illinois. Used with permission.

and . . . the control that comes with ownership. To diminish control is to dilute ownership, and on the desire for and responsibility of ownership we premise a great many of our notions about man and his community. Freedom of contract is a necessary part of the social mechanism of ownership, and when a society of workers can dictate who may be hired and at what price, the employer's freedom of contract, his freedom to use the traditional power of his property, is impaired.

What the courts did, and said they were doing, was to put to one side the interests and aspirations of the employees who desired to act as a group. To these interests and aspirations, society today attaches a very high value indeed.[4]

The late nineteenth century was imbued with the spirit of entrepreneurial capitalism, and the role of government in legislative and judicial areas was largely one of abstention. Yet the collective interests of laborers grew increasingly apparent as this period saw the birth of early labor organization with the Knights of Labor and the early American Federation of Labor. By the turn of the century nearly 6 percent of nonagricultural workers belonged to a labor organization.[5] The clash between a Darwinist social philosophy and labor class identification and organization led to a violent period of labor unrest in the latter part of the century, including destructive strikes and retaliatory employer measures in the railroad, coal, and steel industries. One of the more notorious conflicts was the violent union-breaking actions of the Carnegie Steel Company at the Homestead plant in which 10 men were killed and 60 wounded and the National Guard was utilized to regain control of the plant from the workers.[6]

At the turn of the century, President William McKinley formed the United States Industrial Commission to search for a new conception of industrial government. A massive report by this commission endorsed employer acceptance of unions to prevent workers from turning to socialism for achieving an "element of democracy in industrial life."[7] The report particularly supported the development of labor agreements through collective bargaining, noting the following advantages: better mutual understanding of the conditions, positions, and motives of each party; early identification and correction of misunderstandings and sources of conflict; and development of longer-term understanding and respect between labor and management. These beliefs about the role of collective bargaining, endorsed as early as 1900, became national policy through enactment of far-reaching labor legislation in the mid-1930s. Several moderate government goals proposed by this commission were ultimately accepted: to ensure workers' rights to organize and to strike, to emphasize conciliation and voluntary arbitration, and to define labor practices fair to both employers and laborers.

The Present System of Labor-Management Relations

These concepts of workplace governance ebbed and flowed with the national and international developments of the first third of the twentieth century. The advent of industrial humanism, the challenge of socialist ideology, a world war, mass production manufacturing, and the Great Depression favorably affected public attitudes toward unions. By the mid-1930s Congress passed a series of labor laws that have provided the basic framework of industrial relations until today. The key piece of legislation was the National Labor Relations (Wagner) Act of 1935, which established the legal right of employees to organize and join, or not join, a union. The act made it illegal for management to interfere with this right in any form and required good faith collective bargaining between union and company representatives.

Labor policy in the United States not only has legitimized unions and collective bargaining but also has recognized the inevitability of disputes in the industrial setting. Through statutes and other regulatory actions, government attempts to aid the resolution of disputes. Government establishes the "rules of the game" and a forum for appeals on questions of (1) whether a group of workers chooses to be represented by a union, and if so, which union; (2) the process of collective bargaining on a work contract; and (3) problems and disputes arising from the implementation of the contract.

While dictating the objectives and general structure of employer-employee relations in these areas, the government and the courts have consistently honored the private and decentralized nature of the employment relationship. The National Labor Relations Board, an independent governmental commission created by the Wagner Act, provides a source of appeal for charges by either party of a violation of the rules for union elections and collective bargaining, and the federal courts provide a final recourse on the application of the law. Union legitimacy and management noninterference are explicit and closely regulated, but within this broad structure numerous union elections are held, thousands of private negotiations are conducted, and terms of work for millions of employees are agreed upon. The system of private and decentralized contract negotiations generally functions effectively. When negotiating positions are sufficiently divergent that negotiations and voluntary arbitration fail to produce a contract, the more costly method of the labor strike becomes involved. While it may be tempting and politically attractive for government to reduce the social costs of a strike by dictating or forcing a settlement, the integrity of private settlements has been adhered to. The importance of this system of collective bargaining to the preservation of a free enterprise system is emphasized by labor expert Thomas Kennedy:

> If government becomes involved in the determination of
> labor contract terms in order to avoid strikes, it may not be

able to stop there. With our democratic political structure
it would be impossible, I believe, to prevent compulsory
settlement of wages for union members from leading to
government decisions concerning salaries, professional
fees, and, finally, prices and profits. So long as free collective bargaining is permitted, it forms an outer perimeter of
defense against government regulation in other areas. If it
fails, the possibility of more regulation in the other areas
becomes much greater.[8]

In arriving at a work contract, parties are responsible for their own negotiating positions and strategies. Management is free to calculate the point
at which the cost of a settlement is less than the cost of a work stoppage,
and unions independently decide on the merits and limitations of a present
settlement against the costs of a work stoppage. The possibility of a strike
is an incentive toward settlement for both parties; no one looks to outside
protection, and the most directly interested parties negotiate their differences and live with the results.

The Function of Labor Arbitration

A frequent area of dispute pertains to the application or implementation
of the labor agreement. Here again, an important key to maintenance of
the system of private dispute resolution is the availability to both parties of
an informed, unbiased, and independent decision maker: an arbitrator.
The joint commitment to participate in an arbitral process often forms part
of the labor agreement itself and constitutes an essential element of industrial self-governance.

   Sociologist Philip Selznick has thoroughly traced the development
of labor arbitration and its contribution to industrial relationships.[9] He
views the institution of arbitration as a creative process — one that is flexible and inductive and that has evolved a set of emergent principles for
industrial justice. Arbitrators, drawing upon the formal collective contract,
the reservoir of common law principles such as due process and admissi-
bility of evidence, and the reality of social relationships in the firm, have
gradually developed general principles of fairness in employment relations. Among the emergent principles identified by Selznick are the
following:

*   The collective contract creates an inherent barrier to arbitrary action
    by an employer;
*   Industrial justice should not be applied so as to undermine the legiti-
    mate objectives of the firm;
*   Long service creates a legitimate claim to the mitigation of punitive
    rules; and

- Discipline should be (1) reasonably related to the gravity of the offense and (2) corrective whenever feasible.[10]

These are not surprising or startling principles; in fact their very reasonableness suggests their utility as a basis for making fair judgments with respect to employees and employers. These principles show how the contribution of an independent institution of arbitration reinforces the private system of collective bargaining. The role of the government and the courts has been to create and support the broad framework of decentralized and private employment agreements.

Forms of Worker Participation

The general contribution of unions to American society has been to preserve the corporation as an institution in the face of growing economic class differences. Collective labor action opened the corporation to worker participation in setting the conditions of work. Institutionalization of participation through unionization may be credited, in part, with fostering sufficient integration of labor and management interests to protect the private enterprise system from the threat of radical political movements.

The role of unions in industrial governance grows less clear in this day of mature industrialization. Table 9.1 shows that while total union membership has increased in absolute numbers since World War II, organized labor has suffered a decline as a percentage of the total labor force. Of course, aggregate statistics mask smaller trends that run against the general pattern. In this case, while private sector unions just maintained their membership levels since 1960, public sector unions have more than doubled their numbers of members, and in 1980 over 40 percent of government employees were organized. By 1984, 25 states had enacted laws that permitted their employees to bargain collectively, and this number is expected to increase over time. American Federation of State, County and Municipal Employees (AFSCME) union efforts to enhance the working conditions and wage levels of public workers have been, in some areas, well publicized and quite successful.

Unlike the public sector, the private sector is facing a decline in union membership for reasons that are multiple and complex, including changing needs of the labor force and greater employment in the nonmanufacturing sector. An analysis of several forces affecting organized labor in the private sector by several labor relations experts is presented in Insert 9.B. The uncertain role of the unions in the course of the economy may make it difficult for the existing system to provide needed *new* sources of energy for future integration of employer-employee interests in corporations. One recent integrative attempt to satisfy the concerns of unions, workers, and employers alike is being tried out in a contract between the International Union of Electric Workers and General Motor's Packard

TABLE 9.1 *Union Membership as a Proportion of the U.S. Labor Force, 1977–80, 1983–84*

Year	Total Employment (thousands)	Union Membership (thousands)	Percentage Union Membership of Total Employment
1977[a]	81,334	19,335	23.8
1978[b]	84,968	19,548	23.0
1979[b]	87,117	20,986	24.1
1980[c]	87,480	20,095	23.0
1983[d]	88,290	17,717	20.1
1984[d]	92,194	17,340	18.8

[a]U.S., Department of Labor, Bureau of Labor Statistics, *Earnings and Other Characteristics of Organized Workers,* Report 556, (Washington, D.C.: U.S. Department of Labor, May 1977.)
[b]Unpublished data, Bureau of Labor Statistics.
[c]U.S., Department of Labor, Bureau of Labor Statistics, *Earnings and Other Characteristics of Organized Workers,* Bulletin 2105, (Washington, D.C.: U.S. Department of Labor, May 1980.)
[d]U.S., Department of Labor, *Employment and Earnings,* (Washington, D.C.: U.S. Department of Labor, January 1985.)

Electric division. Their 1984 contract incorporates the idea that current employees will receive lifetime jobs and income guarantees in exchange for the union's agreement to accept a lower-cost, two-tiered wage system in the immediate future.[11] To date, lifetime employment guarantees are quite uncommon; however, additional mechanisms of participation that may ultimately supplement the union role in industrial governance — namely, QWL programs and employee ownership — are in operation in numerous American firms.

Quality of Work-Life Programs

A fairly recent movement in the United States, labeled as worker participation or QWL, has caused some substantial changes in the domain of industrial governance. Robert Guest defined QWL as "a process by which an organization attempts to unlock the creative potential of its people by involving them in decisions affecting their work lives."[12] This process may take a variety of specific forms: joint labor-management committees for problem solving on the plant floor; labor participation in plant design, speed of work flow, or quality control; and worker involvement in production planning, productivity measurement, and a host of other administra-

Insert 9.B

CHALLENGES TO UNION ORGANIZING STRENGTH [QUOTATION]

For all of their limitations the data on union membership unambiguously document an ebb in the percent of the workforce affiliated with construction and manufacturing unions. . . . Even allowing for the fact that 1974 and 1976 were recession years, the decline is still evident. . . .

Much of this decline has been traced to product market or labor market shifts among organized businesses: companies have folded; plants have closed and either relocated abroad or shifted to the less organized South and West. Sometimes these organized firms have simply lost business to nonunion firms. . . .

Declining membership has also been due to interindustry shifts in employment. Where manufacturing employment has grown it has been in new high-technology industries not as easily organized as the older, heavy manufacturing industries. Particularly, we are referring to products such as computers, technical and scientific instruments, and some petro-chemical products.

A third factor influencing membership statistics in manufacturing is the change in the occupational mix. Even though employment is growing, it is growing among the less easily organized white-collar segment. Consequently, union security clauses, which historically contributed to growth in union membership as production worker employment expanded, are decreasing in importance. . . .

There has been increased management resistance to unionization in manufacturing and construction. . . . This wave of resistance is consistent with the long-standing preference and ideology of American business to operate nonunion. In this regard, the bitter debate over labor law reform showed how little consensus we enjoy among labor and mangement on national labor policies. Management believes that they are entrepreneurs, and as the risk takers they want to retain control of the business. . . .

Management has also become more sophisticated in understanding why workers organize and more aggressive within the framework of the law in getting their side of the story across to the employees. . . .

Insert 9.B   continued

The changing nature of the workforce has slowed down union organizing. Women, the better educated, and younger workers have long been more difficult to organize.

[Finally,] the rapid expansion in job rights through legislation has made it more difficult to organize workers. Simply put, the historical fear of the AFL against government involvement in employee relations was correct: public policy gives employees a free ride in areas where the union was the sole provider of benefits. Furthermore, this expansion in such programs as Equal Opportunity, Occupational Safety and Health, and pension plan security (ERISA) has contributed to employer resistance in two ways. Regulatory programs contribute to operating costs and curtail managerial discretion, underscoring the desirability of remaining nonunion and increasing the level of management sophistication in personnel practices, possibly alerting the small employer to this function for the first time.

SOURCE: Myron Roomkin and Hervey A. Juris, "Unions in the Traditional Sectors: The Mid-Life Passage of the Labor Movement," Industrial Relations Research Association, *Proceedings,* August 29–31, 1978, pp. 213–19. Copyright 1978 by the authors. Used with permission.

tive processes. In some plants worker teams function as autonomous work units, scheduling their own production and hiring their own team members. In other plants individual workers maintain authority to shut down an entire line upon seeing a continuing quality defect in product quality.

There are many reasons why American workers may be gaining more involvement in decisions affecting their jobs. One source may be the emphasis on personal dignity and the questioning of traditional authority that was part of society in the 1960s and 1970s. A steadily rising level of education in the work force and a consequent increase in the expectations of workers for more democratic work settings have also played a role in this change. In addition Richard Walton comments on the role the traditional institutions of church, school, and family have played in transforming worker attitudes and values: "These socialization agencies have promoted individual initiative, self-responsibility and self-control, the relativity of values, and other social patterns that make subordinancy in traditional organizations an increasingly bitter pill to swallow for each successive wave of entrants to the U.S. work force."[13]

Finally, economic, technological, and competitive pressures external to the firm are a major source of the attention to quality of work. In an economic environment that is global in its competitive reach, corporate policy that better utilizes human resources is mandatory. Survival and growth require a work force integrated into the goals of the firm, and, as pointed out by one eminent social scientist, "collaboration rather than competition is a basic requirement."[14]

While individual and organizational benefits are important goals of the young movement toward improving work quality, perhaps the greatest potential contribution of the QWL movement lies in its potential for reconciling a contradiction in the way the American worker is governed at work and the way that society in general is ruled. As the Health, Education, and Welfare (HEW) *Work in America* study stated:

> Participative management (one aspect of QWL) permits the worker to achieve and maintain a sense of personal worth and importance, to grow, to motivate himself and to receive recognition and approval for what he does. It gives the worker a meaningful voice in decisions in one place where the effects of his voice can be immediately experienced. In a broader sense, it resolves a contradiction in our nation — between democracy in society and authoritarianism in the workplace.[15]

These social and economic pressures suggest the need for revision in the traditional work structure and style of supervision. Yet American organizations have, for the most part, been slow to explore the implications of concepts such as QWL. One obstacle to this revision may lie within management itself. Worker participation intrudes on historical management prerogatives and calls for substantial effort to change institutional ideologies and practices. One QWL program at a General Foods plant in Topeka, Kansas, was eventually dismantled. *Business Week* offered the following explanation:

> The problem has not been so much that the workers could not manage their own affairs as that some management and staff saw their own positions threatened because the workers performed almost too well. One former employee says the system — built around a team concept — came up squarely against the company's bureaucracy.[16]

Moreover, it is difficult to reverse historical worker distrust for the motives of management. Workers may feel that QWL programs are merely management ploys to speed up the line or squeeze out more work. They will obviously resist changes seen as causing unemployment rather than a greater sharing of economic benefits. It may be difficult for workers to accept management as the sole economic beneficiary of productivity improvements resulting from improved worker-management cooperation.

Finally, union endorsement of worker participation has not been strongly forthcoming, as union leaders may often be suspicious that such management-sponsored programs are simply another technique for undermining their presence. Historically, union-management relations have been marked by adversity in the United States, and it is not an uncommon belief among unions that conflict resolution in this traditional mode serves the interests of the worker best. Insert 9.C is one interpretation of the stance of the union movement toward the work quality concept.

Quality circles, first brought to America from Japan by Lockheed management in 1974, have received mixed reviews after a decade of use in the United States. Insert 9.D illustrates the range of current corporate opinions on this form of employee participation. However, employee involvement programs are still on the upswing in American firms, and organizations such as the International Association of Quality Circles and the American Society of Quality Circles have been formed to advance this employee participation concept. Studies of firms that utilize quality circles state that successful programs share some critical characteristics, whereas unsuccessful programs were more likely to be found in firms lacking the following attributes:

- Top management was committed to the concept of quality circles;
- Top management created a *vision* of desired improvements within the organization to be achieved through quality circles;
- Leaders of quality circles were able to focus the group on clearly established priorities and provide assistance as needed;
- Progress made toward quality circle goals was reviewed on an ongoing basis; and
- Accomplishments were acknowledged and new goals were set.[17]

While quality circle experts generally agree that such programs are best used as a means toward a fairly tangible end such as improved assembly techniques, companies have implemented quality circles for a variety of reasons. Firms cited increasing employee contribution and involvement most often as the reason for initiating quality circles.[18] Improvements in services, products, and/or productivity were given as the reason for creating quality circles only slightly less frequently. Other reasons mentioned included improving trust, communications, and morale, and a few respondents noted their desire to avoid unionization through the use of quality circles.

Some issues pertaining to American quality circles have yet to be resolved by many companies involved in this employee participation movement. First, unlike Japanese workers, it is believed that American workers will require financial compensation if they are expected to generate consistently profitable ideas for their company over an extended period of

---

Insert 9.C

QWL: THREAT TO UNION STRENGTH? [QUOTATION]

Workers and trade unions have their own set of problems with worker participation initiatives. They are often reluctant to engage in these experiments because of suspicions about management's goals, and because of the lack of advantage they perceive in it for themselves. Some workers are uninterested in workplace reforms and seek their satisfaction outside the workplace. Among others, participatory experiments are seen as aimed solely at improvements in productivity, which they believe would bring greater unemployment, not greater shared wealth. Certain types of worker participation (job enrichment, for example) are often seen as management efforts to weaken the role of the union.

Even when workers are offered the prospect of greater control over major decision-making, their response is often negative. The idea that labor should accept a significant responsibility for the efficient operation of an enterprise runs counter to the belief of more American unions that institutionalized conflict is the best means of protecting their members' interests, and that major decision-making should remain in the domain of management. Many trade unions believe that to blur the distinction between employees and managers would interfere with the collective bargaining process. As Thomas Donahue, the executive assistant to the president of the AFL-CIO, has said, "We do not seek to be a partner in management — to be most likely the junior partner in success and the senior partner in failure."

SOURCE: Karl Freiden, *Workplace Democracy and Productivity* (Washington, D.C.: National Center for Economic Alternatives, 1980), p. 44. Used with permission.

---

time. Rewarding viable ideas developed in quality circles does not seem to pose an insurmountable problem to companies; however, it may prove more difficult to develop complementary financial rewards for employees who might also have profitable ideas yet are not quality circle members.

Second, experts also suggest that a company must assess the overall effect that quality circles might have on the organization. A quality circle

Insert 9.D

QUALITY CIRCLES: U.S. CORPORATE SURVEY RESULTS

In an effort to forecast the probable longevity of quality circles in American firms, Merle O'Donnell and Robert O'Donnell sent 2,000 questionnaires to corporate members of the Organizational Development Division of the American Society for Training and Development. They received 417 usable responses.

Quality Circle Usage

Response	Number of Organizations	Percentage of Sample
Not using	207	49
Yes, using	187	45
Used, but discontinued	7	2
Almost ready to begin	16	4

Effectiveness of Quality Circles

Category	Number of Organizations	Percentage of Sample
Extremely successful	37	20
Moderately successful	80	43
Average	14	7
Poor	4	2
Failure	7	4
Too early to tell	45	24

SOURCE: Merle O'Donnell and Robert O'Donnell, "Quality Circles — The Latest Fad or a Real Winner?" *Business Horizons,* May-June 1984, pp. 49, 51. Copyright, 1984, by the Foundation for the School of Business at Indiana University. Used with permisssion.

program is apparently capable of dividing or unifying an organization — depending upon the corporate culture already in operation. One of the major reasons cited by companies who considered their quality circle programs to be failures was that the basic tenets of the concept clashed with their company's existing management style.[19] Finally, few companies have developed an accurate method of measuring the costs and benefits associated with quality circles.

A full trial for QWL in the United States is in progress; the ultimate role and contribution of this concept in the industrial workplace remain uncertain. Its ultimate place will be determined, in part, by economic competition, by the degree to which quality circle contributions can be effectively measured, and by the degree to which management and labor can reconcile these newer practices with past ideologies and institutional relationships.

Employee-Owned Firms

The stake of labor in the performance of American industry is substantial: employee pension funds alone accounted for over $550 billion of investment in 1980 and are expected to provide nearly a half of all external capital raised by American corporations in 1990.[20] Pension fund investments and stock-benefit profit-sharing plans in corporations are indirect mechanisms of integration for employee and firm interests.

Increasing attention is being focused on more direct forms of employee ownership — cases in which employee ownership and employee control are substantial. By general definition, employee stock ownership plans (ESOPs) are designed as a trust fund set up by the company, which primarily invests in the company's stock. This stock is then periodically distributed to employees according to the method outlined in the company's benefit program. Ideally, increased employee productivity will, in turn, increase the value of the stock; thus an employee's financial well-being is tied in part to the firm's economic health. ESOPs have been in existence since the 1930s; however, only in recent years has the concept been in the public limelight. According to the National Center for Employee Ownership, approximately 500 companies are at least 51 percent owned by their employees.[21]

A systematic study of the impact of employee ownership on the economic performance of the firm was conducted at the University of Michigan several years ago.[22] The profitability of 30 employee-owned firms for which data were available were analyzed in comparison with the average profitability of companies in their industries: pretax profits-to-sales for each company was compared with this ratio for each firm's industry. The authors found that the profit-to-sales ratio for employee-owned firms was 70 percent higher than the industry ratio.

In further analysis the researchers discovered that the single most important factor of the ownership structure affecting the profitability of a given firm was the percentage of worker equity. The general configuration of factors for more profitable employee-owned firms consisted of a high proportion of equity held by workers, the presence of worker representatives on the board, and voting rights for employee owners. The study suggests high ownership and control offer the best conditions for integration of worker and management interests. But these conditions are rare; a more common pattern is widespread employee ownership of a relatively small part of the firm's equity. This usually means minimal worker ownership, the absence of worker or employee board representatives, and the absence of voting rights for employee owners.

While the number of examples of truly employee-owned firms is small, the appeal of the idea as a matter of policy in industrial governance is great. Governmental agencies such as the Small Business Administration and the Farmers Home Administration look favorably upon these and other agencies support this development financially.[23] In 1976 Congress passed tax legislation making company contributions to ESOPs tax deductible, and the Senate Finance Committee has studied and actively promoted the concept. In 1981, tax treatment for ESOPs was made even more favorable. The potential of employee ownership may be promising, but it is far from automatic; the change in philosophy and structure is a dramatic departure from traditional concepts and practices. A description of the firm that many consider to be the largest employee-owned corporation in the United States is presented in Insert 9.E.

Insert 9.E

AMERICA'S LARGEST EMPLOYEE-OWNED FIRM: WEIRTON STEEL CORPORATION

Prior to the 1920s, Wierton Steel Company operated under local ownership in Weirton, West Virginia. During the 1920s a number of small steel companies, including Weirton, were merged into National Steel Corporation and remained that way till National sold the Weirton steel mill to local owners in September 1983. However, unlike the previous Weirton owners, the new buyers would have two roles — as workers and owners.

National Steel had determined in 1982 that its investment in Weirton would be sharply curtailed and believed that an eventual closing of the plant would be in the offing. In light of these facts, National Steel proposed that employees of the facility purchase the specialty steel mill. The final price tag for the mill included: (1) $75 million in cash (payable upon closing the deal); (2) $119.2 million in notes payable — spanning a 15-year time period; and (3) assumption of $192.3 million in existing liabilities.

Other conditions of the sale included employee compensation cutbacks and the delineation of old/new owner responsibilities. Overall, Weirton's union members (Independent Steelworker Union) would have their compensation reduced by 19.6 percent. COLA's would be eliminated immediately and replaced with profit sharing down the road. The new worker-owners also agreed to a six-year contract with a provision that prohibited strikes during the lifetime of the agreement. Three Weirton union

Insert 9.E   continued

members would assume seats on Wierton Steel Corporation's 12-member board of directors. National Steel, unlike some other owners involved in employee buyouts, agreed to maintain major pension benefit obligations accumulated at the time of the sale and accepted some responsibility for future employee benefit obligations.

Both partners to the employee buyout deal claimed to have satisfied their objectives. National Steel wanted to reduce the size of its steel division while focusing on a "leaner and meaner" philosophy. A simple shutdown of Wierton steel mill operations would have ostensibly aided this strategy, yet the closure cost of such a move was pegged at $800 million. Selling of the facility to employees purportedly allowed National to take advantage of favorable tax laws and reduce its obligations to the employees.

Once the agreement was finalized, the 26,000 residents of Weirton were able to banish, at least temporarily, any fears of becoming a ghost town. At the time the deal was signed, the Weirton mill employed 7,000 local townspeople, and the community was experiencing a 16 percent unemployment rate. Therefore, it came as no surprise when employees ratified the deal in September 1983; the margin of acceptance did surpass the most optimistic estimates with 6,203 votes in favor of employee ownership compared with a mere 774 nay sayers. Clearly, many employees felt the buyout was their best alternative if they desired any measure of long-term job security. For the time being, most Weirton Steel Corporation employees are guaranteed wages approximating $20,000 or more and some degree of ownership in the firm, buttressed by visions of receiving a portion of the nation's eighth-largest steel mill's future profits.

The employee takeover of the Wierton mill formally occurred in January 1984, and by August the statistics were encouraging. According to Corey Rosen, executive director of the National Center for Employee Ownership, "Weirton Steel has brought back 1,000 workers. The company is quite proud of that." However, recent layoffs have reduced that number to 700 rehired employees. Furthermore, the reported profits, by November 1984, totaled $48 million, and Weirton's profits per ton of steel surpassed the nation's top six steel companies.

SOURCE: Thomas O'Boyle, "National Steel Workers at Weirton, W. VA. to Vote Sept. 23 on Accord to Buy Division," *Wall Street Journal,* August 24, 1983, p. 6; "Weirton's Workers Vote 89% in Favor of Plan to Buy Mill," *Wall Street Journal,* September 26, 1983, p. 16; Howard Banks, "Who Guards the Public Interest?" *Forbes,* April 11, 1983, p. 40; Thomas W. Gardel, "Worker Capitalism," *Cleveland Plain Dealer,* November 6, 1984, p. C1.

EMPLOYEE RIGHTS AND THE CORPORATION

Recent years have witnessed the development of a uniquely modern dimension of employer-employee relationships in which the degree of employee protection from unjust dismissal or unhealthy working conditions and the extent of employee free speech, privacy, and freedom of association outside the job have received substantial attention. The phenomenon of "employee rights" is a contemporary manifestation of the enduring American commitment to individualism. Born of the affluence and mobility of modern society and encouraged by expressions of the egalitarianism of the 1960s and 1970s, this development consists of efforts to protect and enhance freedom of individual action vis-à-vis the potentially arbitrary exercise of employer power. Table 9.2 provides a sample of state laws enacted to protect employees, or potential employees, from possible discriminatory employer actions. This area is raising new issues of public policy that will influence corporations and that will require greater managerial understanding of the role of justice in the governance of the corporation. The remainder of this chapter examines these issues — first, examining the evidence for the increasing role of employee rights in corporations and, second, considering the meaning and nature of *organizational due process.*

Growth of Employee Rights Issues: Social Legislation

For a long time civil service rules and appeal procedures have protected governmental employees from unjust and arbitrary treatment of supervisors. Similarly, the collective labor agreement and established grievance procedures have afforded union members substantial protection from unjust employment practices. Now, several developments indicate these con-

TABLE 9.2 *A Sample of Antidiscrimination Laws Enacted by States*

Area of Discrimination	Number of States
Handicap	44
Arrest records	18
Marital status	21
Lie detector tests	22

SOURCE: Reader's Digest, *You and the Law*, (Pleasantville, N.Y.: Reader's Digest Association, 1984), pp. 450–53. ©1984 the Reader's Digest Association, Inc. Used with permission.

cepts are being extended into the previously untouched managerial, professional, and nonunion areas of the work force.

First among these developments is the burst of social legislation of the 1960s and 1970s that influences the employer-employee relationship. Social justice was addressed in the Civil Rights Act of 1964 and its 1972 amendment giving individuals legal recourse against employer discrimination. After a period of conflict, controversy, and court challenge, it now appears that recruiting, hiring, promoting, and dismissal practices have been permanently altered by this law. For example, in a widely publicized Supreme Court decision in 1978, the Court upheld the policy of the University of California Medical School at Davis to take race into consideration in admission decisions.[24] Allan Bakke, a white male, was not admitted to the program, whereas several minorities with lower admission scores had been admitted. His claim was that the use of race as an admission criterion discriminated against him and was a violation of the Civil Rights Act of 1964. While the Court found the use of strict quotas illegal, it also found race could be used as one factor in admissions decisions, concluding that "the school's interest in attaining a diverse student body is substantial enough to suggest the use of a suspect classification such as race." A year later, the Court again found that an affirmative action program at a Kaiser Aluminum plant did not violate the Civil Rights Act even though black employees were given some preferential job opportunities over white employees with more seniority: the Court declared the legality of "private, voluntary, race-conscious affirmative action plans."[25]

The right of employees to receive equal pay for work of *comparable* value is emerging as an employee rights issue of the 1980s. By strict interpretation, it is not necessarily a male-female issue; yet job categories that are considered to be underpaid, according to job value assessment methods used in lieu of the usual market rate, indicate that traditionally female jobs command a lower rate than complementary jobs typically held by male employees. Considered an unacceptable workplace inequity by some unions, AFSCME and other public sector unions are beginning to challenge this alleged sex discrimination in the courts. Insert 9.F illustrates AFSCME's most successful endeavor, to date, in this area. Taking their cue from the results of the AFSCME/Washington State case, Minnesota, New Mexico, and Idaho have appropriated monies to rectify sex-based wage discrimination policies existing in their government job positions; meanwhile, a larger number of states have commissioned studies of the issue of comparable worth.[26]

In a 1984 decision, which some considered a retrenchment from previous decisions related to affirmative action, the Supreme Court upheld the long-standing labor tradition of "last hired, first fired" in a case concerning layoffs of Memphis, Tennessee, fire fighters. The start of this Memphis controversy began in 1980 when black fire fighters and city officials formally agreed on an affirmative action hiring plan to increase the number of future black fire fighters. By 1981 the Memphis fire depart-

Insert 9.F

COMPARABLE WORTH: A $320 BILLION CONCEPT?

The concept of *comparable worth,* also known as *pay equity,* refers to the payment of equal wages for jobs of comparable value. The "going rate in the marketplace" method for valuing jobs would, under the comparable worth concept, be replaced by a point system to measure the degree to which a job requires a specific level of worker skills, effort, responsibility and to weigh, to some degree, the surrounding working conditions. By itself, the concept is quite controversial and becomes even more highly charged when the issue of unequal pay due to sex bias is factored in. Providing a backdrop for the 1983 landmark comparable worth case involving AFSCME and the State of Washington are some arguable facts relevant to male-female pay rates.

- Women have, since 1950, earned less than $0.70 for every $1.00 earned by men.
- Domination by women in a given job category is a strong indicator of a relatively lower pay scale for those jobs (about $42 per year less in wages for each additional percentage point of women employed in that category).
- At least half the male-female wage gap cannot be explained by anything but sex discrimination, according to the National Academy of Sciences.
- A nationwide switch from paying the "going rate" to payment according to the comparable worth rate would cost approximately $320 billion and increase inflation by 10 percent.
- The value or worth of jobs cannot be determined by scientific methods. Hierarchies of job worth are always, at least in part, a reflection of values — National Academy of Sciences.

AFSCME used a 1974 job evaluation study, which measured the worth of various state jobs using the four previously mentioned criteria, as a cornerstone in its case against Washington State. Overall, the independent study concluded that job categories employing a majority of women paid 20 to 30 percent less than male-dominated job categories receiving the same number of "value points."

In its defense, Washington State argued that it paid its employees wage rates equivalent to what they would have received in the private sector. In support of Washington State, White House policy development analyst Peter Germanis remarked, "If women prefer nursing to tree trimming, resulting in an oversupply of nurses relative to tree trimmers and a relatively low wage, . . . that does not mean that employers are responsible and should be penalized."

AFSCME, on the other hand, argued that the state had practiced wage discrimination in violation of the federal civil rights law and the state law. Union lawyers alleged that the state discriminated against women by setting wage rates for traditionally "female" job categories far below the actual value of the job and cited the study as proof that sexual discrimination existed. Denying the acceptability of the market rate, pay equity advocates claim that the traditional system has merely institutionalized the pay bias against women; therefore, the more objective comparable worth point system should be used.

After hearing both sides, U.S. District Court Judge Jack E. Tanner held that the State had violated federal laws by "direct, overt and institutionalized discrimination" that was "intentional" and is "continuing now." Winn Newman, AFSCME attorney, predicted, "This decision could well break the back of sex-based discrimination and should stimulate an avalanche of private litigation on behalf of the victims of discrimination."

Meanwhile, estimates of the additional monies needed by Washington State to pay back wages for some female employees and raise the wage rates in the "female" job categories range from $400 million to $1 billion. The case is under appeal and expected to wind up in the Supreme Court, where justices there may find themselves making a $320 billion decision.

SOURCE: Tamar Lewin, "A New Push To Raise Women's Pay," *New York Times,* January 1, 1984 p. F15; Marilyn Marks, "State Legislators, Judges and Now Congress Examining Comparable Worth," *National Journal,* September 8, 1984, p. 1666; Harry Bacas, "Measuring the Value of Work," *Nation's Business,* June 1984, p. 32; Jim Drinkhall, "Washington Ordered to Start Payments in Suit," *Wall Street Journal,* December 15, 1983, p. 4; Jay Mathews, "State Ordered to Increase Women's Pay," *Washington Post,* December 15, 1983, p. A2.

ment was facing a dilemma concerning which fire fighters to lay off. Some black fire fighters felt that adhering to the traditional application of seniority as the determining factor in layoffs violated the agreed-upon affirmative action decree, whereas the fire fighters' union maintained that their labor contract required the use of the seniority system in this situation.

After hearing both viewpoints, a U.S. district court issued an injunction to stop fire fighter layoffs that were based solely on seniority; the court held that this criterion violated the earlier affirmative action plan, as black fire fighters were disproportionately represented in the "last hired" category. The case was further appealed, and finally in a 6-to-3 decision the Supreme Court upheld the union's position and issued the following excerpted majority and minority opinions:

As our cases have made clear . . . Title VII protects bona
fide seniority systems and it is inappropriate to deny an
innocent employee the benefits of his seniority in order to
provide a remedy in a pattern or practice suit such as this.[27]
[Majority opinion]

The power of the District Court to enter further orders to
effectuate the purposes of the [affirmative action hiring
plan] was part of the agreed remedy. The parties negotiated for this and it is the obligation of the courts to give it
meaning.[28] [Dissenting opinion]

Employee rights have also been provided in the administration of private
pension and welfare systems; individuals have statutory rights to pension
information and knowledge about administrative decisions and have the
right to enforce these powers in court. In addition virtually all major pieces
of health and safety legislation — clean air and clean water acts, coal mine
safety and industrial health laws — provide protection from reprisal for
the employee who cooperates with a federal agency in the investigation of
a possible company violation of the law. An individual can sue his or her
employer for taking punitive actions because the employee provided information to the regulatory agency.

These are unprecedented pieces of legislation that directly limit employer actions toward employees, rather than work indirectly to legitimize
an institutional structure, such as a union, to negotiate employer-employee
relationships. Perhaps this more direct government role has been a result
of the social importance of the issues that have arisen, the difficulty of
envisioning private mediating institutions in these areas, and a perceived
sense of urgency in guaranteeing specific rights.

Public Support for Employee Rights

Public interest appears to be mounting to address additional issues of employee rights. Observers ask why the same civil liberties people enjoy in
their roles as private citizens must be left at the plant gate or the office
door.[29] One difficult issue in this area concerns the employee's duty of loyalty versus the employee's freedom of speech. Determining when an employee should publicly disclose information that may show harm to consumers, employees, or the public involves difficult questions: Should the
corporation be given a chance to correct the problem before public disclosure? Under what circumstances should managers apply reprisals to persons who are not strictly loyal? Do individuals need protection for actions
of conscience? Another issue poses the employee's freedom from invasion
of privacy against the employer's need for job-related information and
right to maintain security and control. Insert 9.G presents employee and

Insert 9.G

ATTITUDES TOWARD PRIVACY

In late 1978 Sentry Insurance Company commissioned a national survey of attitudes toward privacy, including a representative cross section of American adults and a sample of business employers, such as corporate personnel officers. The following are answers of these groups on a series of questions about privacy in the employer-employee relationship in which a fair degree of disagreement was expressed.

	Percentage Responding Yes	
	Employees (612)	**Employers (200)**
A. Should it be illegal?		
Listening in on conversations of employees to find out what they think about their supervisors and managers		
Should be forbidden	84	70
Should not be forbidden	14	28
Not sure	2	3
Installing closed-circuit television to obtain continuous checks on how fast workers perform		
Should be forbidden	69	45
Should not be forbidden	27	51
Not sure	4	4
Asking a job applicant to take a psychological test		
Should be forbidden	50	25
Should not be forbidden	40	69
Not sure	10	7
B. Should employees have a right of access?		
To supervisor's reports as to whether the employee is suitable for promotion		
Should have right	88	74
Should not have right	9	26
Not sure	4	1

Insert 9.G   continued

	Percentage Responding Yes	
	Employees (612)	**Employers (200)**
To the personal notes a supervisor keeps about the employee's performance		
Should have right	65	46
Should not have right	31	53
Not sure	4	2
C. Should there be a law?		
Should employers decide what rights employees have regarding access to their personnel files or should a law be passed to specify these rights?		
A law should be passed	70	33
Left to employers	23	64
Not sure	7	3

SOURCE: Louis Harris and Associates, Inc., and Alan F. Westin, *The Dimensions of Privacy: A National Opinion Research Survey of Attitudes toward Privacy* (Stevens Point, Wisc.: Sentry Insurance, 1979), pp. 35–41. Used with permission.

employer views on several subjects pertaining to employee privacy. The survey results below show that opinions vary substantially on these issues.

While seeking to maintain a delicate balance of these requirements between employee and employer interests, the apparent directions of public sentiment and state and federal legislative action appear to be moving toward broader definitions of individual rights. Alan Westin of the Educational Fund for Individual Rights draws the following conclusion from a survey of state legislation concerning employee rights:

> In the past few years, eight states have enacted employee-right-of-access and confidentiality laws for personnel records, and bills are currently pending in a dozen other states. Twenty states have passed laws forbidding the use of the polygraph as a condition of employment, and four states also cover the use of psychological stress evaluators.

> Since 1978, over 20 states have enacted laws forbidding
> employers to fire employees for engaging in various kinds
> of civic and political activities, or claiming various kinds of
> employee benefits or rights. Six states now require employ-
> ers to give employees access to information about hazard-
> ous substances used in the workplace. . . . Such state legis-
> lation actions are politically popular, have been designed to
> be relatively low in regulatory duties and administrative
> costs, and are therefore likely to continue despite the "no
> new regulations" stance from Washington.[30]

Further expanding state policy in the employee rights arena, Connecticut
prohibited the termination of private sector employees in 1983 — if their
dismissal stemmed from an exercise of their right to free speech.[31] As of
1984 five states have passed Whistle Blower Protection laws, allowing employees fired for reporting alleged illegal conduct to public authorities to
bring a court action for unjust discharge.[32]

Changing Views of the Courts

The judicial system is another source of change in the employer-employee
relationship. Common law, written and administered on the state level,
largely determines the rights of employees and employers. While some
areas of employee relations have been subject to legislative action — collective bargaining, nondiscrimination, pension rights, and cooperation with
regulatory agencies — all other areas, which are numerous, are covered by
the principles that have evolved over time from the judicial decisions in
hundreds of specific cases.

Common law concerning the conditions of employer termination is
changing. Historically the state courts have applied a concept of "mutuality
of obligation" in which either employee or employer is free to terminate
the employment relationship. In the absence of a written contract, the
courts have accepted the employment relationship as an entirely private
matter and have declined to review or set conditions on the employer's
motives in discharging an employee. This historical common law position
has been referred to as the "employment-at-will" doctrine.

Recently, attention has been drawn to "unjust" dismissal and the lack
of protection or remedies available to most of the private sector work force.
Public sentiment appears to run heavily in favor of reinstatement for individuals who have lost their jobs because of refusal to record customer
telephone calls secretly, because of protests about a new product's safety
defects, or because of unwillingness to falsely declare oneself unavailable
for jury duty.[33] Since more than 70 percent of the private nonagricultural
labor force, or 63 million persons, is not covered by collective bargaining
agreements, the magnitude of this issue might take on substantial dimen-

sions. One researcher estimates that each year a minimum of 6,000 to 7,500 nonunion employees are discharged who would have been found to be discharged unfairly if their cases had been arbitrated, and another 300,000 discipline and discharge cases would be resolved through union grievance procedures if they would have been available to the whole work force.[34] At least one observer emphatically calls for a constitutional amendment to prohibit unjust dismissal.[35]

The state courts appear to be moving away from an employment-at-will doctrine and may be endorsing the concept of "wrongful discharge" more frequently. In a landmark case in New Hampshire in 1974, the state supreme court found that a termination motivated by employer "bad faith or malice or based on retaliation is not in the best interest of the economic system or the public good and constitutes a breach of the employment contract."[36] In his recent survey of employee due process protections, Alan Westin states that "fourteen of the 50 states now reject the termination-at-will doctrine, and will examine discharges to see if the judges believe those violate 'public policy.' Seven other states say that they may swing from the older rule."[37] Westin cites several specific cases in which state courts have found employers subject to legal action by employees for wrongful discharge:

- A West Virginia bank employee who attempted to force his employer to comply with consumer credit laws;
- An employee in California who allegedly refused to participate in a price-fixing scheme for retail gas prices; and
- An employee in New York who was found to be discharged in order to deprive him of his pension benefits.[38]

In each of these cases the court found violation of a public interest or public policy.

Finally, the state courts appear to be increasingly receptive to relying upon company personnel documents as statements of the employee relationship. Stated policies or procedures to be followed in discharging an employee, or even verbal assurances that employees will be retained as long as they do their jobs, may be taken as a right to continued employment in the absence of just cause for dismissal.[39] In a 1980 case the Michigan Supreme Court explicitly referred to an employee handbook as a form of employer-employee contract and stated that the court "could see no reason why an employment contract which does not have a definite term cannot provide job security" for the involved employee.[40]

While court decisions of this nature have been evolving slowly and erratically, the courts are taking a heightened interest in the relationship between employment policies and public policy/interest. Another recent, albeit weak, movement has been toward the development of state and/or federal statutes requiring employers to dismiss employees *only* for just cause, subject to certain limitations such as an employee probationary period where the employer would not be held accountable for demonstrating that the dismissal was for just cause. These trends have led one legal observer to conclude that

> employers would be well advised to examine their policies and procedures for terminating employees so as to guard against arbitrary, malicious, and unfair termination. Although subjecting an employer to liability for an improper termination may do violence to traditional notions of contract law, such a development is taking place and it should be considered in defining the employment relationship.[41]

THE ROLE OF ORGANIZATIONAL DUE PROCESS

The direction that society appears to be taking in the area of employee rights implies that organizations will be called upon to clarify policies with respect to internal dissent, privacy, and termination. If a corporation seeks to attract and retain top-level personnel, or if it seeks to minimize litigation and complaints to regulatory agencies, then policy definition and control in these areas will be increasingly important.

Due process is a shorthand term, perhaps overly legalistic for the employment context, that has come to represent fair procedures in dealing with employees in general and with employee rights issues in particular. While procedural due process has very specific elements — timely notice of charges, right of cross-examination, right to counsel, and the like — in the context of criminal law, it signifies a serious effort to provide fair hearing and appeal procedures to an employee who feels victimized by a wrongful supervisory action.

Insert 9.H presents a statement by Peter Drucker on the importance of jobs and the emergence of "job rights" in Western industrialized nations today. If this is a valid trend, employers appear to be faced with two choices: (1) to wait until the public sector enacts job protection laws that make personnel reductions (and therefore expansions) expensive and risky or (2) to develop policies and procedures to deal internally with human and personnel issues resulting from business plans and activities. Drucker succinctly states the nature and importance of due process and argues that the "job as property" is compatible with capitalism and the market system: "It may thus be the effective alternative to the 'state capitalism' of the totalitarians which, under the name of 'communism,' makes government into absolute tyranny, and supresses both freedom and rationality."[42]

Due Process as an Administration System

The design of due process procedures in organizations is far from an established and stable aspect of management knowledge and managerial practice; at the same time, it is an area of substantial interest and experimentation. Let us begin with the description of one person who apparently successfully played the role of corporate ombudsman.

For two and half years Frederica Dunn was ombudsman in the Aircraft Engine Group at General Electric, reporting to the executive in charge of this business sector.[43] Her job description consisted of (1) reviewing and improving procedures for handling complaints, (2) improving management-employer communication so as to reduce complaints based on policy misunderstanding, (3) seeking reversal of unfair decisions, and

---

Insert 9.H

EMERGENT JOB RIGHTS AND CORPORATE POLICIES [QUOTATION]

In modern developed societies . . . the overwhelming majority of the people in the labor force are employees of "organizations" — in the U.S. the figure is 93% — and the "means of production" is therefore the job. . . . Today the job is the employee's means of access to social status, to personal opportunity, to achievement and to power.

For the great majority in the developed countries today, the job is also the one avenue of access to personal property. Pension claims are by far the most valuable assets of employees over 50, more valuable, indeed, than all his other assets taken together — his share in his house, his savings, his automobile and so on. And the pension claim is, of course, a direct outgrowth of the job, indeed part of the job. . . .

How can modern economies cope with the emergence of job property rights and still maintain the flexibility and social mobility necessary for adapting quickly to changes? At the very least, employing organizations will have to recognize that jobs have some of the characteristics of property rights and cannot therefore be diminished or taken away without due process. Hiring, firing, promotion and demotion must be subject to pre-established, objective, public criteria. And there has to be a review, a pre-established right to appeal to a higher judge in all actions affecting rights in and to the job.

SOURCE: Peter F. Drucker, "The Job as Property Right," *Wall Street Journal,* March 4, 1980, p. 24.

(4) offering an impartial outlet for employee grievances. The ombudsman position in general is an alternate and more direct means to the chain of command for seeking redress of an administrative action.

But what functions did Dunn find herself actually providing in this position? Primary was the correction of situations caused by management oversight or poor communication: the inappropriate denial of a medical insurance claim or confusion about one's responsibilities after an organizational change. Another function was the creation of greater supervisory accountability for understanding and applying company policy. "The mere existence of the ombudsman," Dunn wrote, "encourages managers to be sure they can justify their actions." A final role the office played was to identify systemic employee relations problems — deficient supervisory skills, inadequate performance appraisal, lack of disclosing internal promotional opportunities — where supervisory capabilities were deficient or organizational procedures were inconsistent. Many cases sharing a common origin would identify a policy problem for the organization and spur concerted management effort to improve the area.

Other literature on organizational due process reinforces some of these points and adds a few more. A comparative study of nonexempt, nonunion, fair hearing and appeal procedures in three urban hospitals identified problem correction, education-prevention, and policy development as benefits from due process, although the hospitals relied on procedures other than the establishing of an ombudsman.[44] One hospital was particularly receptive to the use of complaints for general hospital improvement. For example, one nurse's complaint of salary inequity led to an examination, evaluation, and change of salary for a whole class of nurses. While the other two hospitals limited the issues that could be raised in the system or that could be pursued to higher levels in the procedures, this hospital placed no limits on the employee's right to appeal.

Limitations of Organizational Due Process

It is also important to recognize the limitations of due process systems and the importance of having conflict resolution contribute to the basic economic mission of the corporation. Frederica Dunn states explicitly that an ombudsman cannot please people whose idea of justice is having their own way, change managerial styles, or replace the basic need for an honest employer-employee relationship.[45] One advocate of corporate due process, David Ewing, has outlined the limits to the employee rights movement, indicating ways in which due process systems should not function. An employer's policies and appeal system should adhere to the following principles:

• An individual should not be able to divulge information that must be confidential to do the organization's job efficiently;

- No individual has the privilege to make personal slurs and accusations;
- No employee is permitted to make public statements that fail to reflect a conviction of wrongdoing;
- No employee has grounds for objection to supervisory actions in everyday work decisions that do not pertain to legal or moral management reponsibilities; and
- No employee can have unsatisfactory work performance override free speech — one cannot hide poor performance behind public criticism.[46]

These limits seek to ensure fairness to the employer as well as to the employee. They underscore the legitimacy of the objectives and authority of the employer. Fair process procedures seek to channel problems into open, constructive forums and should support the disciplinary actions of a good supervisor while making evident the errors of a poor one. A valid interpretation of the employee rights movement envisions the fulfillment of institutional as well as individual values.

Managerial Responses to Problems of Conscience

Another possible area of organizational contribution of due process lies in the ability to deal with ethical concerns of employees. In this area a corporate action, such as investment in a country seriously violating human rights, may not affect the direct work environment of the employee as much as the employee's moral self-image and general relationship with the employer. Citicorp is one corporation that has given considerable thought and effort to this problem. A variety of programs and procedures are available to employees of this company for airing problems and gaining a hearing for redress of specific complaints. With the recognition that mechanisms for handling conventional job-related problems may not be adequate to respond to ethical issues, special procedures have been developed to deal with problems in this area. In the words of William Spencer, Citicorp president, "The employer and employee who differ on the morality of a business practice or the social benefit of a particular transaction are hard pressed to find a mutually acceptable yardstick to measure the matter. . . . An 'official arbiter' is needed to offer informed guidance on what is or is not good corporate conduct in particular cases."[47]

The specifics of the Citicorp procedures, described in Insert 9.I, are less significant than the fact that the corporation has developed a responsive and integrative device as a matter of policy rather than ad hoc movement from problem to problem. The possible variations for due process development — open door policies, use of arbitrators, peer review committees, management committees, ombudsmen — are nearly endless; the real questions are the intent and function management wants any system to serve. Only when management's commitment, the desired functions of an appeal system, and the types of conflicts to be addressed are clarified should the question of system development be approached.

Insert 9.I

PROTECTING AND PROCESSING EMPLOYEE ETHICAL DISSENT AT CITICORP

Since 1975 at Citicorp all issues of conscience or employee ethical concern have been referred to a five-member committee called the "committee on Good Corporate Practice." Four of its members are part of a larger top management policy group that directs the worldwide activities of the corporation. All members are believed to have enough visibility, credibility, and clout to make their decisions stick.

Any employee questions about or conflicts with corporate actions can be taken directly to the chairman of the committee or are referred to this individual by others. No restrictions are placed on the right to question, and the issue may or may not personally affect the employee. The process of reviewing an employee challenge is managed by the committee chairperson, who may review the problem with the committee, conduct a personal investigation, or request an investigation and evaluation by the head of personnel. The head of personnel may, after investigation, close the issue, refer it to other relevant officers for review, or present findings and recommendations back to the committee chair. The committee chair again decides whether to accept the recommendation, close the issue, extend the investigation, or bring the matter before the whole committee. When convened, the committee reviews the issue at hand and arrives at a decision.

Beyond dealing with particular cases, the committee meets regularly to evaluate present policies, to review conflict-of-interest problems, and to develop new corporate policies. It reports on its activities to the corporate board of directors annually.

SOURCE: William I. Spencer, "Recognizing Individual Rights Is Good Business" (Speech presented to the Third National Seminar on Individual Rights in the Corporation, Washington, D.C., June 12, 1980), pp. 8–12.

IN CONCLUSION: GOVERNANCE AS FIRM INTEGRATION AND ADAPTATION

This chapter has emphasized the need for employer-employee integration — a need arising from a changing economy and labor force structure and from the fresh expression of traditional American individualism in employee relations. Industrialization has historically created recurring pressures on the employer-employee relationship. This chapter has examined available structures — unions, QWL projects, employee ownership, and due process procedures — for their actual and potential contributions to fostering essential integration of employee needs and employer goals. Because each of these structures and mechanisms implies a redistribution of corporate power in particular ways, the issues are bascially questions of workplace governance.

In addition to this emphasis on governance and integration, the topic of corporate responsiveness to change, or the firm's adaptive ability, has been a subtheme in these discussions. A strong case can be made that governance through a wider base and more numerous forms of employee participation creates a greater receptivity and responsiveness to change on the part of organization members and opens more channels of information, offering early identification and response to internal or external threats. As a firm's environment becomes more complex and subject to rapid and unpredictable change, its best strategy for adaptation is to decentralize — place decision making closer to the sources of change and develop feedback mechanisms that initiate clear signals when the firm is deviating from its intended course. QWL projects, employee ownership, and due process mechanisms of the type described by Dunn and Spencer may have the potential for fulfilling exactly this latter adaptive function.

While "integration" and "adaptation" are abstract concepts and relatively unfamiliar in the day-to-day corporate world of work, they are significant long-term social issues and represent future questions of public policy and enterprise competitiveness. The employee relations area is one example of how a managerial perspective can address future relations among business, society, and government in a context other than solely by identifying the virtues or evils inherent in government regulation. The achievement of a general and long-term view may determine the degree of private, voluntary responsiveness in this area and may, ultimately, influence the degree of governmentally-ensured employee protection.

DISCUSSION QUESTIONS

1. How do unions, QWL projects, employee-owned firms, and due process procedures offer potential for employee-firm integration? In your view, which of these has the highest potential for contributing to corporations? What are the limitations of each?
2. How would you characterize the employee rights movement? Is this a social development that is likely to grow or fade in significance in the coming years?
3. What is the task of employee governance in today's large corporations? What are some lessons for management of developments in employee relationships throughout this century?

NOTES

1. Harry H. Wellington, *Labor and the Legal Process* (New Haven, Conn.: Yale University Press, 1968), pp. 27–28.

2. Karl Marx and Friedrich Engels, *The Communist Manifesto* (New York: Monthly Review Press, 1964).

3. Wellington, *Labor and the Legal Process*, p. 27.

4. Ibid., pp. 11, 12.

5. Milton Derber, *The American Idea of Industrial Democracy, 1865–1965* (Urbana: University of Illinois Press, 1970), p. 106.

6. Robert Green McCloskey, *American Conservatism in the Age of Enterprise* (Cambridge: Harvard University Press, 1951), pp. 146–53.

7. Derber, *The American Idea*, pp. 87–91.

8. Thomas Kennedy, "Freedom to Strike Is In the Public Interest," *Harvard Business Review*, July-August 1970, pp. 56–57.

9. Philip Selznick, *Law, Society and Industrial Justice* (New York: Russell Sage Foundation, 1969), pp. 154–78.

10. Ibid.

11. "Innovative Labor Accord Is Expected at GM," *Wall Street Journal*, December 14, 1984, p. 3.

12. Robert H. Guest, "Quality of Work Life — Learning from Tarrytown," *Harvard Business Review*, July-August 1979, pp. 76–77.

13. Richard Walton, "How to Counter Alienation in the Plant," *Harvard Business Review*, November-December 1972, p. 72.

14. Eric L. Trist, "Collaboration in Work Settings: A Personal Perspective," *Journal of Applied Behavioral Science* 13 (1977): 272.

15. U.S., Department of Health, Education, and Welfare, *Work in America*, Report of a Special Task Force to the Secretary of Health, Education, and Welfare (Washington, D.C.: HEW December 1972), p. 84.

16. "Stonewalling Plant Democracy," *Business Week*, March 28, 1977, p. 78.

17. Darwin Gillett, "Better QC's: A Need for More Manager Action," *Management Review*, January 1983, p. 24.

18. Merle O'Donnell and Robert J. O'Donnell, "Quality Circles — The Latest Fad or a Real Winner?" *Business Horizons*, May 15, 1984, p. 138.

19. Ibid.

20. Karl Freiden, *Workplace Democracy and Productivity* (Washington, D.C.: National Center for Economic Alternatives, 1980), p. 7.

21. William Baldwin, "The Myths of Employee Ownership," *Forbes*, April 23, 1984 p. 108.

22. Michael Conte and Arnold S. Tannenbaum, "Employee-Owned Companies: Is the Difference Measurable?" *Monthly Labor Review*, July 1978, pp. 23–28.

23. Freiden, *Workplace*, p. 9.

24. *Regents of the University of California* v. *Allan Bakke*, 438 U.S. 265 (1978).

25. *United Steel Workers of America and Kaiser Aluminum & Chemical Corporation* v. *Brian F. Weber*, 443 U.S. 193 (1979).

26. Daniel Seligman, "Pay Equity Is a Bad Idea," *Fortune*, May 15, 1984, p. 138.

27. "Excerpts from the Supreme Court Decision in the Seniority Case," *New York Times*, June 13, 1984, p. B12.

28. Ibid.

29. David Ewing, "Winning Freedom on the Job: From Assembly Line to Executive Suite," *Civil Liberties Review* 3 (July-August 1977): 8.

30. Alan F. Westin, Chairman's address presented to the Third National Seminar on Individual Rights in the Corporation, Washington, D.C., June 12, 1980.

31. Alan L. Otten, "States Begin to Protect Employees Who Blow Whistle on Their Firms," *Wall Street Journal,* December 31, 1984, p. 11.

32. Ibid.

33. David Ewing, "What Business Thinks of Employee Rights," *Harvard Business Review,* September-October 1977, pp. 81–94.

34. Cornelius I. Peck, "Unjust Discharges from Employment: A Necessary Change in the Law," *Ohio State Law Journal* 40 (1979): 10.

35. Clyde W. Summers, "Protecting All Employees against Unjust Dismissal." *Harvard Business Review,* January-February 1980, pp. 132–39.

36. John D. Feerick, "Erosion of Rule on Employment at Will," *New York Law Journal,* November 7, 1980, pp. 1, 4.

37. Westin, Chairman's address.

38. Ibid.

39. Feerick, "Erosion," p. 4.

40. Wesley M. Wilson, *The Employment At Will Issue; Know Your Job Rights,* (Homewood, Illinois: Dow Jones-Irwin, 1976), p. 58.

41. Feerick, "Erosion," p. 4.

42. Peter F. Drucker, "The Job as Property Right," *Wall Street Journal,* March 4, 1980, p. 24.

43. Frederica H. Dunn, "The View from the Ombudsman's Chair," *New York Times,* May 2, 1976, p. C17.

44. John D. Aram and Paul F. Salipante, Jr., "Internal Mechanisms for Resolving EEO Complaints," (Speech presented to the Third National Seminar on Individual Rights in the Corporation, Washington, D.C., June 12, 1980).

45. Dunn, "The View," p. 17.

46. David Ewing, *Freedom inside the Organization: Bringing Civil Liberties to the Workplace* (New York: McGraw-Hill, 1977), pp. 108–10.

47. William I. Spencer, "Recognizing Individual Rights Is Good Business" (Speech presented to the Third National Seminar on Individual Rights in the Corporation, Washington, D.C., June 12, 1980), pp. 4, 8.

Quality of Work Life
Learning From Tarrytown

INTRODUCTION

This is the story of the General Motors (GM) car assembly plant at Tarry-town, New York. In 1970 the plant was known as having one of the poorest labor relations and production records in GM. In seven years the plant turned around to become one of the company's better run sites.

Born out of frustration and desperation, but with a mutual commitment by management and the union to change old ways of dealing with the workers on the shop floor, a quality of work life (QWL) program developed at Tarrytown. "Quality of work life" is a generic phrase that covers a person's feelings about every dimension of work including economic rewards and benefits, security, working conditions, organizational and interpersonal relationships, and its intrinsic meaning in a person's life. A distinguishing characteristic of the process is that its goals are not simply extrinsic, focusing on the improvement of productivity and efficiency per se; they are also intrinsic, regarding what the worker sees as self-fulfilling and self-enhancing ends in themseves.

TARRYTOWN — THE BAD OLD DAYS

In the late 1960s and early 1970s, the Tarrytown plant suffered from much absenteeism and labor turnover. Operating costs were high. Frustration, fear, and mistrust characterized the relationship between management and labor. At certain times, as many as 2,000 labor grievances were on the docket. As one manager puts it, "Management was always in a defensive posture. We were instructed to go by the book, and we played by the book.

Reprinted by permission of *The Harvard Business Review,* "Quality of Work Life — Learning from Tarrytown" by Robert H. Guest (July-August 1979). Copyright © 1979 by the President and Fellows of Harvard College; all rights reserved.

The way we solved problems was to use our authority and impose discipline." The plant general superintendent acknowledges in restrospect, "For reasons we thought valid, we were very secretive in letting the union and the workers know about changes to be introduced or new programs coming down the pike."

Union officers and committeemen battled constantly with management. As one union officer describes it, "We were always trying to solve yesterday's problems. There was no trust and everybody was putting out fires. The company's attitude was to employ a stupid robot with hands and no face." The union committee chairman describes the situation the way he saw it: "When I walked in each morning I was out to get the personnel director, the committeeman was shooting for the foreman, and the zone committeeman was shooting for the general foreman. Everytime a foreman notified a worker that there would be a job change, it resulted in an instant '78 [work standards grievance]. It was not unusual to have a hundred '78s hanging fire, more than 300 discipline cases, and many others."

Workers were mad at everyone. They disliked the job itself and the inexorable movement of the high-speed line — 56 cars per hour, a minute and a half per operation per defined space. One worker remembers it well, "Finish one job, and you always had another stare you in the face." Conditions were dirty, crowded, and often noisy. Employees saw their foreman as insensitive dictators, whose operating principle was "If you can't do the job like I tell you, get out."

Warnings, disciplinary layoffs, and firings were commonplace. Not only did the workers view the company as an impersonal bureaucratic machine — "They number the parts and they number you" — but also they saw the union itself as a source of frustration — "The committeeman often wrote up a grievance but, because he was so busy putting out fires, he didn't tell the worker how or whether the grievance was settled. In his frustration, the worker would take it out on the foreman, the committeeman, and the job itself."

In the words of both union and management representatives, during this period "Tarrytown was a mess."

Beginnings of Change

Because of the high labor turnover, the plant was hiring a large number of young people. The late 1960s was the time of the youth counterculture revolution. It was a time when respect for authority was being questioned. According to the plant manager, "It was during this time that the young people in the plant were demanding some kind of change. They didn't want to work in this kind of environment. The union didn't have much control over them, and they certainly were not interested in taking orders from a dictatorial management."

In April 1971 Tarrytown faced a serious threat. The plant manager saw the need for change and also an opportunity. He approached some of the key union officers who, though traditionally suspicious of management overtures, listened to him. The union officers remember liking what they heard, "This manager indicated that he wanted to create a philosophy of management different from what had gone on before. He felt there was a better way of doing things."

The plant manager suggested that if the union was willing to do its part, he would put pressure on his own management people to change their ways. The tough chairman of the grievance committee observed later that "this guy showed right off he had a quality of work life attitude — we didn't call it that at that time — inside him. He was determined that this attitude should carry right down to the foremen, and allow the men on the line to be men."

The company decided to stop assembling trucks at Tarrytown and to shuffle the entire layout around. Two departments, Hard Trim and Soft Trim, were to be moved to a renovated area of the former truck line.

At first the changes were introduced in the usual way. Manufacturing and industrial engineers and technical specialists designed the new layout, developed the charts and blueprints, and planned every move. They then presented their proposals to the supervisors. Two of the production supervisors in Hard Trim, sensing that top plant management was looking for new approaches, asked a question that was to have a profound effect on events to follow: "Why not ask the workers themselves to get involved in the move? They are experts in their own right. They know as much about trim operations as anyone else."

The supervisors of the two trim departments insisted not only that plans *not* be hidden from the workers but also that the latter would have a say in the setup of jobs. Charts and diagrams of the facilities, conveyors, benches, and materials storage areas were drawn up for the workers to look at. Lists were made of the work stations and the personnel to man them. The supervisors were impressed by the outpouring of ideas: "We found they did know a lot about their own operations. They made hundreds of suggestions and we adopted many of them."

Here was a new concept. The training director observes, "Although it affected only one area of the plant, this was the first time management was communicating with the union and the workers on a challenge for solving *future* problems and not the usual situation of doing something, waiting for a reaction, then putting out the fires later." The union echoes the same point: "This demonstrated how important it is to solve problems before they explode. If not solved, then you get the men riled up against everything and everybody."

Moving the two departments was carried out successfully with remarkably few grievances. The plant easily made its production schedule deadlines. The next year saw the involvement of employees in the complete rearrangement of another major area of the plant, the Chassis Department. The following year a new car model was introduced at Tarrytown.

Labor-Management Agreement

In 1973 the UAW and GM negotiated a national agreement. In the contract was a brief "letter of agreement" signed by Irving Bluestone, vice-president for General Motors Department of the United Automobile Worker Union (UAW), and George Morris, head of industrial relations for GM. Both parties committed themselves to establishing formal mechanisms, at least at top levels, for exploring new ways of dealing with the quality of work life. This was the first time QWL was explicitly addressed in any major U.S. labor-management contract.

In the past, it had not been uncommon for strike action to be taken during contract negotiations. The manager and the union representatives asked themselves, "Isn't there a better way to do this, to open up some two-way communication, gain some trust?" The union president was quick to recognize "that it was no good to have a 'love-in' at the top between the union and management, especially the Personnel Department. We had to stick with our job as union officers. But things were so bad we figured 'what the hell, we have nothing to lose.'"

The negotiations were carried out in the background of another effort on management's part. Delmar Landon, director of organizational research and development at General Motors, had been independently promoting an organizational development effort for a number of years. These efforts were being carried out in many plants. Professionally trained communication facilitators had been meeting with supervisors and even some work groups to solve problems of interpersonal communcation.

What General Motors was attempting to do was like the organization development (OD) programs that were being started up in many industries and businesses in the United States. But, as with many such programs, there was virtually no union involvement. As the training director put it, "Under the influence of our plant manager, the OD program was having some influence among our managers and supervisors, but still this OD stuff was looked upon by many as a gimmick. It was called the 'happy people' program by those who did not understand it." And, of course, because it was not involved, the union was suspicious.

Nevertheless, a new atmosphere of trust between the union and the plant manager was beginning to emerge. Local negotiations were settled without a strike. There was at least a spark of hope that the Tarrytown mess could be cleaned up.

THE TESTING PERIOD

In April 1974, a professional consultant was brought in to involve supervisors and workers in joint training programs for problem solving. Management paid his fees. He talked at length with most of the union officers and committeemen, who report that "we were skeptical at first but we came to trust him."

The local union officials were somewhat suspicious about "another management trick." But after talking with Solidarity House (UAW's headquarters), they agreed to go along. Both parties at the local level discussed what should be done. Both knew it would be a critical test of the previous year's preliminary attempts to communicate with one another on a different plane. Also, as one union person says, "We came to realize the experiment would not happen overnight."

Management and the union each selected a coordinator to work with the consultant and with the supervisors, the union, and the workers. The consultant, with the union and the management coordinators, proposed a series of problem-solving training sessions to be held on Saturdays, for eight OD hours each day. Two supervisors and the committeemen in the Soft Trim Department talked it over with the workers, of whom 34 from two shifts volunteered for the training sessions that were to begin in late September 1974. Management agreed to pay for six hours of the training, and men volunteered their own time for the remaining two hours.

Top management was very impressed by the ideas being generated from the sessions and by the cooperation from the union. The regular repairmen were especially helpful. Not long after the program began, the workers began developing solutions to problems of water leaks, glass breakage, and molding damage.

Layoff Crisis

In November 1974, at the height of the OPEC oil crisis, disaster struck. General Motors shut down Tarrytown's second shift and laid off half the work force — 2,000 workers. Men on the second shift with high seniority "bumped" hundreds of workers on the first shift. To accommodate the new schedule, management had to rearrange jobs and work loads the entire length of the two miles of main conveyors, feeder conveyors, and work stations. A shock wave reverberated throughout the plant, not just among workers but supervisors as well. Some feared the convulsion would bring on an avalanche of '78s — work standards grievances — and all feared that the cutback was an early signal that Tarrytown was being targeted for permanent shutdown. After all, it was one of the oldest plants in General Motors and its past record of performance was not good.

However, the newly developing trust between management and the union had its effects. As the union president puts it, "Everyone got a decent transfer and there were surprisingly few grievances. We didn't get behind. We didn't have to catch up on a huge backlog."

In spite of the disruption of plant operations, the quality of work life team, the plant manager, and the union officials were determined not to give up. Reduced to a small group of 12 people during 1975, the team continued to work on water leaks and glass breakage problems. This group's success as well as that of some others convinced both parties that quality of work life had to continue despite a September 1975 deadline, after which management would no longer foot the bill on overtime.

During this period all parties had time to reflect on past successes as well as failures. The coordinators (one from the union and one from management) had learned a lesson. They had expected too much too soon: "We were frustrated at not seeing things move fast enough. We got in the trap of expecting 'instant QWL.' We thought that all you had to do was to design a package and sell it as you would sell a product."

Also, during this period, the grapevine was carrying a powerful message around the plant that something unusual was going on. The idea of involving workers in decisions spread, and by midyear the molding groups were redesigning and setting up their own jobs. Other departments followed later.

At this time everyone agreed that if this program were to be expanded on a larger scale, it would require more careful planning. In 1975 a policy group made up of the plant manager, the production manager, the personnel manager, the union's top officers, and the two QWL coordinators was formed. The program was structured so that both the union and management could have an advisory group to administer the system and to evaluate the ideas coming up from the problem-solving teams. Everyone agreed that participation was to be entirely voluntary. No one was to be ordered or assigned to any group. Coordinators and others talked with all of the workers in the two departments.

A survey of interest was taken among the 600 workers in the two volunteering departments; 95 percent of these workers said they wanted in. Because of the large number that wanted to attend, pairs of volunteers from the ranks of the union and management had to be trained as trainers. Toward the middle of the year, a modified program was set up involving 27 off-time hours of instructional work for the 570 people. Four trainers were selected and trained to conduct this program, two from the union and two from management.

A second crisis occurred when the production schedule was increased to a line speed of 60 cars per hour. Total daily output would not be enough to require a second shift to bring back all the laid-off workers. Instead, the company asked that 300 laid-off workers be brought in and that the plant operate on an overtime schedule. Ordinarily the union would object strongly to working overtime when there were still well over 1,000 members out on the street. "But," as the union president puts it, "we sold the membership on the idea of agreeing to overtime and the criticism was minimal. We told them the survival of the plant was at stake."

Full Capacity

Despite the upheavals at the plant, it seemed that the quality of work life program would survive. Then, a third blow was delivered. Just as 60 workers were completing their sessions, the company announced that Tarry-town was to return to a two-shift operation. For hundreds of those recalled to work, this was good news. Internally, however, it meant the line would have to go through the same musical chair game it had experienced 14 months earlier when the second shift was dropped.

Workers were shuffled around according to seniority and job classification. Shift preferences were granted according to length of service. With a faster line speed than before, the average worker had fewer operations to perform but those he did perform he had to do at a faster pace. In short, because of possible inequities in work loads, conditions were ripe for another wave of work standards grievances. Happily, the union and management were able to work out the work load problems with a minimum of formal grievances.

But again the small, partially developed QWL program had to be put on ice. The number of recalled workers and newly hired employees was too great, and turnover was too high among the latter for the program to continue as it had been. Capitalizing on the mutual trust that had been slowly building up between them, management and the union agreed to set up an orientation program for newly hired employees — and there were hundreds of them. Such a program was seen as an opportunity to expose new workers to some of the information about plant operations, management functions, the union's role, and so forth. At one point, the union even suggested that the orientation be done at the union hall, but the idea was dropped.

The orientation program was successful. Some reduction in the ratio of "quits" among the "new hires" was observed. The union president did feel that "we had set a new tone for the new employee and created a better atmosphere in the plant."

BRAVE NEW WORLD

Early the next year, 1977, Tarrytown made the "big commitment." The QWL effort was to be launched on a plantwide scale involving approximately 3,800 workers and supervisors. Charles Katko, vice-president for the division, and UAW's top official, Irving Bluestone, gave strong signals of support. The plant manager retired in April and was replaced by the production manager. The transition was an easy one because the new manager not only knew every dimension of the program but also had become convinced of its importance.

The policy committee and the quality of work life coordinators went to work. In the spring of 1977, all the top staff personnel, department heads, and production superintendents went through a series of orientation sessions with the coordinators. By June all middle managers and first-line supervisors (general foreman and foremen) were involved. Thus by the summer of 1977 more than 300 members of Tarrytown management knew about the QWL approach and about the plans for including 3,500 hourly employees. All union committeemen also went through the orientation sessions.

Also, during mid-1977, plans were under way to select and train those people who would eventually conduct the training sessions for the hourly employees. More than 250 workers expressed an interest in becoming trainers. After careful screening and interviewing, 11 were chosen. A similar process was carried out for supervisors, 11 of whom were subsequently selected as trainers, mostly from among foremen.

The 2 coordinators brought the 22 designated trainers together and exposed them to a variety of materials they would use in the training itself. The trainers conducted mock practice sessions that were videotaped so they could discuss their performance. The trainers also shared ideas on how to present information to the workers and on how to get workers to open up with their own ideas for changing their work environment. The latter is at the heart of the quality of work life concept.

The trainers themselves found excitement and challenge in the experience. People from the shop floor worked side by side with members of supervision as equals. At the end of the sessions, the trainers were brought together in the executive dining room for a wrap-up session. The coordinators report that "they were so charged up they were ready to conquer the world!"

Plantwide Program

On September 13, 1977, the program was launched. Each week, 25 different workers (or 50 in all from both shifts) reported to the training rooms on Tuesday, Wednesdays, and Thursdays for nine hours a day. Those taking the sessions had to be replaced at their work stations by substitutes. Given an average hourly wage rate of more than $7 per attendee and per replacement (for over 3,000 persons), one can begin to get an idea of the magnitude of the costs. Also, for the extra hour above eight hours, the trainees were paid overtime wages.

What was the substance of the sessions themselves? The trainee's time was allocated to learning three things: first, about the concept of QWL; second, about the plant and the functions of management and the union; third, about problem-solving skills important in effective involvement.

The presentation covered a variety of subjects presented in many forms with a heavy stress on participation by the class from the start. The work groups were given a general statement of what quality of work life was all about. The union trainer presented materials illustrating UAW Vice-President Bluestone's famous speech, and the management trainer presented a speech by GM's Landen stressing that hourly workers were the experts about their own jobs and had much to contribute.

The trainers used printed materials, diagrams, charts, and slides to describe products and model changes, how the plant was laid out, how the production system worked, and what the organizational structures of management and the union are. Time was spent covering safety matters, methods used to measure quality performance, efficiency, and so forth. The work groups were shown how and where they could get any information they wanted about their plant. Special films showed all parts of the plant with a particular worker "conducting the tour" for his part of the operation.

To develop effective problem-solving skills, the trainers presented simulated problems and then asked employees to go through a variety of experimental exercises. The training content enabled the workers to diagnose themselves, their own behavior, how they appeared in competitive situations, how they handled two-way communications, and how they solved problems. By the final day "the groups themselves are carrying the ball," as the trainers put it, "with a minimum of guidance and direction from the two trainers."

Trainers took notes on the ideas generated in the sessions and at the end handed out a questionnaire to each participant. The notes and questionnaires were systematically fed back to the union and management coordinators, who in turn brought the recommendations to the policy committee. The primary mode of feedback to their foremen and fellow workers was by the workers themselves out on the shop floor.

Continuing Effort

Seven weeks after the program began in September 1977, just over 350 workers (or 10 percent of the work force) had been through the training sessions. The program continued through 1978, and by mid-December more than 3,300 workers had taken part.

When all the employees had completed their sessions, the union and management immediately agreed to keep the system on a continuing basis. From late December 1978 through early February 1979, production operations at Tarrytown were closed down to prepare for the introduction of the all-new 1980X model. During the shutdown, a large number of workers were kept on to continue the process.

In preparation for the shift, managers and hourly personnel together evaluated hundreds of anticipated assembly processes. Workers made use of the enthusiasm and skills developed in the earlier problem sessions and talked directly with supervisors and technical people about the best ways of setting up various jobs on the line. What had been stimulated through a formal organized system of training and communication (for workers and supervisors alike) was now being "folded in" to the ongoing planning and implementation process on the floor itself.

In the early periods, the trainers were nervous in their new roles.

Few of them had ever had such an experience before. Many agreed that their impulse was to throw a lot of information at the worker trainee. The trainers found, however, that once the participants opened up, they "threw a lot at us." Although they understood intellectually that participation is the basic purpose of the QWL program, the trainers had to experience directly the outpouring of ideas, perceptions, and feelings of the participants to comprehend emotionally the dynamics of the involvement process.

But the trainers felt rewarded, too. They describe example after example of the workers' reactions once they let down their guard. One skeptical worker, for example, burst out after the second day, "Jesus Christ! You mean all this information about what's going on in the plant was available to us? Well, I'm going to use it." Another worker who had been scrapping with his foreman for years went directly to him after the sessions and said, "Listen, you and I have been butting our heads together for a long time. From now on I just want to be able to talk to you and have you talk to me." Another worker used his free relief time to drop in on new class sessions.

Other regular activities to keep management and the union informed about new developments parallel the training sessions. Currently, following the plant manager's regular staff meetings, the personnel director passes on critical information to the shop committee. The safety director meets weekly with each zone committeeman. Top union officials have monthly "rap sessions" with top management staff to discuss future developments, facility alterations, schedule changes, model changes, and other matters requiring advance planning. The chairman of Local 664 and his zone committeemen check in with the personnel director each morning at 7:00 A.M. and go over current or anticipated problems.

AFTER THE DUST SETTLES

What are the measurable results of quality of work life at Tarrytown? Neither the managers nor union representatives want to say much. They argue that to focus on production records or grievance counts "gets to be a numbers game" and is contrary to the original purpose or philosophy of the quality of work life efforts. After all, in launching the program, the Tarrytown plant made no firm promises of "bottom line" results to division executives or anyone else. Getting the process of worker involvement going was a primary goal with its own intrinsic rewards. The organizational benefits followed.

There are, however, some substantial results from the $1.6 million QWL program. The production manager says, for example, "From a strictly production point of view — efficiency and costs — this entire experience has been absolutely positive, and we can't begin to measure the savings that have taken place because of the hundreds of small problems that were solved on the shop floor before they accumulated into big problems."

Although not confirmed by management, the union claims that Tarrytown went from one of the poorest plants in its quality performance (inspection counts or dealer complaints) to one of the best among the 18 plants in the division. It reports that absenteeism went from 7.25 percent to between 2 and 3 percent. In December 1978, at the end of the training sessions, there were only 32 grievances on the docket. Seven years earlier there had been upward of 2,000 grievances filed. Such substantial changes can hardly be explained by chance.

Does this report on Tarrytown sound unreal or euphoric? Here are the comments of the most powerful union officer in the plant, the chairman of Local 664:

> I'm still skeptical of the whole thing but at least I no longer believe that what's going on is a "love-in" at Tarrytown. It's not a fancy gimmick to make people happy. And even though we have barely scratched the surface, I'm absolutely convinced we are on to something. We have a real and very different future. Those guys in the plant are beginning to participate and I mean really participate!

By May 1979 the Tarrytown plant, with the production of a radically new line of cars, had come through one of the most difficult times in its history. Considering all the complex technical difficulties, the changeover was successful. Production was up to projected line speed. The relationship among management, union, and the workers remained positive in spite of the unusual stress conditions generated by such a change.

As the production manager puts it, "Under these conditions, we used to fight the union, the worker, and the car itself. Now we've all joined together to fight the car." Not only were the hourly employees substantially involved in working out thousands of "bugs" in the operations, but plans were already under way to start up QWL orientation sessions with more than 400 new members hired to meet increased production requirements.

Tarrytown, in short, has proved to itself at least that QWL works.

DISCUSSION QUESTIONS

1. What do you feel are the essential conditions necessary for a successful QWL project? What barriers might you anticipate?
2. How would you evaluate the potential of QWL projects as a mechanism of employee-firm integration? What are its limitations? How important would QWL seem to be relative to other available mechanisms?
3. What do you think will be the ultimate utilization of QWL as a concept and as a program in American industry? Why?

John D. Aram

Affirmative Action
Touching the Nerves of Individualism and Equality in America

The civil rights movement of the early 1960s drew national attention to inequality of opportunity between blacks and whites in the United States in virtually all public and private institutions. Employment opportunities were identified as one particular area of race discrimination that, if equalized for blacks, could be a significant factor in breaking the vicious cycle involving poor education, low income, and inadequate housing and health care. To change long-standing and institutionalized employment practices toward equalized opportunity would be a mammoth undertaking and would involve a period of transition, perhaps quite long, in which established practices such as basing employment opportunities on previous job seniority might need to be altered. If providing remedies for past discrimination based on race required changing past practices, then some interests (and former expectations) of whites might suffer in the broader cause of social justice for blacks. Postponing or altering traditional employment reliance on seniority, for example, was bound to create conflict for individuals who had attained seniority in the past.

As a matter of public policy, employers are required to take "affirmative action" to correct imbalances in their work force and to set employment objectives for minorities and women by job classification. Employers are required to report to governmental agencies their employment levels of minorities, women, and other disenfranchised groups and to report their plans and actions to achieve employment levels similar to the composition of these groups in the local labor force. It follows that to raise the level of minority employment in a particular job category minority persons would need to be selected over whites where other factors were reasonably equal (preferential hiring or promotion), and certain traditional job rights, such as seniority, would have to be subordinated for the transition period.

In the course of this transition, some whites' claims to jobs, valid in terms of past institutional practices, would not be met. In a sense some whites would have to be discriminated against to bring participation of minorities, who would not qualify according to past practices, to standards of social justice. On the other hand, the Civil Rights Act of 1964 outlawed discrimination "against any individual." Consequently, employers were presented with a paradox: Could they comply with public policy to redress employment discrimination for blacks without discriminating against whites? And if it is against the law to discriminate against any individual, can remedies for past discrimination against blacks be effective? This paradox ultimately had to be resolved in the courts and is the context in which a major court challenge to the affirmative action program of Kaiser Aluminum and Chemical Corporation was made by Brian Weber, a white male.

BACKGROUND

In 1974 the United Steelworkers of America (USWA) and Kaiser Aluminum and Chemical Corporation entered into a large-scale collective bargaining agreement covering terms and conditions at 15 Kaiser plants. The agreement included an affirmative action plan designed to eliminate conspicuous racial imbalances in Kaiser's almost exclusively white craftwork forces. The company agreed to work toward this goal by reserving 50 percent of the in-plant craft training openings for black employees until the percentage of black craftworkers in a plant was commensurate with the percentage of blacks in the local labor force of each plant.

In the Kaiser plant in Gramercy, Louisiana, only 1.83 percent of the skilled craftworkers were black prior to 1974, whereas the local work force was approximately 39 percent black. Pursuant to the union-company collective bargaining agreement, Kaiser established a program to train its production workers to fill craft openings in this plant, rather than continuing its practice of hiring trained workers from the outside. Trainees were selected on the basis of seniority with the above stipulation that at least 50 percent of the trainees were to be black until the percentage of black skilled craftworkers in the plant approximated the percentage of blacks in the local labor force.

During the plan's first year of operation, a number of black and white workers were selected from the plant's production work force to be craft trainees. As a result of Kaiser's efforts to achieve the 50 percent balance of black and white trainees, the most senior black trainee had less seniority than several white production workers whose bids for selection were rejected. At this point Brian Weber, one of the white production workers denied admission, instituted a class action suit in federal district court. Weber charged that he and other similarly situated white workers had been discriminated against in violation of the provisions of Sections

703(a) and (d) of Title VII of the Civil Rights Act of 1964. The general thrust of these portions of the act makes it unlawful to "discriminate . . . because of . . . race" in hiring and in the selection of apprentices for training programs.*

DECISIONS OF THE COURTS

Both the District Court of Louisiana and the Court of Appeals for the Fifth Circuit held that Kaiser's affirmative action plan discriminated against Weber and did indeed violate Title VII, and Kaiser was ordered to terminate the program. This decision was rendered on the grounds that "all employment preferences based upon race, including those preferences incidental to bona fide affirmative action plans violated Title VII's prohibition against racial discrimination in employment."[1]

Neither Kaiser nor the USWA was satisfied with this outcome, and the case was brought before the U.S. Supreme Court. In June of 1979 the lower court decision was reversed, and the Supreme Court held that Title VII's prohibition against racial discrimination did not condemn all private, voluntary, race-conscious affirmative action plans.[2]

To support its decision the Supreme Court argued that a literal interpretation of Title VII was inappropriate; rather, the pertinent sections should be read against the background of the legislative history of Title VII and the historical context of the act. The Court stated that

------

*Section 703(a) reads as follows:

> It shall be an unlawful employment practice for an employer — (1) to fail or refuse to hire or discharge any individual, or otherwise to discriminate against any individual with respect to his compensation, items, conditions, or privileges of employment, because of each individual's race, color, religion, sex, or national origin; or (2) to limit, segregate, or classify his employees or applicants for employment in any way which would deprive or tend to deprive any individual of employment opportunities or otherwise adversely affect his status as an employee, because of such individual's race, color, religion, sex, or national origin. [78 Stat. 255, as amended, 86 Stat. 109]

Section 703(d) reads as follows:

> It shall be an unlawful employment practice for any employer, labor organization, or joint labor-management committee controlling apprenticeship or other training or retraining, including on the job training programs to discriminate against any individual because of his race, color, religion, sex, or national origin in admission to . . . any program established to provide apprenticeship or other training. [78 Stat. 256]

examination of those sources makes clear that an interpretation of sections 703(a) and (d) that forbids all race-conscious affirmative action would bring about an end completely at variance with the purpose of the statute and must be rejected. Congress' primary concern in enacting the prohibition against racial discrimination in Title VII was with the plight of the Negro in our economy, and the prohibition against racial discrimination in employment was primarily addressed to the problem of opening opportunities for Negroes in occupations which have been traditionally closed to them.[3]

The Supreme Court offered further support for Kaiser's affirmative action plan. The Kaiser plan, they found, did not involve the discharge or *absolute* denial of admission to whites. This fact seemed to reduce Weber's charge of discrimination against him. Furthermore, the plan was only a temporary measure designed to correct an obvious racial imbalance in Kaiser's work force. This also appeared to mitigate the charge of discrimination.

The Supreme Court decision, composed of the opinions of nine justices, was not unanimous. Several felt that the Court had overstepped its boundaries in its interpretation of Title VII. In the words of Chief Justice Warren Burger, one of the dissenters:

I cannot join the Court's judgment because it is contrary to the explicit language of the statute and arrived at by means wholly incompatible with long-established principles of separation of powers. . . . The quota embodied in the collective-bargaining agreement between Kaiser and the Steelworkers unquestionably discriminates on the basis of race against individual employees seeking admission to on-the-job training programs.[4]

Indeed, the majority decision acknowledged discrimination against Weber but found it justified on the basis of its intent to rectify past discrimination and to correct a social imbalance.

The issue of one form of discrimination being more justified than another is the central theme of the Weber case and the cause of substantial controversy. Does the goal of social equality warrant some forms of discrimination and its inevitable suppression of individual rights?

INDIVIDUALISM VERSUS EQUALITY: A MODERN DILEMMA

The Weber case represents a general dilemma of modern society anchored in strong values placed on individualism *and* placed on the improvement of conditions of social life. Individualism permeates American ideals and experience; it is manifest in psychological attitudes of self-reliance, social patterns of geographical and class mobility, and constitutional guarantees of political rights. There is no more widely shared value in American society.

However, twentieth century America awoke to another side of the individualistic ethic. Injustice was present when workers lacked rights to organize and bargain collectively with employers. Harmful products and unsafe working conditions could be an unintentional outcome of individualistic action. The physical environment was found to be deteriorating at an alarming rate. Sociologist Nathan Glazer states that the face of individualism emphasizing economic freedom carried a certain "indifference" to the environment or to those who fell behind in the economic race.[5] Economic inequality, unhealthy working conditions, unsafe products, and environmental degradation were felt to be out of character with the American value emphasizing improvement of social condition, and they fueled government reform in the twentieth century.

The last 20 years in particular have witnessed efforts to balance individualism and provide redress where the individualistic ethic left injustice and unacceptable social conditions. Inevitably, efforts to redress social conditions restrain and restrict current freedoms and expressions of individualism, creating a tension between these two values. Glazer, among others, is led to question the role of individualism in today's society:

> In the late 1960s and early 1970s we suddenly acquired a new batch of regulatory legislation, reflecting a sharply rising concern for minorities and women, for the environment and the consumer of industrial products, and for the worker in industry and agriculture, which quite transformed the face of American industry. . . . They have undoubtedly helped us to move in some degree toward their espoused objectives: equality for minorities and women, protection of the environment, protection for workers and consumers. Each has also spawned great volumes of regulations, new bodies of law, worked out, as is the nature of government agencies, in pedantic and humorless detail, and often to ridiculous extremes. This development raises questions in many minds as to whether it is still reasonable to consider the United States a country in which individualism prevails.[6]

The Brian Weber case was a single incident that became escalated into national attention because it struck at the heart of the conflict between improvement in employment opportunity for blacks and the individual's right to personal advancement. In this case the Court would not back down from supporting the intent of the Civil Rights Act to redress social injustice existing for blacks, even if it meant to violate the letter of the law that prohibits any discrimination.

This tension among values appears to be an inherent characteristic of modern society, and a general reconciliation of the issue may not be possible. The conflict will undoubtedly be experienced on countless settings and expressed in numerous issues. If Glazer is correct in saying that both sides are permanent fixtures of American society and both "are really on the side of the angels," the dilemma is one that will become increasingly familiar.

DISCUSSION QUESTIONS

1. What were the issues in balance in this court case? What issue was represented by Brian Weber's interests? What issue was represented by the Kaiser–United Steelworker's agreement?
2. What may be the risks for the society of a decision against Weber in this case? What may be the risks for society of a decision against Kaiser and the United Steelworkers?
3. What reasons did the Supreme Court use to mitigate the effect on Weber of its support for the Kaiser-USWA affirmative action plan? Do you see other criteria that may help define the point at which social objectives, such as redressing social imbalance, should or should not override individual choice?

NOTES

1. *United Steelworkers of America and Kaiser Aluminum & Chemical Corporation* v. *Brian F. Weber,* 563 F.2d 216 (1977).
2. *United Steelworkers of America and Kaiser Aluminum & Chemical Corporation* v. *Brian F. Weber,* 443 U.S. 193 (1979).
3. *U.S. Supreme Court Reports,* 61 L Ed 2d 484.
4. *United Steelworkers of America* v. *Brian F. Weber,* 443 U.S. 216, 217 (1979).
5. Nathan Glazer, "Individualism and Equality in the United States," in *On the Making of Americans: Essays in Honor of David Riesman,* ed. Herbert J. Gans, Nathan Glazer, Joseph R. Gusfield, and Christopher Jencks (Philadelphia: University of Pennsylvania Press, 1979), p. 129.
6. Ibid., pp. 129–30.

The Plastichem Corporation

BACKGROUND

The Plastichem Corporation is a plastics and chemicals firm, employing about 12,000 people worldwide, with its main headquarters in Chicago. One of the firm's plants produces isocyanate, a reactive component used in the manufacture of polyurethanes. Plastichem's isocyanate production plant is relatively old by industry standards; while it is not considered to be obsolete, neither is it state of the art. This particular plant is located in Termonia, Illinois, a small company town about 85 miles southwest of Chicago.

The plant employs 300 people, about 20 percent of the town's population, and runs on a continuous three-shift basis every day of the year. Though geared primarily for production, a small technical service group is assigned to the plant with five professionals (chemists/engineers). The plant is run quite independently of Chicago, and minimal communication exists between Termonia and the home office.

Termonia is a tightly knit community in which everyone seems to know each other. In the past few months rumors have been circulating around town that the main office is considering closing the Termonia operations and building a larger, more efficient facility somewhere in the South. Termonia's citizens are quite concerned about the likelihood of this occurrence and its effect on the town's economy. Workers at the plant know very well that they cannot afford any down time, since the operation is being evaluated for production efficiency (pounds of isocyanate produced per day) by the home office. Plant expenses also must be maintained at the bare minimum to convince the Chicago office of the utility of the plant.

PRECAUTIONS IN THE USE OF ISOCYANATES

The Termonia plant products TDI, or toluene diisocyanate, which is considered to present the greatest hazard of the commonly used industrial isocyanates. Through the application of suitable safety measures, no apparent harmful effects should result. Occupational Safety and Health Administration (OSHA) regulations govern the industrial usage of this chemical. The American Conference of Governmental Industrial Hygienists (ACGIH) and the American Standards Association have determined the threshold limit values (TLVs) and maximum acceptable concentrations for isocyanates. OSHA has agreed with these values and is responsible for publishing them. A TLV is the level under which all workers may be continuously exposed without the occurrence of adverse physiological effects. The maximum acceptable concentration is a ceiling level not to be surpassed under any circumstances. The TLV for TDI has been set at 0.005 parts per million (ppm) for a time-weighted average eight-hour working day, while the maximum acceptable level concentration is 0.02 ppm for any continuous 20-minute exposure. Tests have determined that the least detectable odor of TDI occurs at 0.5 ppm, indicating that if a worker smells the TDI, a hazardous condition already exists.

Since the odor cannot be detected at low concentrations, elaborate monitoring systems have been developed by two companies: ADM Scientific and MER Incorporated. These systems are coupled with alarm units that trigger a loud horn when the TLV is exceeded and shut the entire production line down when the maximum acceptable concentration is exceeded for more than 20 continuous minutes. The Plastichem plant has such a monitoring/alarm system.

Inhalation of TDI vapors normally results in severe irritation of the mucous membranes in the respiratory tract. Short exposure at concentrations near the ceiling value can cause progressive disabling illness (analogous to breathlessness or reduced pulmonary functioning). Massive exposure has lead to bronchitis, bronchial spasm, and/or pulmonary edema. Liquid TDI splashed directly in the eye can result in irritation or possible damage to the cornea. Contact with the skin due to liquid spills can result in reddening, swelling, and blistering.

Adequate mechanical ventilation is mandatory to control TDI vapor levels. Periodic maintenance of the exhaust system should be done according to OSHA and local air pollution regulations. The Termonia plant has a system that is enclosed and ventilated as specified by OSHA. Termonia also requires that chemical safety goggles and adequate skin protection be used in areas where there is a potential for spills or line ruptures. In addition, the Termonia plant has eyewash fountains and safety showers strategically located about the plant in case of an emergency. Personnel are trained in basic safety procedures.

Finally, TDI is not considered a serious fire hazard, but in the presence of an open flame or extreme heat, it can burn. TDI is sensitive to moisture. It is possible for uncontrollable isocyanate polymerization to occur in the presence of water, resulting in extreme heat generation and pressure buildup, with the possibility of an explosion if it is sealed in a container.

SCHNALL'S DILEMMA

Jared Schnall, a chemist in the technical service lab, is well aware of the plant closing rumors. Actually, they are more than rumors. At a recent meeting held three months ago with his supervisor (the head of the lab), a few of the top manufacturing officials, and the liaison from the Chicago office, the corporate liaison explained that the threat of closing down the plant was real. The liaison mentioned that the day-to-day operating data were being monitored carefully so that the main office could make a decision. The key variables were plant expenditures and output rates. They were also told that a decision would be made eight months from the time of the meeting.

In the three months since the meeting with the Chicago liaison, Schnall had become aware of some questionable activities at the production plant. He felt these activities were a direct result of the cost-cutting and output-increasing efforts of the production workers. Owing to their fear of the plant closing, they had undertaken measures that would be considered questionable under normal operating circumstances.

The first activity noticed by Schnall initially occurred two months ago and was repeated on three subsequent occasions. One morning as he was walking back to the tech-service lab through the plant control room, the MER monitoring system began to signal, indicating the TLV had been exceeded. Under normal circumstances, the horn would blow until the TDI leak was found and secured. If the ceiling level was reached during this period and persisted for 20 minutes, the plant would be automatically shut down and evacuated. However, on this occasion and the other three that Schnall witnessed, a worker in the control room "tripped" a circuit to stop the horn's blowing and to prevent the automatic shutdown of the plant, even if the ceiling level was reached. Having been there when the alarm had gone off on other occasions, Schnall had always heard the continual blowing of the horn, and he had even witnessed a few temporary plant shutdowns. Plant shutdowns are extremely undesirable because it can take anywhere from two to eight hours to locate the leak, to secure the leak, to restart the line, and to reach equilibrium acceptable output conditions.

Wondering why the practice of "tripping" had begun, he asked a friend of his in the control room about it after work. His friend explained to him that this practice had begun when they found out about the possibility of the plant closing. Instead of letting the alarm system shut the plant down temporarily and lower output data, the workers in the control room felt it was better to "trip" the circuit and fix the leak while the system continued to run. They believed their jobs were on the line, and they were willing to take the risk. Schnall was not sure if all of the plant workers were aware of the tripping practice.

Schnall asked his friend if he was concerned about the health conditions on the plant floor during these situations. His friend declared, "Sure I'm concerned, but what else can we do? Besides, the worst thing that has happened so far is a few guys coughed a little and a couple of 'em had to step outside and get some fresh air 'cause their eyes were burning. Listen, Jared, our jobs are on the line. Once we get the word from Chicago that they'll keep the plant open, things'll get back to normal. You'll see!"

Another questionable activity that Schnall discovered pertained to inspection and maintenance procedures. In an effort to keep costs down, two inspection practices had been "temporarily" eliminated. The first was the inspection of waterlines leading into the safety showers and the eyewashes as well as to the actual showers and washes. Schnall was worried that should these fixtures become unknowingly inoperative, owing to lack of inspection and maintenance, someone could have irreparable harm done to them in an emergency situation.

Inspection and maintenance of the air ventilation and circulation system was the other practice that had become nonexistent over the past few months, also in an effort to reduce expenses. In this case, Schnall strongly believed that a steady deterioration of the exhaust system could lead to ineffective removal of dangerous vapors in the event of an emergency. In addition, he knew that an inferior exhaust unit would cause the alarm system to be triggered more often than in normal circumstances. In any case, the lack of inspection and maintenance was in direct violation of OSHA regulations and local air pollution standards.

Schnall was not sure if other questionable practices were being carried out besides the ones he knew about, nor was he sure exactly what he should or could do about this situation. He first consulted with his supervisor, the head of the lab, but his boss did not give him a direct answer. By the time he finished talking with his boss, he realized that his boss was already aware of the situation but was willing to "ride it out" like his friend in the control room.

Still being confused, Schnall began to weigh his alternatives:

1. Ignore it, like his boss.
2. Question or complain to the top management in the production facility. However, Schnall was concerned about how his questions or complaints might affect his permanent working relationship with the production people. His own work schedule was very dependent on the availability of production people and their equipment for trial runs. If they wanted to make work difficult for him, they could. Schnall was especially afraid of confronting the top management because he felt they were probably the ones who initiated the activities in the first place.

3. Go over the production people's heads and contact the Chicago liaison. In this case, working conditions would probably become unbearable for Schnall. He might have to be transferred, but he still feared being stuck with the label of a "spy" wherever he might go in the company. He could contact the Chicago office anonymously and hope that something is done about the safety situation.

4. Contact OSHA if alternatives (2) and (3) are undesirable or are proven fruitless. This alternative could be dangerous, too. Schnall knows that, on the one hand, the home office may have to close Termonia if OSHA is brought in and the normal output levels are determined to be unacceptable. On the other hand, even if OSHA decides to keep the plant running, it might be an uncomfortable working environment for him. Schnall also knows that he is protected by at least three governmental acts. For example, OSHA regulations contain the following statement about employee rights and protection:

> No person shall discharge or in any manner discriminate against any employee because such employee has filed any complaint or instituted or caused to be instituted any proceeding under or related to this Act or has testified or is about to testify in any such proceeding or because of the exercise by such employee on behalf of himself or others or any right afforded by this Act.[1]

It goes on to say in the following section: "Any employee who believes that he has been discharged or otherwise discriminated against by any person in violation of this subsection may, within thirty days after such violation occurs, file a complaint with the Secretary alleging such discrimination."[2] In a final section the following statement is made: "Within 90 days of the receipt of a complaint filed under this subsection the Secretary shall notify the complainant of his determination."[3]

5. Quit. That is, refuse to be a part of these activities but let the workers take the risk if they so desire.

There were a few other items that bothered Schnall. First, he felt that there was no opportunity within the company for someone like himself to question or complain about company practices. He did not feel it was safe for an employee to speak out. In essence, there was no neutral office or third party within the company with whom he could speak.

   Second, he knew his job was at stake in more ways than one. Almost no matter what choice he made, other than ignoring the situation, he felt he would end up fired, transferred with a negative label attached to him, laid off, or working under undesirable or uncomfortable conditions. He was not pleased with the choices.

   The third question that concerned him was the reality of the threat of closure. Was the Chicago liaison using this threat as a ploy to improve the Termonia plant output and efficiency? Was he trying to scare them into working harder? Was he doing this without his supervisor's knowledge?

A final dilemma that perplexed Schnall regarded what would happen if he remained quiet and the home office did decide to keep the plant running. Was it fair for him to withhold information from the main office that would reveal that Termonia people were artificially keeping output high and costs lower under potentially dangerous health conditions? Could this false information lead to the home office making the wrong choice? Also, is the home office not responsible for the safety of the Termonia people whether they are aware of the triggering activities? Should Termonia be run so independently of the home office? Should there be more communication than just through the liaison?

DISCUSSION QUESTIONS

1. What actions would you recommend to Jared Schnall and why? What factors should he weigh in coming to a decision about what to do?
2. What action would you as chief executive officer of Plastichem Corporation want Jared Schnall to take? What is the likelihood that Jared would act in this manner?
3. Is Jared's dilemma likely to be a significant issue in American industry either now or in the future? What are the lessons for managers of U.S. corporations from experiences like Jared's? What reservations might managers have about reacting to problems such as his?

NOTES

1. "The Occupational Safety and Health Act of 1970, Section 11(c)," *Labor Relations Expediter* (Washington D.C.: Bureau of National Affairs, 1971), p. 6213.
2. Ibid.
3. Ibid.

Public Policy, Private Management, and Economic Development

Previous chapters have addressed many dimensions of business-government relations. For example, ways in which public policy influences relationships between employees, customers, and investors and the firm have been explored. We have reviewed the origins of government policy, alternative policy approaches, as well as the advantages and disadvantages of current public policy in these and other areas.

The institutions of government have also entered into our analysis of current issues. The legislative and executive branches of government — Congress, the president, and the regulatory agencies — have been indispensible elements of these reviews. In addition the role of the judicial system has often been a paramount factor in defining the public policy environment of the firm.

One important focus of public policy has been conspicuously absent from our discussions about the process of policy-making, regulation, and corporate governance. In actuality much government attention is focused directly on policies for economic growth and development, namely, how government can foster an environment that creates employment, contributes to investment, and generally increases the standard of living. This section delves into this question.

The first chapter that follows, Chapter 10, directs our attention to business-government relations at the state and local levels, arenas of public policy not strongly emphasized in earlier chapters. In the interests of urban and regional economic development, however, the policies and actions of local authorities assume major importance. Our objective in Chapter 10 is to review and analyze historical policies for local economic development and to discuss ways the challenges of growth are being addressed at this level.

In addition to a greater awareness of local responsibilities for development, a wide appreciation for the roles of technological innovation and entrepreneurship is evident in the United States. Recent decades have witnessed the emergence of scientific support for these processes in our national well-being, resulting in greater impact on national policy. The importance of a policy environment conducive to innovation and new venture development, as well as specific policy instruments directed toward improving this environment, composes the substance of Chapter 11.

Finally, the close tie between our national economy and worldwide trade and investment is an indisputable reality for the United States. The global economy is a vital context for understanding economic growth, and public policies bearing upon business's role in global markets is a critical topic for discussion. Chapter 12 reviews public policy issues arising, first, in the context of international trade and, second, in the process of foreign direct investment of U.S. firms overseas.

Chapter 10

The Business Role in Urban and Regional Development
Governmental Relations in the Context of Community Development

A community and its business sector have a symbiotic relationship. The community benefits from the presence of business through the creation of jobs, an expanded tax base, the provision of services and products, and the presence of prestigious national and international firms. Moreover, community institutions often benefit from charitable activities of successful individuals and firms, and numerous nonprofit organizations draw upon the voluntary experience and energies of persons employed in the business sector.

Similarly, business benefits from the attractiveness and image of the community in which it is located. The community affects the business sector through its ability or inability to supply needed personnel as well as efficient public sector leadership and services.

Business-community relations are undergoing two simultaneous trends. On the one hand, the increased size and diversity of many corporations give them a national and international, rather than a local, scope. Professionalization of management, often identified with increased size and public ownership of firms, may be accompanied by greater mobility among corporate officials. Manufacturing and distribution for a single firm are often widely dispersed, and it is not uncommon for a large firm to do a significant part of its business in foreign countries. These facts can lessen the mutual dependence of the firm and the immediate surrounding community.

On the other hand, interest in creating new employment, often through the hope of participating in fast-growing, high-technology industries, has heightened awareness of common business-community interests at the local level. Plant closings, headquarters relocations, consolidations, and job loss in some areas have made many persons more aware of how business can be the economic lifeblood of their communities.

In addition to changes in the size and diversity of corporations and the economics of local communities, population changes also affect business-community relationships. Racial and economic trends since World War II have created concentrations of poverty, heavily black, in the inner cities. The growth of the metropolitan areas and their segregation by income and race constitute major problems of unemployment and low capital base, often called the urban crisis. Restoring the vitality of urban centers has led to new public-private relationships at the local level.

A more recent movement of population and jobs from the Northeastern and North Central regions to the South and West poses an additional challenge to business and government leaders. Some communities experience the "boomtown" phenomenon of rapid and uncontrolled growth with consequent high demand for public services. Other communities declining in population, or increasing at a low rate, face problems of maintaining an employment base or of generating new employment and investment possibilities. A general movement toward local responsibility and problem solving and awareness of the importance of business to community development has set off an intense competition for location of existing businesses and for new business development. Local and state policy toward economic development has emerged as a major area of business-government relations.

The United States is experiencing dramatic transitions among geographical regions, between manufacturing and service industries, and within the mix of skills needed in today's work force. Each of these transitions creates social dislocation in addition to new opportunities.

Changes affecting local economies are sufficiently vast and powerful that leaders are often at a loss to identify manageable solutions. Yet because the quality of urban and rural life is important and because America seeks not to become socially, economically, regionally, and racially divided, many corporate managers and public officials are dedicating themselves to finding methods for economic redevelopment.

This chapter delineates several issues of business-community relationships and discusses responses by corporations as well as public bodies. The three primary topics of consideration are federal policy and urban development, regionalism and economics, and local and regional planning for economic development.

FEDERAL POLICY AND URBAN DEVELOPMENT

The following are well-known gradual changes in the population distribution (see Insert 10.A) of the United States over the last 25 or 30 years:

- A shift from agricultural to nonagricultural employment. While this trend began far earlier than World War II, it has continued since that period. In 1965, 6.4 percent of the civilian work force was employed in agriculture; in 1980 this figure was reduced to 3.4 percent. The growth of urban areas was, of course, a consequence of migration out of agriculture. In 1980, 63 percent of the population lived in urban settings; in 1980, 75.8 percent lived in urbanized areas.

- The movement of blacks out of the South and to the West, Northeast, and North Central areas between 1940 and 1960. Population trends show a relatively stable population of whites by regions, except for the West, which also experienced dramatic increases for whites in these areas.
- A more rapid growth in the "urban fringe" than in the central cities.
- A more rapid increase of minorities in the central cities.
- The existence of large income differentials between inner-city and sur-burban locations and between blacks and whites.[1]

A complex cycle of events has to a great extent converted cities into racially isolated centers of poverty. The causes of this pattern lie in economic, sociological, and political relationships, and they involve racial fears and isolation, municipal mismanagement, inadequate and counterproductive federal policies, and capital shortage. John Kain of Harvard University states that "the dominant problems of the cities are (1) discrimination, (2) poverty, (3) obsolescence of urban capital, and (4) outmoded fiscal and governmental structures."[2] Other analysts add factors of poor educational facilities, job shortages, political corruption, and a host of other causes.

In recent years some cities have experienced a revival of commercial investment in their downtown areas and are witnessing a process of housing rehabilitation — often termed *urban homesteading.* However important these trends, they only begin to address the many facets of urban decline; they impact minimally upon low-income and low-skilled groups and may result more in the relocation than in the reduction of poverty.

Whatever the historical patterns and causes, the interdependent problems of poverty, housing, health, education, and economic development directly affect the private business sector in terms of (1) employment opportunities provided minorities, primarily blacks and hispanics, and (2) availability of business capital for inner-city economic activity. While the

---

Insert 10.A

CITY-SUBURBAN AND WHITE-MINORITY POPULATION DIFFERENCES SINCE 1970

Central cities in the United States represent, and also illustrate, many of its most serious social and economic problems. The following statistics about

Insert 10.A   continued

cities, race, education, and income convey a tragic picture and several challenging policy issues:

1. Between 1970 and 1980 the urban fringes of American cities (suburbs) have gained in relative population, and the cities have lost population.

| | Percentage of National Population | |
	1970 (percent)	1980 (percent)
Central cities	31.4	29.6
Urban fringes	26.8	31.8

2. The percentage of minority persons has increased in both the central city and the urban fringe.

| | 1970 | | 1980 | |
	Percentage Minority	Percentage Non-minority	Percentage Minority	Percentage Non-minority
Central cities	22.5	77.5	30.8	69.2
Urban fringes	5.7	94.3	22.6	88.4

3. In 1982, wide differences persisted between blacks and whites in education, employment, housing, and income.

	Black	White
Percentage completing up to eight years of elementary school *only* (of persons 7 to 25 yrs).	24.7	14.7
Percentage completing four years of high school *only*	32.5	38.8
Percentage completing four years of college	8.8	18.5
Percentage persons unemployed	11.3	5.5
Percentage persons living in owner-occupied housing	47.2	70.2
Median income		
In central cities	$12,798	$22,884
Outside central cities but in metropolitan area	$17,718	$27,156

SOURCE: U.S., Department of Commerce, Bureau of Census, *Statistical Abstract of the United States 1984* (Washington, D.C.: Government Printing Office, 1984), pp. 27, 37, 38.

"business system" does not act by itself, it can be one participant in society-wide patterns of institutionalized discrimination.

There is little question that residential movement of the middle class, primarily white, in the 1950s and 1960s and the subsequent growth of services and employment opportunities in the suburbs made jobs relatively inaccessible to inner-city minorities. Housing discrimination persists today in many neighborhoods, further limiting access to outlying jobs. Decline in the urban tax base and weak capital investment in the cities adversely affects the income of the cities and the quality of schools. Thus concentrated poverty is a social illness that is self-aggravating. Numerous governmental programs in the last several decades have been designed to respond to different aspects of urban decline. Many past public policies were intended to intervene at the point at which social processes appear to aggravate the vicious cycle of concentrated poverty among disenfranchised minorities. Efforts to break the strength of institutionalized barriers to jobs and investment have been the focal point of public policy in this area.

Since 1980 federal urban policy has emphasized problem solving by states and municipalities and funding programs that give grants to local governments for use in specific projects rather than having local governments apply to national agencies for funding on a project-by-project basis. This approach to urban policy is termed *New Federalism*.

The following discussion reviews policies where the philosophy of New Federalism bear particularly on business decisions; in addition, it touches on other approaches to urban development such as minority contracting, bank lending practices in low-income neighborhoods, urban enterprise zones, and voluntary giving.

New Federalism

As the federal government became more and more involved with urban problems after World War II, funding programs became more specialized; for example, funding for housing, job training, community development, nutrition, and other problems became more centralized. Federal agencies came to carry immense power over local projects owing to their control of the purse strings of federal programs. Upon Ronald Reagan's initial election as president in 1980, the historical trend toward specialization and centralization of urban policy changed. A new belief held that solving local problems could best be done at state and local levels. Consequently a new thrust was created in an attempt to alter the long-standing relationship of the federal government to urban issues.

The largest and perhaps most significant program of the new philosophy was called *revenue sharing*. In fiscal year 1980 funds from a variety of specialized programs were collapsed into a single fund amounting to $6.9 billion. This money was then apportioned to about 39,000 local governments based on a formula that accounts for total state population, urban population, per capita income, and tax rates.[3] The funds could then be used for local projects, with few federal strings attached.

Other programs follow a similar effort to yield significantly greater local control over expenditures. Grants money destined for a variety of housing and development projects is given to states, cities, and urban counties by a formula comparable with revenue sharing. In fiscal 1984, $3.8 billion was distributed under this community development program.

In 1977 a major program called the Urban Development Action Grant (UDAG) program was authorized by the Congress to stimulate commercial activities in urban areas. The UDAG program is designed to compensate for higher costs — land prices and deteriorating structures and services — in communities meeting criteria concerning income levels, unemployment, age of housing, and the number of new jobs to be created by the project.

This program makes grants directly to municipalities that have endorsed certain projects. UDAG grants are given as low-interest, subordinated debt to the project developer who must raise two and a half dollars of private money for the project for every dollar of public funds invested. UDAG funds, then, attempt to increase the competitiveness of cities for private investment and stimulate economic development. In fiscal 1980 the UDAG program was funded at $675 million.

In each of these cases local control has been increased under the philosophy of New Federalism. Not only do states and communities have more control over the use of the funds, but supposedly the costs of federal administration also are saved. On the other hand, urban programs, like many social programs, were vulnerable to reductions in the rate of government spending in the early 1980s. Revenue sharing, which began at $6.9 billion in 1980, was reduced to $4.6 billion by 1984. Community development grants saw nearly a 10 percent reduction over this time period, and the UDAG program had been reduced nearly 35 percent.[4] While decentralization made sense to local authorities, major reductions in funds available for cities have not. Insert 10.B describes federal policy toward job training, another area bearing upon urban development that has likewise been influenced by the New Federalism as well as federal spending reductions.

Minority Contracting

Revenue sharing and other programs of the New Federalism make federal money available at the local level for social and economic development. Given the high percentage of minorities in central cities, opportunities for minority economic development are influenced strongly by the size of the programs. The requirement for federal contractors to make efforts to place a percentage of subcontract works with minority-owned businesses is an effort to expand opportunities for minorities in economic activity. For ex-

Insert 10.B

JOB TRAINING THROUGH PUBLIC-PRIVATE PARTNERSHIPS

Between 1973 and 1982 job training policy in the United States was implemented through a program termed CETA — Comprehensive Employment and Training Act. CETA had a turbulent history; it could point to a few successes but suffered severe criticism for failing to prepare individuals for long-term employment in meaningful jobs. The program was also subject to frequent charges of mismanagement and improper use of funds.

In 1982 CETA was replaced with the Jobs Training Partnership Act (JTPA), which represented a significant departure in the philosophy of job training. JTPA's task would be large — the Department of Labor estimated that between 25 and 35 million people were eligible to receive training under the act. Major innovations in the ideology of job training included the following:

- The federal role in overseeing employment training was greatly diminished, and state responsibilities were correspondingly increased.
- Considerable latitude for program emphasis was left to local service delivery areas.
- Responsibility for local training was vested in organizations called private industry councils whose membership was required to be at least 51 percent businesspersons.
- All training activities would be performed by contract with local PICs (private industry councils). Contracts would be let on the basis of the contractor's performance in successful job placements.

One readily sees how this program is directed by local organizations, strongly influenced by the business sector, and driven by the training needs of employers.

How well the program would meet the needs of the target populations of unemployed and underemployed persons might be another question. First, JTPA suffered greatly diminished resources; where CETA was funded at $9.4 billion in 1979, JTPA was initiated with a budget of $3.6 billion. The Department of Labor estimated that only between 800,000 and 900,000 persons would be served, a participation rate of less than 4 percent. Second, given the program's focus on providing local companies with employees suited to firms' long-term needs, matching people with jobs across service areas would be difficult.

SOURCE: James E. Delaney and James B. Hyman, "Proposal for Fiscal Year 1985 Program Support" by the Private Industry Council of Cleveland/Cuyahoga County. Undated.

ample, the following pieces of legislation address the role of minority enterprise in federal procurement policy:

- 1971 Federal Procurement Regulations contained a clause encouraging
  contractors on federal contracts above $5,000 to utilize minority
  businesses.
- The Public Works Employment Act of 1977 requires that 10 percent
  of each federal construction grant be awarded to minority businesses.
- The Railroad Revitalization and Regulatory Reform Act of 1977 establishes that a goal of 15 percent of purchases made by recipients of financial grants and subcontractors be awarded to minority businesses.
- PL 95–507, passed in 1978, requires that bidders for federal contracts
  above $500,000 ($1 million for construction contracts) submit, prior to
  the contract award, a plan including percentage goals for participation
  of minority businesses. These plans are to be considered, along with
  price, quality, and delivery, in the awarding of contracts.[5]

In fiscal 1983 minority business received $4.8 billion under federal con-
structing requirements. Although an increase of $700 million from two
years earlier, this sum actually represented a decrease in the minority share
of all federal contract money from 3.4 percent to 3.1 percent.[6]

  In addition defense appropriation bills for many years have contained a clause that directs defense contractors to give subcontracting work
to businesses in "labor-distressed areas" when possible. Usually a bonus is
awarded to the contractor who achieves or exceeds subcontracting goals
negotiated with the defense procurement agency. Government procurement policy explicitly favors areas of high unemployment and implicitly
favors small and minority-owned businesses. Under this program subcon-
tracts do not necessarily have to go to the lowest bidder, and it is often
assumed they do not. In fiscal 1983 the minority share of defense prime
contract money was 2 percent, down 1.1 percent from fiscal 1981.[7]

Accountability for Community Reinvestment

By the mid-1970s charges of financial institution "redlining" were becoming increasingly common, and calls from community groups for public intervention to control alleged areawide discrimination in lending patterns
were strong. Redlining is an alleged practice of lending institutions to deny
residential loans to inner-city residents owing to a belief that the central
city was financially risky as a whole. Withdrawing institutional support
meant that the valid credit needs of the area could not be adequately met,
causing or accelerating the neighborhood's decline. Critics of lending institutions were not asking lenders to give higher-risk loans but only to accept the normal-risk loan request of the neighborhoods. Proponents
sought and received from Congress in the passage of legislation known as

the Community Reinvestment Act endorsement of the principle that credit be given on the merits of individual cases and that prejudicial areawide practices be discontinued.

The Community Reinvestment Act attempts to counter discrimination in lending (1) by requiring federally regulated lending institutions to define their market areas and their services and to take actions to meet local credit needs in the community in which they solicit deposits; (2) by requiring institutional regulators — the Federal Reserve, the Comptroller of the Currency, the Federal Home Loan Bank Board, and the Federal Deposit Insurance Corporation — to include an assessment of the institution's performance in meeting the credit needs of the entire community during the course of the regular examination of the institution; and (3) by giving the regulatory agencies power to deny an institution's requests for branch expansion, office relocation, branch closings, deposit insurance, merger, or acquisition on the basis of a failure to meet the credit needs of its community in a nondiscriminatory manner.[8] The latter provision explicitly gives a community group the right and opportunity to challenge institutions on proposed expansion plans. The federal agency with jurisdiction for an institution that has been challenged investigates, mediates, and ultimately decides the grievance.

How is the record of a lender to be known and judged? Practically no information was available on an institution's loan practices until 1975, when Congress passed another law, the Home Mortgage Loan Disclosure Act, requiring public disclosure of mortage loan data. Even now, however, easy success in establishing bank responsibilities to their communities is prevented by several difficulties: What is an adequate performance record in meeting the community's credit needs? What are the community's credit needs and how are they expressed? Does such aggregate data constitute proof of redlining, or does this conclusion require documentation of specific cases of discrimination? The absence of standards, the quality of housing stock, the terms of mortgages, the types of mortgages generally preferred in a community, the market strategy of a particular bank, and the bank's image as a lender will all affect the perception of credit needs and the possibility of discrimination. Also, the aggressiveness of a bank toward expansion may influence its exposure to community challenges.

Despite these obstacles, the Community Reinvestment Act appears to be having an effect as a large number of proposed bank mergers have given community groups the opportunity to use the requirements of the act to support their interests. A report from Chicago, for example, indicates that a central city community group, the Chicago Reinvestment Alliance, was prepared to challenge the proposed acquisition of Chicago's American National bank by the First National Bank of Chicago, which was the country's tenth-largest bank.[9] First National reportedly decided to negotiate with the Alliance and finally agreed to grant $120 million in loans to buy and rehabilitate apartment buildings and single-family units and to purchase Small Business Administration (SBA) guarantees. The agreement was apparently the largest package of this type known to have been made by a U.S. bank. One report states:

> To avoid hostile testimony the Alliance threatened to give before the Federal Reserve Board, First National officials quickly agreed to develop a neighborhood-reinvestment program. In two months, the bank faced Alliance in nine negotiating sessions. Particularly pivotal were two neighborhood tours during which First National's top negotiator was shown successful nonprofit housing rehabilitation projects and commercial-industrial redevelopment, all marked by high quality workmanship and management.[10]

The Alliance negotiated a similar agreement with Chicago's Harris Bank, in the process of takeover by the Bank of Montreal, for a $35 million loan package. Not long afterward, another agreement was finalized with the Northern Trust Company of Chicago for an investment of $18 million in similar projects throughout Chicago.[11] Also, community groups in Boston, Philadelphia, New York, Richmond, and Berkely have used this law to capture investment from the major financial institutions of their communities for housing rehabilitation and improved living. The loosening of banking regulation as well as market and technological changes in the financial services industry may have a strong impact on urban development through the ability of community groups to utilize the Community Reinvestment Act.

Urban Enterprise Zones

A market-based concept is currently being considered as an alternative solution to the economic distress of urban centers. The idea of *urban free enterprise zones* was initially approved in nine British cities under the Thatcher administration and has been endorsed by the Reagan administration as a major component of U.S. urban policy. The enterprise zone concept proposes reductions of government taxes for firms located in designated economically distressed areas whose employees comprise at least half of the residents from within the designated zone. One plan proposes reducing business income taxes by 15 percent and reducing capital gains by 50 percent for firms operating in the zone.[12] Accelerated depreciation and favorable accounting rules would be permitted for businesses within the enterprise zone. Other plans involve the waiver of safety, environment, and minimum wage laws, but these appear to have less support.

While enterprise zone legislation has been under consideration in Washington, D.C., at least 23 states have passed their own legislation for enterprise zones, and at least 16 are in operation.[13] Connecticut, for example, is reported to have designated six zones that offer temporary property tax abatement, sales tax exemptions, income tax reductions, and job training reimbursement. Nearly $100 million is said to have been invested under this program in two years.[14]

Potential federal benefits are considered to be about five times as lucrative as state and local tax breaks. If enacted, the concept promises to move federal urban development policy closer to the free market context that provided the original economic growth model of the United States. Being closer to the free market is not the same as the free market, however, as the cost to the government of the first five years of the program are estimated to be $3.4 billion.[15]

Voluntary Corporate Giving to Community Institutions

A final public policy position toward urban and community development might be termed *private sector initiatives*. This position reflects a view that responsibility for local economic development lies with the individuals and institutions most directly affected in particular communities. This philosophy is also part of an aspect of the New Federalism, which looks to the private sector, rather than the government, for solutions to society's problems. Philanthropy, individual and corporate, is thus called upon to fill the gap created by reduced government commitment to local economic development. A discussion of the level of corporate philanthropy in the United States, as well as several points of view about corporate responsibility for solving social problems, is presented in Insert 10.C.

REGIONALISM AND ECONOMICS

The pattern of population migration from rural areas to cities after World War II aggravated postwar urban problems. This social change has been supplemented by a different pattern of population migration in the 1970s and 1980s — the shift in population and employment from the northern industrial states to the South and the West. Just as the earlier population shifts created unprecedented issues of employment and investment in urban areas and led to new developments in public policy, the present changes raise new issues and stimulate fresh proposals for public policy. Specifically the idea of limiting business mobility, such as by plant closing restrictions, is a reaction to the relative economic decline of manufacturing activity in the Midwest and Northeast. This section addresses the dimensions of this regional change and the challenges it presents for business-community relationships.

Insert 10.C

CORPORATE PHILANTHROPY

The National Conference Board, a business research organization, has reported that corporate philanthropic efforts have been steadily increasing throughout the 1980s. The following figures represent corporate cash, and noncash, donations to not-for-profit organizations in recent years:

Year	Total Corporate Donations
1983	$3.0 billion
1982	$2.8 billion
1981	$2.5 billion

Many social activists believe that charitable corporate donations reflect business's "responsibility" to society at large. Business leaders, however, often view their company's social responsibility more narrowly. According to American Express executive Jerry Welsh, "The wave of the future isn't checkbook philanthropy. It's a marriage of corporate marketing and social responsibility." Standard Oil Co. contributions manager Charles E. Taylor seems to hold a similar viewpoint on corporate philanthropy: "I don't give our company's money away. I invest it."

Other corporate executives have stressed that their company's contribution policy is based on "enlightened self-interest." Noncash donations made by major high-tech companies to schools and universities illustrate this type of corporate outlook. According to one corporate philanthropy consultant:

> Intense competition is developing among companies to get their computer hardware, or equipment, into the leading universities. Companies are being more aggressive because they recognize they likely will be influencing people who will be in the market in later years for such equipment.

American Express Company's support of the Statue of Liberty/Ellis Island restoration project may be considered another example of corporate philanthropy stemming from enlightened self-interest. During the fourth quarter of 1983, American Express promised to donate a percentage of corporate profits to the restoration project for each new credit card issued and for every credit card purchase. By the end of the quarter, American Express had contributed $1.6 million toward the restoration of Ellis Island and the Statue of Liberty. Meanwhile, the dollar volume of American Express credit card purchases was up 30 percent and the number of new cardholders increased 50 percent, when compared with the company's previous fourth quarter.

Insert 10.C   continued

Although a seemingly noncontroversial topic, corporate philanthropy has triggered a few sharp criticisms. According to some economists, philanthropic corporate investments represent a misallocation of corporate profits. They argue that a corporation's primary social responsibility is limited to improving the social welfare of its shareholders. In order to fulfill this responsibility, national economist Milton Friedman claims that corporations are morally obligated to give their profits directly to shareholders. Individual investors may then determine whether they choose to assume various social responsibilities. Yale economist Paul MacAvoy suggests that the use of corporate profits to advance social clauses does not satisfy the corporation's responsibility to its shareholders and may not be in society's best interest either. From MacAvoy's viewpoint:

> The corporation's essential contribution to social welfare is maximization of long-term shareholder gain . . . Government, not the corporation, is structured to solve the demands of competing constituencies and to identify and set social policy objectives.

Meanwhile, the Presidential Task Force on Private Sector Initiatives has urged U.S. corporations to double their philanthropic contributions. National Conference Board analysts estimated that philanthropic corporate contributions increased by over 30 percent in 1984, totaling $4.2 million.

SOURCE: Tamar Lewin, "Corporate Giving Fails to Offset Cuts by the U.S.," *New York Times,* February 15, 1985, p. A1 ; Roberta A. Reynes, "Gift Horses and Hobbyhorses," *Barron's,* March 28, 1983, p. 38; Jeffrey L. Kovach, "Charitable Investments," *Industry Week,* October 1, 1984. P. 29

The Shift

The average population increase for the United States as a whole has remained at about 1.1 percent annually at least since 1970. However, population by the major regions of the country differs significantly from this overall average. Table 10.1 shows the number of people in the Midwest, a region extending from Ohio through Nebraska and the Dakotas, increased only 0.1 percent between 1980 and 1983, an average annual increase of 0.033 percent. In these same years the West, including the Mountain and Pacific states, increased 6.5 percent in population, an average of 2.17 percent per year, nearly double the national average and 65 times higher than the population increase in the Midwest for the same years. Between 1980 and 1983 the South and West together captured 94 percent of the country's 7.4 million increase in population.[16]

TABLE 10.1 *Percentage Increase in Population, by Region: 1980–83 and 1970–80*

Region	1980–83	1970–80
United States	3.3	11.4
Northeast	0.8	0.2
Midwest	0.1	4.0
South	5.5	20.0
West	6.5	23.9

SOURCE: U.S., Department of Commerce, Bureau of Census, "Estimates of the Population of the States: 1970–1983," *Current Population Reports,* Population Estimates and Projections, Series P-25, no. 957, p. 1.

One interesting result in Table 10.1 is the increase in population growth in the Northeast states, extending from New England through the mid-Atlantic states. Having the lowest rate of population growth between 1970 and 1980, this region increased substantially in population growth in the early 1980s. This population change naturally coincides with a revival of the economy of that region.

Population changes are determined by natural increases (births minus deaths) and by migration of persons between regions. A major factor in the regional differences since 1970 is due to people moving from one region to another. Between 1970 and 1980, for example, a net migration of over 300,000 persons moved annually from the Northeast/Midwest to the South/West.[17] During the 1980–83 period the pace of migration appeared to have slowed to about half this rate.[18]

These population changes are closely matched by relative percentage changes in regional employment. The nationwide increase in employment between 1970 and 1980 was 24.1 percent: the Northeast had a rate of employment increase 50 percent below this national average, and employment in the North Central region was 40 percent below; however, the South increased in employment 33.2 percent above this national average, and employment in the West increased 81.4 percent above.[19] As had been widely publicized, regional population and employment shifts have been dramatic.

Two factors appear to be involved in these changes. One is a trend within the structure of the economy: employment has moved away from manufacturing toward services industries. Table 10.2 shows a ten-year change in employment for different employment sectors. The largest decline is in manufacturing, and the largest gains are in services and trade.

If it is true that the economy of the Northeast and Midwest has a

TABLE 10.2 *Distribution of Employment by Major Industry, 1970 and 1980* (In Percent)

Employment	1970	1980
Agriculture	4.4	3.1
Nonagricultural wage and salary	88.3	89.4
Private household	2.2	1.2
Government	15.8	16.3
Other private	70.2	71.9
Mining	0.6	1.0
Construction	4.5	4.4
Manufacturing	25.7	21.3
Transportation and public utilities	5.7	5.5
Trade	16.4	18.2
Finance and services	17.3	21.5
Self-employed	6.6	7.1
Total (in thousands)	78,627	97,545

SOURCE: U.S., Department of Labor, Bureau of Labor Statistics, "Annual Average Area Supplement," *Current Population Survey,* 1970 and 1980. Data supplied by the Department of Labor.

larger portion of manufacturing relative to services, these industrial areas have therefore experienced a slower rate of job increase than other regions. Table 10.3 shows the changes in regional share of national employment in the major industry categories. Whereas manufacturing employment declined overall, the South and West increased their shares of the employment base, and whereas trade and services became more important in the national economy, the Northeast and North Central regions lost relative shares of national employment in these industries.

Obviously, population and employment shifts go hand in hand; people move to where jobs are opening up, and jobs become located where labor skills are available. A more significant question, to which we now turn, is why such a trend first started.

Reasons for the Shift

Frank E. Morris, president of the Federal Reserve Bank of Boston, attempts to explain this migration by isolating factors that often differ substantially between areas.[20] Energy costs, for example, have become more significant in total manufacturing; the cost of energy used in manufactur-

TABLE 10.3 *Average Annual Percentage Change in Employment in Major Sectors by Region, Between 1970 and 1980*

	Northeast	North Central	South	West
Manufacturing	−0.6	−0.5	+1.1	+2.6
Trade	−2.3	−2.8	+5.0	+5.1
Finance and services	−3.8	−4.2	+6.8	+7.9
All nonagricultural employment	−2.0	−2.6	+4.7	+5.9

SOURCE: U.S., Department of Labor, Bureau of Labor Statistics, "Annual Average Area Supplement," *Current Population Survey,* 1970 and 1980. Data supplied by the Department of Labor.

ing in New England in 1974 was 84 percent higher than the average cost of energy in the rest of the United States, putting New England industry at a substantial disadvantage.

Labor rates and per capita state and local taxes can also vary widely. Morris states that the average annual increase in manufacturing wages in the early 1970s for the East–North Central areas was more than 20 percent higher than the increase in the Western Pacific region. On the other hand, the Western Pacific states had an increase in per capita taxes over 8 percent higher than the East–North Central states over the same years. The Western Mountain states furthered their cost advantage in these years with a manufacturing wage increase nearly 7 percent below the national average and an increase in state and local taxes 24 percent lower than the national average.

Of course, the influx of people and business into western and southern areas may eventually create a more competitive and perhaps better organized labor force and a more rapid relative increase in wage rates. In addition more people and larger cities may also increase the need for public services and cause upward pressure on state and local taxes. Similarly, older, less rapidly expanding areas can adapt to regional economic competition, by slowing rises in wages and services, essentially taking a reduction in standard of living compared with other regions.

Costs of energy, labor, and taxes are only a few of the important factors influencing aggregate flows of investment. The availability of labor has been mentioned as a factor; its productivity is also important. The quality of roads, bridges, and transportation facilities is significant; and of course access to raw materials and user markets plays a major role in business location decisions.[21]

Another explanation for the shift in population and employment described above is the impact of federal fiscal policy, whose significance came to light in the late 1970s. In essence each of the four major regions of the country can be seen in terms of inflows and outflows of federal dollars spent on defense installations and contracts, general federal procurement, highway construction, agriculture, water resource projects, and hundreds of social programs in which allocations are based on population, income level, unemployment, or number of college students. Prime military contract awards, for example, appear to contain a regional bias, with the South and West profiting from their concentrations of high-technology industries. The percentage change in prime military contracts per capita for the four major regions between 1951 and 1976 was −29.5 for the Northeast, −45.8 for the North Central region, +109.0 for the South, and +32.1 for the West.[22] These programs represent sources of federal money flowing into a state or region. On the outflow side are federal taxes, where the states differ as well. For example, in 1975 the South had a lower relative per capita income level and was taxed 14 percent below the national average, whereas federal taxes in the Midwest were 5 percent above the national average.[23]

Regional imbalances in these net dollar flows can be substantial. In 1975 the five Great Lakes states had an $18.6 billion deficit or net outflow with respect to the national government, whereas the 16 states of the South enjoyed an $11.5 billion surplus.[24] The single greatest beneficiary of these policies in 1975 was the state of New Mexico — 27 percent below the national average in federal tax burden and 40 percent higher than the national average in federal spending. Little wonder one sees in Congress the organization of political groups — such as the Midwest-Northeast Coalition and, more recently, the Sunbelt Coalition — that scrutinize federal programs for adverse impacts on their constituencies and attempt to bring regional interests more explicitly into policy-making.

Federal fiscal policies have a significant economic impact, which is both a cause and a consequence of regional population and employment shifts. At the same time, the redistributive impact of federal policies may not be as simple as implied above. One comparison of 14 southern states and 11 northern industrial states shows a mixed picture with respect to the regional impact of federal fiscal policies.[25] Furthermore, regional redistribution of national wealth may be desirable. The Sunbelt-South states, for example, have historically lower per capita income, a greater proportion of the poverty population, and lower per capita family income than the industrial northern states. Given this historical discrepancy and the view that one implicit objective of fiscal policy is to close the gap between "the rich" and "the poor," some might argue that government should serve to redistribute income between geographic regions.[26]

A footnote to this discussion is the differential impact that prices of energy — oil, natural gas, and coal — will have upon regional and state economies. Certain states have energy surpluses, and some states are energy impoverished. It is common for exporting states to place a severance tax on sales of natural resources to other states — such as seven cents per thousand cubic feet of natural gas or a tax of up to 30 percent of the value of coal.[27] While the effect does not match regional boundaries exactly, the Northeast and Midwest are energy importers, and parts of the South and most of the West are net energy exporters. The favorable economic effect of energy resources not only is felt in terms of severance taxes and royalty payments, but it also tends to increase personal and business incomes and, of course, to create a competitive advantage to businesses located near cheaper energy.

A third explanation for the regional shifts in population and employment deals with personal attitudes toward the desirability of living in different regions. A survey taken in 1973/74 studied the desires of people in different regions to live somewhere else.[28] The study suggests that people preferred at that time to move out of the East and Midwest and to the South and West, which is exactly what the data show happened in those years.

Another study of reasons for people actually changing regional residence in the 1973–76 period showed employment to be the cause of the move for about 60 percent of the persons sampled.[29] Surprisingly strong, though, was the reason of "wanting a change of climate." Less than 8 percent of the people moving to the Northeast and less than 2 percent moving to the North Central areas had this reason for their change of location, whereas 8.5 percent of those moving to the South and 10.6 percent of those moving to the West gave this reason as the cause of their move.[30] Personal preference for a particular type of environment appears to be a significant factor underlying regional population shifts. The increase in population in the Northeast between 1980 and 1983 mentioned earlier may, however, indicate changes in some attitudes of the last decade.

REGIONAL ECONOMIC DECLINE: TWO DEFINITIONS OF THE PROBLEM

Problem Definition: Corporate Flight

One way to explain the regional differences in rates of employment and job growth is to blame corporations for closing plants in the North and building new ones in the South and West. According to this theory of regional migration, corporations pursue nonunion labor and tax abatements in the South rather than maintaining responsibility to their historical labor force and communities in the North.[31] This belief defines job loss as the source of the comparatively weak performance of the North and East in employment statistics.

Some dramatic instances of plant closings support this view: the closing of the Youngstown Sheet and Tube Campbell Works after acquisition by the conglomerate Lykes Corporation is a celebrated case that unions and community groups use as a example of corporate irresponsibility. Lykes shut down Youngstown Sheet and Tube reportedly after failure to use Youngstown's cash flows for reinvestment and in order to take a tax loss write-off of several hundred million dollars, putting over 4,000 people out of work.[32] Few cities of the Northern Industrial Belt have not been touched by some instance of plant closing or facility relocation in the past decade. When plants are closed, hardship is placed on employees and the communities in which they live.

Concern over negative repercussions of plant closings has resulted in proposals by congressmen for legislation to limit business mobility. For example, Congressman William Ford of Michigan submitted the National Employment Priorities Act, subsequently relabeled as the Employee Protection and Community Stabilization Act. The main provisions of this proposed legislation were the following:

- notification to affected communities and employees of a plant closing or transfer one year in advance;
- authorization of the secretary of labor to hold hearings and issue a report on a plant closing upon the request of the employees or community;
- employee rights to comparable work in the transferred operation, with a relocation allowance; and
- severance pay for employees not relocated of 85 percent of salary for one year and for two years for employees above 55 years old.[33]

The bill also includes programs of loan guarantees and technical assistance to the threatened firm as well as to other firms affected by plant closings.

Reaction to such proposed legislation has been varied. Unions support the initiatives of Congressman Ford and has colleagues. Those wanting to restrict employers' actions on plant closings lean heavily upon the economic, social, and psychological setbacks endured by the individual worker and the community as a result of such closings. In a congressional hearing Marc Stepp, vice-president of the United Automobile, Aerospace, and Agricultural Workers of America, expressed the following view concerning the consequences of plant closings.

> There are devastating effects upon the individual worker's physical and mental well-being. In a study released by the National Institute for Occupational Safety and Health . . . , it was found that workers laid off as a result of their plants having been shut down suffered greater likelihood of heart disease, increased risks of diabetes, peptic ulcers and gout, as well as increases in arthritis and hypertension. . . . The suicide rate reflected in this study was 30 times the rate for the general population. . . .

> When plants relocate or close, and when worker's jobs
> are lost, the community faces losses in tax revenues, losses
> in sales by local merchants and reductions in property val-
> ues as workers are forced to sell homes and move to other
> areas in an effort to find new jobs.[34]

However, many have objected to the proposed legislation, primarily the business community. One of the more compelling objections is the disincentive plant closing laws would provide to new business development. One industry participant in a series of Senate committee hearings on plant closing legislation stated it this way:

> It [the proposed legislation] would encourage manufactur-
> ers to continue their outmoded and unprofitable opera-
> tions using obsolete manufacturing methods. Since ven-
> ture capital flows to opportunity, this legislation would chill
> the enthusiasm for badly needed private investment.
>
> Businesses start small — they earn profits which are the
> basis for re-investment to create new jobs. Businesses grow
> and new companies break off to start the cycle again. This
> legislation would help break this chain.
>
> The effect could be to retard growth of business by pro-
> viding disincentives to expansion. It would restrict the en-
> try of capital which is desperately needed.[35]

Another concern of those opposing the proposals is the creation of an entirely new federal bureaucracy with all of its associated costs to administer such laws.

At least 12 states were considering plant closing legislation in the early 1980s, although only two — Wisconsin and Maine — passed laws requiring advanced notice of a closing.[36] Philadelphia is reported to be the first city to require 60 days notice before a plant closes. Employees have the right to sue for wages for any time short of this period.[37]

The proposed legislation seems unlikely to become federal law in the foreseeable future, and business opposition is also strong in the states. Yet it is equally unlikely that the heated debate will cease on this issue, which represents a trade-off between known personal dislocation and suffering in the short term against hoped-for long-range and general economic benefits.

Problem Definition: New Job Creation

A second way of viewing the problem of the northern and eastern states is the *absence of new jobs created,* especially at lower-skilled levels, rather than jobs lost. This view of regional differences in jobs and population maintains that there is always a certain degree of plant closings, business failure, and business out-migration in any area and that even though these are visible and difficult events, regional differences of their frequency are far less important than the level of new business start-ups and expansions of existing businesses within a region. Where this theory is accepted, public policies tend to concentrate more on positive incentives for business development, such as lower corporate income tax rates to expand capital availability, and a favorable, entrepreneurial small business climate.

Strong evidence supports this view of regional differences in business growth. Table 10.4 presents summary data from a well-known study of the employment changes between 1970 and 1972 for 3.5 million firms. If this sample of firms is representative, the problem of the Northeast and North Central regions is one of start-ups and expansions, not one of failures and contractions. In the latter category the two regions are no worse off than the other regions, nor are the differences between in- and out-migration significant between the "superregions" of Northeast-North Central and the South-West. The single-most important factor between the Frostbelt and Sunbelt regions in the faster rate of employment change from start-ups and expansions in the South and the West. The authors of this study conclude that the degree of interstate migration is far less than generally suspected:

> A surprising finding is the exceedingly low rate of interstate migration — less than .5% of employment for most states and most employment types. This contradicts much conventional wisdom, and suggests that the support of existing businesses and the fostering of new ones is a far more sensible economic development strategy than attempting to lure existing businesses from other parts of the country.[38]

Other studies corroborate this viewpoint. One study, analyzing the sources of business expansion in the Dallas–Fort Worth area between 1960 and 1975, identified local growth, rather than interstate competition, as the primary source of new employment. In this time period 37 percent of new plants were business start-ups, 34 percent were expansions, 13 percent were acquisitions, and 16 percent were relocations; a similar analysis in Houston found that less than 10 percent of new plants were relocations.[39] The predominance of new economic activity appears due primarily to locally generated forces. The author of this study concluded that "growth in the South does not necessarily imply decline in the Northeast."

Over a five-year time period 400,000 firms were analyzed in another attempt to learn about plant relocation effects. These researchers concluded that less than 0.6 percent of the firms moved far enough to change their telephone area codes.[40] These studies are not conclusive; they were conducted in earlier time periods that may not reflect present causes of

TABLE 10.4   *Percentage Change in Employment by Region and Source of Change, 1970–72*

	Start-Ups and Expansions	Failures and Contractions	In-Migration	Out-Migration	Net Change
Northeast	15.8	−22.0	0.4	−0.5	−6.3
North Central	16.6	−19.8	0.2	−0.2	−3.2
South	21.7	−21.6	0.3	−0.2	0.2
West	22.6	−24.6	0.2	−0.1	−1.9

SOURCE: Adapted from Peter M. Allaman and David L. Birch, "Components of Employment Change for States by Industry Group 1970–72" (Working Paper no. 5, Joint Center for Urban Studies of MIT and Harvard University, September 1975), p. 15.

migratory patterns; and they fail to account for relocations of corporate headquarters, which, to some communities today, may be a greater threat than plant closings and relocations. Yet they do provide information indicating that expansions and start-ups are significant factors in a realistic understanding of the process of regional economic development.

CHANGING STRUCTURE OF THE LABOR FORCE

Shifts in population, investment, and employment from some regions to others is part of a long-term transition in the United States. Another large-scale force that affects the prosperity of regions is change in the structure of the work force. The relative shift of employment from manufacturing to services industries, plus the process of modernization within labor-intensive, manufacturing industries, dramatically influences the employment and income prospects of particular states and regions. For example, a study by the Upjohn Institute for Employment Research published in 1983 found that 27 to 37 percent of the jobs for production painters in the auto industry would be displaced by robots by 1990.[41] For the auto industry as a whole, the study anticipated aggregate job displacement of 6 to 11 percent of the blue-collar work force in the auto industry, whereas less than 1 percent would be eliminated for the United States as a whole.[42] Judging from this study, the impact of automation on employment will be very specific to certain industries and to particular jobs in those industries.

The consequences of robotization will be more dramatic for some regions and states than others. Since a primary application for robots is in the production of autos, states of the upper Midwest will experience the brunt of job displacement from this technological change. Michigan, for example, can be expected to lose 5 to 9 percent of its 1978 employment in semiskilled and unskilled jobs owing to robot installation by 1990.[43] Southeast Michigan, the location of the majority of automotive employment, is anticipated to experience 87 percent of this job displacement. Thus the impact can be highly specific regionally.

Several caveats are in order when considering such projections. First, attrition rather than unemployment will account for most of the positions eliminated by robotization. Automation involves a long-term transition, and natural processes of turnover and retirement will usually accommodate employment impacts.

Second, while many jobs are eliminated by new technologies, others are created. For the total U.S. economy, between 100,000 and 200,000 jobs now performed by persons will be done by robots. However, new positions in robot manufacturing, in supplier firms to robot manufacturers, in robot systems engineering, and in corporate users will add from 32,000 to 64,000 jobs by 1990.[44] Moreover, the jobs eliminated are often low skill, dirty, and potentially dangerous, whereas the new jobs created often require more technical training and are more satisfying.

These redeeming factors do not address the concerns of persons who would have had a job, whatever the skill, and are not working because of automation. They also fail to respond to the community that suffers attrition or unemployment due to robots and that may not participate to any substantial extent in the new occupations resulting from this shift. Personal and community dislocation is a natural result of large-scale shifts in technology and occupational mix.

The importance of new job creation to the economic vitality of states and regions is widely accepted in the thinking of public and private sector leaders today. In fact, as judged by a fierce competition between states and regions for jobs and investment, the strategy of new job creation has virtually become conventional wisdom. The next section examines several general approaches by leaders at the state and local levels to the challenge of economic development.

STRATEGIES FOR LOCAL AND REGIONAL ECONOMIC DEVELOPMENT

In the last decade most states, counties, and individual communities have come to realize their economic futures cannot be taken for granted — it is too important to leave the dictates of changing industry economics, and it may well be unwise to depend on federal assistance programs. While the impact of local action on the large-scale process of economic development may be limited, many positive actions can and should be undertaken. In fact it has become increasingly clear that the state or region that does not plan may be left far behind in the intense race for development. This realization has led to a plethora of local efforts involving the public sector, the private sector, and often cooperative programs between them. In general, local and regional approaches to economic development can be classified into programs that (1) seek to revitalize and retain an existing industrial base, (2) attempt to attract existing industry into the region, and (3) aim to strengthen or diversify a local economy by developing new investment from within the area.

Revitalization and Retention Strategies

These efforts are, naturally, concentrated in the older industrial region of the northern and eastern United States. The mature industries of that part of the country — for example, automotive, steel, machine tool, and transportation equipment — involve markets that have been strongly penetrated by foreign competitors. These industries have been facing simultaneous pressures to consolidate capacity, improve efficiencies, and increase quality. With unstable or poor earnings, high investment requirements for modernization, and limited access to capital markets due to already highly leveraged balance sheets, companies in these industries and the communities in which they are located have been facing a rather dismal outlook. In many areas the impact of job and revenue loss to the community has stimulated considerable review about the strengths and weaknesses of the particular region and its prospects for revitalization.

Special programs in public sector investment financing are common in states and communities facing these problems. Industrial revenue bonds and public sector guarantees for loans used to purchase plant or equipment compose a common instrument giving existing companies access to capital below market rates.

Poor union-management relationships are legion in the heavy, maturing industries of the country. Realizing this, many communities have initiated programs to establish improved communications between the leaders of labor and industry. In addition, training and assistance programs dedicated to improving work quality and productivity through collaboration in quality of work life, quality control, and profit-sharing systems are relatively common at the local level in communities in the northeastern United States. Insert 10.D describes the effort of one community in Upstate New York to utilize cooperation from business, labor, and academia to improve competitiveness of local industry.

Planning on a regional level is also a more common occurrence throughout the country. Information about trends in population growth, mix, and distribution as well as information about employment will likely become collected more systematically and be available to the public. In addition strategic questions about regional competitive strengths and weaknesses for business can, and should, be explicitly asked. These are relatively straightforward tasks, and studies of this nature are frequently sponsored by private institutions, such as foundations, or joint public-private task forces. A more difficult task is the creation of community consensus about

Insert 10.D

BUSINESS-GOVERNMENT-UNIVERSITY COOPERATION AT THE LOCAL LEVEL [QUOTATION]

Courageous and imaginative local political leaderships can do a great deal to promote labor-management cooperation in increasing productivity and thereby enhancing their city's competitive position. The example of Jamestown, New York, where Mayor Stanley Lundine . . . was able to persuade management and unions to explore together ways by which costs could be reduced and effectiveness increased is one that should be studied by every political leader who is seriously interested in maintaining and increasing the competitive position of his or her city. Not only political leadership but labor and management as well have much to learn from the Jamestown story. Their relations do not have to be those of a zero-sum game. What Lundine did was to persuade the unions that productivity did not have to be euphemism for a speed up, and he persuaded management that the unions might have a number of good ideas as to how costs could be cut. Lundine was able to persuade unions and management to form a joint committee and add to it industrial engineers from the universities with the object of seeing how best to restore the competitive position of Jamestown's industry. As a result of these efforts Jamestown was transformed from a town with a bad labor image, in three years unemployment was cut in half and the situation changed from one of net disinvestment to one of net investment. What Lundine did in Jamestown is in principle doable elsewhere.

SOURCE: Norton E. Long, "Public/Private Coalition: Hope for Urban Survival," *National Civic Review* 69 (October 1980): 1488. Used with permission.

---

goals concerning population growth and economic development. Perhaps the most difficult task is the mobilization of fragmented and competitive governmental authorities to coordinate policies for realizing regional objectives.

One apparently successful instance of a long-term, comprehensive planning and development effort took place in northeastern Pennsylvania in the late 1960s and early 1970s. This region faced economic decline and deterioration from loss of employment in coal mining and fast population growth from the expansion of tourism and recreation industries. The region needed simultaneously to revitalize large pockets of unemployment and poverty and to plan and channel forces for growth.

Utilizing both public and private funds, an agency called the Economic Development Council of Northeastern Pennsylvania was formed. Its board of directors included county commissioners of all seven counties in the region and representatives from a cross section of the region's banks, utilities, realtors, and industries.[45] One participant in this endeavor described the integrative result of the agency's effort:

> The development agency concept involves an effort to bring together various public and private agencies within northeastern Pennsylvania to hear the views of local groups on problems and areas of major concern facing the region. Such meetings have brought together chambers of commerce, agricultural interests, human resource agencies, mining interests, historical groups, tourist promotion agencies, housing agencies, educational institutions, and business firms. The meetings are more than just general gatherings; they represent first attempts at developing a consensus as to the strategy the region should follow in reaching for new opportunities to encourage sound economic and physical growth, with a meaningful input of local views.[46]

The goals outlined by this coordination effort included:

- Programs to raise per capita income,
- Individual and community action to improve the physical environment,
- Simplification of the fragmented system of local government,
- Development of human resources, and
- Promotion of a more up-to-date district image.

In addition to working toward these goals, the agency serves as a clearinghouse and point of coordination for local needs and development effforts. It sponsored an outside study of economic diversification that led to more focused promotion of the area, and it has stimulated planning and interchange in the region in areas such as needed graduate educational programs, trends in economic development and labor-management relations, and assessment of opportunities to exploit domestic spin-offs from space and defense technology.

The potential benefits from such large-scale coordination of public and private institutions are great, but the process requires patience. It is often difficult, laboriously slow, and frustrating. The threshold requirements for successful effort may discourage widespread use of this model. However, the increasing need for multisector joint planning at the regional level may make it an obvious and more frequently undertaken challege.

Inducements by States and Localities to Attract Existing Industry

Promotional and advertising campaigns extolling the benefits of particular areas as sites for plant expansions or relocations are common tools in the armamentarium of local and state economic development agencies. The more aggressive programs of business recruitment involve overseas as well as domestic visitations, multimedia presentations, and personal involvement by the most visible private and public sector leaders in an area. A high degree of marketing professionalism has entered the competition for industry.

In addition to promotional and personal appeals for new industry, a variety of inducements or incentives are utilized by state and local governments to attract new firms or to aid in the expansion of existing businesses. According to studies in the 1970s:

- 45 states were offering tax-free state and local revenue bond financing to industry,
- 29 states offered other types of low-interest loans,
- 25 states did not collect sales taxes on newly purchased industrial equipment, and
- 38 states did not place inventory taxes on goods in transit.[47]

In addition, there is wide use of public industrial development bureaus and a variety of financial incentives — such as tax credits, tax abatements, and rapid depreciation.

Research on the most important business factors in location decisions has assigned mixed results to the importance of state and local taxes. For example, several investigators have concluded that financial incentives have only minor significance:

> Indeed, the patterns of regional economic growth and business development would probably not look much different in the absence of the existing plethora of developmental incentives. . . . In the main, government is subsidizing firms for undertaking investments that would likely have been made in any case. Furthermore, when one considers that any incentive designed to reduce a company's state or local tax bill will increase that firm's federal tax liability — due to the deductibility of state and local taxes in computing federal net taxable income — the superfluidity of fiscal incentives becomes even more apparent.[48]

Strategies for Developing New Industry from within a Region: The High-Tech Scramble

A third discernible strategy for local economic development assumes that an existing capability for invention and innovation within a specified region can be a major source of new industry and new employment. The absence of risk capital, technical expertise, and entrepreneurial management are often assumed to restrain meaningful participation in emerging growth and advanced technology industries. Numerous state and local programs in place today are intended to overcome these perceived obstacles to future investment and growth.

State funding for new technology-based ventures has made a dramatic emergence as an instrument of public policy. By mid-1984 at least 20 states were known to have implemented a program in venture finance, and many states were expected to follow this pattern.[49] Some states, for example, Indiana and Iowa, raised venture capital funds by giving a tax credit to corporations for their investments in the state fund. Others, such as Michigan, New York, Ohio, Oregon, and Washington, liberalized their pension regulations to allow limited venture investments. In 1983 these five states had committed $237 million in venture financing.[50] As nearly $300 billion in assets are held by local government retirement systems, the amount dedicated to fostering new ventures is expected to rise.

The Connecticut Product Development Corporation is perhaps one of the best known and most successful state programs in fostering new enterprise development. Formed in 1972, this organization pays for the cost of developing new products in small, high-technology companies in the state in return for a 5 percent royalty on the product's sales. Between 1980 and 1983 the corporation reported a 15 percent return on its investments, and since 1976 it claims to have created 1,300 jobs.[51]

A publication of the Office of Technology Assessment (OTA) in 1984 identified 153 government programs at the state level designed to promote technological innovation and high-technology development.[52] Half of the programs submitted to detailed analysis involved financial assistance. Assistance in finding venture capital and provision of long-term loans or loan guarantees were common. About a third of the programs were training programs, usually tied to monies available from federal sources. Partnerships with universities for high-technology education programs were another important focus of activity.

Universities and local governments have also spawned a range of economic development programs aimed toward technology-based industries. Universities have built research and science parks, actively sought collaborative research relationships with industry, and embarked on entrepreneurial training programs and various types of venture or seed capital investments of their own. Local governments are participating in this movement through land-use planning, vocational training, incubator facilities, and a variety of other initiatives. University and local government programs are often the result of community-wide efforts involving the active participation and support of local industry. Insert 10.E presents the con-

---

Insert 10.E

FACTORS CONTRIBUTING TO THE SUCCESS OF LOCAL HIGH-TECHNOLOGY DEVELOPMENT STRATEGIES

> No single factor explains why some communities and regions have been more successful than others in nurturing and benefiting from high-technology development. For every locational determinant identified in economic theory or implicit in government practice, examples can be provided of cities that have several or all of the ingredients but have not yet achieved success. A strong research university, skilled labor pool, available financing, the presence of corporate headquarters, transportation, good climate, cultural amenities — all may be desirable or necessary preconditions, but they are not always enough.

One factor that turns out to be an additional consideration is the nature of local cooperation and leadership. The OTA report continues:

> States and communities that have benefited most . . . have three characteristics in common:
>
> - an organizational culture that promotes a *common civic perspective* and a positive attitude about the attributes and prospects of the region;
> - an environment that nurtures *leaders, both public and private,* who combine an established track record for innovation and entrepreneurship with a broad view of their community's resources and promise; and
> - a network of *business/civic advocacy organizations* that attracts the membership of top officers of major companies and receives from them the commitment to work on efforts of mutual concern, including cooperation with the public sector.

SOURCE: U.S., Office of Technology Assessment, *Technology, Innovation, and Regional Economic Development: Encouraging High-Technology Development — Background Paper # 2* Washington, D.C.: Congress of the United States, OTA-BP-STI-25, February 1984), p. 53.

clusions of this study about the most important factors contributing to success of such efforts.

IN CONCLUSION

Relationships and responsibilities between businesses and communities played no role in original premises of free enterprise and the market system; economic efficiency and the well-being of society were best served by unhampered movement of labor and capital. While this principle still guides economic policy in a general and abstract sense, a mature industrial economy presents problems unanticipated by the precepts of capitalism. When the question becomes one of the large-scale shifts of jobs and investments, social criteria — such as maintaining the cities as vital economic units and striving for a racially and economically open society — need to be included in the formulation of public policy. In addition, human criteria — such as creating job opportunities for disenfranchised groups and minimizing the suffering associated with job loss — must also be figured into the calculus of social policy. On the one hand, society must cope with problems of a declining manufacturing base, fewer unskilled jobs and a large unskilled labor force, economic and racial isolation, and the human and social cost of economic change. On the other hand, solutions to these national problems, including mobility and efficient utilization of capital, need to fit the overall framework of a market system as well as possible.

This chapter has reviewed several facets of this complex problem. With respect to urban areas and geographical regions, discussion has identified the importance of jobs and investment and has reviewed governmental actions and public policy proposals to redirect resources into declining areas. The discussion also pointed out the intimate relation that race, education, skills, and economic class appear to have to urban crisis, and it has taken the view that these problems are in part institutional, for which institutional solutions are needed. The two primary areas of business-government interaction — urban revitalization and regional development — appear to require innovative concepts of economic recovery and broader, more encompassing interinstitutional cooperation. The need for civic leadership in defining and fostering these paths is obviously great.

DISCUSSION QUESTIONS

1. What do you see as the main dimensions of the urban crisis and urban economic decline? What are major sources of revitalization?
2. What national priority would you assign to urban development? What are the dangers or risks or doing nothing?
3. What are feasible policies for the public sector in relation to urban development? What role can managers and corporations play?

4. What issues are raised for business in the light of interregional shifts of population, employment, and investment? How can business leaders be best prepared to deal with these issues?

NOTES

1. These data are taken from U.S., Department of Commerce, Bureau of the Census, *Statistical Abstract of the United States: 1984* (Washington, D.C.: Government Printing Office, 1983) pp. 9–38, 415.

2. John F. Kain, "Urban Problems," in *Social Responsibility and the Business Predicament,* ed. James W. McKie (Washington, D.C.: Brookings Institution, 1974), pp. 217–46.

3. Marilyn Marks, "The Urban Agenda: The Focus Is On Helping Cities Help Themselves," *National Journal,* August 11, 1984, p. 1514.

4. Ibid.

5. Larry C. Giunipero, "Developing Effective Minority Purchasing Programs," *Sloan Management Review* 22 (1981): 33–42.

6. Cathy Trost, "Minority Firms Get Smaller Share of U.S. Contracts under Reagan," *Wall Street Journal,* April 10, 1984, p. 31.

7. Ibid.

8. Thomas M. Buynak, *The Community Reinvestment Act, Economic Commentary* (Cleveland, Ohio: Federal Reserve Bank of Cleveland, December 26, 1978).

9. "Bank Mergers Carry Unlikely Fallout," *Public Administration Times* 7 (July 15, 1984): 12.

10. Ibid.

11. Ibid.

12. "Urban Enterprise Zone Plan Stresses Business Tax Breaks," *Congressional Quarterly Report,* May 9, 1981, pp. 805–9.

13. Joann S. Lublin, "States Expand Enterprise Zones Despite Lack of Federal Incentives," *Wall Street Journal,* July 31, 1984, p. 33.

14. Ibid.

15. Ibid.

16. U.S., Department of Commerce, Bureau of Census, "Estimates of the Population of States: 1970–1983," *Current Population Reports, Population Estimates and Projections,* Series P-25, no. 957, p. 1.

17. U.S., Department of Commerce, Bureau of Census, *Statistical Abstract of the United States 1984* (Washington, D.C.: Government Printing Office, 1984, p. 15.

18. U.S., Department of Commerce, Bureau of Census, "Geographical Mobility: March 1982 to March 1983," *Current Population Reports, Population Characteristics,* Series P-20, no. 393 (October 1984), p. 2.

19. U.S., Department of Labor, Bureau of Labor Statistics, "Average Area Supplement," *Current Population Report,* 1970 and 1980. Data supplied by Department of Labor.

20. Frank E. Morris, "Changing Opportunities — Why Business Moves" (Speech presented to the Conference on Alternatives to Confrontation: "A National Policy toward Regional Change," Austin, Texas, September 26, 1977).

21. Philip L. Rones, "Moving to the Sun: Regional Job Growth, 1968 to 1978," *Month Labor Review* 103 (March 1980): 15.

22. Ibid., p. 16.

23. "Federal Spending: The North's Loss Is the Sunbelt's Gain," *National Journal,* June 16, 1976, p. 883.

24. Ibid., p. 878.

25. C. L. Jusenius and L. C. Ledebur, *A Myth in the Making: The Southern Economic Challenge and Northern Economic Decline,* prepared for the Office of Economic Research, Economic Development Administration, U.S., Department of Commerce (Washington D.C.: Government Printing Office, November 1976).

26. Ibid., p. 28.

27. Richard Corrigan and Rochelle L. Stanfield, "Rising Energy Prices — What's Good for Some States Is Bad for Others," *National Journal,* March 22, 1980, pp. 468–74.

28. David J. Morgan, *Patterns of Population Distribution: A Residential Preference Model and Its Dynamics* (Chicago: Department of Geography, University of Chicago, 1976) p. 22.

29. Rones, "Moving," p. 17.

30. Ibid.

31. See, for example, Ed Kelley and Lee Webb, eds., *Plant Closings,* (Washington, D.C.: Conference on Alternative State and Local Policies, 1979), p. 2.

32. Karl Frieden, *Workplace Democracy and Productivity* (Washington, D.C.: National Center for Economic Alternatives, 1980), p. 55.

33. U.S., Congress, Senate, *Employee Protection and Community Stabilization Act of 1979,* 96th Cong., 1st sess., S. Rept. 1609, 1979.

34. U.S., Congress, Senate, *Hearing before the Subcommittee on Labor Standards of the Committee on Education and Labor,* on H.R. 76, 95th Cong. 2nd sess. August 15, 1978, pp. 66–67.

35. U.S., Congress, Senate, *Hearing before the Subcommittee on Labor and Human Resources on S. 1609,* 96th Cong., 2d sess., March 7, 1980, pp. 222, 224.

36. Archie B. Carroll, "When Business Closes Down: Social Responsibilities and Management Actions," *California Management Review* 26 (Winter 1984): 127.

37. Ibid.

38. Peter M. Allaman and David L. Birch, "Components of Employment Change for States by Industry Group, 1970–72 (Working Paper no. 5, Joint Center for Urban Studies of MIT and Harvard University, September 1975), pp. 1–8.

39. John Rees, "Manufacturing Change, Internal Control and Govern-

ment Spending in a Growth Region of the U.S.A.," in *Industrial Change: International Experience and Public Policy,* ed. F. E. Ian Hamilton (London: Longman, 1978), pp. 155–74.

40. H. Craig Leroy, "The Effects of Plant-Closing Legislation," *Journal of Contemporary Studies,* Summer 1983, p. 78.

41. H. Allan Hunt and Timothy L. Hunt, *Human Resource Implications of Robotics* (Kalamazoo, Mich.: Upjohn Institute for Employment Research, 1983) p. 79.

42. Ibid., p. 82.

43. Ibid., p. 89.

44. Ibid., p. x–xi.

45. Howard J. Grossman, "Regional Development Districts: A Case Study of Northeastern Pennsylvania," *Growth and Change,* October 1973, pp. 4–9.

46. Ibid., p. 5.

47. Bernard L. Weinstein and Robert E. Firestine, *Regional Growth and Decline in the United States* (New York: Praeger, 1978), p. 139.

48. Ibid., p. 134.

49. Carol Steinback and Robert Gusking, "High-Risk Ventures Strike Gold with State Government Financing," *National Journal,* September 24, 1984, p. 1767.

50. Ibid., p. 1769.

51. Ibid., p. 1768.

52. U.S., Congress, Office of Technology Assessment, *Technology, Innovation, and Regional Economic Development* (Washington, D.C.: Government Printing Office, 1984), p. 11.

Enterprise Zones
Fact or Fantasy for Urban Development?

Enterprise zone legislation has gained the support of conservative and liberal federal legislators, yet languishes in legislative limbo — leaving individual states to develop their own enterprise zone programs. This different approach to improving the quality of life in decaying or depressed areas originated in England under the sponsorship of Sir Geoffrey Howe (an experienced British public official). Proving to be a somewhat elusive concept, enterprise zone legislation typically offers a combination of relief measures from constraints to businesses if they choose to locate in depressed areas of the country. Legislators and President Ronald Reagan have concentrated proposed relief from constraints in one or more of the following four areas: taxation, regulation, local services, and community involvement. It was believed by some persons that depressed areas (particularly declining inner cities) could, once again, prove attractive as business locations if the federal government provided the right combination of incentives.

These incentives would be available to businesses only if they located in areas designated as enterprise zones by the federal government. Areas likely to qualify as enterprise zones would typically have chronically high unemployment levels and/or large numbers of inhabitants living near poverty level standards. Older Frostbelt cities would be prime candidates to qualify for enterprise zone status.

LEGISLATIVE ATTEMPTS

On June 12, 1980, Congressmen Jack Kemp (Republican, New York, representing the Buffalo area) and Robert Garcia (Democrat, New York, rep-

---

Based upon a previous case written by Darrell Kelly and Carol J. Fritz that appears as Case 8.A in the first edition.

resenting the South Bronx) introduced H. 7563, a bill to establish enterprise zones in areas with high unemployment and poverty. The legislation focused upon small business development, rather than attracting major industry to the inner cities.

Along with its Senate counterpart, S.2823, introduced by Republicans Rudy Boschwitz (Minnesota) and John H. Chaffee (Rhode Island), this bill tested the political waters in order to identify provisions that would have difficulty passing and those upon which to base a 1984 bill to be introduced into the new 97th Congress. Provisions that drew the most fire, and were subsequently dropped in the 1981 version, included the requirement that local governments cut property taxes in these zones, that social security payroll taxes on employers and employees be reduced 50 to 90 percent — depending upon the age of the employee, and that a subminimum wage rate be established to stimulate employment among young and unskilled workers. The latter two provisions were strongly opposed by organized labor and also by liberal Garcia, who stated that the bill would be weakened by any provision detrimental to labor or minorities.[1]

In June 1981 the revised bills were introduced into the House and Senate by the previously mentioned sponsors. As introduced, the bills contained provisions for a more flexible approach to demonstrate local commitment and paid more attention to the needs of newly developed small businesses, including bigger tax incentives and a provision for start-up capital. Efforts to bring enterprise zone proposals to a legislative vote were frustrated, as the bill became stalled in the House Ways and Means Committee. In addition to some congressional support for enterprise zones, President Reagan has also avidly supported the general concept since his 1980 campaign. In 1982, after a tour of revitalized Baltimore, Reagan announced, "We've seen a vision today and it works." He then defined "what works" as private initiative in lieu of direct federal funding to cities.[2] Baltimore's Mayor William Schaefer quickly pointed out to Reagan that in fact much of Baltimore's revitalization was directly underwritten by the federal government.

However, despite strong executive support and some congressional support, no enterprise zone legislation was passed in Congress in 1981. In 1982 and again in 1983, Reagan sought legislative approval of the enterprise zone plan, describing it as a "free market approach to our nation's urban problems."[3] The Reagan enterprise zone program contained four basic elements that sought to improve the economic lot of businesses and inhabitants of enterprise zones. Each element was supported by specific incentives available only to persons, entities, and businesses existing within the boundaries of an enterprise zone:

- Reduced federal, state, and local taxes for enterprise zone businesses.
    — 10 percent tax credit for construction and/or rehabilitation of commercial, industrial structures.
    — 10 percent tax credit to employers for payroll paid to bona fide

zone employees in excess of wages paid to such employees in the prior year.

— Elimination of capital gains taxes for qualified property.

— Relief from tariff and import duties to designated foreign trade zones within certain enterprise zones.

— Excess tax credits allowed to be carried back three years and forward for the life of the zone.

- Regulatory relief at the federal, state, and local levels for enterprise zone businesses.

— State and local governments may request enterprise zone relief from any federal regulation (barring regulations (1) that are required by a statute or (2) that protect the public from significant environmental/safety risks).

- Plans to improve local services, including experimentation with private alternatives to provide those services.

— Not provided for directly by federal enterprise zone plan. However, states and/or local governments may improve local services in an effort to satisfy enterprise zone designation criteria, which require local governments to demonstrate commitment to the program prior to being selected as an enterprise zone.

- Neighborhood involvement so that local residents participate in the economic success of their zones.

— 5 percent tax credit for capital investments in personal property.

— 10 percent tax credit for the construction of rental housing structures.

— 50 percent wage tax credit to employers hiring disadvantaged individuals (50 percent available for initial three years and 10 percent for every year afterward).

— 5 percent tax credit, $525 limit per employee, given to qualified zone employees.[4]

The bill was approved by the Senate Finance Committee, yet it never reached the Senate floor in 1982. Strong opposition to the bill existed in the Democrat-controlled House, and no hearings were held on the president's enterprise zone proposal.

Undaunted, Reagan resubmitted his enterprise zone proposal, entitled "The Enterprise Zone Employment and Development Act of 1983," to Congress in March 1983. Changes from the previous year included a requirement that one third of the designated zones be in rural areas, reduced qualifications for small communities seeking enterprise zone status, and a provision for coordinated state and federal tax incentives.[5]

As in previous proposals, up to 75 enterprise zones could be designated by the Department of Housing and Urban Development (HUD) over a three-year period. While many more areas may apply for such favored status, applications would be evaluated on state and local efforts to revitalize the distressed areas. In theory a state could choose to concentrate its efforts in (1) reducing regulations and (2) improving services in potential federal enterprise zone areas while refusing to provide tax relief and still be eligible for enterprise zone status. Individual enterprise zones would receive favored treatment for as long as the state/local government chose or up to 20 years — whichever time period elapsed first. This act also provided for a four-year phaseout period.

By January 1984 both the House and Senate had developed bills reflective of the president's enterprise zone proposal (H. 1955, S. 863). The House Ways and Means Committee chairman, Dan Rostenkowski (Democrat — Illinois), had expressed concern about the bill, consequently scheduling no action on the bill in the committee.[6] The House bill appeared doomed; however, enterprise zone legislation was proposed for inclusion in Senate and House tax bills. Once again, the House blocked such a move and Rostenkowski claimed that a time of high budget deficits was not the time to create new tax breaks.[7] The Treasury estimated that the lost tax revenues from enterprise zone legislation would be approximately $3.4 billion after five years into the program.[8]

Reagan, obviously frustrated with Democratic resistance in the House, complained, "If [the Democrats] really wanted a future of boundless opportunity for our citizens, why have they buried enterprise zones, over the years, in committee?"[9] In response to the president's denouncement, some Democrats have echoed familiar criticisms of the enterprise zone concept. They question, Would any *new* jobs in fact be created, or would businesses simply transfer their current employees to job positions in enterprise zones? In addition some legislators claim the zones to be a method for giving out tax deductions without strings attached. According to Congressman Fortney Stark (Democrat — California), "There's no way to control it [enterprise zones]. It's a very sloppy loophole."[10] In fact there appears to be no clear-cut answer to these and other concerns relevent to enterprise zone goals.

ENTERPRISE ZONES — PROS AND CONS

Theoretical Issues

Debate over creation of enterprise zones exists on theoretical and pragmatic levels. At a theoretical level enterprise zone controversy reflects the ongoing debate over whether it is more efficient for the government to expand employment opportunities by moving people to jobs or jobs to people. Most government efforts to date have followed the former approach — giving people education, job training, or transportation to help them move up job ladders or across boundaries into long-term employment. The enterprise zones plan follows the other course, enticing existing or incipient enterprises to locate in areas of high unemployment.

Another, somewhat theoretical, concern addresses the possible repercussions resulting from a highly successful enterprise zone program. If these zones do attract thriving businesses, what will happen to the surrounding property values? A dramatic increase in property values could trigger a large hike in rental rates, effectively forcing out the very inhabitants the program had intended to help.

Moreover, in theory enterprise zones may violate some American views on fairness and equality. Is it right to allow some businesses to create possibly more pollution, pay less than their "fair share" in taxes, and generally be subject to less federal and local regulatory scrutiny than their competitors across the street in nonenterprise zones? Some observers respond by claiming that "the ends justify the means," whereas others insist there are different methods for achieving the same results without forsaking values of fairness and egalitarianism.

Finally, a critical question arises: Is the true thrust of enterprise zone proposals focused on increasing the competitiveness of low-income persons in the job market, or is the program more directly aimed at gentrification? If it is the latter, then it would be the cities, not their present inhabitants, who would be "saved" by enterprise zone legislation. While either goal may be desirable, they are not necessarily accomplished in tandem.

Pragmatic Issues

In all debates over pragmatic enterprise zone issues, the use of tax incentives receives considerable attention. Both opponents and supporters of enterprise zones make similar arguments. The net result is that both sides appear to be able to "have their cake and eat it, too." Pro–enterprise zone persons claim that lowering tax rates for businesses willing to locate in the zones will serve as a powerful incentive to attract businesses to the area. Meanwhile, other advocates of enterprise legislation suggest that it will cost the government little in lost tax revenue, as new businesses are rarely profitable for the first few years. While both results are attractive benefits, it is difficult to imagine that they would operate simultaneously.

Arguments against tax incentives suffer from the same flawed reasoning. Some antagonists claim that new businesses will not be lured into enterprise zones with tax relief bait, as these new ventures are not likely to generate a taxable profit in the near future. Other antagonists claim that the program will be too costly, in terms of deferred tax revenues.

There is some evidence that tax incentives will only marginally impact on a business's decision concerning where to locate. Some 78 managers of Fortune 500 companies and smaller companies were interviewed on the subject. A summation of interviews led to the conclusion that "taxation and financing schemes developed by government entities have only a minimal effect on the selection of new plant locations."[11] However, the tax incentives with which these managers were familiar were not as substantial as the proposed combination of federal, state, and local tax incentives.

Sabre Foundation, a policy and public philosophy study foundation, interviewed state officials as to the impact of tax and other incentives on state-designated enterprise zones and came to quite a different conclusion. Sabre claimed that tax incentives in part contributed to the creation/savings of tens of thousands of jobs and attracted nearly $2 billion in private investment.[12]

The ability of enterprise zone programs to create/save jobs has been highly publicized and seriously questioned. First of all, it has proved quite difficult to clarify what constitutes a "saved" or "created" job. Often analysts have had to rely on each individual business's assessment of whether or not they would have created the job elsewhere if an enterprise zone did not exist. A "no" answer would ostensibly characterize a particular job as a "created" job. Similarly, an individual business would have to evaluate whether it would have kept a specific job if it were not in an enterprise zone. Obviously, assessments in both areas must be quite subjective.

Supporters of enterprise zones claim that bringing businesses into these areas will provide numerous jobs for persons who are unable to commute to work outside their neighborhood. In response to a concern that, perhaps, enterprise zone business will "import" employees from outside the zone. Sabre's Dick Cowden suggests, "People outside the neighborhood are reluctant to go to the neighborhood."[13] Others believe that the tax credits available for employers hiring disadvantaged zone inhabitants will more than offset any employer's inclination to hire from outside the neighborhood.

Critics of enterprise zones claim that in fact such legislation will create and/or save few jobs for low-income persons. The tax credit incentive to employ local workers is just one of many tax credits available to enterprise zone businesses. Therefore, critics question whether a surfeit of accessible tax incentives would allow businesses to avoid local hiring without any reduction in their income. Dan Henson, adviser to Baltimore's major business association supports this view. According to Henson, "I don't want a tax credit for hiring and training people if it's going to hassle me. There's not that much tax incentive in the world."[14]

Skepticism of the program's ability to generate new jobs is also shared by uninvolved outsiders. The Congressional Research Service, an extension of the Library of Congress, stated in a report, "There is no empirical evidence that the administration's enterprise zone proposal would create economic activity, without the added stimulus of public investment."[15] Garcia and others had intended enterprise zones to operate in conjunction with other federal programs to revitalize urban centers; however, Reagan has eliminated or reduced other federal support programs in this area.

At the end of 1984 the future of federal enterprise zone legislation appears to be up for grabs. Optimists suggest a few reasons why proposed enterprise legislation might fare better in Congress in 1985. During 1983 and 1984, it was felt by some that Democrats were unwilling to support Republican legislation that would help their constituents back home. As the presidential and other national elections passed, Democrats might be more amenable to bipartisan efforts to pass the proposal.[16] Others suggest that enterprise zone legislation might pass owing to a dearth of alternatives. As National Urban League official Maudine Cooper acknowledged:

> We all know that this administration is not going to be pouring money into the cities, so what else is there? Folks are looking for answers, and anything new will get some support. We're grasping at straws.[17]

Meanwhile, Garcia suggests another reason why the proposal might survive: "The old ideas didn't work. We have nothing to lose in trying a new one."[18]

Those who believe the bill has no future frequently point to increasing federal deficits. Admittedly, federal enterprise zone programs have no proven track record in the United States. Therefore, no one really knows how much federal revenue, which otherwise might serve to shrink the deficit, will be sacrificed to support zone legislation. Further hampering the success of enterprise zone legislation is the fact that no one knows how many jobs will genuinely be created or saved as a result of this legislation. Without answers to these basic questions it is unclear what the cost-per-job-created-or-saved might actually be. It has been suggested by some that zone legislation might be the equivalent of "shooting an elephant to make mouse stew." Therefore, federal legislators might remain reluctant to approve the president's proposal. Meanwhile, individual states continue to enact their own versions of enterprise zone programs.

STATES' ENTERPRISE ZONE ACTIVITY: A SPECIAL REPORT

Tired of waiting for Congress to take definitive action on federal enterprise zone legislation, states have increasingly decided to take matters into their own hands. (See Exhibit 1.) As of October 1984, 18 states had active enterprise zones and 6 more states had passed, but not yet acted on, zone legislation.[19] In part, states have created enterprise zones in response to pressure applied by officials in their cities. For some local officials enterprise zones may appear to be a progressive answer to local economic-related woes. However, other city planners simply feel their city must be targeted as an enterprise zone in order to compete for jobs effectively. According to Harold L. Wolman, research associate at the Urban Institute, "A lot of cities feel they can't afford to be the only ones without a [enterprise zone] package."[20]

EXHIBIT 1   *Profile of a Typical State Enterprise Zone*

Area	5.3 square miles
Months of Operational Zone	8.7
Zone Residents Seeking Work	2,026
Characteristics Since Activation	
Number of Start-up Businesses	1.9
Number of Business Expansions	1.1
Number of Business Renovations	1.1
Number of New Jobs	54
Number of Planned Jobs	99
Number of Jobs Saved	48
Number of New Jobs for Disadvantaged	26
Amount of New Investment	$6,132,000

SOURCE: Richard Cowden, *Enterprise Zone Activity in the States* (Washington, D.C.: Sabre Foundation, November, 1983). Used with permission.

To date, apparently only one organization has actually surveyed the impact of state-sponsored enterprise zone legislation in different communities. In 1983 the Sabre Foundation, whose mission emphasizes public philosophy and policy studies, attempted to measure the effect that enterprise zones had on employment, new investment, and fiscal issues in nine states. Three qualifying conditions limit any attempts to draw broad-based conclusions from the survey results: (1) there was heavy reliance on subjective data (each zone provided all the relevant statistics); (2) most enterprise zones had been operational for less than one year; and (3) different criteria was used by states in determining which areas would qualify as needing enterprise zone relief. Qualifying conditions notwithstanding, Sabre proclaimed, "The message of the data is clear: enterprise zones are delivering results."[21]

EMPLOYMENT

Measurement of changes in enterprise zone employment conditions was divided into four categories: jobs created, jobs saved, jobs planned, and jobs "pending." A job, in this survey, was defined as "created" if a new job opening developed in the region after the area was designated as an enterprise zone. The term *created* raises some questions, as no attempt was made to determine whether the company already had planned to develop that position elsewhere. If so, perhaps *transferred* would be a more accurate term. *Planned jobs* refers to positions predicted to be filled by a company within three years of operating within a zone, whereas *pending jobs* refers to positions that city officials believe a company will eventually establish within an enterprise zone.[22] (See Exhibit 2.) Information pertinent in determining whether planned and pending jobs would have been created elsewhere is also lacking.

The Sabre survey also indicated that a proportionately high number of disadvantaged persons were recipients of the created and/or saved jobs. Five cities that tracked hiring practices stated that disadvantaged workers accounted for 23 to 100 percent of the "new hires" in their zone.[23] Taken at face value, this statistic might appear to support the claim that enterprise zones do serve the economic needs of low-income and no-income persons. However, over 100 communities did not track hiring practices within their area triggering doubts as to whether improving the economic lot of zone inhabitants is, indeed, a high priority overall.

In response to the question, Do enterprise zones lead to the creation of new jobs?, the Sabre Foundation responded, "In the state and local experience the answer is clearly yes."[24] The study's lack of ability to determine definitively (1) whether employment gains within the enterprise zones are offset by an equal number of employment losses outside the zone and (2) whether zone inhabitants are the typical beneficiaries of newly created jobs, however, serves to underscore the concerns of some congressional legislators and urban analysts.

NEW INVESTMENT

Private investment in new construction, expansion, or renovation is classified as new investment. (See Exhibit 3.) Between 1981 and September 1983, rural and urban enterprise zones reported that a combined total of $450 million was invested by private organizations in the above-mentioned areas.[25]

By category the retail industry represented the largest portion of new enterprise zone business (48 percent). Manufacturing followed next with a 29 percent share of the increase. Service industries represented 18 percent of the new business, whereas miscellaneous industry comprised the remaining amount.[26] Rural areas held an attraction for new manufacturing businesses, whereas urban areas received equal economic stimulus from all sectors.

According to the Sabre Foundation, this growth in enterprise zone activity did not generally stem from business relocations. In fact the foundation noted only one *reported* instance (in Toledo, Ohio) of any noticeable relocation of business caused by the creation of an enterprise zone. Typically, growth was attributed to expansion of existing industries within the

EXHIBIT 2 *Expansion in Enterprise Zone Employment,*
1981–September 1983

Category	Number
Jobs created	4,601
Jobs saved	4,085
Jobs planned	8,477
Jobs "pending"	3,108
Total	20,271

SOURCE: Richard Cowden, *Enterprise Zone Activity in the States*
(Washington, D.C.: Sabre Foundation, November, 1983). Used with
permission.

EXHIBIT 3 *Business Start-up/Expansion/Renovations*

Category	Number	Percentage of Total Projects
Start-ups	160	46
Expansions	91	26
Renovations	97	28

SOURCE: Richard Cowden, *Enterprise Zone Activity in the States*
(Washington, D.C.: Sabre Foundation, November, 1983). Used with
permission.

zone and the creation of completely new small businesses. These conclusions were drawn from telephone interviews and questionnaires addressed
to state and local officials.

FISCAL ISSUES

Sabre, in its survey of state enterprise zone activity, concluded that many
fiscal assumptions made by the Treasury Department were inaccurate.
Moreover, the Sabre report claimed, conjectures on the part of the Treasury Department consistently *overestimated* the costs associated with enterprise zones and *underestimated* the benefits to be derived from zone activity.

Sabre stated, contrary to the Treasury Department opinion, that all activity in the zones would not have occurred in another, less favorable business climate. Reports from state officials, received by Sabre, indicated that zone incentives had a major influence on at least 50 percent of the new activity within the enterprise zones.[27] It seems questionable to conclude, however, that the removal of enterprise zone relief as a major influence would have halted that portion of new activity. Perhaps, more appropriately, it might be said that enterprise zone measures enhanced the likelihood of those business activities transpiring within zone boundaries.

Treasury Department estimates of the expected federal enterprise zone costs were not adjusted to account for reduction or elimination of government transfer payments to unemployed and disadvantaged persons. Sabre's report on enterprise zone activity in the states suggested that increases in enterprise zone employment rates would reduce the outflow of government monies represented by welfare payments, unemployment compensation, et cetera. This seems to be a valid supposition, yet few zones actually monitor the degree to which transfer payment recipients are securing jobs within the targeted zones; therefore, the fiscal impact of zone activity in this area can not be measured with any accuracy at this time.

One further Treasury Department assumption, challenged by the Sabre survey, relates to the department's estimates of business tax revenues that would be foregone if federal enterprise zones were created. According to Sabre research, 46 percent of all new business activity within state enterprise zones was represented by new business start-ups.[28] These new businesses, typically unprofitable in their first years, would not be required to pay taxes regardless of their location; this runs contrary to the department's assumption that companies choosing to locate in enterprise zones would have paid taxes had they opted to operate outside of enterprise zone boundaries. Criticisms of Treasury Department estimates in this area, made by Sabre, seem reasonable, yet the proposed federal enterprise zone relief measures are more potent than the current state measures; thus businesses operating at a profit outside of enterprise zones may be more readily enticed to relocate if federal zones were created.

Although the Sabre report unhesitatingly forecasts a promising future for areas designated as enterprise zones, these conclusions appear only partially substantiated by an impartial documentation of facts. Actual fiscal employment and investment results stemming from the creation of enterprise zones have proved to be more elusive than the concept itself.

DISCUSSION QUESTIONS

1. If you were a congressperson or senator who would vote on the proposed legislation, how would you vote, and why? Indicate the provisions that you most favor? What changes, if any, do you feel would strengthen the law?

2. In what manner do you feel enterprise zone legislation would be most likely to induce business development in the inner cities — through relocations, expansions, or start-ups? How long do you anticipate waiting for the impact of this program to be felt?

3. Is government intervention in the operation of the free market justified by the goal of urban development? What do you consider to be the limits of the government's role?

4. Are there other provisions that must be incorporated in the law in order to ensure that the needs of low-income persons are served? Or would additional provisions needlessly complicate the issue? Explain.

NOTES

1. Nadine Cohodas, "Urban Enterprise Zone Plan Stresses Business Tax Breaks," *Congressional Quarterly*, May 9, 1981, p. 807.
2. James Traub, "Urban Enterprise Fraud," *New Republic*, October 18, 1982, p. 11.
3. "Urban Aid Programs," *Congressional Quarterly*, February 5, 1983, p. 283.
4. "Reagan Sends to Congress Message on Enterprise Zones," *Congressional Quarterly*, March 26, 1983, p. 634.
5. "Boxscore," *Congressional Quarterly*, March 12, 1983, p. 533.
6. "Housing/Community Development," *Congressional Quarterly*, January 21, 1984, p. 85.
7. "Housing/Development," *Congressional Quarterly*, July 7, 1984, p. 1611.
8. Susan Smith, "Finance Committee Revives Enterprise Zone Proposal," *Congressional Quarterly*, May 21, 1983, p. 1022.
9. Robert Rothman, "House Democrats Still Stymie Reagan Enterprise Zone Plan," *Congressional Quarterly*, September 29, 1984, p. 2368.
10. Ibid.
11. Fred Withans, "Will Enterprise Zones Work?" *Journal of Business Management*, July 1984, p. 10.
12. Dick Cowden, "Enterprise Zones Escape a Political Twilight," *Wall Street Journal*, October 31, 1984, p. 32.
13. Rothman, "House Democrats Still Stymie Reagan Enterprise Zone Plan," p. 2371.
14. Traub, "Urban Enterprise Fraud," p. 12.
15. Rothman, "House Democrats Still Stymie Reagan Enterprise Zone Plan," pp. 2369–70.
16. Ibid., p. 2369.
17. Ann M. Reilley, "Can Urban Zones Work?" *Dun's Review*, February 1981, p. 55.
18. Ibid.
19. Cowden, "Enterprise Zones Escape a Political Twilight," p. 32.

20. Marilyn Marks, "The New Urban Agenda: The Focus Is On Helping Cities Help Themselves," *National Journal*, August 11, 1984, p. 1516.
21. Richard Cowden, *Enterprise Zone Activity in the States* (Washington, D.C.: Sabre Foundation, November 1983), p. 1.
22. Ibid., p. 14.
23. Ibid., p. 21.
24. Ibid., p. 26.
25. Ibid., p. 1.
26. Ibid., p. 12.
27. Ibid., pp. 20–21.
28. Ibid., p. 21.

Greenhouse Compact
Rhode Islanders Issue "No Confidence" Vote

Rhode Island's economic development plan seemed to contain all the key ingredients considered necessary for successful implementation. The state's citizens and leaders realized (1) Rhode Island (RI) faced severe economic problems, (2) compromise among interest groups was necessary and possible, and (3) remedial action was capable of improving RI's economic future. The plan for Rhode Island's economic future, eventually named the Greenhouse Compact (GC), was developed by the Rhode Island Strategic Development Commission. In fact even the composition of the commission was carefully constructed in a manner thought to enhance the success of their proposals.

The 19 members of the commission and their accompanying 50-member advisory committee were handpicked by Governor J. Joseph Garrahy in September 1982. Garrahy, serving a fourth and final two-year term as governor, wanted to leave an economic policy as a legacy of his gubernatorial career.[1] This intended legacy ultimately was formulated as Rhode Island's most ambitious and comprehensive economic endeavor ever attempted. Acknowledging the need to develop a plan acceptable to the state's interest groups, business, finance, organized labor, higher education, public service, and environmental leaders were actively sought by the governor to become members of the commission and the advisory committee.[2] In general these state leaders willingly accepted roles of responsibility within the commission. Given the cooperative spirit of the commission, combined with an emphasis on generating apolitical solutions to RI's economic problem, the prognosis for Rhode Island's economic future began to look more encouraging.

The commission, intended by the governor to operate with considerable autonomy, spent one year gathering relevant data concerning RI's economic status. The results of this study were published in a voluminous

---

report along with the commission's recommended action plans in October 1983. A consensus plan had been developed, and it was generally accepted by all parties that some sacrifices would have to be made by each of the interest groups in order to advance Rhode Island's economic development.

Commission members felt the GC would be well received by voters, in part owing to three big "plus" factors incorporated in the plan. Multi-partisan involvement in developing the plan would lead to a broadly based sponsorship of the plan. Therefore, the first and most obvious plus factor was in place. Union members would be reassured by their leaders' endorsement of the plan, and members of the business community would hopefully be influenced by their company's executive support of commission proposals. Students would be made aware of their university's confidence in the commission's plans, and the general public could read about all the advantages of the commission's economic proposals in their local newspapers.

Another factor, considered a plus by the commission, centered around the broad scope of the GC. A plan of this size could accomplish far more than individual programs, instituted by state legislation, in a piece-meal manner.

A final plus involved the proposition that major funding for the Greenhouse Compact would *not* come from the voters' pockets. Only a relatively small portion would be underwritten by additional tax monies. The programs, in large part, were planned to be self-sustaining, supported by existing businesses or fueled by a new business tax base created through economic expansion.

In fact, identification of these factors as positive would be hotly contested in the following months by GC opponents. Some state politicians, anticipating this reaction, suggested that the GC goals would be best served (1) if individual programs were gradually phased in, (2) if financial support of programs were gained through state budgetary processes (not requiring voter approval), and (3) if a referendum vote were avoided.[3] The underlying inference suggests that politicians believed the public would not vote in its overall best interests; therefore legislators must "slip in" progressive economic legislation piece by piece.

PERCEPTIONS OF RHODE ISLAND

A major problem alluded to in the GC was the negative self-image held by the state's populace. Chairman of Fleet Financial Group, J. Terrence Murray, remarked, "We continuously shoot ourselves in the foot."[4] Apparently local and national business executives agreed with the state's collective self-assessment. RI's economic base has been declining since the early 1970s, and the GC predicted no net job creation within the state during the 1980s under the existing conditions.[5]

Numerous reasons were cited to explain business's apparent disinclination to build, relocate, or remain in RI. In 1971, 428 manufacturing firms employing 50 persons or more existed in RI. By 1982, 177 of these firms had shut down, relocated, or reduced their operations, resulting in a loss of up to 40,035 jobs for Rhode Islanders.[6] Furthermore, most existing firms planned to expand outside of RI. One of two explanations was typically offered by involved manufacturers: inefficient RI management or belief that other states were more attractive places to locate.

The GC claimed that frequently businesses did not seem to have specific complaints about RI but, rather, felt that the state had a negative attitude toward business, whereas other states would actively court them. In a few cases energy costs and poor labor-management relations were stated as disincentives for building or maintaining business operations in RI.

Further reinforcement of RI's undesirable business atmosphere came from outside sources. The influential Alexander Grant Study, which evaluates the business climates in different areas, ranked RI's business climate as the second *least* desirable in the continental United States. The Conference of State Manufacturers also considered RI to have the second-worst business environment nationwide.

EVALUATION OF RHODE ISLAND ECONOMIC STATUS

While the New England economy appeared to be on the upswing in 1983 through 1984, Rhode Island was expected to be excluded from the general trend. In 1983 Rhode Island lagged behind the national economy and was expected to have a disproportionately high unemployment rate at the end of 1984.[7] For those who remain employed, Rhode Island offered the lowest average civilian manufacturing wage rate in the nation. Industries considered to be in the declining sector employ over 50 percent of RI's industrial employees. (See Exhibit 1.)

The commission determined that only 19 percent of Rhode Islanders were employed in possible growth industries, and 26 percent of the state's employees were in industries considered to be stable. For the remaining 55 percent of employed persons, prospects for job security were not encouraging.[8] The Greenhouse Compact summarized Rhode Island's economic position — if action was not taken:

> Overall, the prospects are bleak. Industries which are likely
> to lose employment or at best stay stable far outweigh those
> with growth prospects. Those companies with growth pros-
> pects often plan to expand out of state.[9]

Although quite a negative statement about the state of economic affairs in Rhode Island, it was not strongly disputed by Rhode Island leaders or the general public. In light of the apparent consensus among the business, labor, government, and general public sectors that Rhode Island was ailing,

EXHIBIT 1 *Economic Forecast for Major Rhode Island Industries*

Major RI Industry	Possible Level of Growth	Explanation
Textiles	Stable or decline	Foreign imports High energy costs
Jewelry	Decline	Outsourcing Mature market
Wire and cable	Stable	Mature market Outsourcing
Fishing	Slight growth	Ecological concerns Foreign competition
Tourism	Growth	Existing but untapped potential
Ports	Undetermined	Excess capacity Infrastructure restrictions
Wholesaling	Decline	Inventory taxes
Defense industry	Slight growth	Competitive bidding
Metalworking	Varied	Successful market "niching" Fragmented industry structure
Retail	Growth	Not given
Higher education	Slight growth	High out-of-state enrollment
Electronics	Slight growth	Successful market "niching"
Health care	Stable	Industrial expansion out of state

SOURCE: Rhode Island Strategic Development Commission, *The Greenhouse Compact, Executive Summary* (Providence, Rhode Island: Rhode Island Strategic Development Commission, November, 1983).

the commission put forth an economic development package (Greenhouse Compact) in October 1983.

GREENHOUSE COMPACT PROPOSALS

Rhode Island's Strategic Development Commission prepared the most comprehensive economic analysis of a U.S. state in existence. This report and its recommendations were spawned, in large part, from interviews with local and neighboring businesspersons. It was obviously an effort to generate pragmatic, rather than theoretical, economic solutions. The results of the report seem to reflect an underlying philosophy of the commission that in order for Rhode Island to prosper "all groups in society must sacrifice, abandon old prejudices, and, most importantly, work together."[10] To this end, the GC outlined programs to provide tax and other financial incentives, research programs, job training, government support, changes in the law, risk capital, a science academy, and the continued existence of the commission for seven years.

Tax and Financial Incentives

Firms would be encouraged to increase their employment levels in Rhode Island through relocation or local expansion. In return for increased employment levels, Rhode Island would fund a specific percentage of the employment through a 12-year grant/note. Applicable interest rates would be below market rates.

However, to be eligible for the grant/note, firms would have to create jobs with a total higher average wage rate (at time of application for the loan) than the current average wage rate in Rhode Island. If the promised number of jobs are created with the requisite higher average wage rate, the loan would be considered a grant. All firms would be required to pay the interest payments for the first four years, regardless of job creation levels.

New product efforts by established firms would also get a financial boost in Rhode Island. The state would provide matching funds to assist a firm in developing untried products or new markets. If the endeavor was successful, the loan would be repaid; if not, the loan would be erased.[11]

In order to stop the financial hemorrhaging of troubled Rhode Island firms, the state would establish a "stabilization fund" to provide financial relief. Financial institutions would actually supply the funds; however, they would be rewarded for their efforts with tax credits. These funds would only be available to businesses believed capable of eventually succeeding independently and which exhausted all other sources of private financing. Furthermore, specifically targeted industries (tourism, wholesaling, boat building, et cetera) would be recipients of financial incentives tailored to their individual needs.

Entrepreneurs would have tax incentives available to them as enticements to set their businesses up in RI. Tax incentives would also be available to industries that support improvements in higher education. The commission claimed these tax incentives were in special areas that would stimulate economic growth. The more general tax incentives, already in operation in Rhode Island, would be eliminated. It was believed that the state had gained little in return for deferring tax revenue under its existing system.

State-Supported Research

While some economic experts claim that governments are ill-equipped to identify business opportunities with *any* accuracy, the GC held a more optimistic view. The commission considered itself unable to predict *all* areas where business opportunities might arise; therefore, provisions were made for research "greenhouses." The purpose of the greenhouses would be to promote applied research likely to lead to the creation of new industries within Rhode Island. In theory the greenhouses would be able to draw from isolated research efforts in local businesses, hospitals, and universities, then put the "research pieces" together into a commercially marketable product or service.

To complete the picture, a venture capital fund would operate to link viable greenhouse products with entrepreneurial management and supply the necessary financing for the ventures. Eight local areas of expertise, which were thought to lend themselves most advantageously to greenhouse research, were identified. Clinical drug testing, geriatric products and services, robotics, and thin film materials (used in semiconductors) were among the eight contenders for greenhouse research.[12]

Job Training and Education

The Greenhouse Compact realized that many efforts to stimulate business would have much less impact if Rhode Islanders were not adequately trained or educated for the newly created jobs. Therefore, up to $500 per new job created would be provided for businesses intending to expand in Rhode Island. Businesses, in turn, would be required to apply this money to training costs associated with hiring new employees. Special pilot programs would be developed to address more general problems such as illiteracy and discrimination.

One of the more ambitious GC proposals focused on the creation of the Rhode Island Academy of Science and Engineering. The academy would serve as a hub for all scientific and technical matters. It would facilitate specialized discussions between researchers and educators, promote math and science classes in the school systems, advise the commission, and guide research at various RI institutions.

Changes in Existing Laws

One of the reasons cited by business in support of their statements that RI was "antibusiness" involved payment of strikers' benefits. The state law currently provided unemployment compensation benefits to strikers, beginning six weeks after a strike had been called. According to the GC, this did not seem to promote strikes but did leave Rhode Island with a negative image within the business community.

To rectify this image problem, the compact suggested a change in the law. The strikers would be disqualified from state benefits if substantial "work stoppage" occurred due to a strike. Workers not called back to work one week after the end of a strike would be qualified to receive unemployment compensation. These proposed legal revisions were intended to prevent state subsidization of a normal strike yet allow for unemployment compensation if a worker was involuntarily unemployed.[13]

In addition to the preceeding proposals, the Greenhouse Compact included a variety of state "support programs." One example of a support program would be the rebuilding of the state's infrastructure in critical areas such as ports and certain roadways. Other incentives would be developed to encourage the Public Utilities Commission to operate more efficiently, thus reducing energy costs. Winter tourism programs would be developed along with numerous other programs to encourage the development of specific industries. Finally, the commission itself would be in business for seven years. During that time period, well-functioning programs would be spun off to existing government agencies, and all programs would be provided a permanent governmental "home" at the end of seven years or discontinued.

RECEPTIVITY TO THE GREENHOUSE COMPACT

The compact's aggressive goals intrigued many factions within the state. Heavy emphasis on improving the average hourly rate in all industries, including manufacturing, along with the intention to create 60,000 new jobs clearly appealed to organized labor. The AFL-CIO responded with a pledge to support the program despite the curtailment of strikers' benefits.[14] In reference to the GC, AFL-CIO state president Ed McElroy stated, "There will be larger slices of the pie for the workers and everyone will be a winner."[15]

Providence, Rhode Island's major newspaper (*Journal-Bulletin*) wrote editorials supporting the compact's creation of economic opportunities.[16] Rhode Island government, mainly Democratic, was quite enthused about the project starting with the governor's initial action to create the commission. Charged with the responsibility for nominating two lawmakers to serve on the commission during its expected seven-year lifetime, both the state Senate majority leader and the House majority leader responded by naming themselves to the commission.[17] State Republican leaders had some reservations about the $40 million, one-time tax increase yet offered no strident opposition.[18]

Business leaders of Rhode Island's major corporations actively supported the GC. A listing of the Strategic Development Commission membership appeared to be a microcosm of "Who's Who" in Rhode Island. In fact, one of the project's leading promoters, Ira Magaziner, had previous experience advising the governments of Sweden and Japan. Not to be overlooked, all major universities within the state were also represented on the task force.

EDUCATING THE PUBLIC

Once the Greenhouse Compact was completed in October 1983, supporters launched an intense lobbying effort to persuade the general public to
approve the $700 million project. Of that amount, $500 million was to be
attained through private sector investment. A majority of the compact's
programs stipulated a specific percentage of private investment from a
firm before that company would be eligible for compact funds. For instance, the compact required companies to commit two dollars toward job
training for every dollar they received from the compact for that purpose.
Portions of the remaining $250 million would self-financed by the Green-
house Compact's commission. For example, $120 million would be raised
through bond issuance. Bonds would be repaid through revenue derived
from the commission's successful programs.[19] Another $30 million would
be given in tax credits. The remaining $60 million would also come from
sources other than the general public; public pension fund investments,
new federal funds, and so on, were among the potential revenue sources
under serious consideration.

However, $40 million was slated to come directly from the public.
Two methods were to be used to raise the necessary millions. A one-time,
$15 million personal income tax surcharge would be levied. The remaining
$25 million would be derived from a one-time payroll tax levied against
employers.[20]

Owing to the size, cost, and method of financing involved in implementing the GC, the package in its entirety would be voted on by Rhode
Islanders in a special June 1984 election. This allowed Greenhouse Compact supporters and opponents approximately seven months to present
their case to the people. In a state only 48 miles long with a population
totaling 958,000 (by comparison, Dallas, Texas, population — 947,000),
this did not seem an insurmountable task.

Union and business supporters underwrote a $300,000 campaign to
promote the GC. Some 17 members of the commission, representing all
interest groups, crisscrossed the state in an effort to explain the program
and gain grass roots support. An estimated 800 appearances were made on
behalf of the Greenhouse Compact to knitting groups, senior citizen
groups, assemblies of workers, and anyone else who would listen.[21]

The message given to the people was at once both simple and complex. The stated reasons and advantages of the Greenhouse Compact were
not difficult to grasp, yet an explanation of the various components could
be quite confusing. "Rhode Island right now is like Chrysler three years
ago. . . . we have to do a little more," explained Telesis president Ira Magaziner. Commission chairman J. Terrence Murray opted to emphasize a
more positive aspect of the GC when speaking to community members:

> If we create only half the jobs we expect to create, the extra
> taxes from the new workers will more than pay off the

bonds, and the Greenhouse Compact won't cost you an extra penny. In fact, if we are successful, it should create a broader tax base, and could even lower your taxes.[22]

Other messages focused on a little sacrifice now for a brighter future. As one television ad proclaimed, "Too often our children have to leave Rhode Island now to follow their dreams."[23]

Opposition to the Greenhouse Compact was small by comparison, minimally organized, and underfunded. When the GC was first presented, it carried the image of "motherhood and apple pie."[24] Dissenters faced being considered anti–Rhode Island. Despite this possible stigma, a group against the GC did emerge, calling themselves Common Sense.

Allan Feldman, professor of economics at Rhode Island's Brown University, headed up Common Sense, whose membership included a small number of other university professors, conservative businessmen, and some students. Funding to advance their message totaled approximately $30,000.[25]

Common Sense's message was simple also. One television ad suggested, "A $300 million tax increase. . . . Big tax breaks for wealthy investors. . . . What's in it for you?"[26] The group argued that the program was not likely to succeed, but voters would still pay the tax increase and eventually be saddled with repayment of the bonds. When questioned about the feasibility of the Greenhouse Compact, Brookings Institution analyst Charles Schultze commented, "I can't talk about Rhode Island's plan specifically, but in general, you don't create Silicon Valleys by passing a bill and setting up a few tax incentives."[27]

By late spring 1984, controversy over the GC began to heat up, and the issue had lost its "motherhood and apple pie" image. Common Sense advocates pressed on. The economic analysis underlining the GC was termed faulty by another Brown University economics professor, George Borts; he claimed that the analysis overstated the potential advantages offered by the GC programs and understated the associated costs.

Furthermore, antagonists of the GC claimed, the state should not be in the business of trying to pick industrial winners. Although promoters of the compact had consciously avoided any reference to "industrial policy," opponents of the proposals had no such reservations when referring to the project.

Antagonists of the Greenhouse concept also landed heavily on the politically sensitive issues surrounding the proposal. The commission, in charge of administering the programs over the long term, was touted as being able to "operate independent of politics." As Rhode Islanders had suffered a number of recent political corruption scandals, this quality was considered critical for voter acceptance.

But, opponents suggested, the commission would not be politically independent. They noted that two Democratic legislators had already named themselves to the commission. This did not sit well with the Republican gubernatorial candidate, who began to make "politicization of the Greenhouse Compact" a campaign issue. To negate these claims, two Republican lawmakers were then included on the commission.[28] This response, in turn, did not sit well with the voters, further reinforcing public opinion that the commission would not be an apolitical governing body. To underscore questions about the commission's integrity, a short television pitch cautioned voters, "Those big shots in Providence have another plan to pick your pocket."[29]

BUSINESS-GOVERNMENT-LABOR COALITION FAILS

Other states closely watched how Rhode Islanders received the Greenhouse Compact and were quite interested in the outcome of the upcoming issue in the June 1984 referendum vote. As economic responsibility during the Reagan administration shifted largely from the federal government to state governments, new and innovative ideas generated locally were closely scrutinized. By February 1984 Ira Magaziner had already received 25 to 30 greenhouse-related inquiries from various states. Rhode Island voters, responding to a poll taken early in 1984, indicated a 2-to-1 preference for the proposal.[30]

However, public sentiment began to turn against the Greenhouse Compact as the referendum date neared. Telephone polls, sponsored by GC supporters in April 1984, brought forth startling results. According to these voter opinion tallies 20 percent of RI voters were pro Greenhouse Compact, 20 percent were anti Greenhouse Compact, and 60 percent of the people polled were unsure.[31] Common Sense had successfully triggered public skepticism. During local meetings, people began to voice their doubts: Who would control the money? Why haven't banks wanted to finance greenhouses before? Other people commented that they didn't know much about the idea but knew their friends were against it.[32] One worker appeared to sum up the feelings of many Rhode Islanders:

> They make it sound good, but I'm against it. I don't believe
> it wouldn't cost us anything and I'm tired of taxes. You
> can't trust politicians when they say it won't cost anything.[33]

Although the local polls showed opinion to be fairly evenly divided on the greenhouse issue in June 1984, it was defeated by a 4-to-1 margin.[34] In fact, Rhode Islanders went out of their way to indicate their negative opinions on the GC. Normally, 8 to 12 percent of the state's voters turn out for a special election, yet the Greenhouse Compact drew 29 percent of the state's eligible voters to the polls.[35] If the previously surveyed pro–Greenhouse Compact voters remained supportive, then virtually all the "unsure" voters had decided that the "plus" factors concerning the compact actually belonged in the "minus" column. The Greenhouse Compact Commission declared themselves to be out of business while Rhode Island leaders and others speculated on the reason for the voters's unequivocal decision.

People have become turned off to government involvement. [Ira Magaziner][36]

The plan was perhaps too bold. [Governor Garrahy][37]

The [Greenhouse Compact] demonstrated the difficulty of selling a complex program. [Howie Kurtz, *Washington Post* writer][38]

The GC . . . sounded kind of cold, complicated, intellectual. [F. W. Schweke, vice president — Corporation for Economic Development][39]

Voters believed the programs were for the wealthy and politically influential. [Allan Feldman][40]

Positive factors proved to be major liabilities. . . . expenditures frightened people. [Bill Mutterperl, council to the commission][41]

Citizens and leaders of Rhode Island still believe the state faces definite economic problems. The cooperative spirit of interest groups, critical to integrated economic planning, existed. No one in Rhode Island has denied that remedial action would improve the state's economic status, yet voters obviously felt the GC would not serve their interests well. Financially supporting an untried, grand plan when the resultant benefits could prove quite nebulous appealed to few voters.

Common Sense's message, casting doubt on government's ability to create a commission resistant to pork barrel politics, was heard clearly by Rhode Islanders. Moreover, it was a message that seemed to rouse the voters' underlying suspicions that any plan, program, or organization with political roots cannot or will not operate apolitically. Meanwhile, other states have proposed limited versions of the Greenhouse Compact, leaving supporters of the GC to wonder if Rhode Islanders had shot themselves in the foot again.

DISCUSSION QUESTIONS

1. How do you appraise Rhode Island's Greenhouse concept as a plan for economic development? Is it appropriately ambitious, comprehensive, results-oriented?
2. Is it ever realistic to propose a long-term development program with a tax increase and expect the proposal to pass? If so, what conditions must exist?
3. What lessons might other states gain from the GC when planning their economic development strategies?
4. As a citizen of Rhode Island, how would you have voted? Why?
5. Was it a mistake to allow voters to decide the Greenhouse Compact's

fate? Are legislators better equipped to make long-term economic decisions for the populace?

NOTES

1. Howard Kurtz, "Tiny Rhode Island Maps a Grandiose Plan," *Washington Post,* November 26, 1983, p. A3.
2. Rhode Island Strategic Development Commission, *The Greenhouse Compact: Executive Summary* (Providence, R.I.: Rhode Island Strategic Development Commission: November, 1983), p. 6.
3. Bill Mutterperl, Council to the Commission, Excerpts from a telephone interview, November 19, 1984.
4. Stephen P. Morin, "Rhode Island Blues Won't Go Away, But Summer Is Nice," *Wall Street Journal,* June 28, 1983, p. 21.
5. Rhode Island Strategic Development Commission, *The Greenhouse Compact,* p. 10.
6. Ibid., p. 16.
7. Michael Doan, "How Businesses Will Fare In Your Region," *U.S. News & World Report,* January 16, 1984, p. 35.
8. Rhode Island Strategic Development Commmission, *The Greenhouse Compact,* p. 25.
9. Ibid., p. 24.
10. Ibid., p. 4.
11. Ibid., p. 26.
12. Ibid., pp. 30–31.
13. Ibid., p. 35.
14. Kurtz, "Tiny Rhode Island Maps a Grandiose Plan," p. A3.
15. Bruce G. Posner, "The Little State that Could," *Inc.,* October 1983, p. 151.
16. "Industrial-Policy Revolt?" *Wall Street Journal,* June 25, 1984, p. 26.
17. Mutterperl, Excerpts from a telephone interview.
18. Peter W. Berenstein, "States Are Going Down Industrial Policy Lane," *Fortune,* March 5, 1984, p. 112.
19. Rhode Island Strategic Development Commission, *The Greenhouse Compact,* p. 38.
20. Ibid., p. 39.
21. Tamar Lewin, "Putting Industrial Policy To a Vote," *New York Times,* June 10, 1984, p. D4.
22. Ibid.
23. Howard Kurtz, "A 'New Idea' Fizzles On Launch," *Washington Post,* July 15, 1984, p. B5.
24. Tamar Lewin, "Cynicism Cited In Plan's Loss," *New York Times,* June 14, 1984, p. D2.
25. Kurtz, "A 'New Idea' Fizzles On Launch," p. B5.
26. Ibid.

27. Lewin, "Putting Industrial Policy To a Vote," p. D4.
28. Mutterperl, Excerpts from a telephone interview.
29. Lewin, "Putting Industrial Policy To a Vote," p. D4.
30. "Blueprint for Industrial Policy," *Dun's Business Month,* February 1984, p. 28.
31. Mutterperl, Excerpts from a telephone interview.
32. Kurtz, "A 'New Idea' Fizzles On Launch," p. B5.
33. Lewin, "Putting Industrial Policy to a Vote," p. D4.
34. David Purcell, "Rhode Islanders Uproot 'Greenhouse' Plan," *Christian Science Monitor,* June 14, 1984, p. 3.
35. Brian C. Jones, "Greenhouse Defeated in All 39 Communities," *Providence Journal-Bulletin,* June 13, 1984, p. 1.
36. Purcell, "Rhode Islanders Uproot 'Greenhouse' Plan," p. 3.
37. "Industrial-Policy Revolt?" p. 26.
38. Ibid.
39. Kutz, "A 'New Idea' Fizzles On Launch," p. B5.
40. Ibid.
41. Mutterperl, Excerpts from a telephone interview.

Chapter 11

Government Action and Economic Growth

Policy Issues Affecting Technological Innovation and Small Business Development

Few processes will affect the future of the United States more than its course of economic development. Economic growth is essential for fulfilling human economic needs and for achieving noneconomic social goals.

Governmental influence on economic development is an immense topic that, in its full scope, is broader than the specific focus of this book on business and government interactions. However, several particular areas of government action in the field of economic policy — technological progress and entrepreneurial development — bear directly upon business-government relations.

It is difficult to overstate the modern importance of technological development, which performs the following essential functions: it improves individuals' abilities to communicate, to learn, even to live; its stimulates employment and raises the standard of living; and it helps to maintain worldwide economic strength and a reasonable balance of economic power. In the context of long-term national interests, perhaps no other issue of the governmental role and relationship to business deserves more emphasis.

Earlier chapters discuss ways in which governmental policy encourages or inhibits industrial innovation and technological change. For example, health and safety risks to industrial workers, community members, or consumers were discussed as serious by-products of technological change. In certain circumstances government regulations designed to deal with these side effects may divert capital away from research and development and discourage innovative activities; in other cases regulation may create new markets for technical advances. As argued in Chapter 4, highly concentrated industries and conglomerate-type corporate acquisitions may create institutional obstacles to business innovation. Government policies that ignore these impediments to innovation also fail to respond to the public interest. In various ways public policy indirectly bears upon the technological capability and performance of the business sector. This chapter discusses the various options and consequences of governmental policies *directly* addressed to technological progress.

Governmental encouragement or discouragement of small business development strongly influences the public sector's commitment to technology. Statistics released by the National Science Foundation have shown that small businesses are 2.5 times as innovative as larger businesses and, on the average, require one-third less time to introduce their innovations on the market.[1] A commitment to small business also appears to be a commitment to technological development. Small business is especially important in the earlier, less costly stages of innovation and in industries where innovation is generally less expensive.

However, the contributions of small business to national economic goals do not stop with new technology. Relatively more jobs created are, by and large, a result of more innovative small business activity. One study found that 66 percent of new employment comes from businesses with 20 employees or less and that 86.7 percent of new jobs in the private sector between 1969 and 1976 were created by businesses with fewer than 500 employees.[2] In contrast, the *Fortune* 1,000 companies created only 1 percent of new private sector jobs over this same period.[3]

In addition, while small businesses appear to contribute little to the nation's exports, a great potential is present, notably in the innovative part of the small business population. The Commerce Department has estimated that at least 20,000 additional small companies could, with adequate policy guidance, export their products and greatly aid the country's balance of payments.[4]

The theme of small business development is presented in earlier chapters primarily as a tangential or secondary topic; to this point the importance of small businesses to national economic goals has been overlooked. Owing to its importance as a source of new technology, and because entrepreneurship has a significant standing in relation to economic development in its own right, policy questions bearing directly upon small businesses are considered in this chapter.

ECONOMIC GROWTH AND TECHNOLOGICAL COMMITMENT

The study of the sources and processes of economic growth is the focus of extensive economic research and ongoing theory formulation. Technological innovation has been found to determine more than half of national or international economic growth.[5]

Contributions of Technology to Economic Growth

Technology influences economic growth by means of several mechanisms. Technological advancement may lead to the creation of entirely new industries; for example, television, jet aircraft, and digital computers comprise significant industries today, whereas none of these existed in commercial form prior to 1945.

Technology also stimulates growth through the modification and improvement of existing products. Construction of home appliances with greater energy saving devices or higher performance components are types of product improvements. Color television sets, microwave ovens, or refrigerators with automatic ice makers are innovations that contribute to economic growth in this manner. The combined effects of new industries and of new or improved products account for up to half of economic growth.[6]

Productivity improvements that can be traced to technological advancement account for the other half of new economic growth. These improvements generally cause changes in manufacturing operations that lead to higher output per unit of labor input. Some studies place the contribution of technological change to productivity improvements as high as 85 or 90 percent.[7]

Substantial attention has been given to the relatively poor standing of the United States in recent years compared with major industrialized competitors Japan and West Germany. Insert 11.A provides recent information on ten-year trends of productivity, wage, and unit labor cost increases from 1973 to 1983. Compared with these two countries, the United States has done poorly, illustrating the reason for renewed attention to technological development.

Advances in Knowledge

Economist Edward Denison, in several studies sponsored by the Brookings Institution, provides a widely respected analysis of the contribution of science to economic growth. The Denison studies can be used to assess the impact of advances in knowledge on economic growth through productivity improvements. Denison first studied the sources of economic growth between 1929 and 1969 and between 1948 and 1969.[8] He studied determinants such as the amounts of labor and capital committed, increased worker education, and improved resource allocation as well as advances in knowledge. The latter variable included managerial and organizational technologies and contributions of the physical sciences and engineering to new products and processes.

The study showed that 31 percent of the increase in economic growth between 1929 and 1969 and 34 percent of the growth between 1948 and 1969 resulted from improvements in knowledge. In fact, this factor

Insert 11.A

RECENT COMPARATIVE PRODUCTIVITY AND UNIT LABOR COST CHANGES FOR THE UNITED STATES, WEST GERMANY, AND JAPAN

Productivity increases result from a variety of sources: overall indexes do not indicate the contributions of any single factor. New technology is certainly one important source, but other factors that should be taken into account include labor skill and effort, capital investment, capacity utilization, energy use, and managerial skill. The following figures from the Department of Labor show that the United States lagged behind West Germany and Japan in overall productivity gains from the mid-1970s through the early 1980s while at the same time experiencing a faster rate of wage increase. The combined effect of low productivity rates and high wage rates is captured in the United States' high average unit labor cost.

Average Annual Percent Rates of Change, 1973–83

	Output per Labor Hour	Hourly Compensation	Unit Labor Costs in National Currency
United States	1.9	9.2	7.2
West Germany	3.3	7.9	4.5
Japan	7.3	8.6	1.2

SOURCE: U.S., Department of Labor, Bureau of Labor Statistics, *Manufacturing Productivity and Labor Cost Trends in 1983 in 12 Countries* (Washington, D.C.: Department of Labor News Release, December 31, 1984), p. 2.

was the single most important contributor to economic growth in either period. In a later analysis of why economic growth had declined in the 1973–76 period, Denison again found advances in knowledge to be the single most influential factor.[9]

These studies are not without some qualifications. The advances in knowledge variable, for example, includes all other unmeasured determinants of economic growth. Consequently, other unknown factors, such as changes in the quality of management or rises in energy costs, are present in this variable, although these are considered to be either unmeasurable or insignificant. After all qualifications are taken into account, the studies confirm that which has been found by other researchers: the contribution of knowledge advances to economic growth is great.

Organized Research and Development

Technology's importance to economic growth raises the question of how to increase knowledge and technological improvements. Comprehension of how, why, and when knowledge advances is not well developed. Certainly the sociopolitical climate helps determine the probability of technological advancements. Others attribute economic growth largely to cyclical shifts in emphasis from basic science to applied science.[10]

A more directly measurable and controllable factor is the level of organized R & D activity; here one assumes that higher levels of research will advance knowledge more rapidly, which in turn will lead to technologically improved products and processes and to new industries. A group of leading economists have supported this conclusion in a report to the National Science Foundation:

> Although what we know about the relationship between R & D and economic growth productivity is limited, all available evidence indicates that R & D is an important contributor to economic growth and productivity. Research to date seeking to measure this relationship . . . points in a single direction — the contribution of R & D to economic growth/productivity is positive, significant and high.[11]

U.S. investment in research and development is higher than most countries, but in recent years the United States has lost relative ground to Japan and West Germany.[12] For example, in 1970 R & D expenditures as a percentage of gross national product were 2.64 in the United States, 2.18 in West Germany, and 1.79 in Japan. Only the Soviet Union had a higher percentage than the United States at 3.23. Preliminary percentages for 1983 indicated that West Germany's ratio had risen to 2.68 while the U.S. ratio had declined to 2.45 percent.

The focus of U.S. scientific activity is also noteworthy. In 1980 the largest sector for research and development in the United States was national defense, with 47 percent of all expenditures. Space exploration and health research were second and third in importance with 14 and 12 percent, respectively. By 1984, national defense R & D was expected to consume 70 percent of all federal R & D dollars. West Germany and Japan both emphasized general R & D or R & D spanning several fields; moreover, these countries placed more emphasis on research for economic development such as agriculture, energy, and industrial growth than did the United States.

Finally, the balance of business and government involvement is quite different in the United States, where the government plays a more dominant role. In 1979 nearly 33 percent of R & D performed in the U.S. private sector was funded by government; in West Germany approximately

21 percent of industrial research was based on public funds; and in Japan an amazingly low 1.4 percent was funded by the government.

Overall, these figures show the United States has a major commitment to R & D, but one that has declined, especially in relation to major industrialized countries. Also, business-government relationships in research are quite different in the United States. The U.S. government funds a higher proportion of private R & D, and the country is relatively more committed to defense and space research and relatively less committed to research in areas related to economic growth, such as manufacturing and transportation.

Increases in Capital Formation

The Denison studies identified capital increases as a major source of economic growth, accounting for about 16 percent of the 1929–69 growth rate and nearly 22 percent of postwar growth between 1948 and 1969.[13] An increase in capital intensity more capital relative to employment is important to raise national income per person employed and thus to increase national wealth.

Similar to productivity, the recent rate of increase in capital formation in the United States has been low compared with that of previous periods of U.S. history and that of other industrialized countries today. Table 11.1 presents international comparisons, prepared by the Department of Labor, of capital investment and growth in manufacturing output. The correlation of capital investment with productivity increases, especially at the extremes of investment, shows the importance of capital input to output growth. For the period from 1960 to 1972 the United States was far behind its trading competitors in capital investment in proportion to gross domestic product. Relatively less U.S. fixed capital investment was bound to cause lower rates of productivity increase. The second column, output per labor hour, is a standard measure of productivity, which demonstrates this relationship.

Why would one country have a lower or greater rate of capital investment than another country? Capital available for economic investment comes from two primary sources: personal savings and corporate profits. On neither count has the United States performed as favorably as its international counterparts. Personal savings in the United States since 1960 have consistently been below 8 percent of disposable personal income and less occasionally fallen below 5 percent.[14] European countries' savings rates are often at least double this figure, and the Japanese people save at approximately four times this rate. U.S. industry is also low in terms of the rate of reinvestment of corporate profits. Between 1960 and 1973, for example, 11.2 percent of U.S. manufacturing output was reinvested, whereas this figure was 13.6 percent for the United Kingdom, 17.1 percent for Swe-

TABLE 11.1   *Increases in Capital Investment and Changes in Manufacturing Output Among Industrialized Countries*

	Fixed Capital Investment as a Percentage of Gross Domestic Product, 1960–72	Output per Hour in Manufacturing, 1960–83
United States	13.8	2.6
United Kingdom	14.8	3.5
Italy	15.1	5.6
Denmark	15.6	5.9
Belgium	15.7	7.1
France	16.2	5.8
Germany	17.0	5.0
Sweden	17.1	4.8
Canada	17.2	3.5
Netherlands	18.4	6.9
Japan	26.0	9.1

SOURCE: U.S., Department of Labor, Bureau of Labor Statistics, *Manufacturing Productivity and Labor Cost Trends in 1983 in 12 Countries* (Washington, D.C.: Department of Labor News Release, December 31, 1984), p. 6.

den, and 24.4 percent for Japan.[15] These differences are due, in part, to differing public policies of corporate taxation, allowances for depreciation, and taxation of dividends, which affect capital available for business reinvestment.

PUBLIC POLICY DIMENSIONS OF TECHNOLOGY AND CAPITAL FORMATION

Justification for public sector involvement in the process of industrial innovation stems from belief that the free market underallocates capital to areas in which the public interest is high. For example, large financial commitments necessary for some areas of research and development, such as new and alternative energy sources, are so great relative to the size of most firms that underinvestment relative to social needs will occur.[16] In addition, the uncertainties implied by the longtime horizon of large-scale projects may create a disincentive to investment.

Moreover, the market seems unable to allocate an appropriate level of benefits to the innovator. If financial returns to private investors are substantially lower than economic returns to society as a whole, the private system misallocates resources away from innovative activity. The problem of capturing or internalizing benefits of innovative activity may be particularly acute in basic research or in public health research,[17] where the results of innovation are least controllable. (See Insert 11.B.)

In Chapter 6 governmental attempts to assign social costs of pollution, product safety, and occupational health to the firm were discussed as a problem of the internalization of external costs. In innovation, however, the problem is one of internalizing benefits rather than costs, and this may be an even more difficult problem. Many undesirable social consequences of business activity, like pollution, are visible, and most "victims" are easily identified; in contrast the absence of innovation leads to benefits that will not occur — certainly a less visible problem and one without a well-defined constituency of victims. The lack of benefits is diffused widely, and because we are unknowing victims, the case for redirecting policy is weak.

Fig. 11.1 presents a classification of governmental roles in the process of technological development. One basic distinction is between a direct governmental role of initiating specific R & D projects and an indirect governmental role of attempting to create a favorable general environment for innovations. The former is often referred to as a "mission-oriented" policy and the latter as a "nonmission-oriented" policy.

In addition to the direct/indirect distinction, governmental action can emphasize the resource side of innovative effort-supplying capital through tax reductions and through human resources necessary for innovation. Or, public policy can create a market for new technologies or products; the best example of this policy orientation is governmental purchases aimed at stimulating or inducing superior technology. The former emphasis might be termed a *technology supply* and the latter a *technology demand* emphasis. Let us consider each of the cells in this framework more closely.

Direct Government Role, Technology Supply

The technology supply strategy consists of a number of financial instruments that governments can use to stimulate and encourage specific projects. For example, U.S. policy to support the commercialization of synthetic fuels technology in the late 1970s relied upon $1.5 billion in direct federal loans and loan guarantees (assurance to a private lender in case a company defaults on a loan) to reduce the risk of new and costly technologies to the private sector.[18] Government financing was available for construction of physical facilities and purchase of land and mineral rights, equipment, or transportation facilities necessary for the project.

Other governments rely more on financing tools of this type than does the United States. West Germany, for example, has adopted an innovations policy that includes direct government cost sharing with industry

Insert 11.B

SOCIAL AND PRIVATE RATES OF RETURN FROM INDUSTRIAL INNOVATIONS

In the early 1970s economist Edwin Mansfield and colleagues attempted to measure the social and private rates of return from a sample of innovations. Funded by the National Science Foundation, the study examined 17 cases of innovations by business firms located in the Northeast: innovations used by firms, product innovations used by households, and process innovations. The following table specifies both the industry producing the innovation and the type of innovation involved.

Innovation	Type of Innovation	Type of User	Rate of Return (percent)	
			Social	Private
Primary metals	Product	Firms	17	18
Machine tool	Product	Firms	83	35
Control system component	Product	Firms	29	7
Construction material	Product	Firms	96	9
Drilling material	Product	Firms	54	16
Drafting	Process	Firms	92	47
Paper	Product	Firms	82	42
Thread	Product	Firms	307	27
Door control	Product	Firms	27	37
Electronic device	Product	Firms	Negative	Negative
Chemical product	Product	Firms	71	9
Chemical process	Process	Firms	32	25
Chemical process	Process	Firms	13	4
Major chemical process	Process	Firms	56	31
Household cleaning device	Product	Households	209	214
Stain remover	Product	Households	116	4
Dishwashing liquid	Product	Households	45	46
Median			56	25

While Mansfield cautions us on the difficulties of information gathering and measuring encountered during his research, the results documented in the table have several important implications.

First, they indicate the social rate of return, or economic value to society as a whole, from these 17 innovations is very high. The median estimated social rate of return is about 56 percent.

Insert 11.B   continued

Second, the results indicate the private rates of return from these innovations have been substantially lower than the social rates of return. The median private rate of return (before taxes) was about 25 percent, although the dispersion of returns around this point was quite large.

Finally, the results indicate that in a substantial number of cases the private rate of return was so low that no firm, given the gift of hindsight, would have invested in the innovation. On the other hand, from society's point of view the rate of return from the investment was well worthwhile.

SOURCE: Edwin Mansfield, John Rapoport, Anthony Romeo, Samuel Wagner, and George Beardsley, "Social and Private Rates of Return from Industrial Innovations," *Quarterly Journal of Economics* vol. 9 (1977): 221–40. Used with permission.

on specific projects. Interest-free, forgivable loans by which the government finances 50 percent of the cost of commercial development of a new technology constitute another West Germany program, as are government guarantees for equity capital placed by German banks in innovative enterprises.[19] England maintains a National Research Development Corporation, which can pay development costs of promising projects outright, license technology from public sector universities and research councils, or enter into joint ventures directly with private companies.[20]

A final type of direct federal funding program is federal support for basic research. The largest basic research commitment in 1983 was by the Department of Health and Human Services. It was estimated that this agency committed over $2 billion to research, accounting for 35 percent of all federal basic research funds. The second, third, and fourth largest funding agencies for research in 1983 were the National Science Foundation, the Department of Defense, and the National Aeronautics and Space Administration (NASA) with an estimated 17, 13.5, and 12 percent of federal basic research funding, respectively.[21] By 1984 the Congressional Budget Office estimated the NASA's R & D programs, which directly benefitted the aeronautics industry alone, would total $504 million.[22] Other examples of the government's close R & D relationship with the aeronautics industry are illustrated in Insert 11.C.

Since 1970 federally sponsored funds have constituted nearly 70 percent of the basic research funds of universities and colleges.[23] On the other hand, federal support for basic research in industry is substantially lower, estimated at about 23 percent in 1978. This portion is similar to federal support for applied research (25 percent in 1978) but is substantially lower than the portion of federal support for development efforts in industry (38.5 percent in 1978).[24] Overall government commitment to de-

FIGURE 11.1   *Classsification of Public Policies Toward Technological Development*

	Policies Affecting the Supply of Technology (Resource Emphasis)	Policies Affecting the Demand for Technology (Market Emphasis)
Direct Governmental Action (Mission-Oriented)	• Subsidies/Cost Sharing • Loans, Loan Guarantees • Public Venture Capital • Federal Research Laboratories • Grants for Development of Basic Research	• Technology Procurement • Technology "Forcing" Regulations
Indirect Government Action (Nonmission-Oriented)	• General Tax Policies • R & D Tax Incentives • Manpower Training and Development Grants • Patent Laws	• Guarantee of Market at Certain Prices • User Subsidies

velopment is further evidenced by estimates that in 1983 some 61 percent of all federal R & D funding was dedicated to this area.[25] In summary the government's impact appears greatest on basic research in health and science and on industrial projects close to commercialization.

Exemplifying the government's interest in funding technology development within industry was an industrial technology bill (representing a merger of two separate bills) introduced by Congressmen Slade Gorton and Don Fuqua in 1984. Under this bill's provisions the government would underwrite over $200 million in R & D costs associated with the development of new, high-technology manufacturing in general and robotics in particular.[26]

Of course, in addition to funding research projects the federal government owns and manages a large system of research laboratories that conduct basic research. This, as well, is direct involvement on the supply or resource side of technology. The combined 1984 expenditures of these 755 laboratories were expected to total $15 billion — an amount representing one third of the government's total 1984 R & D expenditures.[27]

Direct Governmental Role, Market Emphasis

The billions of dollars of goods and services the federal government purchases each year can be used to create a "demand pull" on new technology.

Insert 11.C

GOVERNMENT SUPPORT OF AIRCRAFT RESEARCH IN THE AERONAUTICS INDUSTRY

The government has maintained a high profile in the aircraft industry over the years. A study done by David Mowry and Nathan Rosenberg outlines some of the impact that government R & D policy has had on this industry. According to the authors, the aircraft industry has been able to attract governmental support to a degree not found in other industries. At the same time, the aircraft industry has also been the beneficiary, to an unprecedented degree, of technological breakthroughs in other related industries such as the metals industry. Listed below are some of the actions taken by the government over the years to spur rapid technological innovation in the commercial and military aircraft industries.

- The government funded the National Advisory Committee on Aeronautics (originally NACA, later renamed NASA) beginning in 1915. An initial major purpose of this agency was to fulfill the needs of aircraft designers. To this end, NACA paid for the building of costly infrastructures necessary for aircraft design testing.
- The U.S. government subsidized the development of air transportation designed to transfer mail in addition to their other functions (McNary-Waters Act of 1930).
- After World War II, NACA sponsored fundamental research in aeronautics.
- The U.S. military underwrote all jet engine R & D costs.
- The U.S. government subsidized approximately 80 percent of all aircraft R & D expenditures throughout the 1960s.
- Government creation of the Civil Aeronautics Board led to fixed prices within the industry, which, in turn, caused airline carriers to purchase aircraft designed with technological innovations that would reduce the craft's operating costs.

The net result of the U.S. government's willingness to absorb aeronautical R & D costs has been the continuous development of air transporters that are on the leading edge of technology and are a large export item.

SOURCE: David C. Mowry and Nathan Rosenberg, "The Commercial Aircraft Industry," in *Government and Technical Progress.* ed. Richard R. Nelson (Elmsford, N.Y.: Pergamon Press, 1982), 3:128–49.

The process of inducing technology through procurement has been especially important in some high-technology fields in which U.S. industries have worldwide leadership. One pair of reviewers notes that an example of this impact is the field of electronics, where procurement, in concert with other government policies, is considered to have played an important role:

> In order to stimulate innovation in the electronics industry, the U.S. government used various instruments such as financial support for R & D and procurement incentives, and it created a general climate favorable to innovation. The mix of these three instruments was the most important reason for the success of the project. Direct R & D subsidies were given, and companies were sure to find a willing purchaser. Companies even funded several times as much R & D support as from the Department of Defense, due to the fact that the government considerably reduced uncertainty on the demand side.[28]

The role of defense procurement particularly in transforming engineering knowledge and capability into usable technology has been a critical factor of development in many industries. The dominance of American aircraft manufacturers in jet transportation, for example, has been profoundly influenced by defense contracts. A large order for a military tanker version of the Boeing 707 paid part of the development and tooling costs for that airplane,[29] and American rearmament for the Korean War gave the industry funds to develop large jets when the European aircraft industry was shrinking.[30]

The pursuit of national objectives in space exploration has also caused advances in technology that are commercially applicable. A major impact of the U.S. space effort is being felt in communications capabilities. One observer describes the benefits presently achieved or within reach owing to advances in communications technology:

> A whole new spectrum of communication services — cable television, direct-broadcast satellites, global search-and-rescue capability, remote medical diagnostic services, business communications, personal "wrist radios," navigation aids, electronic mail, and package locations — and a host of other esoteric applications have been proclaimed as not only technically feasible but economically practical within a decade or so.[31]

Space research has also enhanced knowledge about aviation, metals and materials, human physical processes, and the solar system; it has furthered development of pharmaceuticals, electronics, and specialty glass and promises knowledge about alloys resulting from eventual zero gravitational manufacturing in space.[32]

Another direct, market-oriented role of government involves its influence as a regulator. However, the impact of health, safety, and environmental regulations on process and product innovations is ambiguous. On one hand, "technology forcing" regulations may stimulate industry to manufacturing and commercial innovation, such as the development of pollution control businesses or the creation of industries for disposing of toxic wastes; in other instances regulations appear to divert R&D funds away from innovative activity. There is some evidence that safety and environmental regulations can have a positive stimulus in relatively mature, concentrated industries[33] and are more costly and inhibitive for small firms. However, as one group of researchers notes, it is difficult to generalize about the costs and benefits of regulation on technology across industries, across types of regulation, and across firm size:

> The effects of regulation can be positive or negative. For example, positive effects may often occur when regulatory requirements complement some existing market force (for example, in the case of fuel economy regulations in the auto industry) or where a new or ignored area of development can be exploited. Regulatory constraints, however, may hamper innovation by blocking certain new technical options by decreasing the resources available for new product development. Of particular concern is the fact that the regulation may hurt the competitive position of small firms.[34]

Indirect Government Role, Technology Supply

A third broad public strategy toward technological progress involves establishing the long-term financial and human resources necessary for a favorable environment for innovation. One of the foremost policy tools in this area is the multifaceted impact of tax policies on research and development and on capital expenditures. The election of Ronald Reagan in 1980 saw a significant shift in the role of government in promoting economic development, a shift that emphasized creation of incentives for expansion and modernization of production rather than direct government stimulation of demand.

This policy position is in contrast to demand-side economics, often called *Keynesian economics,* emphasizing government spending to increase demand for goods and services, which in turn spurns business investment. Credit is made available by keeping interest rates as low as possible by expansion of the money supply, thus facilitating business investment, economic growth, and productivity increases. This orientation toward economic policy was successful in pulling the economy out of the 1930s depression and adjusting to the economic cycles in the period of relative economic stability until the 1970s. Perhaps triggered by the drastic step-function increases in energy costs, or perhaps brought on by the cumulative effect of easy credit, government deficits, and high taxes, the inflationary side of demand economics made itself evident in the 1970s. The demand side of the economy was discovered to be running wild: high government spending and an insatiable demand for personal and business credit put unprecedented pressures on the demand for goods and services. High taxes, low personal savings, and financing of government deficits created a scarcity of investment capital and rapid inflation.

Supply-side emphasis is an alternative framework that may offer greater opportunity to break the pattern of inflation. In this scheme, inflation is attacked by monetary policy, allowing interest rates to go high enough to slow credit expansion. Personal and business taxes are reduced to create incentives for savings, investment, and work effort. These policies attempt to reduce inflation, maintain price stability, and provide an economic climate conductive to long-run capital investments and confidence in research and development. They also seek to provide capital — internally generated by lower taxes and faster depreciation and externally generated by higher savings — for business modernization, capital improvements, and productivity increases. Finally, reduction of government spending further cuts the demand for goods and services, allowing the public budget to move toward greater balance and alleviating the inflationary pressures of high government deficits. Supply-side tax assumptions were embodied in the Economic Recovery Tax Act of 1981 advocated by President Reagan. Insert 11.D describes the major components of this bill concerning capital formation.

Insert 11.D

PROVISIONS OF A SUPPLY-SIDE TAX CUT BILL

In August 1981 Congress passed and the president signed a tax reform bill that included major administration recommendations for economic recovery. The basic aim of this bill was to lower tax rates to allow capital to remain in the private sector where it could be put to economic use and stimulate national growth. The new tax laws were anticipated to lower federal tax revenues $1.5 billion in 1981, $38 billion in 1982, $150 billion in 1984, and $268 billion in 1986. Here are several major provisions of the bill:

1. Individual tax reductions
   a. Reduction of individual marginal tax rates 5 percent in October 1981, 10 percent in July 1982, and another 10 percent in July 1983.

Insert 11.D   continued

     b. Reduction of the highest rates on investment income from 70 percent to 50 percent, the existing maximum for earned income.

     c. Reduction of the maximum rate on capital gains from 28 to 20 percent.

2. Corporate tax reductions

     a. Established as of January 1, 1981, new depreciation rules for business for investments previously having depreciation over their "useful" life:

         (1) Three-year depreciation for autos, light trucks, R & D equipment, and certain pollution control equipment. A 6 percent investment tax credit is allowed.

         (2) Five-year depreciation for all other machinery and equipment. A 10 percent investment tax credit is allowed.

         (3) A 10- or 15-year depreciation for buildings, depending on the type of structure. A 10 percent investment tax credit is allowed.

     b. Allowed accelerated depreciation of assets — taking a disproportionate amount of depreciation in the assets' early years.

     c. Allowed immediate deduction by small businesses of the cost of machinery and equipment up to certain limits.

     d. Made sales of investment tax credits and accelerated depreciation benefits from unprofitable companies that could not use them to profitable companies that could more easily.

     e. Created a 25 percent tax credit for new spending on research and development above the average expenditure for the past three years.

3. Savings incentives

     a. Increased the amount an individual can deduct from taxes for contributions to an individual retirement account.

     b. Doubled the amount a self-employed individual can deduct for his or her own retirement plan.

     c. Allowed depository institutions to offer a one-year savings certificate (to earn interest at 70 percent of the one-year Treasury bill rate) and allowed taxpayers to exclude interest ($1,000 for individuals, $2,000 for couples) from the certificates from taxes.

     d. Increased from 15 percent to 25 percent of payroll tax deductions for employers for contributions to an Employee Stock Ownership Plan (provided the payroll contributions go toward paying off an ESOP loan to buy company stock).

SOURCE: "Reagan Tax Plan Ready for Economic Test," *Congressional Quarterly Weekly Report,* August 8, 1981, pp. 1431–36.

Apparently supporting the philosophy that supply-side measures effectively serve to stimulate technological innovation, in 1984 the House Republican Task Force on High Technology Initiatives issued their intended legislative agenda. Some of their supply-side proposals are included in the following:

- A permanent 25 percent R & D tax credit;
- Stronger patent laws;
- Tax incentives to encourage corporate donations to educational institutions;
- Amendment of antitrust laws to remove disincentives pertaining to corporate joint research ventures; and
- Substantial reductions in current and projected federal deficits.[35]

The strength of supply-side economics may be the ability to break the inflationary cycle and promote long-term economic growth and stability. Its weakness may be that it proves a less effective tool for overcoming economic downturns or recessions than a demand-stimulus approach. Also, commitments to social objectives, such as income equalization, and to important social programs of food assistance, housing, and health care may be drastically reduced.

In addition to general tax incentives, offered by supply-side economics, a variety of specific tax policies have existed for economic and technological development. Such policies have included the investment tax credit in which businesses are permitted to deduct 10 percent of the cost of a new investment in plant and equipment from their federal income taxes. Similarly, all costs for research and development, short of prototype plant construction, have been allowed to be taken as expenses in the year they are incurred, even though their results are expected to accrue over a longer period of time. These provisions, intended to aid the immediate cash flow of the corporation by reducing its taxable income, were placed into some uncertainty by the administration's tax reform plan introduced in early, 1985.

There are a variety of other proposals to provide selective tax incentives for research and development activity. Special depreciation allowances or tax credits for first-of-a-kind facility construction, tax credit for support of university research, and a special tax credit for investment in R & D facilities would aim specifically at stimulating R & D activity.[36] One study sponsored by Texas Instruments estimates that a continuing 25 percent tax credit on R & D expenditures initiated in 1966 would have added about $2 billion annually to R & D in 1966–77, about $5 billion in 1978–87, and about $11 billion in 1988–97.[37] The results from these investments could be quite dramatic; the study estimated average annual productivity gains of 0.2, 0.3, and 0.4 percent for each of the respective ten-year periods, and average annual GNP growth of $4 billion, $36 billion, and $102 billion. A policy that would have a short-run cost of about $20 billion to the federal treasury in tax income foregone would be more than compensated by additional tax receipts in succeeding decades. Assuming this study is valid, it shows the dynamic long-term impact of public policy favorable toward economic and technological progress.

Other major programs for indirect governmental involvement in supplying technology concern manpower training, development activities, and patent policy. In one sense federal research awards to colleges and universities are human resource development programs because they often support the education of graduate students in scientific fields. In addition, major research funding agencies such as the National Institutes of Health or the National Science Foundation maintain special scholarship funds for master- and doctoral-level work and for research projects of young faculty members. However, governmental policy toward scientific manpower development appears to fall short of a comprehensive strategy, such as the strong Japanese governmental emphasis on technical education and training of highly skilled personnel for industry.[38] In fact, one analysis of U.S. governmental policy concludes, "The United States today has no conscious manpower policy specifically designed to strengthen the environment for technological innovation and to respond to the needs of workers in a technologically changing economy."[39]

Indirect Governmental Rule, Technology Demand

Indirect governmental policies that pull technology are rare, although examples of public policy impact are available. The general movement of the state courts toward strict manufacturer liability for consumer injuries due to defective products is a public policy that may induce new technology in consumer products. The government also encourages new technology indirectly by forcing certain products off the market by consumer regulation.

Another tack taken by government to stimulate indirectly an increase in demand for technology involves government subsidization. A recent NASA charter amendment by Congress called for the agency "to seek and encourage, to the maximum extent possible, the fullest commercial use of space."[40] In an effort to accomplish this goal the government has chosen to subsidize corporate space shuttle payloads. The corporate price per full payload is set at a fixed rate of $71 million through 1988 — a level below the government's breakeven point for a space shuttle mission.[41]

The availability of tax credits for users of energy-efficient heating systems or home insulation is another example of indirect government action working on the demand side of new technology.[42] By providing an economic incentive to users of energy, government hopes that a market pull is exercised on the development of energy-saving technology. While a potentially useful tool in the repertoire of policies supporting technological progress, indirect, demand-oriented policies appear rarely used and may warrant more consideration.

Several observations are in order to summarize this discussion of Fig. 11.1. First, policy approaches to technological progress are numerous and probably work best in concert. That is, indirect *and* direct governmental roles and emphasis on technology supply *and* technology demand are all vital policy tools. Second, indirect and supply-oriented policies may be considered to have the more powerful general and long-term effects on national objectives of productivity improvement and economic growth. This observation places particular importance on the policies identified in the lower left window of Fig. 11.1 and suggests the importance of working to create a favorable environment for research and development.

At the same time that policies addressed to the environment of R & D have a vital long-term role, they lack the ability to promote more immediate and specific innovations. This, of course, is the strength of actions based on direct government involvement in technology and on market-based or demand-oriented policies. If these assumptions are correct, it is not surprising that government procurement has played an important role in some of the significant technological advances in this century.

Finally, it should be noted that other industrialized nations, our economic competitors in the international arena, appear to be making strong and explicit public commitments to the advancement of science and technology. If these efforts are successful, the level and direction of U.S. commitment will be increasingly challenged and the strategies of public policies discussed here, and others, will likely become a more central focus of business-government relations.

THE ROLE OF ENTREPRENEURSHIP IN THE UNITED STATES

Small business is as synonymous with America as individualism and personal freedom. In the early years of the country, all businesses were small businesses, and the roots of independence and entrepreneurship remain influential today as small businesses account for about 40 percent of our gross national product. Some observers, in fact, report a resurgence of the spirit of entrepreneurism in America and expect the 1980s to be the "entrepreneurial decade." In April 1980 the White House Commission on Small Business noted this resurgence:

> There is a tide in the spirit of individual enterprise in America, and it is rising. More and more Americans are eager to start small, independent businesses. More and more are deciding that only through ventures of their own can they achieve the kind and quality of life that they envision. According to Dun and Bradstreet, 427,827 new businesses were incorporated in 1978, and late in 1979 the annual rate was running at more than 520,000 — 63%

greater than the number of new incorporations five years before.[43]

This section examines the importance and ramifications of the small business economy in the United States. We will view ideological, economic, and technological roles of entrepreneurship and review salient public policy issues affecting small business development.

The Ideological Role of Small Business

Small business organization represents more than the original structure of the U.S. economy. It also embodies the ideals of opportunity and personal advancement. Entrepreneurship presents the chance for autonomy, economic self-sufficiency, and personal self-expression. It is the economic mechanism for maintaining a fluid social structure and for achieving upward progress on the economic ladder; it is perhaps one of our greatest opportunities to integrate minorities and women into the economic mainstream. Small enterprise can be a means to reward invention and creativity, it can be a chance to recover from past mistakes or to redirect one's life and ambitions, and it can be an escape from subordinancy and stifling bureaucracy.

Without a viable means of showing enterprise, the American values of individualism and independence would be hollow slogans. And, of course, without the deep roots of individualism, the opportunity for entrepreneurship would be useless. Individualism and entrepreneurship form an inseparable ethic in the American economic and social system.

Finally, a vital small business sector provides insurance against political tyranny achieved through economic concentration. A strong and independent small enterprise system disperses economic power, localizes economic decision making, and protects democratic processes. The diffusion of economic responsibility and participation in the economic system is necessary to democracy, a point well made by the White House Commission on Small Business:

> Small Business is, in a deep sense, our Birthright Economy. It is through individual enterprise that we seize those rights of liberty and opportunity that we cherish — the freedom to take our lives into our own hands and pursue prosperity by our own lights; the chance to take risks on our own behalf. And the more people who assume risk and responsibility, the more citizens there will be with a direct stake in fortifying democratic government.[44]

The United States, as a matter of public policy, has been committed to assist and protect the interests of small businesses. The major governmental agency to implement this policy is the Small Business Administration (SBA), an independent regulatory commission. In many ways this agency promotes small business interests in the United States. Insert 11.E provides an overview of its function and some of its activities.

The Economic Role of Small Business

It is estimated that over 14 million corporations, partnerships, and proprietorships in the United States are "small" businesses.[45] This group is a paradox because on the one hand, these businesses dominate the business sector — they comprise 99.7 percent of all companies and employ approximately 47.8 percent of the private, nonfarm work force.[46] They have also played a major role in employing U.S. workers during a recent economic downturn. Between 1980 and 1982 small businesses produced 2.65 million new jobs as compared with an overall loss of over 1.66 million jobs in larger industries during the same period.[47]

Insert 11.E

THE SBA — ITS MANDATE AND ACTIVITIES

The fundamental purpose of the Small Business Administration (SBA) is to aid, counsel, and protect the interests of small business. Utilizing a number of programs to accomplish its mission, the SBA incurred administrative expenses totaling over $297 million in fiscal 1983. The following are several of its major programs:

1. *Financial Assistance.* The SBA provides guaranteed, direct, or immediate participation loans to small business concerns to help them finance plant construction, conversion, or expansion. The loans may also be used by small businesses to acquire equipment, facilities, or supplies. Special loan programs exist for small businesses that hire the handicapped, that make energy conservation devices, or that invest in distressed urban areas.

   Loans may be provided to small businesses that have sustained substantial economic injury resulting from natural disasters such as floods. Assistance may also be given to small firms located in designated areas of economic dislocation or to those adversely affected by urban renewal or highway construction programs.

   In fiscal 1983 the SBA guaranteed or partially guaranteed over 19,000 loans made to small businesses. The total of these loans surpassed $2.5 billion.

2. *Management Assistance.* The SBA sponsors courses and conferences,

prepares informational leaflets and booklets, and encourages research into the management problems of small business concerns. The agency also counsels interested small firms on major aspects of importing and exporting. During fiscal 1983 the SBA reached over 137,000 persons through counseling or training sessions.

3. *Minority Small Business.* The main objective of this program is to help close the gap in business ownership between minority individuals and other Americans. To this end, the SBA supplies the necessary technical and financial assistance to minority individuals or enterprises.

4. *Procurement Assistance.* The SBA provides a wide range of services to small firms to help them obtain and fulfill government contracts. For example, it sets aside suitable government purchases for competitive awards to small business concerns.

   In fiscal 1983 the SBA facilitated procurements to small business totaling $2.3 billion. The SBA-sponsored "Breakout" program has successfully provided small business an entry into the Defense Department's spare and repair parts procurement program. Additionally, the SBA furnished over 8,000 potential small business sources to contractors in fiscal 1983. Computer services provided by the agency allow registered small firms to have their capabilities immediately reviewed when requests are made for small business sources.

5. *Policy and Planning.* The SBA evaluates the impact of agency programs and planning and recommends policy for program direction and for the allocation of agency resources.

6. *Investment Assistance.* The SBA licenses, regulates, and provides financial assistance to small business investment companies and licensees. The sole function of these investment companies is to provide venture capital to small business concerns. Over the past quarter century approximately 47,500 small firms have received over $4.5 billion in financing through this program.

7. *Advocacy.* The SBA initiates, coordinates, and develops the agency's position as the government's principal advocate of small business: it ensures appropriate representation of small business interests in official channels. For example, as an advocate of small business, the agency evaluates whether the regulations of other federal agencies cause an unnecessary hardship on small businesses. If so, the SBA may recommend that an agency make particular regulatory changes — in accordance with the Regulatory Flexibility Act.

SOURCE: U.S., Small Business Administration, *Annual Report FY 1983,* vol. 1 (Washington, D.C.: Government Printing Office, 1984); James C. Sanders. "GOP's Concern for Small Concerns." *Wall Street Journal,* May 31, 1984, p. 23.

On the other hand, small businesses represent a falling share of national income and corporate profits. Some estimates place the small business share of GNP at 55 percent after World War II; today this share has declined to approximately 38 percent.[48] Parallel to these results, the share of manufacturing assets held by companies with $10 million or less in assets fell by 19.6 percent in 1960 to 11.1 percent in 1976.[49] Moreover, the Federal Trade Commission (FTC) reports that large companies (assets of more than $250 million) increased their share of corporate profits from 59 percent to 73 percent between 1960 and 1976. The share of profits of small- and medium-sized companies over this period dropped from 41 percent to 27 percent.

Whatever the causes of this decline, future growth and economic well-being are clearly tied in large part to the vitality and strength of the small business sector. For example, it is estimated that 14 million new jobs will be needed in the economy in the 1980s to accommodate increases in the labor force and to achieve a 4 percent level of unemployment. Since small business generally accounts for a substantial portion of all new jobs, great effort might be made to foster prosperity in this sector.

The Technological Role of Small Business

New, small technology-based firms appear to have done much to create new industries and economic growth in the United States, an advantageous phenomenon for the United States in worldwide economic competition. The scientific and management consulting firm Arthur D. Little published in 1976 an analysis of the impact of new technology-based firms since 1950 on the economies of the United States, West Germany, and Great Britain.[50] The study found these businesses had a significant impact in the United States but played only a minor role in Germany and England. Thousands of technology-based firms founded since 1950 having billions of dollars of sales were identified in the United States. By contrast, 200 or less such firms with little total contribution to national income were found to exist presently in each of the other countries. Insert 11.F presents the factors found in the United States to affect favorably the opportunities for new technology-based businesses, demonstrating the importance of individualistic values and social mobility.

Other studies of inventions and innovations in the United States have reached similar conclusions about small business as a source of economic progress through new technology. A review of the literature on inventions in industry in the United States in this century found the percentage of invention by small firms or independent inventors was never observed to be lower than 50 percent and, depending on the industry and period of time studied, was occasionally 100 percent.[51] Similarly, a report by the Office of Management and Budget of the U.S. government disseminated the results of a study that found that more than half of the techno-

Insert 11.F

SMALL BUSINESS AND TECHNOLOGY IN THE UNITED STATES: A COMPETITIVE CHANGE

A dramatic difference in the role and impact of new technology-based firms in the United States compared with other industrialized countries was observed in an extensive analysis of the origin of current industry across nations. The following were considered to be unique factors favoring the formation and growth of new technology-based business in the United States.

- A very large domestic market conducive to rapid growth and development;
- The availability of private wealth as a source of seed capital for starting new ventures;
- A fiscal framework that encourages the flow of private risk capital into new ventures;
- An active market for trading of shares in new ventures, that is, the over-the-counter (OTC) market;
- A prevailing attitude in society at large which encourages entrepreneurship;
- High mobility of individuals between academic institutions and private industry;
- The behavioral and attitudinal character of American scientists, many of whom are willing to establish their own business in order to exploit their technical knowledge;
- A large and active government expenditure program to provide significant opportunities for [new technology-based firms] endeavors, particularly through government procurement programs.

SOURCE: "New Technology-Based Firms in the United Kingdom and the Federal Republic of Germany," Report prepared for the Anglo-German Foundation for the Study of Industrial Society, in *Technological Innovation: Government/Industry Cooperation,* ed. Arthur Gerstenfeld (New York: Wiley, 1979), p. 84. Used with permission.

logical advances in this century — including xerography, insulin, penicillin, the jet engine, the helicopter, air-conditioning, cellophane, and many others — arose from individual inventors and small companies.[52] Finally, a study of 380 important innovations produced in five countries between 1953 and 1973 conducted for the National Science Board arrived at these conclusions:

- Small firms contributed about a third of important innovations in this period.
- Small businesses' contributions were greatest in the United States, followed by France, West Germany, Great Britain, and Japan.
- In the United States small firms evenly produced three different types of innovation: radical breakthroughs, major technological shifts, and improvement innovations. Small firms in other countries tended to produce either all radical breakthroughs (England) or very few radical innovations (Germany, France, Japan.)[53]

All studies indicate that small business contributes vital energy to economic advancement through technological invention and innovation (Insert 11.G).

PUBLIC POLICY AND THE SMALL BUSINESS SECTOR

The unique size and national character of the United States create an environment in which the contribution of small business to national employment and economic growth goals is large. Characteristics of the U.S. economy offer the best opportunity for continued economic regeneration based on the formation of new enterprise. There are numerous ideas about public policy orientations to small business development. Many of these can be classified either as (1) proposals to eliminate apparent biases against small business in public policy or as (2) proposals to give small business preferential treatment.[54]

Eliminating Apparent Bias against Small Business

There may be areas of government action in which small businesses suffer disadvantages for no other reason than their smallness. Examples might include (1) tax and accounting, (2) government regulations, (3) financing, and (4) federal agency procurement, especially concerning R & D expenditures. Each of these will be briefly considered.

Tax and Accounting

Tax and accounting practices occasionally become complex enough to penalize small companies that cannot afford large staffs to take advantage of cost information and filing procedures for maximum benefit. One example from the White House Conference pertains to capital recovery through different allowable methods of calculating asset depreciation. Analysis of corporate tax filings show that 94 percent of large corporations take advantage of the opportunities for capital recovery provided by the complex system of figuring asset depreciation, whereas only 0.5 percent of small

---

Insert 11.G

THE CONTRIBUTION OF SMALL BUSINESSES TO INNOVATION AND JOB CREATION

The claim that small businesses make a disproportionately large contribution to innovation does not lack substantiation. A recent study by the National Science Foundation determined that in the post–World War II period firms with less than 1,000 employees were responsible for half of the "most significant new industrial products and processes." Firms with 100 or fewer employees produced 24 percent of such innovations. In addition, the cost per innovation in a small firm was found to be substantially less than in a large firm, since small firms produced 24 times more major innovations per research and development dollar expended as large firms.

The significant role played by small innovative businesses is underscored in a study conducted by the Massachusetts Institute of Technology Development Foundation. The foundation calculated the compounded average annual growth in sales and jobs for the following three groups of companies (1969 to 1974):

Type of Companies	Growth in Volume of Sales (percent)	Growth in Jobs (percent)
Mature	11.4	0.6
Innovative	13.2	4.3
Young, high-technology	42.5	40.7

In this study, mature companies were Bethlehem Steel, DuPont, General Electric, General Foods, International Paper, and P&G. Examples of innovative companies used were Polaroid, Xerox, and Texas Instruments. Young, high-technology companies included the likes of National Semiconductor and Marion Laboratories.

SOURCE: U.S., Department of Commerce, "Advisory Committee on Industrial Innovation — Final Report" (Washington, D.C.: Government Printing Office, September 1979), p. 259–60.

---

companies (less than $5 million in assets) avail themselves of these procedures. Consequently, large companies deduct depreciation equal to about 3.6 percent of their receipts, and small companies deduct about half this amount.[55]

The Tax Equity and Fiscal Responsibility Act, passed by Congress in 1982, has negatively impacted on the financing problems of small businesses in a different manner. Under this act firms are required to pay 90 percent of their tax liability — a 10 percent increase from the previous rate. Moreover, the Tax Equity Act repealed the 200 percent Accelerated Cost Recovery System and the Safe Harbor provision that allowed firms to sell unused tax benefits: the net result of these repeals has been increased cash flow difficulties for the smaller business.

Government Regulations

Second, government regulation may often create greater financial hardship for small enterprises than it does for large firms. For example, one survey by the SBA of 1,000 small firms found these firms, collectively, had to complete 305 million government forms asking 7.3 billion questions per year.[56] In the chemical specialty industry alone, another survey reported that these firms had to increase their annual operating costs by $95,806 on the average, in order to comply with EPA regulations; the average annual outlay for capital expenditures associated with EPA compliance totaled $268,056.[57] These results led the surveyors to conclude that artificial economies of scale are introduced by such requirements — the larger firm can pass along increased costs with less increase in per unit prices.[58]

Behind criticisms of the impact of regulation on small businesses lies the belief that these businesses are unreasonably penalized for their smallness. The same number of specialized staff people are simply not available in these businesses to devote their full attention to the vast number of government regulations. Murray Weidenbaum makes this point in a broad analysis and criticism of government regulation:

> Government regulation, often unwittingly, hits small business disproportionately hard. Most of the impact is unintentional, in that the standardized regulations typically do not distinguish among companies of different sizes. But in practice, forcing a small firm to fill out the same specialized forms as a large company with highly trained technical staffs at its disposal places a significantly greater burden on the smaller enterprise. That general point is supported by data and examples from such different government regulatory activities as the Environmental Protection Agency, the Employment Retirement Security Act, the National Labor Relations Board, the Occupational Safety and Health Administration, and the Securities and Exchange Commission.[59]

Small business proponents argue for the review and revision of regulatory requirements to alleviate the disproportionate burden imposed on small business. These revisions would include provisions for greater small business input into rule making, substantially more flexibility in applying rules to small enterprises, and much greater use of small business exemptions.

To some extent the government has been responsive to the pleas of small businesspersons. Congress has enacted both the Regulatory Flexibility Act and the Paper Reduction Act, in part to reduce compliance costs. All federal rule-making agencies must allow alternative (less cumbersome) methods of regulatory compliance for small firms. The Paper Reduction Act has attempted to minimize the federal paperwork burden for a number of entities — including small businesses.[60]

While these legislative efforts may be encouraging to the small businessperson, little attempt has been made to reduce the *financial* burden so often associated with regulatory compliance. Moreover, lack of information about the impact of rules and regulations on small business operations may constitute a hidden and unplanned cost to the smaller operator.

Financing

Small businesses also appear to operate at a disadvantage in the financial markets. It has long been recognized that small businesses have "limited access to long-term debt and equity markets" and when the economy declines, so does the ability of the small firm to obtain and afford the capital it needs.[61] Governmental actions appear to have exacerbated the difficulties of small business in this area. National reliance on the savings pool to finance deficits has raised the cost of capital and severely limited the access of small firms to needed financial resources. It has been asserted that the small business entity will "usually pay anywhere from 1.5 to 4 points above the stated prime rate."[62]

Aware of the above-mentioned financing problems, the federal government again attempted corrective measures. Small Business Investment Companies were created to funnel a combination of private and public funds into small business ventures. Long-term financing opportunities were created through federal efforts to increase the small firm's access to industrial revenue bonds, federal loans, and equity markets. Creation of the SBA 503 loan program has provided small enterprises with long-term, fixed-asset financing in an effort to create jobs in certain designated areas.[63] Federal efforts in this area have no doubt improved the financial situation of some small firms; however, the positive impact has been limited as available public funds have been frozen at $160 million for three years and obtainment of industrial revenue bonds requires substantial administrative effort on the part of the involved small business.[64]

Federal Agency Procurement

Finally, small businesses appear to receive a disproportionately smaller piece of the federal procurement pie — relative to their critical role in industrial invention and innovation. Federal procurement dollars may flow to businesses in two familiar ways: a business may be awarded a contract to produce goods/services for the government or federal monies may be given to a firm to be used for desired federal research and development. Small businesses have been excluded, to some degree, from both areas. Procurement procedures and policies may be largely to blame in this instance. The Office of Federal Procurement Policy of the Office of Management and Budget surveyed 19 agencies and identified the following facts about the federal procurement system:

- ·485 offices regularly issue procurement regulations.
- 877 different sets of regulations exist.
- 64,000 pages of regulations are in effect.
- 21,900 new or revised pages are issued each year.
- Proliferation is greatest in large agencies with multiple authority levels.
- 83 percent of all regulations are issued by levels below agency headquarters.[65]

The procurement policies of the Department of Defense (DOD), which account for almost 80 percent of all federal procurement dollars, illustrate the technical problem for small businesses. The DOD normally issues contract solicitations in excess of 100 pages and routinely refers to "standard form clauses" that are not printed in the text of the solicitation. The result is time-consuming research on the part of the small business or a costly fee for an expert to make sense of the solicitation.[66]

Small business also appears to face special difficulties in federal R & D procurement. Although the small business sector contributes about 40 percent of the country's gross domestic product, it receives about 22 percent of federal procurement dollars and less than 4 percent of federal R & D expenditures.[67] Relative to its important role in industrial innovation, small business receives proportionately fewer R & D dollars.

Reasons for these low percentages are not typically clear-cut but probably include the following: the greater relative cost to public agencies to identify and fund small concerns; the relative lack of information, familiarity, and time of small business people to compete for federal R & D funds; bureaucratic inefficiencies associated with the difficulty of changing policy directions; and political and ideological barriers to altering national policy. Further hampering the participation of small businesses in federal procurement programs is the government's payment schedule. A study by the American Consulting Engineers Council found that government paid its small businesses 2.5 months late, necessitating relatively expensive short-term borrowing on the part of the small firm to meet immediate cash needs.[68]

Government efforts to rectify the above inequities have likely been helpful but are not comprehensive. The Office of Federal Procurement Policy is charged with developing procurement processes that will increase small business involvement in this area, and to date a few successes may be noted. A program called Breakout is one attempt to open up the spare parts procurement processes to small concerns; the DOD can solicit small distributors, suppliers, and manufacturers directly if quality standards are not at issue. A recent report by the Defense Department described the success of the Breakout program: "To date, approximately 2,329 items have been successfully 'broken-out' for competition.... Documented savings are $43.8 million."[69]

The Small Business Innovation Development Act in 1982 was enacted by Congress to serve a four-fold purpose; to stimulate technological innovation, to use small businesses to complete federal R & D projects, to help minority-owned enterprises, and to increase private sector commercialization derived from federal R & D. Included in this legislation is a requirement that major federal agencies allocate a certain percentage (normally 1.5 percent) of their research and development funds to small businesses.[70]

To spur federal agencies into developing expeditious payment policies, Congress passed the Prompt Payment Act of 1982. Agencies that are tardy in their payments must now pay an interest penalty to their creditors. During the first year, 20 agencies monitored by the government paid $1.46 million in interest payments.[71]

Federal efforts to reduce or eliminate biases against small businesses in the areas of tax and accounting, regulatory compliance, financing, and federal procurements have satisfied some interest groups. Meanwhile other groups insist that further biases should be eliminated, and still other groups promote preferential treatment as the most satisfactory solution to address the problems of small businesses in these areas.

Giving Preferential Treatment to Small Business

Reasons cited for giving preferential treatment to small businesses rather than confining government actions to eliminating biases are numerous and debatable. One argument for preferential treatment centers around the claim that innovative ability may be inversely related to firm size; therefore, government should concentrate incentives around small enterprises, as they are most likely to be innovative. As early as 1967 a government study indicated that more than half of the technological innovations in the twentieth century — including xerography, insulin, the jet engine, airconditioning, and others — were made by small businesses or individuals.[72]

Moreover, advocates of preferential treatment suggest that small-scale firms frequently possess a combination of three other desirable characteristics not typically clustered in larger firms:

- *Marketing.* The small firm usually targets a specific market in which it is the leader.
- *Dynamic Entrepreneurial Management.* The small technology firms, in particular, have a greater ability to seize an opportunity.
- *Internal Communications.* Companies are small enough that communication among various staff members is easier.[73]

The existence of these and other desirable traits, including small business's purported ability to better satisfy the nation's employment needs during economic downturns, has led proponents of preferential treatment for small businesses to propose one or more of the following changes in current legislation:

- Allow small businesses to deduct from income at least two times the level of R & D allowed for large businesses;
- Reduce corporate income tax at lower corporate income levels;
- Allocate federal R & D monies to small businesses at a greater rate;
- Offer special tax allowances for new types of debt instruments particular to small businesses; and
- Augment and emphasize programs of public credit to small businesses.[74]

At this point in time, public policy is characterized by an incremental, piece-meal, and often internally inconsistent approach to small business. It has also proved to be politically more acceptable to remove biases *against* small businesses than to legislate biases *for* small businesses. Furthermore, the effects of recent legislation — which has removed some biases — has yet to be thoroughly evaluated as to its impact on this business sector.

   Judgment of existing and proposed policies depends on the assessment of the small business sector's social and economic importance. Traditionally, legislators have steered away from enacting policies preferential to a single firm, industry or business sector, although various industry-specific programs, such as the tobacco growers' subsidy, do exist, and procurement policies have favored development of industries such as aircraft engines or computer manufacturers. Business-government relations in this context still remains an open area for public policy development.

A CONCLUDING COMMENT

Many, if not most, areas of contemporary business-government relations in the United States are fraught with controversy. Often, government finds itself attempting to influence and reform the role of business in society, and business largely finds government an unwanted and coercive regulator of its affairs. At best there is mutual ambivalence in the relationship; at worst there is overt hostility. The major policy issues of the day — antitrust; corporate governance; health, safety, and environmental protection; community relations; corporate political involvement; and multinational country relationships — are filled with conflicts between public values and private actions and pose strong challenges for the integration of business, government, and society.

The area of economic growth, particularly with respect to technological development and small enterprise growth, gives welcome respite from this pattern of tension in business and government affairs. Here, public interests largely match private incentives and capabilities; the public welfare requires productivity growth, technological superiority, and a strong and vital environment for entrepreneurship. These are functions that business best provides. Consequently, the difficult problem of adapting corporate policies and social policies, where public and private interests are distinct and possibly inconsistent, is largely reduced in this area.

The real question is whether, or to what magnitude, economic growth and technology development policies can be adopted. One risk is that the climate of adversity and suspicion present in other policy areas will carry over into these dimensions of economic policy, thus threatening the opportunity to capitalize upon mutual public and private interests. If technology policy can be developed and is not, the public interest will not be well served.

However, the more basic risk is not that a positive growth policy will fail owing to neglect or oversight but that other national objectives will compete for national resources, detracting from the pursuit of economic objectives. A few of these — greater equalization of income and health and safety investments — have been briefly touched upon in this chapter. These, also, are important national objectives with deep roots in American ideology and strong political constituencies. The challenge to national interests in technology and small business development comes from conflicting national goals, not from differing perspectives of business and government on the importance of technology. The test of our commitment to economic goals will be our persistence in finding ways to integrate successfully our multiple national objectives.

DISCUSSION QUESTIONS

1. What roles do technological innovation and small business development play in America's economic goals? How are the two processes related?
2. What governmental policies, if any, toward the development of technology do you feel are most effective and vital? Why?

3. Do you favor preferential national policies toward small business? What other business sectors or interests may compete with small business for preferential policy treatment?

NOTES

1. National Science Foundation, National Science Board, *Science Indicators 1982* (Washington, D.C.: U.S. Government Printing Office, 1983), p. 104.
2. David L. Birch, "The Job Generation Process," MIT Program on Neighborhood and Regional Change, Cambridge, Massachusetts, 1979, p. 9.
3. U.S., White House Commission on Small Business, *America's Small Business Economy: Agenda for Action,* Report to the President (Washington, D.C.: Government Printing Office, April 1980), p. 20.
4. Ibid., p. 22.
5. Robert A. Charpie, "Technological Innovation and the International Economy," in *Technological Innovation and the Economy,* ed. Maurice Goldsmith (New York: Wiley-Interscience, 1970), p. 3.
6. Ibid., pp. 3–4.
7. Roy Rothwell and Walter Zegweld, *Industrial Innovation and Public Policy: Preparing for the 1980s and 1990s* (Westport, Conn.: Greenwood Press, 1981), p. 24.
8. Edward F. Denison, *Accounting for United States Economic Growth, 1929–1969* (Washington, D.C.: Brookings Institution, 1974), p. 131.
9. Edward F. Denison, *Accounting for Slower Economic Growth: The United States in the 1970s* (Washington, D.C.: Brookings Institution, 1979), p. 2.
10. Gerhard Mensch, *Stalemate in Technology* (Cambridge: Ballinger, 1979).
11. Leonard L. Lederman, "Government Policy and Innovation in the United States," in *Technological Innovation: Government/Industry Cooperation,* ed. Arthur Gerstenfeld (New York: John Wiley & Sons, 1979), p. 160.
12. Statistics in this section are all drawn from National Science Foundation, National Science Board, *Science Indicators 1982,* (Washington, D.C.: Government Printing Office, 1983) pp. 40, 195, 199–200.
13. Denison, *Accounting for United States Economic Growth,* p. 132.
14. U.S., Department of Commerce, Bureau of the Census, *Statistical Abstract of the United States* (Washington, D.C.: Government Printing Office, 1980), p. 44.
15. Alfred C. Neal, "Immolation of Business Capital," *Harvard Business Review,* March-April 1978, p. 77.
16. Center for Policy Alternatives, *Government Involvement in the Innovation Process,* prepared for U.S., Congress, Office of Technology Assessment (Cambridge: Massachusetts Institute of Technology, 1978), p. 3.

17. Ibid.
18. "Bill Gives Synfuels Push to Private Industry," *Congressional Quarterly Weekly Report* 38 (June 21, 1980): 1693.
19. Center for Policy Alternatives, *Government Involvement*, p. 46.
20. Ibid., pp. 44–45.
21. *Science Indicators 1982*, p. 245.
22. Richard Corrigan, "Federal Government Getting Into the High-Tech Research and Development Act," *National Journal*, September 15, 1984, p. 1718.
23. *Science Indicators 1982*, p. 305.
24. National Science Foundation, National Science Board, *Science Indicators 1978* (Washington, D.C.: Government Printing Office, September 1979), p. 208.
25. National Science Foundation, *Science Indicators 1982*, pp. 238, 241.
26. Leon E. Wynter, "Congress Is Debating Federal Role in Setting Technological Priorities," *Wall Street Journal*, August 1, 1984, p. 1.
27. Corrigan, "Federal Government Getting Into the High-Tech Research and Development Act," p. 1719.
28. Rothwell and Zegweld, *Industrial Innovation*, p. 112.
29. Ronald Miller and David Sawers, *The Technical Development of Modern Aviation* (New York: Praeger, 1968), p. 262–63.
30. Ibid., p. 279.
31. Jerry Grey, "Implications of the Shuttle: Our Business In Space," *Technology Review* 84 (October 1981): 38.
32. Ibid., p. 40.
33. Arthur Gerstenfeld, *Technological Innovation: Government/Industry Cooperation* (New York: John Wiley & Sons, 1979), p. 183.
34. Center for Policy Alternatives, *Government Invovlement*, p. 59.
35. Ed Zschau and Don Ritter, "Encourage Innovation Instead of Industrial Lemons," *Wall Street Journal*, August 1, 1984, p. 18.
36. Committee for Economic Development, *Stimulating Technological Progress, Statement by the Research and Policy Committee of the Committee for Economic Development* (New York: CED, January 1980), p. 71.
37. Ibid.
38. Center for Policy Alternatives, *Government Involvement*, p. 44.
39. Ibid., p. 61.
40. M. Michael Waldrop, "Space Commerce: The Quest for Coherence," *Science*, August, 1984, p. 1.
41. Ibid.
42. Center for Policy Alternatives, *Government Involvement*, pp. 66–67.
43. U.S., White House Commission on Small Business, *America's Small Business*, p. 9.
44. Ibid., p. 12.
45. U.S., Small Business Administration (SBA), "President's Report on the State of Small Business," *SBA Fact Sheet*, March 1984, p. 2.
46. Ibid., p. 1.

47. Ibid.
48. Ibid.
49. All statistics in this section are from U.S., White House Commission on Small Business, *America's Small Business,* pp. 9–23.
50. Gerstenfeld, *Technological Innovation,* pp. 80–92.
51. Rothwell and Zegweld, *Industrial Innovation,* p. 185.
52. U.S., White House Commission on Small Business, *America's Small Business,* p. 21.
53. Rothwell and Zegweld, *Industrial Innovation,* p. 188.
54. Much of the material for the remainder of this section is excerpted from John D. Aram and Jeffrey S. Coomes, "Public Policy and the Small Business Sector," *Policy Studies Journal,* in press.
55. U.S., White House Commission on Small Business, *America's Small Business,* p. 27.
56. Ibid., p. 31.
57. Kenneth W. Chilton and Murray L. Weidenbaum, "Government Regulation: The Small Business Burden," *Journal of Small Business Management* 20 (January 1982): 1–7.
58. Ibid.
59. Murray L. Weidenbaum, *The Future of Business Regulation: Private Action and Public Demand* (New York: ANACOM, 1980), pp. 51–52.
60. PL 96–511 U.S. Code, Paperwork Reduction Act of 1980.
61. Allan Disman, "State Capital Formation and Small Business Needs," *Governmental Finance* 12 (December 1983): 13.
62. Small Business United, "Creating Jobs for America's Future (Paper presented at Small Business United: A National Network for Legislative Action, Washington, D.C., May 1 and 2, 1984), p. 5.
63. Aram and Coomes, "Public Policy."
64. Lee Kravitz, "Why SBICs Want to Break From the SBA," *Venture,* October 1984, p. 64.
65. U.S., Office of Federal Procurement Policy, *Proposal for a Uniform Federal Procurement Policy* (Washington, D.C.: Government Printing Office, 1982).
66. President of the United States, *The State of Small Business: A Report of the President* (Washington, D.C.: Government Printing Office, 1984), p. 328.
67. U.S. White House Commission on Small Business, *America's Small Business,* p. 20.
68. President of the United States, *The State of Small Business,* p. 330.
69. U.S., Office of Procurement Policy, *Review of the Spare Parts Procurement Practices of the Department of Defense* (Washington, D.C.: Government Printing Office, 1984), p. 39.
70. PL 97–219 U.S. Code, Small Business Innovation Development Act of 1982.
71. President of the United States, *The State of Small Business,* p. 330.

72. U.S., White House Commission on Small Business, *America's Small Business*, p. 21.

73. Roy Rothwell and Zegweld, *Innovation and the Small and Medium Sized Firm* (Boston: Klurer, Nighoff, 1981), p. 45.

74. Drawn from U.S., White House Commission on Small Business, *America's Small Business*, pp. 50–56; and U.S., Department of Commerce, *Advisory Committee on Industrial Innovation: Final Report* (Washington, D.C.: Government Printing Office, September, 1979), pp. 264–69.

National Goals and the Biotechnology Industry
What Direction for U.S. Public Policy?

The biotechnology industry[1] in the 1980s has been compared with the computer industry in the 1960s. Similar to the early days of the computer industry, the United States has been largely responsible for pioneering basic research in this technology; advanced knowledge in the early research stages has enabled the United States to gain an initial international lead in the critical development and commercialization stages.

Tremendous growth and profit potential is anticipated within this field, and yet few products currently generate positive financial returns. To date, the industry has successfully marketed a hair-dissolving drain cleaner, animal vaccines, and artificial snow, but only a small number of biotech products have even reached the market.[2]

Nevertheless, the future of the biotech industry is extremely promising as the number of potentially profitable products is virtually unlimited. Genetically engineered animal hormone growth products may generate sales totaling $515 million in 1985, whereas the biotech health product market is expected to exceed $17 billion by 1995.[3] According to Assistant Commerce Secretary Bruce Merrifield, the market for various biotech products will be worth billions of dollars by the later 1990s.[4] Others suggest that control of the biotech industry will eventually rival dominance of the semiconductor market as an important measure of an industrialized nation's economic health. Unfortunately, from the American viewpoint, analogies between the two industries do not stop at this point.

American biotech analysts predict that Japan is, once again, threatening to capitalize on American basic research "breakthroughs" and take over the lead in the race to commercialize biotech products. According to the U.S. Office of Technology Assessment (OTA):

> Japan has a very strong bioprocess technology on which to build, and the Japanese government has specified biotechnology as a national priority. The demonstrated ability of the Japanese to commercialize developments in technology rapidly will surely manifest itself in biotechnology.[5]

Underscoring its designation of biotechnology as a "national priority," Japan's Ministry of International Trade and Industry has initiated, and partially financed, interindustry biotechnology endeavors. Furthermore, the Japanese government has channeled a major portion of its research funds toward projects that are focused on eliminating commercialization "bottlenecks"; this research strategy facilitated Japan's successful entry into the international semiconductor market.

European nations have also increased and consolidated their efforts in genetic engineering commercialization. Great Britain changed its investment policy in 1979, allowing tax write-offs for individuals investing in small companies. As a result Britain's venture capital market is second only to the American venture capital pool.[6] The West German government has shared sponsorship of biotech projects with interested German industries. Moreover, the ten members of the European Economic Community have considered funding a five-year, $134 million biotech program in order to stimulate a European "Common Market in Technology."[7] Given Europe's intensified efforts in the international genetic engineering area, the United States cannot even be assured of a "second place" standing in the biotech race without a continued national commitment to the promotion of this technology.

The United States achieved its position as the world leader in genetic engineering as a result of the combination of three critical factors: a national commitment to basic research, and a commitment to entrepreneurial spirit, and the willingness of private investors to finance high-risk biotech ventures.[8] However, these factors will not guarantee U.S. dominance in commercialization. The central questions are (1) whether the U.S. government should do more for this industry and (2) if so, what?

EXISTING PUBLIC POLICIES

The American government has exhibited an interest in U.S. dominance of the biotech market. In order to maintain America's lead in biotech commerce, Congress requested the OTA to conduct an analysis that would provide answers to two critical questions: What factors will impact future U.S. competitiveness in biotechnology? and What, if any, policy changes are needed to promote U.S. commercialization of biotechnology? The following sections discuss major points of study.

Tax and Financial Incentives

By international standards the United States is considered to have the most favorable tax environment for biotech ventures. In 1983 over $1 billion of private investment flowed into genetic engineering ventures. Biotech firms have received monies from R & D limited partnerships, sales of stock, and venture capital organizations.[9] Individual investors appear to be attracted by the low capital gains tax rates, whereas industrial investors are interested in gaining R & D tax credits. Furthermore, American corporations and individual investors seem ready to continue funding high-risk bioventures if high potential investment gains exist. European and Japanese governments have not chosen to support biotechnology through incentives; consequently, commercialization of foreign bioventures has typically been funded by established companies or by the government at lower levels than present in the United States.

Governmental Support of Biotech Research

The federal government has placed an emphasis on basic research in this industry. In 1983, federal funding of biotech research and development projects totaled $517.4 million.[10] Less than 7 percent of the federal funds were devoted to applied research, whereas basic research received the remaining amount.[11] Limited federal funding for applied research projects has, in turn, restricted the supply of a critical manpower area: applied biotech researchers. According to the OTA study, the United States does not have more than a "handful" of biotech training programs and does not sponsor training in applied biotech research.[12]

Some biotechnologists believe that this unbalanced research focus may cause the United States to eventually relinquish its position as the world leader in biotech commercialization. Currently the United States has been unable to transform basic knowledge into marketable products in this industry.[13] Generic applied research focuses on the resolution of technological and scientific problems commonly faced by a number of genetically engineered products.

Japan parlayed national funding of applied semiconductor research into successful semiconductor commercialization and is expected to apply the same research strategy to biotechnology in the 1980s. Europe has also realized that generic applied research may be a major key to their competitiveness in biotechnology. The proposed European joint biotechnology program plans to stimulate commercialization of biotechnology by researching solutions to "technical and scientific" bottlenecks.[14] One might ask whether product development is the Achilles heel of U.S. competitiveness in growth industries.

Federal Regulation

Appropriate and adequate regulation of the biotech industry has been the topic of extensive debate since the first gene was cloned in 1973. In a 1984 congressional hearing, Senator Dave Durenberger's questions underlined some common public concerns: "Do we really understand the consequences of these powerful new tools? In our haste to gain the obvious benefits, might we cause unintended harm?"[15] An earlier congressional staff report on biotechnology acknowledged: "While there is only a small possibility that damage could occur, the damage that could occur is great."[16]

Until recently, genetic experimentation was conducted in controlled laboratory settings; scientists contend that genetic products now require "realistic" testing in outdoor settings. Environmentalists and others fear that genetically engineered microorganisms could cause tremendous and irreversible damage to an environment that lacks a natural immunity to man-made new life forms. Questioning whether harmful organisms can be "recalled" from the environment, one congressional aide asked, "If you can't shoot it or plow it under or poison it, how do you get it back in the jar?"[17] Biotech researchers claim that cruder genetic engineering has been performed on plants, animals, and microorganisms for many years without mishap.[18] Virtually all interested groups agree that genetic engineering endeavors require some regulatory controls; however, biotechnologists have objected to some existing regulations, and environmentalists are lobbying for stringently controlled biotech experimentation.

To date, the National Institutes of Health (NIH), the Environmental Protection Agency (EPA), and the Food and Drug Administration (FDA) have assumed major biotech regulatory roles. NIH is responsible for setting overall experimentation guidelines, whereas the EPA has begun to assert itself in the regulation of biotechnology field tests. Meanwhile, the FDA determines whether genetically engineered food and chemical additives are safe for human consumption.

Biotech producers would like FDA regulations to be relaxed. Currently, products under FDA jurisdiction must receive the agency's approval before they are introduced in foreign markets. The laborious and time-consuming FDA approval process, according to industry advocates, has limited their competitiveness in world markets. Conventional drug manufacturers have leveled similar criticisms at the FDA, claiming that the tedious approval process has substantially delayed the release of innovative drugs created to benefit mankind. Unable to gain expeditious FDA approval of their products, biotech firms have been forced to sell product technology instead. Singular sales of technology, in lieu of multiple and ongoing product sales, reduces the industry's profit potential. When questioned about the effects of existing FDA product regulation, biotech lobbyist Stephen Lawton commented:

That's hard on emerging industries that have to compete
in Japanese and European markets with Japanese and European firms. It is compelling, just absolutely compelling,
that the law be changed. In our view it's absolutely critical
to our industry. In the scheme of things [new biotechnology companies] are a bunch of itty-bitty guys. We've got to
start selling products, not technology.[19]

Congress is expected to allow FDA-unapproved products to be exported to
industrialized nations. Concerned about the potential "dumping" of unsafe
products in unsophisticated markets, Congress has not considered further
modification of the law to include Third World nations.[20] Although the
biotech industry is likely to overcome this particular regulatory hurdle,
stiffer challenges are surfacing.

Intellectual Property Rights

By OTA standards, "the U.S. intellectual property system offers the best
protection for biotechnology of any system in the world."[21] "Intellectual
property" includes trade secrets, patents, and breeders' rights.[22] In the
1980 *Diamond* v. *Chakrabarty* decision, the Supreme Court definitively concluded that patent rights could be issued to the creator of a genetically
engineered, oil-consuming microbe.[23] This decision eliminated previous
doubts pertaining to the patentability of new life forms. Currently, biotech
innovators may select the legal mechanism that offers the highest degree
of protection for their particular product for any of the three available
areas.

  The ability to protect intellectual property adequately serves a twofold purpose in the genetic engineering industry. Able to maintain possession of their ideas, innovators have been willing to start their own small
biotech firms. Industry observers have attributed American dominance in
the biotech field, in large part, to the innovative abilities of small firms.
According to Rod Raynovich, president of one small biotech firm, "A giant
company is like a large ship in the ocean — it maneuvers slowly. We're able
to mobilize and maneuver faster, and our overhead expenses are lower."[24]

  The ability of U.S. firms to protect their existing and future innovations has also been perceived as valuable by individual and corporate
investors, leading to the availability of seed money for bioventures. In 1983
larger, established firms invested approximately $500 million in small
firms' R & D projects; in return corporate investors received "first rights"
to the manufacture and sale of some of the small firms' newly developed
biotech products.[25] As small firms are believed to be the best environments
for innovation and larger firms are better equipped to market biotech
products, the United States's protective intellectual property system has
performed a critical role in linking the two business segments.

Academic-Industrial Affiliations

U.S. biotechnology producers have demonstrated an interest in funding basic genetic engineering research within American universities. Established firms, unable to explore all biotech research avenues, have added their financial resources to existing governmental research grants. In return genetic research carried out in university laboratories has increased the U.S. biotech knowledge base while preparing a steady supply of biotech basic researchers for entry into the labor force.

Neither Japan nor Europe has developed strong university-industry biotech research ties.[26] Again, the United States' capacity for linking parties that perform critical roles in the commercialization of biotechnology has proved to be an advantage in the international market.

Trade Policies

Restrictive provisions in U.S. antitrust laws and trade policy may discourage U.S. biotech commercialization. Strict U.S. antitrust laws effectively ruled out R & D joint venture agreements among biotech companies in the earliest days of biotechnology research. In 1984 Congress passed the National Cooperative Research Act in an effort to encourage industrial research.[27] Biotech firms may now apply for governmental antitrust protection for joint R & D ventures under this act. Small firms may no longer fear the imposition of triple damages from losing an antitrust case, but the lengthy process of obtaining governmental approval for multicompany research projects remains an obstacle to collective research efforts.

Some industry observers believe that the absence of trade protection may seriously undermine U.S. biotech commercialization efforts. The President's Commission on Industrial Competitiveness recently indicated that tolerant or nonexistent U.S. trade policies have already weakened American trade balances in semiconductor, consumer electronics, and communications equipment industries.[28] According to the commission, the federal government has allowed foreign governments to restrict U.S. imports while flooding the American market with exported goods.[29] As a direct result of this liberal trade policy, the American biotech market is vulnerable to penetration by Japanese and European biotech firms. The OTA study on biotech commercialization concluded:

> Foreign exchange and investment control laws help prevent access to domestic markets and technology by foreign firms. The United States has the fewest controls, whereas Japan and France have the most control mechanisms. Thus, the U.S. markets are the most accessible to foreign firms and therefore the most vulnerable to foreign competition.[30]

American free trade policy has not yet impacted biotech firms as few genetically engineered products have proved to be commercially viable. However, it predicted that the biotech industry may eventually rival, or surpass, the semiconductor industry in economic importance. Japan's swift and highly successful entry into the semiconductor industry has not been forgotten, leading some biotech advocates to suggest that the U.S. genetic engineering industry may require strict new trade laws to forestall a similar Japanese penetration of the U.S. biotech market.

Public Acceptance

Public support for bioventures is considered an influential factor in U.S. biotech commercialization. Public perception of the biotech industry is in turn influenced by environmental concerns mentioned earlier and ethical concerns. The tremendous potential of biological technology has led to discussions concerning socially "acceptable" and "unacceptable" new life forms. To some persons, genetically engineered plants seem only a few scientific steps away from genetically engineered people.[31] Biotech researchers typically view these fears as unrealistic and consider genetically engineered humans to be scientifically impossible for many years.

Little legislative action has been taken on numerous congressional bills that were designed to reduce the public's environmental and ethical fears. After a period of concern in the mid-1970s scientists are now fairly unified in their claim that biotech research is conducted in a responsible manner. Moreover, public sentiment has shifted toward deregulation, or limited regulation, rather than increased regulation of industries. The lack of restrictive regulations has allowed biotechnology experimentation to flourish. The OTA warns that continued public acceptance of genetic engineering is critical to U.S. competitiveness in this arena and might be significantly reduced "in the event of an accident or perceived negative consequence of biotechnology."[32]

POLICY RECOMMENDATIONS

The U.S. Office of Technology Assessment recommendations for maintaining the American lead in biotechnology commercialization focused on enacting more effective biotech trade and research policies.[33] First, training programs for biotech researchers need to be upgraded and expanded. Increasing the number and skills of biotech researchers will enable the United States to resolve recurring biotech problems and move genetically engineered products into the commercialization stage more rapidly.

Second, antitrust laws need to include revisions designed to facilitate joint research ventures among biotech firms. In particular, expediting the governmental joint venture approval process would encourage more biotech firms to combine their research resources, leading to accelerated biotech product development.

Next, the United States needs to limit the flow of genetic engineering technology from U.S. firms to foreign countries. American biotechnology firms would prefer to sell biotech products rather than technology; therefore, the transfer of biotechnology would decrease if export trade laws were modified to facilitate product sales. In addition the OTA suggested that U.S. biotechnology outflows should be formally regulated by the American government.

Stricter import trade laws should be created to preserve the U.S. biotech market for American genetic engineering firms. The accessibility of U.S. markets has already contributed to an estimated semiconductor trade deficit that approached $3 billion in 1984, as compared with a trade surplus two years earlier.[34] Trade laws that deterred foreign bioproduct sales in U.S. markets would give impetus to U.S. biotech commercialization as a domestic genetic engineering market would be reasonably assured.

Suggestions of this type are not unfamiliar to Congress, and in fact, many manufacturing and some high-tech lobbying groups have already pressed for protective trade laws and less restrictive antitrust laws for their industries. Meanwhile, tight U.S. budget constraints combined with a general reluctance to promote specific industries has stalled congressional action on these recommendations. Either Congress must face angry lobbyists from other industries if the biotech industry is singularly exempted from existing trade and research policies *or* broad-based, potentially costly policy changes must be enacted in an effort to facilitate the commercialization of one U.S. industry.

DISCUSSION QUESTIONS

1. If additional federal spending on biotechnology research must be offset by reduced federal spending in another area, would you allocate federal monies for new biotech personnel training programs? Why or why not?
2. Would you favor stricter biotech research regulations in order to prevent potential environmental hazards? What are some possible costs and benefits associated with your decision?
3. In your opinion, is the U.S. biotech industry in the 1980s directly comparable with the U.S. semiconductor industry in the 1960s? What, if any, significant differences exist? To what extent should the United States develop policies to support biotech commercialization?

NOTES

1. Occasionally labeled the "new scientific frontier," biotechnology typically includes three scientific techniques: gene splicing, cell fusion, and bioprocessing. Gene splicing and cell fusion techniques are used to alter the composition of a cell in an effort to produce an organism with unique or enhanced characteristics. Aspartame, human insulin, and new medical diagnostic kits are among the few biotech products currently on the market. *Bioprocessing* refers to production processes that substitute genetic techniques for traditional manufacturing processes. Production of vitamins and steroid compounds is simplified when bioprocessing is substituted for conventional chemical processes. See James David Spellman, "Small Firms Are Big in Biotech," *Nation's Business,* May 1984, p. 78, and U.S., Office of Technology Assessment, *Commercial Biotechnology: An International Analysis Summary* (Washington, D.C.: Government Printing Office, January 1984), p. 10.

2. Joseph Alper, "What's New in Biotechnology," *New York Times,* November 18, 1984, p. F13.

3. Spellman, "Small Firms Are Big in Biotech," p. 76.

4. John M. Barry, "Biotech: Will the U.S. Lose Its Edge?" *Dun's Business Month,* August 1984, p. 58.

5. U.S., Office of Technology Assessment, *Commercial Biotechnology,* p. 25.

6. David Dickson, "Boom Time for British Technology?" *Science,* April 13, 1984, p. 136.

7. David Dickson, "Europe to Boost Biotechnology?" *Science,* June 1, 1984, p. 963.

8. U.S., Office of Technology Assessment, *Commercial Biotechnology,* p. 3.

9. Ibid., p. 18.

10. Ibid., p. 19.

11. Ibid.

12. Ibid., p. 20.

13. Ibid., p. 19.

14. Dickson, "Europe to Boost Biotechnology?" p. 963.

15. Elizabeth Wehr, "Congress to Consider Impact, Problems of Gene Engineering," *Congressional Quarterly,* December 15, 1984, p. 3095.

16. Ibid., p. 3094.

17. Ibid., p. 3096.

18. Ibid.

19. Barry, "Biotech: Will the U.S. Lose Its Edge?" p. 59.

20. Ibid.

21. U.S., Office of Technology Assessment, *Commercial Biotechnology,* p. 21.

22. Ibid.

23. Elizabeth Wehr, "Slow Move From Laboratory to Market," *Congressional Quarterly,* December 15, 1984, p. 3094.

24. Spellman, "Small Firms Are Big in Biotech," p. 76.

25. Ibid.

26. U.S., Office of Technology Assessment, *Commercial Biotechnology,* p. 22.
27. "Research Venture Gets U.S. Approval on Computer Work," *Wall Street Journal,* March 5, 1985, p. 46.
28. John W. Wilson, "America's High-Tech Crisis," *Business Week,* March 11, 1985, p. 58.
29. Ibid.
30. U.S., Office of Technology Assessment, *Commercial Biotechnology,* p. 23.
31. Robert C. Cowen, "Needed: A Major Study to Resolve Worries over Biotechnology," *Christian Science Monitor,* August 23, 1984, p. 21.
32. U.S., Office of Technology Assessment, *Commercial Biotechnology,* p. 24.
33. Recommendations in this section are all drawn from U.S., Office of Technology Assessment, *Commercial Biotechnology,* pp. 25–26.
34. Wilson, "America's High-Tech Crisis," p. 59.

Chapter 12

The Internationalization of Business
Trade and Direct Foreign Investment

A trend toward global economic interdependence since World War II has accelerated in the last decade. Today the economies of the world — developed and developing — are intertwined in important and lasting ways. "We used to be an isolated agricultural economy," says an official of a U.S. agricultural association, "but now what happens in Europe, Brazil, and Southeast Asia affects what happens on Rural Route 2 in Iowa."[1] This comment has become a way a life in many manufacturing, service, and agricultural industries in the United States, and the converse is equally true: events in other parts of the world depend on what happens in the United States. The importance of economic development to all countries and the advent of a global economy combine to make tade and foreign investment key issues of business-government relations.

The degree of interdependence creates unprecedented and unknown relations between sectors of the world. By the end of 1984, annual foreign investment in the United States had reached $833 billion, a doubling in five years.[2] The vast majority of these funds were invested in U.S. stocks, bonds, and government securities or were private deposits in U.S. banks. In 1984, foreign capital constituted 26 percent of U.S. corporate capital spending and was generally credited with providing sufficient funds to the American economy to keep interest rates low in the face of a nearly $200 billion U.S. government deficit.[3] As is well known, a great deal of the debt of developing nations is owed to private banks in the industrialized countries, and a considerable amount of the hundreds of billions of loaned dollars are deposits from profits on sales of petroleum by a relatively few countries to the West and Japan. The market for capital is truly worldwide for both the private and public sectors.

International trade is another source of economic interdependence. Rapid growth in world trade occurred from the mid-1950s through the

1970s and was expected to continue throughout the 1980s. Over the former period world trade grew at an average annual rate of 7.3 percent compared with growth in real world output of under 5 percent per year.[4] Such heightened trade is important as a source of increasing worldwide standards of living. Not only are countries led to specialize in products and services that are relatively cheaper for them to produce, but expanded markets allow unit costs to be reduced and thus goods to be produced and purchased more inexpensively. Benefits of international trade accrue to both partners in a transaction. For example, 33 percent of the growth in Canada's economy in 1984 has been estimated to have resulted directly from its boom in exports to the United States.[5] Clearly, this trade aided the Canadian economy. Likewise, it was not all bad for the United States either. Goods are imported into the United States primarily owing to lower prices; the growth of imports into the United States between 1981 and 1984 is estimated to have keep inflation at 4 percent versus a projected 7 percent without lower-priced imports.[6] Of course, the drawback for the importing country is loss of jobs to foreign producers.

Foreign direct investment is a third force leading to tighter integration of the economies of the world. Investment in foreign production follows from the need to locate facilities close to overseas markets and to establish overseas production centers that serve as export locations. It may be less costly for an American manufacturer, for example, to build a manufacturing operation in Brazil, both to serve the Brazilian market and to export to other South American countries, than it would be to export to all of South America from U.S. operations.

The low cost of transportation for many articles and a highly competitive cost of manufacture overseas have led American producers in various industries to manufacture items offshore for sales into the U.S. market. Thus the Brazilian subsidiary of a U.S. company may also be exporting product components or entire products into the United States. U.S. direct foreign investment amounted to $226 billion in 1983, a 2 percent increase from 1982.[7] Three fourths of this investment was in the so-called developing nations and a fourth — $51 billion — was in the developing countries. The income from this investment in 1983 amounted to nearly $21 billion.[8]

Because of the size of the American market, considerable foreign investment is made in the United States each year as well. Foreign direct investment in the United States at the end of 1983 — $135.3 billion — was approximately 60 percent of American investment overseas.[9] In 1983, 11.7 billion new dollars were invested by foreign sources in business assets in the American economy. While considerably smaller than the absolute amount of U.S. direct foreign investment, the growth rate has been significantly faster; from 1978 through 1982 foreign direct investment in the United States grew an average annual rate of 30 percent.[10] All but 15 percent of this investment originated in Canada, Europe, or Japan. Investments overseas and in the United States by foreign sources both represent huge capital flows. These figures again indicate the interdependence of the world's national economies and the arrival of the global economy.

These worldwide economic developments have several implications for public policy and private management. First, heightened international competition places a premium on each country's industrial competitiveness. Loss of domestic and international market share by American firms in the last several decades has led to considerable reflection about American management methods and about public policies that may impede innovation and productivity in U.S. industry.

Second, global interdependence means that a country's economic prosperity is closely tied to its balance of exports and imports. Consequently, trade policy has become a focal point of business-government relations. Significant policy changes occurred in the United States in the early 1980s attempting to boost exports, and in the light of dramatic increases in imports, pressures mounted for the government to limit imports in many industries. Likewise, the government has sought to open foreign markets to U.S. products through multilateral trade agreements and by direct negotiations with single countries, most notably Japan.

The first part of this chapter discusses international trade from the standpoint of U.S. export and import policies. We will review ways the government seeks to promote exports and ways that it restricts or controls them. We will also discuss pressures for import protection that have arisen in numerous industries in the light of severe international trade competition and review actions taken by the government in response. Finally, we examine the relation of U.S. multinational firms to host governments in the context of foreign direct investment. This relationship, pregnant with economic, social, and political dimensions, is an important testing ground for managerial capabilities in a complex, multivalued world.

GOVERNMENTAL TRADE POLICIES

Export Promotion

It is difficult to overstate the importance of export trade to the United States's economy. In the early 1980s one out of every eight manufacturing jobs and one out of every four agricultural jobs was tied to exported products, and these figures are bound to increase as the economies of the world become more intertwined.[11] A $19 billion increase in exports, for example, has been estimated to increase private investment in the United State by about $4 billion a year, owing to the need to expand capacity to meet additional product demand.[12] Moreover, this same increase in exports would lead to the direct employment of an additional 400,000 people and the indirect employment of about another 500,000 to 600,000 persons.[13] Federal tax receipts would increase more than $9.5 billion per year, and additional state and local tax income could amount to $2.7 billion a year.[14] Export promotion has every reason to be a major focus of public policy toward business.

The following sections review several major dimensions of U.S. export policy. While governmental policy undoubtedly has an influence on the level of the country's exports, other factors also determine flows of trade. A dramatic rise in the value of the dollar between 1980 and 1985 provided a great stimulus to exports from other countries into the United States and created a serious impediment to American export trade. The exact causes for the meteoric rise in the dollar are unknown. Certainly, record budget deficits and high interest rates were factors. The political stability of the United States is an oft-mentioned cause. Some economists believe pure economic speculation became a root cause.[15] Whatever the underlying causes of changes in currency exchange rates, the balance of trade for the United States is considered, in part, to be a function of governmental export policies, to which we now turn.

Multilateral Negotiation of Tariff Reductions

Since 1947, significant tariff reductions have occurred under the auspices of a multicountry organization called the General Agreement on Tariffs and Trade (GATT). GATT rules specify that a party granting a trade advantage to one country must grant the same advantage to all contracting parties. Agreements achieved by this organization have affected tariffs on thousands of products. For example, the ratio of duties collected to free imports was 7.4 percent in the late 1960s and had fallen to 3.5 percent in 1979.[16] The most recent round of negotiations, the Tokyo Round, in the mid-1970s involved 99 countries and was the most far-reaching trade negotiation ever held.[17] Tariff rates on manufactured goods in the major industrial countries were expected to fall from around 11 percent to 7 percent over a decade, a reduction of over 35 percent.[18]

GATT treaties have achieved considerable success in the worldwide reduction of import tariffs and have acted to restrict direct export subsidies by participating countries. Nontariff barriers have emerged in recent years, however, as major obstacles to international trade and have become the focal point for much debate and negotiation. The following policies for encouraging exports and impeding imports have drawn attention in recent years:

- Import quotas and voluntary restrictions on imports,
- Restricting governmental procurement to national companies,
- Using product standards as barriers to trade,
- Domestic subsidies to production in exporting industries, and
- Preferential credit and other nontax incentives for exports.[19]

The Tokyo Round of GATT negotiations began to attack nontariff barriers to trade. For example, that agreement calls for nondiscrimination among member nations in government procurement, an action that could open a $20 billion market to U.S. exporters.[20] In addition, agreements were reached on subsidies, antidumping, and product standards and certification systems. The implementation of these agreements may be more difficult than enforcement of direct import tariffs, however, and the type and range of nontariff obstacles to trade may be much greater. Insert 12.A describes how foreign aid and export assistance are occasionally tied together as export promotion policy by several European governments. This practice, referred to as *mixed credit financing,* is advocated by some in the United States as a necessary policy to combat aggressive foreign competitors.

Bilateral Trade Negotiations

In addition to multilateral agreements, of which GATT is the outstanding example, the U.S. government negotiates specific trade agreements on a country-by-country basis. One of the most conflicted trade relationships in the 1980s, and the primary focus of U.S. bilateral trade negotiations, is with Japan. Japan has often been accused by business leaders, government officials, and the media in the United States of unfairly protecting its home markets from foreign competition. In the light of a $125 billion trade deficit in the United States in 1984 and a $35 billion trade surplus for Japan in the same year, discussion on the openness of Japanese markets was a major point of contention with our closest Asian ally.

     At the end of 1984 a study prepared for the Senate Foreign Relations Committee by the State Department and the Office of the U.S. Trade Representative claimed that in the three previous years the Japanese had failed to fulfill promises to give more access to foreign firms. Reductions in both tariff and nontariff barriers were described as "too small" and "quite shallow."[21] For their part in this conflict the Japanese are seen as feeling that Western complaints reveal a sign of weakness and an attempt to change the rules of the game when the Japanese are winning.[22] Specific areas of contention and continuing negotiation involve sales of American cigarettes; citrus, beef, and other agricultural products; telecommunications equipment; computer software; medical diagnostic equipment; and financial services.

Export Financing Policies

The Export-Import Bank (Eximbank) is the major U.S. governmental agency designated to assist export financing. The Eximbank usually supplements private sources of export financing with loans or loan guarantees

---

Insert 12.A

ON THE FRONTIERS OF EXPORT FINANCING: COMBINING GOVERNMENT LOANS AND GRANTS TO FOREIGN BUYERS

For a number of years the U.S. government has provided credit to domestic companies to finance exports, as have other industrialized countries. Each developed country has also maintained a foreign aid program that gives development grants to low-income countries. A new tactic in the competition for international trade, however, is to tie together export financing to the domestic firm with a grant to the importing company for the purchase of the same project.

For example, Mitsui & Company of Japan won a contract to build a $300 million ammonia plant in Indonesia over an American competitor, the M. W. Kellogg Company of Chicago. Because the Japanese government offered the Indonesians financing to pay for the project in addition to export financing for Mitsui, the cost of the project was reduced below that of the American firm, which did not have such an elaborate financing package organized by its government.

The Organization for Economic Cooperation and Development (OECD) estimates that $2 billion in mixed credits was given by all countries prior to 1982. This figure had risen to $3.2 billion in 1983 alone and totaled over $5.2 billion for the first three quarters of 1984. Mixed credits, as this practice is called, appears to be one of the hottest items in the competition for international trade.

In addition to creating distortions in trade, mixed credit programs are accused of shifting development funds to Third World countries with higher incomes. Only 3 countries receiving mixed credits from 1980 to 1983 — Burma, India, and Kenya — had per capita incomes classified as low-income countries, the other 15 countries receiving this form of aid could not be so classified.

The United States appears to have two main policy options to address the influence of such governmental policies on international trade. First would be to create a mixed credit "war chest" advocated by some to counter the aggressive actions of foreign competitors. The second approach is to negotiate terms for such packages among the major competing nations. The United States, for example, has proposed making the grant element of the package a minimum of 50 percent of any deal, drastically increasing the cost to the government involved. U.S. proposals to an OCED conference in late 1984, however, failed to be discussed.

SOURCE: Bruce Stokes, "Latest Trade Enticement Combines Government-Financed Loans with Grants," *National Journal*, December 12, 1984, pp. 2433–35.

due to the length or size of the financing needed by an American company. It also works with private insurance companies to provide insurance for U.S. exporters against payment default by foreign buyers and against nationalization of assets by foreign governments. In 1980 the bank's credit and insurance programs participated in approximately 20 percent of U.S. manufacturing exports.[23]

Inside the United States the Eximbank has been criticized for favoring large, established companies with reliable access to private export financing at the expense of small- and mid-sized firms. One noted economist, Robert Wescott, describes the focus of the Eximbank in these terms:

> Since about 1977, it is fair to say that the Eximbank has increasingly aided large U.S. aircraft, telecommunications, and power-generating-equipment manufacturers. Of the total dollar value of the bank's fifteen largest loans in 1980, 44 percent was for aircraft, 31 percent for power-generating equipment, 13 percent for telecommunications equipment, and 9 percent for energy-development projects. Seven of the bank's thirteen biggest loans were to support aircraft sales — mainly for just two companies, Boeing and McDonnell-Douglas. Westinghouse, Western Electric, Hughes Communications, Combustion Engineering, and Lockheed have been other principal beneficiaries.[24]

Public policy toward the Eximbank is subject to contradictory forces. On the one hand, this agency has fallen prey to the interest of federal deficit reductions; the bank's direct lending portion of its total lending authorization was cut to $4 billion in 1984 from a high of nearly $6 billion in 1981,[25] and elimination of all direct loans was proposed by the Office of Management and Budget for fiscal year 1986.[26] On the other hand, other governments appear to be strengthening, not weakening, their own export financing programs. For instance an evaluation study for a subcommittee of Congress's Joint Economic Committee in the late 1970s determined that the U.S. Eximbank compared favorably with governmental support for exporters in Canada and Italy but compared unfavorably in interest rates and degree of credit support to comparable institutions in France, England, West Germany, and Japan.[27] On the domestic side, exports as a policy priority will need to be determined and its claim on the national budget clarified; in the international context the long-run interest of the United States lies in avoiding an uncontrolled international export financing war by taking the initiative for negotiated agreements with trade competitors.

In 1971 the U.S. government enacted a special tax incentive for exports by allowing companies to establish exporting organizations called Domestic International Sales Corporations (DISCs). A DISC was allowed several tax advantages. First, the Internal Revenue Service allowed companies to charge a higher price to its DISC for the product than would normally be allowed by intercompany pricing rules. This practice allowed a higher level of profit to be generated in the DISC as opposed to the parent corporation. Second, and most important, the government allowed a DISC to retain, free of current income tax liability, up to one half of its annual income, provided it was used in export development activities. The beneficial tax treatment of DISCs thus created a means for public subsidy for export activities. One report indicated that 73 percent of all U.S. exports passed through DISCs in 1978, and that exports were up to $3.6 billion higher owing to their presence.[28]

Not surprisingly, the DISC policy was strongly opposed by trading competitors, particularly European countries, as an unfair, illegal export subsidy and as a violation of the GATT treaties. Retaliation in the form of increased tariffs and decreased quotas on U.S. goods was threatened by European leaders.[29] During 1984, then, the United States responded to foreign pressures; Congress passed a law converting the DISC organization into a more acceptable organization form called a Foreign Sales Corporation (FSC) as of January 1, 1985. Under this law U.S. companies will have to show an actual presence in the nations where they do business, and at least one foreign member is required on the FSC board. Finally, FSCs are allowed to exclude only 17 percent of export income from taxes instead of the previous 50 percent figure. As DISCs went out of business, Congress did, however, permit transfer of an estimated $24 billion in tax-deferred income held in DISCs to parent corporations, forgiving approximately $13 billion in anticipated taxes.[30]

Export Trading Companies

One of the most startling differences between the private system of trade in Japan as opposed to that of the United States is the presence of trading companies in Japan. A trading company is an enterprise dedicated to importing and exporting a wide range of goods that, because of its specialization, can achieve greater volume in given products, offer a broader range of products and services, and provide greater private financing of trade activities. Traditionally dealing in commodity-type products where economies of scale are important factors, the Japanese companies have played a large role in that country's success in international trade. In 1980, trading companies were estimated to have transacted $278 billion in sales, about one fourth of Japan's gross national product.[31] The nine largest companies accounted for 54.5 percent of Japan's import and 48.2 percent of its exports.[32]

Until 1984 the United States had no comparable mechanism, owing primarily to antitrust prohibitions against firms in the same industry combining together for any business dealings. As early as 1918 a law entitled the Webb-Pomerene Act permitted limited antitrust exemptions for firms forming associations to export. Unfortunately, Webb-Pomerene never fulfilled its promise; in 1979, for example, 33 associations accounting for less than 2 percent of U.S. exports existed.[33] Major limitations have been perceived in this legislation; service industries were not covered by the law, and participating companies could never be assured beforehand that their activities would not be challenged for antitrust violations.

In 1982 Congress passed a broader law allowing the formation of export trading companies, including stronger antitrust exemptions. Preclearance from antitrust prosecution for exporting can be given to a company formed under the act. Thus competitors can join together for export purposes and cannot be sued for engaging in any activity previously approved by the secretary of commerce.[34] Moreover, banks, previously prohibited from investing in and making loans to the same company, are now permitted to invest up to 5 percent and loan up to 10 percent of their capital and surplus in an export trading company.[35]

The untapped potential for export of U.S. products and services is considered great; only 10 percent of American firms are estimated to participate in international trade, and at least 20,000 more companies than participate today are considered to have products competitive in price and quality for foreign markets.[36] Perhaps other, smaller countries may have a natural sensitivity to the benefits of international trade because of their dependency on foreign supplies and customers. The position of U.S. exports in an increasingly international economy appeared sufficiently weak and Congress was sufficiently worried about international competitiveness to break long-standing traditions in the fields of antitrust and banking regulation. Support for export trading companies stands as one example of necessary adaptation of public policy to changing economic conditions.

U.S. Export Controls

In some cases the United States overtly prohibits the overseas sale of certain goods by American companies. A case in point was President Reagan's imposition of export controls on oil and gas equipment sales to the Soviet Union in December 1981. Stating that the Soviet Union carried a "heavy and direct responsibility" for imposing martial law in Poland, the president declared that no American-made equipment or components would be used in the construction of the Siberian gas pipeline to Western Europe.[37] Six months later the U.S. government escalated the issue by attempting to prohibit U.S. subsidiaries and licensees from selling oil and gas equipment to the Soviet Union or even from fulfilling already signed agreements.

National security export controls have been in operation in the United States since 1940, when controls were intended to ensure adequate supplies during world War II.[38] In the Soviet pipeline incident President Reagan was acting under the Export Administration Act of 1979, which authorizes controls necessary to restrict the export of goods and technology which would make a significant contribution to the military potential of any country or combination of countries which would prove detrimental to the national security of the United States.[39]

The extensive U.S. embargo on American firms', subsidiaries', and licensees' sales of oil and gas equipment to the Soviet Union raised a furor and was immediately disavowed as an infringement of international law by European foreign ministers and was overtly violated by several firms with full support of their governments. Ultimately the U.S. attempt to control European firms was rescinded under an agreement between the United States and several European countries to study the problems of East-West trade more extensively and develop a common policy approach.

The Siberian pipeline controversy points to some of the ambiguities in the 1979 export control act. Can export sales be denied based on very general, rather than specific, national security interests? To what extent should foreign policy interests be permitted to influence trade opportunities? Are there adequate safeguards against presidential misuse of trade as a tool of diplomacy? How should benefits to intangible values such as national security be weighed against the concrete costs of lost trade in making export control decisions?

Export controls of product sales to the Soviets have generated controversy in other areas as well. President Jimmy Carter suspended sales of U.S. grain to the Soviet Union after the invasion of Afghanistan in 1979. Later, when trucks from the world's largest automotive manufacturing facility at the Soviet Kama River plant appeared in Afghanistan, the Carter administration placed controls on parts and components for U.S. truck engine assembly lines destined for the USSR.[40] Finally, consistent with his opposition to the Soviet presence in Afghanistan and the U.S. boycott of the 1980 Olympics, President Carter established controls on all exports except medicine and medical supplies intended for use or sale in the 1980 Moscow Summer Olympics.[41] It is an open question whether diplomatic benefits outweighed costs in the loss of trade in these circumstances.

Even when exports are intentionally limited, their justification may be ambiguous and their impact questionable. In addition to protesting martial law in Poland, for example, the embargo of oil and gas equipment might have been interpreted as an attempt (1) to prevent European dependence on Soviet natural gas, (2) to impede general Soviet economic development, (3) to protest the use of political prisoners as labor in the project, or (4) to deny the Soviets hard currency earnings from the gas sales.[42] Military, diplomatic, and economic consequences become intertwined as export controls enter the realm of public policy, and it is at least as hard to decipher their motives as their effects. Insert 12.B illustrates policy problems in attempting to regulate the sale of advanced technology to the Soviet Union.

Insert 12.B

TRADE EXPANSION VERSUS NATIONAL SECURITY RISKS IN HIGH-TECH EXPORTS

The U.S. competitive position for technologically advanced products is quite important to the American economy. Exports of computer and semi-conductor products alone amounted to $132 billion in 1983, 11 percent of all U.S.-manufactured exports and 30 percent of all goods sold by those industries. The value of U.S. high-tech goods licensed for export rose over threefold between 1979 and 1983. While the United States suffers in the competition for goods with known technologies, the country has a relative trade advantage in products containing leading-edge science and engineering knowledge.

However attractive a source of exports, however, state-of-the-art technology also carries potential national security risks. The U.S. government is aware of a large-scale, organized, and often successful effort on the part of the Soviet Union to obtain proprietary American technology, in large part defense technology, through the guise of export trade. The U.S. Customs service foiled an elaborate attempt to disguise the sale of a so-phisticated minicomputer to the USSR. Built in Massachusetts, the computer was sold to a New York exporter and shipped to South Africa. From there some components were shipped to West Germany and others to Sweden, where they were destined to be shipped separately to the USSR. It is not possible to estimate the value of technologies transferred to the Soviet Union through such circuitous routes, although the number of known thefts and theft attempts is substantial.

The United States has a licensing system for highly advanced systems, and the DOD maintains a list of militarily critical technologies for which exports are controlled. National security may advise tightening of license requirements for high-tech exports. Such actions, however, may make world markets easier for competitors to capture — such as the Japanese in supercomputers — who are not restrained by parallel government regulation. Too restrictive an attitude may also negatively affect international technical cooperation between the U.S. and Japan and Europe, which is not in the long-run interests of the United States. There is no obvious way to draw the line between free trade in scientific knowledge and technology-based products versus ensuring national security.

SOURCE: Monci Jo Williams, "How Not to Capture the Export Trade," *Fortune,* August 6, 1984, p. 69; Orr Kelly, "High-Tech Hemorrhage from U.S. to Soviet Union," *U.S. News & World Report,* May 7, 1984, pp. 47–48; David Pauly, "High Tech's Keystone Cops," *Newsweek,* February 6, 1984, p. 64.

A series of laws passed by the U.S. Congress for moral or social purposes often are argued to constrain foreign trade unintentionally. An example is the Eximbank, which is restricted from making loans for export to countries deemed to be violating human rights or failing to meet freedom-of-emigration criteria designated by the U.S. Congress.[43] Similarly, the bank can only be involved in transactions with South African firms certified by the secretary of state as complying with the practices designed to reduce apartheid — known as the Sullivan Principles.[44] Other laws emphasizing moral or ethical principles in international business, such as the Foreign Corrupt Practices Act or Antiboycott Regulations, are also argued to inhibit American exports. These laws are briefly mentioned in a later section describing the social and ethical impacts of direct foreign investment by U.S. multinational firms.

Finally, the reach of U.S. antitrust extends across national borders and may influence this country's international trade position. First, the courts have established that conspiracies — such as price fixing — involving American firms conducted outside of the United States are illegal if they have economic consequences inside the United States.[45] Moreover, the prohibition against mergers that may lessen competition "in any section of the country" has been interpreted to include import and export activities as well as whether such mergers may limit "potential competition" inside the United States. For example, foreign acquisitions may be challenged where an American company is seeking to buy a foreign entrant into the U.S. market.[46]

The main impact of antitrust regulations is on the competitive position of U.S. firms in the international marketplace. Other industrialized countries actually favor concentrated domestic industries, cartels, and monopolies and emphasize competition in external markets. By comparison U.S. antitrust policies against concentration and cooperative trade relations may limit the potential of U.S. industry to compete in the international context; uncertainty about the application of antitrust laws to international transactions may lead U.S. companies to seek and exploit export opportunities less actively.

Defenders of antitrust respond that the best way to position ourselves in the international arena is to have strong competition at home, which provides incentives to keep cost low, modernize plants, upgrade worker skills, and stay on the forefront of innovation. As one official of the antitrust department said, "A firm that has trouble competing in Columbus or Cleveland is going to have an even harder time in Munich or Milan."[47]

U.S. Policies Restricting Imports

The logic of free trade is compelling, and the United States has long endorsed this ideal as official policy. As seen in discussions of other issues, however, public policy is a matter of political economy, not necessary solely of economic ideals, and owing to strong forces, the United States is occasionally unable to live by a strict free trade ideology. Special interests can and do introduce protectionism into U.S. trade policies.

In several large and visible industries, such as autos and steel, the United States has a recent history of establishing agreements with major exporting countries that essentially allocate the U.S. market among domestic and foreign producers. Called *orderly marketing agreements* or *voluntary export restraints,* the U.S. government insists on these agreements in order to buffer national industries from international competition. Between 1981 and 1984 Japan agreed to limit its export of autos into the United States to 1.7 million units per year. In 1984/85 a series of bilateral negotiations were concluded to limit worldwide imports of steel to about 21 percent of the U.S. market for a period of time, a policy that was said to carry an $18 billion price tag over a five-year period for the American consumer.[48] While preserving American jobs that would otherwise be lost to foreign workers and aiding the profitability of U.S. firms in these industries, import restraint practices lead to higher prices throughout the American economy, costing jobs and weakening competitiveness in many related industries.

In spite of the progress the trading nations of the world have made in reducing direct tariffs and the efforts of the U.S. government to open foreign markets to American products, the United States appears susceptible to quotas, marketing agreements, and other import restraints. In summer 1984 *Newsweek* presented evidence that the worldwide trend is toward more restrictive trade and concluded:

> When Ronald Reagan, an ardent free trader, took office, 20.3 percent of manufactured goods sold here came under some kind of import restraint other than tariffs. That figure now threatens to jump above 40 percent. Europe, Canada, and Japan are equally restrictive.[49]

Another form of import restraint, domestic content legislation, has been proposed but never enacted in the United States. Organized labor and some parts of the auto industry have supported legislation requiring a certain percentage — usually above 80 percent — of American labor and parts in cars sold in the United States. In effect, producers would be required to manufacture in the United States in order to sell here.

Any import restrictions are imposed through an elaborate bureaucratic procedure in which affected industries file complaints with the International Trade Commission, (ITC), an independent fact-finding agency. Upon finding that a domestic industry is being injured by foreign competitors, the ITC suggests remedies to the president, who is free to accept or to ignore them. Occasionally, congress and the president will enact tariffs directly through legislation, or as in the case of the copper industry, congress may instruct the executive branch to negotiate voluntary import restraints for specific products.[50]

Beginning in 1962 the government granted financial assistance to unemployed workers and to firms affected by imports. The Trade Adjustment Assistance Program sought to reduce internal political opposition to free trade, ease transitions away from internationally uncompetitive industries, and compensate for injury due to imports. In its height in the late 1970s, this program annually assisted roughly 150,00 workers and well over 100 firms at a cost of about $350 million.[51] It was hoped, of course, that the advantages of allowing imports in the affected industries far exceeded the cost of this program. The subject of much controversy, this program finally failed to survive congressional budget cutting in 1984.[52]

We have seen that international trade involves economic policy, tax laws, antitrust enforcement, foreign policy objectives, internal employment problems, and national security questions. Public policies concerning international trade involve many more industries, diplomatic relations with foreign countries, and social issues than mentioned in this brief review. However, the values expressed in the issues addressed and the political economy of trade practices remain fairly constant across the many policy questions arising in this area.

In addition to the complexities of trade policy, the economic, social, and political dimensions of direct foreign investment compose another realm of business-government relations in the international area. Managers of multinational corporations are particularly affected by company-host country relations, the subject of the next section.

MULTINATIONAL CORPORATIONS IN A GLOBAL ECONOMY

International investment is a visible example of corporate action that is subject to multiple social, economic, and political forces. The last 25 years have seen the emergence of multinational corporations, with their great financial resources and influence on worldwide economic processes. The last quarter century has also witnessed the emergence of over 100 new nations, many of which are still "developing" economically. These nations are often imbued with strong nationalism and a distrust for the multinational corporations of the industrialized free world. In addition, the rise to power of socialist governments in Western Europe create adverse conditions for foreign investment in these more developed societies.

The multinational corporation, both cause and consequence of a more integrated and interdependent world economy, can become the focus of hopes, fears, and frustrations of developed and developing societies alike. Desired for its ability to bring capital, jobs, and technology, and disliked for its autonomy and potential indifference to national goals, the multinational corporation in a politically diverse and economically interdependent world often prompts controversy.

Benefits to world economic activity from foreign investment are enormous: capital and technology are transferred from relatively well-off nations to poorer nations, raw materials are converted to finished products, and standards of living are improved for both home and host countries as resources are concentrated in areas of their greatest economic advantage. The multinational corporation is often the agent through which such constructive developments occur.

However, foreign investment is often a mixed blessing; virtually every economic decision can have undesirable effects. Foreign investment can reduce work opportunities for unskilled laborers in the host country, it may create a drain on a host country's foreign exchange through repatriation of capital, or it may threaten the viability of national industries. In addition, recipient countries may fear the loss of important sectors of their economies to foreigners, or they may be ideologically opposed to the principle of private capital. Nor do objections to foreign investment arise only in host countries — persons in the home country may view overseas investments as the exportation of jobs or as support of totalitarian political regimes. In an international context of disparate political orientations, changing social structures and values, and great differences of national wealth, no economic action is neutral; investments often have mixed economic effects and substantial social and political implications.

Any discussion of multinational corporations must be general enough to address overall patterns and strategies of international business and their implications for both the company and the host country. Yet no rules apply to every case or every country. International business is an area of continual change; the relationships between multinationals and countries throughout the world vary on a country-to-country, company-to-company, project-to-project, day-to-day basis.

An Overview of Multinationals

What is a "multinational" corporation? How is it different from many businesses having sales and perhaps even some operations overseas? While the lines may not always be clear, a multinational corporation has major investments in several countries; its future depends on more than one economy. One scholar in this area states that the MNC (multinational corporation) is a business "where operations are in two or more countries on such as scale that growth and success depend on more than one nation, and where decisions are made on the basis of global alternatives.[53] In other words a firm with substantial export business or even worldwide distribution is not a multinational corporation, but a firm with foreign investment at a level sufficient to give it an international economic perpsective is a multinational corporation.

U.S.-based multinationals play a leading role in worldwide business activity. In 1979, 44 percent of the world's largest industrial corporations were U.S. firms, and as much as half of the world's total foreign investment was accounted for by U.S.-based companies.[54] While the dominant role of the United States among large multinational corporations has declined in the past 15 years, U.S. companies are still an important factor in world business. In 1979 the United States had more than 3.5 times the number of the largest multinational industrials than any other single country, and among the ten largest companies in the world, U.S. firms outdistanced firms from other countries by substantial margins in sales, assets, and number of employees.[55] The sales of the ten largest U.S.-based multinationals alone constituted nearly 20 percent of the U.S. GNP in 1979.[56]

HOST COUNTRY PERSPECTIVES ON ECONOMIC AND TECHNOLOGICAL ISSUES

The attractiveness of MNCs to host countries stems from their potential contribution to national economic goals; whether developed or developing, the host country stands to gain from foreign investment. Capital is made available, managerial and technical know-how is transferred, employment is increased, and balance of payments is often aided. One study of foreign investment in Spain supports this view:

> Companies with foreign equity are far more productive, buy and sell more goods, and employ more people than other companies. On average, foreign equity companies sold eight times more goods and created six times more jobs in 1977 than the typical Spanish concern without foreign capital.[57]

In short, foreign investment can aid in the development of widely shared goals: industrialization, a rising standard of living, and general economic development.

On the other hand, some observers look critically at foreign investment in developing nations. Theorists and social critics have argued that international trade keeps weaker states in dependent positions, that international trade leads to division of labor with developing nations performing menial tasks, or that integration into a world market in a dependent position poses an obstacle to development of weaker states.[58] Multinational corporations are often seen as a means of maintaining subordinate positions for Third World countries; they are sometimes called agents of economic imperialism or neocolonialism.[59] The nature and implications of this view, widely referred to as *dependency theory*, are further described in Insert 12.C.

Insert 12.C

DEPENDENCY THEORY IN THIRD WORLD THOUGHT

Originating in Latin America in the 1960s and spreading to other parts of the Third World, dependency theory states that major problems of developing nations result from their subordination to the economies of the major industrialized countries. This view is related to Leninist concepts of imperialism that depict foreign investment exploitations of the Third World's natural resource and agricultural base for the benefit of affluent societies. The institutionalization of underdevelopment for the developing world results.

Strict adherents to this view advocate total nationalization of foreign investment as a means of reducing dependency and eliminating exploitation. Others, reformists in this movement, opt for selective nationalization, stronger state action within the Third World, and reduced ties to the industrialized West. In any case this theory has given Third World leaders a common reference point and will undoubtedly be a major point of debate within North-South relations in coming years.

Summarizing the origin of this theory in Latin America, political science scholar Paul Sigmund writes:

> The broad appeal of the dependency analysis lay in its mixture of Marxist tools of analysis with nationalistic goals of self-determination and a greater share in the benefits of economic development. It gave a form and direction to the generalized resentment by Latin Americans of their underdevelopment, and in both its radical and reformist versions it identified foreign, especially United States, economic influence as the principal obstacle to Latin American development.

SOURCE: Paul E. Sigmund, *Multinationals in Latin America: The Politics of Nationalization* (Madison: University of Wisconsin Press, 1980), pp. 32–33.

From General Theory to Pragmatic Negotiations

While groups of theorists may disagree about the general advantages and disadvantages of direct foreign investment, international capital flows generated by multinational corporations are an ongoing reality. The ownership of the investment, the technology it uses, and its impact on imports and exports can lead to sharp, pragmatic differences between MNCs and host countries. One of these problems, for example, is the degree to which MNC profits are repatriated to the home country. Multinational corporations often repatriate more from developing countries than they invest there in new capital. While this appears to convey an exploitative relationship, additional considerations must be taken into account. First, the investment base that generates income is many times larger than the repatriated income each year. Second, new investment often replaces imports to the host country or generates new exports that can save substantial amounts of critically short foreign exchange. Third, substantial benefits accrue to the host country in the form of higher wages, lower consumer prices, and larger tax revenues.

Conflict in MNC–host country relationships stems from the fact that the MNC may consider the economic welfare of the corporation before considering the welfare of host countries — a perspective opposed to that of the leaders of a given host nation, which places highest priority on the economic benefits of MNC investment in the country. There are several areas in which a divergence of interests may arise:

- Local governments would prefer to see MNCs purchase supplies locally to the maximum possible extent. From the MNC perspective, however, a system of centralized supplying may be more efficient and reliable for attaining standard parts, and overall MNC profitability may be aided by purchase of supplies from the parent corporation or from one of the other affiliates abroad.
- A multinational corporation may rationalize its distribution of sales and optimize its profitability by restricting the exports of an affiliate from a given country or by limiting its exports to designated areas. From its perspective, restricting sales to the Andean countries from a Colombian affiliate and restricting sales to all other South American countries from an affiliate in Argentina may be most profitable for the MNC. From the perspective of either Colombia or Argentina, however, exporting to all of South America would be preferred. In the extreme case a MNC with many affiliates might restrict all exports to prevent interaffiliate competition.
- A MNC may see advantages in centralizing R & D activities — if not in the home country, at least in a single or a few locations. Host countries, on the other hand, prefer the employment and investment advantages of locally based R & D. In addition, higher intrafirm charges for technology from the parent can limit an affiliate's competitiveness and sales potential.[60]

While investment appears positive for the host country on a general level, the specific investment may diverge substantially from host country interests. The main point of tension is captured in one observer's statement: "It is the global basis of decision making that results in the tendency . . . to shift decision making . . . outside a country."[61]

The presence of conflicting interests may be exacerbated by a difference between a host country's standard of living and that of the MNC's home country. Investments from affluent nations in developing countries are especially susceptible to conflict, owing to the greater appearance of exploitation of the poorer by the wealthier. Tension in the relationship may also be greater where the MNC investment is in nonrenewable extractive industries, such as mining or oil production, than where the MNC establishes local manufacturing operations.

It should be pointed out, however, that most U.S. foreign investment is located in developed rather than developing countries: 80 percent of total assets of U.S. manufacturing affiliates and 67 percent of petroleum affiliates are located in developed countries.[62] These facts, though, do not mitigate the highly visible and complicated character of MNC–developing nation relations, nor do they reduce the desire for governments of developing nations to maximize their gain from foreign investments.

International focus was placed on MNC–developing country relations by the explosion of a Union Carbide pesticide plant in Bhopal, India, at the end of 1984. Insert 12.D presents some of the questions arising from this incident.

The Importance of Technological Gaps between Countries

Large differences between the relative technological capabilities of different countries create fears and special challenges about MNC activities that transfer technology across borders. In the 1960s strong reservations were expressed in Europe over America's technological lead and American companies' increasing dominance in European markets for aircraft, space equipment, and electronic products. In recent years there are fears in the United States that technological leadership and control of many domestic markets is being assumed by Japanese firms. The multinational firm is the agent for transferring benefits of advanced technology across borders, but a large imbalance in this capability touches the nerves of national pride and independence. Dominant foreign ownership of prestigious high-technology industries such as electronic chip manufacturing or consumer electronics may be hard to accept. For reasons of national employment, self-de-

---

Insert 12.D

MNC AND HOST COUNTRY RELATIONS: LESSONS FROM THE BHOPAL DISASTER

Escape of poisonous gas from a Union Carbide plant in Bhopal, India, that killed over 2,000 people on December 3, 1984, led to a series of questions about relations between host countries and foreign corporations.

Insert 12.D   continued

India is one country that imposes strong restrictions on foreign firms. Foreign exchange regulations in 1973 generally limited foreign equity participation to 40 percent of an investment. Based on a large export business from the Bhopal plant, however, and its high level of technical sophistication, Union Carbide had convinced the Indian government to allow the company 50.9 percent participation.

Given that it was a majority owner, the government still did not give Union Carbide complete freedom to manage the operation. In fact, the firm was required to use local labor, materials, and equipment. The plant was managed entirely by nationals at the time of the accident.

Reviews of the situation that came to light after the disaster indicated that worker training often failed to convey a basic understanding of the reason behind procedures. Maintenance persons routinely signed work permits they could not read, and critical pressures gauges for toxic chemicals were broken. The frequency of safety audits was determined by local management, and the plant had not been inspected for 2.5 years.

What lessons are possible for governments and corporations from this tragic event? First, is it wise for countries to insist on ownership or management control when the human resources for proper administration of the firm are in short supply? Also, will the local government be able to enforce safety standards through inspection and enforcement programs? At the time of the accident India had a federal environmental department staff of 150. The U.S. Environmental Protection Agency has a headquarters staff of 4,400.

Should corporations undertake investments where they do not have management and ownership control? IBM and Coca-Cola, for example, have decided not to do business in India for this reason. Also, what actions can and should a firm take to ensure proper management of a foreign facility? Is local adaptation always a matter of meeting national requirements, or can adaptation indicate the cost-cutting, profit-maximizing attitude that some critics assert? Union Carbide admitted there was no direct authority link with the Indian facility. Reporting relationships would seem to lie within the discretion of the parent, even given local restrictions, and would seem to be in the best interests of the corporation.

SOURCE: Cathy Trost, "Chemical-Plant Safety Is Still Just Developing in Developing Nations," *Wall Street Journal,* December 13, 1984, p. 1; Stuart Diamond, "Disaster in India Sharpens Debate on Doing Business in Third World: Corporations Forced to Reconsider Practices and Reassess Risks," *New York Times,* December 16, 1984, p. 1; Thomas M. Gladwin and Ingo Walter, "Bhopal and the Multinational," *Wall Street Journal,* January 16, 1985, p. 20.

fense, or simply national prestige, host governments carefully examine trends and proposals for MNC investment from a perspective of the control of technology.

Appropriate Technology for Developing Nations

Differences in technological capability are, of course, even greater between industrialized and developing nations, and they generate a series of expectations for MNCs. On the one hand, some developing countries may prefer high-technology foreign investment as a development strategy. Others may desire modern technology as a sign of prestige and may resent the utilization of second-best equipment in their countries by MNCs. On the other hand, host countries may perceive a mismatch of MNC preference for capital-intensive technology and their own preference for more labor-intensive technologies.

The recipient country closely scrutinizes the labor requirements of an investment in relation to the available supplies of manpower in the country. Investment in a developed nation with a surplus of skilled and managerial workers may be appealing to that country, whereas the same investment is less attractive to a developing nation with shortages in these groups, and a surplus of low-skilled labor. Since employment is always a social objective, labor-intensive technology may be preferred by some host countries to more capital-intensive operations. Review of this issue led one noted economist to state, "Unfortunately, much of the new science and technology being produced today is largely irrelevant to the needs of the developing countries. What is needed in many of the developing countries is relatively old technology — i.e., old from the point of view of the industrialized nations — which does not require relatively sophisticated skills or much capital."[64]

Host countries often question whether MNC products are appropriate to their social and institutional structures and whether products and processes from industrialized nations are likely to have negative consequences for the host country. Harvard professor Raymond Vernon identifies some of the problems that arise in marketing products across cultures:

> Automobiles and tractors are designed on the assumption that their worn-out parts will be replaced instead of repaired, a preference that reflects the relatively high costs of repairmen and low costs of capital in the advanced countries. New drugs are developed on the assumption that they will be administered under the supervision of doctors. Baby foods are formulated for a typical middle-class kitchen rather than for cooking facilities in an urban slum.[65]

To the extent inappropriate assumptions prevail in producing and marketing Western industrial products in developing nations, the role of the MNC risks being controversial and contentious.

Beyond the capital-labor intensity of the investment, the form of the investment can be an issue. Naturally, beginning a new business is usually preferred by the host government to the acquisition of an existing business. If the MNC proposes to enter a country by acquisition, host country government officials may be interested in knowing its commitment to expansion, or modernization, and to personal training and development. Whether the investment is by a new facility or a purchase arrangement, the local government is usually interested in determining whether the MNC will supplant or stimulate business developments in these specific and related industries. The level of technology transferred in the course of MNC operations is a complex problem in which MNC–host country relations are influenced by the specific technology, the development goals of the country, the form of the investment, labor availability, and the sociopolitical climate of the recipient country.

Host Country Adjustments

In recent years host countries have generally developed stronger, more extensive policies toward direct foreign investment. In a recent analysis of this development one pair of researchers classifies host country restrictions as either (1) limitations to strategic freedom, such as in the selection of technology, or (2) threats to managerial autonomy, such as the requirement for joint ownership.[66] This development is a natural outgrowth of the dual forces discussed earlier: desires to reap the positive general benefits of foreign direct investment and to overcome problems caused by specific differences in interest between the host country and the multinational corporation. In the case of Mexico, for example, government carefully manages foreign investment to maximize benefits to the host economy and minimize disadvantages or threats to national industries:

> The current [Mexican] administration welcomes foreign investment, especially when it creates new jobs, generates exports, brings in new technology, and locates outside highly congested urban areas. But some sectors are reserved exclusively for the Mexican government, such as hydrocarbons, basic petro-chemicals, power generation, and several others. In sectors where foreign investment is permitted, the investment law generally limits foreign ownership to a maximum 49%. But, under some circumstances, for example if a company exports all its output, 100% foreign ownership is allowed.[67]

A more active and assertive stance of recipient countries like Mexico toward foreign investment is an attempt to claim the benefits of foreign investment without suffering its drawbacks. This movement is also consistent with the acceptance in many countries of an activist role of government in stimulating, supporting, or protecting elements of the private sector. Of course, the ultimate weapon of host countries for influencing foreign investment is nationalization, an action that is likely to influence the investment climate for many years. Particularly the dramatic change of government in Iran and nationalization of foreign investment in 1980 have given new importance to developing methods of political risk assessment for foreign direct investment.[68]

There are several types of host government policies, short of nationalization, commonly found today:

- Screening and approval processes may be used to evaluate investment impact on national goals of employment, exports, growth of supplying industries, development of R & D activity, and other factors of national interest. Control of entry into a country allows the host government to negotiate its best set of specific investment conditions.
- Requirements for local equity participation may be placed on the foreign investment. Minority, or occasionally majority, involvement may be a condition necessary for government approval. Also, joint ventures may be encouraged, or the host government may require a certain degree of local participation in management.
- Certain sectors of an economy — banking, communications, public utilities — may be protected by a flat prohibition on foreign investment. Restrictions may also be placed on investment by acquisition. Of course, where high public sector ownership or a state monopoly exists, opportunities for foreign investments are reduced substantially.
- Host governments have become more involved in the evaluation and determination of transfer prices — prices charged by one subsidiary or unit of a firm for services or products delivered to another unit — with the MNC. In addition, taxation and allowed repatriation of profits are universal areas of host government policy. Some countries limit repatriation of profits to as low as 10 to 15 percent of the investment.[69]

The MNC–host country relationship is not confined to entry policies. Substantial pressure can be applied to existing foreign businesses to increase export earnings, augment local R & D, or reduce component purchases from the outside.

On the other side of the ledger, incentives to channel investment into certain areas are sometimes offered in addition to, or in place of, restrictions on direct foreign investment. For example, government-sponsored indigenous training programs or special infrastructure development, such as facility construction, may be provided. The following description outlines positive incentives recently developed by the Spanish government toward foreign investment:

> The major incentives for the big companies are the Madrid government's liberalization measures and the Spanish market itself. One liberalizing move was the removal of limits on repatriation of capital. Before 1977, only about 8% of a Spanish subsidiary's capital could be repatriated to the parent. But that limit no longer applies. . . . Taxes are also lower in Spain that in most other European countries. Income tax is 30% on all companies in Spain, foreign or national, and tax incentives are available to foreign companies that invest in a depressed region, such as Andalusia in the South, or in projects that create jobs. . . . This year, the Spanish government has taken steps to simplify the formalities for foreign investors and to facilitate financing in Spain.[70]

We have seen evidence that the world is moving toward a "global economy" — many businesses have become multinational by taking an international posture in operations as well as sales. Moreover, host country governments are also taking an increasingly active and forceful role in determining conditions of foreign investment. Given these premises, there is little doubt that the international dimension of business-government relations stands to grow in importance for corporate managers in coming years. Corporate managers will have to be sensitive to a wide variety of economic and technological issues that may influence the acceptability of an investment overseas and may determine its success once it is made. They will often have to combine this sensitivity with negotiating skills to reconcile divergent interests of the corporation and host governments. The skills required for participating in multicultural management teams constitute an important frontier of corporate and managerial development.

Thus far we have examined the implications of the corporation's *economic* roles overseas. While these economic roles compose a leading edge of management practice, they still lie within the bounds of normal business activities and practices. At the same time, there are also *social* and *political* dimensions, at home as well as overseas, to MNC actions that are, perhaps, less familiar and less tractable than the economic ramifications of direct foreign investment. The international context of business adds another level of complexity to investment decisions and to business-government relations. Issues in the public eye have affected MNC investment in South Africa, for example, or the promotion of infant formula in developing countries, or the role of International Telephone and Telegraph (IT&T) in Chilean domestic politics. These are difficult and elusive issues but ones that must be considered as potentially critical influences on MNC activities.

These types of issues and some corporate responses to them are the subject of the next section.

SOCIAL AND POLITICAL DIMENSIONS OF MNC ACTIVITIES

A New Managerial Challenge

The role of financially powerful multinational corporations in the internal political affairs of developing countries has been a subject of social criticism for some time. The classic illustration may be the role of the fruit companies in the Central American "banana republics." Here, the common belief is that American corporations have influenced internal political processes by giving financial support to political candidates or officials in return for favorable investment and trade policies. Thus the MNC might become an external, narrowly interested, and invisible factor in domestic politics of host countries. The absence of any effective control on MNC actions is the major reason why the "sovereignty" of multinational corporations has become a public issue in the last several decades.

One of the most famous cases of MNC intentions to interfere in a developing country's domestic politics is that of IT&T and its alleged attempts to prevent the ascension to power of socialist Salvador Allende in 1970 in Chile. Events of those years, unraveled through later Senate subcommittee hearings, showed the intention of IT&T officials to provoke economic and civil disorder that would alter the direction of electoral affairs.[71] Up to a million dollars was apparently offered for efforts of this type to be organized by the foreign intelligence arm of the U.S. government. Although no programs of this nature were actually mounted, the actions of IT&T were overt enough to prevent the company from successfully claiming losses from its insurance company for property later expropriated by Allende.[72] As the information of IT&T's interest in Chilean political involvement came to light, the company and MNCs in general became the focus of bitter criticism by Allende and other leftist spokespersons; the whole episode generated substantial politicalization about multinational corporation accountability. If there is a silver lining to the event, it might be the greater sensitivity of corporate executives and country officials to the explosive implications of MNC involvement in the internal political affairs of host countries.

Short of direct involvement of multinational corporations in domestic policies, participation in the economy of a nation may be interpreted as endorsement of that government's political orientation and social policies. For example, one might challenge investments in countries with rightist authoritarian governments because such governments often have poor records on human rights. On the other hand, it would be consistent to challenge, equally forcefully, investments in socialist or leftist totalitarian states.

It is convenient to believe that economic investment is neutral, that is, independent of politics. Investment may play only a negligible political role, but it hardly ever *appears* negligible and it probably is never completely neutral to political and social factors.

Worldwide consciousness of social and political issues confronts managers of multinational corporations with new and complex policy problems. Days of unhampered and uncriticized actions abroad are long past. Managers need to address the broader ramifications of investing in a given country, of continuing to invest, or of not investing. They need to accept public accountability for considering the impact of their investment on social and political freedoms within the host country in addition to its impact on employment levels and foreign exchange.

Infant Formula in Developing Nations: A Case in Point

The marketing of infant formula in developing countries shows the urgency of considering the social impact of MNCs. In addition to being a widely publicized and controversial issue, this topic has the advantage of being closely and systematically researched by an independent team of investigators.[73]

The primary issue is whether food and pharmaceutical companies act responsibly in the mass promotion of infant formula in Third World countries. For reasons of infant nutrition and immunity from diseases, it is well established that breast feeding is a superior method of infant feeding in societies or segments of societies in which sanitation is substandard and hygienic use of bottle feeding is, at best, difficult. The lower expense of breast feeding also makes it a more viable method of infant nutrition. Not all mothers, however, can breast-feed their infants; in some cases formula substitutes can save lives. Where the alternatives may be cornmeal or sugar and water, formula may be very appropriate. Nor do personal circumstances lead all mothers to want to breast-feed, giving nutritional substitutes an important role in any society.

In the early 1970s public attention began to focus on the promotional tactics used by MNCs for infant feeding in developing countries and the association between high childhood morbidity and mortality and the decline of breast feeding. The issue has been punctuated by boycotts, congressional hearings, shareholder resolutions, and international conferences. In May 1981, 119 nations approved a voluntary international code to restrict the promotion of infant formula. The United States was the only nation voting against this resolution, an action that led both the House and the Senate to pass resolutions overwhelmingly criticizing this stance.[74] The controversy has led to strong attacks and defenses of corporate action and, as much as any other single issue, demonstrates the complexities of MNC and host country relationships (see Insert 12.E).

The infant formula controversy represents an emergent dimension of the international environment of business. Citizen groups in developed

Insert 12.E

INFANT FORMULA MARKETING AND COLOMBIAN NATIONAL INTERESTS

Especially in economically advanced nations, better conditions of sanitation make the option of formula feeding important and viable. Higher levels of income and education also make these populations less vulnerable to inappropriate use of formula substitutes. These social factors tend to reduce the risk of product misuse in developed nations and may balance commercial advertising and mas promotion. Although infant formula *can* similarly be mass promoted to societies not sharing these characteristics, the question is whether it should be.

The problem arises if a company's interest in sales expansion overrides consideration of the best alternative in the interest of mother and infant. Company advertising and direct contact promotions serve a significant educational function to physicians and mothers about when formula feeding is appropriate and how to use the specific product properly. Yet adveritising to the public and to health professionals is primarily a sales mechanism. In addition, "milk nurses," individuals dressed to give an appearance of medical personnel who visit new mothers in hospitals and give free formula samples, may deceive many mothers. Advertising suggesting that good health depends on formula, as opposed to breast milk, may be considered unfair. Direct sales contact with professionals and sponsorship of professional trips and conferences for physicians may bias their recommendations to mothers.

An extensive field study of infant formula marketing and governmental response in Colombia, South America, identified childhood malnutrition as a serious problem; infants less than one year represented 2 to 4 percent of the country's population but accounted for 25 to 30 percent of all deaths. Two thirds of all lower-class children under age six had some degree of malnutrition, a condition known to be an important factor associated with childhood death from disease.

The Colombian government had identified malnutrition as an urgent national problem and had developed corresponding programs. The two MNCs selling formula in Colombia were not engaged in public advertising. Rather they both emphasized maintaining relationships with physicians and other health professionals.

The authors identified a series of steps that would seem to lie within the ability of the particular corporations in Colombia and that would substantially close the gap between company practices and national goals: modified labeling, reform of the nature and intensity of promotion, and efforts in product development. While the researchers appeared optimistic about such a convergence of corporate and public policies in Colombia, they also recognized the perhaps exceptional nature of that country and of the companies operating there. The following statement indicates substantial pessimism about universal integration of corporate practices and host country goals: "Incredibly, there are still some sellers of infant formula in the international industry who seem not to have learned anything from the controversy and continue to market — and view markets — in old ways."

SOURCE: Adapted from James E. Post and Edward Baer, "Analyzing Complex Policy Problems: The Social Performance of the International Infant Formula Industry," in *Research in Corporate Social Performance and Policy,* ed. Lee E. Preston (Greenwich, Conn.: JAI Press, 1980), p. 174.

and developing nations alike have placed corporate practice under close, critical review, giving rise to a stream of accusations and organized consumer action. Issues are emotionally charged, the line between use and abuse of the product is often hard to draw, and verifiable facts are exceptionally rare. This situation may be a prototype of the array of economic, social, and political forces that can converge upon an international business practice. It also illustrates the expansion of awareness and philosophy necessary to navigate the multinational corporation successfully in the waters of international affairs.

Impact on American Labor

A strident, politically oriented criticism of U.S.-based multinational corporations arose from American labor in the 1960s and 1970s. In the mid-1970s leaders of the U.S. labor movement were claiming the loss of nearly a million jobs over a five-year period, owing to MNC movement of operations overseas.[75] These decisions have cost not only jobs, say members of organized labor, but result in the exportation of technology and decline in the rate of U.S. economic growth. This, of course, is the converse of major reasons — employment and technology — why host nations are receptive to MNC investment; there is a worldwide competition for industrial investment, touching many charged issues of economic development, nationalism, and protectionist sentiment. In fact, in 1971 the Burke-Hartke Act, which would have restricted outflows of capital and technology from the United States, was proposed, intensely debated, and ultimately rejected by the U.S. Congress.[76] A related argument charges multinational corporations with reducing the U.S. portion of world manufacturing.[77]

The impact of MNC expansion overseas on employment in the United States is hard to study empirically. It is indisputable that displacement of some jobs has occurred and that new and different employment opportunities result from international movements of capital and people.

As Raymond Vernon sums up the available research in this area, it may be that short-term dislocations are balanced by longer-term issues:

> [A] common result emerges from these studies: Whatever the direct and immediate effects of the multinational structure may be upon employment totals in the United States, aggregates produced by such statistical exercises are small. The estimates range from a few hundred thousand jobs added to the U.S. economy to a few hundred thousand jobs lost; and the estimates at the extremes are on the whole less plausible than the estimates in the middle. On the present evidence, therefore, the question of aggregate employment effects in the United States is a secondary issue.
>
> More certain than the change in the total number of U.S. jobs is the change in the mix: the number of jobs available for the unskilled has been reduced, while the number available to the skilled has been increased. In social terms, that shift is hard to evaluate, for it may burden the present generation while offering new promise to the next.[78]

Social and Ethical Impacts

Some of the issues concerning MNC activities and impact are ethical questions. Corporations are variously charged with economic exploitation of host countries, unwarranted political and social interference at home and abroad, inequitable returns provided to home nations, and unfair exporting of jobs and technology. Perhaps because its global orientation coincides neatly with immediate interests of neither home nor host nations, the multinational corporation is subject to an unusual amount of criticism. While this criticism can, as we have seen, be phrased in economic, political, and social terms, it also involves ethics.

Regardless of the pros and cons of these general lines of criticism, there are several areas in which government policy toward U.S. international businesses has had its primary origin in ethical concerns. A prime example is the revelation of widespread business bribes and payoffs to overseas officials by U.S. multinationals that came to light in the mid-1970s during the Watergate investigations. The consequence of these disclosures was a law nearly unanimously passed in the U.S. Congress, the Foreign Corrupt Practices Act of 1977, to strictly prohibit bribes or payoffs to foreign officials. This law carries the threat of criminal prosecution and substantial financial penalties.

Since the enactment of this law, U.S. business has claimed that its economic consequences are substantial. Not only is the law unclear, it is argued, but literal compliance places American business at a severe disadvantage in competition for contracts overseas, where usual business practices often involve some degree of patronage to government officials. Currently under review, it is likely that the foreign payments provision of the Foreign Corrupt Practices Act will be clarified and relaxed. In late 1981 the Senate approved by voice vote a bill that exempted from penalties individuals who made good faith efforts to end illegal payments in their firms.[79] The bill also defines as noncorrupting gifts and payments to a foreign official if they are lawful in the official's country, constitute a courtesy, are a necessary expense, or are needed to fulfill an existing contract. However, this law would continue to prohibit any action expressly designed to direct or authorize a bribe, including nonverbal signs of approval such as shrugs or winks.

Another piece of legislation that might be said to have ethical origins (but with political overtones) is a U.S. law banning cooperation with the Arab boycott of Israel. After the Arab-Israeli war of 1973, Arab nations strengthened their long-standing boycott of U.S. firms doing business with Israel or conducting business with Jewish groups or Jewish-owned corporations in the United States. The law, the Export Administration Amendment of 1977, makes it illegal for firms to discriminate against individual corporations or groups in the United States; thus conformance with the boycott is illegal for U.S. corporations. Whether this law has much of an economic impact is unclear, but it stands as a statement of governmental moral principle in the realm of international business.

A CONCLUDING COMMENT

This chapter has reviewed important points where public policies influence the exporting of U.S. goods and services and the importing of the goods and services from foreign countries. Because of the singular importance of world trade to the prosperity of this and other countries, business-government relations in the context of international trade assume major significance. While the ultimate success of U.S. firms in the sphere of international trade depends only in part on public policy, the role of government is visible and often controversial.

As for many other topics, international trade implies economic change and dislocation within the United States. The economics of some industries and the skills of its firms' managers will lead to relative success in the arena of international competition. Inevitably, other industries will falter and decline in the face of global economics and managerial weakness. The constant challenge, risk, and change due to international pressures induce numerous questions about import and export controls, export financing, and industrial policy for international trade. Should the government act either to prevent or to ease the ensuring transitions in the domestic economy? Should it act in partnership with specific industries to establish international dominance in world trade? The answers to these questions appear to depend on one's economic interests as much as on ideology. Needless to say, business-government interactions on the stage of international trade will be a prime feature in the repertoire of public policy issues in the coming decades.

This chapter has also reviewed the prevalence of the multinational corporation in the world economy. Issues stem from the transnational scope of the multinational corporation and a realization that its actions may at times conflict with specific interests of either host or home country. Given the considerable economic impacts of international investment, managers are well advised to understand the implications of global decision making in a private corporation and to know where this process converges with and diverges from interests of national sovereignties.

The intertwining of social, economic, and political dimensions in the actions of multinational corporations is a foremost example of the complex nature of the present-day managerial environment. There is no clear and simple way to segment the economic implications of business activity from social and political, and at times ethical, consequences; because investment occurs within a particular social structure and under a given governmental system, it appears to favor some social groups or political ideologies over others.

These conclusions should carry lessons for present and future managers. First, host countries have a different view of the legitimate and desirable role of government in private sector decision making, and managers of U.S. multinationals will need to learn to operate within that perspective. Special skills and effort are required to work successfully within the framework of the host country *and* to achieve an integration of host country requirements and company objectives.

Second, realization that investments are social, political, and ethical, as well as economic, requires that a manager grapple directly with substantial complexity and assume responsibility for meeting objectives in multiple areas. The freedom and autonomy of the multinational corporation as an economic institution may depend on the extent to which its managers are able to integrate broader, longer-term social consequences into its decision-making processes.

DISCUSSION QUESTIONS

1. Review reasons why either import or export controls have been implemented in the United States. In your view, do these reasons override the case for free trade?
2. Recommend a U.S. policy toward financing domestic exports.
3. What factors might explain the rise in the numbers and extensiveness of multinational corporations in recent decades?
4. What do you see as the points of conflicting and of compatible interests between MNCs and host countries? What policies or actions would you recommend to MNCs?

NOTES

1. Robert A. Rosenblatt, "Imports Storm Citadels of U.S. Economy," *Cleveland Plain Dealer,* September 23, 1984, p. F9.

2. James Sterngold, "A Nation Hooked on Foreign Funds," *New York Times,* November 18, 1984, p. F1.

3. Ibid., p. F24.

4. Jack Carlson and Hugh Graham, "The Economic Importance of Exports to the United States," in *The Export Performance of the United States,* ed. Center for Strategic and International Studies (New York: Praeger, 1981), p. 41.

5. Sterngold, "A Nation," p. F4.

6. Rosenblatt, "Imports," p. F9.

7. Ned G. Howenstine, "U.S. Direct Investment Abroad in 1983," *Survey of Current Business* (U.S., Department of Commerce, Bureau of Economic Analysis) 64, no. 8 (August 1984): 18.

8. Ibid.

9. R. David Belli, "Foreign Direct Investment in the United States in 1983," *Survey of Current Business* (U.S., Department of Commerce, Bureau of Economic Analysis) 64, no. 10 (October 1984): 26.

10. Ibid., p. 27.

11. U.S., Department of Commerce (DOC), *Report of the President on Export Promotion Functions and Potential Export Disincentives* (Washington, D.C.: Government Printing Office, Transmitted to the Congress in September 1980), p. 1.

12. Carlson and Graham, "Economic Importance of Exports," p. 89.

13. Ibid.

14. Ibid., p. 92.

15. Lester C. Thurow, "The Great Dollar Bubble: Hurting American Exports," *Technology Review* (January 1985): 10.

16. Robert F. Wescott, "U.S. Approaches to Industrial Policy," in *Industrial Policies for Growth and Competitiveness,* ed. F. Gerard Adams and Lawrence R. Klein (Lexington, Mass.: D.C. Heath, 1983), p. 134.

17. U.S., DOC, *Export Promotion Functions,* p. 5-1.

18. Carlson and Graham, "Economic Importance of Exports," p. 110.

19. Ibid.

20. U.S., DOC, *Export Promotion Functions,* p. 5-1.

21. *Cleveland Plain Dealer* December 29, 1984, p. B9.

22. Ron W. Napier, "Troubling Trade Signals From Japan," *New York Times,* December 30, 1984, p. F3.

23. Wescott, "U.S. Approaches to Industrial Policy," p. 138.

24. Ibid., pp. 139–40.

25. Ibid., p. 139.

26. "Reagan's Wish List of Domestic Spending Cuts," *National Journal,* December 29, 1984, p. 2457.

27. Wescott, "U.S. Approaches to Industrial Policy," p. 140.

28. U.S., DOC, *Export Promotion Functions,* pp. 6–18.

29. Laura Saunders, "Trying It Their Way," *Forbes,* October 22, 1984, p. 176.

30. Ibid., p. 181.

31. Jack G. Kaikati, "The Export Trading Co. Act: A Viable International Marketing Tool," *California Management Review* 27 (Fall 1984): 61.

32. Ibid.

33. Ibid., p. 64.

34. Ibid., p. 63.

35. Ibid., p. 65.

36. Ibid., p. 59.

37. U.S., Congress, Office of Technology Assessment, *Technology and East-West Trade: An Update* (Washington, D.C.: Government Printing Office, 1983), p. 31.

38. U.S., DOC, *Export Promotion Functions,* p. 7-1.

39. Ibid.

40. U.S., Congress, Office of Technology Assessment, *Technology and East-West Trade,* p. 34.

41. Ibid.

42. Ibid., p. 88.

43. Wescott, "U.S. Approaches to Industrial Policy," p. 141.

44. Ibid.

45. C. Fred Bergsten, Thomas Horst, and Theodore H. Moran, *American Multinationals & American Interests* (Washington, D.C.: Brookings Institution, 1978), p. 257.

46. Ibid., p. 261.

47. Donald I. Baker, "Merchantilism and Monopoly — Alternatives to a Competitive America," in *Multinational Corporations and Governments: Business-Government Relations in an International Context,* ed. Patrick M. Boorman and Hans Schollhammer (New York: Praeger, 1975), p. 117.

48. Thomas F. O'Boyle, "U.S. Consumer Is Seen As Big Loser in New Restraints on Imported Steel," *Wall Street Journal,* January 7, 1985, p. 19.

49. Eric Gelman, Thomas Rich, and Doug Tsurouka, "Playing Politics with Quotas," *Newsweek,* July 23, 1984, p. 56.

50. "Wide-Ranging Trade Package Clears Congress," *Congressional Quarterly,* October 13, 1984, p. 2671.

51. J. David Richardson, "Trade Adjustment Assistance under the United States Trade Act of 1974: An Analytical Examination and Worker Survey," *Import Competition and Response,* ed. Jagdish N. Bhagwati (Chicago: University of Chicago Press, 1982), p. 328.

52. "Wide-Ranging Trade Package," p. 2671.

53. Thomas G. Parry, *The Multinational Enterprise: International Investment and Host-Country Impacts* (Greenwich, Conn.: JAI Press, 1980), p. 1.

54. John Hein, "The World's Multinationals: A Global Challenge," Information Bulletin no. 84 (New York: Conference Board, 1981), pp. 3–4.

55. Ibid., pp. 8–9.

56. Hein, "The World's Multinationals," p. 10.

57. "Spain Still Attracts Foreign Investors," *Wall Street Journal,* May 20, 1981, p. 27.

58. Robert T. Green and James M. Lutz, *The United States and World Trade: Changing Patterns and Dimensions* (New York: Praeger, 1978), pp. 17–24.

59. Ibid., p. 21.

60. Parry, *The Multinational Enterprise,* pp. 9–15.

61. Ibid., p. 9.

62. U.S., Bureau of Economic Analysis, News Release, "New Major Study of U.S. Multinational Companies Released," Department of Commerce, June 2, 1981, p. 2.

63. Jean Jacques Servan-Schreiber, *The American Challenge* (New York: Atheneum, 1979).

64. Edwin Mansfield, "Technology and Technological Change," in *Economic Analysis and the Multinational Enterprise,* ed. John H. Dunning (New York: Praeger, 1974), p. 158.

65. Raymond Vernon, *Storm over the Multinationals: The Real Issues* (Cambridge: Harvard University Press, 1977), p. 52.

66. Yves L. Doz and C.K. Prahalad, "How MNCs Cope with Host Government Intervention," *Harvard Business Review,* March-April 1980, p. 150.

67. "Sound of the Economy," Citibank Special Report on Mexico, printed document, July 1980, p. 13.

68. Thomas L. Brewer, "Political Risk Assessment for Foreign Direct Investment Decisions: Better Methods for Better Results," *Columbia Journal of World Business,* Spring, 1981, pp. 5–11.

69. Robert Black, Stephen Blank, and Elizabeth C. Hanson, *Multinationals in Contention: Responses at Governmental and International Levels* (New York: Conference Board, 1978), pp. 14–22.

70. "Spain Still Attracts Foreign Investors," p. 27.

71. U.S., Congress, Senate, *Hearings before the Subcommittee on Multinational Corporations of the Committee on Foreign Relations,* 93d Cong., on "The International Telephone and Telegraph Company and Chile, 1970–71," p. 1, March-April 1973.

72. Anthony Sampson, *The Sovereign State of ITT* (New York: Stein and Day, 1973), p. 273.

73. James E. Post and Edward Baer, "Analyzing Complex Policy Problems: The Social Performance of the International Infant Formula Industry," in *Research in Corporate Social Performance and Policy,* ed. Lee E. Preston (Greenwich, Conn.: JAI Press, 1980), 2: 157–96.

74. "Congress Criticizes Infant Formula Vote," *Congressional Quarterly Weekly Report* 39 (June 20, 1981): 1092.

75. Black, Blank, and Hanson, *Multinationals in Contention,* p. 65.

76. Ibid.

77. Richard J. Barnet and Ronald E. Müller, *Global Reach: The Power of the Multinational Corporations* (New York: Simon and Schuster, 1974), pp. 215–17.

78. Vernon, *Storm over the Multinationals*, p. 116.

79. "Senate Passes Legislation to Relax Key Provisions of Foreign Bribery Statute," *Congressional Quarterly Weekly Report* 39 (November 28, 1981): 2370.

The Role of the U.S. Government in Establishing International Trade Equity

In 1984 the United States trade deficit was $123 billion, the largest in history.[1] The trading deficit with Japan alone was $37 billion, and some persons estimated that it could reach $40 billion or more by the end of 1985.[2] Business and political leaders viewed the growing deficit with concern, and as President Ronald Reagan began his second term, pressure was mounting for him to do something. Ensuring the entry of U.S. exports into foreign markets and stemming the flood of Japanese imports into U.S. markets were of particular interest to American business.[3]

Since World War II the United States has pursued a policy of free international trade. As the world reached mid-decade in 1985, two events served to underscore the trade problems faced by the United States. The vulnerability of the U.S. economy to many foreign products was highlighted by Reagan's decision not to seek an extension of the Voluntary Restraint Agreement (VRA) with Japan governing the import of automobiles. Second, the increasing strength of the U.S. dollar was exacerbating an already weak U.S. export position.

In March 1984 the Reagan administration chose not to seek a renewal of the four-year-old VRA with Japan. The administration believed that it was necessary, at least officially, to end government sanctioning of import quotas for automobiles manufactured in Japan. The agreement had limited Japanese imports to 1.85 million units for the year ending March 31, 1985.[4] This decision was greeted with mixed reactions. For the U.S. consumer the decision was hailed as a milestone. Some analysts calculated that the VRA had cost the American consumer an additional $400 per auto.[5] Others, like Chrysler's chairman Lee Iacocca, called it a sad day for the American worker.[6]

The international trade debate also highlights U.S. fiscal and monetary policy. An overvalued dollar serves to make imports more attractive in the domestic market and to make U.S. exports unattractive to consumers abroad because the higher dollar adds costs to goods entering foreign markets. As the dollar increases in value, international competition becomes that much more difficult for U.S. firms, many of which are already competing in highly competitive markets. IBM, one of the nation's and the world's strongest businesses, reported in early 1985 that its profitability was being adversely affected by the increasing value of the dollar.[7]

While these events served to highlight problems in international trade, the role of the U.S. government had yet to be defined. Should the role of the government be restricted to negotiations? In that role the government has sought to negotiate "fair" agreements that not only protect or assist U.S. companies in their efforts to compete internationally but also maintain the overall theme of opening international markets. Or, should the role of the government be more aggressive and possibly punitive? A bill introduced into Congress in early 1985 requiring a 20 percent surcharge on all imports was an example of a more aggressive and retaliatory role.[8]

The purpose of this case is to examine the role of government in international trade. Current trade frictions between the United States and Japan will be used to illustrate the complexity and difficulty of achieving trade equity. The case provides a general overview of the issues from both U.S. and Japanese perspectives. Several possible U.S. policy options toward international trade are outlined in a final section.

INTERNATIONAL TRADE IN PERSPECTIVE

The last decade has witnessed considerable activity to reduce and even eliminate restrictions that inhibit the flow of goods among nations. Much of that activity has included Japanese markets, which had remained relatively isolated even into the mid-1970s.

When World War II ended in August 1945, the United States was the only major economy not ravaged by the war. The United States then developed major development programs such as the Marshall Plan in Europe to rebuild the economies of its allies and its enemies.[9]

The occupation of Japan lasted until 1952, during which time the U.S. government effected changes that created a British parliamentary-style government and an American-type judicial system.[10] Part of the reconstruction of Japan called for the isolation of its markets from foreign competition. It was believed that the Japanese economy needed an opportunity to redevelop without the pressure of foreign competition.[11]

As a result of its unique economic position, the United States ran trading surpluses with its trading partners throughout the 1950s and 1960s and naturally assumed a leadership role among the free economies. The development of the cold war conflict in 1947 only served to heighten the U.S. role as leader of the non-Communist industrial world.[12]

By the mid-1960s the world economy began to realign; redevelopment in Europe and Japan became apparent as these economies began to perform more effectively. The combination of new equipment and greater trade opportunities served to lessen disparities among the economies. In 1966 the United States registered its first trading deficit with Japan. By the end of the decade it would either register deficits with the major European economies or states of parity would be reached.

This historical context provides a focal point for U.S. international trade strategy. As the world economy strengthened, the United States intensified its pursuit of free trade — it generally sought to remove protectionist barriers that inhibited the free flow of goods.

In large part the U.S. effort has been multilateral — negotiating multicountry agreements to lessen barriers to trade. The most common vehicle has been the General Agreement on Tariffs and Trade (GATT), a multinational association with the responsibility of negotiating international trade reductions. The last concluded round — the Tokyo Round — was somewhat successful for the United States since it effected reductions in tariff barriers of almost 50 percent by the Japanese.[13] While these reductions would not completely go into effect until 1987, they represented meaningful reductions in tariffs.

The other means of negotiation is bilateral talks. The United States has engaged in negotiations with Japan and other nations separately to address perceived or actual trade barriers.

THE U.S. VIEW: HOW OPEN IS OPEN?

While the goals of U.S. trade policy have been to negotiate free trade, the negotiation process has at times been frustrating for the government and for the nation as a whole. Although specific instances of accommodation on the part of the Japanese and other trading partners can be cited, sentiments within the nation were typified by Special Trade Representative William Brock's remarks:

> People don't think we're getting a fair shake abroad.
> They're coming to the conclusion that it is going to take a
> two-by-four to get other countries' attention.[14]

Despite the success of GATT and bilateral trade talks, there is still a feeling that foreign markets are not as open to American goods as American markets are open to foreign goods. Particularly with the Japanese, there may be some justification for that concern. In March 1985 the Japanese announced an increase of 25 percent in the number of automobiles exported to the United States, increasing the number exported to 2.14 million units.[15] While government and business leaders were dismayed by this decision, the relative difficulty in penetrating Japanese markets angered them more. More leaders could readily cite instances where U.S. exporters of agricultural products, forestry products, telecommunications products, and services were denied access to the Japanese domestic market.[16]

Exporting Agricultural Products to Japan

Agricultural products constitute one example of where the United States could point to specific tariff and nontariff barriers inhibiting trade.[17] During the last decade, the United States and Japan have been involved in agricultural disputes involving citrus and beef products,[18] which seem to typify conflicts on agricultural problems between the two nations.

The barrier to U.S. exports is a complex system of price supports that Japan uses to sustain its agricultural markets and its agricultural work force. The fact that most nations have some form of agricultural protection system does not lessen the perceived inequity by Americans. In the case of agriculture Japan has created a complex quota system. According to one report:

> Through import quotas on a great many commodities, the Japanese government effectively determines the size of excess demand so that domestic market prices remain high. Imports are less, as a result of both higher domestic production and consumption foregone.[19]

The impact on prices has been severe. Beef and butter, which are part of the complex quota system, sell for approximately three to four times the current world price.[20]

Nontariff barriers such as health and quarantine restrictions are just as effective. Use of the "clean area principle" — which "allows authorities [to] quarantine an entire country if a pest is discovered anywhere within its frontiers"[21] — led the Japanese to ban exports of broccoli from California until 1979 because of beetles in Colorado, and California cabbage is still restricted for the same reason.[22] The medfly incident several years ago had a similar effect on the California citrus industry's ability to export to Japan.

Telecommunications

Telecommunications present similar problems for U.S. manufacturers. While there was a bilateral agreement reached in 1980 that essentially "opened" the telecommunications market, there have been feelings among U.S. businesses that it is an agreement in name only. The major thrust of the 1980 agreement was that Japan's giant public corporation, Nippon Telegraph and Telephone (NTT), would buy more of its equipment from U.S. manufacturers.[23] Some U.S. firms are now claiming that the market really is not open at all.

For instance, four years after the agreement companies like GTE Corporation have seen little improvement. GTE went to the trouble of setting up a Japanese subsidiary — GTE International — and attempted to construct a deal with NTT.[24] The deal is yet to be completed, and GTE now faces what many other American firms face in the Japanese telecommunications market: the uncertainty of deregulation. Deregulation, which went into effect on April 1, 1985, was supposed to generate a more competitive environment. Yet the rules developed for the industry "struck most companies as still another attempt by the Japanese to stack the deck against foreign competitors."[25]

Another instance with IBM Japan illustrates what appears to be resistance on the part of the Japanese to U.S. participation in the domestic telecommunications market. Since NTT does not have a research and new product development arm like its American counterpart AT&T, the Japanese government set out to create a research consortium — the NTT family — that could provide the advanced telecommunications that NTT would need to provide technologically advanced service. In the course of creating the consortium, IBM Japan was excluded without any explanation.[26] Events like this serve to fan trade tensions between the nations.

Americans tend to view their markets as open. In addition to loss of domestic market share in automobiles, Americans can readily identify losses in television, cameras, calculators, and textiles. If U.S. markets are open to foreigners, the argument goes, then so should foreign markets be open to U.S. firms.

THE JAPANESE VIEW: A MATTER OF PERFORMANCE, NOT PROTECTION

The Japanese view the growing trade imbalance in different terms. It is more a question of performance than preferential treatment from their perspective. In their view Japan has simply been more effective in competing in a world that the United States created.

Performance can be defined in terms of national economic policy and business strategies. The economic argument holds that Japan's economic policies allow it to compete better in the present world economy. The strategy argument holds that Japanese managers have the patience and persistence required by longer periods of entry into new markets. The result is a growing dominance in market share and trade identification.

The Economics of Japanese Trade

Over the past few years there has been a growing Japanese awareness of becoming a significant economic power. For example, of all the economies in the free world, Japan's was among the hardest hit by the oil shortage that disrupted the Western economies in the early 1970s. Yet, of all the major economies, Japan's has singularly adapted to, and recovered from, the changing energy environment.[27]

As a result of its growing economic strength Japan may take a more active role internationally. In fact, Japan's ambassador to the United States in 1984, Nobuo Matsunaga, stated that Japan was so strong that the United States and Western Europe "can't compete at all" under present tariffs.[28] The new ambassador was urging his government to take an active role in a new round of international trade talks designed to address the changing realities of the world economy.[29]

The growing economic strength of Japan relative to the United States is linked to radically different economic policies. A unique combination of government direction and commercial focus have led some to characterize the Japanese phenomena of the postwar period as "Japan, Inc."[30] However, such labels do little to describe how Japan's development affects the way it operates in the international economy.

Government has played a major role in the development of the Japanese economy by pursuing economic policies that promote export and saving. Japan's easy money and tight fiscal policy[31] have enabled it to maintain a depressed yen, which makes Japanese goods more attractive in foreign markets. The undervalued yen plays a major role in Japanese economic policy, particularly when there is an economic slowdown in the domestic market. When a domestic slowdown occurs, the Japanese are more likely to increase their ability to export.[32]

Contrasting the economic policy of Japan with that of the United States illustrates major differences. The United States has pursued tight money and easy fiscal policies,[33] resulting in a large deficit. The large deficit, in turn, creates pressures on capital markets, since the government is borrowing more and more money to finance the growing deficit. This very process has led to high interest rates and an increase in the value of the dollar. These in turn make U.S. goods less competitive in foreign markets.

There is also a strong defense to the argument that the Japanese protect their markets with tariff and nontariff barriers. While there is little doubt that government regulations, bureaucracy, and a more complex distribution system present considerable difficulties for foreign firms, most trade experts say Japan has fewer trade barriers than many other industrial countries.[34] For example, when the last round of GATT-negotiated tariff reductions goes into effect in 1987, the average Japanese tariff on industrial imports will be 2.8 percent, compared with 4.4 percent in the United States and 4.7 percent in the European Economic Community.[35] Japan has been shown to have no more quotas on imports than its major trading partners, and a recent study concluded that major nontariff barriers applied to 22.1 percent of Japan's manufactured imports. Comparable figures for the United States and France were 45.1 percent and 36.5 percent, respectively.[36]

Finally, the Japanese have pursued policies contributing to overall economic growth, whereas the United States has pursued policies to improve the quality of life. One author concludes that the impact on economic performance is significant:

> Improving the quality of life, however, is a costly undertaking. It involves more consumption, higher wages, and more imports to provide consumers with domestically unavailable goods and/or lower prices. In this sense, for example, while free trade had for years contributed to the United States high quality of life, it also brought with it a deterioration in the trade balance. In other words, an improvement of the quality of life can actually contribute to the intensification of trade frictions.[37]

Strategy: Patience and Persistence

Another perceived difference between the United States and Japan is the short-term orientation of many American managers. It would be fair to state that the Japanese do not understand the impatience of American firms that wish to do business in Japan.

Understanding the way in which the Japanese do business in the United States helps to clarify the Japanese position. A Japanese firm is often willing to assume considerable losses before it achieves success in a new market. A summary of that strategy might be: "Target. Invade. Seek dominance."[38] The difficulties of NEC, a Japanese computer company that has lost a lot of money in its attempt to penetrate the U.S. computer and telecommunications industry, is a good example.[39] The company persists, similar to Toyota Motor Corporation's persistence in the early 1960s[40] and Sharp's success in products from calculators to small computers in the 1970s and 1980s.[41]

American firms do not seem to demonstrate a comparable patience. To compete effectively in Japan, the American exporter must create an association or a long-lasting impression of market staying power. One author has noted, "The successful exporter to Japan is often the one who has entered into a joint venture or some reasonably permanent kind of tie-up with a Japanese company."[42] This is essential for success, since the exporter needs to gain the confidence of the consumer and the distributor.[43] Consumer surveys in Japan attribute customers' reluctance to buy foreign products to "cost, uncertainty about service, incomprehensible instructions, and inappropriate sizes of products or other details that do not fit Japanese conditions."[44]

The telecommunications instance mentioned earlier is an example of this point. Whereas GTE international went into Japan on its own and failed to secure a large segment of the market, other companies that have shown the willingness to set up joint ventures have met with some success.

McDonnell Douglas has a joint venture with Marubeni, a Japanese trading company, to offer computer time-sharing services.[45] Rolm International, a subsidiary of IBM, has met with great success after the 1980 telecommunications agreement. Since 1980 it has sold "more than 100 digital PBX systems in Japan, including a $2 million reservations system for Japan Airlines."[46]

From the Japanese standpoint, then, the problem is not nontariff or tariff barriers but the attitude of U.S. firms. It is difficult to claim that the telecommunications market, for instance, is not open when firms like Rolm and McDonnell Douglas are making some progress.

One other area of strategy involves the changing world economy and the fact that the United States has yet to readily adapt to and embrace it. Newly industrialized countries like South Korea, Brazil, and Indonesia are able to produce goods more cheaply than the United States or Japan. They have a good supply of inexpensive labor and advanced capital equipment. While the Japanese have been pursuing joint ventures in these countries, the United States has been hesitant. Only General Motors Corporation has pursued any type of joint venture. It recently concluded an agreement with Hyundai, one of South Korea's largest trading groups, to work together on a joint venture to manufacture small automobiles.[47]

From the Japanese standpoint, then, the United States has simply not met the challenge of a new economic order. Its economic policies stress consumption rather than growth. Consumption leads to increased imports, whereas growth leads to increased exports. Moreover, when the United States does have opportunities for market penetration, its lack of success is due to a lack of patience and a failure to study the market.

REACHING TRADE EQUITY

Since the Japanese and the United States have such differing views on the state of the world economy and on the state of their trade relations, continued negotiations in an atmosphere of trade friction is likely to ensue. The intensity and the direction of the relationship will be influenced by the role the United States chooses to adopt.

Multilateral Negotiator: Continuing with GATT

One option for the United States is to continue negotiating through the prevailing international system. In this role the United States would stress redressing of trade barriers through international agreements, primarily GATT.

The last concluded GATT round was in 1979. Since that time, the United States's view of the world economy has changed. According to William Brock, special U.S. trade representative until March 1985:

> There is damn little equity in the trading relationships that we have with other countries. . . . The United States, which has less than one-third of the industrial world's gross national product, is taking 58 percent of the products manufactured for export for all the developing countries. . . . Japan is slightly half the size of the U.S. economy and they are taking less than one-seventh as much as we are. . . . Trade is an economically valuable tool for growth, but it is absolutely unsustainable if it is not reciprocal, if it is not balanced.[48]

Brock argues that the United States is taking negotiating positions that will "get the attention of countries to the urgency of multilateral progress."[49]

Bilateral Negotiations

In addition to continued multilateral negotiations the United States could place greater emphasis on bilateral trade talks. Rather than seek to address trade barriers in the multilateral arena, the United States could direct its negotiating efforts toward specific nations — such as Japan — to eliminate bilateral differences.

This stance has been one of the approaches used by the United States toward Japan. For example, the Commerce Department was involved in revising regulations governing the "opened" Japanese telecommunications market.[50] Prime Minister Yasuhiro Nakasone and President Reagan had a series of meetings at mid-decade to discuss U.S.-Japanese trade relations in an effort to improve relations through a bilateral process.

Imposing Import Restrictions

The United States could also adopt more aggressive strategies to redress perceived inequities. One alternative is the imposition of trade restrictions such as VRAs that protect U.S. markets.

This strategy has been used by the United States with some frequency in recent years. One observer described the situation as follows:

> The pattern has been drearily repetitive. Japanese exports of a certain product category began to penetrate the United States market, rapidly resembling a "torrential downpour." The affected United States producers react by exerting pressure on Congress to enact protective measures. The United States government urges the Japanese to curb exports "voluntarily," with a hint of reprisal if the request is not met. After rounds of hurried negotiations a

political compromise is reached in the form of an "orderly marketing agreement" or "voluntary trade restraint." A temporary calm prevails until, a year or so later, the next "torrential downpour" strikes.[51]

Complicated VRAs or import quotas have been used on several occasions by the government to protect domestic markets. According to a 1983 report, nearly 40 percent of manufactured goods sold in the United States fell under some kind of import restriction, including textiles, steel, and motorcycles.[52]

Tariffs and Market Closure

Even with considerable import restrictions on foreign products, many American businessmen still claim that Japanese markets are not as open as U.S. markets. One study illustrated that the United States could reduce its trading deficit with Japan by $10 billion if certain market areas — telecommunications, computers, forestry products, and medical products — were opened to U.S. firms.[53]

A lack of progress on reducing trade frictions could lead to a more retaliatory stance by the United States. A bill before Congress in early 1985, for example, called for a 20 percent surcharge on all imports to the United States.[54] However, there appeared to be no support within the Reagan administration for such a measure because of its inflationary impact and the likelihood of a damaging trade war.[55]

Punitive unilateral action on the part of the United States may not be improbable. The so-called Nixon shock of August 1971 is an example where the United States did act unilaterally to stabilize the world trade system. In an attempt to curb projected deficits in world trade payments of almost $30 billion, Nixon imposed a 10 percent surcharge on imports, devalued the dollar, and created special tax legislation to promote exports.[56]

For example, in spring 1985 the Senate Finance Committee approved legislation that would require President Reagan to take steps within 90 days to offset the increase to the U.S. trade deficit expected from Japan's decision to increase the number of new autos its ships to the United States.[57] If such legislation were passed into law, the president could convince the Japanese to buy more U.S. goods, or he could restrict the number of goods the Japanese ship here.[58]

DISCUSSION QUESTIONS

1. Assess the relative impact of each of the following factors in the U.S. trade deficit:

   a. U.S. fiscal and monetary policies.

   b. Tariff and nontariff barriers in countries such as Japan.

   c. Attitudes of U.S. business toward entering foreign markets.

2. Depending on the analysis of factors in the previous question, what should be the general U.S. policy toward foreign trade? What specifically should be the position of the U.S. government toward trade with Japan?

3. What lessons for U.S. business might be drawn from the shift in the balance of U.S. trade in the last several decades?

NOTES

1. Art Pine, "Rapidly Rising Dollar, Big Trade Deficit Stir More Pleas for Help," *Wall Street Journal,* February 12, 1985, p. 1.

2. Kathy Robello, "Arguments Growing between Longtime Partners," *USA Today,* March 29, 1985, p. B5.

3. Thomas Brazaitis, "Dole Warns Japanese on Trade," *Cleveland Plain Dealer,* March 30, 1985, p. A4.

4. Urban C. Lehner, "Speculation on Easing of Auto-Import Curbs Has an Impact on Stocks, Especially Subaru's," *Wall Street Journal,* February 11, 1985, p. 37.

5. "Car Quotas: End of the Road," *Newsweek,* February 18, 1985, p. 65.

6. Thomas J. Brazaitis, "Reagan to Allow More Car Imports," *Cleveland Plain Dealer,* March 2, 1985, p. 1.

7. John Marcom and Dennis Kneale, "IBM Unveils First Models of Sierra Line," *Wall Street Journal,* February 13, 1985, p. 2.

8. Pine, "Rapidly Rising Dollar," p. 1.

9. Chikar Higashi, *Japanese Trade Policy Formulation* (New York: Praeger Special Studies, 1983), p. 13.

10. T. J. Pemperel, *Policy and Politics in Japan* (Philadelphia: Temple University Press, 1982), p. 15.

11. Higashi, *Japanese Trade Policy Formulation,* p. 13.

12. Ibid.

13. Mary Sasso and Stuart Kirby, *Japanese Industrial Competition to 1990* (Cambridge, Mass.: Abt Books, 1982), p. 70.

14. Pine, "Rapidly Rising Dollar," p. 1.

15. Kathry Robello, "Trade War: Auto Curbs May Backfire," *USA Today,* March 28, 1985, p. 1.

16. Brazaitis, "Dole Warns Japanese," p. A4.

17. Ibid.

18. United States–Japan Advisory Commission, *Conflict and Comity: The State of Agricultural Trade Relations between the United States and Japan* (Washington, D.C.: U.S.–Japanese Advisory Commission, 1984), p. 4.

19. Ibid., p. 28.

20. Ibid.

21. Ibid., p. 30.
22. Ibid.
23. Douglas R. Sease, "U.S. Firms Assert Japanese Aren't Giving Them Fair Access to Big Telecommunications Market," *Wall Street Journal,* March 20, 1984, p. 32.
24. Ibid.
25. Ibid.
26. United States–Japanese Advisory Commission, *U.S. and Japanese Industrial Policies,* (Washington, D.C.: U.S.–Japanese Advisory Commission, 1984), p. 21.
27. "U.S. Out of Race, Japanese Asserts," *Cleveland Plain Dealer,* February 22, 1985, p. B11.
28. Ibid.
29. Ibid.
30. Isiah Frank, ed., *The Japanese Economy in International Perspective* (Baltimore and London: Johns Hopkins University Press, 1975), p. 4.
31. Robert S. Ozaki, "United States–Japanese Economic Relations," *Current History,* November 1983, p. 392.
32. Frank, *The Japanese Economy,* p. 67.
33. Ozaki, "United States–Japanese Economic Relations," p. 392.
34. Nicholas D. Kristof, "Japan's Quotas, Tariffs Fewer Than Other Countries," *Cleveland Plain Dealer,* April 5, 1985, p. C9.
35. Ibid.
36. Ibid.
37. Higashi, *Japanese Trade Policy Formulation,* p. 26.
38. E. S. Browning, "A Top Japanese Firm Finds U.S. Market Difficult," *Wall Street Journal,* March 25, 1985, p. 1.
39. Ibid.
40. Ibid.
41. Merlin Stone, "Competing with Japan — The Rules of the Game," *Long Range Planning,* April 1984, p. 42.
42. Sasso and Kirby, *Japanese Industrial Competition,* p. 68.
43. Ibid.
44. Kristof, "Japan's Quotas, Tariffs," p. C10.
45. Sease, "U.S. Firms Assert," p. 32.
46. Ibid.
47. "Toyota, Nissan, Honda — Watch It," *Newsweek,* February 11, 1985, p. 57.
48. Bruce Stokes, "Bill Brock Sees 'Damn Little Equity' in America's Trading Relationships," *National Journal,* December 15, 1984, p. 2397.
49. Ibid.
50. Sease, "U.S. Firms Assert," p. 32.
51. Ozaki, "United States–Japanese Economic Relations," p. 358.
52. Eric Gelman, Thomas Rich, and Doug Tsurouka, "Playing Politics with Quotas," *Newsweek,* July 23, 1984, p. 56.
53. Robello, "Arguments Growing," p. B5.

54. Pine, "Rapidly Rising Dollar," p. 1.

55. Ibid.

56. Thomas Horst, *Income Taxation and Competitiveness* (Washington, D.C.: National Planning Association, 1978), p. 4.

57. Art Pine, "Senate Panel Approves Anti-Japan Bill Despite Administration's Trade Talk," *Wall Street Journal*, April 13, 1985, p. 14.

58. Ibid.

Atlas Copco's Gamble in Bolivia

The experience of Atlas Copco AB, the Swedish-based engineering transnational company in Bolivia, illustrates the problems and risks that can beset companies setting up manufacturing operations in a developing country.

When the Andean Pact, a regional grouping of South American countries that includes Bolivia, was created at a meeting in Cartagena, Colombia, in 1969, Atlas Copco had been doing business in the region for years.

The pact has since allocated different kinds of industrial production to different member countries. Bolivia, with its prominent mining industry, was awarded the production of rock drills, larger compressors, and pneumatic tools.

Atlas Copco faced a dilemma. The pact would establish a tariff barrier around the member countries, which originally comprised Bolivia, Ecuador, Colombia, Peru, and Chile. If the company failed to take advantage of the chance to manufacture within the region, it would find itself excluded from well-established markets and might see competitors taking its place. On the other hand, substantial investment in Bolivia involved considerable risks. The country has seen nearly 200 changes of government in the past 150 years.

Atlas Copco decided that production in Bolivia was something it could not forego, however, both as a contribution to the country's development and so that it could stay and do business.

Therefore, when Bolivia asked about 100 foreign firms if they were interested in setting up a plant to make mining equipment, the Swedish company was among the ten applicants.

Atlas Copco signed a contract with Bolivia in February 1974. A local subsidiary, Atlas Copco Andina SA, was founded in May the same year, and in the spring of 1975 operations started in rented temporary premises.

Practical problems soon became apparent. Construction of a new plant in the capital, La Paz, was much delayed because, the company says, local building know-how was not up to the standard required.

It was almost impossible to find workers with industrial experience in Bolivia to operate the plant. Also, the company had to recruit Bolivian expatriates abroad and train them for management positions.

The agreement with Bolivia specified rapid progress toward the plant's products having 75 percent local content. Progress toward that goal has been slow because of what the company calls "the unsatisfactory industrial infrastructure" in Bolivia.

The most serious uncertainties, however, concern the Andean Pact itself. Headquartered in Lima, Peru, it was intended to create an integrated market of 70 million people in the western part of South America to act as a counterweight to the economic power of Brazil and Argentina. In fact, Chile soon announced its intention of leaving the pact, believing that it could attract more foreign investment on its own.

Commercially, the pact's attraction for Atlas Copco was that it was provided a guaranteed, protected market. But regional groupings are only effective if all the members stand together. Chile's secession from the pact in 1976 moved the balance of power away from the west coast toward the more northerly member, Venezuela, which joined in 1973.

In 1977 Bolivia reexamined its own rather weak position within the pact. It remained a member. However, in July of last year [1980] general Luis Garcia Meza seized power. Atlas Copco worried that his tough, unpopular regime might compromise Bolivian membership of the pact.

Meanwhile, there have been delays in arriving at a common tariff. Some public sector bodies have gone outside the region to purchase from Atlas Copco's competitors, thus negating the company's chief reason for manufacturing in Bolivia.

Although the pact is still alive, and the region has great natural resources, including oil, there is a tendency for transnationals to look with greater favor on Chile and Brazil, where conditions for investment are considered less restrictive.

Atlas Copco counts its blessings. It is still doing business in the region and claims that it has made more progress under the Cartagena agreement than any other mechanical engineering company.

On the other hand, the company could produce the output of its Bolivian plant by running its plant at Antwerp, Belgium, for only three to five hours of overtime each week.

If it is in luck, Atlas Copco's Bolivian venture will eventually make a profit. But it may not succeed in doing so before Atlas Copco Andina has passed into Bolivian hands, as it will do eventually under the terms of the agreement with Bolivia.

DISCUSSION QUESTIONS

1. Given the high degree of economic and political uncertainty often surrounding direct foreign investment, why would a company like Atlas Copco want to participate overseas? How should a multinational corporation view opportunities such as those offered by the Andean Pact?

2. In retrospect, was the decision of Atlas Copco to compete for the opportunity to build a plant in Bolivia wise?

3. A variety of problems can serve as disincentives to foreign investment. What approach toward foreign investment would you recommend for a Third World country with ambitious development goals? How politically acceptable within the Third World would your proposal be?

Policy Making
Public and Private Sector Roles for Business

Previous chapters have spanned a wide range of topics and issues in the public policy environment of business. Our review of business-government relations has led us to consider such disparate subjects as, for example, antitrust policy and local economic development, environmental protection and international trade, and corporate governance and small business development. Nearly every action of business, representing a vast array of topics, in some way is touched by a public policy issue. The spectrum of public-private sector interactions is as extensive as business activities themselves.

In spite of this diversity two perspectives have been present in our discussions. First, we have been concerned consistently with the development of social policy concerning a particular issue. What are relevant criteria for intelligent public policy? What are alternative policy designs? What effects might be anticipated from alternative courses of government action? The process and substance of public policy development have constituted a continuing focus of analysis.

Second, discussion of each issue has invariably explored implications for private sector managers. As each topic on society's agenda involves some expectations for the firm, managers' understandings and their preparation and skills in dealing with issues are crucial elements in corporate policy development. While the issues may often gain more attention in the arena of public policy, corporate changes in response to them are no less important.

The two chapters in this section reflect these two perspectives on the field of business and public policy. Because corporate political action and private corporate management span all of the particular topics addressed earlier, chapters dealing with these dimensions are combined in this final section. Chapter 13 discusses the private sector's role in electoral and governmental politics, a role having consequences for public policy in all areas. The final chapter, Chapter 14, summarizes the author's views on the challenges and requirements of private sector leadership for managing the current public policy environment of business.

Business and Politics
The Changing Role of Corporations in Public Policy and Campaign Finance

In 1976 the First National Bank of Boston and other business interests conducted an advertising campaign opposing a state referendum in Massachusetts to authorize a graduated personal income tax. The attorney general of Massachusetts, Francis X. Bellotti, challenged the bank's actions in court, citing a state law prohibiting corporate expenditures on matters not materially affecting the assets of the corporation. The bank argued that this Massachusetts law was a violation of the corporation's First Amendment right to freedom of speech; the state argued that prohibiting the use of corporate resources to influence a referendum was necessary to protect shareholders whose views differed from the "corporation's" view.

In 1978 the U.S. Supreme Court decided that the corporation indeed had First Amendment rights and found the Massachusetts law unconstitutional.[1] The majority opinion stated that shareholders are competent to protect their own interests, that through "procedures of corporate democracy" they posses significant mechanisms to influence company policy and protect their own interests.[2] Corporations cannot be denied a right to free expression on matters of public interest.

The *Bellotti* decision is a notable event in business-government relations in several respects. First, it reaffirms the long-standing role of business in political affairs in the United States. A close historical examination of the corporation in American politics by scholar Edwin Epstein in 1969 illustrated the nature of corporate political involvement from colonial times through the postwar period. Epstein concluded that "both governmental [influence on governmental policy] and electoral [support for candidates and election issues] activities of corporations have been part of American political history from the very beginnings of this country."[3] In this context *Bellotti* reinforces an important historical strand of business-government relations.

In a second respect the *Bellotti* decision demonstrates a heightened public policy role for the corporation today. While business participation in politics is not new, corporate involvement has accelerated and expanded since 1970. The pervasive impact of governmental actions on management decisions during the past several decades has alerted corporate leaders to the importance of participation in public affairs as business people as much as private citizens. "CEOs of the future must have an expanded capacity to cope with the expanding social forces that play on their enterprises," states David Rockefeller, chairman of Chase Manhattan Bank. This will require "plunging into the rough and tumble waters of the hearing room and the press room."[4]

This new attitude is manifested by corporate programs in business-government relations and by expanding efforts at influence, not only through traditional governmental lobbying but also through the use of new techniques for influencing public opinion and taking political action. In addition to the support for corporate activism given by *Bellotti*, new laws governing the financing of political campaigns — laws permitting corporations and other interests to form political action committees (PACs) and to solicit and disperse campaign contributions — have been passed within the past decade. These reforms represent a landmark for business participation in electoral politics; they offer the opportunity for unprecedented corporate roles in public affairs.

While few would argue that corporate political involvement is "an inherent characteristic of a pluralistic democracy,"[5] the expanded forms of business participation stimulate questions about the appropriate balance between business interests and the interests of other social groups — labor, consumers, communities, or environmentalists — in the process of public policy formulation. The impact of corporate involvement, especially in campaign finance, has become a focal point for analysis in business-government relations in which the basic question is how democracy may be aided and how it may be hindered by heightened corporate involvement.

This chapter explores the forms and consequences of business participation in political affairs. We begin with corporate activities designed to influence governmental policy and public opinion such as trend monitoring and analysis, lobbying, and advocacy advertising. This area of governmental politics leads to discussion of the social power of corporations and to the question of whether business has been an overly dominant actor in public policy development.

A second focus of the chapter examines corporate participation in campaign finance, or what Epstein calls "electoral politics." Recent experience with PACs in national elections is reviewed, and questions about the impact of corporate involvement are discussed.

BUSINESS INVOLVEMENT IN GOVERNMENTAL DECISION MAKING: ORGANIZING FOR INFLUENCE ON PUBLIC AFFAIRS

Business organizations are arriving at a new level of involvement in their management of government affairs activities; such activities are more explicit, widespread, and organized than they were just a decade ago. There are several identifiable elements of this movement: the monitoring and analysis of political trends, direct lobbying, indirect lobbying through grass roots issue campaigns, advocacy or public interest advertising, chief executive officer (CEO) involvement, and the creation of corporate public affairs offices.

Monitoring and Analysis of Political Trends

Government affairs activities within an individual organization can be quite diverse and complex. Major corporations often maintain a government relations unit at their corporate headquarters to monitor and report major trends in legislation and regulation. It is not uncommon for large corporations to employ specialists in public policy analysis who prepare position statements for the corporation on public issues. Corporate executives use such reports to become informed about the public policy environment of the firm and as an aid in preparing speeches and in meeting with government officials and external groups.

Corporate public policy or public affairs offices are most common in firms with $1 billion or more in sales; only about 50 percent of smaller corporations have an in-house office. Firms more frequently tending to have governmental affairs offices are firms in highly regulated industries, such as utilities and communications, and those subjected to public scrutiny, such as businesses dealing with foods (labeling and additives), chemicals (toxicity and disposal), and petroleum (distribution and pricing).[6]

Direct Lobbying

Many corporations maintain an office in Washington and perhaps in one or more state capitals to maintain personal contact with policymakers and agency administrators. A large part of the work of the individuals in these offices is to facilitate the flow of information — from Washington to company managers and from the company to government officials — about the problems and needs of the company and the industry. Of course, Washington representatives also express the company's views on proposed pieces of legislation and attempt to influence the government process in ways favorable to the corporation.

Washington offices may be staffed with corporate personnel, or they may utilize the services of trade associations and/or professional lobbyists. A recent study indicated that most firms with corporate government affairs offices also use external resources to help maintain activity on several fronts — monitoring and analysis, direct and indirect lobbying, public interest advertising — simultaneously.[7]

Indirect Lobbying

Indirect or grass roots lobbying utilizes the efforts of employees and retirees of the firm, shareholders, customers, and even sympathetic citizens to contact legislators at the local level, to speak at public meetings, and to generate large volumes of mail to appropriate government offices when issues of vital concern emerge. It is not uncommon for several hundred people to be identified by a corporation as its indirect lobbying, or grass roots, organization.

To initiate a grass roots program, the organization first must identify a network of individuals who share the interests of the company. Contact people within the network are selected at key locations either because of their position within the organization or because of their political awareness and interest. Orientation and training may be provided by means of company manuals, formal workshops that include public speaking and letter writing skills, or meetings with company spokespeople and legislators.

Once the network is in place, information on vital issues is provided periodically through newsletters, reports to stockholders, and meetings of employees and community groups. It is increasingly common for corporations to hold regional stockholders' meetings to provide opportunities for speakers to inform those gathered on issues of current importance.

Calls to action are requested from the network when needed. At such times the services of the network members are crucial to the success of the response. These calls may come at any stage during the legislative process or when the regulations for the implementation of legislation are being written. Knowing that it is easier to initiate than to change bills and regulations, most sophisticated firms become involved as early as possible.

A report issued by the Conference Board in 1979 stated that 54 percent of 390 large corporations included formal grass roots programs in their government relations programs.[8] Of these, 61 percent started between 1975 and 1978, and 26 percent began between 1970 and 1974. Only 12 percent had begun prior to 1970. The report concludes that "there appears to be no question about it; grass roots is the approach that business is currently emphasizing . . . and finding effective."[9]

Advocacy or Public Interest Advertising

Advocacy or public interest advertising is a highly visible and increasingly popular form of political activity. This approach, in which the corporate position on issues of public interest is stated in its advertisements, seeks to add "to the supply of fact, opinion, and interpretations from which the public shapes its own conclusions," according to one prominent agency executive.[10]

The Mobil Oil Corporation has been a leader in this field, presenting a direct counterattack against those who blamed oil companies for the energy crisis. This campaign in newspapers and magazines and on television stressed the presence of a worldwide shortage of crude oil and the need for increased exploration.

In January 1974, six U.S. senators and representatives petitioned the Federal Trade Commission (FTC) to undertake a significant enforcement effort aimed at the regulation of environmental and energy-related claims in "corporate image" advertising.[11] Mobil expressed its opposition in April of that year in a memorandum to the FTC stating that "the Constitution and a legion of decisions by the courts have made it clear that such an intrusion cannot be permitted because of its chilling effect on the free expression of ideas."[12] An excerpt from the memorandum appears in Insert 13.A.

The FTC eventually agreed with Mobil's right to free expression and responded unfavorably to the petition. In its opinion the commission reaffirmed the significance of corporate free speech:

> The Commission shares the Supreme Court's view that the First Amendment embodies the "profound" national commitment to the principle that debate on public issues should be uninhibited, robust, and wide-open. The Commission believes that the free speech guarantee requires that government regulation allow breathing room to the expression of views on public issues.[13]

Involvement by the CEO

The above developments have naturally led to greater direct involvement by the nation's CEOs. As one CEO said, "The CEO, by virtue of the office he occupies, starts off with a stockpile of political ammunition."[14] Citing a survey of chief executives, this individual reported that nine of ten executives speak publicly on issues related to their company's specific interests

---

Insert 13.A

MOBIL'S JUSTIFICATION OF ADVOCACY ADVERTISING [QUOTATION]

> Mobil feels that the need for a complete and open discussion regarding the environment and energy is particularly acute at this time and that the petition is thereby of an extremely injurious nature to the public interest. Unlike the major issues that have been before the public in recent times, i.e., Vietnam, Civil Rights, disarmament, this is the

Insert 13.A   continued

first instance in more recent history in which an issue of universal public importance and concern focuses on one private sector of the economy, namely the oil industry. The energy crisis, which has had such profound effects, has led to a public debate on the legitimacy of the operations of particular companies such as Mobil. . . .

As a corporation, Mobil is deeply concerned that the avalanche of news on the energy crisis, emanating from the television networks, is simplistic and therefore inaccurate. Moreover, Mobil believes that such news is peculiarly misleading because emphasis is placed on charges made by critics who do not have an in-depth understanding of an extremely complex industry. The news media have thus given undue circulation to what Mobil regards as the uninformed and inaccurate view that the oil companies should be blamed for the energy shortage and the ensuring discomfort of the public. At the same time, because of the complexity of the situation and the limitation of time on television and space in newspapers, Mobil believes that many viewpoints relating to this crisis are currently denied entry into the marketplace of ideas. Unless the public can obtain a better comprehension of this highly complex problem, Mobil believes there will be adverse effects on the future of the nation. An inadequately informed public opinion could lead to the adoption of counterproductive measures which would only serve to lengthen the energy crisis. . . .

Mobil's advertising . . . is but one effort on the part of our company to express another viewpoint which should be considered if the nation is to avoid these adverse consequences. Mobil asks the Commission to continue to support measures, such as counter-advertising, which would permit the fuller dissemination of ideas to the public. In any event, the petition should be dismissed as inappropriate and contrary to the fundamental policy of promoting unfettered debate on an issue of crucial public and political significance.

SOURCE: U.S., Congress, Senate, Subcommittee on Administrative Practice and Procedure of the Committee on the Judiciary of the U.S. Senate, *Sourcebook on Corporate Image and Corporate Advocacy Advertising* (Washington, D.C.: Government Printing Office, 1978), pp. 1367–69.

and that 80 percent have taken stands on broader public issues. He said that these figures reflect a dramatic change from the past when a typical businessman asked if our greatest national political problem was ignorance or apathy answered, "I don't know and I don't care."[15]

Changes in the structure and complexity of society and in the multifaceted role of government policy on corporate action have awakened corporate officials to a new level of business political involvement. Closer and more immediate relationships among business, society, and government seem to force acceptance of an expanded role of corporate leadership; many executives believe that business leaders must be valid participants in the formation of public policy — or become victims of it.

On the other hand, the current political emphasis on deregulation and reducing the role of government may raise questions about the need for business leader involvement in public affairs. The corporate counsel of a major corporation recently asked, "Aren't we now in a deregulatory period? Do we still need to be concerned about how to get across our ideas and views to our government representatives?"[16] The present political mood suggests a lack of new initiatives for government in social areas and the loosening of government controls on government actions in areas already legislated. However, neither of these developments indicates a dramatic reversal concerning the role and visibility of the corporation in society. On the question of whether to continue efforts to get business views across to government, the same corporate counsel responds, "'Yes,' is the simple answer. . . . It would be a mistake to conclude otherwise." Along similar lines, one close observer of business-government relations draws these conclusions:

> Public support for the basic social objectives of laws such as equal employment opportunity, occupational health and safety, pension protection, and protection of the environment remain quite strong. These laws will not be repealed or turned 180 degrees away from their purposes. What will be changed will be their administration — less extensive government regulatory rules; more options for managements to demonstrate essential compliance through their choice of means; more cost-benefit analysis and risk assessment formulas used in determining what requirements are reasonable to impose by law; and a lessening of federal inspection activities and pattern-violation test cases through the means of budget cuts and staff reductions.[17]

PUBLIC AFFAIRS AND ISSUE MANAGEMENT AS CORPORATE FUNCTIONS

The above discussion illustrates a growing number of interactions between electoral and governmental politics and the private economic sector, and it indicates the increasing involvement of managers with multiple aspects of governmental decisions. Where complex, controversial, and potentially threatening issues can unexpectedly arise in the corporate environment, one might expect to see the evolution of corporate structures designed to allow a deliberate and managed response. Consistent with these trends, 90 percent of the companies in a 1983 study of 400 large and medium-sized firms had public affairs offices. The recent importance of public policy issues was demonstrated by the fact that more than one half of the units were created since 1970.[18]

What do public affairs offices do? In the national survey mentioned above, the most frequent areas of activity were community and governmental relations; 85 percent of the companies assigned these activities to the public affairs unit. Other frequently mentioned responsibilities include corporate contributions, media relations, and stockholder relations; beyond these fairly common areas, activities of public affairs units diverge considerably.[19]

To a certain extent the public affairs function often routinizes and regularizes the firm's interactions with external constituencies. Many activities come to represent maintenance functions: membership on community-based committees, centralization of philanthropic decisions, preparation of news releases, and so forth. These are staff functions of any large organization; they serve to channel and to conduct the normal, everyday transactions of the corporation with specialized groups.

Another potential function of a public affairs office has come to be referred to as *issues management.* In concept at least, this is a more active, anticipatory role in relating the firm to its social, legal, and political environment. Authors of the above study refer to three functions of a public affairs office.[20] The first consists of gathering social and political intelligence where issues of importance to the firm are identified, analyzed, and prioritized and social and political positions of the corporations are formulated. A second function is the development of external action programs based on these positions. Lobbying, public issue advertising, and political organization and action are potential outcomes in this area. Finally, internal communications — helping managers and employees to understand the context and substance of external issues — is thought to be a third public affairs function. In general the belief is that this office serves to establish better two-way communication — from the corporation outward and from the outside environment into the firm.

At its most general level of description, issues management runs parallel to, and contributes to, strategic planning.[21] First, adaptation to discontinuities in the environment — the public policy *or* the competitive environment — should be an overall corporate capability. Second, processes of issue management and strategy development both must integrate the diverse views of decentralized operating units. And third, each should be an aid to decision making for executive and line managers. Table 13.1 lists corporate managers' responses when surveyed on the link between public

TABLE 13.1   *Public Affairs Contribution to Corporate Planning*

Activity	Percentage of Respondents	
	Yes	No
Identify public issues for corporate attention	80.9	19.1
Set or help establish priorities for public issues at corporate level	68.1	31.9
Provide forecasts of social/political trends to corporate planning office	64.5	35.5
Identify public issues for department, division, or subsidiary attention	64.5	35.5
Provide forecasts of social/political trends to departments, divisions, or subsidiaries	63.0	37.0
Review corporate plans for sensitivity to emerging social and political trends	60.5	39.5
Set or help establish priorities for public issues at department, division, or subsidiary level	56.4	43.6
Prepare a narrative section regarding future social/political trends, which includes directions for preparation of corporate plans	50.0	50.0
Review department, division, or subsidiary plans for sensitivity to emerging social and political trends	48.0	52.0

SOURCE: James E. Post, Edwin A. Murray, Jr., Robert B. Dickie, and John F. Mahon, "The Public Affairs Function in American Corporations: Development and Relations with Corporate Planning," *Long Range Planning*, April 1982, p. 15. Used with permission.

affairs offices and corporate planning within their firms. One pair of corporate issues managers at the Atlantic Richfield Company introduce the purpose of the office as follows:

> An issues management process . . . can help a company to realize its business objectives by helping it anticipate and respond to changes in its external environment. Properly conceived and executed, issues management is a process to organize a company's expertise to enable it to participate effectively in the shaping and resolution of public issues that critically impinge upon its operations.[22]

While the concept of issues management has been well developed, its actual practice may not have yet fulfilled such high aspirations. The recent survey of 400 firms showed little evidence of the institutionalization of this function in its most ambitious form, which involves sophisticated planning and integration with the strategic process; rather, the more mundane, short-term, and reactive functions actually seem to prevail. The authors of the study summarize three reasons why public affairs concerns often fail to be elevated to a policy level:

1. A less threatening regulatory environment under the Reagan admin-istration, plus the need for cost reductions through the recession of the early 1980s, led to a deemphasis of the role and the budget of many public affairs offices.
2. The broader objective of relating public affairs and issues management to corporate strategy was rarely considered when many offices were established in the 1970s. Most corporations created offices in haste to respond to specific issues, and few corporate offices have succeeded in expanding their subsequent roles.
3. The pressing importance of public affairs issues, when they occur, leads to high involvement by senior officers of many firms. Then, when external issues are not pressing and the CEOs' attention is otherwise directed, only weak administrative structures are left to continue the function. "In some companies," state the authors, "the preoccupation of CEOs with public affairs has left the public affairs department by-passed, frustrated, undercut, and administratively underdeveloped."[23]

Undoubtedly the public affairs function has been incorporated into stan-dard corporate practice in its more routine and mundane tasks. Whether it will ever attain an influential role at the policy level of corporate func-tioning on a widespread and consistent basis depends first on the relative threat posed by the public policy environment to the private sector. A com-prehensive role seems unlikely without a rather dramatic shift in the phil-osophic approach of business to the relevance and need to achieve higher levels of integration of the firm and its environment.

BUSINESS INVOLVEMENT IN PUBLIC POLICY: A POWER ELITE?

Evidence of a Power Elite

Various sinister incidents, such as the Teapot Dome scandal in the early 1920s and revelations of illegal corporation contributions to the Nixon Committee to Reelect the President, have created a fear, or at least a sus-picion, that business interests have had an undue influence on public pol-icy. Several analyses document an apparent decision-making structure that favors business interests. For example, a landmark study of the power structure of Atlanta, Georgia, concludes that significant community projects and policies were formulated by a small group — individuals from industrial and commercial settings, financial owners, and top executives of large firms.[24] This study was one of a series of efforts in a political science tradition that views communities as highly stratified and concludes that decisions are controlled by a small power elite.

Other writers have argued that business interests have disproportionate influence on national policy issues. Political scientist Charles E. Lindbloom is a recent spokesperson for this point of view. Lindbloom traces the role of business in today's democratic societies and finds public or governmental authority strongly influenced by the needs and responses of businesspersons.[25] Governmental actions are profoundly shaped and constrained by adverse business actions that can cause undesirable social consequences such as unemployment. Because public officials are concerned about business performance, corporate leaders have disproportionate access to public policymakers and undue influence on governmental policy. Lindbloom finds such a privileged role of business not only in the United States but in all societies having electoral political systems.

Studies of business influence on specific public policy issues became popular in the 1970s. Insert 13.B illustrates the analysis of one political scientist writing from the perspective of undue business influence. His point is to expose hidden business influence on the formulation of energy policy during the Nixon administration.

Insert 13.B

A VIEW OF BUSINESS, GOVERNMENT, AND THE ENERGY INDUSTRY [QUOTATION]

> Throughout his campaign, in speeches and private meetings, Nixon made one thing perfectly clear to the oil industry — his complete reliability on specific issues of concern (including antitrust, regulation, foreign expropriation, and, of course, the depletion allowance) and his general deference to wealth and power. In return he received heavy campaign backing from corporate leaders, the independents and newer entrepreneurs. As always, Rockefeller, Mellon, and Pew family contribution provided the solid foundation. . . .
>
> Once elected, he insisted that basic energy decisions, including those dealing with the mandatory of import program, belonged in the White House. For a while, Peter M. Flanigan, an investment banker from Dillion, Read and Company with tanker investments, imported liquified nat-

ural gas interests, and oil ties and sympathies, was considered "the man to see" in the executive office on oil matters, including the keeping down of oil import quotas despite rising demand. Governor Walter J. Hickel of Alaska was nominated secretary of the interior. This was at the urging of oilmen, including Robert O. Anderson, chairman of the board of Atlantic Richfield [Arco] who was also Republican national committeeman from New Mexico and a substantial contributor. Arco was eager to have Alaskan oil flowing. Hickel was an ambitious developer who had been a natural gas utility executive and held oil leases. John B. Connally, increasingly active as a business consultant to oil corporations since his service in the Kennedy cabinet and as governor of Texas, and also a counsel for International Telephone and Telegraph, was later to join Nixon's administration as secretary of the treasury. . . .

Nor was it to be overlooked that the incoming president and his attorney general, John N. Mitchell, came from a New York law firm (Nixon, Mudge, Rose, Guthrie, Alexander, and Mitchell) that had been representing El Paso Natural Gas, a giant pipeline system dominating the West Coast and closely linked to major oil, coal, and gas interests. El Paso had been negotiating with a host of federal agencies for clearance to import liquid natural gas from Algeria to the East Coast. This quest raised tangled questions concerning relations with a "third world" nation which had nationalized American oil interests, the impact on the Federal Power Commission's ability to maintain the lower prices of domestic natural gas, and the safety of the new tankers required. El Paso had also long been involved in complex antitrust litigation, resisting court attempts to lessen its monopoly control by divestiture of some of its acquisitions. Once in office both Nixon and Mitchell made clear their disdain for such actions. The Justice Department immediately dropped an El Paso merger suit. The law firm had also been retained by Atlantic Richfield in connection with its complex takeover of Sinclair Oil, which coincided with the accession to office of the new administration.

SOURCE: Robert Engler, *The Brotherhood of Oil: Energy Policy and the Public Interest* (Chicago: University of Chicago Press, 1977), pp. 59–60. Used with permission.

Evidence of Pluralistic Decision Making

Not all studies of public policy formulation conclude that communities are governed by power elites nor that business has disproportionate influence on government. Eight years after the study of Atlanta's power structure was published, Robert Dahl of Yale University published an extensive analysis of policy formation in New Haven, Connecticut. Dahl concluded that community power was more fluid, fragmented, and changeable than viewed in the Atlanta study.[26] Other studies find not a covert or conspiratorial involvement but an interactive and mutually adaptive institutional relationship between business and government. After a detailed review of community power and decision-making studies, widely respected scholar Nelson W. Polsby concluded:

> Careful analysis of the evidence at hand seems to indicate that elites are freest in their power to commit the resources of the community when decisions are relatively routine and innocuous; other kinds of decision making — of a nonroutine, unbureaucratized, or innovative variety — seem to require special consent by citizens who fall outside the small decision-making group.[27]

One particular study concerning the influence of business on U.S. tariff policy should be cited as an example of the pluralist basis of governmental decision making on the national level.[28] Through extensive fieldwork the authors of this study examined the role of the economic self-interest of businesspeople (namely, how their firms would be affected) in determining their attitudes toward tariffs and free trade, and how attitudes were converted into attempts to influence national policy. This study found little support for a belief in the primacy of economic interests. Rather, the authors found personal interests to be broader and more complex than simple economic motives, and they found perceptions of self-interest to be influenced considerably by external communication. Likewise, the process of influencing national policy could not be simplified into uniform, monolithic business interests. Studies such as this argue against a tendency to oversimplify the impact of business on public policy.

Today, business is more visibly organized than ever before to influence public opinion and governmental decision making. For example, the Business Roundtable has emerged as a visible and influential organization that expresses the public policy interests of big business. Likewise, other organizations such as Small Business United are focal points for the expression of interests of small business people on public policy questions. Corporations and business associations, however, are far from alone in the attempt to influence government officials and the public through organized means. The lobbying system is crowded with representatives of educational organizations, agricultural interests, organized labor, physicians and other health professionals, and many, many other groups with their own "business" interests.

Also, it is difficult to identify any unified "business interest" lobby on specific issues. Issues create divisions within the business community. In establishing oil policy in the 1970s, small domestic oil producers were at odds with large international suppliers, as well as with large companies with substantial domestic supplies. Savings and loan institutions favored the removal of interest rate restrictions on deposits, whereas the home-building industry favored maintaining them. Large shippers supported deregulation of trucking and truckers opposed it. Several large American auto manufacturers favored limitations on imports, whereas businesses that sold steel and other products to the Japanese opposed such restrictions. Although business involvement in governmental politics may be large and growing, it is by no means monolithic.

The Role of Public Interest Organizations and Citizens' Lobbies

A number of public interest organizations have been formed, many in the late 1960s and 1970s, to promote causes for which no institutionalized base exists. Generally these organizations are in the areas of consumerism, safety, health, and environmental concerns and oppose policies believed to be influenced by well-organized economic interests. These organizations receive support from like-minded individuals and respond to policy issues on their behalf. Organizations such as Friends of the Earth, the Environmental Defense Club, Congress Watch, and the Sierra Club exemplify groups of this type.

Public interest, in this case, means the interests of significant elements of the public who are not otherwise organized and represented, and it does not necessarily mean the interest of the entire public. Other organizations exist primarily to inform the entire public and provide open and responsive government. Common Cause and the League of Women Voters fall into this second category. To avoid confusion it has been suggested that these groups be called "citizens' lobbies."[29]

Public interest lobbies conduct and disseminate the results of studies, initiate or attempt to block legislation, seek to influence rule making, instigate court action, and file court briefs on critical decisions. Their presence affects business-government relations since the issue orientation of special interest groups may conflict with the interests of specific businesses or industries, or with the economy as a whole.

Many special interest groups active in the 1960s and 1970s had a liberal orientation and may have been a significant factor in the passage of much social regulation in these years. More recently, conservative groups have increased in visibility and strength. For example, Harbridge House, the Hoover Institution, the Center for the Study of American Business, the American Enterprise Institute, and the National Legal Center for the Public Interest conduct research and disseminate analyses favorable to business on questions ranging from macroeconomic policies to single issues.

If, as de Tocqueville observed, the American tendency to form associations of like-minded persons is a strength of democracy, then the high level of political organization and intense lobbying are beneficial elements to society. They are also certainly consistent with the American individualist tradition. The best standard for assessing these developments is whether the system of influence is open equally to all parties — a basic precondition for public policy to reflect a proper balance of interests among social groups.

The financing of political campaigns is one key element in the process of exercising influence on government. Here, rules and practices have changed dramatically over the past decade or so and are still in a state of flux. Let us turn to examine the system of campaign finance as it has evolved and as it exists today.

CAMPAIGN FINANCING: RULES OF THE GAME

Until recently, campaign financing was accomplished primarily through political parties, with party funds solicited directly from individuals. Organized participation of business and labor in electoral politics was constrained by U.S. law; corporations and unions were both prohibited from expending organizational funds for political purposes. This prohibition was based on the twin beliefs that assets of unions and corporations ought not to be spent for purposes beyond normal profit-making activities without the assent of all members or stockholders (a view similar to that struck down in *Bellotti*), and that this prohibition would protect the political process from dominance and control by concentrations of economic wealth.[30]

Corporate political committee activity, neither frequent nor strong, was limited mainly to a few industrywide groups. Most corporation-generated money entered the political process through private contributions made by wealthy individuals. Without disclosure regulations such money was difficult to identify.

The Emergence and Growth of Political Action Committees

To maximize political muscle the labor movement initiated political action committees (PACs) as early as the 1930s, using the device of small voluntary contributions from many union members, rather than union funds per se. In 1955 the newly formed American Federation of Labor and Congress of Industrial Organizations (AFL-CIO) created its Committee on Political Education (COPE), which later became the model for the more formal committees of the 1970s.[31]

Fearing that an upcoming court case might find a particular union local guilty of compulsory and union-financed activity, the labor movement encouraged federal legislation permitting the formation and administration of separate funds in organizations for use by PACs. Thus an amendment was incorporated into the Federal Election Campaign Act (FECA) of 1971 that institutionalized PACs and cleared the way for them to become a mechanism whose importance in federal campaign financing has increased not only for labor unions but also for business corporations and for trade-professional associations. Because labor and business interests had operated so distinctly until 1971, union leaders may not have been fully aware of the precedent that PAC creation would establish for the business community.[32]

Following the Watergate revelations concerning illegal corporate involvement in federal political campaigns, the role of PACs was clarified and strengthened through a series of legislative, judicial, and regulatory actions. The FECA amendments in 1974 and 1976, a comprehensive Supreme Court decision in 1975, and regulatory rulings of the Federal Election Commission have formulated the main guidelines for campaign financing used today:

- Corporations, unions, membership organizations, trade associations, cooperatives, and nonstock corporations can establish and administer PACs.
- Corporate PACs are limited to soliciting contributions from stockholders and management personnel and their families; labor PACs are limited to soliciting contributions from union members and their families; these two groups can solicit funds from the other's constituency twice a year, using an independent third-party agent.
- Corporations and labor unions that have government contracts are free to form PACs.
- Payroll deductions for union PACs are allowed if the employer's PAC uses this plan.
- Proliferation of PACs sponsored by a single firm or union is discouraged by means of contribution limits on individual campaigns.
- PAC titles must include the name of the sponsoring organization.[33]

Individual members of organizations, such as General Motors or the United Automobile Workers (UAW), may organize and act collectively in the political arena, making it possible for substantial sums of money to be collected from small donors, often geographically dispersed but homogeneous in interests. In addition to the business-and-union-related efforts previously mentioned, membership organizations such as the National Association of Realtors or the National Association of Life Underwriters have been established around common interests, collecting funds through direct mailings to individuals identified as potential contributors through membership lists of their organizations.

The growth of PACs has been so dramatic that the term *PAC phe-*

nomena has been used to describe the process.[34] Between December 1974 and June 1984, the total number of PACs increased from 608 to 4,243.[35] Labor, corporate, and trade/membership PACs have each experienced growth in absolute numbers; the rate of growth across different PAC types has varied significantly. Since the mid-1970s, corporate PACs have multiplied most rapidly and now dominate labor PACs by a four-to-one ratio. Prior to 1974, labor PACs outnumbered business and trade membership PACs. Table 13.2 illustrates some recent trends in PAC membership affiliations and political contributions.

Contribution Limitations

National office contribution limits set for individuals, political parties, and PACs are outlined in Fig. 13.1. The possibility of individual prominence in campaign financing has been substantially reduced by a $25,000 annual limitation on total contributions and by a $1,000 ceiling on contributions to a candidate for each election. The greatest allowance for individual contributions is through intermediary groups — PACs and party committees at the local, state, and national levels. For federal elections, multicandidate state and local party committees have a limit of $5,000 per candidate per election, whereas national party committees have higher limits.[36] Discussion of several proposed changes in these limits and thus in the comparative strength of individuals, party committees, and PACs in total campaign financing will follow in a later section of this chapter.

Independent Expenditures

Another element in campaign finance is the growth in importance of *independent expenditures*, advertisements taken on behalf of candidates without their direction and without any direct communication. The Federal Election Campaign Act of 1974 had placed a limit of $1,000 on expenditures of this type, but in 1976 the Supreme Court found this to be an interference with the right to freedom of speech in support of a congressional candidate (in 1985 the Court struck down this limitation on PAC contributions on behalf of presidential candidates on the same freedom of speech grounds).[37] This decision is consistent with the emphasis on corporate freedom of speech in *Bellotti*. Furthermore, in 1981 the Court again reinforced the value placed on individual freedom of speech in electoral politics. In this case a community group, Citizens against Rent Control, challenged a city ordinance that placed a $250 limitation on contributions to committees organized to pass or defeat ballot measures in Berkeley, California.[38] The Supreme Court found the Berkeley law to be a violation fo the First Amendment's guarantee of free speech and struck it down. Thus the Court has consistently refused to limit PAC or individual campaign contributions

TABLE 13.2 *Percentage Increases in PAC Affiliations and Contributions,*
1977–84

PAC Affiliation	Increase in Number of PACs	Increase in Dollars Contributed
Corporate	147	727
Labor	67	243
Trade/member	38	289

SOURCE: Federal Election Commission, "FEC Releases 18-Month PAC
Study" (News Release, FEC, Washington, D.C., October 26, 1984), p. 1.

that support political beliefs and do not appear to unduly influence or corrupt a political candidate.

Independent expenditures can be used to campaign against, as well
as for, a candidate. For example, a journalistic report in early 1980 stated
that the National Conservative PAC expected to spend $700,000 in media
publicity against five Senate candidates. This "campaigning" was taking
place before any primaries and in some cases, prior to the identification of
opposing candidates.[39] Of the five liberal senators targeted by the National
Conservative Political Action Committee, four — Birch Bayh of Indiana,
Frank Church of Idaho, George McGovern of South Dakota, and John
Culver of Iowa — were defeated for reelection. In the 1984 presidential
campaign the AFL-CIO and the National Conservative PAC conducted
costly independent-expenditures campaigns in support of Walter Mondale
and Ronald Reagan, respectively. The AFL-CIO's Committee on Political
Education spent an estimated $18 to $20 million in Democrat voter turnout
drives, voter registrations, and other efforts intended to aid Walter Mondale. All PAC's independent expenditures on Ronald Reagan's behalf totaled $15 million compared with about $600,000 for Mondale; an additional $1.5 million was spent on an anti-Mondale campaign effort.[40]

THE IMPORTANCE OF PACS

Advantages of PACs to Individual Contributors

A nonparty PAC provides an attractive means of financial political involvement for individuals because the PAC establishes a direct relationship between a donor's particular interest and candidate support, PACs allow like-
minded campaign contributors to combine their small donations into
larger, and hopefully more influential, campaign contributions. Further-

FIGURE 13.1 *Federal Election Campaign Act Limits on Campaign Financing*

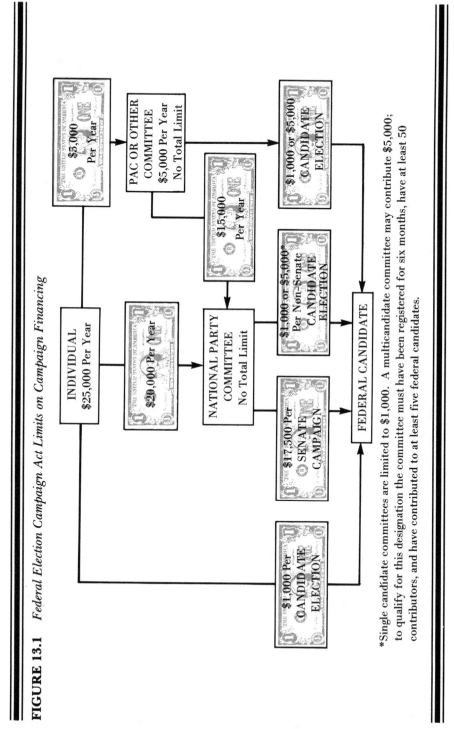

*Single candidate committees are limited to $1,000. A multicandidate committee may contribute $5,000; to qualify for this designation the committee must have been registered for six months, have at least 50 contributors, and have contributed to at least five federal candidates.

more, PACs selectively support candidates after extensive research on their voting records and positions, enabling individuals to target their campaign contributions with a minimum of time and effort. The PAC mechanism is attractive to candidates as well as to contributors since it is possible to solicit funds from numerous small sources that would be difficult or expensive to reach by direct means.

Although many firms consider PACs an excellent way to express corporate opinion to government and to counter labor movement initiatives, several large corporations have declined to utilize the PAC mechanisms. Reasons for nonparticipation in PACs include the fear of a potential boomerang effect: adverse publicity may result, alienating both government and consumers. Some corporations have learned that employees do not like to be solicited for funds and that they prefer to make contributions directly to candidates or to a political party of their choice.

The PAC Role in Political Participation

In addition to providing means for a broad range of dispersed individuals to channel their political interests, the new campaign finance rules sanction interest group representation on an organization-affiliation basis, legitimizing campaign contributions previously shrouded in secrecy and opening the financing system to public inspection. Cutting across professional, occupational, and organizational groups, PACs offer the possibility of more citizen involvement in voter registration, get-out-the-vote drives, and communication about public issues. These activities are increasingly common dimensions of PACs, supporting the premise that a democratic political system should structure opportunities to increase the likelihood of citizen participation in the process.

To the extent that PAC money augments and broadens contributions through political parties and contributions given directly to candidates, it strengthens the political system. To the extent that it supplants political party fund-raising and weakens the ability of candidates to raise significant money outside of the PAC system, it may be harmful to the political process by redistributing political strength away from ideologically broad political parties and toward ideologically extreme groups and/or economic special interests. The power of PACs relative to party organization is illustrated by the fact that in the 1978 congressional campaign the two major parties contributed $6.4 million to Senate and House candidates and spent another $4.8 million on their behalf, whereas PACs contributed $35.2 million to these candidates.[41] In 1978 these PAC contributions of $35 million represented nearly 18 percent of all federal campaign contributions.[42]

In the 1979/80 election cycle, political parties contributed $6 million to Senate and House campaigns and spent another $9.2 million on their behalf. In this election PACs contributed $55.2 million to national candidates, over 23 percent of all contributions.[43] The PAC contributions to Senate and House candidates in the 1984 election year surpassed $100 million dollars and constituted 27.3 percent of all campaign monies raised from January 1983 through September 1984.[44]

In 1979 a Harvard report on the impact of the Federal Election Campaign Act concluded that many unforeseen consequences had developed. Prepared for the Administrative Committee of the U.S. House of Representatives, the report stressed that growth of campaign finances through PACs was weakening political parties since candidates often found it easier to campaign independently from their political party.[45]

Such a weakening of political parties may constitute a threat to the public interest. Political parties act to integrate diverse interests within broad competing philosophies and to prevent splintering and polarization of political interests. If PACs become too strong and too successful, stable political coalitions under general party philosophies could become untenable, and extremism could become more dominant in American politics. Insert 13.C summarizes the views of this report on the impact of the present system of campaign financing strength of political parties.

Opinions differ on the point at which PACs would overreach their constructive and legitimate role and begin to undermine the political process. Edwin Epstein places the danger point at 25 percent of total contributions to candidates; PAC contributions to congressional candidates exceeded this percentage by the final months of the 1984 election campaign. In addition, Epstein warns that (1) the greater inherent power of business and labor and (2) a Federal Election Commission ruling that allows the administrative expenses of these PACs to be paid by the sponsoring organization give them advantages over other social interests (such as environmental and consumer groups) that may create disproportionate political power.[46]

PAC Financing and Government Influence

Underlying concerns of undue PAC influence is the belief that campaign financing is closely tied to lobbying influence, that an elected officeholder is more responsive, if not more indebted, to interests playing a major role in financing the campaign of the politician as candidate. Therefore, as PAC, or special interest, financing grows in the system, elected officials will be more responsive to narrow interests. This is suspected to be the most fundamental and pernicious consequence of electoral reforms of the 1970s; it is a view supported by findings showing a higher incidence of PACs among regulated industries and industries that are more obvious targets of possible congressional action.[47] If the growing strength of PACs means a substantial increase in special interest access and influence in government, then recent campaign reforms may contribute to the predominance of narrow and short-term interests in government over the pursuit of more global and long-term interests.

Insert 13.C

POLITICAL PARTIES AND ELECTION INFLUENCE: A DECLINING ROLE

In 1979 the Committee on House Administration of the U.S. House of Representatives published an extensive analysis of the impact of federal election campaign legislation from 1972 through 1978. The following excerpt shows that one major conclusion of this study was that campaign finance reform was a factor weakening already declining national political parties.

> The American party system is weaker today than at any time in recent American history. Voter allegiance to the parties is down. Party leaders and workers have less and less to say about candidate selection and play only minor roles in most contemporary campaigns. The consequences of this decline include lower voter turnout, increased voter alienation, and a growing inability of party leaders to ensure accountability of office holders and candidates.
>
> There are many reasons for this decline in party strength. . . . an unintended consequence of the implementation of the Federal Election Campaign Act has been to impose further constraints upon the ability of our parties to operate. In fact, the act has had the practical effect of actually encouraging rival and competing organizations to parties: that is, political action committees and candidate organizations.
>
> Because of declining capacities of party institutions, candidates are forced to turn to special interest groups for support, financial and volunteer. Candidates who emerge from primaries, moreover, are more likely to appeal to constituencies both more transitory and less stable than those composing a party organization. . . . The American party system should be strengthened wherever possible, ties between a candidate and his party should be increased rather than lessened, and parties [should be] the cement that provides stability within the American electoral system.

This report made several recommendations to strengthen the role of political parties. First, a separate $50 tax credit for contributions to policial parties was suggested, whereas no tax credit would be allowed for contributions to PACs; second, party committees would be allowed to contribute more to congressional and senatorial races than PACs; and third, require-

Insert 13.C   continued

ments for reports of contributions by state and local committees would be loosened for political parties and not for PACs.

Congress has not acted on these recommendations but will likely reevaluate them as more recent information on the roles of political parties and PACs come to light.

SOURCE: U.S., House, Committee on House Administration, *An Analysis of the Impact of the Federal Election Campaign Act, 1972–78,* 96th Cong., 1st sess., H. Rept. 51–403, 1979, pp. 12–13 (prepared by the Institute·of Politics, John F. Kennedy School of Government, Harvard University).

In one citizen's lobby estimation, PACs may already be too influential. According to Common Cause president Fred Wertheimer, large congressional campaign contributions from anti–tax reform PACs may stall congressional action on this issue:

> A historic opportunity now exists for fundamental reform of our tax system. The major barrier to tax reform, however, will come from special interest groups . . . fighting to protect their special tax preferences."[48]

Further discussion concerning the effects that PAC contributions may have on tax reform is presented in Insert 13.D.

Special interest campaign financing may reinforce the protection of specific groups at the expense of legislative initiatives benefiting large numbers of people. Lee Sherman Dreyfus, former governor of Wisconsin and spokesperson for electoral reform, sees a relationship between the structure of campaign finance and an elected official's ability to make cuts in governmental spending:

> Any time that there has been a move to cut state spending, there are one or more lobbyists saying don't tread on me and my people. Whatever part of government is cut, there surfaces a special interest group, a lobbyist group with dollars to support any candidate opposing the cut and oppose any candidate supporting the cut. The incumbent fears losing campaign contributions. The incumbent fears the newsletter, the mailings, the phone calls opposing him with only a small, underfunded political party to rise to his defense.[49]

Perhaps the most consistent source of criticism of campaign contributions and governmental influence is the public interest organization Common

Insert 13.D

PAC DONATIONS AND TAX REFORM

Two public interest organizations, Congress Watch and Common Cause, claim that sizable PAC contributions to members on congressional tax reform committees — House Ways and Means and Senate Finance committees — may undercut any major congressional drive to reform the U.S. tax structure. The unequal distribution of 1984 PAC monies among congressional incumbents, Ways and Means and Finance committee members, and their 1984 political opponents is cited by Congress Watch and Common Cause as proof that PAC contributions were not intended to merely support particular political candidates. Instead, Congress Watch contends that PAC monies were intended to influence congressional committee members to vote against tax reform measures that corporate PACs believe to be detrimental to business. According to Congress Watch lawyer Jay Angoff:

> The huge amount of money given by special interest groups to senators and congressmen is a major reason why the deficit is so big, why the tax code is so complicated and unfair, and why Congress is unlikely to do much about either.

1984 average PAC campaign contributions were as follows:

	House	**Senate**
Committee members — all	$186,962	$710,513
Incumbent candidates	142,906	612,112
Opponents of committee incumbents	10,927	115,279

National Association of Realtors PAC official Randall Moorhead has denied allegations that PAC contributions are used as a tool by special interest groups to influence particular congressmen. As spokesman for the largest PAC contributor during the 1983/84 campaign, Moorhead stated, "Our PAC contributions are not designed to influence legislation in particular committees. They are designed to elect people whom we support."

Congress Watch, however, has questioned whether "support" was the only motive behind large PAC contributions to Ways and Means Committee members in virtually uncontested congressional races. In 1984 PACs contributed over $200,000 to eight committee members who captured more than 70 percent of the vote in their districts. Only four other House candidates received equivalent PAC support under similar conditions.

Many congressmen share Common Cause and Congress Watch skepticism on Congress's ability to mount any successful tax reform effort. Democrats and Republicans have frequently acknowledged that strong presidental leadership on this legislative issue is necessary. When the Treasury Department circulated a tax simplification proposal in November 1984, 14 House Ways and Means Committee members expressed their objections to the Treasury Department's plan to eliminate investment tax breaks in a letter sent to the President. As of February 1985 the Senate Finance Committee had not made plans to review the Treasury's tax reform proposal.

SOURCE: "Candidates Receiving $200,000+ Increase 1800%" (News Release), Public Citizen, Washington, D.C., January 3, 1985; p. 29, Pamela Fessler, "Members Await Details of Tax Code Revision," *Congressional Quarterly,* February 16, 1985, pp. 301–2, Steven Pressman, "Members of Tax-Writing Committees Reap PAC Money," *Congressional Quarterly,* February 16, 1985, p. 302.

Cause. Studies done by Common Cause on particular legislative issues establish a correlation between campaign contributions and legislative results. Wertheimer states:

> More and more, Congress faces struggles where the particular interest of an organized segment of our society is pitted against the more generalized interest of those less directly involved. In this kind of political equation PAC contributions, which normally represent only the organized interest, take on an exaggerated importance. Also, organized interests do not "balance" each other off in the political system. Which organized interest groups, for example, compete on an ongoing basis with the dairy interests on agriculture policy, the realtors on housing policy, the maritime unions on maritime policy, the truckers and teamsters on transportation policy?
>
> We see more and more cases of special interest groups exercising increasing power to determine or veto policies that affect their own interests. The veto power is of special significance because it is easier to block legislation in the congressional process than to pass it. With growing constraints on government resources, painful choices need to be made on how to distribute more limited resources. With groups unwilling to sacrifice government favors the veto power gains even greater weight. The result has been growing paralysis in government.[50]

Michael Malbin, another spokesperson on the PAC phenomenon, argues that there is no substantive evidence of a close and consistent tie between the new broadly based PACs and governmental influence. He argues that "PACs and the connection between their gifts and congressional policy are a good deal less significant than we have been led to believe." In support of his statement Malbin pointed out that PAC contributions as a percentage of total congressional receipts did not increase from 1976 to 1978, as would be expected if the proportion of PAC contributions could be directly correlated with PAC political influence. However, PAC contributions in the following years have steadily increased as a percentage of total political contributions. In Malbin's opinion, reformers should concentrate on the direct mail specialists who typically appeal to narrowly based extremists at the ends of the political spectrum and raise money for both electoral candidates and issue lobbies in a manner that further polarizes the political process.[51]

PAC INFLUENCE: PRESERVATION OF THE STATUS QUO OR FORCE FOR CHANGE?

One issue concerning PAC giving is whether organized interest groups will use the opportunity for candidate political support to seek favor with incumbent political figures or whether challengers for public offices will also be supported. If PACs assume a strategy of low political risk, they will tend to reinforce the status quo of political directions and make politics less, rather than more, competitive. This effect, if it were to occur, would be unfortunate, since strong competition for office and good financial backing for challengers help keep politicians in touch with public sentiment and more accountable to their constituencies.

Table 13.3 presents information about contributions to incumbents, challengers, and open seat races for all candidates in the 1983/84 election campaigns by types of PACs. As shown, 79 percent of PAC giving went to incumbents by July 1984. Later statistics indicated that PAC contributions to incumbents, covering the entire 1984 campaign period, averaged 73 percent of total PAC contributions.[52] This proportion represents a sharp increase from the 1978 and 1980 elections. During those two campaigns, incumbents received approximately 60 percent of all PAC contributions. In 1982 incumbents received 66 percent of total PAC campaign donations.[53]

Table 13.3 also shows that support is by far the greatest for incumbents among all types of PACs. Four years earlier, "no-connected organization" PACs, such as the National Conservative PAC, targeted only 32 percent of their contributions toward incumbents, whereas other PACs have always shown a consistent preference for supporting incumbent candidates.

The overall distribution of PAC contributions indicates a clear "incumbency" effect only hinted at in 1980. If the 1982 and 1984 PAC-giving statistics indicate the beginnings of a trend, then PAC contributions will comprise an increasing portion of total campaign contributions and will

TABLE 13.3 *Contributions by Different Types of PACs to Incumbents, Challengers, and Open Races, January 1983–July 1984*

	Number of PACs	Candidate Contributions (millions of dollars)	Incumbent Average (percent)	Challenger Average (percent)	Open Races Average (percent)
Corporate	1,322	21.5	87	5	8
Labor	235	12.7	70	18	12
Trade/member/health (not business related)	468	13.8	86	6	8
No-connected	392	6.8	60	26	14
Other (cooperatives and corporations without stock)	124	2.1	89	5	6
Total	2,541	56.9	79.8	10.7	9.5

SOURCE: Federal Election Commission, "FEC Releases 18-Month PAC Study" (News Release, FEC, Washington, D.C., October 26, 1984), p. 2.

definitely favor incumbent politicians. The combination of these two factors may cause the political system to be less responsive to candidates who may represent changing public sentiment.

PROPOSALS FOR CAMPAIGN FINANCE REFORM

Are modifications of the present system of political finance warranted? If so, what should be changed? Obviously, determination of whether PACs supplement or supplant other campaign finance mechanisms is essential. In addition, judgment about the degree and importance of the "incumbency effect" in PAC financing, the upper percentage of PAC-funded dollars in congressional campaigns relative to individual and party contributions, and the degree of connection between campaign financing and influence on governmental decisions enters into one's view of the importance and urgency of further campaign reform.

A number of reforms have been proposed, several of which are the following:

• Reduce the allowed limit of a single PAC contribution to a congressional candidate and the total funds by all PACs to a given candidate;

- Increase the allowed limits for direct individual contributions to political candidates and increase income tax credits for gifts to candidates and parties; and
- Provide for government matching of small private contributions for candidates who raise a threshold level of financial support and limit the total expenditures of candidates receiving partial public support.

The first proposal would serve to limit the PAC role in congressional campaigns, but it may be an unconstitutional restriction of freedom of speech and association. The second would seek to balance PAC influence by broadening the channel of direct contributions to candidates, thus reducing the proportional size of PAC contributions. It may have the drawback of permitting undue individual visibility and influence in campaign finance. Regarding the third proposal, partial public finance would restrict PAC influence at the national level. Provision of public subsidies would help challengers and make races more competitive, but at the same time, a ceiling on total spending by candidates is considered to favor incumbents.[54]

In 1983 a bill incorporating many of the above reform measures was introduced in the House of Representatives. Sponsors of the bill were unable to muster strong support for the reform measure, although the highly disputed section requiring public financing of House campaigns was eventually withdrawn.[55] Large PAC donations to incumbent representatives was speculatively cited as one likely explanation for House opposition to the bill. Congressman Jim Leach, a leader in the House effort to curb PAC campaign expenditures, predicted, "This is a classic issue in which members of Congress will have to be coerced by public pressure to do the right thing."[56]

A second focus of reform would be to constitute stronger disclosure regulations with respect to lobbying activity. Accountability for lobbying is, at best, weak. A law passed in 1946 requires individuals and organizations whose "principal purpose is to influence legislation" to register and file reports with officials of the House and Senate. Yet a lobbyist is not required to disclose the major sources of contribution, nor is a lobbyist obliged to report on activities undertaken to influence government officials. Viewing the overall accountability of lobby regulation, the *Congressional Quarterly* states:

> The 1946 Federal Regulation of Lobbying Act (PL 79–601) requires paid lobbyists to register with the clerk of the House and the secretary of the Senate and to file quarterly financial reports with the House clerk.
>
> However, large loopholes in the law exempt many interests from registering. . . . The act does not seriously limit the objectives of lobbyists, especially those interest groups whose lobbying activities do not fall under the narrow definitions of the law.[57]

The argument in favor of stricter regulation of lobbying maintains that greater accountability for influence of public officials will allow more accurate expression of the "public interest" in government policy. A counterargument urges the need to maintain the constitutional right of all citizens to petition the government. To the extent disclosure discourages some individuals from expressing their views to public officials through organized lobbies, it may interfere with the citizens' rights. Voting and lobbying are private expressions of one's beliefs and, according to this view, ought to be similarly protected.[58]

A CONCLUDING COMMENT

Changing roles of business leaders have been identified in various previous chapters of this book. In the context of corporate governance we identified forces leading the corporate executive to understand and manage institutional structures and relationships for integrating multiple constituencies with the corporation. Discussions of health, safety, and environmental quality found business leaders developing mechanisms for deliberate, planned adaptation to societal attitudes, values, and perceived needs. Finally, in the context of multiple dimensions of business-community relations, aspects of business leadership responding to minority employment, urban redevelopment, and plant closing were stressed.

Corporate political involvement is another sphere in which the role of business and government has been subject to recent change. While business has been involved in politics since colonial days, the business role in public policy has been altered in the past decade owing to a confluence of factors: the increasing burden of regulation of the 1960s and 1970s, popular acceptance of economic problems — inflation, low growth, reduced competitiveness, unemployment, lower relative productivity — as major public issues, and Supreme Court rulings favorable to business free speech and campaign finance reform. These factors, a mix of threat and opportunity, have led to a precedent-setting growth in the involvement of corporations in political processes and public decision making. There is little doubt that political action is one of the major points of interface between business and government.

If political action is significant, several implications arise. First, consistent with the direction and pressures of other trends we have discussed, the corporate manager of the future will need to be much more than a competent decision maker in business. The enlarging intersection of business and society will require a familiarity with public issues and an ability to analyze and draw conclusions from a perspective broader than apparent corporate interests. Skills of understanding and analysis are not all that will be required, as action will also be at a premium. David Rockefeller makes this point in saying that "the chief executive in the year 2000 will have a personal responsibility for advocacy, activism, and outspokenness."[59]

Previously, business interests were expressed in the political process as contributions and involvements of individual managers and employees; what is new is the legitimacy of the political role of the *institution* of business and business associations. The history of business-government relations is replete with controversies about whether the institution of government should affect the institution of business. Now the situation allows for increased influence of business on government, and a dimension of potentially far-reaching importance has developed.

Finally, this new relationship to government is not without risk for business. While it is an opportunity, it is also a potential liability. Business might become so dominant that other social interests, also perceived as legitimate, are unduly weakened; the political power of business might be misused to promote narrow purposes outside of widely felt national interests; or business statesmanship of high quality may not be broadly achieved in society. If these conditions develop, public trust in the political process will be damaged and the concept of corporate rights might be altered. The changing roles of corporations and their leadership in the political sphere is an example of the necessity for responsibility to accompany power in the interests of all sectors of society. The area of corporate political involvement is another area that demonstrates the need for professionalism in management.

DISCUSSION QUESTIONS

1. What are the principal forms of business participation in nonelectoral governmental affairs? Why have such business roles appeared to increase in significance in recent years? Which forms of participation do you see as most viable and effective?
2. What is a political action committee? Why does one see apparent rapid growth in the number of PACs in the United States?
3. What constructive effects might PACs have as elements of election finance? Where might the PAC system become dysfunctional to the democratic process? In your opinion, are the benefits or the risks of the present rules of campaign finance greater?

NOTES

1. *First National Bank of Boston* v. *Bellotti*, 435 U.S. 765 (1978).
2. Ibid., pp. 794–95.
3. Edwin M. Epstein, *The Corporation in American Politics* (Englewood Cliffs, N.J.: Prentice-Hall, 1969), p. 35.
4. David Rockefeller, "The Chief Executive in the Year 2000," *Vital Speeches of the Day*, January 1, 1980, p. 164.
5. Epstein, *The Corporation in American Politics*, p. 36.

6. Phyllis S. McGrath, *Redefining Corporate-Federal Relations* (New York: Conference Board, 1979), p. 57.

7. Ibid., p. 58.

8. Ibid., p. 37.

9. Ibid., p. 35.

10. John E. O'Toole, "Advocacy Advertising — Act II. Highlights of the 1974 Fortune Corporate Communications Seminar, *Fortune Magazine,*" in *Sourcebook on Corporate Image and Corporate Advocacy Advertising,* Subcommittee on Administrative Practice and Procedure of the Committee on the Judiciary of the United States Senate (Washington, D.C.: Government Printing Office, 1978), p. 302.

11. "Petition of FTC of Bayh, McIntyre, Moss, Aspin, Rosenthal, and Young," *Sourcebook* 5 (January 9, 1974): 1091–48.

12. "Memorandum of Mobil Oil Corporation in Opposition to Petition to Extend the Advertising Substantiation Resolution of the Federal Trade Commission," *Sourcebook* 5 (January 9, 1974): 1366–88.

13. Commerce Clearing House, "Corporate Image Advertising," *Trade Regulation Reports* 950 (August 25, 1975): 141–42.

14. William F. May, "CEOs and the Public Business," *Vital Speeches of the Day,* May 15, 1980, p. 458.

15. Ibid., p. 456.

16. Leland J. Adams, Jr., Senior Corporate Counsel of the Gillette Company, "Some Do's and Don'ts in Communicating Effectively with Government" (Annual Meeting of Home Economists in Business, Atlantic City, June 20, 1981).

17. Alan F. Westin, Chairperson's Address, Third Annual Seminar on Individual Rights in the Corporation, Washington, D.C., June 1980.

18. James E. Post, Edwin A. Murray, Jr., Robert B. Dickie, and John F. Mahon, "Managing Public Affairs: The Public Affairs Function," *California Management Review* 26 (Fall 1983): 136.

19. Ibid.

20. Ibid., pp. 138–39.

21. C. B. Arrington, Jr., and Richjard N. Sawaya, "Issues Management and Corporate Strategy," *California Management Review* 26 (Summer 1984): 148–60.

22. Ibid., p. 148.

23. Post et al., "Managing Public Affairs," p. 138.

24. Floyd Hunter, *Community Power Structure* (Chapel Hill: University of North Carolina Press, 1953), p. 109.

25. Charles E. Lindbloom, *Politics and Markets: The World's Political-Economic Systems* (New York: Basic Books, 1977), pp. 170–88.

26. Robert A. Dahl, *Who Governs? Democracy and Power in an American City* (New Haven: Yale University Press, 1961), pp. 85–86.

27. Nelson W. Polsby, *Community Power and Political Theory* (New Haven: Yale University Press, 1963), p. 128.

28. Raymond A. Bauer, Ithiel de Sola Pool, and Louis A. Dexter, *American*

Business and Public Policy: The Politics of Foreign Trade (New York: Atherton Press, 1964), pp. 107–229.

29. Andrew S. McFarland, *Public Interest Lobbies: Decision-Making on Energy* (Washington, D.C.: American Enterprise Institute for Public Policy Research, 1976), p. 43.

30. Edwin M. Epstein, "Business and Labor under the Federal Election Campaign Act of 1971," in *Parties, Interest Groups, and Campaign Finance Laws,* ed. Michael J. Malkin (Washington, D.C.: American Enterprise Institute for Public Policy Research, 1980), pp. 110–11.

31. Ibid.

32. Ibid., pp. 111–12.

33. Edwin M. Epstein, "The PAC Phenomena: An Overview," *Arizona Law Review* 22 (1980): 358–59.

34. Ibid., p. 356.

35. Federal Election Commission, "FEC Releases 18-Month PAC Study" (News Release, FEC, Washington, D.C., October 26, 1984), p. 1.

36. Federal Election Commission, "Campaign Guide for Congressional Candidates and Committees," printed document (Washington, D.C.: FEC, August 1980).

37. *James L. Buckley* v. *Francis R. Valeo*, 424 U.S. 1 (1976); Stephen Wermiel, "High Court Rejects Limit on Spending by PACs to Aid Presidential Nominees," *Wall Street Journal*, March 19, 1985, p. 16.

38. *Citizens against Rent Control* v. *City of Berkeley*, 102 S.Ct. Reporter 434 (1981).

39. "Liberal Incumbents Are Main Targets of TV Ads as Political-Action Groups Exploit Court Ruling," *Wall Street Journal*, January 25, 1980, p. 40.

40. Wermiel, "High Court," p. 16.

41. Epstein, "The PAC Phenomena," p. 361.

42. Epstein, "Business and Labor," p. 139.

43. Federal Election Commission, "FEC Releases Final Statistics on 1979–80 Congressional Races" (News Release, FEC, Washington, D.C., March 7, 1982), p. 3.

44. Steven Pressman, "Campaign Spending Could Top $400 Million," *Congressional Quarterly*, October 27, 1984, p. 2776.

45. U.S., House, Committee on House Administration, *An Analysis of the Impact of the Federal Election Campaign Act, 1972–1978*, 96th Cong., 1st sess., H. Rept. 51–403, 1979, p. 2 (prepared by the Institute of Politics, John F. Kennedy School of Government, Harvard University).

46. Epstein, "Business and Labor," p. 149.

47. Bernadette A. Budde, "Business Political Action Committees," in *Parties, Interest Groups*, ed. Malbin, pp. 11–12.

48. Steven Pressman, "Members of Tax-Writing Committees Reap PAC Money," *Congressional Quarterly*, February 16, 1985, p. 302.

49. Lee Sherman Dreyfus, "People or Money . . . Which Will Rule the State?" *Vital Speeches of the Day*, April 1, 1980, p. 366.

50. Fred Wertheimer, "The PAC Phenomena in American Politics," *Arizona Law Review* 80 (1980): 615.
51. Michael J. Malbin, "Campaign Financing and the 'Special Interests,'" *Public Interest*, no. 56 (Summer 1979), pp. 21–42.
52. Congress Watch, "Candidates Receiving $200,000+ Increase 1800%" (News Release, Congress Watch, Washington, D.C., January 3, 1985), p. 29.
53. Federal Election Commission, "FEC Releases New PAC Spending Figures for '80 Elections" (News Release, FEC, Washington, D.C., March 29, 1981), p. 1.
54. Gary C. Jacobson, "Public Funds for Congressional Campaigns: Who Would Benefit?" in *Political Finance*, ed. Herbert E. Alexander (London: Sage Publications, 1979), 5: 99–127.
55. Dennis Farney and Albert R. Hunt, "Backers of Public Funding of House Races Drop Idea, Will Seek New Curb on PACs," *Wall Street Journal*, September 16, 1983, p. 6.
56. Ibid.
57. Congressional Quarterly, *Weekly Report* 39 (March 7, 1981): 434.
58. Congressional Quarterly, *Almanac* 34 (1978): 782–87.
59. Rockefeller, "The Chief Executive in the Year 2000," p. 164.

The Business Roundtable

> We business people are usually at our best when we are
> making something, or selling something, or servicing
> something — and competing with other companies at
> every step along the way. We thrive on competition. We
> know more about it than anyone else. We're experts. We
> live and and breathe competition every day.
>
> That's when we're competing in the conventional mar-
> ketplace of goods and services. But there is another mar-
> ketplace out there — the marketplace of ideas and public
> issues. This is a marketplace which we haven't penetrated
> nearly so well — not as well as we should have and not as
> well as we *could* have. The truth is that we have been clob-
> bered. As a result, we have not been able to do our best in
> the more traditional areas of competition as well. Our free-
> dom of action has been too restricted.

The speaker was Thomas A. Murphy, chief executive officer (CEO) of
General Motors and newly installed chairman of the Business Roundtable,
an association of 190 CEOs of major American corporations. The date was
June 12, 1978, and the occasion was the Roundtable's annual meeting in
New York. Murphy was warming to his theme, and his focus on the new
role of the CEO struck a responsive chord with his distinguished audience.
Murphy continued:

> John deButts [CEO of AT&T] once said that no one should
> be considered for a chief executive officer's job unless he
> has first spent at least a year working in Washington. John
> may have been indulging a little hyperbole, of course —

but not as much as we might have thought a decade ago. For it should be crystal clear that the day of the cloistered chief executive is long past. If the walls of our executive suites have not already been opened up to this new arena of competition they should be. And standing there in the middle of this arena should be our very best competitors, our chief executive officers.

It makes no difference whether the CEO is comfortable in this new arena. It's where the action is, and it's where we have to go. It's been this way for some time, but business was slow to recognize it. We can't, we must not, be isolated from the realities of the political process. Look at what Irv Shapiro [CEO of du Pont] and Reg Jones [CEO of General Electric] have been doing — making the rounds of Washington, from the President on down; visiting state capitals; sitting down to talk with mayors. They haven't been delegating these tasks to others. They should serve as models for top management throughout the business community.

They, along with John Harper [chairman of the Executive Committee at Alcoa and a founder of the Business Roundtable] and others who preceded them, have made the Roundtable the premier business organization in our country run by chief executive officers themselves. Under such leadership, the Roundtable has been highly selective in choosing and developing issues that are in the *public* interest as well as in our own. Then these issues have been translated into carefully reasoned positions that have been communicated to government personally — forcefully — one-on-one. . . .

If further reasons must be given for placing such new and heavy demands on our chief executives, then let me conclude by reminding you that people respond best to other people — not to "things" like a corporation. They respond best to government when they see it in the person of a President they admire, or of a local Congressman or mayor they know on a first-name basis. The union movement to them is not a button or a slogan — it's George Meany or Doug Fraser. And I hardly need mention who the consumer movement is most frequently identified with.

So, the inescapable fact is that today's chief executive officer, too, must be a public figure. He must be ready to assume all of the risks and all of the difficulties that up-front visiblity entails. Many of us are not comfortable in the spotlight — or on television. But, since we are intent upon developing a healthier relationship of mutual respect and confidence with the government and the public, it is the individual — the flesh-and-blood man who exhibits such qualities himself — who must humanize the corporate image. Through us, the public must see corporations in the same human terms that they see the President, George Meany, or Ralph Nader.

HISTORY OF THE ROUNDTABLE

The content of Murphy's remarks — indeed the very fact that he was addressing them to an assembly of 190 CEOs of America's largest corporations — signaled a remarkable change in the role of the CEO as perceived by the business community and a much broader shift in the context of American business-government relations.

In some ways, of course, business participation in politics was old hat. Special interest lobbying by business, labor, and other groups had been conspicuously evident in Washington and state capitals for decades. Just as New York had long led American cities as the site of corporate headquarters, Washington, D.C., which ranked last among major cities in corporate headquarters, had for many years led the nation as the location of trade associations. By 1978, *Business Week* estimated, more than 1,500 such associations were headquartered in Washington. Individual corporations, of course, could belong to several different associations. Dow Chemical, to take an extreme example, paid annual dues totaling several million dollars to the more than 700 associations to which it belonged. The leading trade associations such as the American Petroleum Institute have an annual budget of $30 million based on 350 corporate members; others like the National Association of Home Builders, have 96,000 members with a smaller budget of $11 million.[1]

Hundreds of corporations also had "Washington reps," and their number was growing rapidly in the late 1970s. (One estimate held that the number of corporations with Washington reps had grown from about 100 in 1968 to about 500 in 1978.) In one sense, then, the Business Roundtable was just another combination of trade associations and Washington reps lobbying for its own special interests, monitoring Capitol Hill and the White House for possible threats and opportunities.

In a second important sense, the Roundtable was a type of research organization. Its stated overall purpose was to "examine public issues that affect the economy, develop positions that reflect sound economic and social principles and make these positions known to the public and its representatives in government." Just as there were lots of trade associations, there were plenty of research organizations, too, in Washington. One, for example, was the venerable Brookings Institution, a generally liberal, privately endowed agency that produced scholarly books and articles on topics in economics and foreign affairs. Another was the American Enterprise Institute (AEI) for Public Policy Research, which was frequently referred to as "a right-wing Brookings," and which in the late 1970s became a leading center for the promulgation of free market economics and philosophy. Unlike Brookings and AEI, however, and unlike some of the "public interest" research organizations associated with Ralph Nader, the Business Roundtable had no independent endowment income and published no books and no articles. It was a research organization whose products were circulated privately, among its members.

Basically, however, the Roundtable was neither a trade association nor a research organization but an entirely new type of phenomenon: a relatively small group whose *membership was restricted to CEOs of major American corporations.* These CEOs were themselves the shock troops performing the chosen missions of the Roundtable, and it was this small size and heavy concentration on the personal role of the CEO that set the Roundtable clearly apart from the National Association of Manufacturers or the U.S. Chamber of Commerce.

The organization had come into existence in 1972, in a merger of three smaller but similar groups: the Construction Users Anti-Inflation Roundtable, whose mission was to combat rising construction costs; the March Group, which aimed to get the viewpoint of business more space in the media and more influence in government; and the Labor Law Study Committee, which had been working to counterbalance the political influence of Big Labor. Within a very few years after its founding, the Roundtable had achieved a series of successes that surprised even its founders, and that brought it to the attention of the media. Roundtable members had mixed feelings about this recognition of its clout. Originally they had very deliberately struck the lowest possible profile (refusing, for example, to disclose their membership) to minimize their vulnerability to attack. When their surprising success made continued invisibility no longer possible, they became more forthcoming about what it was they were trying to do.

How their missions were interpreted in the press is evident from the titles of several articles devoted in whole or in part to the Roundtable. These included "Big Industry Gun Aims at the Hill" (*New York Times,* March 7, 1975), "The Business Roundtable: New Lobbying Arm of Big Business" (*Business and Society Review,* Winter 1975/76), "Business' Most Powerful Lobby in Washington" (*Business Week,* December 20, 1976), and "Business Is Learning How to Win in Washington" (*Fortune,* March 27, 1978). Each of these articles noted the unusual structure of the Roundtable, with its elite membership, its tiny permanent staff (10 to 15 persons, split about evenly between New York and Washington), and its division into task forces oriented around particular issues or problems. In 1977 the task forces and their chairmen were as follows:

1. Accounting Principles (Thomas Murphy, General Motors)
2. Antitrust (Donald Seibert, J.C. Penney)
3. Consumer Interests (James Ferguson, General Foods)
4. Corporate Constituencies (Walter Wriston, Citibank)
5. Economic Organization (Robert Hatfield, Continental Group)
6. Corporate Organization Policy (J. Paul Austin, Coca-Cola)
7. National Planning and Employment (Lewis Foy, Bethlehem Steel)
8. Energy (Ray Adam, NL Industries)
9. Environment (Frank Milliken, Kennecott Copper)
10. Field Support (Robert Hatfield, Continental Group)
11. Government Regulation (Frank Cary, IBM)
12. Labor Legislation (Richard Riley, Firestone Tire & Rubber)
13. National Health (Charles Pilliod, Goodyear Tire & Rubber)
14. Taxation (Reginald Jones, General Electric)
15. Wage-Price Controls (William Sneath, Union Carbide)

Overall Roundtable strategy was directed by a rotating 40-member policy committee, which met several times a year under a chairman and two co-chairmen. In 1977 the chairman was Irving Shapiro of du Pont, and the cochairmen were Thomas Murphy of General Motors and Reginald Jones of General Electric. These three, together with John D. Harper of Alcoa, had been the acknowledged leaders in the early years of organizing the Roundtable, and their own personal prestige had helped immeasurably in the success of the effort. (See Appendix A to Case 13.A for a full list of the policy committee.)

Financial resources for the Roundtable's work came from annual dues assessed on member corporations according to gross sales (these dues totaled between $2 million and $3 million, from sliding assessments of $10,000 to $35,000). A much more important factor, however, was the internal staffs and resources of the member corporations themselves. That is, most of the research work of the Roundtable was done by corporate staffs, at the direction of the CEO. This obviously gave such work the highest priority, and it meant that the capability of the Roundtable for doing certain types of tasks was practically unlimited.

In categorizing the Roundtable's work, and its allocation of resources to the several tasks it set for itself, one outside observer estimated that during the organization's first six years perhaps two thirds of its efforts went into lobbying and related research efforts and about one third to internal self-reform by corporations. A small residual went to an apparently one-shot campaign of advocacy advertising on behalf of the "free enterprise system." (Each of these three efforts is described below.) A second outside analyst contended that the real significance of the Roundtable was in educating its own membership on the importance of political activism and on specific issues of significance to business. This line of thought contended that the implicit priority of the Roundtable was to raise the consciousness of top management and to promote the notion that the "CEO of the future" must inevitably be a public figure, not a "private" executive.

LOBBYING AND RELATED RESEARCH EFFORTS

Each of the Roundtable task forces was engaged in more or less continuous research into issues of concern. Often corporate staffs were tapped for the bulk of the research, but occasionally outside contracts were let to expert consultants trained in the relevant issues. Usually the task forces' managers, the corporate staffs, and the consultants worked in close harmony to produce the desired report. The report itself could be very brief and narrow, addressed to some specific short-term lobbying needs, or it could be longer, addressed to some perennial problem in business-government relations.

Typical of the major, long-term study was a project on the problem of inflation. The results of this study appeared in a short but hard-hitting pamphlet mailed out to Roundtable members in June 1978. The purpose of this document, and many others like it on other topics, was to supply reliable information for the Roundtable's own orchestrated lobbying campaign, for the individual lobbying efforts of the member corporations, and for the public speeches of the corporate CEOs. The recommendations — fairly specific for a document on a slippery subject, cooperatively produced, and implicitly endorsed by the CEOs of 190 diverse corporations — were as follows:

First, courageously tell the people that government cannot do everything at once. Some worthwhile programs must be postponed. Some problems are better left to private-sector solutions. We cannot demand too much, too fast, of our economy without paying the price of inflation.

Second, reduce the proposed $500-billion federal budget request for fiscal 1979 by $10–$15 billion — a 2 to 3 percent reduction. Thereafter, increases in federal government expenditures (both budget and off-budget items) should be no greater than the rate of inflation.

Third, in accordance with our budgetary recommendation, the rate of monetary expansion must be gradually reduced to a rate of growth that is consistent with the potential real rate of growth in the economy. This is fundamental to the achievement of price stability.

Fourth, reduce the tax burden on individuals and business. Inflation-induced increases in both personal and corporate income taxes are adding to the already heavy burden of rapidly rising prices and costs, and stunting the growth of the private sector.

Fifth, re-evaluate government regulations for their inflationary effects. We welcome the President's move in that direction. A deceleration in new government regulations that mandate costly expenditures in the private sector would be a useful first step.

Sixth, continue to remain firm in the rejection of mandatory wage and price controls. Wage and price controls, with their potential for distortion, only deal with the consequences — rising wages and prices — but not the causes of inflation — government monetary, fiscal, and regulatory policies.

Seventh, develop a comprehensive program to keep U.S. industry competitive in world markets. Efforts must be made to expand exports, reduce our dependence on imported oil, and negotiate away the artificial barriers to U.S. products abroad.

Eighth, encourage every business firm, large and small, to minimize waste, reduce costs, and offer more value for the customer's dollar. This the Roundtable companies pledge themselves to do.

Ninth, encourage cooperation by organized labor in holding down business costs — and thus prices. By helping to improve productivity, labor helps to keep U.S. industry competitive at home and abroad, and thus increases job opportunities and real income.

Inflation was only one of several complex topics studied by the Roundtable. A second task force undertook a long-term study of the equally complicated question of U.S. tax policy. Again, the purpose was to provide members with ammunition both for lobbying and in "going public" within their own communities. The study on taxation was especially revealing of the Roundtable's overall approach; 53 pages in length, it contained a detailed discussion of all major subcategories of the tax question, then brief digests of each recommendation, presented in 14 pages of summaries. These summaries were easily adaptable for use in lobbying and public speeches by CEOs. (See Appendix B to Case 13.A for the cover letter accompanying the pamphlet on taxation and Appendix C to Case 13.A for the Summary Statement on the tax aspects of capital formation.)

EFFORTS OF THE ROUNDTABLE TO INFLUENCE PUBLIC POLICY

All this information on inflation, tax policy, and other topics went directly to the CEOs and to the Washington office of member corporations. There it was put to appropriate use in direct lobbying efforts and in *building broad coalitions of other business groups, Washington reps, and trade associations.* In several estimates of Roundtable effectiveness, various analysts listed these examples of cases in which the Roundtable appeared to have played a major role:

1. Convincing President Ford to say that he would veto a consumer protection agency bill, should Congress pass one then under consideration,
2. Building strong support in Congress for deregulation of natural gas prices,
3. Keeping a bill that would provide for an audit of the Federal Reserve System tied up in the House Rules Committee,
4. Delaying the progress of three major antitrust bills — two in the House and one in the Senate,
5. Gumming up labor reform legislation in 1978,
6. Softening the wording of one of the Clean Air acts, and
7. Deleting a reference to antitrust legislation from President Carter's 1979 State of the Union message.

Critics pointed out that each of these "achievements" was negative and that a better Roundtable strategy would be to use its significant access to policy makers to support positive, affirmative programs. This line of thought, in turn, raised fundamental questions about whether business should under any circumstances support increased government activity, and whether such positive programs as were advocated should be confined to the Roundtable's efforts at business self-regulation. (See the Roundtable Statement on Boards of Directors, discussed later in this case.)

HOW THE LOBBYING IS CARRIED OUT

Regardless of negative or positive programs, the method of lobbying itself was a topic of intense interest to Washington observers. For the campaign against a new consumer protection agency, for example, the Roundtable employed a public relations firm that sent out cartoons and canned editorials to 3,800 newspapers across the United States. This material depicted the proposed new agency as just another parasitic bureaucracy, unnecessary and expensive.

The major effort, however, was not in the hinterlands but in Washington itself. *Fortune* magazine introduced a story about corporate political activity with the following description of a scene in the Roundtable's Washington offices, as staffers mapped out their strategy against the consumer protection agency:

> Just a few blocks from the White House, in Room 811 of one of Washington's least memorable office buildings, this conversation is going on between two men, one of whom is holding a list of Congressmen in his hand:
>
> "Henry Gonzalez of San Antonio ... should we use Sears? We have problems with Jake Pickle on this, I'm not

sure we can get him . . . OK, let's ask Sears about Gonzalez . . .

"Delaney of Long Island . . . well, Delaney's a character, still he was helpful as chairman of the Rules Committee . . . Bristol Myers is close to Delaney, let Bill Greif handle that . . .

"Steed of Oklahoma . . . he hasn't committed himself, maybe Phillips should call him . . . ask the Chamber of Commerce . . .

"Gaydos of Pennsylvania . . . ask Alcoa if they'll do it, John Harper was very enthusiastic about this one . . . Hatfield of Continental could to it but I hate to ask him . . .

"Marks of Sharon, Pennsylvania . . . ask Ferguson of General Foods to call Kirby of Westinghouse about Marks . . .

"Gore of Tennessee . . . Carrier Corp. and TRW . . . do we really have a chance with Gore? We really think we do? Ask Lloyd Hand of TRW . . .

"Let's be careful . . . but if we haven't done our job by now . . . but we have, we've got the votes and we know it."

The Roundtable's efforts, *Fortune* added, "were right on target: despite the support of the Carter Administration and a broad coalition of consumerists, the bill was smashingly defeated in the House of Representatives last month. The agency is now only a ghostly heap of rubble — a war memorial to the new firepower of business on Capitol Hill."[2]

The dialogue quoted above suggests again the fundamental reason for the Roundtable's success and the difference between the Roundtable and older business groups such as the Chamber of Commerce. That difference was in the direct involvement of the CEO. When a CEO called, the congressman or senator accepted the call. If the legislator was out of the office, the call was soon returned. If the CEO decided on a personal visit, he typically took along one or more of his division or plant managers from the congressman's home district. This built the kind of constituent or grass roots pressure that has become increasingly important in Washington.

SINGLE-ISSUE POLITICS

As to why such pressure has become more important — indeed why an institution such as the Roundtable should appear and enjoy such success in the 1970s as compared with some earlier period — the simplest and most accurate answer may be found in the fashionable phrase "single-issue politics."

One reason for the emergence of single-issue politics was the remarkable success in the 1960s of coalitions built around one goal, such as civil rights, aid to education, and medical care. These issues — somewhat like national defense, the greatest example of single-issue politics in U.S. history — commanded support that transcended party lines. Such issues typically attracted cadres of workers tirelessly devoted to the promotion of their programs. These workers and their supporters often seemed totally uninterested in all other programs except as such programs might help or hurt their own.

On the other side of the lobbying relationship, what was happening in Congress also promoted the rise of single-issue politics. This was the remarkable decline of party discipline, indeed of any sort of discipline. Washington observers had long contrasted the American legislative system with that of, say, Great Britain, in which party discipline was strictly enforced and in which (at least for Britain and other parliamentary systems) there was no formal separation between the legislative and executive branches. Whereas the British prime minister was by definition the leader of his party and a member of Parliament, the American president (or state governors, for that matter) might well confront opposition majorities in both houses of the legislature. This had happened repeatedly in recent times, with Presidents Wilson, Hoover, Truman, Eisenhower, Nixon, and Ford being stymied time and again by recalcitrant congressional majorities in the hands of the opposition party.

Once the parties themselves began to fragment, the American government became even more difficult to predict or to control. In the early years of the fragmentation, that is, from about 1938 into the 1960s, new coalitions grew up, such as that between southern Democrats and northern Republicans. But even these sorts of coalitions began to disintegrate before such issues as civil rights and economic competition between the Sunbelt and the Frostbelt.

The upshot of these trends was that the American political system was already under great strain when it suddenly received two extraordinarily severe blows. These, of course, were the Vietnam War followed by the Watergate tragedy.

From the point of view of individual congressmen, therefore, the situation as of the middle and late 1970s suggested that the wisest possible course was one of independence, a strategy of every person for himself. Some even quit altogether. Bewildered by it all, numerous senior legislators, including some ousted committee chairmen, simply retired or resigned, wearied by a pace of change that had left them powerless to affect events.

With party discipline now a meager force (at least in comparison with what it had been in earlier times), with few seats in any district any longer "safe," and with the role of government continually expanding legislators found themselves in need of reliable data on which to base their votes and reliable indicators of what their constituents wanted. This was one reason behind the huge recent growth in the size of congressional staffs. If such organizations as the Business Roundtable could stir up strong constituent support for one position or other, and provide hard data about complex issues such as inflation or taxation, then the staffs and the legislators would likely be receptive. Such organizations as Common Cause and the "public interest" groups associated with Ralph Nader had already demonstrated that the field was now ripe for this stort of lobbying. If one could mobilize or appear to mobilize public opinion, and if one could construct a powerful and intelligible case for a particular program, the odds for success were pretty good, irrespective of the ideology behind the lobbying.

Some analysts attributed just this type of pattern to the success of such new programs as the regulation, in the automobile industry, of engine emissions, fuel economy, and safety. The onset of thoroughgoing regulation in an industry that had been almost totally free of governmental interference prior to about 1964 demonstrated that single-issue politics could have rapid and decisive results. Numerous other examples came readily to mind — the Occupational Safety and Health Act, the Consumer Product Safety Commission, and so forth. Perhaps the most arresting example of the suddenness with which single-issue poliics could strike was the revolution in mandatory personnel retirement, which passed both houses of Congress in 1978 with practically no debate at all. This remarkable turnabout in what had been a national policy for many years demonstrated two things: first, the speed with which support could be mobilized behind a single issue that transcended party politics; and second, the fact that single-issue politics could almost as easily get the government out of something as into it.

Of course, one way to keep government out was to remove the reason for it to get in. With this thought in mind, the Roundtable did not restrict itself to research purely for the purposes of lobbying but undertook two additional missions. The first was the promotion of business self-regulation and internal reform; the second, an experiment in advocacy advertising on behalf of free enterprise.

THE ROUNDTABLE, INTERNAL BUSINESS REFORM, AND THE "WHITE PAPER" APPROACH

One method used by the Roundtable in its effort to address important business problems was the "white paper" — a careful statement on an important subject, addressed both to Roundtable members and to American corporations in general. A good example both of the process and the results of this approach was the Statement on Boards of Directors, issued in 1978.

The Roundtable took up this issue in part because the Securities and Exchange Commission (SEC), the Federal Trade Commission, and several committees of Congress had begun inquiries of their own, and additional regulatory laws seemed a real possibility. This attention in the public sector had arisen as a result of a wave of scandals. These included the numerous illegal corporate contributions to the Nixon reelection campaign of 1972, the foreign bribery cases of Lockheed and other corporations, and a series of other unpleasantries that raised the overall issue of "corporate governance."

Taken together, the scandals seemed to demonstrate a situation already well known to critics of the corporation: that some corporate boards were feckless, impotent, and largely ceremonial bodies. Overpaid and underinformed, many board members knew little of what went on inside their companies and were silent partners in what was in some instances a mere charade played out within the American economy. The real power, most analysts knew, resided with professional management. Indeed, many boards had a majority of "inside" directors who were themselves officers of their own corporations, which meant that management was in effect supervising and ruling itself.

Given this interesting situation, the Roundtable undertook to formulate and publish a position on the issue of boards of directors.[3]

The first step was to assign responsibility to the Task Force on Corporate Organization Policy, whose chairman at the time was J. Paul Austin of Coca-Cola. Austin appointed a steering committee of three business school deans and two senior professors, and these five in turn conducted a Scholars' Symposium in May 1977 at the Harvard Business School. Kenneth Andrews of Harvard, one of the 17 participants and a leading student of corporate boards, described the symposium:

> The gathering of academicians, as you would expect, generated a variety of views ranging all the way from the minority position of the American Enterprise Institute that nothing much needs to be changed (except back) to the assertion that more research into board practices and problems is required before students and critics of boards will really know what they are talking about (my own position). Although a few participants had no board experience and approached the issues from the theoretical background, for example, of economics, most of the persons present were themselves members of corporate boards and had considered earlier the agenda issues.
>
> The three topics generating the most spirited interchange were (1) the proper contribution of outside directors in determining corporate policy, (2) the creation and function of a board "strategy committee," and (3) the appropriateness of the chief executive officer's serving as chairman of the board.

The numerous ideas and proposals generated by the symposium were discussed a few weeks later in New York at a conference of CEOs, most of whom were themselves members of the task force. Detailed criticism and discussion continued at a later meeting of the same group, this time in

Atlanta. The participation by the CEOs at all meetings was reported to have been much more active than usual, and their comments on the successive drafts submitted by Roundtable staff members demonstrated that here was an issue they really cared about. Finally, both the task force and the policy committee of the Roundtable (see Appendix A to Case 13.A for a roster of the policy committee) approved the statement, and it was formally issued in January 1978.

The statement itself was 25 pages long, dealt mainly with general issues of broad interest, and presented a program for gradual reform, quite in contrast to some of the more radical proposals coming from regulatory agencies. (SEC Chairman Harold Williams, for example, had suggested that CEOs should be the only "inside" directors on corporate boards, that they should not be chairmen, and that interested "suppliers," such as investment bankers for and outside counsel to the corporation, not be included on the board.) The Roundtable report did endorse the proposition that boards have majorities of "outside" directors, and it did enumerate a long list of procedural reforms, such as more reliable flow of information to the board and better use of existing board committees.

In the larger sense, as Andrews remarked, the real value of the report "is not so much substantive as it is catalytic. Its positive contribution will turn on what behavioral response it produces among the members of the Roundtable, all of whom have it in their power, if they would, to move their boards in the directions of the letter and spirit of these recommendations." At the very least, argued Andrews, "The report is at the leading edge of normal good practice," and the statement itself "is a political achievement" insofar as it reconciled widely divergent opinions on a subject about which Roundtable CEOs fell particularly well informed. As for more concrete results, the Roundtable began to track the response to the report and to measure changes in board practice. (See Appendix D to Case 13.A.) Nobody within the Roundtable or elsewhere could predict with much confidence whether serious change would come about. As in so many other areas, however, one choice did seem clear. Either business could put its own house in order, or it could wait passively for the government to step in and do the job itself. At bottom, what was involved was a major Roundtable theme, indeed one of the oldest themes in the history of business-government relations in America: that of voluntarism versus coercion.

ADVOCACY ADVERTISING BY THE ROUNDTABLE

In 1975 and 1976, Roundtable companies paid about $1.2 million for an experimental series of advertisements that ran in the *Reader's Digest*, a magazine that boasts the largest circulation in the world. Each of the ads was three double-column pages in length, and each contained a simplified discussion of complex issues affecting the American economy. The tone of the ads was very much in keeping with that of *Reader's Digest* articles in general, characterized by appealing leads, apt illustrations, and broad interest for almost any literate citizen. They were comparable in some respects to the much bigger campaign run by the Mobil Oil Corporation, though the message of the Roundtable ads was a bit less strident and a bit less sophisticated in argument. Themes of the series were evident from some of the titles of the ads: "Free Enterprise — Is This Any Way to Live?"; "Whatever Happened to the Nickel Candy Bar?"; "Who Cheers When Products Work?"

Occasionally, a Roundtable ad would take explicit issue with government policy. During the controversy over new antitrust legislation, for example, one ad entitled "Too Big or Not Too Big?" argued the virtues of scale economies and equated bigness in general with efficiency. In another ad, the Roundtable took direct aim at government spending. The subject was inflation, and the text was entitled "The 'Secret Tax' American Can't Afford."

One of the strategic issues faced by Roundtable planners was whether to resume this method of getting its message across. The impact of such advertising was exceedingly difficult to measure, and some CEOs believed that the whole arena might best be left to individual corporations.

THE QUESTION OF VULNERABILITY

In the euphoria of their early successes, some Roundtable members seemed insufficiently aware of the extent to which their organization might be vulnerable to shifting patterns of public opinion, or the shifting fortunes of the American economy.

Other members, however, had given thought to these matters. It seemed to them that the Roundtable's vulnerability fell into two broad categories. One range of issues was simple to diagnose but not so easy to cure. This was the fact — at once a source of pride and of potential vulnerability — that the membership, including all the "business statesmen" such as Irving Shapiro, obviously represented Big Business. The 190 CEOs who made up the Roundtable all came from companies whose sales were measured in hundreds of millions of dollars. One potential challenge that might arise, therefore, was from within the business sector itself: from small businesses whose interests in many respects diverged from those of Roundtable companies. This problem was a variant of one inherent in the Roundtable itself (the problem of building a consensus even among Big Business firms whose interests diverged); but some viewed it as a more serious issue because of the question of image. The American populist strain and the very strong popular preference for "the little guy" and "the small businessman" as against "the giant faceless corporation" meant that the Roundtable was in effect living in a glass house and had better select very carefully the stones it threw.

A related type of vulnerability had to do with the long history in

American politics of scandals or pseudoscandals involving business-government relations. Any college sophomore could quote a litany of such scandals. There was the famous tale, for example, of Senator Daniel Webster's "retainers" from the Second Bank of the United States, the central bank of its day. Webster received a total of $32,000 during his years in the Senate, including $10,000 on the day after he delivered a particularly moving pro-bank speech. And in the years after the Civil War, business-government relations grew so corrupt that the era acquired the nicknames "The Gilded Age" and "The Great Barbecue." Such industrial giants as Jay Gould and John D. Rockefeller became associated with the bribery of legislators, and the term *robber baron* also entered the national vocabulary.

This was only the beginning of an era that continued into the first decade of the twentieth century, when a corps of muckraking journalists made careers of discovering and publicizing business corruption and political influence. The results of their well-known efforts were such books as Upton Sinclair's *The Jungle* (meatpacking), Frank Norris's *The Octopus* (railroads), David Graham Phillips's *The Treason of the Senate* (businessmen and senators), and Lincoln Steffens's *The Shame of the Cities* (businessmen and urban politicians).

One of the interesting things about antibusiness feeling during the era of the muckrakers (the "progressive era") was that it occurred in a context of great national prosperity. The early twentieth century was a time of almost uninterrupted economic growth, and it seemed ironic to many businessmen that the better they did their jobs on behalf of the national economy, the worse they seemed to fare in the minds of the reading public. At any rate, it was not until the time of World War I that the muckraking spirit temporarily died out — a pattern that would repeat itself during World War II, suggesting that wars that had the support of the people tended to quiet economic passions and to dissolve ideological differences between businessmen and their critics.

In the 1920s, American business reached the zenith of its popular esteem. Prosperity roared, and such novel products and services as the automobile, the radio, and the movies introduced a new type of consumer-oriented popular culture. So great was the change in the way Americans lived that the twenties have been called "the first really twentieth-century decade." Businessmen such as Henry Ford became the leading national folk heroes. President Coolidge's maxim — "The business of America is business" — became a cliché, and an accurate one at that.

SAMUEL INSULL AND ELECTRIC UTILITIES: A CAUTIONARY TALE FOR THE ROUNDTABLE?

Yet even in this high tide of business esteem, there occurred an episode — now almost forgotten — that might hold lessons for the Business Roundtable and its attempts to educate public opinion and influence public policy. The setting was the electric utility industry, and the issues were in some ways analogous to those confronting the Roundtable in the 1970s and 1980s. The episode is perhaps best reflected in the career of Samuel Insull, the leading utility executive of the 1920s and an honored "business statesman."

Insull had led the life of a Horatio Alger hero. A penniless lad, he had emigrated to the United States from England and had served for several years as private secretary to Thomas Edison. He had then pioneered the electrification of the Middle West and had made millions in building Commonwealth Edison of Chicago into one of the nation's most innovative utilities. Insull had been an industry leader in marketing, finance, technological innovation, and especially publicity. "I believe," he once said, "it is our duty to the properties we manage, to the stockholders who own them, and to the communities they serve, that we should enlighten those communities on the situation. I believe in doing it not in any gumshoe way, but in every sense openly and boldly." Furthermore, Insull was very active in state, local, and national politics. He was a blue-ribbon businessman, and in November 1929 he achieved the rare honor of appearing on the cover of *Time*.

Meanwhile, two related trends were about to produce disgrace and downfall not only for Insull but for the electric utility industry itself. The first was the stock market crash of 1929, which brought down the pyramids of utility holding companies that Insull had so carefully built up. (An organizational innovator, he himself had been chairman of the boards of 65 different such companies.) The second trend, which ensured the disgrace of the entire industry, was broad reevaluation by numerous critics of the publicity and lobbying efforts of the utility industry. Starting in 1928 (that is, at the high tide of business popularity), the Federal Trade Commission (FTC) conducted an intensive study of the industry's structure, performance, and activities in government and public relations. The investigation was pressed on a reluctant FTC (which had a conservative Republican majority of members owing to the appointments of commissioners by Presidents Harding and Coolidge) by a Senate resolution pushed through by a coalition of Democrats and Progressive Republicans.

The ensuing FTC study was the most systematic and intensive inquiry into a single industry ever to occur in the United States up to that time. It went on for seven years — agonizing years for the industry, as Insull and other leaders watched their critics in Congress and the commission parade an almost incredible series of sins and questionable practices before the American public. Individually and through their trade associations, the utility companies were shown to have engaged in every conceivable form of public relations, much of it bordering on outright propaganda.

The target of the propaganda was municipal and state ownership of electric power facilities. To meet this challenge, the industry had surreptitiously subsidized a few teachers and professors, published numerous books and pamphlets, mailed out countless canned editorials to newspapers across the country, and sent its spokespersons to speak at colleges, schools, churches, and clubs and on radio shows. It had sponsored questionable "customer ownership" movements whereby nonvoting stock could be purchased by residential users of electricity. The entire campaign portrayed the investor-owned American utility industry (which typically charged high rates and had succeeded in electrifying only 3 percent of American farms by 1930) as efficient and innovative — a symbol of free competitive enterprise (despite the fact that the industry is a natural monopoly). Movements for public ownership, by contrast, were characterized as bolshevistic, un-American, and inefficient. In short, the utilities were selling a philosophy. To do it more effectively, they often disguised their own authorship, as with the canned editorials or with ghost-written articles over the signatures of prominent citizens whom they paid for the endorsement. Without the campaign, as one utility publicist put it, "We'd all be in a hell of a shape. . . . Without this, I venture to say that state, municipal and government ownership would have been 100 percent ahead of what it is today."

All of this public relations and lobbying activity was carefully documented by the FTC's study, which was ultimately published by the Senate in 83 large volumes of testimony and exhibits. The revelations, as expected, provided a rich cache of ammunition for antibusiness critics. In addition to the prolonged assault on the industry's abuses, which appeared in magazines and the daily press, at least six books appeared, detailing the whole story. The titles of the books express their tone: *Confessions of the Power Trust, High Power Propaganda, Power Ethics, The Public Pays* (this was by Ernest Gruening, later a U.S. senator), *The Power Fight,* and *Pyramids of Power: The Story of Roosevelt, Insull, and the Utility Wars.*

In the years of this investigation, which coincided with and was obviously related to the economic crisis of the Great Depression, Samuel Insull's reputation plummeted. Whereas he had been a principal symbol and folk hero of twenties prosperity, he now became a symbol of what appeared in the context of depression to be a discredited and morally bankrupt system. As indictments were filed against him for some of his financial dealings, he fled the country in disgrace, only to be apprehended in Greece and extradited back to stand trial in the United States. (He was acquitted, but as in many cases of this type he had already been found guilty by the newspapers.)

The industry itself fared even worse. Franklin D. Roosevelt made it a prime target in his campaign for the presidency in 1932, speaking of electric rates calculated to "rob" the public and pointing out that the customers of Ontario Hydro, the publicly owned Canadian utility just across the border, paid only $3.00 a month for the same amount of electricity that cost citizens of Manhattan $17.50. When Roosevelt became president, such legislation as the Public Utility Holding Company Act, the Tennessee Valley

Authority Act, the Rural Electrification Administration Act, and the Water Power Act showed just how ready Congress and the American people were to punish an industry they perceived as rotten and corrupt. Additional legislation that affected this same industry, such as the Securities Act and the Securities Exchange Act, originated amid even broader public anger, in this case at Wall Street itself, which was seen as having brought on the Great Depression by loose and corrupt management of the stock exchanges and capital markets. Like the utility industry, the securities industry had rapidly gone from very high public esteem to the depths of disfavor. And it was not merely a matter of a tarnished public image but of new and stringent regulatory laws now on the statute books.

Much of this agitation and new regulation could be attributed to the Great Depression itself and to the New Deal spirit that exploited public discontent with the business system. Some historians noted, however, that with the exception of the World War II period business scandals had become virtually independent of economic context and had acquired a life off their own, almost as part of the American routine. Ready examples came to mind, not only for such periods as the Democratic Truman administration (gifts by lobbyists of deep freezes and mink coats to the wives of high administratioan officials) but also for such periods of close government-business cooperation as the Republican Eisenhower administration (the Goldfine–vicuña coat–Sherman Adams scandal). The crucial point, said some observers, was that business-government relations will always be a tricky field on which to play; that despite what the law might or might not allow, public opinion was a force unto itself. Perhaps it could be as fickle in the 1970s and 1980s as it had been with Samnuel Insull and others in the 1920s and 1930s.

ARE ALL INSTITUTIONS NOW MORTALLY VULNERABLE?

Evidence of the vulnerability of particular organizations or individuals was ready at hand, in the experiences of the FBI and CIA and in the ongoing work of such publicists as Jack Anderson, such political celebrities as Ralph Nader, and such television programs as "Sixty Minutes," which in a matter of two or three minutes could demolish the reputation of just about anyone or any organization, public or private. by the late 1960s, and certainly throughout the 1970s, the credibility of virtually all institutions was at a discount. The one-two punch of Vietnam and Watergate had dealt the American polity and the American psyche the most profound blows they had sustained since the Civil War. Roundtable members knew that these trends, these tragedies, were intimately related to the new context of single-issue politics, which made their own work and their own plans potentially more effective than they might have been in the 1940s or 1950s.

THE ROAD AHEAD: TWO SETS OF CRITICAL ISSUES

In other respects, Roundtable CEOs wondered whether the profound national disillusionment that had begun in the 1960s and was persisting into the 1980s was more an advantage or more a disadvantage to what they were hoping to accomplish. Did it represent an opportunity for them to strike a sincere and convincing attitude of responsible business statesmanship and set the Roundtable apart from the countless multitude of self-centered special interests groups? Or was the Roundtable itself really one of these groups, fighting and clawing along with the rest, strictly on the basis of self-interest, for a share in the shaping of public policy?

Thus, despite their satisfaction with the organization's progress during the first six years, and despite the *exhilaration* with active political participation many of them felt, the CEOs wondered in particular about two critical sets of questions for the future. The first set was essentially reactive and defensive: how best to protect themselves and their organization from the kind of attack, and the vulnerability to events, that had inverted the reputations of even such elite *public* agencies as the FBI and CIA; or that long ago had brought down Samuel Insull and the utility industry; or that even longer ago had produced the era of muckraking and explicitly anti-business journalism. To put the question another way, How long might the period of single-issue politics last, and on what conditions was it dependent? And what about the members' own personal vulnerability, as a group of "fat cats" with astronomical salaries, engaged together in an organization that — whatever its merits — was in the literal sense a very exclusive rich men's club.* Put simply, these questions really had to do with how to preserve the legitimacy and credibility of their own participation in the policy-making process. Where, for example, should the line be drawn between what the Roundtable itself did and what its member corporations did using their own staffs and their own budgets? Was there not a serious question of legitimacy here?

The second set of critical issues was separate from, but in part limited by, the first set. Where the first set was reactive and defensive, this second set was active and strategic. These questions were very specific and straightforward:

---

*Just how high executive compensation in American business is in relation to salaries in the public sector is illustrated by the following comparison: "In 1962, when automobile sales had yet to reach record levels, the salaries and bonuses paid the fifty-six officers and directors of General Motors exceeded the combined remuneration received by the President of the United States, the Vice-President, 100 U.S. Senators, 435 members of the U.S. House of Representatives, the nine Supreme Court justices, the ten cabinet members, and the governors of the fifty states" (see Robert T. Averitt, *The Dual Economy* [New York: Norton, 1968], p. 178).

First,   *How to identify those emerging issues which were both important and amenable to Roundtable influence;*

Second,   *How to deploy the resources of the Roundtable so as to achieve an effective match between tools and issues, using the instruments of publicity, white paper statements, and direct lobbying which had made the organization's first five years so replete with success;* and

Third   *How much of the typical CEO's time really could or should be spared for advocacy, lobbying, and other partisan activities? Thirty percent? Forty? Fifty? Was it inevitable that the "CEO of the Future" spend such a major proportion of time on such matters? And was not every minute spent on politics — however enjoyable — a minute subtracted from the primary business of running the corporation?*

DISCUSSION QUESTIONS

1. What is the likelihood that the activities of the Business Roundtable will provide a focus for traditional populist sentiment in American politics and result in more harm than help to the interests of big business? Might some Roundtable activities be more susceptible to public distrust than others?
2. To what extent should self-reform or self-regulation be a primary goal of the Roundable? How great is the potential of voluntary change? How promising is it as an alternative to governmental intervention?
3. What recommendations can you make about issues of managing the Roundtable presented at the end of the case, namely,
   a. How to identify emerging issues?
   b. How to deploy Roundtable resources effectively?
   c. What level of effort to expect from member CEOs?

APPENDIX A TO CASE 13.A

Members of the Policy Committee — 1977*

Ray C. Adams, NL Industries

J. Paul Austin, Coca-Cola

Robinson F. Barker, PPG Industries

William W. Boeschenstein, Owens-Corning

Fletcher L. Byrom, Koppers Co.

Frank T. Carey, IBM

John T. Connor, Allied Chemical

Justin Dart, Dart Industries

John D. deButts, AT&T

James L. Ferguson, General Foods

Lewis W. Foy, Bethlehem Steel

Clifton C. Garvin, Jr., Exxon

Richard L. Gelb, Bristol-Myers

W. H. Krome George, Alcoa

John W. Hanley, Monsanto

Richard A. Riley, Firestone

David Rockefeller, Chase Manhattan Bank

Donald V. Seibert, J.C. Penney

Irving S. Shapiro, DuPont

William S. Sneath, Union Carbide

Edgar B. Speer, U.S. Steel

George A. Stinson, National Steel

Edward G. Harness, Proctor & Gamble

Shearon Harris, Carolina Power & Light

Robert S. Hatfield, Continental Group

Gilbert W. Humphrey, Hanna Mining

Reginald H. Jones, General Electric

Ralph Lazarus, Federated Department Stores

Donald S. MacNaughton, Prudential Insurance

Robert H. Malott, FMC Corporation

Frank R. Milliken, Kennecott Copper

Roger Milliken, Milliken & Co.

Thomas A. Murphy, General Motors

David Packard, Hewlett-Packard

Ellmore C. Patterson, Morgan Guaranty Trust Co.

Charles J. Pilliod, Jr., Goodyear

John J. Riccardo, Chrysler

W. Reid Thompson, Potomac Electric Power

Rawleigh Warner, Jr., Mobil Oil

William L. Wearly, Ingersoll-Rand

Arthur M. Wood, Sears, Roebuck

Richard D. Wood, Eli Lilly

Walter B. Wriston, Citibank

Senior Members
John D. Harper, Alcoa
Howard J. Morgens, Procter & Gamble

Irvin S. Shapiro
Chairman

Reginald H. Jones
Cochairman

Thomas A. Murphy
Cochairman

---

*The Policy Committee is set up to maximize industrial and geographic balance. One fifth of the members are replaced each year by regular rotation.

APPENDIX B TO CASE 13.A

 The Business Roundtable

Irving S. Shapiro
Chairman

Reginald H. Jones
Cochairman

Thomas A. Murphy
Cochairman

NEW YORK
405 Lexington Avenue
New York, New York 10017
(212) 682–6370

G. WALLACE BATES
President

JAMES KEOGH
Executive Director–Public Information

RICHARD F. KIBBEN
Executive Director–Construction

WASHINGTON
1801 K Street, N.W.
Washington, D.C. 20006
(202) 872–0092

JOHN POST
Executive Director

July 7, 1977

MEMBERS OF THE BUSINESS ROUNDTABLE

Tax reform is high on the agenda of both the Administration and the Congress this fall, and the views of the business community are being sought.

Accordingly, the Task Force on Taxation of the Business Roundtable has prepared the attached package of tax proposals. Copies of this package are going to your company representatives in Washington. A co-ordinated distribution to key members of the Congress and the Executive Branch is being arranged.

But this is only the beginning. To get action on these proposals, you personally and your managerial associates should talk them over with your Senators and Representatives. We must also build understanding among employees, share owners, the press, and other audiences. Additional copies are available from the Business Roundtable office in New York. We shouldn't worry about duplicate distribution, because it's important to let our governmental representatives know that this is an industry-wide concern.

Emphasis will change from one to another of these tax proposals, as the legislative and political process moves ahead. But it's important for the Congress to understand that the public interest demands, and the business community wants, positive action on these tax issues.

Reginald H. Jones
Chairman–Task Force on Taxation

Att

POLICY COMMITTEE: Irving S. Shapiro*, *Chairman* · Reginald H. Jones*, *Cochairman* · Thomas A. Murphy*, *Cochairman* · Ray C. Adam* · Frank T. Cary* · John D. deButts* · James L. Ferguson* · John D. Harper** · Robert S. Hatfield* · Frank R. Milliken* · Howard J. Morgens** · David Packard* · Charles J. Pilliod, Jr.* · Donald V. Seibert* · William S. Sneath* · Edgar B. Speer* · J. Paul Austin · Robinson F. Barker · William W. Boeschenstein · Fletcher L. Byrom · John T. Connor · Justin Dart · Lewis W. Foy · Clifton C. Garvin, Jr. · Richard L. Gelb · W. H. Krome George · John W. Hanley · Edward G. Harness · Shearon Harris · Gilbert W. Humphrey · Ralph Lazarus · Donald S. MacNaughton · Robert H. Malott · Roger Milliken · Ellmore C. Patterson · John J. Riccardo · Richard A. Riley · David Rockefeller · George A. Stinson · W. Reid Thompson · Rawleigh Warner, Jr. · William L. Wearly · Arthur M. Wood · Richard D. Wood · Walter B. Wriston

*Executive Committee
**Senior Members

APPENDIX C TO CASE 13.A: BUSINESS ROUNDTABLE SUMMARY STATEMENT

CAPITAL FORMATION

A National Requirement

The United States must increase the share of its resources devoted to capital investment in order to increase productivity and real wages, reduce inflation, and provide jobs for a growing labor force. Other national needs — energy, environment housing, rebuilding the cities, a tax base for social services — also require higher levels of capital investment. The present tax structure is tilted against business investment and must be reformed so as to provide greater *incentives* for capital formation.

Why Action Is Needed

• U.S. lags other nations in investment, economic growth, and productivity growth (1960–73 Study by U.S. Treasury)

	Investment Ratio		Output Growth Rate		Productivity Growth	
	Percent	Rank	Percent	Rank	Percent	Rank
Japan	29.0	1	10.8	1	10.5	1
West Germany	20.0	2	5.5	3	5.8	4
France	18.2	3	5.9	2	6.0	3
Canada	17.4	4	5.4	4	4.3	5
U.K.	15.2	5	2.9	7	4.0	6
Italy	14.4	6	5.2	5	6.4	2
U.S.	13.6	7	4.1	6	3.3	7

• Declining rate of investment in plant equipment is slowing down growth in productivity and real wages.

  – The growth rate in the amount of private plant and equipment (excluding pollution control investments) declined from 4.3 percent per year in the period 1965–70 to 3.3 percent per year in 1970–75 and can be expected to decline further to 2.5 percent per year in the period 1975–1977.

  – Congressional Budget Office study shows growth rate of plant and equipment per worker fell from 2.6% in 1965–70 to 1.6% in 1970–75, and is expected to decline further to 1.0% in 1975–77.

  – Growth rate in worker productivity fell from 2.4% in 1965–70 to 1.0% in 1970–75.

- Slowdown in productivity growth results in slower growth in real wages. Since 1969, real hourly wages have grown by less than 1% a year.

- Jobs for a growing labor force require investment in tools of production.

  - Civilian labor force expected to rise from 93 million in 1975 to 103 million in 1980 and 110 million in 1985.

  - Average annual increase of 1.5 million workers to be equipped.

  - U.S. needs to devote 12% of real GNP to business investment during 1975–80 to reduce unemployment to 5% (and meet environmental and energy needs) according to Commerce Department Study of 1975.

  - However, between 1965 and 1974 business investment averaged only 10.5% of GNP, and during 1975 and 1976 it averaged only 9.3%. Thus, business investment must be accelerated to 13% or more of GNP to reach economic and employment goals.

  - Argument that investment in labor-saving devices reduces employment is not borne out by experience. Capital spending and private sector employment are closely correlated through booms and recessions. Investment up, employment up.

- U.S. will run out of plant capacity before it runs out of unemployment.

  - Unemployment rates when economy runs at "full capacity":

        1968 — 3.4% unemployment
        1973 — 4.8% unemployment
        1978 — 6.0% or more unemployment expected.

- Capital spending is lagging in the present economic recovery. Key weak spot.

  - On March 2, 1977, Arthur Burns testified that real business capital spending only increased 3% during current recovery versus an average of 15% during the previous post–war recovery cycles. Still lagged by 8% in 1977.

- Incentives and means for investment have eroded.

  - Reported profits of nonfinancial corporations, after taxes, have increased 94% since 1965. But when *adjusted for inflation* (underdepreciation and phantom inventory profits) they have actually declined 10%.

  - Real return on investment (adjusted for inflation) has eroded. It was 3.7% in 1976 — hardly an incentive to invest at today's cost of money.

FIGURE 13.2   *Return-On-Investment* After Taxes (Nonfinancial Corporations)*

RETURN–ON–INVESTMENT* AFTER TAXES

Nonfinancial Corporations

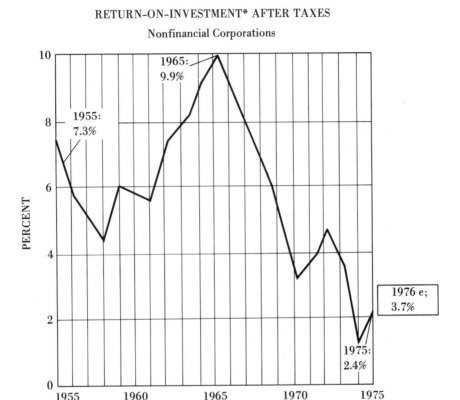

SOURCE: Calculated from Commerce Department data.

- The effective corporate tax rate adjusted for phantom inventory profits and underdepreciation peaked at 59.7% in 1974. The 1975 and '76 rates of 51.6% and 51.2% are otherwise the highest since the 1950's.

  - Corporate tax cuts enacted since 1950's have been insufficient to offset the ravages of inflation.

APPENDIX D TO CASE 13.A

 Roundtable Report

— **published by**
The Business Roundtable

1801 K Street, N.W.	No. 78–9	200 Park Avenue
Washington, D.C. 20006	December 1978	New York, N.Y. 10017
(202) 872–0092		(212) 682–6370

SHAREOWNERS EXPRESS SATISFACTION WITH STRUCTURE, PERFORMANCE OF BOARDS

Owners of shares in the nation's publicly held corporations express basic satisfaction with the composition and performance of boards of directors as now structured and elected.

This is the central finding of a nationwide study of shareowner attitudes conducted by Opinion Research Corporation for The Business Roundtable. In this survey, individual shareowners were asked to make their judgments about the company in which they "own the most stock."

Results of the survey included:

– Eighty-eight per cent are completely or fairly satisfied with the job the Board of Directors is doing.

– Eighty-seven per cent of those who have ever communicated with their company say management is responsive to communication from shareowners.

– Among the seventy-three per cent who know the composition of the Board of Directors, nearly nine in ten feel that it is appropriate.

– The present procedures used for nominating directors are viewed by seven in ten shareowners as fair and just to them as owners.

– A two-thirds majority of shareowners oppose any federal regulation that would require special interest groups to be represented on company boards. Support for such a requirement is higher among those with less education, those having smaller portfolios, and those holding stock in only one company.

– The company's growth record, future of its industry, and the dividend record are of top importance in shareowners' minds when deciding to invest in a company.

– It is the rare shareowner — about one in twenty — who is holding onto his shares in order to vote on management decisions and otherwise take a direct and active role in the company's affairs. Overwhelmingly, the decision to hold onto stock is the expectation of economic gain.

The survey was conducted under the auspices of the Roundtable's Corporate Organization Policy Task Force, headed by John D. deButts, Chairman of American Telephone & Telegraph. The results have special relevance in connection with various proposals on corporate governance being considered in Washington.

NOTES

1. "For Trade Associations, Politics Is the New Focus," *Business Week,* April 17, 1978, p. 107.
2. "Business Is Learning How to Win in Washington," *Fortune,* March 27, 1978, p. 53. Courtesy of *Fortune* Magazine; © 1978 Time Inc.
3. The account that follows is derived from Kenneth R. Andrews, "The Roundtable Statement on Boards of Directors," *Harvard Business Review* 78 (September-October 1978): 24–38. Courtesy of Harvard Business Review; © 1978.

Business and Political Action
To PAC or Not to PAC?

Jessica Smythe, founder and chief executive officer of a chain of 17 hardware and hobby stores in a heavily populated midwestern state, had seen the firm grow in 15 years from a single store on a neighborhood shopping street to a corporation with assets of $9 million and annual sales of $22 million: 12 of the stores were located in large, thriving suburban shopping malls, 2 were in urban neighborhoods undergoing a renaissance, and the remaining 3, including the original store, were in declining urban areas and undergoing a decrease in sales concurrent with a surge in operating expenses.

At its last meeting the board of directors had voted to leave these last three stores in their present locations rather than move them to more profitable settings. This decision to become involved in efforts to rejuvenate the neighborhoods was motivated both by concern for the maintenance of urban neighborhoods and by the knowledge that renovation efforts in the two renaissance areas had produced heavy demand for hardware and other remodeling aids. In fact, Smythe had been able to purchase the paneling, stained glass, and fixtures from buildings scheduled for demolition in these areas and to resell them. Generally, they were sold as quickly as they could be put on display. In brief, neighborhood development was good for the corporation as well as for the city.

Each of the three declining areas had formed a neighborhood association, largely in response to the urging of the local merchants, and had sought public development funds with which to renovate the older buildings. Partly owing to financial entrenchment severely limiting the money available at all levels of government, and partly because of insensitivity to the needs of the communities on the part of their congressional representatives, available federal funds in the form of block grants were not forthcoming. It was apparent that the neighborhood associations had little political clout.

Smythe was certain that these congressmen had enough influence to obtain funding for the deteriorating areas and to have a suitable amount allocated to these development projects.

As Jessica Smythe pondered the insensitivity of locally elected officials to neighborhood interest, she was aware that the next congressional election was just six months away. Most likely, some form of political involvement was needed . . . perhaps in the form of campaign financing.

Smythe would like to see one congressman in particular defeated. Not only had he voted against the enabling legislation for neighborhood development funds, he also had refused to discuss the matter on her recent visit to his local office during the congressional recess.

The other two congressmen were neither antagonistic nor helpful, and Smythe felt that they would listen to reason once the political clout of one neighborhood group was established.

COMMUNITY CHARACTERISTICS

Smythe reviewed the strengths and weaknesses of the neighborhoods. All three were heavily populated with middle-aged and older adults with a common, foreign ethnic origin. They had remained in the neighborhood in which they had settled and raised their children, even though in many instances the children had moved away, leaving a customer base of individuals on fixed incomes. Other less affluent families had been attracted to the neighborhoods in recent years because of their close proximity to the urban center and because rental and home sales prices were reasonable.

Each neighborhood association wished to maintain the identity of the neighborhood; both the older and the more recent residents agreed about this. Furthermore, the residents cooperated with each other in keeping the neighborhood clean and in a modest state of repair. Each could point out specific improvements that had resulted from community effort: one or more homes that had been repainted using volunteer labor and paint supplied by an elderly homeowner, or porch steps replaced in similar fashion. However, the age of the homes and the lack of financial resources clearly indicated that outside funding was needed even to retain the status quo.

Faced with the prospect of seeing the neighborhoods decline further, and of losing the equity the residents and merchants had in their properties (frequently a high percentage of their total worth), everyone involved believed that each neighborhood group would be cohesive and would actively support a group effort. Smythe felt certain of this.

It would be possible to calculate the financial cost to the city of lost property, business, and sales and personal income taxes if local merchants and residents were forced to move from the area. Moreover, there would be increased costs for protection services to avoid property damage, fires in empty buildings, and crime on dark streets. It also was doubtful that any new enterprises could be found to move into the neighborhoods to occupy empty store spaces and to create new jobs.

The best approach appeared to be immediate action directed at elected officials, such as Congressman X.

CORPORATE POLITICAL ACTION

For a political action committee (PAC) to be formed, several things had to occur quickly. Jessica Smythe knew that her firm could provide administrative services for a PAC associated with it. However, she would need the support of the board of directors. Jessica Smythe owned 40 percent of the stock, but approval of the remaining stockholders would be critical.

Smythe knew of a firm of similar size that had raised $50,000 for a PAC, and she wondered how she might be able to accomplish such a goal. Funds could be solicited directly from stockholders and employees. Would employees from suburban areas and nearby cities where branch stores were located be willing to contribute funds? What type of internal network would be needed? Since PACs can solicit funds from individuals outside the parent organization twice a year, the Smythe PAC could approach merchants and residents within the area and appeal as well to civic-minded individuals from a wider geographic region.

If like-minded groups could be identified, such as party committees for candidates the PAC wished to support, the League of Women Voters, and perhaps groups interested in neighborhood preservation, the efforts of the Smythe PAC could be extended. Since the election was just six months away, the PAC might not be able to qualify as a multicandidate committee; therefore it would have to follow the dollar limitations established for individuals and other such groups acting in concert. Each candidate that was supported could receive $1,000 per election (primary, general, runoff); however, $5,000 could be given to any other committee in support of one or more candidates the PAC favored, and $20,000 could be given to a national party committee for use in congressional elections. Adding this together, the PAC could contribute $3,000 directly to the three congressional candidates it selected for the general election, as much as $20,000 to the party of the candidate opposing Congressman X, and $10,000 to two committees that loaned their support to the opposing candidate. Together, this meant that $33,000 could be allocated for contributions, and the remaining money used for the preparation of leaflets and for solicitation expenses.

There were additional considerations. To qualify eventually as a multicandidate PAC and be able to contribute $5,000 per candidate per election another time, it would be necessary to contribute to at least five federal candidates and to obtain funds from at least 50 individuals.

Would it be wise to plan for the long term and to qualify as a multicandidate PAC? Smythe knew that the 17 stores were scattered throughout 12 congressional election districts in the state and that some employees lived in still other districts. How would five candidates be selected for support? Should small amounts be given to a large number of candidates, with larger sums reserved for the three targeted districts? The uncle of one suburban store manager was running in a "safe" election. How much money should be diverted for his campaign? Would a wider dispersal of funds to include the suburbs hinder solicitation efforts from groups interested primarily in urban neighborhood preservation? There were five stores in urban areas, each in a different congressional district.

Of course, other types of PAC organization were possible. Each neighborhood association could form a PAC, but this would prevent the Smythe firm from providing administrative services. There was a national trade association of hardware dealers, but if support was sought from this group, other firms learning of these efforts might try to acquire a large share of the block grant money for areas they serve, even if they provided little support for the association PAC.

On another level the effort could boomerang through negative publicity or through retaliatory action on the part of developers interested in tearing down the buildings and creating large office or apartment buildings.

Would Smythe company involvement in politics truly represent the interests and viewpoints of individual shareholders? To what extent should shareholders and employees decide what candidates to support?

Jessica Smythe had been asked to prepare a report for board consideration by the end of the week. What specific recommendations should she make?

DISCUSSION QUESTIONS

1. What recommendations should Jessica Smythe make to the board of directors? Should a PAC be formed? Why or why not? What other alternatives should be considered, and on what basis do you accept or reject them?
2. If a PAC is formed by a business firm, what criteria should be used in deciding whether to apply for multicandidate committee status, in selecting the candidate(s) to be supported, in soliciting funds from individuals and other groups, and in decided whether to expand the PAC to an organizational level beyond the firm?
3. In evaluating the level of political involvement of a firm, which factors must be considered? When is political involvement in the best interests of the firm? Of the stockholders?

Chapter 14

Generalizations for Managing Business and Public Policy

INTRODUCTION

Each of the topics addressed in previous chapters of this book involves a broad range of managerial and public policy questions. Chapter and case materials have been replete with conflicting ideological positions, opposing sources of information and expertise, and differing desired courses of action. To conclude our discussions of U.S. experience in the realm of business and public policy, it is useful to ask what general conclusions for U.S. managers can be gleaned from this vast diversity of issues and perspectives. What enduring principles for present or prospective managers can be derived from these discussions? The aim of this chapter is to extrapolate beyond specific chapter topics in order to set forth several such generalizations.

THE CENTRAL ISSUE: INTEGRATING BUSINESS AND SOCIETY

Whether the subject is corporate governance, international trade and foreign investment, antitrust enforcement, securities regulation, corporate political action, product safety regulation, or any one of a number of other public policy issues, it is an established fact that complex public questions bear on corporations and the business system. However, values common to all parties within these issues are rarely obvious, and policy directions are not often developed quickly or easily. Multifaceted issues present in prior chapters stand witness to the observation that multiple interests, perspectives, and values have been found to bear upon any particular public policy question. The integration of differing preferences for business behavior is certainly a major task for the society as a whole and for managers of its economic organizations.

Historically, our society has relied upon a brilliant mechanism for resolving conflicting interests. A market-based economic system allows a series of impersonal transactions to integrate differing preferences. Interests are expressed in monetary terms, and prices reflect and direct transactions. The strength of people's preferences dictate how much they are willing to pay for a certain outcome; given existing prices, each person maximizes his or her economic well-being.

Since national outcomes rely on agreements among numerous parties, this historical mechanism has the important feature of decentralized decision making. Large-scale patterns and directions, such as a higher rate of growth for one product or industry over another, emerge solely upon the aggregation of innumerable individual transactions. The absence of a centralized decision-making process concerning the vast amount of economic activity is both a consequence of the core values of freedom and individualism in American society and an assurance for the continuation of these values.

Market processes have been explicit in our consideration of public policy and private management in prior chapters. They alone, however, do not address all of the apparent requirements of society today. The following topics stand out as additional factors present in the larger picture of public and private policy issues:

1. Not all social values are convertible into monetary terms and therefore do not lend themselves to being integrated into private decisions through market-based transactions. Generally, expectations or preferences for equity and justice reside outside the pricing mechanism. Calls for greater health, safety, and environmental quality also appear difficult to place within the calculus of the market.
2. Deviations from desired market functioning are not necessarily self-correcting. The existence of substantial market power by a single firm undercuts premises of decentralized allocation of resources through market-based pricing. Inadequate information about corporate management creates imperfections in capital markets and may lead to loss of institutional credibility as well as economic inefficiencies.
3. The increased size and technological base of many corporations increases their impact on social, political, and ethical behavior. From the degree of safety present for workers and communities affiliated with production of toxic chemicals to the influence of corporations on electoral politics, corporate activities are highly visible and easily become matters of public awareness and debate. Market-based economic transactions do not appear to address fully and adequately the firm's relationship to all aspects of society. A realm for judgments pertaining to the subjective, qualitative, and largely value-based dimensions of this relationship remains.

Our traditional market mechanism for integrating differing interests in society is a vital, effective, and precious — but incomplete — process. Additional values and expectations, not inherently incorporated into the market mechanism, are present.

The political process is, of course, the context in which nonmarket values are expressed, evaluated, and acted upon. Competing views of market performance, the relative importance of economic and noneconomic goals, and alternative beliefs about how to reach a particular goal are issues inevitably placed on the agenda of government. We have seen how at different times, in different ways, and for different reasons the legislative, judicial, and executive branches of government become involved in resolving social differences.

Differing interests are primarily resolved by compromise in political decision making. A wide range and diversity of political interests prevents any single coalition from gaining sufficient power to ignore or override competing interests. Public policies, consequently, typically result from numerous trade-offs among parties where any single interest rarely obtains all of what it wants. This slow and incremental process appears capable of integrating interests sufficiently well to retain the commitment and involvement of all parties. Social cohesion takes precedence over quick decision making, and the maintenance of continuity prevents radical departures from past policy.

Issues placed on the agenda of government call for difficult judgments: How can we balance equally desirable but apparently conflicting values? Can government action supplement the market, or does public action simply compound the problem? What is an appropriate cost to impose on society to reduce the overt manifestations of a particular problem? The political process is the necessary context for addressing conflicts about market and nonmarket values.

Fortunately, the American political process is itself highly integrative — pluralistic, decentralized, and successful in maintaining commitment to the process for all parties. Upon its participants the process places only the requirements of compromise and negotiation — activities that carry the obligation to accept the legitimacy of opposing points of view.

Just as the market mechanism appears to achieve an incomplete integration of all relevant values, political processes do not necessarily satisfy all of the requirements of social integration posed by the growth and development of an industrial society. Government action resulting from political decision making may not resolve underlying issues. Enacting consumer protection laws or increasing compensation to injured parties through product liability cases, for example, is an outcome of governmental decision making that may still fall far short of creating closer, more responsive business-consumer relations. While succeeding to force safety preferences into product decisions, both of these actions have a punitive orientation and encourage compliance rather than adaptation. Long-term adaptation of the firm to safety questions — the basis for true business-consumer integration — may still be lacking. Beyond the frequent inflexibility of public policies, government actions often risk undermining the advantages of the market system without compensatory benefits, worsening the situation by all accounts.

Society depends on the achievement of a continuing integration among differing social and economic interests. Some differences are resolved ideally through market pricing mechanisms. Others do not submit to monetary transactions and arrive in the arena of political decision making where integration is sought by negotiation and compromise. The political process is fully capable of responding to noneconomic values and frequently constrains economic processes by placing requirements on business behavior. Whether public policies achieve adaptive, lasting integration, however, is open to question.

The interdependency of the firm with external social interests is an established fact, and in the final analysis, a large realm of discretion remains for creative and integrative action by private sector managers acting in the interests of their firms. To these needed skills of managers we now turn.

ACTION PARADIGMS FOR MANAGING INTERDEPENDENCIES

Economic transactions are, naturally, the most familiar and common form of relationship between the firm and its direct and indirect constituencies. A large body of management knowledge, largely based on quantitative analysis, has been developed to inform managerial decisions about economic decisions. Analytical decision techniques, in fact, constitute one basis on which to claim that management is a profession.

Our attention in this book has focused on another area of management responsibility: dealing more directly with the public expectations and social values that may be incompletely incorporated into corporate actions by market processes. What concepts or guidelines can managers use to guide their actions in this area? How can they think about their actions, and what are their needed skills? These questions highlight the managerial implications of business and public policy issues; of what consequence to firms and to society is managerial behavior on these issues?

The Advocate Manager

We have seen that issues frequently pose trade-offs between competing interests where a particular firm is an active participant. Court decisions, administrative rulings, and legislative proceedings are processes involving advocacy. In addition, managers are also corporate advocates in private negotiations with unions, consumer or environmental groups, dissident stockholders, and foreign governments in numerous other commercial and noncommercial transactions. Negotiation is an expected and common part of the role of the effective manager. To be effective in these settings, managers need to have a strong understanding of the issues, to draw upon the best information and expertise available, and to be skilled in communication and persuasion.

Trade-offs are often made through negotiation, and advocacy processes call for strong negotiating skills. The necessity of negotiation is dictated by the presence of independent sources of power — differing parties are forced to deal with others whose immediate objectives appear incompatible. In fact, because the two parties are interdependent, compromise is a desirable outcome. This is not to say that each party does not try to get the most favorable outcome it can in any particular incident; of course, each uses all the information, strategies, and powers of persuasion it can muster to influence the terms of the settlement.

The key test of the success of a negotiation, however, is not only whether an agreement was reached in a particular incident but also whether succeeding agreements were more or less difficult to reach. Negotiations that build resentment, anger, or distrust harm both parties' long-run interests. A successful negotiator accepts the legitimacy of the other party's position and recognizes that the ability to achieve his or her goals depends on the other party's parallel ability to experience concrete progress toward its goals. Compromise, therefore, is a necessary part of the process. Negotiation is dictated by the necessity to divide a limited pie; yet successful negotiation is a form of cooperation — finding a solution to the predicament of shared power such that both parties can come back to the relationship in further transactions. The manager who lets advocacy become adversity has usually allowed personal ego to override corporate responsibility.

Uncertainty and Provisionalism in Advocacy

A casual observer of U.S. public policy in recent years would be bound to conclude that there is little certainty in our knowledge about economic events. In the first decade of the 1980s, sustained economic growth has, surprisingly, been achieved amidst unprecedented budget deficits and historically high interest rates. Similarly, record inflows of foreign capital and an unrelenting strength of the dollar were unanticipated events. Surely theories abound to interpret and explain these events in retrospect; there is no shortage of persons that profess to know why something happened. But these are hindsight views. Few persons, if any, understand economic forces sufficiently well to anticipate the direction of events. In fact, being among the world's contrarians — those predicting the opposite of the commonly held view simply on disbelief of popular assumptions — has become a respectable profession. Not infrequently, our assumptions are turned upside down by the course of events, causing a reorganization of our beliefs about the possible and the impossible, about cause and effect.

In addition, beliefs about cause and effect, and even about right and wrong, can be influenced by personal interests or stakes. Ardent free traders may decide to favor import quotas or tariffs on foreign products when they perceive foreign governments subsidizing their competitors, especially when such policies cause lost sales for their firms. Of course, views are relative to one's injury; upon examining the same situation, an unaffected person may suggest allowing foreign governments to subsidize American consumers. Constantly changing circumstances generate new information and alter personal stakes, consequently affecting beliefs about what needs to be done.

This point of view does not suggest discarding all predictive models and discrediting the scientific method. On the contrary it makes pursuit of understanding even more important. To establish cause-effect, right-wrong belief systems is essential to managing institutions. If carried beyond the point at which new information suggests reorganization of beliefs, though, one's beliefs become a disservice.

To the extent managers act as if their beliefs are truth, as opposed to preliminary ways of organizing their experiences and interests, they are taking a risk of acting less effectively than otherwise possible. Assuming higher levels of certainty than actually exist may lead a decision maker to become an adversary rather than an advocate. A healthy commitment to a provisional view of the world need not take anything away from negotiating effectiveness, and it may add to it.

The Positive-Sum Manager

Many managerial situations call for advocacy roles and negotiating processes. Advocacy proceedings nearly always have a short-term time orientation — a relatively specific issue needs immediate resolution. The court will decide in favor of one or another party, the collective bargaining process results in a new labor contract or a strike, the current Congress passes a law or it does not, or the regulatory agency modifies a rule or it does not. Although the issues may continue over a long time, specific incidents have a discrete, nominal character.

To assume, however, that all constituent relations with the firm always call for managerial advocacy may overlook another equally valid alternative. Managers and investors share a community of interests in the long-term prosperity of the firm, as do employees, the surrounding community, consumers, and each other major constituency. In the long run the firm's interest lies in qualitative improvements in its relationships with its constituencies — improvements that are difficult to achieve by an incident-by-incident advocacy approach. Groups having a long-term interest in the welfare and prosperity of the business system and the managers of each firm should, over time, accentuate their common interests and seek to diminish the relative frequency of their advocacy processes. We have repeatedly seen in chapters and cases how clarity of organizational purpose and consistency of organizational design are common requirements in adapting the firm to demanding constituencies and changing circumstances.

Today's manager has a positive-sum role to play that requires commitment to broad, long-term integration of interests. This is a very different process than the short-term corporate advocate and effective negotiator, although the manager may need to foster the latter while participating in the former. We will realize less than the full potential of our diverse society and our free economy if long-term processes are foregone because positive-sum managerial roles are confused with advocacy.

CORPORATE LEADERSHIP: THE BOTTOM LINE OF POLICY STUDIES FOR MANAGERS

The world confronts managers with an increasing number of choices about social aims and actions as well as about strategies and tactics of the firm. In the final analysis the study of business and public policy is about leadership — an intangible, ill-defined quality that indicates the ability to make choices that synthesize differences into purposeful and adaptive directions.

Executive leaders will determine the future of the American economic system in part by their ability to manage pluralistic systems. Human and social differences find expression inside and outside of the corporation. Executives are needed who utilize purpose and values to achieve convergence among different interests. Executives need to understand and contribute to the creation of environments that generate benefits for multiple parties.

There is a strong opportunity in the United States for managers to influence the public policy climate in which business functions. This opportunity can be accepted or ignored.

There is also a great need to manage the corporation in new relationships to customers, employees, owners, and the public. Today no organization or institution has the luxury to function without respect to its interdependence with these constituencies. The need to manage in this new context also can be realized or foregone.

American management runs a great risk of failing to respond to present world challenges. Managers are prone to looking to new techniques for regaining economic competitiveness on a worldwide scale. However, new and better techniques are not the answer. Rather, an answer lies where few managers look: in ways that various constituencies have a stake in the firm's success. This view is an alternative to the attitude that perceives constituent groups as inherently indifferent, if not hostile, to the success of the firm.

A complete understanding of the opportunity and needs confronting the United States today has yet to be achieved by American managers and observers of the U.S. economic system. The current emphasis on managing innovation and change in the firm, widespread present attention to organizational culture, and rebirth of interest in worker participation and labor-management collaboration are a few signs of the interest in finding more effective and adaptive management methods. Recent attempts to discover the elements of excellence in management are other indications. The intense interest in Japanese management philosophy and techniques is another sign, as is the strong movement to consider the role and influence of management ethics.

These efforts, probing and partial statements of today's leadership requirements, represent a rethinking of the role of executive leadership in the firm. Together, they are saying that the manager of tomorrow has part of the responsibility for achieving integration in a pluralistic society. The task of establishing purpose and direction is central, and the need to achieve a common benefit with respect to individual difference is paramount.

In an important sense public policy represents a statement about interdependency — laws, regulations, and court decisions are expressions of expectations about the relationship between the private economic sector and other interests or social values. Sometimes this may be an assertion of the rights between a firm and a person, such as the court's decision in a product liability, worker illness, or job discrimination suit. In other situations policy may represent an attempt to achieve a mutuality of interests. Economic development grants, encouragement of export trading companies, R & D tax credits, and many other public actions constitute statements about the relationship of business actions and a perceived interest in economic growth.

The fact that public policy is an outcome of a political process does not change the basic fact that it establishes an expectation — sometimes a constraint — for business in relation to a group or a value. Policy is, in the final analysis, an expression of an interdependency; politics is simply a method by which to determine which statement of interdependency will be accepted from competing notions.

The view that managers influence the nature of interdependencies both inside and outside the firm is not a typical view of managerial work. When people see managers at work, they are making investment decisions, solving problems, having meetings, giving directions, making speeches, and doing numerous other concrete tasks. Interdependencies are not easily perceived in the flow of everyday events. Yet the premises or assumptions with which managers approach their work will make a difference in whether problems reappear, whether human and financial resources are fully used, and whether goals are achieved. To view the firm's interests either without regard to the interests of other social and constituent groups or, worse yet, as an adversary to other groups is to work against existing social reality.

The culture of a firm is not "managed" directly. The intersection of common interests within and outside of the firm is not identified the same way a plant site is located. Interdependency is an awareness; it is a result of a thousand concrete actions, each based on the premise that joint interests are attainable and desirable as a rule of administration.

The implications for managers of this viewpoint are enormous. First, managerial actions need to be based on the assumption that the corporation does not function autonomously or exist apart from a large variety of social interests and values. Whatever is achieved within our economic system results solely from the mobilization and contribution of energies among various social interests and values.

Second, appreciating and managing interdependency is a task common to the internal environment of the firm as well as to the quality of its external environment. The success of the firm and health of the private economic system depend on the ability of leaders to develop common purpose within a context of social differences.

Social groups — labor organizations, "public interest" organizations, senior citizens groups, environmentalists, various business and trade associations, professional and occupational organizations, and numerous others — are, naturally, highly partial to their own views of what interdependencies should exist between business and the wider society. These views are frequently embued with ideology, values, and emotion; thus the task of achieving convergence on purposes and directions that create mutual benefit is no small challenge.

Finally, leadership consists of creating possibilities for mutual benefits among groups and individuals with divergent interests in a setting in which the firm itself has specific interests. To act only in terms of the immediate interest of the firm and to fail to act fully in the interest of the firm both represent deficient leadership.

Balancing the firm's immediate interests with its long-term interests and balancing the firm's more narrow interests with a community of interests in its wider environment constitute major tasks of leadership in today's corporations. The public policy environment of the firm, including its implications for internal management, is an important context for understanding these leadership tasks.

DISCUSSION QUESTIONS

1. Reviewing the substantive issues discussed in previous chapters, what are your own generalizations or overall conclusions about corporate leadership requirements for the future?
2. Describe the concept of the positive-sum manager and illustrate how this ideal can be realized in management practice. What problems would you anticipate in having this concept adopted widely? What, if any, alternatives to this leadership approach do you see for ensuring the adaptation of our corporations to competitive forces and for achieving their integration with the broader society?

Name Index

Subject Index